Psychoanalysis

and

Psychotherapy

PSYCHOANALYSIS

and

PSYCHOTHERAPY

36 Systems

ROBERT A. HARPER

Jason Aronson, New York

Copyright © 1974 by Jason Aronson, Inc.

LIBRARY OF CONGRESS CATALOGING IN PUBLICATION DATA

Harper, Robert Allan
  Psychoanalysis and psychotherapy.

  Reprint of the ed. published by Prentice-Hall,
Englewood Cliffs, N. J.; with new introd.
  1. Psychotherapy. 2. Psychoanalysis.
RC480.H3   1974   616.8'914   73-18625
ISBN 0-87668-131-3

Copyright © 1959 by Prentice-Hall, Inc.
Manufactured in the United States of America

Preface

This book is an attempt to present the main types of psychological treatment in clear, brief, and simple language. Psychotherapeutic theories and techniques included are those which rely primarily on verbal interchanges between an adult or older adolescent patient (or client) and the agent of treatment (variously called a counselor, therapist, psychiatrist, psychoanalyst, or psychologist). Therapies excluded from our consideration are the physiologically oriented (drugs, shock, surgery, etc.) and the adjunctive and non-verbal methods (such as dance, art, occupational, and play therapies).

Readers who rigorously identify themselves with any one of the many systems of psychotherapy will probably be disappointed with the author's treatment of their particular system. There are at least two reasons for such dissatisfaction: (1) Wide and brief coverage of the many systems means that it is possible to hit only the main points and high spots, not the details and refinements, of any one system. And (2) as a non-adherent of any particular system (although finding much of value in many), the author may miss some of the values apparent only to a faithfully practicing therapist of a system. The first deficiency is intrinsic to any broad survey. The second weakness is an inescapable concomitant of an over-all objectivity and is somewhat comparable to the situation where a person holding no systematized religious convictions makes a survey of the various religions: what is lost in fine and mystical detail is more than compensated for by clarity of general perspective.

Whatever the affiliation or non-affiliation of the reader, this book offers a more complete survey of contemporary systems of psychotherapy than has been previously presented in a single volume. Such a presentation should be of particular interest to students of the behavioral and social sciences as well as to the intelligent layman who has heretofore looked in vain for an understandable map of the psychotherapeutic maze.

While the field of psychotherapy has grown since this was first written, the contemporary systems of psychotherapy are firmly rooted in the principles and procedures described in this book. Many readers have told me that part of the lasting strength of PSYCHOANALYSIS AND

PSYCHOTHERAPY: 36 SYSTEMS is that it presents the essence of major therapeutic schools more succinctly and simply than can be found in separate accounts or in other surveys of the field. Technical words which could not be avoided in accurate descriptions of the systems are defined in a glossary at the end of the book.

R.A.H.
Washington, D.C.

Contents

Psychoanalysis

and

Psychotherapy

CHAPTER 1

Psychotherapy in Modern Society

Psychotherapy as a term, literally means "treatment of the psyche." As we shall see, there are many conceptions of the nature of the psyche and of what constitutes its appropriate treatment. We are interested in the various systems of psychic treatment which depend mainly on verbal interchange, the most important medium of human communication. This does not mean that we shall have no concern about gestures, facial expressions, posture, and other non-verbal transmissions of meaning, but only as parts of systems that are chiefly oriented to verbal interchange.

Verbal treatment of the psyches is generally undertaken only when the patients or their associates consider these psyches in an unsatisfactory condition. Psychotherapy is designed for *disturbed* psyches. What constitutes a state of disturbance so extreme as to warrant psychotherapeutic treatment is also a matter on which varying opinions are available. But, in general, the psychotherapist of any school undertakes to treat the mind and/or emotions of a person after he becomes convinced (by direct observation) that the person is thinking, feeling, or acting in a sufficiently undesirable (or disturbed) way to merit treatment. The therapist must be convinced, furthermore, that the particular type of treatment which he dispenses will be useful in reducing or removing the psychic disturbance of the patient.

Man has known for centuries that verbal communication between or among two or more individuals can have desirable effects on the thinking, feeling, or acting of one or more of the individuals. Both

1

formal and informal education of many types rests on this proposition. Physicians and clergyman have likewise based part of their procedures on this observation. In like manner have politicians, advertisers, and other propagandists. The attempt to induce human beings to behave in what is considered a desirable manner is, in fact, the conscious or unconscious purpose of a very large percentage of human interactions.

Despite the long history of efforts to influence human attitudes and actions through communication, it is legitimate to view psychotherapy, as such, as a very modern phenomenon. Perhaps the clearest point of differentiation between psychotherapy and other forms of attempted behavioral change is the factor of *clear awareness* on the part of both the therapist and the patient that the goal of the whole undertaking is to make the patient's thoughts, feelings, and/or actions more desirable, acceptable, and comfortable to him and his associates. Such clear recognition of the undesirability of existing behavior patterns and clearly stated focus of activity to reduce or remove such undesirability is usually not to be found in other forms of educational or propagandistic endeavors. When education, for example, comes to be an *agreement* between the educator and the student that the goal of the education has become the substitution of desirable patterns of behavior for what has been clearly designated as disturbed thoughts, feelings, or actions of the student, the education has become psychotherapy, the educator has become a therapist, and the student has become a patient.

A certain amount of self-awareness has been achieved by man at other periods in his social history, but never with the extensity and intensity of the contemporary society out of which psychotherapy has emerged as a significant process. The Greeks, after a long period of cosmological speculation, turned their attention to some of the same problems found within the modern disciplines of sociology, psychology, economics, and political science. Then, as now, there were conflicts between old and new values, rapid social changes, and a breakdown of many of the traditional social forms. Social crisis helps focus man's interest on his personal and social being.

Fascinated as we readily become with the activities and utterances of the ancients, we find little among these of direct bearing on the theories and techniques of psychotherapy. Although the Greeks to some degree anticipated modern western man in self-awareness, they never organized specific systems of psychotherapy. Our only historical point here about the Greeks is this: their situation, like our modern one, illustrates the point that *man thinks about himself only when he becomes aware of difficulties about himself.* Thinking is most accurately and simply defined as problem solving. Problems directly related to himself shake man's confidence and threaten his security. Therefore he postpones as long as possible the necessity of facing them. This has been the history of the human race. It likewise tends to be the history of any human individual. When modern man, like the Greeks, could no longer postpone the disagreeable process of examining his problems as a functioning social animal, he began the long journey towards self-awareness. Modern man's look at himself, however, has been longer, deeper, and more systematic than that of any previous human group. He has developed not only scientific observations about himself and his problems, but systematic ways of treating these problems.

It is not our task here to trace the social changes and the scientific discoveries that gradually forced modern western man to become aware of his personal problems and of his need to attempt their solution. First stirrings of understanding that disturbed persons are still human beings and respond to interpersonal relations based on kindness, consideration, and understanding are historically credited to Pinel, who introduced such procedures in the asylums of 18th-century France. Also in the 18th century, Mesmer introduced what may be considered the first specific psychotherapeutic technique by demonstrating the healing effects of hypnosis (which Mesmer mistakenly believed to be "animal magnetism" and which generally came to be called "mesmerism"). But it was not until the latter part of the 19th century that the conscious movement of psychotherapy may be considered to have gotten under way. For all practical purposes, the development of systems of psychotherapy can be dated from the early work of Sigmund Freud. This is in no way intended to belittle some of his forerunners and contemporaries: Charcot, Bernheim, Breuer, Janet, Bleuler, Kraeplin, and others. These men did valuable work (on which Freud in some instances drew) but they were not psychotherapeutic system builders.

Before turning to Freud and his monumental pioneer work, we

shall try to consider in the remainder of this chapter some of the common characteristics of psychotherapy. We thus look at general similarities before considering specific diversities.

In looking for common characteristics among the various systems of psychotherapy, the observer is apt to be reminded of the somewhat facetious syllogism that "all generalizations are false, including this one." There is scarcely a psychotherapeutic theory or technique endorsed today by some reputable therapists which has not been skeptically viewed or seriously questioned by others. Even such a vague generalization as "it is desirable for the therapist to be warm and accepting," will be challenged in some parts of reputable psychotherapeutic literature.

Yet generalizations need not be universally true, to be helpful. As an aid in learning the English language, the generalization that a plural of a word is usually formed by adding "s" serves well. The effectiveness of the generalization is not negated by the ready discovery of exceptions to the rule for forming plurals (datum and data; goose and geese; sheep and sheep; mos and mores).

The beginning student in the survey of systems of psychotherapy should take our presentation of generalizations about psychotherapy in a fashion analogous to rules about the language. In all we say about psychotherapy in the remainder of this chapter the phrase "in general" may be appropriately applied. In later chapters, we shall take cognizance of the many departures from these generalizations.

Psychotherapy begins with a patient who presents himself for help with some problems. He is often partially or totally mistaken about the causes or even the specific nature of his disturbance, but he has been convinced by his own observations or the reports of his associaates that he has a difficult situation or set of situations for which he needs professional assistance. This first characteristic of psychotherapy is then a person (the patient) who has at least some awareness of certain neglected or mishandled life problems and a desire to solve them.

A second component of psychotherapy is the presence of a person who has the task of helping the patient. This person—the therapist —perceives that the patient is in some state of incongruence or distress, knows himself to be in a relative state of congruence or lack of distress, and understands the relationship between himself and the patient as one in which he has the skills and knowledge which will probably enable him to help the patient eventually to reach a state of increased congruence and reduced distress.

More than one person may be involved as patient, as therapist, or both. When more than one patient is involved, the situation and process is referred to as *group psychotherapy*. When more than one therapist is working with one or more patients simultaneously, the term *multiple therapy* is employed.

As the therapy proceeds, a third characteristic appears: namely, a positive regard of patient for therapist and of therapist for patient. This does not mean necessarily any deep love by patient for therapist or vice versa. It does not even mean that patient and therapist come to *like* each other (although often they do). But it does mean that they come to respect one another and to feel comfortable and effective in their psychotherapeutic interactions.

Essential for psychotherapy is conviction on the part of the therapist that he understands and empathizes with the patient in his efforts to face and deal more effectively with the problems of his life. The therapist needs to perceive, for example, that this patient is an immature, emotionally dependent, orally fixated, socially ineffectual character who multiplies his difficulties by pursuing his addiction to morphine. But it is also desirable for him to understand with some feeling how a person might reach a point where he could feel so defeated by life (but not to the extent that he over-identifies and becomes involved in the troubles of the patient). He must also appreciate the difficulties of emerging from such a state, and discover ways of overcoming such difficulties from the vantage point of the patient.

It would appear to be also helpful, in psychotherapy, for the patient to have some degree of perception of the positive regard and the empathic understanding which he and his struggles evoke from the therapist. It is an aid to the therapeutic process for the therapist in some way, through words or actions, to communicate to the patient that he, the therapist, does understand and does care significantly about the patient and his efforts to overcome his difficulties.

The foregoing factors may be viewed as generally desirable conditions under which psychotherapy may proceed. Some therapists (notably so-called client-centered ones) would hold that such factors as those we have described are not only essential, but sufficient content of psychotherapy. Most therapists, however, would maintain that with the relationship established between therapist and patient (as implied by the characteristics we have outlined) the essential work of the therapy remains to be done: namely, by various additional procedures (such as those that follow), by which the patient is helped to more effectively handle his problems.

To reach this goal, the therapist provides information and corrects misinformation about the patient's environment. For the patient to make a better adaptation to the realities of his life, he needs to perceive them more accurately. Whether by direct counsel and interpretations or more deviously—through facial expressions, gestures, questions—the therapist provides the patient with a different outlook on his external surroundings.

In related fashion, the therapist helps to alter the patient's opinion of himself. Although there may be outer expressions of superiority, these are defensive reactions for the patient has basically a low judgment of himself. He secretly and mistakenly perceives himself as an unworthy person, and much of the fundamental help he requires from the therapist is in order that he may come to evaluate himself increasingly as a fully worthwhile person.

Another component frequently found in the psychotherapeutic process is what is generally called *catharsis*. The release of pent-up feelings, the revelation of emotional secrets, in the warm and understanding presence of the therapist are generally helpful to the patient. Disappointment, anxiety, and frustration soon reach intolerable levels in many disturbed persons, and the verbal expression of these feelings sometimes helps to dispel them.

One usually desirable factor in psychotherapy is what may be called "home work." The therapist and the patient agree on certain actions (based on the patient's changed conceptions of himself and his environment) with which he is to experiment between one psychotherapeutic session and the next. The patient reports on his successes and failures regarding these attempted changes in his behavior, and then he and the therapist make plans for additional changes. As the patient experiences gratification from successful accomplishments in new modes of behavior, his self-esteem grows. This, in turn, enables him to execute still more improvements in his behavior.

The successful completion of psychotherapy depends on the gradual reduction of the patient's dependence on the therapist. The patient has achieved his improved personal and social adjustments with the assistance of the therapist and has become almost inescapably fond of and addicted to the therapist and the therapeutic sessions. He must be gradually "weaned" from the therapist in much the same way the child is weaned from the parent. The patient is aided in this endeavor directly by discussing his emotional dependency problems and indirectly by his increased feelings of independent achievement. Some of his action tasks between sessions (his home work) are subtly directed by the therapist toward the end of helping the patient to realize his ability to function effectively without the therapist.

So much for the main processes in psychotherapy. Now for the psychotherapist himself. The first generalization about therapists in theory, but not always in practice, is that they are persons *trained* to do the special kind of work which we have outlined thus far. Training in the skills of psychotherapy is generally undertaken by people within the following major professions: medicine, psychology, nursing, education, social work, and the ministry. Although even the theoretical goals of training vary widely for persons in any of these professions who will undertake psychotherapy, it may be generally assumed that these should include thorough knowledge of the history, major experimental findings, and differing bodies of theory in psychology, sociology, psychiatry, social work, and education, as well as in psychotherapy itself. Added to such knowledge concerning normal and pathological behavior in our society (and some comparisons with behavior patterns in other societies) is the very important technical experience of actual clinical work, under supervision, with patients, of thus integrating observation with theory. And a final significant aspect of the training of a psychotherapist is his submission to intensive psychotherapy in order to learn his own deep anxieties, unfulfilled wishes, defense mechanisms, and limitations. Personal therapy is useful in that the therapist learns to use himself more effectively in his work with others.

The *personality characteristics* needed in a person who is going to be a psychotherapist are also very important to consider. Through having experienced intensive psychotherapy himself, the therapist should have been freed of serious emotional problems. But, since the therapist needs to be an empathic person in order to work effectively with his disturbed patients, it seems safe to say that many successful therapists are persons who have *formerly* had disturbance in their own personalities. To appreciate the turmoil the patient feels in his disturbance and the difficulties to be encountered by the patient in his efforts to change (to be, that is, empathic toward the patient), the therapist may profit from having experienced and successfully worked through perhaps not the same, but at least comparable, problems. He must likewise have the intelligence and the superior self-understanding (derived to some extent from his personal therapy) that will enable him to perceive with sensitivity and objectivity the specific nature of the patient's problems and probable routes toward overcoming these problems. If, to objectivity, intelligence, and empathy, we add a high degree of emotional stability and flexibility, we probably have the principal general personality characteristics essential in a psychotherapist.

There are also certain characteristics of the patient which are essential to effective psychotherapy. The patient should be sufficiently intelligent so that he is able, with guidance, to improve his perception of himself and his environment and to carry out programs of improvement arrived at in therapy. He should likewise be capable of rising above his disturbances enough of the time to make possible a fairly consistent use of his intelligence in communication with the psychotherapist. Persons so disturbed that they cannot communicate effectively usually need some other form of therapy (drugs, shock, etc.) prior to psychotherapy. Importantly linked with intelligence and capability to communicate is the patient's realization of his disturbance and his desire to get well. Because of the difficulties encountered in slowly achieving personality change, only a person with fairly consistent motivation to overcome his disturbance is likely to be a successful patient. A relatively intelligent person, capable of fairly rational communication, who is strongly dissatisfied with the present state of his life and is determined to try to improve his condition: this is a person who is most ready to become a patient in psychotherapy.

We have now discussed the processes of psychotherapy, the nature of the therapist, and the characteristics of the patient. What is lacking for us to envision the general nature of psychotherapy? Only the setting and here our generalization can be simple, indeed. One outstanding desirability for one or more therapists to relate with one or more patients in the processes described as psychotherapy is a full degree of privacy. Other factors are also often considered worthwhile. Among such desirabilities would be comfortable chairs, proper ventilation and heat and lighting, undisturbing decorations, possibly a couch, and so on. If, however, the therapist is undisturbed by the absence of one or more such desirabilities, the patient will soon learn to be. Privacy usually cannot be sacrificed, though, because it is essential for the patient to have full assurance that the difficult and delicate matters related to his effort to overcome his disturbances will never fall into the hands of anyone who can use these matters against him.

In summary, psychotherapy is a form of treatment of persons (patients) with disturbed thoughts, feelings, and/or actions, by other persons (therapists) largely through the process of verbal interchange with the specific goal of which they are mutually aware—reducing these disturbances and encouraging more desirable behavior. Here then, in concise form, are the common components of the psychotherapeutic process: (1) one or more persons (patients) with some awareness of neglected or mishandled life problems; (2) one or more persons (therapists) with relative lack of disturbance who perceive the distress of the patients and believe themselves capable of helping the patients to reduce distress; (3) a positive regard of patients for therapists and vice versa; (4) understanding and empathy of therapist for patient; (5) perception by patient of the positive regard for and empathic understanding of him by the therapist; (6) provision by the therapist of more correct information for the patient regarding the realities of his environment; (7) help that the patient may achieve a better self-evaluation; (8) emotional catharsis; (9) a gradually increasing number of tasks for the patient to perform between therapy sessions in applying new information about himself and his environment; and (10) a gradual process whereby the patient learns to become independent of the therapist. The therapist needs to be trained in the behavioral and social sciences in general and in psychotherapeutic activities under competent supervision in particular. He also needs to undergo intensive personal therapy and to be a person with a high measure of such personality characteristics as objectivity, intelligence, empathy, emotional stability, and flexibility. The patient needs to be sufficiently intelligent and undisturbed to communicate with a considerable degree of effectiveness and to be strongly dissatisfied with his present condition and determined to improve it. These elements, brought together in a setting which assures the highly essential privacy and relative comfort, are the substance and basis of the process of psychotherapy.

Selected Readings

Bernstein, Arnold, *On the Nature of Psychotherapy*. New York: Doubleday, 1954.

Cameron, D. Ewen, *General Psychotherapy*. New York: Grune, 1950.

Dollard, John, and Neal D. Miller, *Personality and Psychotherapy*. New York: McGraw, 1950.

Ellis, Albert, *How to Live with a Neurotic*. New York: Crown, 1957.

Fromm-Reichman, Frieda, and J. L. Moreno (Eds), *Progress in Psychotherapy*. New York: Grune, 1956.

Ingham, H. V., and L. R. Love, *The Process of Psychotherapy*. New York: McGraw, 1954.

Masserman, Jules H., and J. L. Moreno (Eds), *Progress in Psychotherapy*, Vol. II. New York: Grune, 1957.

Mowrer, O. H., *Psychotherapy: Theory and Research*. New York: Ronald, 1953.

Seward, Georgene, *Psychotherapy and Culture Conflict*. New York: Ronald, 1956.

Wolberg, Lewis R., *The Technique of Psychotherapy*. New York: Grune, 1954.

Freudian Psychoanalysis: Early Developments

Both from the standpoints of historical primacy and contemporary influence, it is appropriate to begin our survey of systems of psychotherapy with the psychoanalytic theories and techniques of Sigmund Freud. In Chapter 2, we shall consider Freud's pioneer work. In Chapter 3, we'll take up later developments of psychoanalytic theory and practice by both Freud himself and by analysts who remained fundamentally loyal to the major Freudian framework. Chapters 4 and 5 will deal with major departures from Freudian theories or practices by psychoanalysts who are "non-classical," "neo-Freudian," or "non-Freudian" in their orientations.

Although Freud is sometimes credited with having discovered the "unconscious mind," this assertion does not seem to be historically justified. Freud's first psychoanalytic conceptions seemed to have developed primarily out of his work in hypnosis with Charcot and Breuer, especially the latter. Since Freud did not become closely associated with Breuer until about 1885 and since the drafting of their first paper on hysteria was not undertaken until 1892, a number of authors may be considered forerunners of Freud in the matter of discovering the unconscious.

The early opposition to Freud did not stem so much from professional incredulity regarding the *existence* of unconscious mental processes as from shock and distaste regarding what Freud stated to be the *nature* of these processes. Although some writers preceded Freud in pointing out the existence of the unconscious, none, before

11

or since, has exceeded him in the penetrating originality and rich detail with which he described unconscious psychic phenomena. And all these dynamic unconscious activities—the true instinctive molders of human destiny, said Freud—were a kind of boiling reservoir of unfulfilled sex desires from infancy onward. It was this startling description of the unconscious that brought the professional wrath down on Freud's head in the late nineteenth and early twentieth centuries (and, to a lesser extent, on the classical Freudians of today).

Out of first his work in hypnosis and somewhat later his clinical work in free association (to be discussed later) and in his analysis of his own dreams and those of his patients', Freud built his early theories of human behavior. It is not our purpose to give precise historical landmarks in studying this development. In general, however, the psychoanalytic techniques and theories discussed in this chapter will refer to those practiced and held by Freud and his followers from the last decade of the 19th century until the second decade of the 20th century.

As we have said, Freud first began to develop psychoanalytic concepts in his work with Breuer in treating patients who suffered from hysteria. Hysteria (a term no longer employed in standard psychiatric nomenclature) was then considered a kind of catch-all category of highly variable symptoms—sensory, motor, vasomotor, visceral, and mental. For example, paralyzed limbs, deafness, blindness, and other pathological conditions for which no anatomical or physiological causes could be found. With Breuer, Freud found that a patient with hysteria was helped by encouraging her, under hypnosis, to "talk out" the emotional difficulties that apparently arose from early events which she could not previously remember. Breuer and Freud continued this "talking out" process with the patient in the waking state. The psychotherapeutic technique of allowing the patient to talk about his difficulties came to be called *catharsis*.

Both Breuer and Freud soon abandoned catharsis as a major psychotherapeutic method, but for quite different reasons. As far as we can determine Breuer's motives from a not too clear history, he reacted negatively to two developments of the method. First, he found the increasingly obvious sexual content of the early experiences revealed by the patient personally objectionable; and, secondly, he became uncomfortable with the strong attachment patients developed for the physician while the cathartic technique was being used. Freud, however, seemed to have his creative imagination fired by both these facts and used them as important components of the psychoanalytic system that he moved on alone to build. The predominantly sexual nature of the unconscious, as we have already mentioned, became a major tenet in psychoanalytic theory, and strong attachment to the therapist (positive transference) became part of the curative process in the clinical application of psychoanalysis.

Before proceeding with our analysis of the psychoanalytic technique Freud developed out of the cathartic method, we should pause to recognize two fundamental hypotheses in early psychoanalytic theory from which Freud never departed. These two hypotheses, in fact, often served as basic guides in the understanding of more detailed psychic phenomena later studied by Freud and his followers. The first is the concept of psychic determinism or causality, which holds that each psychic event is determined by the ones which preceded it. Mental phenomena, Freud held, are no more capable of existing without causal connection than are physical events in the external world. This is also true of certain thoughts or actions which are usually misinterpreted as being accidental or meaningless. This principle was fundamental in Freud's constant exploration of what other investigators dismissed as trivial, irrelevant, and meaningless psychic activities. These studies, in turn, led to his important discoveries. The second main hypothesis which served as a guide to all later psychoanalytic explorations was Freud's idea that consciousness is the unusual rather than the regular characteristic of mental processes. Unconscious mental processes, Freud found, are of fundamental significance and frequency in human behavior and are usually the causes of human actions (although other apparent "causes" may be consciously ascribed or the event may be written off as a "meaningless accident" as brought out in the first hypothesis). The two hypotheses may be jointly stated as follows: every behavior pattern of man has a cause, and it is most likely that the cause will be unconscious.

By the later years of the 1890's, Freud had reached the conclusion that catharsis in either the hypnotic or waking state was in itself inadequate as a psychotherapeutic technique for exploring the unconscious. He developed his exploratory method of free association, which really became the basic tool of psychoanalysis. Remnants of both the hypnotic and waking cathartic procedures were observable in the psychoanalytic procedure: the patient reclined on a couch; the analyst (in a role of unquestioned authority like the hypnotist) sat behind the head of the patient; and free association itself was a logical extension of catharsis. In free association the patient was directed to let his mental processes go with as little conscious direction (or censorship) as possible and to tell everything which passed through his mind, no matter how trivial, irrelevant, disconnected, or unpleasant. By reducing the filtering role of the conscious mind, the patient was thus more apt to present the analyst with clues which could lead to the unconscious roots of his difficulties.

As Freud proceeded in step by step soundings of the unconscious sources of his patients' symptoms of disturbance, he became more and more impressed with the sexual nature of these sources. Tracing back the roots of disturbances further and further into childhood, Freud formulated the doctrine of infantile sexuality.

This theory contends that the *libido,* or life force, drives the individual in search of pleasure. While this life force is primarily sexual in nature, it includes all feelings which motivate a person to desire pleasurable contact with others or even with himself. From infancy, Freud hypothesized, the individual is pushed by the libido toward the achievement of mature sexuality. If he meets with no serious obstacles, the individual progresses through certain stages of sexuality. If consistently frustrated, the individual may "fixate" his libido at any of these stages prior to maturity and develop corresponding pathological conditions.

The first stage of sexuality, characteristic of the first year of the child's life, is the *oral* stage. During this phase the libidinal energy of the child is centered in the mouth and gratification is derived through this channel. The second is the *anal* stage, at which time the libido partially transfers itself to the anal zone, and intense pleasures are derived from the retention and expulsion of feces. The child's interests during this period (ages one to three) are largely concentrated on himself (narcissism), and satisfactions are derived chiefly from his own body (auto-erotism). His interpersonal relationships are primitive and directed toward partial objects (for example, the breast rather than the mother as a whole). At about the age of three, the penis (clitoris in the female) becomes the focus of libidinal energy, and this ushers in the last pregenital phase, the *phallic* stage. At first in the phallic stage, interest in the penis (or clitoris) is auto-erotic, but soon sexual interest in the parents develops, and the Oedipus period begins.

The *Oedipus* period (usually thought of as extending from ages three to seven and part of the phallic stage) takes its name from the Greek legend of Oedipus, who unknowingly killed his father and married his mother. Freud pointed out that the child in the Oedipal period of life becomes sexually interested in the parent of the opposite sex and develops a feeling of rivalry toward and a wish to displace the parent of the same sex. Soon learning that such sexual interest in the parent of the other sex is forbidden and feeling hate as well as love for the parent of the same sex, the child develops strong feelings of anxiety and guilt. Expecting punishment for his "criminal" desires, the male child fantasies becoming castrated. A comparable fantasy of genital injury apparently takes hold of the female child. Also because the girl observes that she has a very small "penis," the clitoris, she develops a basic sense of inferiority (penis envy).

The intensity of fear becomes so unendurable in the child that he or she is forced to yield to the powerful rival (the parent of the same sex) by renouncing and repressing sexual feelings toward the love-object (the parent of the other sex). This struggle, called the Oedipus complex, was to Freud the crucial factor in the development of personality. With successful repression and resolution of the conflict, a relatively healthy personality develops. With lack of successful working through of the conflict, serious personality disturbances evolve.

Following upon the Oedipal period (and still within the third and last pregenital stage, the phallic) is the phase of life which Freud designated as the latency period. This period of relative sexual quiescence in the individual begins at about age seven and lasts until the onset of puberty (somewhere around twelve to fourteen years of age). The increased activity of the genital glands at puberty brings a correspondingly heightened libido, which reactivates the old Oedipal interests. If a relatively successful resolution of the earlier Oedipal crisis was achieved, however, the individual transfers his or her sexual interest to persons of the other sex outside the family and goes on to mature sexual fulfillment. The libido thus finally reaches its original goal, the genital stage of development.

We'll return a little later to a consideration of some of the psychopathological conditions which, according to Freud, result from difficulties in resolving the Oedipal conflict. Several other contributions he made to the understanding of unconscious sexuality in normal, as well as abnormal, personality development should be given our attention now. First is his hypothesis of bisexuality of human beings: no male is devoid of some strong wishes of a feminine nature, and no female is without some underlying masculine tendencies. Such homosexual inclinations are very strongly repudiated by most people at the conscious level. Unconsciously, however, bisexuality (and guilt and anxiety regarding it) is of great importance in understanding human behavior.

A second important hypothesis of Freud's regarding human sexuality is the bipolarity of human emotions, a process which has come to carry the name, *ambivalence*. Feelings of a positive nature toward a person or group are, according to Freud's clinical investigations, almost invariably accompanied by feelings of a negative nature. One side of the emotional reaction, often the negative, is usually repressed from consciousness, however, so that the individual is generally aware of only one aspect of his emotional response. The parent, for example, is conscious of loving his child, but is often unconscious of an accompanying hostility toward this same child. Such hostility is nevertheless significantly influencing the parent's interactions with the child and is not infrequently observable to an outside observer. The same is true of the child's feelings toward the parent, of the man's or woman's attitudes toward the mate: conscious love is often mixed with unconscious hate. Ambivalence of other feelings also often occurs—happiness with an underlying melancholy; pleasure with displeasure; joy with anger.

Freud's analysis of human sexuality led to a third significant hypothesis which he called *sublimation*. This theory holds that a certain amount of libido which is originally devoted to a sexual focus may be directed into ostensibly non-sexual channels from which either an esthetic or utilitarian pleasure is derived. Stated differently, sublimation is the unconscious gratification of a sexual desire by a substitute activity which conforms to personal and social definitions of acceptability (in the form of art and/or utility). Out of sublimation, according to this Freudian hypothesis, grew the whole superstructure of human civilization.

The fourth important hypothesis which Freud developed from his clinical observations of human sexuality is what he termed *displacement*. This process, first discovered by Freud in his analysis of dreams, is the representation of a part by the whole, or vice versa. That is, when one idea or image is substituted by another which is emotionally (not necessarily logically) associated with it, displacement has occurred. If, for example, a person has had a very unpleasant experience with a man who happened to have a beard, he may displace his hostility toward this person to all men with beards. A part of one unpleasant experience has come to symbolize the whole, and, illogically and irrelevantly (except in an emotional sense), the presentation of the stimulus (any man's beard) will bring forth the emotional response of hostility.

Displacement functions in a number of important ways in psychoanalytic theory and practice. One is in Freudian dream interpretation, a subject to which we'll soon turn our attention, and another is *transference*. You will recall that we mentioned earlier that one of the reasons Breuer apparently dissociated himself from collaboration with Freud in the treatment of hysteria by the cathartic method was his distaste for the strong attachments patients developed for the therapist in the course of the treatment. Freud, on the other hand, was not only undismayed by this fact, but went on to use his observations about these attachments as one of the corner stones of the evolving psychoanalytic practice. This attachment of patient for analyst was actually a form of displacement. The phrase *object displacement* was used by Freud when a love or hatred for a certain individual was denied consciously by the patient and (though the source of the feeling remains in the unconscious) referred to another person as stimulus "by proxy" for the emotional response. When the psychotherapist becomes the "proxy," that is, when a patient displaces to the analyst in the present, love or hatred unconsciously attached to a significant person (often a parent) in his past, *transference* has occurred. Freud found that the patient, in the course of free association, inevitably displaced many important positive and negative feelings.

When transference became particularly intense, the patient would reproduce and re-enact important childhood conflicts and fears.

The emotional experience of recalling unresolved childhood problems (through free association) and facing them in the transference situation with the understanding and accepting substitute parent (the analyst) may be considered the "dynamic axis" of the curative process in Freudian psychoanalysis. The individual as a child was too weak and too inexperienced to solve these problems, so he pushed them out of consciousness (repressed them). Now helped to be stronger and wiser by both maturity and the analyst, the patient is better able to face these conflicts and to gain the knowledge to solve them.

We spoke earlier of free association as *the* psychoanalytic technique. What we have just said about the importance of transference in no way contradicts this. Through the passive, permissive atmosphere of the psychoanalytic situation, in which the patient is constantly encouraged to say whatever comes to mind, transference is likely to develop. Lying on the couch where he cannot even see the face of the analyst, coming frequently (generally five times a week) into this submission-inducing setting, and being kept quite ignorant of reality factors about the analyst, the patient is further stimulated to call forth strong feelings from the past and to attach them to this almost phantom figure of the analyst. Free association and the psychoanalytic setting are well designed, then, to encourage transference. Psychoanalysis, employing the technique of free association, may be considered *transference analysis*.

So long as the patient continues to associate freely, the psychoanalyst keeps quiet. When strong resistances to free association develop, the analyst will interfere only to the point of helping the patient to overcome the resistance and to start talking again. One important aid to free association that Freud discovered early in his investigations derived from dreams. Freud found that many patients, in the course of freely associating, mentioned their dreams and that, when they were then encouraged to associate on the dream material, much new unconscious feeling was revealed. When associations to other topics broke down, associations to old or new dreams often brought an important "break through." Dream analysis, then, became an important extension of, not substitution for, the technique of free association.

In studying the free associations of his patients (and of himself) on dreams, Freud discovered that certain types of displacements were very common: that is, certain images in dreams very frequently stood for or symbolized objects and desires of the real world. These common symbols of dreams generally referred to the intense interests of childhood: members of the immediate family, body parts (especially sexual ones), bodily functions and experiences (urination, defecation, copulation, eating, anger, weeping, etc.), birth, death, and so on. Some of the more common examples of Freudian symbols in dreams occur quite often: money stands for feces, a journey or absence for death, a king or governor or other authority figure for father, a pair of sisters for breasts, a tree, steeple, necktie, sword, snake, etc., for a penis, a box, ravine, book, purse, etc., for a vagina.

Although Freud felt certain symbols commonly occurred in dreams and were sometimes an aid to the analyst in understanding a patient's dream does not mean that such authoritative dream interpretation was substituted for free association. Freud specifically warned against dream interpretation which was not based on specific knowledge of a particular patient's unconscious conflicts (derived through free association). Such knowledge of common symbols would, however, occasionally help the patient and analyst over an obstacle to understanding (a resistance) of the particular patient's unconscious.

The essential assertion about the unconscious mind which Freud made on the basis of his analysis of dreams was that a dream was *always* a wish fulfillment. By analyzing the highly disguised dream product (the manifest content) for its underlying meanings (the latent content), the precise nature of the patient's deep-seated desires can be understood. Freud felt that the study of dreams led not only to an understanding of general unconscious material ("the royal road to the unconscious"), but especially the repressed desires that (because unfulfilled other than in dreams) were creating the major disturbances in the patient's mental life.

Two other aids to the understanding of unconscious motives of the individual which Freud discovered early in his investigations should be mentioned here. These are the analysis of parapraxes and wit. The former are slips of the tongue and pen and memory and many of the daily mishaps that we call "accidents." Such, Freud ably demonstrated, are not meaningless errors, but revelatory of unconscious desires. The man who forgets a present for his wife on an anniversary or who forgets to introduce her at a social gathering, for example, is not just "absent-minded" or "careless": he is expressing underlying feelings of hostility. The politician who says: "Ladies and gentlemen, a vote for me is a vote against honesty—I mean, ha, ha— a vote against *dis*honesty in government" may be revealing some of his underlying motives and deserves to be watched.

In much the same way, wit and humor offer the individual a way of releasing part of his pent-up energy attached to repressed wishes. These wishes are invariably of a sexual or hostile nature, Freud discovered—wishes which, in a serious and open way, the individual could not express without meeting with disapproval from self and others. An examination of the jokes of any social circle will well bear out Freud's observations: hostility, lust, or desires which combine the two are being fulfilled.

Freud's first description of the mind presented it as analogous to a telescope made up of various psychic components arranged consecutively and stretching from the perceptual system at one end to the motor system at the other, with the various memory and association systems in between. This conception was described in his book on dreams (see "Selected Readings" at the end of this chapter for the best English translation of this, generally considered the greatest of Freud's works), which first appeared in 1900, but was never further elaborated. As described in that book, however, the *wish* is the sole motive force of the whole psychic apparatus. A wish was described by Freud as "a current in the apparatus" (apparently conceived of as a psychic excitation analogous to a nerve impulse) which derived from a tension (unpleasure) and arriving at gratification (pleasure) —that is, the release of tension.

Freud's early view of the mind also included his important formulation of two fundamentally different kinds of mental processes, which he labeled *primary* and *secondary*. The primary process is characteristic of children, of highly disturbed persons, and of the unconscious minds of all people. A wish, by the route of the primary process, seeks *immediate gratification*. It is uninhibited by any reality factors, any logical contradictions, any causal associations, any sense of appropriateness. The goal of a wish via the primary process is to discharge the excitation through any motor exit. If that fails, the primary process will find an unconscious sensory route (notably through dreams in healthy individuals and through hallucinations in pathological persons) via the remembered perception of a previous satisfaction.

In the secondary process, the emphasis is on the ability of the individual to delay the fulfillment of the wish. The more mature and experienced person is able to recognize environmental circumstances which are favorable or unfavorable to discharge of psychic energy rather than discharging regardless of appropriateness and other reality factors (as is the case with the primary process). Psychic energy also becomes much more firmly fixed to certain objects and channels of discharge in the secondary process as distinguished from the ready switch of a wish from one to another object and channel in the primary process.

Secondary process thinking is the mode of conscious thinking we usually attribute to the relatively normal and mature adult. It is largely verbal in nature and follows the rules of syntax and logic.

Primary process thinking is the dominant mode of thinking for the young child and persists in the unconscious in adult life and manifests itself chiefly through dreams, humor, pathology, and a few other ways. It is characterized by the absence of negatives, conditionals, or other qualifications; the replacement of an idea by its opposite; visual or sense impressions often in the place of words; and absence of a sense of or concern with time.

As Freud pointed out, it is essential for the psychotherapist to understand the difference between the secondary process of thinking, with which we are so familiar through introspection of our adult conscious minds, and the primary process, predominantly the activity of the unconscious. Without a realization of the quite different nature of the primary process, the various normal and pathological manifestations of the patient's unconscious remain a mystery to the therapist. Light cast on the unconscious and its operation via the primary process is sometimes considered the most profound contribution Freud made to understanding human behavior and helping the individual to overcome unconsciously rooted disturbances.

With this brief summary of the early Freudian conceptions of how the human psyche is constructed and how it functions and of the major psychoanalytic treatment procedures, we need to try to understand a little more specifically how Freud applied his hypotheses to particular types of emotional disturbances.

When, earlier in the chapter, we talked of the libidinal development of the individual, we described the three pregenital stages through which passage is made on the way to the goal of genital maturity. If, as a result of traumatic experiences, a considerable amount of libido becomes fixated at one or more of these pregenital zones, the individual's development toward maturity will be blocked, Freud contended, and some form of psychoneurosis will occur. Pathological symptoms may not appear until later in life, at which time, under the influence of emotional strain, great quantities of libido will pour back into the points of fixation (oral, anal, or phallic). This is the process of *regression*. It is seen in mild form, for example, in a child of three or four, who, under some such emotional stress as the arrival of a baby brother or sister, will regress to the oral stage of thumb-sucking. An adult example of pathological regression to the oral stage would be a chronic alcoholic. The hysteric patient, according to Freud, represented regression to the phallic stage, and the obsessive-compulsive neurotic is the classical example of anal libidinal fixation.

In terms of these early theoretical formulations, the task of psychoanalytic treatment as conceived by Freud was to release the libido fixated at pregenital points and help the disturbed person to avail himself of this neurotically wasted energy for practical life problems. As a result of successful analysis, the libido was set free to follow its course toward its instinctive goal of genital maturity.

Freud made some distinctions between what he called *actual* neuroses and *psycho*neuroses, but he did little to follow up these differences. He devoted his major clinical interest from 1900 onward to what he called the psychoneuroses (hysteria and the obsessions). One type of patient in the actual neuroses was the neurasthenic, a term Freud limited to persons with such symptoms as fatigue, listlessness, flatulence, constipation, headache, and dyspepsia. He hypothesized that neurasthenia developed from excessive masturbation or nocturnal emissions. The other type of actual neurosis, according to Freud, was anxiety neurosis, a condition which he proposed developed from habitual sexual activity without adequate outlet (lovemaking without orgasm or with inadequate orgasm, as in coitus interruptus). It is now thought by many psychoanalysts that these were mistaken conceptions, and little reference is found to Freud's notion of actual neuroses in recent psychoanalytic literature.

Quite the contrary is true, however, regarding Freud's conceptions of the psychoneuroses. These ideas underwent a steady expansion and revision by Freud and his followers well into the third decade of the 20th century. We shall here consider some of the earlier developments in Freud's beliefs about the psychoneuroses.

As a result of his work with Breuer, the reader will recall, Freud concluded that hysterical symptoms were caused by a forgotten event whose accompanying emotional energy had never been discharged. He soon added to this idea that for any emotional experience to be the source of a psychic disturbance it had to be strongly distasteful to the individual's conscious self. Freud thought this applied not only for cases of hysteria, but also for obsessions and many of the phobias. Since many of these repugnant experiences reported by patients in free association seemed concerned with sex and childhood, Freud proposed the hypothesis that these emotional disturbances were the result of sexual seduction in childhood by an adult or an older child.

This latter hypothesis soon had to be altered by Freud. He came to realize that many of the stories which his patients told him of having been sexually seduced as children were, in fact, fantasies rather than memories. At first discouraged, Freud soon proceeded to develop the theory of infantile sexuality, which we have already discussed.

The evidence that patients were preoccupied with sexual fantasies from early childhood onward through life led Freud to place less emphasis on particular traumatic events as the causation of the psychoneuroses. In a new theory which was formulated about 1905, Freud placed new stress on the importance of the patient's sexual constitution and heredity as sources of psychoneuroses. He did not, however, make such sources exclusively responsible. He believed that constitutional and experiential factors both contributed to the development of psychoneurotic conditions, and that either one in some instances can be predominant.

Further revisions of the Freudian theories of the mental disorders (and of the nature of the psychic apparatus in which these disorders occur) take us into the second decade of the 20th century and beyond. We have reserved discussion of this material for Chapter 3.

Summary

From his work in hypnosis with Breuer, Freud developed the method of mental catharsis. This was a technique whereby the patient "talked out" the nature and sources of his problems and thus (in some instances) overcame his emotional disturbances. Becoming dissatisfied with catharsis as a method, Freud extended the technique into what he called free association. In this procedure, the patient, reclining on a couch, tells the therapist all that passes through his mind. Such uncensored recounting helps the analyst to discover important unconscious sources of the patient's problems.

Freud held to the fundamental hypotheses that all psychic events have causes and that most such causes derive from the unconscious. The sources of mental disturbances, Freud contended, were primarily sexual in nature. In his sexual development the individual passes through four stages: the oral, anal, phallic, and genital. Fixation of too much of the libido (psychic energy, life force) of the individual at any of the pregenital stages brings corresponding pathological psychic conditions. The time of greatest disturbance falls in the Oedipal period (within the phallic stage). At this time the individual struggles with lust for one parent and jealous conflict with the other. Successful resolution of the Oedipal conflict is a prerequisite to normal adulthood (the genital stage).

Other important concepts in the Freudian theory of sexuality include the latency period, bisexuality, ambivalence, sublimation, and displacement (a special form of which is transference). Analysis of the transference relationship, by the process of free association, may be considered the "dynamic axis" of the curative process in psychoanalysis.

Dreams and their interpretation developed as an important aid to the free association process in analysis. Two other such aids were Freud's analysis of everyday slips, which he felt were always unconsciously meaningful, and wit, as revealing of unconscious hostility and sexual desire.

Two different types of processes are at work in the psychic apparatus of the individual, according to Freud: the primary and the secondary. The former is characteristic of the mental life of children, of disturbed persons, and of the universal unconscious. The latter is the usual conscious thinking of an undisturbed adult.

Freud's early applications of his theory to pathological conditions stressed the importance of libidinal fixation and regression. He also developed more detailed hypotheses regarding what he termed the actual neuroses and the psychoneuroses.

Selected Readings

Brenner, Charles, *An Elementary Textbook of Psychoanalysis.* New York: Int. Univs., 1955.

Breuer, Josef, and Sigmund Freud, *Studies on Hysteria* (translated by James Strachey). New York: Basic Books, 1957.

Freud, Sigmund, *The Basic Writings of Sigmund Freud* (translated by A. A. Brill). New York: Modern Library, 1938.

———, *The Interpretation of Dreams* (translated by James Strachey). New York: Basic Books, 1956.

Jones, Ernest, *The Life and Work of Sigmund Freud,* Vol. I. New York: Basic Books, 1953.

CHAPTER 3

Freudian Psychoanalysis: Later Additions and Modifications

As already indicated in Chapter 2, Freud did not view his teachings as complete and final, and throughout his lifetime he continued to modify and supplement them. He frankly acknowledged that he was not always certain himself about the relationships between some of his older and newer concepts. He felt strongly, however, that a desire for consistency should not prevent the recording of insights that an existing system did not readily accommodate. While such flexibility is admirable, the resulting inconsistencies make our understanding of Freudian theory considerably more difficult. At times, in an effort to make certain concepts clear and understandable, we may be guilty of oversimplification.

The first Freudian conception of the human mind as analogous to an optical instrument (presented in 1900 in *The Interpretation of Dreams*) was never, as we mentioned in Chapter 2, further elaborated. In 1913, however, Freud made a new effort to develop a topography of the mind by dividing its contents and operations into three mental systems: Ucs. (unconscious), Pcs. (preconscious), and Cs. (conscious). This differentiation between preconscious and unconscious mental activities is important in psychoanalysis. Thoughts on which awareness is not currently centered (hence, not immediately conscious), but which are recallable by an effort of the will constitute

Pcs., the preconscious. The group of mental processes and contents which make up Ucs., the unconscious, are at least temporarily barred from access to consciousness by some force within the mind itself and cannot be reached by an effort of attention on the part of the individual.

In 1923, Freud proposed a third and final general hypothesis concerning mental systems. This third theory is called the structural hypothesis to distinguish it from the topographic theory just mentioned. In this latest conception, Freud distinguished three functionally related structures of the mind: the id, the ego, and the superego. In general, the id represents the basic drives (instincts), the ego is the mediator between the id and external reality, and the superego comprises the individual's moral precepts and ideal aspirations (roughly, his conscience).

By the time he developed the structural hypothesis, Freud had somewhat changed his point of view regarding the instinctual nature of man. The reader will remember from the preceding chapter that for a long time Freud considered all instinctual manifestations of the individual a part of the sexual drive. Around 1920, however, mainly as a result of his study of masochism and sadism (the former is the pathological enjoyment of receiving pain and the latter of seeing others suffer), he proposed the existence of another basic drive in addition to the sexual: the aggressive drive or "death instinct." He considered the two drives fused in both normal and pathological activities, but in varying amounts and intensities. The term "Eros" (life) was employed to refer to the sexual drive, and the term "Thanatos" (death) to refer to the aggressive drive.

Freud believed that the aggressive drive showed the same capacity for fixation and regression and the same development through the oral, anal, phallic, and genital phases as the sexual drive. The relationship of the aggressive drive and various parts of the body is not so close as for sex, but it is still apparent. Biting, for example, is a characteristic aggressive activity of the infant or of the adult who has regressed to the oral stage. In like manner, soiling or feces retention express aggression in the anal stage of development.

The id, then, became the psychic representation of the sexual and aggressive drives and their many derivatives. These drives are present from birth. The id is considered as comprising the entire original psychic apparatus of the individual. The ego and superego later differentiate themselves, grow out of the id, and become separate functional entities.

Impulses of the id are not fused, organized, disciplined, or controlled. The id is subordinate only to the pleasure principle. A need is at its id source a demand for immediate gratification and operates by the primary process (see Chapter 2).

Freud thought that the superego did not begin to differentiate itself in any clear fashion until the fifth or sixth year of life. The ego, however, gradually starts to develop from about the sixth month onward. Frustration by the external environment is the factor that leads to the growth of the ego functions of the psyche. When the environment has consistently said "no" under certain circumstances to the demands of the id for immediate gratification, the infant begins to differentiate between himself and external reality and between the id impulses which external reality gratifies (pleasure) and the id impulses which external reality frustrates (pain). This "precipitate" of experience, these growing reality perceptions and the infant's adjustments to the perceptions, come to constitute the ego. The ego is the executant for the drives, the mediator between the id and the external environment. It is the "I," the self, the aspect of personality responsible for perceiving, knowing, thinking, feeling, choosing, and the kind of doing that follows perception of the outside world. The ego controls the crude impulses of the id and distributes psychic energy in what are thought by the ego's perceptions to be those ways which will insure maximal pleasure.

Like the ego, the superego is a function of personality which grows out of the id, but not until around the ages of five or six years. More specifically, the superego, according to Freud, develops as a result of the Oedipal conflict. In the pre-Oedipal period the child may be considered largely amoral. He does what he is told to do contrary to his own id impulses only because he (or, in Freudian terms, his ego) perceives the punishing effects of the environment (usually in the form of his parents) as a greater source of pain than the frustration of his id impulses. When threat of punishment from external sources is removed for the pre-Oedipal child, however, his id impulses take over, unrestrained by internal sanctions. But after about the fifth year, morality begins to become an internal matter with the child and proceeds to develop until a point of considerable stabilization is often reached at about the age of ten.

This internalization of the parental point of view by the child comes about through the process of identification with the parents in doing battle with the id impulses which emerge in the Oedipal struggle. Because the child becomes so frightened by his own impulses to kill the one parent and by the anticipated retaliation (castration) for his desire to engage in sexual activity with the other parent, he comes to see no alternative but to join forces with his parents in repressing these dangerous Oedipal urges. As he increasingly does so, the internalized "parent," the superego, comes into being.

As we parenthetically mentioned earlier, the superego corresponds roughly to what we consider "conscience." Contrary to the usual conception of "conscience," however, Freud believed the superego to be largely unconscious. As conceived by Freud, the superego becomes a kind of never-sleeping censor which critically examines the impulses of the id and the various activities of the ego, ready to pounce upon and punish what is judged to be "immoral" and to reward with self-praise and self-love all desirable or virtuous thoughts, feelings, and action.

Since the superego is based upon childish perceptions of reality and is largely the internalization of whatever the parental authority figure seemed to evaluate as "bad," the moral reactions of the individual are likely to contain many irrationalities. An important part of the analyst's role during the process when the patient is reliving his childhood experiences in the analytic setting is to help him to make a more realistic and rational evaluation of morality.

One clinically important aspect of the disapproving superego that Freud pointed out is worthy of special note. It is rather obvious to the individual who feels guilty that he has violated his conscience, his conception of morality. By no means so obvious, however, are inferiority feelings as signals of the violation of superego dictates. Freud showed how such feelings commonly arise from unconscious disapproval of the superego. The individual may consciously give himself all sorts of apparent reasons for a feeling of inadequacy, failure, low self-esteem, but the probable unconscious (and real) reason is that he has violated the instructions of his superego. According to some now unconscious memories of internalized parental dictates, the individual feels inferior as a "bad boy."

The introduction of the structural theory of the psyche led to a number of other changes in Freudian theory and in the emphasis of clinical practice. One of the important theoretical changes was in Freud's view of the nature of anxiety. Anxiety, according to Freud's original theories, resulted from the accumulation of undischarged libido which was then somehow (by a method unexplained) transformed into anxiety. In 1926, Freud abandoned this idea and suggested instead that anxiety appeared in two sets of circumstances, which he referred to as "traumatic situations" and "danger situations." He considered anxiety itself, as a basic reaction pattern, was biologically inherited, not culturally acquired. The first situational instigation of the hereditary reaction of anxiety are the traumatic situations where the psyche is overwhelmed by an influx of stimuli too great to handle. The prototype of traumatic situational anxiety is the birth experience (an idea much more extensively developed later by Otto Rank, who proposed it as the source of all neuroses—see Chapter 4). Other such traumatic instigations could also emerge in the life of the individual, but mainly such experiences are confined to childhood when the ego is relatively weak and undeveloped.

As the ego of the child develops, he learns to recognize and anticipate situations which contain potential trauma and to react to the anticipation of them with anxiety. This type of recognized or anticipated danger (as distinguished from the overwhelming, unhandled influx of stimuli in the traumatic type of anxiety), Freud called signal anxiety. The ego of the child reacts with anxiety to the anticipated danger: thus anxiety is a signal of impending danger for which the ego mobilizes its defenses. Because such anxiety is experienced as strong pain or discomfort (or "unpleasure," as it is often referred to in psychoanalytic writings), the ego is able to command much psychic energy from the id to deal with the situation.

There are a number of typical danger situations which Freud pointed out as occurring in sequence in the child's life and which elicit a great deal of signal anxiety. There are (1) loss of the loved object, (2) loss of the object's love, (3) loss of or injury to the genitals (loosely referred to as "castration anxiety"), (4) disapproval and punishment by the superego. The first danger situation is probably experienced by the child even before he can be said to feel so complex an emotion as love. It is the feeling of anxiety that arises from the possibility of permanent separation from the source of gratification (in the earliest experience of the infant this is the mother and her breast; anxiety probably first arises during frustration of the infant's desire to suckle, which, in turn, brings realization that the breast is separate from himself and his desires and, hence, subject to loss).

The second danger situation is sensed with accompanying anxiety by the child somewhere around the age of 18 months. It comes with the realization by the child that the gratification of his desires is dependent upon the love and good-will of the significant persons in his environment. The discovery of the importance of the love of the significant persons for the continuance of gratification arises, like the earlier form of signal anxiety, out of frustration. In this instance, frustration is perceived by the ego of the child (whether this is objectively true or not) as withdrawal of the significant person's (still, usually, the mother's) love.

Toward the end of the third year of life, as the child moves into the phallic stage of development, the new focus of anxiety becomes his genitals. Frustration and punishment come to center in his newly-discovered source of gratification. He now fears that the significant persons in his environment will destroy this source of pleasure.

The final typical danger situation brought out by Freud comes, of course, with the development of the superego after the age of five or six years. Here the signal of danger comes from within. The threats of punishment which formerly came from the significant persons in the external environment now come from the child's internalization of these persons in the form of his superego.

Freud held that all of these dangers persist unconsciously, at least to some degree, throughout the life of the individual. The relative importance of each danger varies from person to person. Not only is some degree of each type of anxiety found in normal adults, but a high amount of one or more of the types is observable in every emotionally disturbed individual.

With the introduction of the structural hypothesis of the psyche in the early twenties, the main focus of psychoanalysis changed from concentration on the vicissitudes of the libido to centering of attention on manifestations of anxiety. In the earlier theory, as we have brought out, Freud felt that the psychoneuroses were a result of libidinal fixations at the various pregenital stages, and, hence, the principal concern of the clinical analyst was to undo fixations and to help patients adequately to discharge libido through mature, genital channels. Such earlier concern about the activities of the libido has not been entirely displaced by explorations of anxiety, but there is considerably less emphasis on the detailed and almost exclusive tracing of infantile sexual development. Stated in another way, the almost undivided concern of Freud and his followers with unconscious instinctive development (then felt to be entirely sexual) has been broadened to include a great deal of concern with the ego and its failures, especially as manifested through anxiety. What was largely a psychology of the id has been expanded to make room also for a psychology of the ego.

Freud also came to distinguish three types of anxiety: real or objective anxiety, neurotic anxiety, and moral anxiety. In objective anxiety, the source of the danger is external to the individual. He is threatened, for example, with a loss of his job or his wife or his house or his life. In neurotic anxiety, the threat of danger resides in the id. The person is anxious about being overwhelmed by an uncontrollable urge to commit some act or think some thought which his ego defines as harmful. Moral anxiety is identified as a threat from the superego: that is, anxiety about being punished by one's conscience for doing or thinking something which is contrary to the moral standards the person holds.

The foregoing discussion of the Freudian conception of anxiety may be misleading in several ways that we must try to avoid. First, it must be realized that the individual is almost never accurately aware (other than through the help of the therapist in the treatment setting) of the real sources of his anxiety. In neurotic anxiety, for example, the individual may say that he does not care to learn to dance because he thinks dancing is sinful. But unconsciously he may be afraid that in a situation of close contact with a member of the opposite sex, his id impulses (in this case, the sexual impulse) will overwhelm him and lead him to make overt sexual advances. Or, in moral anxiety, the individual may say that he will not learn to swim because it is a futile expenditure of energy. He may unconsciously, however, feel that in such a situation his superego will seize the opportunity of punishing him for his sins by causing him to drown.

Second, such distinctions among types of anxiety (objective, neurotic, moral) were made by Freud largely for the convenience of study and discussion. He realized that in actual life situations, two or more of the types are generally blended.

Third, the emphasis on anxiety in emotional disturbance should not be taken to mean that Freud thought all anxiety was pathological. Quite to the contrary, Freud contended that only by anxiety could the individual learn to become aware of dangers from within and without and thus proceed with normal development. A person without anxiety would be unable to learn how to fend off external dangers and would be at the mercy of every instinctual impulse that arose within him.

The three chief forms taken by what Freud called neurotic anxiety are (1) free-floating, (2) phobic, and (3) panic. The free-floating type of anxiety is characteristic of the "nervous" person who is constantly apprehensive about impending disaster. The anxiety is often vague and unfixed, or, if temporarily centered on something, quite transitory. Such a person, according to Freud's theory, is actually afraid of his own id. He is constantly apprehensive of the possibility that aggressive and/or sexual impulses will overwhelm his ego controls. He is not conscious, however, of this source of his anxiety.

The phobic type of anxiety derives from the same unconscious source (fear of instinctual forces) as free-floating anxiety, but is characterized by specific, intense, irrational fear. The outstanding attribute of the phobia is that the person's anxiety is out of all proportion to the actual danger in the object or situation to which the apprehension is attached. The person may have a phobia about closed places like small rooms, trains, elevators (claustrophobia); open spaces like fields, large dance-halls or auditoriums (agrophobia); high places like tall buildings, cliffs, airplanes (acrophobia); or mice, birds, snakes, water, bugs, and practically every other thing imaginable.

In each instance, the person can give a more or less plausible reason for his phobic reaction to the particular object or situation ("mice bite"; "bugs carry germs"; "elevators break down"; etc.), but the objective danger is either imaginary or very slight in relation to the degree of fear manifested. Freud found in analytical treatment of patients that the particular objects to which phobias are attached represent some temptation to or association with instinctual gratification. An obvious example would be the association of snakes with the phallic symbol: hence, fear of snakes would be associated unconsciously with fear of being overwhelmed by the sexual impulse. Moral anxiety, Freud pointed out, is often an additional complication of the neurotic anxiety of the phobia, for the feared id impulse would be, if expressed, contrary to the moral standards of the individual.

Panic anxiety apparently arises when the individual senses that his id impulses are about to break through the controls he has assembled. The person feels panic when this is about to happen. He may fully act out the sexual or aggressive impulses (for example, commit rape, "shoot up the town," jump in front of a passing automobile), or he may discharge the id impulse in some less extreme way (steal from the corner grocery, "tell off" the boss, get drunk, or use aggressive or sexual language). The person temporarily rids himself of excessive and unendurably painful anxiety by doing (more or less) what the id demands. Such panic reactions (unless the form of acting out is very mild) usually evoke punishment from the environment, but such punishment is often welcomed by the individual who has panicked. The id impulses he was unable to control will now be controlled, he feels with relief, by external forces; and the guilt feelings which arise from his superego regarding his "bad" actions are mollified by punishment. Hence, both neurotic and moral anxiety feelings are thus relieved by the administering of external punishment. The simplest illustration of this is the child who acts out "being bad" until he is punished and then proceeds contentedly with his play after punishment has been administered.

The centering of attention on anxiety and the ego's role in handling anxiety led to a closer examination of the defenses the ego normally and abnormally develops against the id impulses. Freud noted that there were the general defenses, such as a change in focus of attention, the formation of a fantasy, the furtherance of a safer and better-controlled id impulse in place of the feared one, and the neutralization of the energy of the dangerous drive. There are other more specific defense mechanisms used by the ego against the impulses of the id. While lists of these mechanisms vary among

Freudians, some of the most common are repression, rationalization, projection, introjection, regression, turning against the self, isolation, thought dissociation, reaction formation, and denial of reality. All of these defense mechanisms operate to some degree in normal behavioral development and functioning as well as in pathological conditions. Although we shall briefly discuss each mechanism singly, they often function in plurality.

The defense mechanism first recognized by Freud, and still considered the most basic, is repression. Repression is the activity of the ego which keeps the undesirable id impulse (or any feeling, wish, memory, or fantasy associated with it) from entering consciousness. Freud believed that the repressed material continues to be charged with a cathexis of psychic energy which constantly presses toward fulfillment. The ego, on the other side, maintains the repression by a counter-cathexis, an expenditure of energy opposed to the id impulse. If the cathexis increases in strength or the counter-cathexis weakens, the repressed material will emerge into consciousness. This may happen in several ways, one of which we just discussed as panic anxiety. In sleep (in the form of dreams) and in such toxic states as acute alcoholism, there is also a temporary reduction of the ego's counter-cathexis and, hence, the partial emergence of repressed id impulses. Severe frustration can also bring an increase in id cathexis and a decrease in ego counter-cathexis. Puberty is also notable for bringing an increase in the intensity of the sexual drive (and possibly also the aggressive drive) with resulting break-through of id material that had been successfully repressed in childhood.

Another common defense mechanism is rationalization. When an undesirable id impulse moves into consciousness, the ego quickly changes the nature of the thought or feeling in order to make it more acceptable. If, as a result of an aggressive impulse of destruction for a hated business associate, an individual breaks a confidence the associate made to him and gets the associate fired for some misdemeanor, his ego cannot bear to face the real motivation for his action. He rationalizes. That is, he finds ego-comforting things to say to himself (and perhaps others) about his behavior; he finds "good" reasons to substitute for the real reasons: morality comes before friendship; confidentiality should not stand in the way of justice; "it hurt me more than it did him"; loyalty to the company comes ahead of loyalty to a friend; "I did it for his own good, because remaining unpunished would have led him to worse actions in the future"; "he is more fortunate than the rest of us, for we are still stuck in this horrible place"; etc. A rationalization is likely to contain some truth in general and possibly even in the particular situation (otherwise the ego couldn't be convinced of the "truth" of a rationalization). It is, however, not relevant to the person's actual motive for doing something. The ego is thus protected from coming "face to face" with the real motive.

A third type of defense mechanism is projection. Here the individual protects his ego from recognition of an undesirable id impulse by relocating the impulse in another person. *A* is projecting when he imputes to *B* the particular impulse which he, *A,* unconsciously feels. The woman, for example, who is fighting to keep repressed a strong desire to engage in illicit sexual relations may protect her ego from being overwhelmed by such an id impulse by projecting the impulse to men as a group. Every male then becomes for this woman a potential rapist and, hence, to be avoided in all but the most public and protected situations.

Introjection is the reverse of projection. Here the ego defends itself against the unconscious pressures of the id by identifying itself with another person. If our woman of the preceding paragraph identifies herself with a seductive movie actress, for example, she can partially achieve wish fulfillment by this route and thus temporarily reduce her libidinal cathexis. By taking in (introjecting) the sexy actress, she partially fulfills her sex wish by "being" the actress in the embrace of the hero. She still, however, successfully keeps out of consciousness the fact that she even has such a sexual desire.

A fifth mechanism of defense is regression. We have already discussed this process in Chapter 2 in connection with the early Freudian theory of infantile sexuality and accompanying pathological developments. It is, in addition, often employed as a means of protecting the ego from being overwhelmed by id impulses. If the ego is unable because of severe anxiety to handle adjustment problems at the genital level, for example, there may be a reverting of a great deal of libinal energy to, say, the anal stage. Such a person might be one who has repressed all sexual feeling in a genital sense (becoming frigid or impotent), has largely isolated himself from his fellow human beings (especially of the opposite sex), and has devoted himself exclusively to the life of a sculptor. An example of a less extreme and more transitory regression to an oral point of libidinal fixation would be the angry person who "cools off" by smoking a cigarette (thus checking the aggressive id impulse).

A defense mechanism which is generally seen only in children and the emotionally disturbed is called turning against the self. If the child feels an aggressive impulse toward some respected (and feared) person like a teacher or a parent and dares not express (or even consciously admit) such an impulse, he may strike or berate himself. Often introjection accompanies turning against the self. The child is, in effect, temporarily being the hated parent and thus striking the parent as he strikes himself. But the ego is spared, and the aggressive impulse is reduced without being openly directed toward the parent.

Seventh in our list of ego defenses is what Freud called isolation of affect. It may be considered a particular type of repression, where memory or fantasy of some painful past experience is readily accessible to the consciousness, but the feeling (generally pain) has been dissociated. That is, instead of a complete repression of some past event, only the emotion connected with the event is kept out of consciousness. Thus, the ego is protected from the id impulse by having the emotional power of the impulse repressed. By analogy, the usual form of complete repression is to remove from consciousness the whole memory of some "horrible monster" in the id. By the mechanism of isolation, the monster appears in consciousness, but all his horror has been removed.

A somewhat related form of ego defense (which Freud also referred to as "isolation," but for which, to avoid confusion, we use another term) is thought dissociation. It is marked by momentary "mental blankness." When the ego wishes to protect itself from a thought that carries with it dangerous id impulses, it dissociates this thought from thoughts that preceded it and thoughts which follow it. Thus deprived of associations, the dreaded thought will have difficulty re-entering consciousness.

Reaction formation is a ninth and allegedly much more common defense mechanism. As brought out in Chapter 2, ambivalence often exists regarding persons with whom the individual interacts. One of the ambivalent feelings (the feared one) is rendered unconscious and kept that way by an overemphasis on the other. This is reaction formation. The ego is protected from the threatened aggressive impulses of the id toward the child, the parent, the mate, and other significant persons by *conscious* feelings of love, protection, tenderness, gentleness, and so on.

The tenth and final defense mechanism which we shall discuss is denial of reality. Such denial is most readily observable in severe pathological conditions. For example, it is common for persons who have suffered paralysis as a result of a brain injury to deny the reality of their paralysis. Even if the paralyzed limb is brought into their area of vision, they "don't see" the limb at all, or fail to recognize its paralyzed state, or even claim that it is the limb of some person other than the patient. The ego is thus being protected from facing the disagreeable state of reality: namely, the paralysis. Less obviously than in this example of objectively recognizable paralysis, the ego uses the denial mechanism to protect itself from external stimuli that are associated with dangerous id impulses. Denial of reality may be considered a special form of repression that prevents admission to consciousness of external stimuli that point to the existence of dread id impulses.

It is not possible for us to proceed in even summary fashion with the application of the later Freudian theories to the specific pathological conditions met with in the clinic. We must confine ourselves to an indication of the broad outline of change in emphasis that the new theories made in Freudian treatment of emotional disturbances. In general, either excessive frustration or over-indulgence in the early years of life lead to the development of a weak ego, and a weak ego makes for serious pathological difficulties. A strongly frustrated or overindulged ego does not learn its main task of mediating between the id and external reality. In severe and constant frustration, the id impulses are given little opportunity for even indirect satisfaction, and, hence, the full psychic energy available to the ego is utilized in the task of repression. This leaves the ego ineffectual for dealing with external reality. In over-indulgence, the id impulses are easily gratified, and the ego never sufficiently develops. This is true because it is only out of meeting frustration (in moderate amounts) and learning how to handle it that the ego develops its strengths and skills in relation to external reality. The overindulged, like the overly frustrated, id produces a sick, weak ego.

Just as the ego can become seriously incapacitated, problems can develop in the individual's superego. The whole Oedipal struggle may not be successfully resolved. The superego, aware of strong unresolved lust for one parent and destructive tendencies toward the other, may be exceedingly harsh in its judgment of every act of the individual. Such a person is constantly ridden with guilt and inferiority feelings. He tends to be a neurotic perfectionist with a self-evaluation of being a miserable failure (whatever may be his external successes). Or the Oedipal struggle may misfire in the other direction: an unduly lenient superego may develop. This type of individual will develop pathological patterns as a result of insufficient moral standards. The extreme form of this latter malady would be the so-called sociopathic or psychopathic personality.

When a relatively stable balance among the ego, id, and superego is achieved, the existing state, in Freudian terms, constitutes the person's character structure. If the person seems relatively happy and well-adapted to his environment, his character structure may be considered healthy or normal. If his capacity for pleasure is relatively restricted and his adaptation to his environment is relatively impaired, he is said to have a pathological character structure (or a character disorder or a character neurosis).

A psychoneurosis, as distinguished from a character neurosis, may be understood in terms of the later Freudian theories as the ego's failure to control the id impulses. None of the ego's ordinary defenses are sufficiently strong to prevent a break-through of undesirable id impulses. The ego, in the course of an acute and desperate conflict with the id, works out what Freud referred to as a "compromise formation." The compromise formation unconsciously expresses both the id impulse and the ego reaction and constitutes what, in contemporary parlance, is called a psychosomatic symptom. Vomiting, for example, may represent a pregnant mother's unacceptable id impulse to destroy an unwanted child and the ego's partial success in preventing the expression of this impulse. That is, the compromise formation of vomiting gives partial vent to the id's desire to get rid of this child, but also represents the ego's success in curbing full expression of (and even consciousness of) the destructive impulse. (It is not here suggested that there may not be physiological reasons of an entirely different sort for vomiting in some instances of its occurrence in pregnancy.) In addition to such psychosomatic expressions of compromise formations between id and ego in psychoneurosis, there is the intensive and habitual employment of one or more of the special defense mechanisms we have discussed (such as regression, projection, denial of reality, introjection, etc.).

The success of psychoanalysis in the treatment of the psychoneuroses and the character neuroses varies with many factors according to Freud and his followers. In general, the greatest success seems to be obtained with young adults and with persons who feel the greatest dissatisfaction with or discomfort in the neurotic states. Failure is by no means rare even in these groups.

Although Freud's theories grew chiefly out of his observations in the course of an active clinical practice, psychoanalytic therapy also followed the pattern of theoretical development. When Freud first discovered the influence of the unconscious on the behavior of the individual, therapy consisted primarily in bringing repressed material into consciousness. Many psychoanalysts today remain strongly under the influence of the early theory and still insist that the main job of an analysis is that of rendering unconscious content and process conscious. As Freud himself (considerably greater in flexibility than some of his followers) developed the structural theory of the psyche, however, he increasingly realized that the ego must undergo changes in order to become capable of handling the repressed material brought up in the free associations. The emphasis in therapy, therefore, came to be placed more and more on resistance (the ego defenses as they related to the individual's inability to face and handle unconscious wishes which appeared in the course of the analysis) and transference as the means of overcoming such resistance and helping the ego to utilize psychic energy which had been going into the major ego defenses (especially repression). The relationship of the analyst to the patient was increasingly recognized as essential as the effect of the newer Freudian theories came to be felt in psychoanalytic practice. Much of the recent psychoanalytic work has dealt not only with transference (that is, the displacements of feelings from significant persons in the patient's past to the therapist), but counter-transference (that is, the displacements of past feelings of the therapist's relationships with others to the present patient).

Freud in his later work emphasized the corrective influence of the objective, non-evaluative attitude of the analyst. As the patient relives his childhood experiences in the therapeutic situation, change in his attitudes is effected because he has never before experienced objective reactions to his behavior. The patient will be able to face what he formerly repressed because of the censure of significant persons in his past. While insight is still considered important, the corrective emotional experience of the therapy itself has been increasingly stressed as the means whereby the individual's ego can have the strength to handle the formerly repressed material in an integrative fashion.

It should be realized that we have tried to confine our discussion of Freudian psychoanalysis largely to the theories of normal and pathological behavior and to the clinical procedures related to these theories. There are many other theories and applications of psychoanalysis made by Freud and his followers. Freud turned his attention to numerous aspects of society and activities of various groups within society. He and others of his persuasion have made provocative studies of art, science, literature, religion, war, and many other social phenomena. Such matters as these, however, are out of the range of our consideration.

Summary

From 1900 to 1923, Freud developed three somewhat separate theories of the general nature of the psyche. The last of these, called the structural hypothesis, brought about many important changes in psychoanalytic theory and practice. Freud expanded his conception of the basic instincts to include an aggressive drive (death instinct) as well as the sexual drive. The id, according to the structural hypothesis, became the psychic representation of these basic drives or instincts and their derivatives. The ego is the mediator between the id and external reality, and the superego comprises the individual's moral precepts and ideal aspirations. The ego begins to form about the sixth month of life, but the superego does not develop until the fifth or sixth year, as a result of the Oedipal struggle.

Later Freudian theory and practice concentrated much attention on the role of anxiety. Freud proposed that anxiety appeared in two sets of circumstances, "traumatic situations" and "danger situations." The birth trauma stands as a prototype of the former. Typical danger situations which evoke signal anxiety are loss of the loved object, loss of the object's love, loss of or injury to the genitals, and disapproval and punishment by the superego. Freud held that these typical dangers and their accompanying anxiety persist unconsciously throughout the life of the individual. He also distinguished objective or reality anxiety, neurotic anxiety, and moral anxiety. Neurotic anxiety was further subdivided into free-floating, phobic, and panic.

The centering of attention on anxiety and the ego's role in handling anxiety led to a closer examination of the defenses the ego develops against id impulses. Ten special defense mechanisms are considered: repression, rationalization, projection, introjection, regression, turning against the self, isolation, thought dissociation, reaction formation, and denial of reality. All of these defense mechanisms operate in both normal and abnormal behavioral development and functioning.

One of the results of the new Freudian theories was that in practice psychoanalysis became less exclusively a study of unconscious processes and developed increasing interest in the activities of the ego and superego. Many pathologies could now be understood in terms of the malfunctioning of these latter two aspects of personality. In general, distinction was now made in Freudian terms between a character neurosis (where the balance among the ego, id, and superego is such that the person's capacity for pleasure is relatively restricted and his adaptation to his environment is relatively impaired) and a psychoneurosis (partial failure of the ego to control the id impulses). As psychoanalytic clinical practice has proceeded increasingly with applications of ego psychology, more and more emphasis has been placed on the importance of the relationship between the analyst and the patient and on the corrective influence of the relatively objective therapeutic situation itself.

Selected Readings

Fenichel, Otto, *The Psychoanalytic Theory of the Neuroses*. New York: Norton, 1945.

Freud, Anna, *The Ego and the Mechanisms of Defense* (translated by C. M. Baines). New York: Int. Univs., 1946.

Freud, Sigmund, *A General Introduction to Psychoanalysis* (translated by Joan Riviere). New York: Garden City, 1943.

————, *Beyond the Pleasure Principle* (translated by James Strachey). New York: Liveright, 1950.

————, *New Introductory Lectures on Psychoanalysis* (translated by J. H. Sprott). New York: Norton, 1933.

————, *The Ego and the Id* (translated by Joan Riviere). London: Hogarth Press, 1935.

————, *The Problem of Anxiety* (translated by H. A. Bunker). New York: Norton, 1936.

Jones, Ernest, *The Life and Work of Sigmund Freud*, Vols. II and III. New York: Basic Books, 1955 and 1957.

CHAPTER 4

Deviations in Psychoanalysis: I

As we noted in Chapter 3, Freud showed considerable flexibility in his own thinking and was never hesitant to change his theories in the light of newly-discovered facts. But he was often less than generous in the consideration he gave to new and independent hypotheses developed by some of his followers. Some of the men Freud attracted, however, were ill-suited for the role of compliant pupil. The result was a succession of schisms in the psychoanalytic movement. In this chapter, we'll consider six foremost pupils of Freud who departed from his teachings and, in varying degrees, set up systems of their own.

A. ADLER

Alfred Adler was the first of Freud's pupils to break with the master (in 1911). Adler rejected the sexual etiology of neurosis and contended that feelings of inferiority were the true cause. Adler stated that Freud and his followers were misled by the "jargon" of neurotic patients into believing that sex lay at the root of their difficulties. Patients, Adler held, were really expressing a compulsion in the direction of the "masculine goal" by their sexual fantasies and sexual feelings. Masculinity represents strength and power in Adler's system, and femininity symbolizes weakness and inferiority. "Masculine protest" is common in both men and women (but especially the latter) and is a striving for power. Instead of sex, according to Adler, the search for power determines human actions and development.

Everyone develops some sense of inferiority, Adler pointed out, because he is born completely helpless and remains relatively weak and dependent during a long childhood. Such basic inferiority can be exaggerated by body or organ defects (whether real or imaginary), by having older and more powerful siblings, parental rejection or neglect, and by many other factors. One way to cope with feelings of inferiority is by compensatory action: gaining power to overcome the sense of weakness. This aggressive or masculine reaction often leads to considerable success in terms of recognized achievement in some area of life, some accomplishment of power over one's fellows. The second way of coping with feelings of inferiority is more easily recognizable as neurotic: the submissive or feminine patterns of denial or retreat. Such retreat or denial may take the form of fantasies, psychosomatic illnesses, projections, rationalizations, denials of reality, and other defense mechanisms which we considered within the Freudian frame of reference in Chapter 3.

Adler felt that a person's development was conditioned by his social environment rather than by biological forces and insisted that an individual could be analyzed and understood in terms of his present purposes or life goals rather than in terms of his infantile past. Adlerian analysis is undertaken in terms of each individual's "life plan" or "life style." Since everyone's life style is in some ways unique, Adler came to refer to his system as "individual psychology." Once the particular life style of the individual is fully understood, the job of the therapist is to re-educate the patient to what are believed to be healthier patterns and goals. Adler emphasized social feelings and community interests and service as goals that therapy could put in the place of less desirable strivings for power.

Sex to Adler was simply a handy weapon available to the individual in his struggle to gain power over others. He saw the Oedipus complex as being of secondary importance and symptomatic of the struggle of the child (in actuality or in fantasy) to gain power over the parent. Only the pampered child, according to Adler, fails to resolve his Oedipal conflict as a result of his timidity about extending his sexual power to someone other than the over-indulging parent.

Adlerian therapists (of whom a fair number exists in New York, Chicago, Los Angeles, and principal European cities) follow Adler's example in minimizing unconscious forces and in exploring past events only insofar as they cast initial insight on the patient's life style. Just as the unconscious and its sexual manifestations are not stressed, correspondingly less emphasis (than that of the Freudians) is placed on the importance of transference. It is only when strong feelings are displaced from significant persons in the patient's life onto the therapist in a way that blocks therapeutic progress that the individual psychologist gives any attention to transference phenomena.

Adler was the first psychotherapist to place high value on the social relationship between the therapist and the patient. He believed that this relationship could serve as a re-educative bridge to other relationships. He held that all individuals who fail are deficient in concern and love for their fellow human beings, and he devoted most of his energy in therapy to the attempt at increasing the social interest of the patient. The disturbed person, Adler thought, had a private and irrational meaning for life that stops short of deep and positive feeling for others. The therapist's job, then, as Adler saw it, was to help the individual to substitute realistic for unrealistic life goals and to instill social interest and feeling.

As already implied, Adler's treatment procedures were greatly different from those he had learned from Freud. He dispensed with the couch and substituted face to face sitting positions. He assumed an active, teaching role as therapist. He used dream interpretation largely to cast further light on present life style and future life goals. Interruptions of the patient were frequent, for Adler conceived the therapist's responsibility that of pointing out self-deceptive tendencies to the patient. Hence, free association gave way to a therapist-directed interview. Patients were usually seen three or four times a week (compared with the Freudian five or six), and a much shorter total term of treatment (than the Freudian) was the general rule.

B. STEKEL

Wilhelm Stekel broke with Freud after Adler and shortly before Jung. He lacked both the systematic organization in his writings and the temperament in his interpersonal relations to develop a well-knit school of followers. He has, however, had some influence (sometimes uncredited) on the development of psychotherapy in the

United States. Stekel's contributions were primarily in technique, rather than theory, but he made several original theoretical changes in psychoanalysis. Stekel's intuitive skills in dream interpretation influenced Freud in his adoption of various symbols. Stekel was also a pioneer observer and writer on the subject of sex, normal and pathological, and many of his views hold up well in the light of modern sex research.

The patient's current conflicts were as important as past conflicts in the Stekelian approach. Like Adler, Stekel felt that the Freudians were too preoccupied with the patient's past to give proper attention to the present. In some cases, Stekel contended, the patient could be helped without any recourse to the distant past. Even in those instances where past conflicts were important, current conflicts, he felt, also needed a great deal of the analyst's attention.

Stekel anticipated some of the recent Freudian emphasis on character analysis and counter-transference (see Chapter 3). He asserted that the future of psychoanalysis rested in the development of a growing understanding of the character structure of the patient and emphasized a close relationship between the specific personality characteristics of the patient and the main trends and tendencies of his psychoneurotic condition. Although he did not discuss counter-transference as such, Stekel frequently stressed that the personality of the analyst is the decisive factor in the progress of the therapy. He maintained that the personality of the therapist, rather than his particular method, is of greatest curative significance.

Stekel stated that his emphasis on his role as a therapist and his responsibility to try to cure the patients who came to him was the factor that sharply distinguished his procedures from those of Freud. The latter, Stekel said, seemed to be more interested in advancing his theories and techniques than in helping a particular patient. Stekel held that Freud considered himself first a scientist and secondly a therapist and that he, Stekel, had a reversed priority. Freud's guide was mainly: "What can I learn from this patient about the psychological nature of human beings?" Stekel's standard was: "How can I cure this patient?"

However much truth one wishes to place in Stekel's evaluation of Freud, he seemed to have a correct perspective of his own chief focus of interest. His concentration on the curative process as such seems to account for most of his innovations in technique. He came to take a more and more active role in the therapeutic process in an effort to achieve a cure more speedily and effectively. Appropriately enough, Stekel referred to his procedures as "active analytic psychotherapy."

The analyst, as Stekel conceived him, is an active partner throughout therapy. He collaborates from the outset with the patient in the interpretation of his free associations and dreams. He may intervene in the course of the patient's association to suggest more detailed discussion of what the therapist considers a significant point. Or he may recommend the dropping of a certain line of association as nonfruitful or indicative of resistance. Stekel emphasized the importance of intuitive listening in the therapist. He believed that intuition was a combination of sympathy and imaginative insight and could be acquired by special effort and training. By the use of intuition, Stekel maintained, the therapist could be aware of the appropriate timing of interventions to break down the patient's resistances to insight.

Stekel did not even avoid occasional exhortation and direct advice, but he stressed the patient's own responsibility in all decision making. Although Stekel himself was apparently quite authoritarian in his attack on patients' resistances, his followers (of whom Emil A. Gutheil is the best known in the United States) tend to be more permissive and objective in their approach to active analysis.

Much of Stekel's intuitive analysis was focused on the dreams brought in by his patients. He felt that his own demonstrable skill in dream interpretation was no particular gift, but, like other aspects of intuition, something that could be developed by an analyst who devoted himself to the task. Stekel was primarily interested in current attitudes and responses of the patient as revealed in dreams and was concerned with past dream events only in the sense of throwing light on the patient's basic characterological difficulties. His basic agreement with Adler is here apparent.

Although Stekel recognized transference as a part of every analysis, he felt it seldom became a major problem in active analytic psychotherapy because the therapist is constantly demolishing patients' illusions and their childish displacements of emotion. He felt that enough positive transference would automatically develop toward a successful active therapist (simply out of gratitude of the patient for improvements felt by him) to help the patient to face some of the difficult tasks of the analysis. But, since the active analyst foresees a limited relationship (rarely more than six months was required by Stekel's methods), he does not encourage the patient to develop the fantasy of a permanent romantic relationship (which, Stekel held, is often the case in classical psychoanalysis).

As already indicated, present-day followers of Stekel have not held rigidly to his teachings. They have, in fact, contended that the essence of the Stekelian approach is activity and flexibility, that many of Stekel's ideas have been adopted freely into current psychoanalysis of other "schools," and that they themselves feel free to adopt ideas from various non-Stekelian sources. Most contemporary active psychoanalytic therapists do not hold rigidly to the six-month limitation on the length of therapy, are less authoritarian than Stekel in their approach to patients, and place less emphasis on the strictly intuitive aspects of analytic interpretation.

C. JUNG

The deviations of Adler and Stekel were, as we have seen, in the general direction of greater directness and simplicity in theories and techniques than those expounded by Freud. The departure of Carl Jung led to the development of a system more esoteric and complicated than that of Freud.

Jung's complete break with Freud came in 1912, but he had not been as wholehearted in his acceptance of the Freudian views from the very beginning as had some of Freud's followers. Jung's increasingly independent ideas reached a point of irreparable rupture with his publication, in 1912, of a new interpretation of the nature of the libido (*The Psychology of the Unconscious*).

It is interesting to observe that in terms of our own historical perspective a substantial portion of the difference in the Freudian and Jungian conceptions of libido seems to be a matter of words and not basic concepts. The "primal" libido, according to Jung, is undifferentiated energy, a universal "life urge." Early in the history of the human race, however, Jung said, the libido was primarily sexual in nature, but became desexualized in the course of human evolution and could no longer be reconverted into sexual energy. Jung particularly rejected the notion that the sucking of the infant is any way sexual in nature. But Freud had said (see Chapter 2) that there were four stages of development of libidinal fixation, characterized by certain zones in which a major portion of psychic energy (libido) focused: the oral, anal, phallic, and genital. Since, Freud said, the same psychic energy that focuses genitally in the adult is manifesting itself in the three earlier stages, it is proper and convenient to conceive of the libido as sexual from infancy onward. Jung, on the other hand, said that this energy had a neutral quality (as a result of an evolutionary desexualizing process) and took on the characteristics of the zones into which it flowed and fixated itself: hence, the libido was hunger, not sex, at the oral stage. To paraphrase, we have this situation: Freud said the libido is observable in A, B, C, and D stages; since it is the same libido that finally reaches fruition in D (genitally fixated sex), we shall call it D (sex) from the very beginning. Jung said that the libido is an X (neutral) force that flows through various stages and that it is improper to call it by the name of any particular stage. But, by and large, the two men seemed to have the same fundamental life force in mind.

So sensitive was Freud, however, to the many resistances and condemnations of the sexual aspects of his theory that he could not have been expected to accept Jung's desexualized description of the libido. Neither he nor Jung recognized that the differences between their theories were largely semantic. And it may be that Freud was right that Jung and his followers found that a desexualized libido was both personally and publicly more palatable, especially in the concentration of Jungian interest in religious and ethical phenomena.

In like manner, Jung's interpretations of the Oedipus complex and the Electra complex (a term he used to refer to the affection of the girl for her father and jealousy toward her mother) indicate a departure from Freudian thinking which is greater in words than in substance. Jung does emphasize the early hunger-satisfying (not, he contends, sexual) pleasure that the mother provides the child, but he does admit that the love of the child for the mother develops a sexual characteristic as the infant matures. The nature of the Oedipus complex thus becomes very similar in Jung's view to that of Freud's.

Although Jung substantially adopted many of Freud's concepts, his emphasis in both theory and therapy was different from Freud's. Jung was mainly interested in the purposive, goal-striving interpretations of behavior rather than the causative sources. To this extent his point of view resembled Adler. Jung considered the Oedipus complex, for example, along with the whole sexuality of the unconscious, as a symbol with a prospective, not retrospective, reference. Although the behavior of the individual, including his Oedipal strivings, arise from an earlier mode of adaptation to life, it signifies, according to Jung, a step forward on the road to various life purposes. Unlike Adler, however, who sought to understand the specific life purposes of the unique individual, Jung visualized various collective life purposes, which strike most non-Jungians as vague, non-testable, mystical.

Jung observed that the symbolic productions of disturbed persons resembled those of primitive people. From this he speculated that there must be an hereditary portion of the mind that contained the imprints of ancestral experience. He therefore hypothesized the existence of a collective unconscious. Jung thought he could see primordial images, which he called "archetypes," in associations, fantasies, drawings and dreams. The most common of these archetypes, Jung held, were the Animus, the mate ideal of the female psyche, and the Anima, the mate ideal of the male psyche. Along with the collective unconscious (and its contained archetypes), Jung further subdivided the human psyche into the persona (the superficial social mask of the individual which he presents to others in his social relationships) and the ego (a deeper part of the psyche which is reflective of personal experiences and is partly conscious and partly unconscious).

Emotional disturbance develops in an individual, according to Jung, whenever disharmony develops among the persona, the ego, and the collective unconscious and also whenever the masculine Animus gets out of balance with the feminine Anima. Whenever a person becomes too extreme in his personality sub-type of introversion (interests centered in himself) or of extroversion (interests centered in the external world), he is also likely to become emotionally disturbed.

Jung, like Adler and Stekel, used dream interpretations chiefly for an aid to understanding current difficulties and future strivings more than past unconscious sources of psychic problems. Also similarly to the two previous deviants, Jung made free association secondary to specific focusing of the interview along lines considered significant by the therapist. Jung also contended that the quantity and quality of the therapist's interpretations should vary with the personality type of the patient: introverts need extensive, detailed, and refined interpretation, and extroverts are satisfied if the prescribed behavioral change improves their adjustment and are less interested in the dynamic causations of the change.

Jung may, with Stekel, be considered a forerunner of the contemporary emphasis in psychoanalysis on counter-transference, the analyst's own problems, and the ability of the analyst to learn from the patient. He likewise anticipated Rank and some of the later deviants in stressing the positive and creative aspects of personality which can be brought out in therapy and in seeing the constructive importance of the therapist-patient interactions.

Probably more than in any other system of psychotherapy, however, it is difficult for the outsider to see how the Jungian theory sheds much light on actual human behavior or how the theory functions in the therapeutic situation. Patients are undoubtedly helped by the interest and constructive suggestions of the Jungian therapist about current life difficulties, and Jungians show for the importance and integrity of the individual patients a respect not always so evident in some other practitioners. But just how the various metaphysical and mystical interpretations of the alleged parts of the individual's psyche contribute help to the patient is not at all clear. The system has the quality of an esoteric religion, and it seems at times to take the patient away from reality and to encourage the development of a mystical fantasy life.

The Jungian analytical psychology did not develop many followers in the United States. Indirectly, however, some of Jung's ideas have become absorbed into contemporary psychotherapy. His influence on Rank, Horney, and Fromm, and their influence in turn on the American psychoanalytic movement, has been considerable.

D. RANK

Otto Rank joined Freud's inner circle of Viennese followers while still a very young student and remained for many years one of Freud's closest associates. Around 1920, however, Rank began to experiment with short-term therapy, activity versus passivity in the analytic situation, and related technical issues. Soon thereafter he began to expound theoretical changes in psychoanalysis that grew out of his clinical innovations. A break developed between Freud and Rank, and Rank moved from Vienna to Paris (and later to New York).

Rank can in some ways be considered, with Stekel, a forerunner of the present-day advocates of short-term psychoanalytic therapy. His theories have also contributed importantly to the Philadelphia or the "functional" (as distinguished from the Freudian-based "diagnostic") school in social casework and to client-centered or non-directive therapy (to be discussed in Chapter 6). Rank's orientation also tended to emphasize social relationships in the etiology of mental illness much more than did Freud's, so he may be considered a precursor of such "dynamic-culturalists" in psychoanalysis as Horney and Fromm.

Rank's most devastating attack on established psychoanalytic theory came with his publication in 1924 of his *Trauma of Birth*. Here Rank introduced a mother-centered conception of fear, anxiety, dependency, and insecurity. He contended that the birth trauma was more important then the Oedipus complex as a source of emotional disturbance. He also questioned the passive role of the analyst in therapy and argued for a more active, flexible, and creative functioning of the analyst.

Central in the Rankian theory is the conception of the will as an expression of the positive, unifying, growing, creative aspects of the individual in his movement toward independence. Blocking the positive will are the dependency strivings of the individual—the pathological tendency to "return to the womb." The Rankian analyst analyzes the birth trauma and thus helps the individual to overcome his pathological womb-returning tendencies and to release his constructive will.

Although Rank felt the analytic hour offered the patient an opportunity to live through past experiences, especially the birth trauma, his emphasis in therapy was on the present rather than the past. The patient was encouraged to assert himself in order to strengthen his own will and, through the mobilization of constructive elements in his personality, to transfer negative expression of will (which corre-

sponds to the Freudian concept of resistance) into positive and creative will.

Like Stekel, Rank reacted strongly against the "interminable"
length of classical analyses. In fact, Rank's experimentation with specific "end-setting" or "time limit" in therapy, together with the accompanying greater activity of the therapist, were the chief technical
changes out of which theoretical deviations developed.

Rank emphasized the flexible, adaptible, individual, patient-
centered nature of the therapeutic process. It was in this way that he
anticipated the later development of client-centered therapy. Rebelling against the rigid, pre-determined notions of the content of each
analysis, Rank held that every relationship between patient and therapist should be a unique and creative process and that the patient,
not the therapist, needed to point the way to his particular method
of achieving self-determination and self-direction.

The degree to which such therapeutic ideals of permissive self-
realization are truly practical in work with highly disturbed persons
has been the subject of much disputation between Rankians and other
therapists. The controversy has grown in intensity and extent with
the advent of non-directive or client-centered therapy (see Chapter
6), and the facts for its resolution are not currently discernible.

E. FERENCZI

Sandor Ferenczi may be considered a Freudian deviant mainly in
method rather than in theory. In his earlier explorations for improved
therapeutic techniques, Ferenczi was closely associated with Otto
Rank. Like Rank, Ferenczi first departed from the classical analytic
techniques by taking a more active role in therapy. In his efforts to
break down the resistance manifested by his patients, Ferenczi extremely extended the Freudian dictum of patient privation while in
analysis. Freud had recommended sexual abstinence for the patient
on the basis that the libido, deprived of sexual outlet, would concentrate itself with greater force in the past emotional experiences that
were being relived in the analytic situation. The genitals, Ferenczi
reasoned, were only one point of focus for the libido of the neurotic.
Privation of other bodily pleasures (which therefore had some libido

attachment) should, Ferenczi thought, bring all the more libido into the emotional experiences related to the analysis. He tried to persuade his patients on the basis of this hypothesis to limit to the absolute minimum such activities as eating, drinking, defecation, and urination, as well as the direct sexual outlets.

This extreme application of the privation philosophy brought violent reaction in Ferenczi's patients, and for a time he thought that the resentment and aggression thus released and directed toward him as therapist had excellent therapeutic value. After a time, however, Ferenczi became disillusioned, for he found that the hostility patients expressed was not tied in with the emotional experiences of childhood, but simply direct reaction to the difficulties of life created in the current therapeutic situation. He carried the method on for a while on a voluntary basis to see if the removal of compulsory sanctions reduced hostility toward the analyst. He finally concluded that the whole procedure was a failure.

About 1927, Ferenczi swung his experiments in psychoanalytic techniques toward the opposite extreme to stern privation: namely, love and permissiveness. In this area of technical innovation, Ferenczi achieved some lasting fame, some following, and considerable disapproval from Freud and other classical analysts. Ferenczi's changed reasoning was to the effect that neurotics are people who have never been properly loved and accepted as children by their real parents. What disturbed people most need then, as he now saw it, is a therapist who, as a substitute parent, will let them relive their childhood experiences in a completely warm, loving, permissive atmosphere.

Ferenczi was like some of the deviants before him in discovering the importance of the therapeutic relationship and of the therapist's role in that relationship. While a greater conformist in theory than the four men we have previously discussed in this chapter, Ferenczi was a greater non-conformist than any of them in some of his techniques. Just as he had been an extremist in the imposition of authoritarian asceticism, he now became an extremist in the technique of love and permissiveness. Freud was right, Ferenczi held, in his basic technique of helping the patient to relive his childhood experiences, but did not sufficiently stress the difference in the therapeutic environment in which the reliving took place. The therapist, Ferenczi said, should set himself up in as sharp a contrast as possible with the "bad" parent in relation to whom the patient developed his neurosis. The therapist should be a "good" parent who accedes to as many of the patient's wishes as possible. The therapist also, by Ferenczi's example, should admit his mistakes, blind spots, and shortcomings to demonstrate to the patient that all parents are not self-righteous, intolerant, "deity-pretending," unloving figures. By his "relaxation therapy" Ferenczi felt he opened a new world of constructive interaction for the patient.

Ferenczi's technique of permissiveness led to his acceptance (and at times active encouragement) of the patient's dramatization of childhood experiences. If the patient wanted to "act out" some phase of early childhood, for example, Ferenczi would treat him as if he were a young child and permit him to play childish games or use childish speech. He was even known to take a disturbed person who was struggling with the dramatization of some childhood conflict into his arms or lap.

As would be expected, such activities drew fire from the classical analysts, who were noted for their formality and detachment in the therapeutic situation. Freud himself was critical of Ferenczi's ideas of encouraging acting out, of giving "love," and of admitting mistakes to patients.

For an observer of today who is relatively removed from wholehearted commitment to any particular set of techniques, there seems to be both positive and negative values in Ferenczi's innovations. As Moreno has independently demonstrated (see Chapter 9), dramatization of emotional disturbances seems at times to be an effective therapeutic technique (especially in group situations). It seems doubtful, however, that its greatest value comes in individual therapeutic situations where the therapist permits himself to get emotionally involved (as Ferenczi apparently often did). The matter of "love" of the patient, too, when carried to a Ferenczi-like extreme, can evidently be a block to understanding as readily as aloofness and frigidity can. Ferenczi apparently did not understand (as Horney was later explicit in demonstrating—see Chapter 5), that love can be neurotically as well as healthily employed by the patient and the therapist. Hence, therapeutically offered "love" will not necessarily heal the patient any more than the hostility engendered by Ferenczi in his earlier methodological experiments.

Ferenczi's extreme emphasis on love, warmth, and permissiveness, did, however, gradually bring a corrective influence in many psychoanalytic circles for the opposite classical extreme of the socially distant, anonymous, coldly mysterious analyst. In like manner, Freud and some of his followers were probably too sensitive about criticism from patients and too quick to assume that any fault of an analyst pointed out by the patient was inevitably resistance and negative transference. Ferenczi did much to bring to the attention of at least some analysts that they are imperfect human beings and that it is possible that the criticism of a patient is reality-oriented. Many contemporary analysts would hold to the view that their admission of mistakes can assist, not necessarily disrupt, an analysis, but that such admission must be done judiciously and in great moderation so that the patient will not be encouraged to make hostile and defensive diversion of the analysis to the therapist's, rather than his own, problems.

Although Ferenczi himself was careful not to develop a separate theory of psychoanalysis and to precipitate an outright break with Freud, a few followers have carried on his techniques and developed some supporting theories. These theories stress the fundamental and over-riding importance of the curative effect of love and of the need of the therapist to provide love and acceptance in the therapeutic setting regardless of the hostile provocations of the patient.

F. REICH

Wilhelm Reich first broke with Freud in 1932 in a controversy over the existence of the death instinct in general and the function of such an instinct in the causation of masochism in particular. In more recent years, Reich proceeded to develop what was variously called *orgone* therapy and *vegetotherapy,* which was not only a radical departure from Freudian psychoanalysis, but from what we in this book consider psychotherapy. We shall, therefore, make no attempt to understand these later theories of Reich and shall confine ourselves to a consideration of his contributions to psychoanalysis in the special area of character analysis.

Under contemporary psychoanalytic circumstances, especially as a result of the influence of such "dynamic culturalists" as Horney, Sullivan, and Fromm, the analysis of the character structure of the patient has become fairly routine procedure. Reich, however, was the first analyst to make character a major focus of his study. Unlike the dynamic culturalists, however, who view character analysis as the main objective of therapy (because malformations of character are believed to be the heart of the neurosis), Reich viewed character analysis as a necessary obstacle-overcoming process prior to the main task of analysis. He felt the "character armor" was the major resistance put up by many patients to the analysis of their unconscious processes. Reich considered the removal of such resistance merely essential preparation for the main analysis, that is, the retracing of the vicissitudes of the libido by the process of free association. Reich, in fact, referred to the analyzing of character resistances as "education for analysis." He felt that penetration of these resistances by repeatedly calling the patient's attention to them and analyzing the sources of such negative and resistant behavior patterns as passivity, ingratiations, and over-aggressiveness, cleared the way for the release of unconscious material.

Reich was the first analyst to make considerable observation of typical postural and other physiological reaction patterns. He also pointed out how characteristic modes of response on the part of the patient (such as cynical withdrawal or acting out tendencies) can prevent effective probing of unconscious data. He showed how the ego could play one id impulse against another, so that the defensive armor could become as instinctually resistant to change and as irrational as a repressed impulse. Far from directly reflecting the libidinal structure of the patient, character by the Reichian view typically represents a reaction against powerful libidinal tendencies and, hence, is a serious block to remove from the path of the analysis.

When Reich felt that the character armor had been broken through, he would return to the more passive role of the classical analyst. In harmony with Freud's earliest formulation of the libido theory, Reich felt that the patient, no longer fettered by his character resistances, could work through the repressed infantile sexual material and thus enable the libido to make a mature (that is, genital) fixation. Reich contended that the real test of the cure of the patient was his achievement of full orgastic potency. This view can scarcely be held today with any scientific validity, for studies of schizophrenics and other highly disturbed patients indicate that some of them have full orgastic potency.

Summary

Six major deviants among the pupils of Freud were Adler, Stekel, Jung, Rank, Ferenczi, and Reich. Adler, the first to break with Freud (1911), developed what he came to call a system of individual psychology, which was based primarily on the contention that emotional disturbance arose from feelings of inferiority and represented an individual's striving for power. Adler de-emphasized sex as a factor in mental illness and stressed present life style and future life goals instead of unconscious past events. Adler also substituted a didactic, therapist-directed interview for Freudian free association with a relatively passive therapist.

Stekel is probably the least celebrated of the deviants, for he never developed a real "school" of followers. His contributions were more in technique than in theory, but he made a few contributions in the latter. From a technical standpoint, he developed what he called an "active analytic psychotherapy" in which he emphasized current as well as past conflicts, the importance of the therapist's personality and factors of counter-transference, the active intervention of the therapist, and a further development of the analytic tool of dream interpretation.

Contrasted with the more direct, simple, didactic types of deviation of Adler and Stekel, Jung's rebellion from Freudian theory and practice went in the direction of greater complications to the point of mysticism. Although bitter denunciation and counter-denunciation broke out between Jung and Freud regarding the former's desexualizing of such important Freudian concepts as the libido and the Oedipus conflict, much of the difference in these areas seems a matter of semantics rather than of substance. Jung's emphasis in both theory and therapy was different from Freud's in seeking the purposive, goal-striving interpretations of behavior rather than the causative sources. In the course of his elaborations of what he called analytical psychology, Jung developed concepts of the collective unconscious, persona, ego, animus, anima, archetypes, introverts, extroverts, etc. A few of

Jung's concepts (notably introversion and extroversion) have been adopted into the general psychological literature, but his chief lasting contribution would appear to be his focus on some of the positive and creative aspects of personality and in his influence on later deviants such as Horney and Fromm.

Rank at first experimented only with technical changes in classical analysis (including short-term therapy), but later broke with Freud and developed a new theoretical system. He made the birth trauma more significant than the Oedipus complex and, hence, centered attention on the mother, rather than the father, as most influential in the development of the individual. Rank also had a social, rather than a biological, emphasis in the theories he held about causation of both pathological and normal aspects of personality. He, like Jung, brought out the positive and creative potentialities of the individual and thought of therapy as offering the opportunity for the patient to release these potentialities (for which he used the term "will"). Rank has had a considerable influence in one framework of social casework (the "functional" school), in client-centered therapy, and, less directly, the dynamic-cultural forces in psychoanalysis.

Ferenczi, unlike the other five men discussed in this chapter, never completely broke with Freud (although Freud publicly and privately rebuked him for his deviations). He experimented at first with a more active form of authoritarianism in therapy, and then he turned to the opposite extreme of love and permissiveness. In this latter procedure, the therapist creates an environment of warmth and acceptance for the patient. This environment, because of its contrast with the neurosis-producing atmosphere of the patient's early parental home, gives him an opportunity to work through his unresolved conflicts to a mature and normal termination. In the course of such permissiveness, Ferenczi encouraged criticism of the therapist by the patient, bilateral expression of "love," and a dramatization ("acting out") of childhood difficulties. His influence has been valuable in "humanizing" the psychoanalytic process, but it is generally thought that he was impractical in his utilization of the techniques to which we have referred.

Reich, the last of the six deviants considered in this chapter, broke with Freud over the death instinct and masochism. He proceeded in later years to develop orgone therapy (vegetotherapy), which departs so radically from not only psychoanalysis, but our conception of psychotherapy, that it is not herein considered. Reich was so well known, however, for his brilliant and original analyses of character structure (done, for the most part, prior to his break with Freud) that his name is worthy of inclusion in our consideration of the non-Freudian developments of psychoanalysis.

Selected Readings

Adler, Alfred, *The Practice and Theory of Individual Psychology*. New York: Harcourt, 1924.

Ansbacher, H. L., and Rowena R. (Eds), *The Individual-Psychology of Alfred Adler*. New York: Basic Books, 1956.

Ferenczi, Sandor, *Sex in Psychoanalysis*. New York: Basic Books, 1950.

———, *Further Contributions to the Theory and Technique of Psychoanalysis*. New York: Basic Books, 1952.

Jung, Carl G., *Modern Man in Search of a Soul*. New York: Harcourt, 1933.

———, *The Practice of Psychotherapy*. New York: Pantheon, 1954.

Karpf, Fay B., *The Psychology and Psychotherapy of Otto Rank*. New York: Philosophical Lib., 1953.

Rank, Otto, *Will Therapy and Truth and Reality*. New York: Knopf, 1947.

Reich, Wilhelm, *Character Analysis*. New York: Orgone Institute, 1945.

Stekel, Wilhelm, *Compulsion and Doubt*. New York: Liveright, 1949.

———, *Technique of Analytical Psychotherapy*. New York: Liveright, 1950.

CHAPTER 5

Deviations in Psychoanalysis: II

In this chapter we shall consider what might be called the latter-day deviants in the psychoanalytic movement. We shall deal with the theories and practices of four so-called "dynamic-cultural" psychoanalysts (Horney, Sullivan, Fromm, and Anderson), with modifications of psychoanalysis in the direction of briefer and more directive treatment (psychoanalytically oriented psychotherapies), and with a new philosophical orientation which has developed especially among theoretical European analysts (existential analysis). The latter two developments will be treated quite briefly because their practical effects on psychotherapy can be briefly and simply stated. The systems of Horney, Fromm, and Anderson will also be handled rather summarily not only because much of their published work which bears directly on psychotherapy can be succinctly expressed, but also because the popularly written works of all three are readily available.

The bulk of this chapter treats the personality theory and psychotherapeutic system of Harry Stack Sullivan. The devotion of the major portion of our space to Sullivan has three justifications: (1) his contributions were brought to a higher and more complicated level of conceptualization than those of the other dynamic-culturalists and seem to be of more widespread and deeper influence in the growing, changing field of psychotherapy; (2) his publications (for the most part posthumous and for the most part transcribed from recordings of his lectures) are not easily understood and digested by the layman; and (3) his work, for both of the foregoing reasons, resists extreme condensation.

A. HORNEY

Karen Horney was trained as a Freudian analyst in Germany and came to the United States in the early 1930's. She soon made a break with the classical psychoanalytic movement and founded a separate association and training institute, which she headed until her death in 1952. Although she considered her theories "corrective" of Freud, rather than a completely new approach, she rejected both his instinct theory and his structural theory of the mind (id, ego, superego).

The underlying determining principle for human behavior, according to Horney, is not Freud's instincts of sex and aggression, but the need for security. When the security of the child in relation to his parents reaches unmanageable proportions, he develops an all-pervasive feeling of the world as a hostile and dangerous place. This feeling is what Horney calls basic anxiety.

The anxious person develops various strategies by which to cope with his feelings of isolation and helplessness. Any one of these strategies may assume the character of a drive or need in the dynamics of the personality. They are irrational (hence neurotic) attempts to find the solution for the problems of disturbed human relationships. Horney speaks of ten such neurotic needs: (1) for affection and approval, (2) for a "partner" who will take over one's life, (3) for restriction of life with narrow borders, (4) for power, (5) for exploitation of others, (6) for prestige, (7) for personal admiration, (8) for personal achievement, (9) for self-sufficiency and independence, and (10) for perfection and unassailability. These ten needs are the sources from which inner conflicts develop. Or, stated somewhat more pointedly, inner conflicts result from the interplay of these neurotic needs. A vicious circle is set up. If, for example, the neurotic asserts his need to be independent, he aggravates his unsatisfied need to be loved and admired.

These ten neurotic needs, Horney felt, fall under three general headings: moving toward people, moving away from people, and moving against people. The normal person also has some degree of conflict among these three broad categories of needs, but achieves a considerable degree of balance and integration among them. The neurotic person, however, tends to create an idealized image of himself in which the contradictory trends presumably disappear (but are actually only repressed).

The neurotic's idealized self-image, according to Horney, is not merely a false belief in his value and significance, but a kind of monster which comes increasingly to usurp his best energies and thus his ability to realize his potentialities. The neurotic becomes bent on actualizing his idealized self, which entails not only a search for worldly glory, but also a dedication to a tyrannical inner system whereby he tries to mold himself into a godlike being. He makes special claims on the world for attention, consideration, and deference, on the one hand, and develops, on the other hand, an unrealistic pride (as distinguished from a healthy self-confidence) which prevents him from doing the things that might achieve for him some of the worldly glory he feels to be his right.

The heart of neurosis, then, as Horney conceived it, is a disturbance in the patient's relation to self and to others. The godlike being (that is, the idealized self-image) is bound to hate the person's actual being (what Horney called the *actual self*). Along with the concepts of the idealized self (the neurotic, prideful, glory-seeking aspects of the personality) and the actual self (the whole personality of the individual as it actually exists at any point in time), Horney spoke of the "real self." By the latter she meant the central inner force of the individual which she believed to be the source of free, healthy development of personality potential. The real self is what the actual self can become by the therapeutic overthrow of the idealized self. The central inner conflict of the neurotic, as Horney saw it, is a battle between the constructive forces of the real self and the obstructive force of the pride system, between healthy growth and the neurotic drive to prove in actuality the perfections of the idealized self.

Horney's main idea of therapy, therefore, became that of giving the disturbed individual help in fighting the idealized self-image (including all the neurotic needs tied in with this image), realistically facing the actual self (seeing himself as he now is), and releasing the real self (that is, replacing the obstructive forces of pride with healthy growth). The idealized image offers a major stumbling block in therapy, according to Horney, because the recognition of these as neurotic trends means for the patient a collapse of what he perceives to be his integrity as a person. Yet it is only by putting the patient therapeutically through this "disillusioning process" and thus weakening the obstructive forces, the therapist helps the patient to release the constructive forces of the real self for healthy growth.

Like some of the earlier psychoanalytic dissidents, Horney believed in a more directive and active therapeutic role for the analyst than did Freud and his classical followers. She felt that the various strategies in relation to neurotic needs, the neurotic trends, the glory-seekings and pride systems of the idealized self-image, should be interpreted to the patient.

B. SULLIVAN

As a system builder in psychotherapy, Harry Stack Sullivan is probably second only to Freud. Sullivan in his later years (he died in 1949) seemed to feel some strong urge to present a well-rounded theory of human behavior. Sullivan was sensitive, too, about being considered a mere deviant from Freudian psychoanalytic theory and seems at times to use neologisms and circuitous explanations in order to appear independent of Freud. (It may be true, however, that he felt he thus avoided ambiguities and misconceptions.) The chief influences on Sullivan, as a matter of fact, were not so much Freud as the psychobiologic psychotherapy of Adolf Meyer (see Chapter 8), the broad humanistic psychiatric teachings of William Alanson White, and his own experience as a clinical psychiatrist.

Sullivan showed a remarkable understanding of not only what goes on inside people, but also what takes place between people as they relate to one another. His major thesis was that the primary concern of psychiatry is the study of interpersonal relations.

Sullivan's conception of interpersonal relations included more than what goes on between two or more people in interaction. He also referred to the relationships a person may have with imaginary people (such as one's "dream girl" or "the man who will some day take me away from all this"), with illusory or fantastic personifications (such as the kind of idealization of one's childhood sweetheart that Dante conjured up with Beatrice; or an illusion of some such personified entity as "the government," with which one interacts).

Whenever, in an interpersonal situation, persons react to a personification existing at least partly in fantasy, what Sullivan called *parataxic distortion* occurs. This would include what the Freudians refer to as transference (displacement of early childhood attitudes toward a significant person onto the therapist), but is more broadly any attitude toward another person based on fantasy or on identification of that person with other figures. Thus, in Sullivan's terms, the patient is interacting with a personification of this childhood person, not realistically with the therapist, and one of the main purposes of therapy, as Sullivan saw it, was to help the patient to see the parataxic distortions which kept him from making secure and satisfying interpersonal relationships.

Sullivan divided the purposes or goals of human behavior into two interrelated classes: the pursuit of satisfactions and the pursuit of security. Satisfactions, as he used the term, refers to biological needs, including sleep and rest, sex fulfillment, food and drink, and physical closeness to other human animals. Security, on the other hand, was used by Sullivan to refer to a state of well-being, of belonging, of being accepted. Most psychological problems, he pointed out, arise in relation to the pursuit of security. At times a society will interfere seriously with the biological satisfactions (most often sex in our society), but generally things go wrong in the formation or in the carrying out of security operations. When the individual has a state of "good feeling," or euphoria, security has been achieved. When he has a loss of euphoria, uneasiness, anxiety, his pursuit of security has been (at least temporarily) unsuccessful.

The process of becoming a human being is, in Sullivanian terms, the process of socialization. From birth onward values of the culture (conveyed in attitudes of persons around him) are transmitted to the child. The child begins to experience feelings of euphoria or security whenever he behaves "correctly" according to the values held by his parents or parent-substitutes and feelings of insecurity whenever he behaves "incorrectly."

Before the infant is even aware of himself as something separate from his surroundings, some of the attitudes of the person Sullivan called "the mothering one" are conveyed to him through "empathy." While Sullivan was not too explicit about what he meant by the term "empathy," he apparently viewed it as a biologically derived means of emotional communication. For example, if the mothering one feels anxiety for any reason around feeding time, this anxiety is somehow communicated to the infant. By such "emotional contagion and communion" from the mothering one, Sullivan thought, the infant first acquired his own feelings of anxiety.

Sullivan considered anxiety a potent, but restrictive, force in the formation of the self. As a result of early experiences of anxiety, human beings become, to varying degrees, "inferior caricatures of what they might have been." (In Horney's terms, the actual self falls far short of the real self.) The existence of large undeveloped areas of personality is most obvious in the highly disturbed, and Sullivan's therapeutic work was directed mainly toward people with severe mental disorders, especially schizophrenics. Much of Sullivan's therapeutic activity was focused on the parataxic distortions which had been produced by, and served to perpetuate, anxiety states in the patient. As a result of his experience of anxiety in childhood, the disturbed person has a highly distorted picture of himself and his relationships with others (these are his parataxic distortions). Such pictures were developed unthinkingly just to remove or reduce anxiety. Because the individual feels deeply, but irrationally, that they continue to provide him the means of avoiding anxiety, they are maintained until the disturbed person can be helped by the therapist to work through these distorted concepts and develop more rational, realistic concepts.

If, in the course of growing up, an individual is fortunate enough to have sound interpersonal relations with his peer group, especially with a close chum in adolescence, he may get some of his parataxic distortions corrected. Life itself, in other words, and not only psychotherapy, can provide corrective experiences. However specifically achieved, such correction, accomplished by comparing one's thoughts and feelings with others, Sullivan called "consensual validation."

In the process of the development of the self, the infant, Sullivan postulated, gradually evolves three personifications of "me": "good me," "bad me," and "not me." The "good me" is an organization of the experiences of the security feelings. The "bad me" is an organization of the experiences related to anxiety states. The "not me" seems to originate from "primitive anxiety," what Sullivan called the "uncanny" experiences of horror, dread, awe, and loathing in infancy. The "not me" feelings generally reveal themselves only in psychotic episodes and in night terrors and nightmares.

If experiences which bring security feelings predominate in the life of the developing child, the "good me" tends essentially to represent his conception of his self. If he meets an unusual number of unfortunate anxiety-producing experiences, he identifies primarily with the "bad me." Put differently, the child evaluates himself in terms of the reactions toward him he sees in the significant persons around him. If the parents and other significant persons show him a great deal of love, respect, and tenderness, he grows up with a conception of himself as worthy of love and esteem (the "good me" prevails). If the attitudes of the significant persons are largely negative, the child grows up without self-love and self-esteem (the "bad me" reigns).

The term "dynamism" is important in Sullivan's system. He defined dynamism as "the relatively enduring pattern of energy transformations which recurrently characterize the organism in its duration as a living organism." It refers to a kind of package of processes—the ways in which energy is organized and channeled in the organism. Sullivan applied the term dynamism to the whole emerging self, but also to part-systems within the developing self-dynamism. The lust dynamism, for example, was analyzed by Sullivan into the following components: (1) a psychobiological integrating apparatus, (2) a system of zones of interaction, (3) a pattern of covert and overt symbolic events, and (4) a system of integrating tendencies.

The emergent self-dynamism determines the aspects of the total available experience that will be utilized and integrated by the individual at any point in his life. Sullivan used the term "selective inattention" for the method used by the self-dynamism to control focal awareness so that what does not make sense in terms of the particular individual's self organization needs to get no attention. Particularly during the juvenile era, when the individual has an opportunity to test his ideas and values with his contemporaries (consensual validation), his self-dynamism develops the guide values for those things which are and those which are not worthy of attention (Sullivan's designation of "the juvenile era" will be given below).

Some things are so threatening to the security of the self, however, that they simply cannot be faced by the individual. The aspects of the individual's experience that lead to acute anxiety tend to be excluded from his awareness before they can bring their attendant anxiety. This mental process is essentially what the Freudians refer to as repression and is what Sullivan called *dissociation*.

Like Freud, Sullivan was interested in the developmental history of the individual and presented his conception of stages. Sullivan's stages of development are not, however, based on the emerging biological needs of the individual, but are characteristically related to the social patterns and the interpersonal relations, of the individual at various points in life. Sullivan's stages of development follow:

1. *Infancy*—from a few minutes after birth to the appearance of articulate speech. 2. *Childhood*—from the appearance of the ability to speak articulately to the appearance of a need for playmates. 3. *Juvenile era*—from the beginning of association with companions until the emergence of a need for an intimate relationship with another person of comparable status. 4. *Preadolescence*—the chum period, which ends with the eruption of genital sexuality and a change of strong interest from a person of one's own sex to a person of the other sex. 5. *Early adolescence*—the patterning of some type of performance which satisfied one's genital drives. 6. *Late adolescence*—from the achievement of such a lust-satisfying pattern until one is able to establish a love relationship in which the other person is nearly as significant as one's self (at which point one enters adulthood).

In discussing the human organism and its interpersonal relations at various stages of development, Sullivan emphasized the child's capacity to deal with various types of symbolization in his reactions to his environment. The goals of human behavior remain the same throughout all the stages: the pursuit of satisfactions (fulfilling biological needs) and the pursuit of security (avoidance of anxiety and attainment of "good feeling"). The means to the goals, however, the methods of pursuing the two basic purposes, depend on the individual's growing capacities in the various stages to understand and manipulate symbols in his social environment.

Sullivan typed people according to their most prevalent interpersonal attitudes. Although he did not offer the list as comprehensive, he said that he had observed ten syndromes, as follows: (1) nonintegrative: the so-called psychopathic personality (the chronic liar, thief, cheat, etc., who seems to lack any strong social feelings); (2) self-absorbed: a person characterized by fantastic, wishful thinking; (3) incorrigible: an individual who is hostile and forbidding toward all people except those whom he can regard as his inferiors (toward whom he has a kind, benevolent attitude); (4) negativistic: people who have given up hope of getting love and approval from others and who have therefore come to settle for attention; (5) the stammerer; (6) the ambition-ridden personality; (7) asocial: the detached, lonely people; (8) inadequate: the clinging-vine type; (9) homosexual (Sullivan considered homosexuality, like the other nine syndromes, a type of adjustment to anxiety and not a problem in itself); (10) chronic adolescent: the person who perpetually pursues, but never finds, the ideal in life.

Most of Sullivan's knowledge of personality was derived empirically from work with schizophrenics and obsessional cases. He learned early that the method of free association did not work well with these patients. Failure of other techniques he tried also led him to concentrate his attention on the communication process and the forces that aid and impede the transmission of meaning between people. In the course of his study Sullivan learned how important are the therapist's own attitudes, ideas, and actions in the therapeutic relationship. Thus derived Sullivan's emphasis on psychiatry as the study of interpersonal relations and on the therapist as a *participant* observer.

Just as the Freudians look for the origin of presenting symptoms in the repressed infantile unconscious of the patient, Sullivanians look for the source of characteristic syndromes in childhood experiences which have brought about massive dissociation in the patient. Sullivan apparently felt that for the patient to realize that his underlying anxieties and hostilities are understandable reactions to childhood hardship and confusion is of considerable assistance in facing the current consequences of such socialization. Unlike Freud (and more like Stekel and Adler), Sullivan felt that the therapist and patient needed to follow up such insight with a *direct attack* upon the old dissociations in order to break them down. Sullivan tried to maintain a back-and-forth movement in therapy between the analysis of the parataxic distortions revealed in the interpersonal relations of patient and therapist, of past situations as the source of these distortions and as a means of opening up dissociated reactions, and of the current life of the patient outside the therapeutic relationship.

For the particular kind of interpersonal relations that take place between the patient and the therapist, Sullivan used the term "psychiatric interview." He divided the interview into four stages: (1) the formal inception, (2) reconnaissance, (3) detailed inquiry, and (4) the termination.

In the inception, Sullivan stated, the interviewer should maintain mainly an attitude of quiet observation, during which he tries to understand the nature of the patient's problems. Sullivan stressed that the therapist should be alert not only to what the patient said, but how he said it (rate of speech, intonations, changes in volume, bodily position, facial expression, etc.). Although the therapist's main job at inception is quiet observation, Sullivan warned that he should not, even in the first interview, carry this role to the point where the patient feels he is simply being observed. The therapist should remember that he is an expert in interpersonal relations, and the patient should feel from the very first interview that he is learning something which will benefit him.

What Sullivan termed reconnaissance is the part in therapy where the therapist collects, by intensive interrogation, a great deal of biographical information about the patient. Although he advocated flexibility in the therapist's approach, he felt irrelevant and trivial matters should be ruled out.

As he moves into the third stage of the interviewing process (detailed inquiry), the therapist should, according to Sullivan, have several varying hypotheses to test out regarding the nature and source of the patient's difficulties. The therapist should realize that there is a constant two-way flow of ideas and feelings between the patient and therapist. Whenever communication becomes blocked, the therapist should ask himself what he has done to increase anxiety in the patient. The therapist needs to be constantly alert to his own attitudes and to control them in the interest of optimum communication.

Sullivan believed that the therapist should bring about a decisive and directive termination of the therapy. The therapist should summarize what he and the patient have learned about the patient and his (the patient's) interpersonal relations and should predict the probable effects of the patient's changed attitudes on his future interpersonal relations.

C. FROMM

Erich Fromm was trained as a psychologist, sociologist, and psychoanalyst in Europe before coming to the United States in 1933. Since his arrival in this country, he has had a great deal of influence on not only other psychoanalysts, but also on psychologists, sociologists, philosophers, religionists, and the general public. He has made no attempt, however, to develop a separate system of psychotherapy. He draws freely upon the concepts of all schools of psychoanalysis, including the Freudian (within which he had his original training), and he criticizes Freud and other analytic theorists only on points where he feels they have made either serious omissions or overemphases. Fromm nevertheless is most closely identified with the dynamic cultural points of view of Sullivan and Horney.

The essential theme of Fromm's writing is man's need to find meaning in his lonely, individuated life. Fromm holds that man can use his unique individual freedom to unite himself with his fellow men in a spirit of loving productiveness to achieve self-fulfillment and to develop a better society, or he can retreat from freedom by submitting himself to the bondage of an authoritarian society.

More specifically than either Horney or Sullivan, Fromm has tried to understand the interrelationships between the individual's psychic forces and the particular society in which he lives. Practically none of his interesting and, at times, profound analysis of these psychological and sociological interrelationships bear *directly* upon either the theories or techniques of psychotherapy. It is not contended that many of his significant historical and socioeconomic formulations, as well as his examination of the nature of individual dynamics, are not applicable to psychotherapy. It is simply stated that, for the most part, such applications have not been made (at least in writing) by Fromm or by anyone who holds to his formulations. It is quite probable, however, that through his stimulating effect on other therapists, through his challenging appeal to readers to overthrow their constricting conformity to irrational authority, and through his functioning as a teacher and therapist, Fromm has had as important an effect on the developing field of psychotherapy as any contemporary.

D. ANDERSON

A psychiatrist of the dynamic-cultural school who has apparently not yet developed a following among therapists, but whose theories have been presented to the public in nontechnical form, is Camilla Anderson. Her point of view does not seem to differ markedly from those of Sullivan, Horney, and Fromm (especially the latter). Trained in classical psychoanalytic techniques and theories, she arrived at her outlook, however, largely independently of the other dynamic-culturalists. We shall not repeat those aspects of her theories which are similar to those we have already considered. Her unique emphasis seems to be that of helping the individual to free himself from all morally judgmental attitudes and to replace them with critical conceptual judgments and realistic appraisals. Pride and guilt are two sides of the neurotic coin, as conceived by Anderson, and the patient needs to be helped to free himself of both in order to function in a practical and satisfying way in his social relationships. Psychotherapy is the process of becoming reality-oriented in place of moral-value-oriented. The therapist's job is to aid the patient in the process of getting acquainted with his own wants, feelings, capacities, and limitations, and then to evaluate the ways to improve his functioning in critically practical rather than moralistic terms.

E. PSYCHOANALYTICALLY ORIENTED PSYCHOTHERAPIES

With the possible exception of Ferenczi (who avoided an open break with Freud on theoretical grounds), all of the deviations from Freudian psychoanalysis we have considered thus far have not only included some alterations in the techniques recommended by Freud, but even more significant variations in theory. The psychoanalysts whose work we shall briefly consider in this section have held rather steadfastly to Freudian theory, but have experimented freely outside the classical psychoanalytic techniques. Probably a majority of psychoanalysts in the United States today have privately experimented with non-Freudian techniques, but relatively few have espoused such variations in public and professional forums. The four most widely known challengers of classical psychoanalytic techniques are (1) Alexander, French, and some other members of the Chicago Institute for Psychoanalysis; (2) Felix Deutsch and his system of "sector therapy"; (3) Benjamin Karpman and what he has called "objective psychotherapy"; and (4) John Rosen and his method of "direct analysis."

Alexander and his followers have attempted probably more than any other psychoanalytic group to subject their procedures to both critical examination and actual scientific experimentation. One of the main technical recommendations to emerge from these studies was the desirability at times to reduce and to interrupt therapeutic contacts with the patient. Interpretations, Alexander found, were often insufficient to counteract regressive dependency tendencies on the part of many patients. Such tendencies were not only combatted by properly-timed reduction of the frequency of interviews and interruptions in the therapy ("vacations" from the therapist during which some of the new insights can be "digested" and incorporated into the patient's behavior patterns), but also by encouraging the patient to undertake new life experiences outside therapy designed to increase his self-confidence.

The Chicago group believes that an intensely anxious individual may still need to be seen daily, especially during periods of great stress, but that less acutely anxious patients may progress quite well on three, two, or even one visit per week. In their experimentation with and without the couch in analysis, these investigators came to feel that it may be beneficial for shy, timid, guilt-ridden patients, but is likely to be a formidable obstacle to the progress in therapy of a hostile patient who cannot give way to his passive needs. The group's stress is on the desirability of having a plan of treatment that is modified as new facts emerge about the patient's personality and the problems he has to solve in his actual life conditions.

In addition to the points we have already mentioned, the Chicago group's technical flexibility includes occasional substitution of direct interviewing for free association, the offering to the patient of advice and suggestions about certain aspects of his life adjustment problems, and the utilization of life experiences that occur in order to advance certain treatment procedures. Greater emphasis is placed on the relationship between the therapist and patient rather than strictly on the transference, but positive transference is encouraged to establish rapport and enhance therapeutic progress and negative transference is analyzed when it blocks therapeutic progress. Stress is also given to the utilization of corrective emotional experiences which occur both in therapy and in the concurrent real life situations of the patient.

The "sector therapy" of Felix Deutsch is based considerably on the patient's associations to key words obtained from his autobiographical social history. While Deutsch does not feel that psychoanalytic treatment can be shortened in order to achieve extensive reconstructive goals, he believes limited goals can be achieved in the analytic interview by his technique of focusing on symptoms and conflicts which the patient's own key words and phrases have revealed. These key words and phrases will usually stimulate free associations in the patient. Deutsch advocates interrupting such free associations, however, when they veer away from the emotionally important material and then guiding the patient back to his key words and phrases. By this method, according to Deutsch, symptoms of present problems of the patient can be linked with underlying conflicts. Present associative chains of the patient are broken up by the therapist's confrontations, and new ones are formed. The patient's ego is thus helped to change its defensive attitudes and to discriminate present realities from past experiences.

In a somewhat related technique, Benjamin Karpman asks the patient, after a few preliminary interviews, to answer a series of questions taken from his own autobiography or from data otherwise secured by the therapist. Three separate series of questions are usually presented and, when written answers to these questions have been received, the therapist prepares a typed memorandum for the patient. Reading material may be given the patient regarding subjects related to his problems, and the patient's reactions in writing are also here requested. Dreams may also be written by the patient, and interpretations returned in writing by the therapist. Brief interviews are also held several times a week with the patient, but a close relationship between therapist and patient is avoided. At termination, a final memorandum as a whole is given to the patient. Karpman feels that this "objective psychotherapy," while more superficial than classical psychoanalysis, is well adapted to institutionalized patients and to persons with mild to moderate emotional disturbances.

Another psychiatrist, John Rosen, has adapted psychoanalytic techniques to his work with deteriorated psychotics. He has termed his procedures "direct analysis," and they consist of his efforts to enter directly into the symbolic worlds of the patients. Rosen takes at different times a series of roles symbolic of the people feared by his patients as expressed in their delusions and hallucinations. Working with excited catatonic, paranoid, and hebephrenic patients, Rosen tries to train his patients to feel that these feared people are now friendly and love the patients. This he demonstrates by helping the patients to do the things that the "voices" have frightened them away from doing previously. Interpretations coupled with strong positive transference and with the therapist's participation in the patient's world of fantasy have profound constructive effects, according to Rosen. He feels that in the treatment of schizophrenics the countertransference must be similar to the feelings that a good parent would have for a highly disturbed child. He contends that the therapist must identify with the unhappy patient in such a way that, like the good parent, he is disturbed by his unhappiness and cannot rest until the patient (child) is again at peace. While Rosen feels that the therapist must make up for the tremendous deficit of love which the patient has experienced in his early life, he does not shrink from vigorous physical contact should he feel, for example, that direct restraint is indicated in order to command the patient's attention or direct the stream of his thought. Although claimed cures have been spectacular, later reports and independent studies indicate considerable relapse.

F. EXISTENTIAL ANALYSIS

Another development of psychoanalysis has been its union with a form of European metaphysics called existential philosophy, and the resulting mixture has been appropriately termed existential analysis.

While the movement has achieved considerable support in Europe and parts of Asia, it has made little headway in the United States. Enough American interest is gradually developing, however, especially among analysts of the William Alanson White Institute and the Washington School of Psychiatry, to justify our giving existential analysis some brief attention.

Perhaps the foremost contemporary exponents of the existential philosophy are Martin Heidegger, Martin Buber, and Jean Paul Sartre. Various factors, including his extreme nihilism, have tended to exclude much of Sartre's point of view from consideration by psychoanalysts. Buber and Heidegger have been the most influential in the psychoanalytic movement. Of the European analysts who have applied the existential point of view to their therapeutic work, Medard Boss, Viktor Frankl, and Ludwig Binswanger are the best known. They follow the point of view of Heidegger.

Existential philosophy represents a European trend away from positivism, functionalism, instrumentalism, pragmatism, and operationalism—all of which tend to be close to the center of the value system of the scientist and of many American therapists. This is one reason for the lack of popularity of existential analysis in this country. Another reason is that existentialism is a philosophy of crisis, and the American scene does not yet reflect the European atmosphere of crisis. In an environment of desperation, man, as the existentialists see him, is striving for his forgotten power to *be;* man's plight is one of despairing for his *spontaneous existence.*

Existential analysts, then, emphasize the importance of the individual's values and goals and direct their attention toward understanding his personal world—his world of values. Their central contention seems to be that other therapists fail to formulate in explicit terms their understanding of the general nature and specific values of man and are therefore guided by hidden philosophical presuppositions which block their understanding of the patient. By analyzing the "meaning-structures" of each patient's personal world of values and by stripping themselves of preconceived notions about the nature and values of man, the existential analysts claim that they have discovered that the essential nature is a basic kind of being or "be-ness" and that the outstanding human value is a human unity, a being-together-in-the-world.

Although his terminology is at points different (and both the intellectual and emotional meanings of the German terms often defy translation into English), Viktor Frankl seems to be striving in the same general direction with his application of existentialism. Frankl emphasizes what he calls the "existential neurosis," which derives from the individual's inability to see meaning in life. Therapy consists largely in helping the patient to find an "authentic existential modality." The task of what Frankl calls "logotherapy" is to reveal the flaws in the patient's world-view (system of values) and to help him to achieve a readjustment of that view.

What does such understanding of the nature and values of man bring to the therapist? It does not, for the most part, lead him to depart from whatever psychoanalytic or psychotherapeutic procedures to which he previously adhered. It will, however, the existentialists assert, greatly change the attitude with which the therapist uses these tools in relating to the patient. If the therapist really understands that man is fundamentally a world-unfolding, world-opening being, he will have a kind of reverent love toward each such human being he encounters as a patient. He will see the patient with his personal world of values in terms of human existence (the be-ness) and the major value of human unity. The therapist will function himself and will try to aid his patient to function with the realization that man's intrinsic task is so to exist that he may help his fellow men most effectively to develop. The therapist will be aided, the existentialists postulate, to stand on the same place with his patients, the plane of common existence. He will relate to the patient as an existential partner in analyzing a reality of a present which is altogether continuous with the past and bears within it the possibilities of a future.

The foundation of the curative process in psychotherapy, according to this point of view, is the fundamental being-togetherness of therapist and patient. From the first encounter of patient and therapist, the latter, if existentially attuned, is together with his patient's way of existing (what other therapists have called "empathy" or "empathic understanding"). Also from the very first, the patient begins to partake of the therapist's way of living. Gradually as the sick patient, feeling understood and cared for by the therapist, gets the courage to emulate increasingly the therapist's healthy mode of existence and thus moves on to health himself by daring to be his own true self.

This, briefly, is the somewhat "spiritual" contribution of existential analysis. It offers no new techniques as such, and its theoretical contributions seem to lie mainly in the area of emphasis of certain values already recognized (albeit perhaps insufficiently practiced) by other psychotherapists.

Summary

The systems of four recent psychoanalytic deviants, the dynamic culturalists, have been reviewed in this chapter. We have also briefly considered psychoanalysts who have varied more in techniques than in theory under the heading of "psychoanalytically oriented psychotherapies." Our final section dealt with existential analysis.

The first of the dynamic culturalists, Karen Horney, considered the underlying determining principle of human behavior to be the need for security. When this need goes unfulfilled, the individual develops basic anxiety. The neurotic individual develops ten different kinds of strategies for handling anxiety, and these strategies themselves come to constitute neurotic needs. There are three characteristic patterns into which these needs fall, and the individual comes to structure his characteristic patterns into what Horney called his idealized self-image. Psychotherapy, in Horney's terms, becomes largely a process of helping the patient to fight his idealized self-image (including all the neurotic needs tied in with this image), to see himself as he actually is, and to replace the obstructive forces of his neurotic pride with healthy growth, thus releasing his real self.

Harry Stack Sullivan offered a much more complicated system of psychotherapy. He divided the purposes or goals of human behavior into two interrelated classes: the pursuit of satisfaction and the pursuit of security. The process of becoming a human being, Sullivan pointed out, is the process of socialization. The main object of the therapist's study should be the interpersonal relations of the patient: past, present (including those with the therapist), and future (for which the therapist must help him realistically prepare himself).

Anxiety, parataxic distortion, selective inattention, dissociation, dynamism, stages of development, and characteristic syndromes are key concepts of Sullivan's which are considered in this chapter, but which cannot be briefly summarized. Sullivan also made some original contributions to therapeutic techniques, which he developed under the heading of "the psychiatric interview."

Erich Fromm, the third dynamic culturalist, has made many important theoretical contributions to the understanding of the individual and his society, few of which, however, have dealt directly with psychotherapy. Fromm's essential theme is man's need to find meaning in his lonely, individuated life, which need he can fulfill only by uniting himself in a spirit of loving productiveness with his fellow men. Only in this way will man, according to Fromm, achieve self-fulfillment and develop a better society.

Camilla Anderson, who has independently developed a dynamic-cultural system that in many ways resembles those of Horney and Fromm, has made an original emphasis on man's need to free himself of all moral judgments and to substitute critical conceptual judgments and realistic appraisals.

The psychoanalytically oriented psychotherapists have largely confined themselves to the development of techniques which will bring greater speed and efficiency to the treatment of individuals who do not seem to need classical psychoanalysis and (in the case of Rosen) to the treatment of psychotics.

The central contention of existential analysis is that therapists fail to formulate in explicit terms their understanding of the general nature and goal of man and are therefore misled by hidden philosophical presuppositions. By stripping themselves of preconceived notions about the nature and goal of man, the existentialists hold, they have discovered that the essential nature is a basic kind of "be-ness" and the goal is a human unity, a being-togetherness. With attitudes derived from this understanding, the existential analyst feels he can be more helpful to his patient.

Selected Readings

Alexander, Franz, *Psychoanalysis and Psychotherapy.* New York: Norton, 1956.
Anderson, Camilla, *Beyond Freud.* New York: Harper, 1957.

Boss, Medard, *The Dream and Its Interpretation*. London: Rider, 1957.

Deutsch, Felix, and W. F. Murphy. *The Clinical Interview* (2 vols.). New York: Int. Univs., 1955.

Frankl, Viktor E., *The Doctor and the Soul; an Introduction to Logotherapy* (translated by Richard and Clara Winston). New York: Knopf, 1955.

Fromm, Erich, *Man for Himself*. New York: Rinehart, 1947.

Horney, Karen, *Neurosis and Human Growth*. New York: Norton, 1950.

May, Rollo, Ernest Angel, and Henri F. Ellenberger (Eds), *Existence: A New Dimension in Psychiatry and Psychology*. New York: Basic Books, 1958.

Rosen, John N., *Direct Analysis*. New York: Grune, 1953.

Sullivan, Harry Stack, *The Interpersonal Theory of Psychiatry*. New York: Norton, 1953.

———, *The Psychiatric Interview*. New York: Norton, 1954.

CHAPTER 6

Client=Centered Therapy

The first system of psychotherapy of widespread prominence that has its roots almost exclusively in American psychology (as distinguished from psychiatry, on the one hand, and European sources, on the other) is what was originally called nondirective counseling and more recently client-centered therapy. The originator and outstanding exponent of the system is Carl Rogers.

Rogers, with a background in liberal theology (Union Theological Seminary) and the progressive educational philosophy of John Dewey, as well as in clinical psychology (Teachers College, Columbia University), brought to his functioning as a counselor and psychotherapist a strong personal and professional predisposition toward permissiveness. In his clinical internship as a counselor, Rogers reacted negatively to what he saw as highly authoritarian psychotherapeutic procedures based on what he believed to be very speculative theories of human behavior (psychoanalysis). On his first full-time job as a counselor (Director, Rochester Guidance Center), Rogers was further influenced by his own experiences in treatment procedures, by his conferences with fellow staff members, and by the deviant psychoanalytic views of Otto Rank into an attitude of total permissiveness of counselor toward client. The permissive attitude rests on the proposition that the client has basic potentialities within him for growth and development. The main function of the therapist is to provide the atmosphere in which the client feels free to explore himself, to acquire deeper understanding of himself, and gradually to reorganize his perceptions of himself and the world about him.

Since leaving Rochester in 1940, Rogers has taught, as well as continuing in clinical and administrative work, at three major universities: Ohio State (1940-45), Chicago (1945-57), and Wisconsin (since 1957). During this period of time, he has trained many graduate students in his basic approach to psychotherapy, has sharpened and modified the details and rationale of client-centered therapy, has developed a theory of personality which corresponds to the therapy, has undertaken and stimulated in others much more research than any other "school" of therapy, and has likewise produced and stimulated others to produce a vast amount of professional literature on client-centered therapy and related topics.

There seem to be many reasons for the popularity of the Rogersian approach to therapy. One is that it fits snugly into the American democratic tradition. The client is treated as an equal, who has within him the power to "cure" himself, with no need to lean heavily on the wisdom of an authority or expert. Second, the client-centered philosophy of the person's potentiality for constructive change also fits in well with the optimistic aspect of American culture: the notion that if he meets the knock of opportunity with determination and good will, each individual can come to a good goal. Third, the client-centered way appeals to the young, insecure, inexperienced, prospective therapist as, at least superficially, the "easy way." It is unnecessary for the therapist to have any great knowledge of personality diagnosis or dynamics, and he takes no real responsibility for guidance of the disturbed client. He simply encourages the client to be more fully himself; he provides warmth and acceptance as the means whereby the client can achieve self-realization. Any permissive, warmly loving person can readily become a therapist via the client-centered system. Fourth, the method, at least in its early years, held promise of being a swifter route to personality change than did psychoanalysis. The fact that client-centered therapy no longer seems so brief may arise from the fact that more disturbed and more difficult patients have turned to client-centered therapists in recent years. And the fifth basic appeal of client-centered therapy has been its attraction for American psychologists who better understand its philosophical postulates, its respect for psychological research methods, and its lack of foreign terms and methods. This latter point has been partially negated, however, by the rapid diffusion (especially in the last decade) of the psychoanalytic point of view among clinical psychologists and the lingering behavioristic influence (especially in the psychology of learning) which views the phenomonological outlook of client-centered therapy as unscientific.

As we have indicated, Rogers' personality theory followed many years after his first developments of the client-centered techniques of therapy. The first written formulations of the therapy were presented in 1940, and the first full presentation of the personality theory did not appear until 1951. In our examination of client-centered therapy, however, we shall reverse the historical process. We shall follow the same procedure we have used in our consideration of other systems: first, a look at the conceptions of human behavior and, then, at the theories and techniques of therapy.

In developing his theory of personality, Rogers drew from the hypotheses of many psychologists (especially Goldstein, Snygg and Combs, Maslow, Angyal, Lecky) and, to some extent, the theories of Harry Stack Sullivan. Most essential in understanding the main theoretical conceptions of personality of Rogers and his associates is knowledge of what is called the phenomenological point of view. By this hypothesis, each person has a phenomenal field, which is a definition of events or phenomena as they appear to him. His behavior, according to the phenomenologists, is entirely determined by his field, and predictions of his behavior demand knowledge of that field.

If, for example, a clinician is trying to understand the behavior of a homosexual, he is wasting his time, according to the phenomenologists, to study statistics about homosexuality, studies of background factors in the development of homosexuals, theories of the etiology of homosexuality, etc. The valid source of information is the particular homosexual himself: how does *he* feel? How does life appear to *him?* What does *he* think about himself in relation to other people? Answers to such questions as these, Rogers and other phenomenologists say, are necessary really to understand the behavior of any individual and to predict how that individual will respond to future situations in or out of therapy.

A person's phenomenal field is limited. Only a small portion of experience can be held in focus at a given time. The phenomenal field becomes constantly restructured according to the person's need.

Freudians would say psychic content moves from the preconscious to the conscious mind, and Sullivanians speak of selective attention and inattention.

Those parts of the phenomenal field which the individual perceives as part or characteristic of himself are of particular importance in the determination of behavior, as understood by Rogers. These include the individual's physical self and his relationships with the cultural and physical worlds. Some of these things the individual considers relatively unimportant, and he leaves them rather vague and unattended. But those aspects of his phenomenal self which are highly differentiated and which he has defined as definite and relatively stable attributes of himself constitute the compelling aspects of his life and form his self-concept. Stated differently, the self-concept, or self-structure, is an organized configuration of perceptions of the self which are admissible to awareness.

It is difficult for a person not immersed in the Rogersian system to see clearly how the self-concept thusly defined differs markedly from Horney's idealized self-image. In psychological maladjustment, the two constructs would seem to be one and the same. Rogers speaks of psychological tension when the organism denies to awareness significant sensory and visceral experiences, which consequently are not organized in the self-concept. Hence, under those circumstances the Rogersian self-concept would strongly resemble the idealized self-image, which, the reader will remember, was a chief neurotic trouble-maker in the Horneyian scheme of things. Presumably Horney's real self (and Fromm's true self) is approximated in Rogers' healthy individual's self-concept: when the concept of the self is such that all the sensory and visceral experiences of the organism are, or may be, assimilated on a symbolic level into a consistent relationship with the concept of the self.

When organic experiences and needs appear which have not been symbolized and which are inconsistent with the self, they are, in Rogers' terms, *disowned* by the individual. This comes close to Freud's idea of repression and Sullivan's notion of dissociation. The unconscious mind itself has no place in the Rogersian scheme of personality.

Rogers has pointed out that the values attached to experiences and those which are part of the self-concept may be either values directly experienced in the past by the organism or values taken over from others, but perceived in distorted fashion as if they had been experienced directly. The values that are taken over in this distorted fashion from others lead to confusion, unhappiness, and ineffectiveness. Such a person does not "know himself," for his organism (that is, his visceral and sensory perceptions) tells him one thing and his self-concept (the values he permits to enter his awareness) tells him another.

Within the framework of the phenomenological theory, the fundamental urge underlying all behavior is the need to preserve and enhance the phenomenal self. Any experience which is out of line with the structure of the self may be perceived as a threat, and the more threats there are, the more rigid the structure of the self to protect and maintain itself.

The reader will notice that Rogers has found it necessary to formulate two opposing systems, the organism and the self, which correspond roughly to Freud's id and ego and Jung's unconscious and conscious. The organism may have visceral and sensory experiences that the self does not let itself perceive because they are inconsistent with the self stucture.

With self preservation and enhancement the basic motivation of human behavior, the individual who is doing what seems (to us) obviously self-destructive acts must mistakenly perceive these acts as routes to self esteem. Therapy, then, consists of helping the individual to find ways of conceiving of himself that will free him of conflicts and which will allow him to function smoothly in his relationships with others. In client-centered therapy, which provides primarily an atmosphere free of any threat to the self-structure, the person can work out a harmonious integration of the self and the organism. In this environment, the individual may perceive, examine, and revise the self-structure to assimilate and include experiences formerly avoided as inconsistent with that structure. Thus assert the client-centered therapists.

The reality with which client and therapist deal, according to Rogers, is the reality of the present as perceived by the client. There is generally sufficient community of experience and sufficient overlapping of phenomenal fields, he believes, beween therapist and client to make possible a meaningful interchange of ideas and feelings. Past and future have relevance in the Rogersian system only insofar as they are conceptualized currently by the client or insofar as they constitute tensions that non-symbolically influence present behavior. Etiology, diagnosis, and prognosis are not matters that should occupy the client-centered therapist's mind. He should be concerning himself with the here and now of the client. Rogers feels that behavior is goal-directed, but needs and goals are part of the present, not the past or the future.

Rogers takes the position that the patient's reports are valid and reliable sources of information about his personality. The central feature of Rogers' conception of personality is the self-as-object, and it is assumed that consciously experienced self feelings can be communicated to the therapist. This position is in marked contrast to the psychoanalytic view that the patient's conscious impression of himself is highly invalid and unreliable as a source of information about true (unconscious) personality motivation. Rogers and his followers show little or no interest in dream interpretations, parapraxes, wit, or free association as routes to unconscious motivation; for, from the practical standpoint of its function in Rogersian therapy, unconscious motivation is non-existent.

As the client enters therapy, according to Rogers, he is likely to have a critical negative picture of himself. He has an idealized image of how he should be and is quite certain he miserably fails to measure up to this ideal. At first in therapy, he is apt to feel even more discouraged and self critical, but he begins to develop an awareness of quite contradictory attitudes toward himself. As he explores these attitudes, in the accepting and approving atmosphere supplied by the therapist, the patient begins more and more to accept himself as he is, including the contradictions. Both self-condemnation and self-approval begin to decrease, and objective observation of himself in action tends to be substituted. As these changes take place, the patient comes to feel himself a more real and unified person. His goals shift and become more achievable, and the discrepancy between his ideal self image and his perceptions of his real self become less and less. The patient's inner life thus becomes increasingly free of tension.

It is pertinent to note at this time that the Rogersian therapists have more objective or near-objective evidence to support their contentions about what happens in successful client-centered therapy than other schools of therapists can produce to support their contentions. Rogers and his followers have made more tape recordings and movies, conducted more research investigations, and opened their procedures more fully to inspection than any other system. It does not mean that their claims are all justified or that their principles and practices are sounder therapeutically than other systems. Our interpolation of comment about research at this point is simply intended to indicate in fairness that assertions regarding what happens to the client in client-centered therapy are not based simply on wishful thinking on the part of therapists of this persuasion. Our critical examination of the Rogersian system, along with all the others, will be reserved for Chapter 10.

The attitude taken by Rogers toward the role of diagnosis in therapy is rather unique. He feels that diagnosis is not only unnecessary, but unwise and detrimental. This attitude applies not only to all psychometric tests, but also to any stated opinions on the part of the therapist about the nature of the patient's problems. Rogers feels that the client may be ill-prepared to handle certain information diagnostically revealed to him and that diagnosis fosters the dependency of the client on the therapist as "the expert." Not only does diagnosis probably have a damaging effect on the attitudes of the client, according to Rogers, but likewise on the therapist. It is not the therapist, but the client who must make the decisions about changes in the client's behavior, and the less the therapist's attitudes are colored by a predetermined point of view the more he will be able to give the client the acceptance and positive regard that he (the client) needs to improve his mental health. Stated differently, the less the therapist thinks he knows as an expert, the less he will interfere with the client's freedom to develop the therapeutic situation to meet his own needs. And Rogers contends, as a final point, that the therapist has enough to do in simply understanding what it is that the client is trying to work through without trying simultaneously to formulate self queries designed to bring him (the therapist) to a point of diagnosis.

From some of the studies that have been made of the therapeutic process, the following characteristic activities of the client-centered therapist have emerged: (1) Strong, consistent effort to understand the client's content of speech and feelings conveyed by words, gestures, expressions, etc.; (2) an effort to communicate this understanding to the client by word or (more often) his general attitude of acceptance; (3) occasional presentation of a condensation or synthesis of expressed feelings; (4) occasional statement of the nature and limits of the therapeutic relationship, the expectancies of the situation, and the therapist's confidence in the ability of the client to handle his problems; (5) when question-answering and information-giving seem relevant to the client's working through of his problems, they are engaged in, but denied when they seem likely to increase the client's dependency; (6) while the therapist may interrupt the client to make sure he understands what the client is saying or feeling, he offers no interpretations other than those which seem to summarize what the client (not the therapist) is feeling; (7) likewise the client-centered therapist does not try to promote insight directly, or to give advice, praise, blame, or to teach or suggest programs of activities, or to ask questions or suggest areas of exploration.

While certain aspects of client-centered therapy are characteristic of most, but not all, of the systems discussed in this book, there is one issue on which client-centered therapy is different from all of the others. That one issue is the leaving of all responsibility for the course and direction of therapy to the client. The choice of topic of discussion, the finding of meanings, the speed or lack of speed with which the client faces certain problems in his life, the frequency and degree of digressions, the follow-up of what seems to be a significant area for exploration—all of these and comparable decisions are made by the client, not the therapist, in client-centered therapy.

When is an individual ready for therapy, in client-centered terms? It is when his organized self-structure no longer effectively meets the needs of the reality-situations in which he finds himself, or when he feels a significantly large cleavage between what he wants to be and what he is. Such a person, either vaguely or clearly feeling anxiety, enters client-centered therapy and, according to Rogers, experiences a kind of freedom which is decidedly new to him. While the patient has been in other situations where he was not directly attacked, he has never before had every aspect of self which he exposed equally accepted and valued. His belligerencies, uncertainties, perceptions of contradictions, discouragements are not challenged, belittled, or contradicted, but are accepted and valued. In this atmosphere of safety and acceptance, Rogers contends, the firm and defensive boundaries of self are relaxed, and the patient is able to consider objectively his contradictory perceptions and experiences and gradually assemble a new personality gestalt.

Client-centered therapy, Rogers says, is a process of disorganization and reorganization of the self. The new organization contains more accurate symbolization of a much wider range of sensory and visceral experience, a reconceptualized system of values based on the person's own feelings and experiences (in place of the old, largely borrowed, second-hand values). The painful dis- and reorganization can be made by the client mainly because his old contradictory attitudes are not only accepted by the therapist, but the new and difficult patterns as well. The client comes to introject the calm acceptance of the therapist and can handle the new and difficult reality perceptions necessary for the reorganization.

As the new self-structure becomes firmer and more clearly defined, it provides the client with a steadier guide for his actual behavior. Positive attitudes increasingly predominate over negative, and the client sees in himself more and more a pattern of behavior drawn from experience, rather than a pattern imposed upon experience. Because the value system is based more on actual experience, it feels more realistic and comfortable and in harmony with the perceived self. Ideals seem more achievable. Also overt behavior is more adjustive and socially more sound, because the assumptions on which it rests are more realistic.

While Rogers admits that some transference attitudes (usually mild, but occasionally strong) appear in client-centered therapy, he maintains that these attitudes do not develop into a transference relationship or a transference neurosis. This, he says, is because the client-centered therapist's reaction to transference is the same as to any other attitude of the client: he tries to understand and accept. Acceptance then leads to the recognition by the client that these feelings are within himself, not in the therapist. The impersonal and secure attitudes of the therapist soon lead the client to abandon a belief that the feelings displaced (transferred) to the therapist belong elsewhere than inside him, the client. Rogers hypothesizes that a transference relationship is most likely to occur when the client ex-

periences the therapist as having a more effective understanding of
his own self than he himself possesses, a situation that cannot develop
in correctly operated client-centered therapy (because the therapist
looks to the client as the true source of information about the client's
self).

In the early development of his system of psychotherapy, Rogers
set certain limitations regarding the sorts of persons who could be
helped by the client-centered approach. These limitations referred
to such matters as age, intelligence, freedom from family control, and
absence of excessive instabilities. More recently he has expressed reluctance about setting arbitrary limits of effectiveness. Work with
mentally defective and delinquent individuals has been negligible,
but success has been obtained with some individuals in almost every
other category of pathology, according to Rogers. Since the nature
of client-centered therapy is such that harm is not likely to result to
any individual not helped, Rogers contends, there is no reason to pre-
clude experimenting with the technique with any type of patient.
This is true, Rogers says, because of the lack of any pressure in the
relationship: the person draws back from subjects too upsetting or
dangerous to face.

Quite recently, Rogers has addressed himself to the question of
what psychological conditions are necessary and sufficient to bring
about constructive personality change. By "constructive personality
change" (he also uses the alternate phrase of "psychotherapeutic
change"), he means an alteration of the personality structure of the
individual in a direction of greater maturity, integration, and energy
utilizable for effective living. The six necessary and sufficient conditions Rogers has presented are discussed in the following paragraphs.

He points out, first of all, that significant positive personality
change does not occur except in a relationship. His first condition,
then, is simply psychological contact: the awareness of both the client
and the therapist of the presence of the other.

Rogers' second condition as necessary for psychotherapeutic
change is that the client is in a stage of "incongruence." The term refers to a difference between the actual experience of the individual
and his self picture. When the individual is even vaguely aware of
such incongruence, he is anxious. When he is not aware, he is nevertheless vulnerable to the possibility of anxiety. A client in a state

of incongruence, either anxious or vulnerable to anxiety, is, then, this second necessary condition.

The third necessary condition for a client's constructive personality change is that the therapist be congruent or integrated in the relationship. Rogers states that this means simply that the therapist must be freely, deeply, genuinely himself, with his actual experience accurately represented by his awareness of himself. This includes being himself in ways that are not therapeutically ideal. He may feel bored, for example, or preoccupied with his own problems, but so long as he does not deny these feelings to his own awareness, he meets Rogers' definition of functioning congruently.

Fourthly, it is necessary that the therapist experience unconditional positive regard for his client, according to Rogers. This means that the therapist must find himself experiencing a warm acceptance of each aspect of the client's experience as being a part of that client. The acceptance can be in no way conditional: it is caring for the client as a separate person, with full permission from the therapist to have his own feelings and experiences.

Rogers' fifth necessary condition is that the therapist must experience an empathic understanding of the client's awareness of his own experience and that he must try to communicate this empathic understanding to the client. The definition Rogers gives of empathic understanding is that of sensing the client's internal frame of reference as if it were his (the therapist's) own without the therapist's losing his own separate emotional existence. It is the ability of the therapist to sense the client's emotions without himself getting emotionally tied up in them. He comes, as Rogers puts it, to move around freely in the client's emotional world, and then to be able to communicate his understanding to the client (including things the client himself has only vaguely sensed).

It is, then, at least the minimally effective communication of both the therapist's empathic understanding and the therapist's unconditional positive regard that is Rogers' sixth and final necessary condition for constructive personality change. The client must perceive that the therapist empathizes and accepts or such attitudes do not exist in the relationship so far as the client is concerned (no matter how deeply the therapist may feel he is experiencing them). Stated differently, the therapist's behavior and words must be perceived by the client to add up to at least some degree of acceptance and understanding of him.

Rogers has unequivocally stated that if the foregoing six conditions are fulfilled, then effective psychotherapeutic results can be achieved. He feels that this is true regardless of the type of emotional disturbance presented by the client and dismisses contentions of other therapists that conditions vary as the therapist attempts to help neurotics, homosexuals, psychotics, etc.

Few, if any, therapists of whatever persuasion would deny that the conditions Rogers lists are desirable. Most would probably even agree that they are necessary. Few other than client-centered therapists, however, would join Rogers in believing that they are sufficient. Some direction out of the maze, following upon the establishment of empathy and positive regard, would be called for in many systems of psychotherapy.

One of the noteworthy omissions from Rogers' list of necessary and sufficient conditions for therapeutic personality change is any professional training or knowledge for the psychotherapist. Any person who gains experience in functioning as an integrated, or congruent, accepting, empathic person could meet Rogers' criteria of an effective therapist. Psychological, psychiatric, and medical knowledge would become not only irrelevant to effective operation as a therapist, but might even be severe handicaps (along the lines already mentioned earlier of making the therapist feel that he is an "expert" and inclined to engage in diagnosis).

The main merit of Rogers' formulations of the necessary and sufficient conditions for effective therapeutic personality change is that they are hypotheses that can be readily tested. Already research is under way to shed some light on the degree of truth that may be contained in these rather radical postulates.

The client-centered point of view has spread far beyond individual psychotherapy. Application of the basic approach has been made in education, play therapy, group therapy, industrial and business administration, various aspects of religious work, in the training of counselors and therapists, and elsewhere. With the exception of group therapy (the Rogersian approach to which is considered in Chapter 9), these applications are beyond the scope of our attention. They are mentioned to give the reader an idea of the extent and impact of what is essentially an ubiquitous development of an American philosophy: the individual who is, by love and acceptance and understanding, helped to become effectively the master of his own destiny.

How well does client-centered therapy work? Despite their unexcelled research, the Rogersians have not supplied us with satisfactory answers to this question. We know little about their successes compared with successes of other therapeutic systems. We know even less about their failures. To say that other schools of therapy have provided us with even less satisfactory answers regarding the effectiveness of their approaches is true enough. To say, further, that Rogers and his followers have challenged *all* psychotherapists to seek more factual proof of their contentions, to re-examine their theories and techniques in the full and open and objective light of science, is an even more pertinent truth regarding the future health and value of the whole field of psychotherapy. It is the very least tribute objectively earned by Carl Rogers and his client-centered psychotherapeutic system.

Summary

Client-centered psychotherapy is based on a phenomenological conception of human behavior. By this view, each person has a phenomenal field, which is a definition of events or phenomena as they appear to him. His behavior is determined by his field, and prediction of his behavior demands knowledge of that field.

Carl Rogers, chief proponent of client-centered therapy, has pointed out that values which become an integral part of the individual's phenomenal field may be derived either from direct experience or taken from others. The values which are taken over in a distorted fashion from others lead to confusion, unhappiness, and ineffectiveness. This type of person does not "know himself," for his organism tells him one thing and his self-concept tells him another. Such an incongruent individual, anxious or vulnerable, is a likely candidate for psychotherapy.

Client-centered therapy, according to Rogers, is a process of disorganization and reorganization of the self. The new organization contains more accurate symbolization of a much wider range of sensory and visceral experience, a reconceptualized system of values based on the person's own feelings and experiences. The painful dis- and reorganization can be made by the client mainly because his old contradictory attitudes are not only accepted by the therapist, but the new and difficult patterns as well. The client comes to introject the calm acceptance of the therapist and can handle the new and difficult reality perceptions necessary for the reorganization.

Rogers has postulated that psychotherapeutic personality change can be and will be effected when the following conditions are fulfilled: a psychological contact between therapist and client, a state of incongruence in the client, a state of congruence in the therapist, unconditional positive regard for and empathic understanding of the client by the therapist, and the client's perception of the therapist's positive regard for and empathic understanding of him. Diagnosis, professional knowledge, and other frequently emphasized characteristics of the therapist are not considered necessary by Rogers and may, indeed, according to him, be obstructive.

Whatever the degree of truth in the client-centered point of view, the empirical researches undertaken by the group and the challenge that this position has offered to other psychotherapeutic systems has been a healthful influence in the general field of psychotherapy.

Selected Readings

Rogers, Carl R., *Client-Centered Therapy*. Boston: Houghton, 1951.
———, *Counseling and Psychotherapy*. Boston: Houghton, 1942.
———, "The Necessary and Sufficient Conditions of Therapeutic Personality Change." *Journal of Consulting Psychology*, 1957, 21, 95-103.
———, and Rosalind F. Dymond (Eds), *Psychotherapy and Personality Change*. Chicago: U. of Chicago, 1954.

CHAPTER 7

A Variety of Systems: I

To this point we have considered psychoanalysis in its manifold variations and the relatively independent development of client-centered therapy. In the next two chapters, we turn our attention to eleven somewhat separate therapeutic developments, some of which are more deserving of the term "system" than others. All, however, have brought an emphasis in theory and/or technique that makes them of at least some significance in understanding the contemporary psychotherapeutic scene.

In this chapter, we shall deal with six systems of psychotherapy: psychobiologic therapy, Gestalt therapy, hypnotherapy, experiential therapy, conditioned-reflex therapy, and psychotherapy by reciprocal inhibition. Psychobiologic, Gestalt, and experiential therapies are systems that are integrative of a number of points of view, with original emphases within each. Hypnotherapy is a system which stresses the value of the particular technique of hypnosis in both short-term, re-educative and long-term, reconstructive therapy. Conditioned-reflex therapy and psychotherapy by reciprocal inhibition are radical departures from other therapeutic systems.

A. PSYCHOBIOLOGIC THERAPY

Adolf Meyer is a psychiatrist who tried to integrate all forms of psychotherapy and the various biological and medical approaches to treatment. Meyer did not discard psychoanalytic procedures, but tended to emphasize the environmental manipulative and supportive approaches. He also put much stress on the securing of complete medical and social histories. Meyer and his students developed a diagnostic classification system based not on diseases, but on "reaction types," or categories by predominant symptoms. The Meyerian system is generally referred to as "psychobiologic therapy" and its characteristic procedures are termed "distributive analysis and synthesis."

As already indicated, Meyer emphasized the importance of obtaining a clear and full understanding of the patient's own views of his problem, and to this end encouraged the extensive recordings of the interviews. Although the patient is encouraged to describe himself, his background, and current difficulties, the psychobiologist does not hesitate to furnish positive assistance whenever the patient indicates a need for help in giving a fully rounded picture of his situation.

The psychobiologist gives great importance to the patient's point of view in his clinical judgments, but he knows that emotional disturbances fall into familiar categories of symptom combinations. He therefore uses his knowledge of these categories in analyzing and synthesizing facts about the patient. The therapist of psychobiological orientation also knows that he himself has been influenced by his culture to accept certain mental patterns and so does not proceed under the illusion that he can be completely unbiased regarding the values held by the patient. Although the psychobiologist does not attempt to function as simply a mirror of the patient's values, he tries to be aware of his own biases and is careful not to inflict these on the patient.

The effort of psychotherapy, as viewed psychobiologically, is to achieve a synthesis of the views of the patient and therapist which will be the most effective and satisfying for the patient. The therapist needs to stress for both himself and the patient that the therapeutic activity is a joint search for a desirable resolution of the patient's problem and is not an "instruction" of the patient by the therapist: The therapist seeks to make sure that the way of life which is the outcome of this co-operative enterprise is indeed better for the patient than the one he had arrived at alone, prior to the therapy.

The chief disturbances of patients, as the psychobiologist sees them, are those which consist of compulsive habits and accompanying emotions derived from childhood experiences. These habits and concomitant emotional attitudes can be set off by both relevant and irrelevant stimuli, and the patient becomes a kind of prisoner of these irrational, childish patterns. The most destructive of these attitudes in the character formation of the individual are self-hate and self-disrespect. The kinds of character difficulties which develop from these self-attitudes can vary from timidity and feeling of inadequacy (which prevent realization of full personality potential) on through the extreme manifestations such as outward-directed hostility of the sociopathic and criminal personality types or to inward-directed hostility conditions, such as morbid fears, paranoid tendencies, and depressive states.

Since the psychobiologist tries to manage the treatment situation to accomplish the best possible collaboration between the particular patient and himself, he remains flexible and eclectic regarding techniques. Unlike adherents of some therapeutic systems, he does not place certain techniques above personality or situational factors. The Meyerian feels he must be ever ready to alter his methods from directive to nondirective, from suggestive to passively receptive, in accordance with the progress of the collaborative effort and in the light of his knowledge of the patient (derived both from the history and from the therapeutic situation).

The psychobiologist at times uses interpretation as one of his therapeutic tools. Meyer conceived of interpretation as the therapist's use of intellectualized concepts to promote the patient's understanding of the situation—hopefully not only in intellectual, but also in volitional and emotional, terms. Interpretation is offered, never forced, by the psychobiologist at a time that he thinks the patient is ready to use it and able to absorb it.

B. GESTALT THERAPY

The contributions of Gestalt psychology have been most notable in the study of perception. One attempt has been made, however, to apply it much more extensively to the whole area of psychotherapy. Three men, Frederick Perls, Ralph F. Hefferline, and Paul Goodman, are co-authors of this work (*Gestalt Therapy*. New York:

Julian Press, 1951). These writers believe that the Gestalt point of view is the natural and undistorted approach to the wholeness of life by human beings. The Gestaltists contend that in the course of his contact with our culture, the average person gets his integrity of thinking, feeling, and acting fragmented. Gestalt therapy is the effort to heal patients of their dualism of being, to redevelop the unitary outlook.

In proceeding with their Gestalt theories of psychotherapy, the authors draw on material from various other psychological and psychotherapeutic points of view (especially psychoanalytic), but feel that they bring new meaning to these selected materials by their differing synthesis.

The German word "Gestalt," the authors point out, lacks an exact English equivalent. Words which most closely approximate the German meaning are configuration, meaningful organized whole, structural relationship, and theme. The "Gestalt" is the meaningful organized whole of a figure and its background. The "ground" in Gestalt psychology is the context against which the element (the "figure") stands out.

The interplay of figure and ground becomes the focus of the Gestalt theory of personality and therapy as presented by Perls and his associates. The healthy person has a permanent, meaningful emerging and receding of figure and ground. Attention, interest, excitement, grace, concentration, and concern are characteristic of his figure/ground formation. Neurotics and psychotics, on the other hand, have either a rigidity (fixation) or a lack of figure formation (repression) as opposed to the healthy person's elasticity of emerging and receding figure and ground. A disturbed individual's figure/ground formation is characterized by confusion, boredom, compulsions, fixations, anxiety, and self-consciousness.

Perls and his co-authors stress that neither the understanding of the functions of the individual nor of his environment cover the total situation for the therapist. He must be aware of the interplay between the individual and his surroundings (the figure/ground), a position comparable to Sullivan's emphasis on interpersonal relations.

The authors go along with the shifting psychoanalytic emphasis from a search for repressed material to an investigation of the repressing forces in the individual (that is, the task of re-organizing the ego structure). Perls and associates point out that the neurotic feels his survival depends upon his continuing to repress, to censor, to defeat the therapist's efforts to penetrate his defenses. The repressing needs of the patient's ego can be reached not by therapeutic attack, the authors state, but by helping the patient and the therapist to understand the overlooked mechanisms whereby such repressing is accomplished. The "unfinished" (hence, neurotic) part of the patient is in the "obvious" functions of his being: the way he moves, talks, breathes, etc. The therapist must help him to understand the overlooked obvious things about himself in order to enable him to finish the Gestalt of his personality. The patient can regain the elastic figure/ground relation, which is the process of growth and maturing, and thus develop his "self" only by therapeutic guidance in re-examining the obvious about himself.

In their approach to therapy, Perls and his co-authors stress the need for a non-dogmatic, experimental situation. They feel that any implicit or explicit demands on the patient are not only likely to be futile, but may possibly be damaging. They present, instead, graded experiments which are designed to bring difficulties to the attention of the patient. What interferes with the effective accomplishment of the task becomes the focus of their work. They feel they thus bring out the patient's resistances and help him to work them through without directly challenging his defenses.

The types of experiments conducted by the authors are amply illustrated in their book. Without the step-by-step instructions for the exercises themselves and the reasoning which leads up to their use, description of them is either meaningless or misleading. It seemed wisest, therefore, not to try to present examples of these experimental procedures.

Unlike the Freudian approach of trying to recover something from the past or of rescuing it from behind character armor (Reich), Perls and his associates feel they lead their patients to make a creative adjustment to the given present situation. To complete the Gestalt in the present situation the patient must destroy and assimilate the unawareness as an obstacle. The therapeutic experiments allegedly bring out sharp delineation and precise verbal description of the disrupting block or void and open up ways to overcome it. The neurotic loses contact with reality and does not know how to regain it. He persists in a course that further removes him from actuality. The therapist helps him to learn (through the experiments) how he (the patient) is out of contact with reality, where and what the actuality now is, and how to keep in contact with it. Once the self of the patient can keep in contact and keep going, the therapy is terminated. A new and elastic figure/ground relation has thus been achieved.

C. HYPNOTHERAPY

Hypnosis has been both accepted and rejected many times by professional circles. One contemporary psychotherapist who has brought hypnotic techniques back to a status of respectability is Lewis R. Wolberg.

Wolberg believes that hypnosis by itself has no permanent psychotherapeutic effect, but that it functions well in conjunction with other therapeutic techniques. The chief values of hypnosis are its increase in the patient's suggestibility and its removal of repressions which (in the waking state) keep certain aspects of the personality from awareness. The former is quite helpful in the short-term, re-educative type of therapy, and the latter may be of assistance in depth-oriented, reconstructive therapy.

One type of therapeutic situation where the use of hypnosis may be advantageous is where a neurotic symptom is so destructive or incapacitating to the patient that it makes progress in psychotherapy difficult or impossible. The symptom can sometimes be at least temporarily removed by hypnosis at the same time that the patient is motivated to accept deeper therapy. Those kinds of symptoms most responsive to suggestive removal are hysterical symptoms (such as tics, paralysis, aphonia, amnesia, visual disorders, and other sensory disturbances) and habit disorders (insomnia, nail-biting, over-eating, and excessive smoking).

In re-educative therapy the goal is to lead the patient to an understanding of his distortions in interpersonal relationships and to help him toward a more harmonious integration with his environment. Hypnosis may be used to inculcate in the patient new adaptive goals and attitudes that are in line with his biosocial needs. Wolberg believes that there are some patients, such as many obsessive-compulsive personalities, who respond better to persuasion via hypnosis than to psychoanalysis. He believes that the substitution of persuasive philosophical precepts for destructive habit patterns is to be considered preferable to no treatment at all.

The use of hypnosis in reconstructive or psychoanalytic therapy (hypnoanalysis) is most helpful in reducing or removing resistance. Wolberg reports that the mere induction of a trance may be sufficient to bring repressed elements to awareness, but generally special techniques are required. Some of the techniques used are dream induction, automatic writing, dramatic acting out, mirror gazing, free association in trance, hypnotic drawing, the induction of experimental conflicts, and regression and revivification.

Wolberg states that transference feelings are often released during hypnosis and that their proper handling can be of great help in increasing the speed and effectiveness of the analysis. The integration of a memory regarding an earlier relationship with a parent (focused now on the therapist) into the patient's conscious life, and the understanding of feelings associated with the memory, can enable the patient to see what is happening in current life situations, according to the theory of Wolberg. In addition he feels that the recovery of traumatic memories may serve as a means of creating an incentive for change.

Hypnoanalysis also has its re-educational uses. An attempt is made to help the patient to gain insight into the dynamic unconscious sources of his difficulties. The chief technique involved here is for the therapist to demonstrate to him the meanings of his symptoms in terms of repressed conflict by inducing experimental conflicts in the course of the hypnotic trance.

Wolberg feels that hypnotherapy has definite limitations, some of which are as follows: not all patients can be hypnotized to the necessary depth; the material revealed may be fantasy and not true memory (and the two are not readily distinguished by the therapist); regression in hypnosis may seriously affect the transference situation; material encountered in the trance must be integrated in the more conscious layers of the psyche; and hypnosis is more useful in such conditions as hysteria and traumatic neuroses, than with character disorders.

D. EXPERIENTIAL THERAPY

Carl A. Whitaker, Thomas P. Malone, and their associates in the Atlanta Psychiatric Clinic have made a number of original contributions to psychotherapeutic theory and practice. They have specified that they are not interested in developing a new school of psychotherapy, but their ideas are sufficiently unified and distinct to be viewed as a "system."

Whitaker and Malone feel that psychotherapy in the broad sense includes any acceleration in the growth of a human being as a person. They limit their psychotherapeutic focus to growth in the sense of integration, and they feel that increased integration is expressed as both more maturity and as greater adequacy. That branch of psychotherapy which most concerns itself with the patient's deficits in maturity is the biologically based, the medical; and that division which concentrates on the deficit in adequacy is the interpersonal, social-scientific. The authors place their emphasis on matters of maturity because they feel this aspect of psychotherapy is currently in need of expansion. Their point of view may in many respects be considered as a return, with a fresh outlook, to the concerns of early psychoanalysis: that which has since been termed, "id psychology."

Although increased adequacy ordinarily develops through an educative social experience (these authors maintain), growth in maturity derives from emotional experiences. Alterations in the person's intrapersonal structures, the increasing ease in the exchange of energies within an individual, are the goal of experiential therapy. The patient who has had his dynamics rendered more flexible by emotional experiences and thus has energy freed from conflict to use in his interpersonal relations will probably need instruction in the more effective utilization of this energy, but Whitaker and Malone are not at this time primarily concerned with the adequacy aspect of therapy (which corresponds to what, in psychoanalytic circles, is called "ego psychology").

The essential dynamics of psychotherapy, according to Whitaker and associates, develop within a current experience. The psychotherapeutic experience modifies the pattern of inter-relationship of

other current experiences and integrates the biological effects of previous experiences on the organization of current experience (hence
the label "experiential therapy"). Such experience is essentially emotional (dealing with the id processes) rather than analytical, historical, genetic and logically causal (ego-level).

When such id-level therapy is functioning effectively, the therapist
sees the patient (emotionally) as the child-self of the therapist. The
needs of the therapist are intrapersonal ones which lead the therapist
to achieve a better integration of his own self through this child-
image of himself (the patient). Thus therapy, as these therapists
conceive it, is really an externalized intrapersonal relationship: the
therapist and a projection of himself. The experience is in this way
isolated from reality for the patient and frees him temporarily from
the roles demanded of him from society. He is able to act out fantasy roles never previously possible, which releases energy formerly
bound in emotional conflict.

The therapist, meantime, is bringing to bear upon the patient the
feelings and motivations from his own experience which he has perceived in a positive light and which he associates with the role of good
parent. This enables the patient to deepen his symbolic involvement
with the therapist. The therapist, seeing the patient as part of himself
and the experience as a means of satisfying his own deeper integrative needs, has a feeling of growing significance and urgency to
accelerate the growth of the patient.

As the therapist and the patient become increasingly emotionally
involved in the therapeutic experience, a point is reached where
each is responding maximally to the unconscious of the other. The
level of communication is primitive (what Freud called the primary
process) and consists essentially of mass body sensations. This stage
of therapy is what Whitaker and Malone call a joint fantasy experience for the patient and the therapist and is, they believe, the point
at which the main therapeutic benefits accrue to the patient. By fantasy they mean a pervasive experiencing of the unconscious in its
totality (which is non-verbal and organic). The patient's acceptance
of his own fantasies and unconscious experiences is facilitated because he has them in the presence of one who implicitly participates
in them. This also, it is believed, leads to the development of a
greater continuity between consciousness and unconsciousness and

an increasing capacity for the realization of the patient's fundamental biological needs. The patient acquires from the therapist the realization that one can be fantastic while, at the same time, having a very adequate reality capacity.

Whitaker and Malone are reluctant to speak of specific techniques in psychotherapy because they feel that these should grow out of the uniquely personal way in which an individual therapist relates to his patients. They do, however, discuss methods they have found useful in facilitating the emotional, symbolic process of psychotherapy.

In the beginning phase of therapy, techniques should be primarily directed toward isolating the therapeutic experience from other experiences in order to hasten the production of symbolic, fantastic, and unconscious meanings. One useful way to achieve this isolation is for the therapist to delete as many realities as possible from the experience (refusal to discuss his real life, to answer the telephone during therapy, to talk over the patient's problems with his family or with the referring physician, etc.).

It is very important that the therapist indicate to the patient his awareness of the patient's maturities, his wellness, as well as his immaturities, his sickness. In this fashion, the patient's conception of his immaturities becomes less threatening.

The therapist should indicate to the patient that he will not permit his own (the therapist's) personal life to be exploited by the patient. It is important for the patient to see that the therapist is a person who has sufficient integrity and cognizance of his own separateness and realness to refuse to sacrifice himself in the fantasy relationship with the patient. Thus the patient's own confidence is increased about eventually emerging well from the fantasy relationship.

The patient also gains confidence for the plunge into fantasy by the therapist's presenting his own limitations and his immaturities. Again the patient is reassured that a healthy distinction between reality and fantasy is made by the therapist and can be achieved in the future by the patient.

Whitaker and Malone feel that most often, in the beginning phase of therapy, the therapist's responses should consist mainly in his implicit understanding of the symbolic meaning of what the patient has said or done. This implicit understanding can best be expressed in silence. Silence is particularly effective in discouraging mere intellectual verbiage which has no real emotional significance for the patient. A non-verbal response by the therapist to the patient serves the purpose of helping the patient to hear his own superficial verbalization most clearly and precipitates the patient into a deeper level of transference. It also aids the therapist in the development of his own fantasy participation in the relationship.

Both aggression in various forms and physical contact can be judiciously used by the therapist, according to the authors. They agree, however, that these techniques are most likely to be abused and should not be undertaken by the inexperienced therapist.

Much emphasis is placed by the authors on the joint fantasy experience as an aid to effective deep level communication between the patient and the therapist. They have utilized such material objects as clay and rubber knives and such techniques as sleeping and dreaming in the therapeutic sessions as means of facilitating fantasy participation. (The therapist will have a dream in the course of therapy which he then, on awakening, recounts to the patient. The dream presumably helps "clear things up" for therapist and patient.)

Perhaps it is fair to summarize the whole philosophy and procedure of experiential therapy with the statement that the therapist says, in depth effect, to the patient: "We are both troubled people; let us see if by entering the world of fantasy together we can help one another to do a better job of fulfilling our true selves and thus to emerge again in the external world more capable of handling the problems of reality."

E. CONDITIONED REFLEX THERAPY

A radical departure from the usual theories and practices of psychotherapy is the conditioned reflex therapy of Andrew Salter. As the term suggests, this therapy is the application of the Pavlovian conditioning process to clinical procedures. Holding that man's behavior is inseparably rooted in his animal nature, Salter feels that neurotic behavior can be rendered healthy by direct re-conditioning (strong positive suggestion). Salter not only finds more refined and intellectualized procedures futile and irrelevant, but likely further to entrench the person's emotional illness.

The basis of life, according to Salter, is excitation. The cause of emotional illness is inhibition. Hence, the role of the therapist is to help persons to overcome their inhibitions and to express their real feelings. The emotionally ill person has, in one way or another, experienced inhibiting conditioning and needs to be encouraged to develop his excitatory reflexes. Although Salter admits that living in society calls for some inhibition, he feels that the inhibiting conditioning aspects of our culture go far beyond the point needed and thus produce emotional illness. The many different forms of such illness, he contends, boil down to the same fundamental deprivation of excitation.

In his therapy, Salter instructs his clients to stop thinking and to start acting on the basis of their feelings. The healthy person, he believes, is one who acts on spontaneous, outgoing feeling: the healthy act without thinking, and the emotionally ill think without acting.

Salter has developed six basic techniques for reconditioning the faulty, inhibitory patterns of earlier life in the direction of excitation. The first of these disciplines, as he refers to them, is feeling-talk. Since man is a word-using animal, his basic means of excitation is through speech. By saying what he feels when he feels it (even at the risk of social disapproval), the patient will recondition himself away from inhibition and toward excitation.

Salter's second therapeutic discipline for his inhibited client is what he calls facial talk. He should, in other words, frankly show his emotions on his face—positive and negative alike.

The third technique in which Salter instructs his clients is that of contradiction and attack. The client is told not to act as if he agrees when he disagrees. Even without supporting evidence, the client should speak up with his feelings of disagreement and thus externalize his feelings.

Salter also tells his clients to use the word "I" deliberately as much as possible. This helps, he contends, in getting out excitatory feelings.

When praised (Salter suggests in his fifth precept), the client should express agreement. If someone says, for example: "That was a good speech you made at the Elk dinner last Friday," the client should reply along the following lines: "Yes, I think I was in top form that night. It seems to me it made a fine follow-up on your excellent

speech of a year ago." Salter suggests the desirability of thus working in a returned compliment for the other person as well as reflecting favorably his praise of the client.

Salter's sixth rule of conduct is improvisation. His clients are
instructed not to plan, but to live for the here and now. Planning
leads to inhibition, he contends, so his already inhibited clients need
rather to improvise actions from moment to moment and day to day
than to encourage further inhibitory reflexes by stopping to think
ahead.

For critics who suggest that excitation can be carried too far,
Salter has the answer of "yes, but not by these inhibited clients."
These overly inhibited people, he believes, need to learn to act as
if they were constantly half-drunk. Then, if after they have become
reconditioned to be excitatory instead of inhibitory personalities, they
later need some toning down, that, Salter feels, is easily accomplished.

Salter holds, then, that the solution to all the problems brought to
the therapist comes from helping the client to disinhibit (unbrake)
his conditioned inhibitory emotional reflexes and thus to develop
excitatory emotional reflexes. The client is thus re-educated to return
to the healthy spontaneity of which his negative life experiences had
deprived him. Such reconditioning of the individual is even deeper
than other types of therapy, Salter holds, because it is more thorough-
going. Maladjustment is malconditioning, as he sees it, and psychotherapy is effective reconditioning.

It is interesting that Salter has apparently developed no following
among even behavioristically oriented psychologists. His methods are
viewed as overly simplified and his claims of cures extravagant. Salter
seems to feel that his critics are blinded to the truth of his theories and
practices by the conditioning they have received from psychoanalysts
and others who have led them to believe a lot of complicated nonsense about the human animal.

F. PSYCHOTHERAPY BY RECIPROCAL INHIBITION

A more recent, careful, and sophisticated application of the theories
of conditioned response learning to the therapeutic setting is what

Joseph Wolpe, the originator, calls *psychotherapy by reciprocal inhibition.* Wolpe took his first psychotherapeutic cue from observations of experiments with animals. He noticed particularly that the neurotic behavior of an animal tends to disappear when the pleasurable experience of feeding occurs in the presence of anxiety-evoking stimuli. He inferred from these and other experimental findings that in general it is possible to overcome a habit by forming a new and antagonistic habit in the same stimulus situation.

Conducting human clinical investigations patterned along the same general lines as the animal experiments, Wolpe emerged with the following principle: if a response opposed to anxiety can be made to take place in the presence of anxiety-evoking stimuli so that a complete or partial suppression of the anxiety responses is effected, the bond between these stimuli and the anxiety responses will be weakened.

Wolpe did not try feeding responses for overcoming human neuroses; he found other responses more convenient: mainly, assertive responses, relaxation responses, and sexual responses. He has also successfully employed respiratory responses, conditioned motor responses, "anxiety relief" (electric shock cessation) responses, and conditioned avoidance responses. He has caused these responses to be called forth, inside and outside the consulting room, under conditions arranged so that the neurotic anxiety will be maximally inhibited by the antagonistic response selected.

For example, with the use of relaxation as the antagonistic response method to be employed, Wolpe first gives the patient preliminary training in relaxation. He also works out a list of stimuli to which the patient reacts with unadaptive anxiety. The stimuli are ranked according to the amount of disturbance they cause. The patient is then hypnotized, made to relax as deeply as possible, and told to imagine the weakest item in the list—what Wolpe calls the "smallest dose of phobic stimulation." In case the relaxation is not impaired by this dosage, a slightly greater one is presented at the next session. After a number of sessions of gradually increased dosage of phobic stimulation, the patient reaches the point, according to Wolpe, where the phobic stimulus can be presented at maximum intensity without impairing the calm and relaxed state. Then, in situations outside the therapeutic setting, the patient will stop reacting with his previous anxiety to the strongest of the once phobic stimuli. Therapy by reciprocal inhibition has thus taken place.

Wolpe offers statistics to support his assertion that his method has an almost 90 per cent efficiency in helping patients as compared with the 50 to 60 per cent credited to psychoanalytic and other methods. He even contends that much of the lesser success of other techniques derives from the *unknowing* application of reciprocal inhibition therapy. In the private interview (under any type of therapeutic procedure), Wolpe points out, the patient often has positive emotional responses as he confidentially reveals and talks about his difficulties to a person he believes to be knowledgeable, skillful, and desirous of helping him. If these emotional responses which tend to be antagonistic to anxiety are of sufficient strength, they will reciprocally inhibit the anxiety responses that are evoked by some of the subject matter of the interview. Therapeutic effects will thus occur. If, however, the emotional response is small (little transference, in analytic terms), positive results will probably not develop. Or, if too much anxiety is aroused by the interview, Wolpe points out, the patient may get worse.

Wolpe also believes that spontaneous cures of neurosis (where patients get over their neurotic symptoms without any form of treatment) are often the result of fortuitous reciprocal inhibition. He believes his system, in other words, more deliberately and efficiently applies the curative procedures that unsystematically take place in other forms of psychotherapy and in life outside the clinical setting. He invites the step-by-step testing of psychotherapy by reciprocal inhibition by other clinicians and says that a certain amount of such experimentation is already in process.

Summary

Six systems of psychotherapy were considered in this chapter: psychobiologic therapy, Gestalt therapy, hypnotherapy, experiential therapy, conditioned reflex therapy, and psychotherapy by reciprocal inhibition. Of the six, three (psychobiologic, Gestalt, and experiential) may be viewed as somewhat eclectic and integrative of a number of points of view, as well as containing original emphases. Hypnotherapy may be looked upon as largely adjunctive to other therapeutic techniques. Conditioned reflex therapy and psychotherapy by reciprocal inhibition are major departures from the general trend of psychotherapy.

In Meyer's psychobiologic therapy, much stress is placed on the importance of obtaining a clear and full understanding of the patient's own views of his problem, obtained by careful history taking. The therapist emphasizes for both himself and the patient that the clinical activity is a joint search for a desirable resolution of the patient's problems. In this search, the psychobiologist tries to remain flexible and eclectic regarding techniques. Much of his attention is directed toward helping the patient to overcome destructive habits and concomitant emotional attitudes (especially those reflecting self-hate and self-disrespect) which have irrationally imprisoned him from childhood.

Perls, Hefferline, and Goodman have tried to use the concepts of Gestalt psychology to work out a new integrative conception of human behavior and of the therapeutic treatment of this behavior. In the course of his contact with our culture, the Gestaltists contend, the average person gets his wholeness of thinking, feeling, and acting fragmented. Gestalt therapy is directed toward restoring this wholeness. While the authors draw on psychoanalytic and other concepts to further their theory and practice, much of their psychotherapy consists of graded experiments which are designed to bring difficulties progressively to the attention of the patient and to help him work out more realistic Gestalts of himself and his environment.

Wolberg uses hypnosis in the course of both re-educative and reconstructive (psychoanalytic) therapy. In the former, hypnosis is used to inculcate in the patient new and adaptive goals and attitudes that are in line with his biosocial needs. In hypnoanalysis the technique is most helpful in reducing or removing resistance. In the course of treating resistance he uses dream induction, free association in the trance, induction of experimental conflicts, regression, and a number of other hypnotic methods. He also feels that hypnoanalysis can be employed to assist the patient in gaining insight into the dynamic unconscious sources of his difficulties. He recognizes definite limitations, however, in hypnotic techniques and does not view them as replacements of other therapeutic methods.

While specifically disclaiming their desire to develop a new system, Whitaker and Malone have made a number of contributions to theory and technique under the heading of "experiential therapy." Their stress is placed on the emotional experiences of therapist and patient in the treatment situation. In this id-level therapy, the authors point out, the experience is isolated from reality, and the patient is encouraged to act out deep fantasy roles never previously possible. The therapist, meantime, brings to bear on the patient the feelings and motivations from his own experience which he has perceived in a positive light and which he associates with the role of good parent (the patient is felt to be a kind of projection of the therapist's own child self). Whitaker and Malone use a number of unusual techniques in their therapeutic procedures, which are a kind of joint venture of the therapist and patient into the primitive fantasy world of the unconscious.

The conditioned reflex therapy of Salter is based on an animalistic conception of man. The role of the therapist is to help persons to overcome their inhibitions (the source of their sickness, according to Salter) and to express their real feelings in an excitatory fashion. Such reconditioning of the individual is even deeper than other types of therapy, Salter holds, because it is more thorough-going. Maladjustment is malconditioning, as he sees it, and psychotherapy is effective reconditioning.

Wolpe's psychotherapy by reciprocal inhibition is similarly based on observations of animal learning by conditioned response, but consists of more careful and sophisticated applications of principles thus derived to the human clinical setting. Wolpe's major therapeutic principle is that the bond between certain stimuli and anxiety responses can be weakened by the simultaneous evoking of responses antagonistic to anxiety. He not only offers considerable support for his own procedures of reciprocal inhibition in therapy, but also contends that much of the success of other psychotherapies and of spontaneous cures derives from the fortuitous occurrence of similar conditioning.

Selected Readings

Muncie, Wendell, *Psychobiology and Psychiatry*. St. Louis: Mosby, 1939.
Perls, Frederick, Ralph Hefferline, and Paul Goodman. *Gestalt Therapy*. New York: Julian Press, 1951.

Salter, Andrew, *Conditioned Reflex Therapy.* New York: Creative Age Press, 1949.

Whitaker, C. A., and T. P. Malone, *The Roots of Psychotherapy.* New York: McGraw, 1953.

Winters, E. C. (Ed), *The Collected Papers of Adolf Meyer* (3 vols). Baltimore: Johns Hopkins, 1950-52.

Wolberg, Lewis R., *Medical Hypnosis* (2 vols). New York: Grune, 1948.

Wolpe, Joseph, *Psychotherapy by Reciprocal Inhibition.* Stanford, Calif.: Stanford, 1958.

CHAPTER 8

A Variety of Systems: II

Five more systems of psychotherapy will be treated in this chapter. These are directive psychotherapy, general semantics, learning theory therapy, assertion-structured therapy, and rational therapy. All of these therapies constitute marked departures from the therapeutic mode of psychoanalysis.

A. DIRECTIVE PSYCHOTHERAPY

The first of these systems which we shall consider is not so much a reaction against psychoanalysis, however, as an antidote to what its originator, Frederick Thorne, considers the unhealthy, cultish popularity of Rogersian nondirective (client-centered) therapy. Thorne, both a clinical psychologist and a psychiatrist, views his approach as eclectic, not a new system in itself. His use of the term "directive" does not mean that he feels there are not times when permissive, nondirective responses are appropriate. But the term emphasizes Thorne's conviction that constant nondirectiveness and passivity are inappropriate and that *direction* of the therapeutic process belongs in the hands of the skilled therapist and not the sick patient.

Thorne points out that, in general, the need for direction is inversely correlated with the person's ability for effective self-regulation. The sicker the personality, the greater the need for direction from the therapist. Because, in the hands of some unskilled therapists, directive procedures have sometimes been misused, nondirectivists have made the mistaken judgment, according to Thorne, of believing that direction in any form is undesirable.

Thorne feels that directive psychotherapy requires the therapist to be trained and able to use every known method, including some recently neglected ones like hypnosis, suggestion, reconditioning, and direct reassurance. He believes in genuine eclecticism which makes possible the use of all technical resources, either directive or nondirective, that are available at the time and place and seem appropriate to the particular patient's needs.

The directive psychotherapist, unlike the nondirective, develops a specific plan of action. He makes adequate diagnostic studies, including complete case histories, clinical examinations, psychometric and projective studies, and laboratory procedures (such as electroencephalography). The directivist also prepares a descriptive formulation of the psychodynamics of each case: etiology, clinical status, personality resources, and prognosis. His plan makes use of the principles of experimental science wherever applicable at all levels of case handling.

Thorne's directive psychotherapy is based on several premises, which may be summarized as follows: (1) When society, family, the school, and the patient himself have failed to condition healthy behavior the therapist steps in as a kind of master educator. (2) The creation of suitable conditions for the patient to learn a new style of life is the first task of the therapist. This involves the establishment of rapport, analysis of past traumatic conditions, release of emotional blocks, and encouragement of the patient in his own problem-solving processes. (3) Science provides the most valid and reliable authority for interference directively in the life of the patient (as contrasted with earlier arbitrary and unverifiable authority of the church, the family, the government, etc.). Broad scientific training provides the highest standards of competence for the therapist, and help for the patient most favorably arises from this source rather than from emotional, intuitive impressions of either therapist or patient.

Thorne objects to the application of the term "client-centered" to therapy which is strictly nondirectively oriented. He states that intelligently conceived directive therapy is more likely to be centered directly upon the client's real needs than therapy which uses the client's own (sick) feelings as the chief guide. The directively oriented therapy must be client-centered, according to Thorne, with the therapist interjecting only as may be needed to keep the client headed in constructive directions.

B. GENERAL SEMANTICS

Problems in communication are observable in most, if not all, forms of emotional disturbance. It is understandable, then, that attempts would be made to apply the findings of semantics to the theories and techniques of psychotherapy. Semantics is the scientific study of the relations between signs (symbols) and what they mean, and of behavior in its psychological and sociological aspects as it is influenced by signs.

Alfred Korzybski and Wendell Johnson are two semanticists who have made serious efforts (separately) to apply their studies to psychotherapy. Korzybski has postulated that neurotic behavior stems from a lack of clear understanding in the use of words and their meanings. Vagueness in phrasing and defects in conceptualization, among other things, are characteristic of the mentally ill person. So long as there is lack of clarity in the use of symbols, the individual is unable to define or think critically about his values and life goals. Therapy consists primarily in teaching the patient the correct word-habits to replace the faulty orientations in language he previously acquired. He then becomes increasingly able to substitute reality-oriented ends and means for self-defeating patterns.

Wendell Johnson points out that the emotionally disturbed person talks and thinks himself into conflicts. The patient's maladjustments are often the product of unrealistic ideals in life which bring about frustration. Consistent frustration leads to demoralization. Part of the difficulty arises from the patient's inability to conceptualize clearly what he wants from life, and he is, therefore, bound to be disappointed with whatever he achieves. The patient's problems are persistent and cumulative, too, because he cannot identify them properly as a result of his poor organization and clarity of language. The use of semantics in therapy, according to Johnson, is to retrain the patient in the meaning of words about himself and his environment.

As the patient becomes capable of conceiving and formulating his problems more clearly, he gains confidence in his ability to communicate with others and, hence, to handle his interpersonal relations with increasing effectiveness.

While the focus of general semantics may be different from other systems of psychotherapy, it obviously must draw upon techniques developed by other systems. Strict concentration on words and their meaning would seem to be unlikely to achieve removal of all symptoms in highly disturbed patients. The semanticist-therapist strives to improve the communication of his patient with himself, with the therapist, and with others. Attention is also necessarily given to rapport, transference, resistance, and other matters common to other therapeutic orientations. The semantic emphasis has, however, brought to the attention of therapists of other systems the need for greater study and work with communication problems of their patients.

C. LEARNING THEORY THERAPY

A number of psychologists have attempted to view psychotherapy in terms of learning theory. We shall not try to list all of the variations in their views or to attach names of psychologists to variations. Instead, we present a broad overview of learning theory therapy. Names of psychologists who have considerably contributed to this type of therapy follow: John Dollard, Neal Miller, O. H. Mowrer, George Kelly, Julian Rotter, and E. J. Shoben, Jr.

Learning is the summarizing name for all the processes by means of which an individual is changed so that at a later time his actions or reactions are not what they would have been without the previous activity. These modifications in the individual may be favorable or unfavorable. Much of what we have variously labeled emotional disturbance, mental illness, neurosis, psychosis, apparently derives from unfavorable learning experiences. All of the things we have considered under the general category of psychotherapy represent attempts (though not always successful) at promoting favorable learning experiences. Learning theory therapists have tried in their various ways, therefore, to apply psychological knowledge of the nature of both favorable and unfavorable learning to the problems of psychotherapy and its treatment of emotional disturbances.

Learning theory shows us in some detail why a maladjusted person does not automatically learn adjustive behavior. The Freudian concept of the pleasure principle is translated into the learning concept of reinforcement. Much of the maladjusted person's behavior may be understood as that of avoiding that which, as a result of learning experience in his past carries with it (for him) painful reactions. He repeats the avoidant behavior patterns which keep him out of the situations or experiences where he could learn more adjustive behavior. Psychotherapy, therefore, becomes primarily a process of leading the individual into new situations and experiences and controlling as much as possible the nature of those new experiences to increase the probability of gratification. Once the patient experiences gratification from the new learning, the new and more adjustive behavior patterns will be reinforced in the same fashion that the old and less adjustive behavior patterns were.

One of the most effective types of reinforcement is anxiety reduction. Since the patient who decides to undergo psychotherapy is generally so filled with anxiety that he has come to realize (often with desperation) that he can no longer manage without help, he is an especially adept subject for unlearning old behavior patterns. This is true because the reinforcing effect of the old patterns has already been reduced by their breakdown in the life situations which led him to undertake psychotherapy. He is also more susceptible to learning new patterns, which, if the therapist is skillful, can be rendered more quickly and efficiently sources of gratification than without such therapeutic guidance.

The psychoanalytic concept of transference can also be largely understood in terms of the learning theory concept of generalization. The individual develops habitual patterns of response by the process of generalization; that is, responses learned in one particular situation are brought out in what are (often childishly and superficially) identified as similar situations. If the child has many frustrating experiences with what he comes to perceive as an unloving, prudish, frustrating, castrating (in the symbolic sense) mother, he is apt (unless he has some strongly corrective experience with another type of woman concurrently) to develop the generalized concept that all women, not just his mother, possess these disturbing characteristics). Many of his maladaptive behavior patterns can then be understood in terms of this generalized learning, and much of the task of the psychotherapist would be that of directing the patient into social experiences that would be conducive to "unlearning" this concept of women and developing a new and more adjustive concept.

In learning theory terms, much of psychotherapy consists in unlearning or "counterconditioning" the anxieties that motivate compulsive, neurotic behavior (that is, self-perpetuating, self-defeating behavior patterns). Maladaptive behavior patterns are considered largely those which temporarily reduce anxiety, but do nothing about changing the conditions that have produced anxiety. The main reason such self-defeating patterns tend to be self-perpetuating is that they offer the means of immediate reduction of anxiety. The disturbed person, confused by his anxiety, is not able to achieve the perspective necessary to see beyond his emotionally confused state. He keeps doing the things that bring a short-run reduction of his anxiety even though he is simultaneously reaping a long-run increase in anxiety. The learning theory therapists have labeled this principle the "gradient of reinforcement," which hypothesizes that the consequences of actions that lie closest in time to their performance will have the greatest effect. Thus, the immediate relief of acutely painful anxiety leads the emotionally disturbed person to do over and over again what (in the long run) is a self-defeating procedure. The chief task of the learning theory therapist is to break up such self-perpetuating, self-defeating procedures and help the individual to find new patterns which will lead him to full self-realization. In one variant application of learning theory, role playing is employed as the chief tool for accomplishing this therapeutic task. By learning a new social role, the patient may develop a new outlook on his problems and thus deal with them more effectively.

Learning theorists are usually quite active and directive in their therapy. Intervention of direct interpretation is usually considered the most effective way of reducing reinforcement of the older, undesirable patterns and of increasing reinforcement of the newer, more adjustive patterns. Emphasis is also placed on the corrective and reinforcing value of experiences between therapeutic sessions, and much of the time in the actual sessions is directed toward improving the expectancy of favorable reinforcement of the newer patterns in the everyday life experiences of the patient.

Probably more than any other group of therapists, learning theory therapists have rested their contentions on inferences about human behavior that derive from scientific studies. As a group, therefore, they tend to be more cautious, less inclined toward broad claims and sweeping generalizations. They point consistently to the need for further study, to the incompleteness of learning hypotheses, to the tentative applications of existing hypotheses to human behavior in general and to psychotherapy in particular. Such therapists do hold, however, that the behavior of greatest interest to the therapist is learned: negatively, in the form of disturbances presented for treatment; positively, in the form of therapeutic procedures to be undertaken. Since such behavior is learned, these psychologists point out, it must be learned in accordance with principles of learning, known or unknown, and not by any special, mystical process. Further collaboration between the experimental learning psychologist and the psychotherapist would, therefore, seem desirable for all parties concerned.

D. ASSERTION-STRUCTURED THERAPY

E. Lakin Phillips is a psychologist who has attempted to bring the theory and practice of psychotherapy more in line with the findings of contemporary academic and experimental psychology. He has deliberately developed a non-depth theory, which he calls "the interference theory," and the therapy based on this view of human behavior he names "assertion-structured therapy."

Phillips contends that behavioral possibilities are selected by the perceiving-acting person to meet the situations that confront him rather than being the function of his "depths," his unconscious mind. The behavior patterns of any person are to be understood in terms of the choices he makes; he lives by what Phillips calls his *assertions* about the situations in which he finds himself. The individual's assertions (the hypotheses by which he lives; the assumptions on which he operates) have varying probabilities of confirmation or disconfirmation. Hence, life is a constant actuarial process; the individual is betting on his assertions and winning (confirmation) or losing (disconfirmation). The neurotic is essentially a person who is constantly betting on a set of assertions that have a high probability of disconfirmation. The neurotic's behavior, in fact, becomes what Phillips calls redundant—that is, he tends to repeat certain patterns in a circular, self-defeating way. The stronger the assertion, the greater the redundancy; the greater the redundancy, the more inflexible is the organism.

When a patient comes to a therapist, he has been experiencing failure in life. He has, in Phillips' terms, been betting on assertions with poor odds in favor of being confirmed in reality. The therapist's main job, then, is to interfere with what the person is doing, with the kind or degree of his assertions, and to teach the patient to bet less or to bet on different assertions—namely, ones that have greater probability of being confirmed.

This type of therapy, Phillips states, can be conducted on a relatively simple, practical, economical, and efficient basis. When the goal is that of helping the patient to shift his behavior patterns from assertions that hold small probability of confirmation to those that hold high probability, no elaborate hypotheses or complicated terms or long periods of time are necessary.

Psychopathology is understood in Phillips' thinking largely in terms of tension which results from conflict. When the person's assertions meet with frequent disconfirmation, the person and his environment are in conflict. The persistence of such conflict brings both physiological and psychological symptoms and syndromes, the presence of which in an individual leads the therapist to classify him as neurotic, psychotic, emotionally disturbed, mentally ill, etc. If the conflict is not soon resolved, and the tension thus continues to grow, the redundancy of behavior referred to earlier results, for the tension narrows the individual's problem-solving potential. The task of psychotherapy is to reduce the redundant condition of disconfirmation and the resulting tension, so that the individual can engage in effective problem-solving and thus be more firmly oriented in reality. And this, as stated above, is chiefly accomplished by the therapeutic process of interference with ongoing behavior and by teaching substitute patterns that hold greater probability of environmental confirmation. Focus on this procedure is the therapist's main job.

E. RATIONAL PSYCHOTHERAPY

Another very recent systematic psychotherapeutic development has evolved from the clinical practice of a New York psychologist and former psychoanalyst, Albert Ellis. Ellis calls his system "rational psychotherapy." Although influenced by his earlier analytic orientation (which was, however, broadly eclectic and critical of the psychoanalytic departures from science), Ellis' theoretical formulations and techniques may be considered to a great extent a repudiation of not only classical psychoanalysis, but of even the more liberalized approaches of the dynamic culturalists. Probably the closest approach Ellis makes to any system associated with psychoanalysis is to the individual psychology of Adler, but the similarities were reached by quite dissimilar routes.

Rational psychotherapy starts with the hypothesis that human emotion is most importantly caused and controlled by thinking. Much of what is labeled emotion, Ellis contends, is a biased, prejudiced, or strongly evaluative type of thought, and thought usually takes place in terms of language. The individual who feels positive emotions, therefore, such as love or elation, is usually saying to himself, consciously or unconsciously, some sentence to the effect that "this is good." In negative emotions, such as anger or depression, the feeling is caused by some form or variation of the sentence "this is terrible." If an adult did not employ, on some conscious or unconscious level, such sentences, Ellis holds, much of his emoting simply would not exist.

If human emotions largely result from thinking, as Ellis suggests, then one may appreciably control one's feelings by controlling one's thoughts. That is, a person may change the nature of his feelings from negative to positive (or neutral) by changing the internalized sentences, or self-talk, with which he largely created the feelings in the first place. This is what the rational therapist teaches his clients to do: to understand exactly how they create their own emotional reactions by telling themselves certain things, and how they can create different emotional reactions by telling themselves other things.

Ellis believes that emotional disturbance essentially arises when individuals mentally reiterate negative, unrealistic, illogical, self-defeating thoughts. He further believes that, for the most part, disturbed individuals are not aware that they are talking to themselves illogically, or of what the irrational links in their internalized sentences are, or of how they can learn to tell themselves saner and more realistic thoughts or sentences. That is why much of the rational therapist's work is helping the client to find out what he is now saying in the way of internalized sentences, to question the rationality of what he discovers he is saying, and to substitute more rational, more realistic, and more positive self-talk.

Athough Ellis grants that some of man's illogical ideas may be rooted in his biological limitations, most of them derive from his upbringing. A person in our society gets most of his irrational self-sentences from his parents, his teachers, his peer group, and his contact with the general culture, especially through mass media. It is virtually impossible, Ellis points out, to grow up in our society today without an over-abundance of illogical ideas and philosophies which inescapably lead to a certain amount of self-defeating patterns or neurosis.

There are many illogical internalized statements that Ellis feels are very commonplace in our culture. He states that usually several of these almost universal, self-defeating sentences (along with some individualized ones) can be found in any patient who reports for therapy. We present here only a few of what Ellis maintains to be commonly held irrational beliefs. The "illogical" idea which leads to human self-defeat and neurosis is presented first (a) and the more reasonable substitute that the rational therapist attempts to inculcate is given second (b).

1. (a) It is a dire necessity for an adult to be approved or loved by almost everyone for almost everything he does. It is most important what others think of one. It is better to depend on others than on oneself, for a self-sufficient person is a selfish person.

(b) It is pleasant, but not necessary, for an adult to be approved or loved by others. It is better to win one's own respect than others' approval. It is more desirable to stand on one's own feet than to depend mainly on others.

2. (a) It is terrible, horrible, and catastrophic when things are

not the way one would like them to be; they *should* be better than
they are. Others should make things easier for one, help with life's
difficulties. One should not have to put off present pleasures for future gains.

(b) It is too bad when things are not the way one would like
them to be, and one should try to change conditions for the better;
but when this is impossible, one had better become resigned to the
way things are and stop pointless complaining. It is nice when others
help one with life's difficulties; but if they don't, that is too bad and
one can confront these difficulties oneself. If one does not often put
off present pleasures for future gain, one sabotages one's own well-
being.

3. (a) It is easier to avoid than to face life difficulties and self-
responsibilities. Inertia and inaction are necessary and/or pleasant.
One should rebel against doing things, however necessary, if it is
unpleasant to do them.

(b) The so-called easier way is usually the much harder way
in the long run, and the only way to solve difficult problems is to face
them squarely. Inertia and inaction are generally unnecessary and
relatively unpleasant: humans tend to be happiest when they are actively and vitally absorbed in creative pursuits. One should do necessary things, however unpleasant they may be, without complaining
and rebelling.

Ellis contends that rational therapy, though usually a briefer procedure than psychoanalysis, is in some respects more depth-centered
and intensive because it seeks to reveal and assail the basic ideas or
philosophies or values which underlie neurosis. Although in that
sense depth-oriented, the rational therapist focuses his attention on
what he believes are the current, not the past, causes of the emotional disturbance. He shows the client that his problems, especially
his negative feelings (such as anger, depression, anxiety, and guilt),
arise not from past events or external situations but from his present irrational attitudes toward or illogical fears about these events and
situations. Thus a client is shown that it is not his Oedipal attachment
which made and keeps him neurotic, but his self-perpetuated illogical
ideas underlying this attachment: his groundless beliefs that he is
wicked for lusting after his mother, that he cannot survive without his

mother's and father's love, that he will be castrated by his father, that it is horrible to have others think him incestuous, etc.

The rational therapist emphasizes *self-interest* in his treatment procedures. One should love one's neighbor, or at least take care not to harm him, not out of any moral authoritarianism, but out of self-interest: namely, only by so doing is one likely to help build the kind of society in which one would best live *oneself*. The rational therapist believes, in other words, that self-interest demands social interest; and that the rational individual who strives for his own happiness will, for that very reason, also be interested in others. Ellis also believes (along with Fromm and others) that the human animal normally and naturally is helpful and loving to other humans, provided that it is not enmeshed in illogical thinking that leads it to self-destructive, self-hating behavior.

Ellis frequently employs the usual expressive-emotive, supportive, relationship, and insight-interpretative techniques, especially early in the therapy, but he considers these methods merely preparatory to his main task. While most therapists directly or indirectly show the client that he is behaving illogically, the rational therapist makes a forthright, unequivocal *attack* on the client's general and specific irrational ideas and tries to *induce* him to adopt more rational ones in their place.

There are two main ways, according to Ellis, that the rational therapist makes a concerted attack on the disturbed individual's irrational positions: (a) the therapist serves as a frank counter-propagandist who directly contradicts and denies the self-defeating propaganda and superstitions which the client originally learned and keeps perpetuating. (b) The therapist encourages, persuades, cajoles, and at times commands the client to engage in some kind of activity which itself will act as a forceful counter-propagandistic agency against the nonsense he believes. Both of these therapeutic acts are consciously performed with the goal of finally getting the client to internalize a rational philosophy of living just as he originally internalized the irrational ideas and attitudes of his parents, siblings, peer group, and general culture.

Rational psychotherapy, Ellis says, is like most other systems in working best with individuals who are not too psychotic, who are fairly intelligent, and who are reasonably young when they come for treatment. The traits most positively related to successful outcome, Ellis has tentatively stated, are a willingness to work, intellectual curiosity, and a willingness to accept direction from the therapist at the beginning. Among those who benefit least from rational therapy, at this point in its development, are clients who will not accept hard work and discipline, who refuse to try to think for themselves, and who dogmatically insist on adhering to some absolutist creed, such as orthodox Freudianism.

Summary

Directive psychotherapy, general semantics, learning theory therapy, assertion-structured therapy, and rational psychotherapy were the five systems treated in Chapter 8. All five constitute marked departures from the psychoanalytic mode.

Thorne's directive therapy is mainly a reaction against what he considers the extremist, nondirective tendencies of client-centered therapy. He emphasizes that the direction of the therapeutic process belongs in the hands of the skilled therapist and not the sick patient. In helping the patient to work out a new style of life, a more effective pattern of living, Thorne believes in drawing upon any technique or resource legitimately available to the therapist. This includes the utilization of various diagnostic tools and a therapeutic plan of action based as nearly as possible on scientific observations of human behavior in general and the patient's behavior in particular.

General semantics consists of the attempt to apply "knowledge of symbols and their meaning and influence on human behavior" to the therapeutic situation. Korzybski has postulated that neurotic behavior stems from a lack of clear understanding in the use of words and their meanings, and his therapy consists primarily in teaching the patient the correct word-habits to replace the faulty orientations in language he previously acquired. In like manner, Wendell Johnson has contended that the emotionally disturbed person talks and thinks himself into conflicts and that therapy is chiefly a matter of retraining the patient in the meaning of the words he applies to himself and his environment. While relatively few therapists consider themselves primarily semanticists, the work of Korzybski, Johnson, and other semanticists has influenced other therapists in undertaking greater study and work with communication problems.

Learning theory psychologists have suggested that much of psychotherapy consists in "unlearning" or "counter-conditioning" the anxieties that motivate the self-defeating, self-perpetuating behavior patterns in neurotics. The major work of the therapist, as thus conceived, is to break up the attitudes that are acting as reinforcements of these self-defeating patterns. Interjection of direct interpretation is usually considered the most effective way of reducing reinforcement of the older, undesirable patterns and of increasing reinforcement of the newer, more adjustive patterns. Emphasis is also placed on the corrective and reinforcing value of experiences between therapeutic sessions.

The main contention of Phillips' assertion-structured therapy is that the behavior patterns of any person are to be understood in terms of the choices he makes. He lives by what Phillips calls his *assertions* about the situations in which he finds himself. When his assertions meet with frequent disconfirmation in his interpersonal relations, he develops the redundant, self-defeating behavior of the neurotic. Therapy consists largely in interfering with these self-defeating patterns of the individual and helping to develop behavior based on assertions that have much greater probability of being confirmed in his day-by-day interactions.

It is Ellis' main thesis, in what he calls rational psychotherapy, that emotion in the adult human being is most importantly caused and controlled by thinking. The disturbed individual has adopted a lot of irrational and illogical ideas that cause him to behave in a neurotic or psychotic fashion. The job of the therapist is to help the disturbed individual to become aware of the verbalizations he delivers to himself in becoming distressed, point out the stupidity of such self-sayings, and help the person to adopt more rational points of view. When this is achieved, according to Ellis, the individual will cease to be emotionally disturbed.

Selected Readings

Dollard, John, and Neal E. Miller, *Personality and Psychotherapy*. New York: McGraw, 1950.

Ellis, Albert, *How to Live with a Neurotic*. New York: Crown, 1957.

————, "Outcome of Employing Three Techniques of Psychotherapy," *Journal of Clinical Psychology*, 1957, 23, 344-350.

Johnson, Wendell, *People in Quandaries*. New York: Harper, 1946.

Kelly, George, *The Psychology of Personal Constructs* (2 vols). New York: Norton, 1955.

Korzybski, Alfred, *Science and Sanity*. Lancaster, Pa.: Science Press, 1941.

Mowrer, O. H., *Learning Theory and Personality Dynamics*. New York: Ronald, 1950.

Phillips, E. Lakin, *Psychotherapy: A Modern Theory and Practice*. Englewood Cliffs, N. J.: Prentice-Hall, 1956.

Rotter, Julian B., *Social Learning and Clinical Psychology*. Englewood Cliffs, N. J.: Prentice-Hall, 1954.

Thorne, Frederick, "Directive and Eclectic Personality Counseling." From James L. McCary, and Daniel E. Sheer, *Six Approaches to Psychotherapy*. New York: Dryden, 1955.

————, *Principles of Personality Counseling*. Brandon, Vt.: Journal of Clinical Psychology, 1950.

CHAPTER 9

Group Psychotherapy

Group psychotherapy was apparently first practiced with patients suffering from pulmonary tuberculosis by a Boston internist, Dr. Joseph H. Pratt, in 1905. One of the first applications of the group technique with psychoneurotics was by a minister (who later became a psychiatrist), L. Cody Marsh, in 1909. Psychodrama, a form of group therapy, was originated in 1911 by J. L. Moreno.

Soon after World War I, Dr. E. W. Lazell began experimental work in group procedures with schizophrenics in St. Elizabeth's Hospital in Washington, D. C. He later carried on this work in the Veterans Administration. The more psychoanalytically oriented type of group therapy began about 1930, grew fairly rapidly during the later thirties, and, along with many other group therapy orientations, mushroomed during and following World War II.

Today practically every type of individual therapy system has had some of its followers turn their attention to psychotherapeutic work with groups. While we can by no means sample all of the wide varieties of group therapy, we shall try to give some attention to most of the major approaches.

A. PSYCHODRAMA AND RELATED TECHNIQUES

J. L. Moreno first began to experiment with group therapeutic techniques with children in Vienna and was one of the early users of various group methods in the United States. The aim of group psychotherapy as conceived by Moreno is the integration of the patient's self against the uncontrolled forces around him. This is done by exploring his immediate environment by a process Moreno calls sociometric analysis and by helping the patient to understand and handle the environmental forces thus revealed. Free and spontaneous interaction is important in this type of group therapy. This includes relations among patients, between patients and therapists, and among therapists (usually more than one is present).

Chief therapist, auxiliary therapists, and patients are all equals in the therapeutic group as Moreno defines it. He feels that the group composition should resemble as nearly as possible a cross-section of the community in age, sex, ethnic characteristics, etc. The therapist has the therapeutic productivity and stability of the group as his main concern, but he also needs to consider himself as an equal patient, according to Moreno.

The interactional type of group psychotherapy was based on spontaneous interaction among members of the group assisted by a therapist, and psychodrama (linked with group psychotherapy by Moreno from 1936 onward) added the acting-out principle. Moreno and his followers consider psychodrama the depth therapy of the group and contend that "therapeutic acting out" in a controlled environment is both a preventive and curative measure against "irrational acting-out" in life itself.

In the course of interactional group sessions, a member of the group may experience an emotional problem of an intensity for which words seem insufficient. He has an urge to act out the situation, and, in psychodramatically oriented group therapy, a stage or specially designated area is provided for him to do so. One or another member of the group (which may be one of the therapists) may become involved in a counter-role and step upon the stage to co-act with the first patient. Others may or may not join in.

Many psychodramatic techniques have been developed through the years. Rules for their procedure are adapted as the group situation dictates and are not rigidly followed. Sometimes the main focus is on the group and sometimes it shifts to individual members of the group. One frequently helpful method for an individual to gain a new perspective of himself and his adjustment is what is called *role reversal:* A becomes B, and B becomes A, in an acting-out situation.

Another technique is that of the double: an auxiliary therapist, for example, joins Mr. X on the stage and plays the role of Mr. X, too. The double is useful in helping the patient to produce new hypotheses for avenues of further understanding. A variation of the double technique is what is called the mirror method. Here another group member plays Mr. X's role while Mr. X watches.

The foregoing are only a few samples of the psychodramatic devices that Moreno and others have developed. The chief value of psychodrama, according to its proponents, is that it takes place in a setting which approximates most closely the problem-producing situations of life. As problems appear, they are dealt with on the spot, and the solutions are extended to significant people and situations of the outer world. Psychodramatists contend that irrational and compulsive patterns are more readily seen and treated, in the situation which involves action rather than just conversation. Distortions of reality by the patients become quickly apparent and can be dealt with in the interpersonal relationships in which they arise. Thus, it is held, psychodrama goes beyond the theoretical insight characteristic of other forms of therapy and provides corrective emotional experience.

B. ANALYTIC GROUP THERAPY

The early work in group therapy by Dr. Lazell at St. Elizabeth's Hospital was undertaken from a psychoanalytic point of view in part, but tended to develop later along lines of inspirational exhortation. Pioneer work of a more clear-cut psychoanalytic variety was undertaken in the mid-thirties by Wender and Schilder. The former stressed insight, patient to patient transference, catharsis, and group interaction as the main factors of the group therapy process. Schilder extensively utilized the method of free association with groups of four to six patients, who were also being seen in individual analysis. The most extensive exploration of the psychoanalytic approach to group psychotherapy has been by S. R. Slavson, founding president of the American Group Psychotherapy Association and editor of that organization's International Journal of Group Psychotherapy.

Slavson has emphasized the importance of the selection of group members on such bases as clinical symptomatology, motivation for treatment, and intelligence. He, like Moreno, stresses spontaneity and feels that the major advantage of the group is that it permits the acting out of instinctual drives, which is facilitated by the stimulating effect of the group situation. Unlike Moreno, however, Slavson feels that it is the individual and not the group that should always be the focus of the therapist's attention. The group to Slavson is unimportant in itself and is simply a means for speeding up individual therapy. Catharsis, insight, transference relationships, reality testing, etc., are dynamic features of the analytic group situation, similar to, but not identical with, those found in individual therapy. In transference, there is what Slavson has called "target multiplicity": that is, the patient can displace feelings not only to the therapist, but to other patients, who often serve as sibling substitutes.

The ultimate aim of analytic group therapy, like individual psychoanalysis, is the facilitation of the fullest possible communication of unconscious material. In this process of making the patient more aware of his own unconscious, the group therapist has his difficulties increased greatly in one sense by having a complex network of transferences to analyze and interpret. In another sense, however, his task is reduced by the greater possibility of demonstrating and interpreting to the patient the unreality of his transference reaction in the group situation, where the patient can observe the differing transference reactions of his fellow group members. In addition, since each patient's transference reactions are distributed among members of the group, the analyst does not need to deal with the full force of transference on him personally as in individual psychoanalysis.

Some psychoanalysts who are inexperienced in group psychotherapy have questioned whether patients would achieve in the group setting the degree of self-exposure and free association which reveal deep unconscious conflicts. Experienced group analysts, like Slavson, contend that self-exposure can be even greater in the group, where the patient has the support and the example of self-revealing fellow patients. Although various types of resistances are encountered in the psychoanalytically oriented group (just as in the individual setting), experienced group therapists hold that they are often more readily overcome. It is believed that in an effectively operating group, the attitudes of fellow members often convince a resistive patient that his repressed feelings are not only acceptable, but that he will help the group and himself gain status and achieve further understanding by revealing them.

Psychoanalytically oriented group psychotherapists differ among themselves in some of their approaches. In general, however, they discourage group meetings held without the therapist (a pattern followed among some non-analytic therapists) or patient socialization outside the group sessions. Some analysts conduct individual therapy with the same patients they are seeing in the group, some refer group members to other analysts for individual therapy, and some hold that the group therapeutic procedures are sufficient without individual therapeutic supplementation. While new patients are frequently introduced into a group early in the history of that particular group, such a procedure is usually believed to be disruptive after a group has been long established.

The application of psychoanalysis to the field of group therapy is still quite new and fluid. It is probably safe to say that practically any group therapeutic procedure that the reader can imagine, as well as many he cannot imagine, has by now been practiced and reported in the literature by at least one psychoanalytically-oriented group therapist.

C. GROUP-CENTERED THERAPY

This system of group psychotherapy is the application of the client-centered therapeutic theories and techniques (see Chapter 6) to the group setting. It is believed that each member of a group needs to find the same feeling of acceptance from other group members, as the client finds from the therapist in individual therapy. The genuine expression of such feeling of acceptance by the group therapist, it is contended, spreads contagiously through the group, but it may take some time for it to do so. When it happens, however, it has more beneficial effects than acceptance by the therapist alone, for it is a more potent experience, according to the Rogersians, to be understood and accepted by several people who are honestly sharing their feelings in a joint enterprise than simply by a professionally understanding therapist.

As a general procedure, prospective group members are interviewed by the therapist prior to the first meeting of the group. At this time the therapist tries to learn something about the person's problems, to describe the way groups operate, to give him an opportunity to decide whether or not he wants to join a group, and to enable the therapist and the prospective member to develop some mutual feelings of security.

Groups are usually made up of about six clients and the therapist with no visitors permitted and no additions to the group after the first meeting. Although special groups are occasionally set up (such as for engaged or married couples), most groups are formed along such broadly selective lines as similarity of age (adults, children, adolescents), and degree of neurosis (there are of course separate groups for psychotics).

There is considerable flexibility regarding frequency and length of meetings for any particular group. The decision as to how often and how long to meet is usually left to the group, but once a pattern is set, it is usually adhered to. The most frequent pattern appears to be two meetings per week of about one hour's duration each, and the total number of meetings per group has tended to average about twenty.

As the reader of the client-centered point of view would assume, the therapist in group-centered therapy does not have prepared material for discussion by the group. The members are free to bring forth for discussion any problems they deem significant. As in individual therapy, the therapist's main role is not active interpretation, but acceptance, reflection, and clarification of attitudes and feelings presented in the group. The therapist is not strictly passive, however, for he intervenes in case he believes that one or more members of the group are blocking or threatening the free expression of feelings by any other member of the group.

The therapeutic role in group-centered therapy often falls to other members of the group than the therapist. Studies made by the client-centered school seem to indicate that in later sessions, group members become adept at assuming the therapeutic role for fellow members. That is to say, they seem to become more permissive and accepting and less inclined to be interpretive, evaluative, and critical. They are thus able more adequately to function in a way that assists other group members to explore their own feelings further.

One of the advantages of group-centered over individual client-centered therapy, according to its proponents, is the immediate opportunity it affords the group member to test the effectiveness of his ability to relate to people and to improve his skills in interpersonal relations. It provides the patient with many relationships rather than simply the one with the therapist. It seems likely (the Rogersians here agree with the Sullivanians) that the most important changes in personality can be worked out only in meaningful interpersonal relations, and the group has the advantage of providing many more opportunities for such interaction than individual therapy.

In general, the group-centered therapist needs qualities similar to the individual therapist. He must possess such qualities as unconditional positive regard for members of the group, empathic understanding of the feelings of group members and confidence in their ability to be responsible for themselves, with the ability to restrain on his part any tendency to intervene on the assumption that his point of view of the situation is superior. Experience in individual client-centered therapy is believed to be the best preparation for a leader of group-centered therapy.

D. FAMILY THERAPY

A somewhat new approach in psychotherapy is to consider the family, rather than the individual, as the unit in which emotional illness occurs and therefore the unit toward which treatment needs to be directed. There have been various independent therapeutic attempts at family treatment, one of which is that of C. F. Midelfort, a Wisconsin psychiatrist.

Midelfort's point of view is that there tend to be balancing and opposing psychopathologies within a family. A patient with obsessive-compulsive neurosis, for example, is likely to have a family in which some members will have patterns similar to his and other members will have impulsive, acting-out behavior. The latter family members are expressing directly what the obsessive-compulsives are concealing and controlling by their rigidity. Husband and wife, Midelfort states, often show these opposite traits, and their children as well. If the first child is obsessive-compulsive, the second will be like the other parent (impulsive). The third child is likely to be more like the first than the second, and so on in a balancing-opposing pattern.

Each group in a family such as the foregoing is a threat to the other, and one of the roles of the therapist is to remove this threat and help each to become more like the other. In the example presented, the obsessive-compulsive family members are encouraged to feel safe about expressing their impulses more spontaneously, and the impulsive members are helped to exercise more strict controls. A better balance can thus be achieved, and many symptoms can be eliminated. The reason the family cannot do this without therapeutic help is that each group provokes an exaggeration of the existing reaction in the other as a defense against becoming like the other.

In interviews he conducts with families of the type we have described, Midelfort gives assurance and permission for each type of behavior pattern. First he supports the obsessive-compulsive to be the way he is. The impulsive spouse is then encouraged to admit obsessive-compulsive traits within himself. As this formerly very impulsive spouse becomes more obsessive-compulsive (by releasing such tendencies unconsciously there, but previously repressed), the obsessive-compulsive patient can relax and become aware and accepting of his own impulsiveness. The new balance thus established is of less opposing extremes, and the intrapsychic and intrafamily conflict potentials are considerably reduced.

Midelfort takes comparable approaches to the foregoing in dealing with other types of mental illness. The therapist's role, as he sees it, is to analyze the kinds of dynamic interactional patterns in operation in a family, to determine how the therapist can break the circular processes that are handicapping and defeating family members, and to utilize the unconscious accompaniments of existing roles to work out an equilibrium less threatening to each family member.

Individual therapy is used conjunctively with family therapy by Midelfort. He believes, however, that the exclusive use of the former causes a wider gap to form between the patient and his family and may lead to the breaking up of family life. By also using the family therapy technique of bringing the family and patient together in interviews with the therapist, Midelfort believes the family unity can be strengthened. In the family interview, he states, there is a greater objectivity achieved, which leads the family out of its subjective, pathological interactions. The therapist can demonstrate simultaneously for family members an objective and united approach to their problem situations.

Midelfort contends that the main goal of individual therapy is the overcoming of the patient's unconscious and subjective blocks against group activity. When such blocks are sufficiently removed or reduced, the patient then needs to learn to make real and objective those activities that satisfy his social needs. This he can learn to do through group participation. Since the group to which the patient most urgently needs to learn to relate with less disturbance and greater effectiveness is his own family, and since usually the other members are themselves in need of education in more effective interpersonal functioning, family therapy is often the most desirable form of group therapy.

E. OTHER ORIENTATIONS

A psychologist, George R. Bach, has made a serious effort to combine the field theory of Kurt Lewin (essentially Gestalt psychology applied to the study of groups and termed "group dynamics") with a psychoanalytic orientation in developing his system of group psychotherapy. He feels that many of the approaches to group psychotherapy have been simply the application of individual therapeutic techniques without thorough knowledge of the structure and function of groups themselves. While we cannot summarize the intricate interweavings of psychoanalytic and group dynamic theories and practices made by Bach, we shall point out a few of his practical suggestions regarding the operations of group psychotherapy.

Five types of patients, Bach believes, should be excluded from groups: those with insufficient reality contact (psychotics), the cultural deviants (homosexual or criminal, who function best in groups that are composed of individuals with similar symptoms), the extremely dominant and monopolistic personalities, the psychopathically defensive and impulsive, and those with acute environmental crises (recent divorce, death of a child, etc.). Certain types of persons may be acceptable in one group and not another, according to Bach. One group, for example, may have an opening for an aggressive male, while such an individual would be quite disruptive in another group. Bach also cautions against too great heterogeneity of backgrounds (religion, age, etc.), but feels that broadly representative social experiences should be included as much as possible. The range of intelligence should not be too great for ready communication.

Bach holds that the group leader should play the following procedural roles: (1) reflection of group-originated communications with some simplification and facilitation of understandability when needed; (2) some interpretation of group emotions linked with occasional summaries; (3) occasional functioning as an expert to familiarize the group with techniques that may be utilized (such as dream association, psychodrama, and projective drawing). The therapist should also encourage members of the group to act on the principle that while there are no secrets inside the group, all group activities should be kept confidential. In practice this means that everything anybody says, thinks, or does which involves another member of the group is open to discussion in the group, but that each member will feel secure about his behaviors not being a topic of discussion by outsiders.

The group's goal, as Bach sees it, is free communication on a nondefensive, personal, and emotional basis. He feels that the group leader cannot push the group in its progress, but can merely act as a facilitator or catalyst. In general, each member will obtain benefit to the degree of his own efforts. Members who communicate to the group their feelings, association, and perceptions with openness and consistency will, in the long run, find the group a therapeutically effective medium.

Hubert S. Coffey and associates have taken a Sullivanian approach to the study of group therapy. They have made the specific assumption that the problems of the emotionally disturbed person lie in the conflict between the patient's conception of himself and what he communicates to others. This often amounts to the difference between the patient's conscious and unconscious social roles, and the group therapeutic situation, according to Coffey, offers him the best opportunity (if properly conducted) to see these two sets of roles in relation to each other.

Coffey and associates have distinguished three phases of group development: (1) the period of defensiveness and resistance, in which the patients act out the conflicts between conscious and unconscious roles that have caused them difficulty in their other interpersonal relations. In this first phase, the role of the therapist is largely one of allowing free description of their views of themselves and their problems by group members. (2) The next phase is one referred to as that of confiding. In this period much emphasis is given to discussion of dreams, fantasies, early experiences, and less anxiety is shown regarding maintenance of conscious social roles. The therapist in this phase mainly supports testing out of unconscious roles and revelation of their possible sources and provides supporting and clarifying data from the first period of the group's development. A close interpersonal bond tends to develop in this second phase of the group. (3) The last period is referred to as the integrative-prospective. Interpretations from both therapist and group members become more integrative and extensive. Comprehensive summaries for each group member are allowed for in the sessions of this third stage (the last seven of a total of 24 sessions). If the therapy has been successful, the patient now sees the conflict between his conscious and unconscious roles, becomes aware of his rigid social techniques, and, with the group's help, develops new views of himself and his relations with others.

A didactic or pedagogical approach to group therapy has been developed by J. W. Klapman and others. In this approach the lecture material is the main basis of organization and orientation. A series of lectures is presented on such topics as the nature of the common attitudes toward mental illness, types of neurotic conflict, relationship of the mentally ill person to society and vice versa, mechanisms of defense, forms of resistance to therapy, spontaneous resurgence to mental health, and so on. Along with the lectures, readings are assigned and discussed, autobiographies are written and presented, controversial subjects are debated, special readings are assigned to group members for oral presentation to the group, etc. In short, as the term didactic group therapy implies, these are classes in mental health for the mentally ill.

The last type of group psychotherapy that we shall mention is one developed in a state hospital. Its goals are to help patients to gain realistic perspectives regarding their problems and to develop confidence in themselves and in the helping attitudes of others in working out satisfactory solutions to their problems. The therapy, referred to as round-table psychotherapy, is based on the premise that a patient will gain better self-understanding by trying to understand and help others.

Round-table therapy is set up in such a way that a panel of seven patients discuss the problems of one of the seven in front of an audience of eighteen (the remainder of the patients on the ward). The therapist becomes the eighth, but relatively inactive, member of the panel. The therapist has a pre-panel discussion, however, with each of the seven participants. The procedure is one of encouraging the six patients to induce the seventh to discuss his problems freely and to help him solve these problems. The panel is also given considerable authority in making recommendations regarding the treatment of the patient whose problems are discussed.

Variations in the foregoing procedures have been undertaken in other hospitals. Increasingly group therapeutic techniques of various types are employed in hospitals to improve the effectiveness of individual therapy (of both the psychological and medical varieties) and raise the morale and esprit de corps of the hospital patients and staff.

Summary

Group psychotherapies of various kinds have developed rapidly since World War II. The types dealt with in this chapter are psychodrama, analytic group therapy, group-centered therapy, family therapy, the orientations of Bach and Coffey, the didactic approach, and round-table psychotherapy.

The aim of group psychotherapy, as conceived by Moreno, is the integration of the patient's self against the uncontrolled forces around him. He feels free and spontaneous interaction is important in achieving this goal. The "depth" type of such interactional group therapy, according to Moreno, is therapeutic acting out, called psychodrama.

The psychoanalytic point of view has been applied to group psychotherapy by many workers, most notable of whom is Slavson. Catharsis, insight, transference relationships, reality testing, and the like are dynamic features of the analytic group situation, similar to those found in individual analysis. Both special difficulties and special aids are found in group analytic, as compared with individual analytic, therapy. The ultimate aim of the two is the same, however: the facilitation of the fullest possible communication of unconscious material.

Group-centered therapy is the application of the Rogersian approach to group psychotherapy. Feelings of acceptance are stressed in group-centered as in individual client-centered therapy. While difficulties are sometimes encountered in helping each member of the group to be positively accepting of every other member, the effect, when achieved, is considered even more valuable than such acceptance by the therapist in individual therapy. One of the advantages of group-centered over individual client-centered therapy, according to its exponents, is the immediate opportunity it affords the group member to test the effectiveness of his ability to relate to people and to improve his skills in interpersonal relations.

The family is the group treated in a type of group psychotherapy developed by Midelfort. His point of view is that there tend to be balancing and opposing psychopathologies within a family. By treating the whole family, instead of just an individual family member, Midelfort believes he can more effectively help each member to better mental health by bringing about a more realistic, less repressed equilibrium in family interactions.

Bach has combined the field theory of Kurt Lewin with the psychoanalytic orientation in his form of group psychotherapy. The group goal, as Bach sees it, is free communication on a nondefensive, personal, and emotional basis. The group leader can facilitate the group's reaching this goal by various techniques Bach discusses.

Coffey and associates have made an application of some of Sullivan's ideas to group therapy. They assume that the problems of the emotionally disturbed person lie in the conflict between the patient's conception of himself and what he communicates to others. The main function of group therapy is to help the patient to see his unconsciously operating social roles.

In didactic or pedagogical group therapy the stress is placed on communicating mentally healthful concepts to members of the group through lectures, readings, symposia, special reports, and other edu-

cational devices. Round-table psychotherapy is a method developed
in a mental hospital whereby a panel of patients discuss the problems
of a fellow patient, in the presence of a therapist.

Selected Readings

Bach, George R., *Intensive Group Psychotherapy*. New York: Ronald,
1954.

Coffey, Hubert S. "Group Psychotherapy." From L. A. Pennington, and
I. A. Berg, *An Introduction to Clinical Psychology*, 2nd ed. New
York: Ronald, 1954.

Hobbs, Nicholas, "Group-Centered Psychotherapy." In Carl R. Rogers,
Client-Centered Therapy. New York: Houghton, 1951.

Klapman, J. W., *Group Psychotherapy: Theory and Practice*. New York:
Grune, 1946.

Midelfort, C. F., *The Family in Psychotherapy*. New York: McGraw,
1957.

Moreno, J. L., *Psychodrama*. New York: Beacon, 1946.

Powdermaker, Florence B., and J. D. Frank, *Group Psychotherapy*.
Cambridge, Mass.: Harvard, 1953.

Slavson, S. R., *Analytic Group Psychotherapy*. New York: Columbia,
1950.

CHAPTER 10

Critique and Overview

In this final chapter, our difficult task is to try to ascertain, in as clear and objective a manner as possible, what the various systems of psychotherapy each have to offer.

Let us make a broad division of the various schools into two main categories: A. the emotionally oriented, or affective, therapies and B. the intellectually oriented, or cognitive, therapies. Group A constitutes the great bulk of psychotherapeutic systems: all types of psychoanalysis, with the exception of Adler's individual psychology (which is discussed as a form of psychoanalysis more for historical than content purposes), client-centered therapy, Gestalt therapy, hypnotherapy, experiential therapy, conditioned reflex therapy, therapy by reciprocal inhibition and all of the group psychotherapies except didactic group therapy. At times the dynamic culturalists (especially Sullivan and Fromm) veer in the cognitive direction, but most of their therapeutic efforts, like those of the rest of Group A, are directed toward what may be called emotional reconditioning.

Group B may be considered therapeutic nonconformists. The psychobiologic therapists belong primarily in this group, even though they pay some token respect to certain psychoanalytic techniques and theories. Adlerians, who have frankly developed what they refer to as an educational type of therapy, may be considered cognitive therapists. The entire group in Chapter 8 are mainly oriented toward intellectual reconditioning. And that, with the addition of the already mentioned didactic group therapists, is the whole of Group B. None of the therapists in this group have an extensive following.

It would seem, therefore, that Group B is swimming against the therapeutic current, and so it is in some ways. Yet actually the affective vs. cognitive issue is not so simple as it at first appears. Not only have the dynamic culturalists brought increasing emphasis on ego instead of id in deviant psychoanalytic circles, but even the classical analytic group has in practice spent more and more of its time and attention in analysis of the ego defenses, rather than prolonged unwinding of the id impulses. This is a trend in the direction of greater attention to the cognitive, the executive, the less deeply unconscious (if not actually conscious) aspects of the personality.

The client-centered therapists are deep within the affective division of therapy. They speak almost exclusively of feelings, emotional experience, acceptance, emotional safety, love, positive regard, empathy, and similar topics of affect. The Rogersians are actually relying, in final analysis, on the ability of the patient to emerge from the warm, accepting atmosphere of therapy with more rational. logical, efficient, realistic ego structure. They feel that the cognitive aspects of the personality can function adequately once the emotional blocks are dissolved by the accepting therapeutic environment. Although the Rogersians conduct much rationally oriented research, the weight of the influence of their therapeutic system strikes this writer as being in the reactionary tradition of mysticism and art rather than in the direction of advancing rationality and science.

The experiential therapy of Whitaker and Malone, though startlingly "radical" in some of its techniques (such as the occasional use of aggression and therapeutic sleeping), is even more reactionary in its impact, for it advocates a return to the early psychoanalytic emphasis on the deep unconscious forces (the id impulses). These therapists direct their whole effort toward removing the rational, cognitive ego functions from the treatment situation and concentrating on primary processes of communication: fantasy relationships between therapist's id and patient's id. Such activities by their very nature tend to rule out the application of the rational tools of science. We must, however, acknowledge a further factor. It is quite apparent that much of the work undertaken by Whitaker and Malone is with very sick persons, for the most part psychotics. A rational, realistic approach is considerably less effective with a person who has renounced rationality and has escaped from reality than with a neurotic who is simply exhibiting various self-defeating patterns of reality. Understood in this sense, experiential therapy may be a necessary therapeutic departure from rationality for the purpose of meeting and helping the psychotic in his own world of unreality.

The Rogersians, on the other hand, are dealing primarily with mildly disturbed patients, and their rejection of a cognitive approach to their patients' needs to be understood in another frame of reference.

Client-centered therapy, it seems to me, is most clearly and objectively perceived as a historical correction. Rogers developed his emphasis on permissiveness as a reaction to a kind of totalitarianism which had developed in the field of psychotherapy in the late thirties. The Freudians in the twenties and early thirties were the unrecognized minority in the psychiatric fraternity. By the late thirties they had not only won their battle for legitimate recognition among psychiatrists and the general public, but were experiencing a wave of high prestige. Psychoanalysis was being much sought after as a kind of general cure-all for social, as well as personal, problems. As is true of many minorities who newly acquire power, arrogant and dictatorial attitudes were not uncommon among psychoanalytically trained psychiatrists. These attitudes are still to be encountered, but there is a growing realistic humility today regarding the limitations of both the techniques and theories of psychoanalysis among many analysts.

This atmosphere of totalitarianism in psychotherapy in the thirties was further strengthened by the attitudes of psychiatric social workers who came to function in ancillary roles to psychiatrists in clinics, hospitals, and private and public agencies. The service concept was so effectively drilled into most social workers of at least that generation that most of them functioned in devoted, unquestioning servitude (a servitude which was further enhanced by the fact that most psychiatrists were men and most social workers were women). The psychoanalyst's utterance was the not-to-be-disputed word of authority.

It required an intelligent, emotionally independent, male psychologist, free of any feeling of need to be beholden to the psychiatric group or the psychoanalytic sub-group, to lead a successful rebellion against the father figure of the psychoanalyst. The need for such a psychologist was filled by Carl Rogers, and the way he rebelled was naturally structured by his personal and professional predispositions.

His method can be fairly compared to the route taken by Ghandi and his followers in achieving Indian independence of the British. Like Ghandi, Rogers brought about no head-on clash of bristling authority with bristling counter-authority. He quietly emulated Ghandi by non-violently resisting the dictates of authority. He demonstrated in theory, in practice, and in research that people can be just as effectively helped without the complicated psychoanalytic superstructure of technique and mythology of theory. His non-violent rebellion gathered momentum by being joined not only by many other psychologists, but by dissatisfied elements in other professions: ministers, educators, sociologists, social workers, and even a few psychiatrists. As we discussed early in Chapter 6, part of the strength of the client-centered approach was drawn from its appeal to factors deep within the American culture.

The psychotherapeutic revolutionary war would seem to have been won by the rebels. Psychologists and others than psychiatrists and psychoanalysts are increasingly practicing psychotherapy of their own individual choosing.

But some of the post-independence problems of psychotherapy seem resistive to solution by the methods of the revolution. Just as the Indians have found that passive non-resistance does not solve difficulties that they have had to face since the departure of the British, the realistic psychotherapist must admit that not all therapeutic problems respond to emotional permissiveness in the clinical setting.

What Rogers has recently suggested as the necessary and sufficient conditions for psychotherapeutic personality change (see the latter part of Chapter 6) may be what he has labeled them for some *slightly* disturbed patients. Such conditions may even be necessary and sufficient for some moderately to severely disturbed patients whose main problem has been a feeling of being unloved and unaccepted. But this writer shares the point of view of other non-Rogersian clinicians that there are many quite disturbed patients for whom unconditional positive regard and empathic understanding, however well communicated, are insufficient to effect psychotherapeutic personality change. While awaiting the research for which Rogers calls to test these and other therapeutic hypotheses, many clinicians join Thorne (see Chapter 8) in emphasizing the need of many patients for therapeutic direction, diagnosis, and recovery plans based increasingly on the tools of rationality.

In a sense, the client-centered therapeutic atmosphere is the best possible recapture of the uterine environment for the patient. Although Rogers admits his partial dependence on Otto Rank, it is doubtful if he would approve our harking back to the heart of Rankian theory: emotional disturbance mainly traceable to the birth trauma. But the patient who experiences an approximation of unconditional positive regard for and empathic understanding of all his characteristics is getting the closest he will ever get in adult life to the completely satisfying, undemanding environment of prenatal life. To a considerable degree (but perhaps not always to what sounds like an overly seductive, Rogersian degree), acceptance and reassurance may be considered helpful *pre*-conditions to the serious, often cognitive, sometimes directive business which then needs to follow, as many non-Rogersian therapists would see it. This "further business" of therapy is the help needed by an individual who has seriously failed to adapt himself to life as an adult. A brief sojourn in the womblike atmosphere of Rogersian therapy may give such a person the recuperative strength he needs to face the job of learning how to handle the problems of the very unwomblike, non-therapeutic world of adult reality. But many such persons need direct guidance, specific education, in how to utilize their energies in effective, rational, realistic adaptation to interpersonal actualities. Thus it seems, at least, to a non-Rogersian.

What are the most valuable forms of direct guidance and specific education? Much would seem to depend upon specific diagnosis in each instance. But it must be admitted that the best of current psychological and psychiatric diagnostic methods, from Sullivanian analysis of early interpersonal acculturation through psychometric tests to Freudian dream interpretation via free association, are crude, largely unvalidated, and often unreliable tools. This brings us back to the undeniable realization that much more research is needed. But we cannot wait for the results of research in order to proceed to meet the psychotherapeutic needs of many members of our society. Meantime, a number of rational, though not yet scientifically established, guides can be explored by therapists who are willing to experiment with some unfamiliar approaches (a notable example of which is the rational reconditioning process suggested by Albert Ellis).

Such experimentation calls for less rigid adherence to any particular system of psychotherapy, and one wonders if the time has not arrived for greater emphasis on eclecticism, synthesis, flexibility in the use of differing therapeutic techniques. The dogmatic schools of psychotherapy were perhaps historically necessary for various desirable changes of public and professional climate (of which the Rogersian revolution was simply the most recent). It seems likely now, however, that further progress is more blocked than enhanced by clinging to psychotherapeutic "religions." There are two characteristics of rigid systemists: (1) their closed minds about points of view and outright facts which fail to fit their system and (2) their manifestation of what the psychoanalysts call "reaction formations." Let us illustrate these two assertions.

First, we have the current ruling class in psychotherapy: the Freudians. Although, as indicated earlier, humility is beginning to become a part of their personalities, there is still a persisting tendency among many in this group to believe they have the *only* valid answers to the nature of the human psyche and the treatment of psychic disorders. The more rigid and fanatic of the Freudians react roughly in the fashion of religious fundamentalists. Tell a fundamentalist that you think many Biblical stories are to be viewed as allegories and myths, and he has had enough of you. Tell a fundamentalist Freudian that you question the efficiency of free association, the universality of the Oedipus complex or the three stages of infantile sexuality, and his reaction is much the same. He does not care what brand of the devil you have assumed—dynamic culturalist, client-centered therapist, Adlerian, Jungian, or psychobiologist—he knows that your understanding of human behavior is *superficial* (the Freudian equivalent of Satanic) and that your resistance to Freudian doctrine is a manifestation of your own ego defenses against psychosexual truth. Such defensiveness, such repression of the point of view of the "enemy," would indicate in the Freudians, by their own analytical theories, feelings of insecurity. For the patient to admit hate, as well as love, for a parent, is an intolerable ego threat. For an orthodox Freudian to admit doubt in, as well as faith and acceptance of, classical psychoanalytic theory, may be a similarly intolerable ego threat. Such unswerving Freudian faith is suspiciously symptomatic of a reaction formation.

Closed minds and reaction formations are equally evident in fanatics of other persuasions. The psychoanalysis-hating Salter, the Freud-biting Horney, the Freud-repressing Sullivan, the Freud-rejecting Adler and Jung (and those who orthodoxly follow these and other therapeutic messiahs) show an unwillingness to listen objectively and to consider the possible merit of opposing positions. Because of their permissive exterior, such dogmatism is, though present, less evident, in the Rogersians. They are quite fearful of and incapable of dealing adequately with strong, opposing points of view and with authoritarian figures because of their anxiety about their own repressed tendencies toward dictatorial behavior. A Salter who violently overthrows *all* Freudian procedures and theories as utter nonsense must be, by the hypothesis of reaction formation, fighting down some pro-analytic tendencies inside himself that frighten him. The client-centered therapist who pushes down *all* therapist direction, *all* diagnosis, *all* functions of the therapist other than exudence of positive regard and empathy for the omnipotent client, must, by this same hypothesis, be repressing strong authoritarian impulses in himself that he fears and doubts that he can handle. In fairness, it should be pointed out that those therapists who emphatically reject everything the Rogersians have to offer are undoubtedly afraid of soft, accepting, love-giving tendencies in *their* repressed psyches.

While we await research findings (and for definitively helpful results, it is bound to be a long wait), it would appear that many therapists and their patients are likely to profit from a flexible repertoire of therapeutic techniques, rather than from a rigid adherence to a single system of psychotherapy. It is encouraging to observe a growing trend of eclecticism among therapists of many persuasions. (This trend is being fought, however, by some classical analysts, some Rogersians, and others.)

Phillips and Ellis are two cognitively oriented therapists whose writings to date in support of assertion-structured therapy and rational psychotherapy, respectively, give the appearance of anti-eclecticism. It is possible, however, that at least part of their denunciation of other systems is designed to attract greater attention to their own genuine contributions. Both have made significant eclectic contributions prior to the development of their own therapeutic systems, and there is every reason to believe they will do so in the future. Meantime, their systems of psychotherapy serve as an effective challenge to psychoanalysts, client-centered therapists, and others that concentrate largely on emotional reconditioning.

Wolpe brings, in some ways, an even stronger challenge to the theoretical superstructures and the elaborate techniques of many of the therapies in both groups A and B. While it seems likely at this point that his system is based on an oversimplification of human behavior, emotional disturbance, and the therapeutic process, new experimental testing of therapy will be stimulated by his theories and techniques.

The coolest eclectics and rationalists to date in this warm, emotional springtime of psychotherapy would seem to be the learning theory therapists, the psychobiologists, and Thorne. The latter two are eclectics in the full sense of the term, and their major influence in the whole field has been that of pointing out neglected techniques and theories of aid in treating all types of disturbed persons. The learning theory therapists have made their main emphasis that of clearing away mysticism from many varieties of approaches and offering ways of testing by future research many of the hypotheses about human personality, its pathological developments, and methods of treating these pathologies (to this point, however, their actual research production falls considerably below that of Rogers and associates). Thorne and the psychobiologists have likewise underlined reliance on the products of science in the training and functioning of therapists.

The general semanticists have made a contribution which has begun to be absorbed into the general therapeutic stream: namely, the focus of much more careful attention on the whole communicative process, both inside and outside the treatment setting. Much more needs to be learned here, but even now the therapist can function more effectively (whatever other techniques he uses or theories he holds) by devoting a considerable portion of his perceptive skills to his and the patient's transmission of meaning.

The experiments or exercises offered by the Gestaltists need to be explored much more carefully by therapists of many differing points of view. Without necessarily holding to all of the theories of Perls and his associates, the eclectic therapist may find here a technique for rendering more effective the attitude change of some patients.

Hypnosis is being re-explored in a number of therapeutic settings. Caution is needed here, as Wolberg has pointed out, because of the magical aura associated with the technique in the minds of many people. As a tool to be selectively employed, however, hypnosis is part of the legitimate equipment of the skilled therapist.

While Whitaker and Malone may in a sense lead us further away from a rational, scientific approach to psychotherapy by their emphasis on id communication, their techniques have certainly had a healthful effect in challenging *any* rigid, dogmatic assumptions about what will or will not work in psychotherapy. Other imaginative and instructive techniques (including the use of multiple therapists, a method not discussed in our book) continue to emerge from the Atlanta psychiatric center. Future therapeutic developments must certainly take into account the experimental proceedings of Whitaker, Malone, and associates.

The simple technique outlined by Ellis of getting patients to understand the self-verbalized perpetuations of their negative emotions and to learn to substitute more rational and realistic thought which will (allegedly) produce neutral or positive emotional conditions needs much further investigation and therapeutic experimentation. Research which will pit the accepting, affective approach of Rogers, for example, against the directive, cognitive techniques of Ellis should prove valuable. It is encouraging to report that both Rogers and Ellis have independently indicated strong interest in such research.

The group psychotherapies not only offer new ways for helping patients to facilitate the development of greater insights into personality characteristics that they have tended to repress, dissociate, or disown, but also present a practice situation in which the patient can develop his skills in interpersonal relations. To this point, enthusiasm for systems and particular techniques have followed to some extent the route of individual psychotherapy. However, the group experience itself is destructive of dogmatism and rigidity in the therapist, and so a great deal of imaginative trial-and-accidental-success learning has tended to ensue. This has made some contribution to the flexibility of individual therapeutic practices. It is hoped that at least some of the future experimentation in group psychotherapy can develop along systematic research lines which encourage scientific reduplication.

What, then, of psychoanalysis? It seems indisputable that at this point in the development of psychotherapy many of the Freudian theories (especially with certain of the more moderate "corrections" of the dynamic culturalists) are still the best available for an over-all working hypothesis regarding the functioning of the human personality. The more thinking of Freud's critics draw heavily (as many of them admit) upon his insights even in the course of their criticisms. In the writer's opinion, the most sagacious eclectic therapists of at least this generation are likely to be theoretically, and to some extent technically, psychoanalytically oriented. Meantime, many of the psychoanalytic hypotheses can be reformulated (as some already have) in operational terms and tested, along with other hypotheses in large, co-ordinated research projects (still largely in a fantasy stage).

What is the common ground of all these therapies we have considered? How can people be helped by such divergent procedures as those of the classical analyst or the client-centered therapist, on the one hand, and those of the rational therapist or the assertion-structured therapist, on the other?

The following observations about common aspects of psychotherapy are in terms of *effects,* as distinguished from the techniques which were discussed in Chapter 1. They are presented in the form of assertions, but are to be considered tentative hypotheses to be tested by future research. Not all of these observations apply to all patients at all times with all forms of psychotherapy, nor are these common effects the totality of results of any particular system of therapy. They are simply current conceptions of frequently occurring results of the work of many therapists with many of the patients with whom they seem to have success.

First of all, weak egos (those of the patients) at least temporarily gain support from strong egos (those of the therapists). Stated differently, persons with initially low self-esteem gain in this area through intimate association with persons of generally high self-esteem. "*He* (the self-respecting therapist) likes and accepts and gives attention to and cares for and is concerned about *me*. I, therefore, must be better, more worthwhile, less hopeless, etc., than I had thought."

The first effect can be achieved in numerous ways. It can be done by a very non-directive method of largely listening, non-critically feeding back what the patient has said, showing infinite patience and acceptance. Or it can be done relatively impersonally behind the couch on which the patient rests, but with occasional interpretations which demonstrate that the analyst has been listening carefully and that the patient has a fascinating and complicated unconscious (otherwise, the patient feels, why would the analyst consider it worthwhile to spend three or four hours per week listening and interpreting?). Or it can be done by rational instruction, emotional reconditioning (including Wolpe's point of reciprocal inhibition), confirmation and disconfirmation, sharing of fantasy experiences, and consideration of alleged symbols of an alleged collective unconscious. Any of these methods and many others give the patient attention at the very minimum and often understanding, acceptance, and love. As with the child (and in any therapeutic system this is the role the patient at least temporarily takes), even punitive attention from the parent (therapist) brings the feeling that "I am at least worthy of this strong person's time and energy, and I am, hence, of some importance."

The second common effect of psychotherapy is that less rational and less reality-oriented persons (patients) at least temporarily learn more realistic ways of handling life problems from more rational and reality-oriented persons (therapists). They can be specifically told how better to deal with reality, or they can gradually come to imitate the examples set by the therapists over a period of time. But directly or indirectly they are taught (yes, *taught*—though this is a rejected word in many a therapist's vocabulary, the process goes on) by therapists how to behave less disturbedly in confronting their life activities.

Third, patients also learn (again, the methods may be very direct or very devious) that a lot of the things that they have fretted, stewed, or panicked over are not as important as they thought. (The observation that psychotherapy is the process whereby the unbland learn to be led by the bland into becoming bland has some truth in it.) In one way or another, successful therapy reduces anxiety by communicating to the patient that his concerns about what his neighbors think, his guilt feelings about not having been nice to his mother before she

died, his worries about not being acceptable to the members of a social club, etc., are at best unnecessary and at worst idiotic. He is
directly taught such things, or he indirectly comes to "catch on" to
them by associating with a person who is quite bland about such matters.

Fourth, patients learn patience. One of the most frequent difficulties of persons with emotional immaturity and certain forms of
emotional disturbance is a low tension capacity. The very process of
going through the long and tedious process of therapy week after
week, discussing the frequently recurring problems and hearing or
otherwise sensing the same suggested ways of handling these difficulties, develops the person's tension capacity, his ability to be patient.
Stated differently, patients gradually learn to be less childish, more
adult. They learn to insist less on immediately satisfying goal-
responses and to put up with tensions necessary to achieve long-term
goals. They learn sometimes by instruction, sometimes by example
—usually by both.

Fifth, patients learn new sets of myths (a "new faith"), which at
least seem to be more scientific, more closely related to contemporary
social reality, than their old sets of myths. The myths the patients
adopt are their perceptions of the therapists' beliefs. Whether or not
the therapists and the patients are aware of the myth-adopting process
seems to have little effect on its efficiency. Therapists of a few of the
systems (Ellis, Phillips, Salter, and the Adlerians, for several examples) would seem to be frank propagandists: they admit they are
attempting to instill their systems of value in their patients. But
others, including the most non-directive of the Rogersians and the
most classically impersonal of the Freudians, have their patients as
evidence that they, too, transmit their values. Patients even come
to dream the kinds of dreams, in some instances, that they feel are
most appreciated by their therapist.

Since it is very likely that even the most unrealistic myth system
of a fairly healthy therapist will function more effectively (at least for
a time) than the probably quite confused myth system the patient
brought with him to therapy, improvement is likely to ensue from the
change in values for the patient.

Sixth, patients gain perspective about their emotions and their
interactional difficulties from talking about them and hearing the

therapist talk about them. Such talk in itself tends to objectify fears, anxieties, feelings of inadequacy, and so on. The patient finds it gradually more difficult to react with intense fear to, say, open spaces, after all the angles of the nature and possible causes of his phobic fear have been discussed at length by the therapist and himself. Another patient who has always been late to appointments, who postpones other responsibilities, and lies late abed each morning begins to lose his neurotic satisfaction from such tactics of avoidance after he and the therapist have conversationally dealt with these and related factors at great length. The personal privacy, the hidden subjectivity, of various aspects of neurosis can be removed by talk alone (even if the talk is devoid of insight into causation and does nothing other than expose the problems to objective discussion), and sometimes the emotional disturbance loses its power with its privacy.

Seventh, by focusing so much attention on present anxieties while in therapy, patients are likely to find future anxieties less threatening. Not only have the old problems lost a lot of their ego-damaging punch (for such reasons as those discussed in the foregoing points), but new problems often seem weak, pale, and manageable in contrast to the former anxiety investments in the problems subjected to the tedious inspection of psychotherapy. "Nothing can throw me after I live through this" is a sometimes valid reaction of the patient in the process of therapy.

Patients often emerge from therapy with the feeling that the therapist is a part of them and, hence, life will never again be so lonely or so difficult. This intense emotional experience derives from the personal, intimate, problem-inspecting process with even a relatively cold and impersonal therapist. "He's there; he understands; he thinks I am worthwhile. I am not alone; I have some of his strength; I can handle whatever lies ahead."

The points we have just brought out are, we think, observable in psychotherapy as a whole. It should be understood, however, that some systems may more consistently and efficiently achieve these and other important effects. And some therapists, regardless of system affiliation or lack of same, achieve much better results than their colleagues. With any therapist and any system, such results as those we have discussed are by no means inevitable—failures seem at least as plentiful as successes.

Psychotherapy is, if we may now generalize from our list of common effects, a contemporary means for individuals with poorly functioning value systems to find the support of an apparently strong and successful person in learning a new value system and how to live more effectively thereby. None of these value systems learned in therapy may be considered totally satisfactory for meeting the problems of present-day social turbulence. They are varyingly successful stopgap measures for persons who no longer get sufficient ego strength and relationship support from such long-standing institutions (value systems) as the church, the school, marriage, and the family.

We use the term "stopgap measure" advisedly, for it seems quite evident that as the ever-brighter light of science increasingly penetrates psychotherapy, all the systems of this make-shift institution will reveal more fiction than fact, more myth than science. The day may not be too distant—with the advances of biochemistry, physiology, and biophysics, as well as psychology itself—that what we now call psychotherapy will relate to the scientific treatment and prevention of behavioral disorders as astrology now relates to astronomy.

While we look to that day, however, much work must be done with the present primitive tools of psychotherapy. Blunt instruments are surely rendered no sharper by rigidity, dogmatism, and fanatic adherence to a particular system. Young therapists in training should be encouraged to expose themselves to the full range of therapeutic theories and to experiment with the complete repertory of therapeutic techniques. Such therapists, in this period which is hopefully a prelude to more scientific procedures, are more likely, we firmly believe, to be helpful to a great number of patients than therapists conditioned in one theoretical orientation and its limited techniques.

But this is the outlook of an eclectic, and an eclectic is often less acceptable to fanatics than even fanatics of opposing persuasions. Scorning the wrath of the faithful of all systems of psychotherapy, we offer this book as an introduction to therapeutic eclecticism. We are saying, in effect, throughout: look around, reserve judgment for a while and then make it tentative, and experiment with many theories and techniques. Until science brings us definitive answers—if science does—let us try to avoid commitment to a rigid religion of psychotherapy. Let us learn from and constructively employ the arts of many therapies.

Glossary

Words italicized in the definitions are themselves defined in their alphabetical order.

acting out: performing in a new setting the *behavior* learned from and appropriate to another social situation.

active analytic psychotherapy: the term applied to the deviant form of *psychoanalysis* developed by Wilhelm Stekel (see Section B of Chapter 4).

affect: emotion, feeling, mood, feeling tone, temperament. Affect is sometimes employed as a quantitative term to express the person's emotional capacity and the degree of his reaction to given situations and sometimes rather loosely interchanged with other words which refer to either general or specific emotional conditions.

aggression: bold and energetic pursuit of one's ends; often used in the negative sense of expressing hostile and destructive action; sometimes interchanged with *aggressive drive* in the psychoanalytic literature.

aggressive drive: one of the two inherited urges (or instincts) hypothesized by Freud as providing the raw material of all mental life of human beings; frequently referred to as the *death instinct* (*Thanatos*) and thought to give rise to the destructive components of human behavior in contradistinction to the *sexual instinct* (*Eros*).

ambivalence: the bipolarity of feeling; that is, the tendency to be drawn in opposite emotional directions, as between love and hate, acceptance and rejection, denial and affirmation.

analytical psychology: the term applied to the deviant form of *psychoanalysis* developed by Carl Jung (see Section C of Chapter 4).

analytic group therapy: the theories and practices of *group therapy* of those who have a general psychoanalytic orientation (see Section B of Chapter 9).

anima: in Jungian analysis, the feminine component of the *psyche*.

157

animus: in Jungian analysis, the masculine component of the *psyche.*

anxiety: a feeling of a dreadful or fearsome threat, usually of such a vague nature that the person cannot correctly identify its specific source. In the Freudian literature, *"objective anxiety"* is the term used for apprehensiveness with a cause clearly identified in external reality. In Horneyian discussions, the term *"basic anxiety"* is employed to refer to the universal, childhood-derived feelings of loneliness and helplessness. Sullivan, on the other hand, generally employed the term *anxiety* to refer to a general, potent, restrictive force in the development of the individual, first "caught" by a process of contagion (which Sullivan called *empathy*) from the *mothering one* during infancy. *Anxiety,* in short, is a much used and variously defined word in the psychotherapeutic literature.

assertion-structured therapy: the term applied to the system of *psychotherapy* developed by E. Lakin Phillips (see Section D of Chapter 8).

behavior: while variously (and sometimes unclearly) used in psychological and physiological writings, the term is usually employed in the psychotherapeutic literature to refer to anything a human being does: that is, any act or succession of acts.

birth trauma: the damaging effect on the *psyche* of the transition from uterine to extrauterine environment. In the Rankian literature, the *birth trauma* is treated as the fundamental *anxiety* experience out of which most subsequent neurotic conditions of the individual grow.

catharsis: the release of tension and *anxiety* by recounting and/or *acting out* past experiences.

cathexis: in *psychoanalysis,* the amount of psychic energy which is directed toward or attached to the mental representative (that is, memories, thoughts, fantasies) of a person or thing. For example, *cathexis* is high in the *fantasy* a man has of his absent sweetheart (in this case much *libido* is channeled into his mental representation of his loved one; in other instances, *aggression* may be the chief form of psychic energy which is cathected).

character: sometimes used as a synonym of *personality,* but more often distinguished from the latter by its emphasis on volitional and moral aspects of human *behavior:* namely, the relatively consistent behavior tendencies of the individual in relation to moral issues and decisions affecting his relationships with others.

character armor: the term first employed by Wilhelm Reich for the system of *ego defenses* used by patients to resist the psychoanalytic probing of the sources of their *neuroses.* These resistances generally consist of such "good" *character* traits as obedience, co-operation, punctuality, and earnestness behind which the patient "hides" the traits which are likely to lead to the root of his troubles.

character neurosis: a type of psychic pathology or disorder relatively so stable and fixed that it seems an inseparable part of the individual's *personality*. Distinguished from a *psychoneurosis* (frequently referred to simply as a *neurosis*).

character structure: the sum and patterning of *character* traits; in Freudian theory, these traits are developed in the process of the *superego's* efforts to control the *id*.

classical analysis (or *psychoanalysis*): used in two senses—(1) to distinguish the psychoanalytic theories and practices of the earlier Freudian period (with emphasis on unraveling the *unconscious* blockings of the *libido*) from those of the later Freudian period. In this sense, Chapter 2 treats *classical psychoanalysis*, and Chapter 3 deals with later Freudian developments. (2) The term is also sometimes employed to refer to the hypotheses and techniques of Freud and his followers as opposed to those of all psychoanalytic deviants. With this latter meaning, Chapters 2 and 3 may be considered *classical psychoanalysis*. (The first interpretation is the more common.)

client-centered therapy: the term applied to the system of *psychotherapy* developed by Carl Rogers (see Chapter 6).

collective unconscious: in Jungian theory, that part of the individual's *unconscious* which is hereditary and which the individual shares with other human beings. Sometimes called the *racial unconscious*.

compromise formation: (1) in Freudian dream interpretation, the consciously perceived (or manifest) dream, which represents an accommodation between the effort of a wish which has been repressed to seek fulfillment and the effort of the *ego* to defend itself against this disapproved impulse from the *id;* (2) in the Freudian theory of psychoneurosis, a similar adjustment between the incompletely repressed id impulse and the not fully effective *ego defenses* brings about a *psychosomatic symptom*.

compulsiveness: the tendency to repeat over and over inappropriate *behavior* and to be unable to keep from doing so (see *obsession* and *obsessive-compulsive reaction*).

conditioned reflex therapy: the term applied to the system of *psychotherapy* developed by Andrew Salter (see Section E of Chapter 7).

conditioning: the process whereby a form of behavior is elicited by a stimulus other than the originally effective (or natural or unconditioned) stimulus. The classical example (after Pavlov) is the dog which originally salivates with the presentation of food, has a bell rung with such presentation, and is soon conditioned to salivate upon hearing the bell alone. The term is sometimes used loosely to refer to all learning, but is seldom encountered in other psychotherapeutic writings than those referred to in Sections E and F of Chapter 7.

congruence: in the writings of Carl Rogers, the *personality* state in which the individual's actual *behavior* is in harmony with his self perceptions; the term is used to convey the notion of a *personality* which is genuine and integrated, as opposed to false and disturbed (see *incongruence*).

conscious: in *psychoanalysis,* a division of the *psyche* which includes those parts of mental life of which the person is at any moment aware; distinguished from the *preconscious* and the *unconscious.*

consensual validation: in the writings of Sullivan, the corrective experience for an individual's *parataxic distortions;* the process whereby a person reaches a more realistic point of view by comparing his thoughts and feelings with those of his associates.

death instinct: in the later writings of Freud, a basic drive of similar importance to the *sexual instinct;* also referred to as the *aggressive drive, aggression,* and *Thanatos.*

defense mechanism: any psychological instrumentality by which the individual protects his *ego* from *anxiety*-inducing *id* impulses; mechanisms commonly discussed in the Freudian literature include *repression, rationalization, projection, introjection, regression, turning against the self, isolation, thought dissociation, reaction formation,* and *denial of reality.* These mechanisms are also often termed *ego defenses.*

denial of reality: the *ego defense* which prevents admission to consciousness of external stimuli that point to the existence of feared *id* impulses.

depth-oriented therapy: any form of *psychotherapy* which professes to treat the *unconscious* sources of an individual's problems; often, more specifically, some form of *psychoanalysis.*

direct analysis: the term applied to the system of *psychotherapy* developed by John Rosen (see Section E of Chapter 5).

directive psychotherapy: the term applied to the system of psychotherapy developed by Frederick Thorne (see Section A of Chapter 8).

disowning: in the writings of Carl Rogers, the process whereby the individual avoids being aware of experiences and needs which have not been symbolized and which are inconsistent with the *self.* Roughly comparable to Freudian *repression* and Sullivanian *dissociation.*

displacement: in *psychoanalysis,* the substitution of one idea or image by another which is associatively connected with it.

dissociation: in Sullivanian theory, the process whereby the individual excludes from awareness those aspects of his experience which lead to acute *anxiety* (see *repression*—Freud, and *disowning*—Rogers).

distributive analysis and synthesis: the phrase applied to the characteristic procedures of *psychobiologic therapy.*

dynamic culturalists: the term applied to the psychoanalytic theories and practices of those who deviate from the teachings of Freud by placing less emphasis on the instinctive and more emphasis on the changing social sources of human *behavior* (see Sections A through D in Chapter 5).

dynamism: in Sullivanian theory, a relatively enduring configuration of energy found in interpersonal relations—sometimes applied to the whole *self* (self *dynamism*) and other times to patterns of energy organized around specific needs (lust *dynamism;* oral *dynamism*).

ego: in psychoanalysis, that part of the *psyche* which is the executant for the drives, the mediator between the *id* and the external environment.

ego defenses: see *defense mechanisms.*

Electra complex: in *psychoanalysis* (but rare other than in Jungian writings), the repressed desire of a female for incestuous relations with her father and for the destruction of her mother; the female version of the *Oedipus complex.*

empathy: (1) the acceptance and understanding of the feelings of another person, but with sufficient detachment to avoid becoming directly involved in those feelings; (2) in Sullivanian theory, a kind of vague, biologically derived process whereby the infant senses the emotions of the mothering one through "contagion and communion."

Eros: in psychoanalysis, the *sexual instinct* or *libido;* contrasted with *Thanatos,* the *death instinct.*

euphoria: an emotional attitude or feeling tone of health and vigor—"all is well."

excitation: the process whereby activity is set up in a nerve or in a muscle by nerve action; generalized in Salter's theory to refer to a state in the individual in which he is ready for vigorous action (opposed to *inhibition*).

existential analysis: the term applied to the system of *psychotherapy* which combines some of the teachings of existential philosophy with some of the theories and practices of *psychoanalysis* (see Section F of Chapter 5).

experiential therapy: the term applied to the system of *psychotherapy* developed by Carl Whitaker and Thomas Malone (see Section D of Chapter 7).

extroversion: an attitude of interest in things outside oneself rather than in one's own thoughts and feelings; opposite of *introversion.*

facial talk: a method used by Salter in his system of *conditioned-reflex therapy* to help a patient to overcome his *inhibitions* by learning to frankly show his emotions on his face.

family therapy: a type of *group therapy* undertaken with families (see Section D of Chapter 9).

fantasy: imagining a complex object or event (existent or non-existent) in concrete symbols or images, usually in the pleasant sense of a wish-fulfillment.

feeling-talk: a method used by Salter in his system of *conditioned-reflex therapy* to help a patient to overcome his *inhibitions* by saying what he (the patient) feels whenever he feels it.

free association: the chief therapeutic method developed by Freud—the patient is asked to begin with some remark or dream item and to state whatever comes to mind. The associative activity is (ideally) free of both the suggestions of the analyst and the *suppressions* of the patient.

genital maturity: in Freudian psychoanalysis, the goal toward which the developing *libido* is striving; distinguished from the *pregenital stages.*

Gestalt: a German word with approximate English equivalents of configuration, meaningful organized whole, structural relationship, and theme.

Gestalt therapy: the term applied to the system of *psychotherapy* developed by Frederick Perls, Ralph F. Hefferline, and Paul Goodman (see Section B of Chapter 7).

group-centered therapy: the term applied to the system of *group therapy* developed by Carl Rogers and associates (see Section C of Chapter 9).

group therapy: any form of *psychotherapy* in which several persons are treated simultaneously (see Chapter 9).

hostility: tendency to feel anger toward and to seek to inflict harm upon a person or group.

hypnoanalysis: *psychoanalysis* carried on while the patient is under *hypnosis.*

hypnosis: a state characterized by greatly heightened suggestibility, usually attained by bodily relaxation accompanied by concentration on a narrow range of stimuli presented by the hypnotist.

hypnotherapy: *psychotherapy* which utilizes techniques of *hypnosis* (see Section C of Chapter 7).

hysteria: a kind of catch-all form of *neurosis* in which patients manifest such variable sensory, motor, vasomotor, visceral, and mental symptoms as paralyzed limbs, deafness, blindness, and other pathological conditions for which no anatomical or physiological causes could be found. Such patients were much more numerous in the latter part of the 19th and early part of the 20th centuries than currently. The term is not included in the most recent standard psychiatric nomenclature.

id: in *psychoanalysis,* that part of the *psyche* from which the instinctive impulses (namely, the *sexual instinct* and the *death instinct*) emerge; the *id* contains the blind, impersonal, primary emotions from which all behavior springs. Part of the *id's* energy is utilized to form the other aspects of the *psyche* (the *ego* and *superego*).

idealized self image: in Horneyian theory, a pattern of perfectionistic strivings and godlike fantasies which constitute the core of a *neurosis.*

id level therapy: any method of *psychotherapy* which proposes to reach the deeper levels of the *unconscious.* Less common as a term than *depth-oriented therapy.*

identification: (1) the process of becoming like something or someone in one or several aspects of behavior; (2) in *psychoanalysis,* as a *defense mechanism, identification* is sometimes used interchangeably with *introjection.*

incongruence: in the writings of Carl Rogers, the *personality* state in which the individual's actual *behavior* and experience is in disharmony with his *self* perceptions. When the individual is aware of such disharmony, he is anxious; when he is unaware, he is vulnerable to *anxiety.*

individual psychology: the term applied to the system of *psychotherapy* developed by Alfred Adler (see Section A of Chapter 4).

inhibition: stopping a process from continuing, or preventing a process from starting, even though the usual stimulus which elicits the process is present; generalized in Salter's *conditioned-reflex therapy* to refer to any restraint in the range, amount, and effectiveness of behavior (opposed to *excitation*).

insight: the process by which the meaning, significance, pattern, or use of an experience becomes clear—or the understanding which results from this process.

instinct: an unlearned and enduring tendency to act in an organized way that is characteristic of a given species; in his later writings, Freud recognized two irreducible instincts: *Eros* (the *sexual instinct*) and *Thanatos* (the *death instinct*).

interference theory: the hypotheses on which *assertion-structured therapy* is based.

interpersonal relations: the interactions between two or more persons, or the characteristic pattern of such interactions; the reciprocal involvements of two or more people. Most commonly employed in Sullivan's writings.

introjection: a *defense mechanism;* the *ego* protects itself against an impulse from the *id* that is *anxiety*-producing by taking in (that is, identifying itself with) another person. The opposite of *projection.*

introversion: an attitude of interest in one's own thoughts and feelings rather than external events; opposite of *extroversion.*

isolation: in *psychoanalysis,* (1) *thought dissociation;* (2) the *defense mechanism* whereby the *affect* connected with a painful past event is repressed.

juvenile era: in Sullivan's writings, the stage in a child's development which begins when he shows a need for playmates and lasts until the emergence of a need for an intimate relationship with another person of comparable status at *preadolescence.*

learning: all the processes by means of which an individual is changed so that at a later time his actions or reactions are not what they would have been without the previous activity.

learning theory: an attempt to state the general nature of *learning.*

learning theory therapy: the term applied to a system of *psychotherapy* developed by several psychologists (see Section C of Chapter 8).

libido: (1) in Freudian *psychoanalysis,* the *sexual instinct, Eros;* (2) in Jungian (and, confusedly, some Freudian) writings, a life force or instinct which has been somehow vaguely desexualized.

life plan: life style.

life style: in Adler's writings, an individual's characteristic and pervasive pattern of *behavior* for dealing with his feelings of inferiority and for gaining status.

manic-depressive psychosis: a *psychosis* of marked emotional oscillation.

masochism: in *psychoanalysis,* the turning of any sort of destructive tendencies inward upon oneself.

mothering one: the term used by Sullivan to refer to the person (mother or mother substitute) who most significantly influences the individual during infancy.

multiple therapy: any form of *psychotherapy* in which two or more therapists simultaneously participate.

need: a tension induced in the individual by the lack of something which, if present, would tend to further his welfare.

neo-Freudian analysis: the psychoanalytic theories and practices of *therapists* who claim to have revised, rather than to have rejected, the teachings of Freud. In practical effect, all psychoanalysts (except Adler, Stekel, Jung, Rank, and their followers) are either Freudian or *neo-Freudian:* the former if they make no major deviations from Freudian hypotheses or procedures and the latter if they do. Some "Freudian loyalists," however, at times seem more revisionist than neo-Freudians.

neurasthenia: a *psychoneurosis* characterized by feelings of weakness and the general lowering of bodily and mental tone; no longer included in the standard psychiatric nomenclature.

neurosis: psychoneurosis. While Freud made a distinction between what he called actual neuroses and psychoneuroses in his early writings, he and his followers later dropped the distinction.

neurotic need: in Horney's writings, a strategy employed by an anxious person to find a solution to the problems of disturbed human relationships and to cope with his feelings of isolation and helplessness; it takes the form of a compulsive demand for certain behavior on the part of others.

nondirective therapy: client-centered therapy.

objective psychotherapy: the term applied to the system of *psychotherapy* developed by Benjamin Karpman (see Section E of Chapter 5).

obsession: an idea, usually associated with anxiety, that persists or frequently recurs and cannot be dismissed by the individual.

obsessive-compulsive reaction: a type of *psychoneurosis* in which *anxiety* is associated with *obsessions* and compulsions (see *compulsiveness*).

Oedipus complex: feelings of rivalry and hostility toward one parent and of incestuous desire for the other parent. Originally the *Oedipus complex* was used by Freud to refer to the desire of the boy for his mother in hostile competition with his father, but the term has been extended to include comparable behavior in the girl (see *Electra complex*). The situation is also sometimes reversed: the child shows sexual desire for the parent of the same sex and jealousy and murderous rage toward the parent of the other sex (termed an inverted Oedipus).

orgone therapy: a term applied to a system of physical therapy developed by Wilhelm Reich. Also called *vegetotherapy.*

paranoid tendency: evidence of grandiose ideas and/or sensitivity to real or apparent criticism. The delusions of persecution and grandiosity may appear in a rare form of *psychosis* called paranoia, in paranoid *schizophrenia,* or in a sufficiently mild and peripheral and socially insignificant form as to be diagnosed as *psychoneurosis* (or even eccentricity).

parapraxis: a minor error in behavior, such as a slip of the tongue or pen, memory blockings, small accidents, misplacing articles, etc. In *psychoanalysis,* a *parapraxis* is never considered accidental, always caused by some *unconscious* conflict. Popularly called "a Freudian slip."

parataxic distortion: a reaction, in *interpersonal relations,* to a *personification* rather than (or in addition to) an actual person; that is, any attitude toward another person based on *fantasy* or on *identification* of that person with other figures. This is a Sullivanian term which includes the phenomena the Freudians call *transference* and many additional forms of *displacement* and *projection.*

persona: in Jungian writings, the mask of conscious intentions and fulfillments of social requirements of the individual behind which he hides (from himself as well as others) his more deeply rooted components of *personality;* the role which a person plays.

personality: (1) all the mental or *behavior* traits of a person; the sum total of psychological traits; the individual's integrated system of traits or *behavior* tendencies; (2) those aspects of the individual's nature which have developed in social relationships and have other persons or social values as their object. Definition (1) more broadly includes all psychological characteristics of the individual, whether or not derived from or relevant to *interpersonal relations*. These two meanings (and many more) are found confusedly interchanged in the literature.

personification: a type of *projection* in which an individual attributes favorable or unfavorable qualities to another person as a result of his own *unconscious* conflicts.

phenomenal field: everything, including awareness of the *self*, experienced by an individual at any moment. Objects physically present, but not perceived, are not part of the *phenomenal field*, and objects not physically present, but thought about, are.

phenomenological point of view: the hypothesis that an individual's *behavior* may be entirely understood and explained in terms of his *phenomenal field;* particularly applicable to the theoretical formulations of *client-centered therapy* and *existential analysis*.

phobia: a morbid, persistent, excessive fear of some particular type of object or situation; the source of the fear is at least partly irrational and *unconscious*. The term has recently become rare in the literature, and the former tendency to compound the word with others of Greek origin (as in acrophobia, agoraphobia, claustrophobia—fear, respectively, of high, open, and closed places) is now even rarer.

pleasure principle: in psychoanalysis, the demand of the *id* for immediate gratification of an *instinct* (see *primary process*). In infancy, the individual is dominated by the *pleasure principle,* but as the *ego* develops, he becomes aware of the demands of reality (see *reality principle*).

preadolescence: in Sullivanian analysis, the chum period in the development of the individual, which follows upon the *juvenile era* and ends with the eruption of genital sexuality and a change of strong interest from a person of one's own sex to a person of the other sex.

preconscious: in psychoanalysis, a division of the *psyche* which includes those parts of mental life which have ready access to consciousness. Any thought which happens to be *conscious* at a given moment is *preconscious* both before and after that particular moment. Compare with *unconscious*.

pregenital stages: see *stages of sexuality*.

primary process: the characteristic functioning of the *id,* whereby there is immediate and direct satisfaction of an *instinct*. The *id,* according to Freud, does not discriminate between fantasy and reality; hence, if an instinct fails to obtain discharge through a motor exit, it will take an unconscious *sensory* route (notably through dreams in healthy individuals and through hallucination in the mentally ill) via the remembered perception of a previous satisfaction. *Primary process* thinking is the dominant mode for the young child and persists in the *unconscious* in adult life and manifests itself chiefly through dreams, humor, pathology (see *secondary process*).

projection: (1) the process of attributing one's own traits, problems, or points of view to others; (2) used as a *defense mechanism*, the individual protects his *ego* from the recognition of an undesirable *id* impulse by relocating the impulse in another person.

psyche: (1) roughly, the mind (or organized totality of all mental processes or psychological activities); (2) the aspect of the human being which performs psychological functions. Some writers use *psyche* and mind interchangeably; some avoid one term or the other; and some make rather unclear distinctions between the two along the lines of meanings (1) and (2).

psychic determinism: the postulate that psychic or mental processes are never fortuitous, but are completely explainable in terms of their causes.

psychoanalysis: (1) the term applied to the system of *psychotherapy* developed by Sigmund Freud (see Chapters 2 and 3); (2) any system of *psychotherapy* so designated either by its proponents or others. Although Karen Horney, for example (see Section A of Chapter 5), gradually developed a system that departed so markedly from Freud's teachings that she was disowned and denounced by many other psychoanalysts, she continued to consider her theories revisionist and, hence, *neo-Freudian analysis.* Alfred Adler, on the other hand, engaged in a process of reciprocal disowning with Freud and developed his system of *individual psychology*, which both he and Freud considered something other than *psychoanalysis.* Still, by popular usage, Adler's system is (at least in the United States) considered a form of *psychoanalysis.*

psychobiologic therapy: the term applied to the system of *psychotherapy* developed by Adolf Meyer (see Section A of Chapter 7).

psychodrama: the improvised enactment by a client of certain roles and incidents, prescribed by the therapist or spontaneously originating in the client. This therapeutic *acting out* is designed to reveal underlying causes of irrational *behavior* and is usually a part of *group therapy* (see Section A of Chapter 9).

psychometric test: any device designed to obtain a quantitative assessment of an individual's psychological attributes.

psychoneurosis: a disorder of *behavior* characterized by *anxiety*, which may be directly experienced or controlled by *defense mechanisms*, in which there is no gross disorganization of *personality* or great distortion of reality perception, and for which *psychotherapy* is often indicated. The disorder is now quite commonly designated as *neurosis;* it should be distinguished from *character neurosis* and *psychosis.*

psychosis: a disorder of *behavior* in which there is considerable disorganization of *personality* and readily recognizable distortion of reality perception and for which medical treatment (and sometimes hospitalization) in addition to *psychotherapy* is often indicated. The chief so-called "functional psychoses" (where no specific organic causes have been established) are *manic-depressive psychosis* and *schizophrenia.* The distinction between *psychosis* and a severe form of *psychoneurosis* is frequently less than clear in a clinical setting.

psychosomatic symptom: a sign of a bodily malfunctioning which is believed to have originated from, or to have been aggravated by, a psychological malfunctioning. Hives, for example, are thought to derive, at times, from a feeling of resentment.

psychotherapy: the use of any psychological technique in the treatment of mental disorder or social and emotional maladjustment.

psychotherapy by reciprocal inhibition: the term applied to the system of *psychotherapy* developed by Joseph Wolpe (see Section F of Chapter 7).

rapport: a reciprocally comfortable and unconstrained relationship between two or more persons, especially between therapist and patient.

rationalization: (1) the process of concocting plausible reasons to account for one's practices or beliefs which actually derive from other sources; (2) a *defense mechanism* in which the *ego* changes the nature of a thought or feeling (which is associated with a repressed *id* impulse) in order to make it more acceptable. Meaning (2) differs from meaning (1) mainly in its use of psychoanalytic terms related to causation.

rational psychotherapy: the term applied to the system of *psychotherapy* developed by Albert Ellis (see Section E of Chapter 8).

reaction formation: a *defense mechanism* (used in situations where *ambivalence* exists) in which the *ego* protects itself from aggressive *id* impulses by the *conscious* emphasis of positive feelings, such as love, protection, and tenderness.

reaction type: a psychiatric diagnostic classification in terms of the preponderating symptom; historically associated with *psychobiologic therapy.*

reality principle: the process by which the *ego* becomes aware of the demands of the environment and works out an adjustment between these demands and the basic *needs* of the *id.* The *reality principle* utilizes the *secondary process.*

reconnaissance: that part of *therapy* characterized by the collection of biographical information about the patient through intensive interrogation (Sullivan).

reconstructive therapy: any *psychotherapy* which professes to effect major changes in the *personality* of a patient. Often associated with *depth-level therapy* and contrasted with *re-educative therapy.*

redundancy: in *assertion-structured therapy,* circular and self-defeating behavior, developed as a result of the individual's persisting in assertions which meet with disconfirmation. The stronger the assertions, the greater the *redundancy.*

re-educative therapy: any system of *psychotherapy* which is believed to help the individual to handle his problems more effectively rather than to reconstruct his *personality.* Contrasted with *reconstructive therapy.* In general, proponents of a system are likely to claim that it is *reconstructive,* opponents are apt to label it "merely" *re-educative.*

regression: in *psychoanalysis,* (1) the process in which the individual, under the influence of emotional strain, returns to *behavior* characteristic of an earlier *stage of genitality;* (2) as a *defense mechanism,* essentially the same process is utilized in a more transitory way as a means of protecting the *ego* from being overwhelmed by *id* impulses.

reinforcement: any circumstance or event that increases the probability that a response will recur in a situation like that in which the reinforcing condition originally occurred; or, quite generally, any condition strengthening *learning.*

repression: the first recognized and most basic of the *defense mechanisms;* the *unconscious* activity of the ego which keeps the undesirable *id* impulse (or any feeling, wish, memory, or *fantasy* associated with it) from entering consciousness.

resistance: in *psychoanalysis,* opposition to any attempt to get at the unconscious; more generally, opposition offered by a patient to the orders, actions, recommendations, or suggestions of the therapist.

sadism: the compulsive tendency to vent *aggression* and destructiveness on another person; overt sexual satisfaction may or may not accompany this *behavior.*

satisfaction: in Sullivanian terminology, the fulfillment of a basic biological *need,* including sleep and rest, sex fulfillment, food and drink, and physical closeness to other human animals. Distinguished from *security.*

schizophrenia: a group of *psychoses* characterized by major disturbances in reality relationships, by blurring of thought processes by fantasy and personal desires, and by marked behavioral disturbances (often with progressive deterioration of the *personality*). Many types of schizophrenia are distinguished clinically, of which simple, paranoid, hebephrenic, and catatonic forms are most common.

secondary process: the characteristic functioning of the *ego* in which it fulfills *id* impulses by indirect routes (contrast with *primary process*) while at the same time meeting the demands of the external environment (see *reality principle*).

sector therapy: the term applied to the system of *psychotherapy* developed by Felix Deutsch (see Section E of Chapter 5).

security: in Sullivanian terminology, a state of *euphoria,* of belonging, of being accepted. Distinguished from *satisfaction.*

selective inattention: not being guided in behavior by an aspect of the situation that is perceived.

self: (1) that aspect of the person which carries out psychological, as distinguished from physiological, activities; (2) the individual revealed to his own observation as the identical and persistent center of psychological processes (Rogers); (3) that part of the personality which has alertness, which notices what goes on (Sullivan); (4) *actual self—* the total psychophysical being at a given moment, including both *conscious* and *unconscious* mechanisms (Horney); (5) *idealized self—*the perfected and glorified person which the neurotic believes himself to be after he unconsciously identifies with his previously imagined *idealized self-image* (Horney); (6) *real self—*the source of the energy that, in each individual, can be mobilized in the direction of constructive and healthy growth (Horney); (7) *true self—*all the potentialities of the individual which might be developed in the most favorable social milieu (Fromm).

self-concept: a person's view of himself; the fullest description of himself that a person is capable of giving at any particular time. This is similar to, if not identical with, meaning (2) of *self.*

self-dynamism: the pattern of the enduring motivations toward *satisfaction* and toward *security* that form the *self-system* (Sullivan).

self-system: the more or less final choice of potentialities that the individual seeks to develop and to integrate as a result of his formative experiences in *interpersonal relations* (Sullivan).

semantics: (1) the science of meanings of words or other signs; (2) *general semantics—*the term applied to a system of *psychotherapy* based on applied *semantics* (see Section B of Chapter 8).

sexual instinct: in *psychoanalysis,* an inconsistently employed term for pleasure-seeking and life-expressing *id* impulses and *unconscious* drives. Originally Freud used *sexual instinct* (and the synonym *libido*) to refer directly or indirectly to sexual craving or erotic desire, but, in his later writings, seemed to veer toward the less specifically erotic meanings of general pleasure-seeking and life-expressing (*Eros*).

socialization: the processes by which an individual acquires sensitivity to the demands of group life and learns to get along with and to behave similarly to other members of the group.

stages of development: (1) *stages of sexuality;* (2) in Sullivanian theory, the periods in the individual's development characteristically related to various patterns of *interpersonal relations* (infancy, childhood, *juvenile era, preadolescence,* early adolescence, late adolescence, and adulthood).

stages of sexuality: in Freudian theory, the developmental periods through which the individual is pushed by the *libido* toward the achievement of mature sexuality. The first period, characteristic of the first year of life, is the oral stage, during which the libidinal energy is centered in the mouth. The second is the anal stage, usually extending from age 1 through age 3, during which the *libido* is partially transferred to the anal zone. In this phase the child derives great pleasures from the retention and expulsion of feces. The third period is the phallic stage, during which interest is first focused on the penis (or clitoris), but soon fastens upon the parents. This third phase is sometimes referred to as the Oedipus period (see *Oedipus complex*). All three stages are called *pregenital stages* to distinguish them from the normal adult state, *genital maturity.*

structural hypothesis, the third and last theory of the *psyche* proposed by Freud, in which he distinguished three functionally related structures of the *psyche:* the *id,* the *ego,* and the *superego.* Distinguished from the *topographic theory.*

sublimation: in Freudian theory, the alteration of the channels of the *libido* in such a way as to bring the expression of the *sexual instinct* within the bonds of conventional approval. For example, the infantile wish to play with feces (expression of the *libido* at the *anal stage*) may be sublimated by playing with mud (and, still later in life, by sculpturing in clay).

superego: in *psychoanalysis,* that part of the *psyche* which comprises the individual's moral precepts and ideal aspirations; it is mainly developed in the Oedipal period and is largely an internalization of parental standards as perceived by the *ego.*

suppression: in *psychoanalysis,* a *conscious* exclusion of disapproved desires; contrasted with *repression,* in which the process of exclusion is not conscious.

Thanatos: the *death instinct.*

therapist: one who conducts treatment procedures; the agent who provides *psychotherapy.*

therapy: psychotherapy.

thought dissociation: a *defense mechanism* by which the *ego* protects itself from a thought that carries with it dangerous *id* impulses—the ego dissociates this thought from thoughts that preceded it and thoughts which follow it. The individual experiences momentary mental blankness; sometimes called *isolation.*

topographic theory: Freud's effort to develop a map of the *psyche* by dividing its contents and operations into three mental systems: Ucs. (*unconscious*), Pcs. (*preconscious*), and Cs. (*conscious*). This was the second of three theories of the psyche formulated by Freud. The first was an unnamed hypothesis which compared the mind to an optical instrument; the third was the *structural hypothesis.*

transference: in *psychoanalysis,* the *displacement* of *affect* from one object to another; specifically, the process whereby a patient shifts feelings applicable to another person (often a parent) onto the psychoanalyst.

trauma: damage or injury to the *psyche;* an experience or set of experiences (plural, traumas or traumata) that inflicts serious injury.

turning against the self: a *defense mechanism* whereby the *ego* (usually of a child) protects itself from a forbidden *aggressive* impulse against another person which it (the *ego*) dare not consciously admit by self-berating or self punishment. The child is, in effect, temporarily being the hated person (often a parent) and thus striking or berating that person by striking or berating himself.

unconscious: in *psychoanalysis,* a division of the *psyche* the contents of which are at least temporarily (and usually permanently) unknown to the individual. This part of the *psyche,* Freud hypothesized, contains the mental processes which are of fundamental significance and frequency in human *behavior* and are usually the causes of human actions. Also see *collective unconscious.*

value: (1) an abstract concept, often merely implicit, that defines what ends or means to an end are desirable; (2) a goal; (3) the degree of worth ascribed to an object or activity.

vegetotherapy: orgone therapy.

will therapy: the term applied to the system of *psychotherapy* developed by Otto Rank (see Section D of Chapter 4).

Index

Cardinal John Cody. Archbishop of Chicago, the most controversial figure in the American Church. Money and questions of morality beset him. Yet, more than any other cardinal, he has an entree to the Vatican, in part because of his old friend Paul Marcinkus.

Bishop Paul Marcinkus. Vatican banker extraordinary. Financial scandal swirls around his towering figure. He dismisses it all and says God knows the truth. And he did John Paul II a favor the pope will never forget—even though it brought the Church closer to confrontation with Russia.

Michele Sindona. Financier, friend of Paul VI. Currently serving a long term in a New Jersey penitentiary, the end result of a career of swindling that almost bankrupted the Vatican.

Cardinal Sebastiano Baggio. The papacy's "hit-man," the ruthless prefect of the Sacred Congregation for Bishops whose most spectacular failure is his attempt to unseat Cody.

Cardinal Giovanni Benelli. Wheeler-dealer prelate who thinks his moment has come when John Paul I becomes pope. He promises himself sweet revenge on his opponents. But before he can strike, he is engulfed in drama.

Cardinal Pericle Felici. Prefect of the Supreme Tribunal of the Apostolic Signatura, the papal appellate court. Knows everybody in the Church who matters. A magnificent manipulator in the name of retaining traditionalism. Even his friends fear him.

Father Lambert Greenan. English-language editor of the pope's newspaper, *L'Osservatore Romano.* Witty, waspish and wise.

Father Sean MacCarthy. Radio Vatican commentator. He cannot quite believe it when he learns that his colleagues have bugged conclave.

Archbishop Gaetano Alibrandi. Papal nuncio to Ireland. A diplomat with unusual links to people and places that diplomats normally steer clear of. But then Alibrandi is no ordinary nuncio.

Father Andrew Greeley. The Church's critic-in-residence.

And sundry other members of the Sacred College of Cardinals, the Curia and the Church at large.

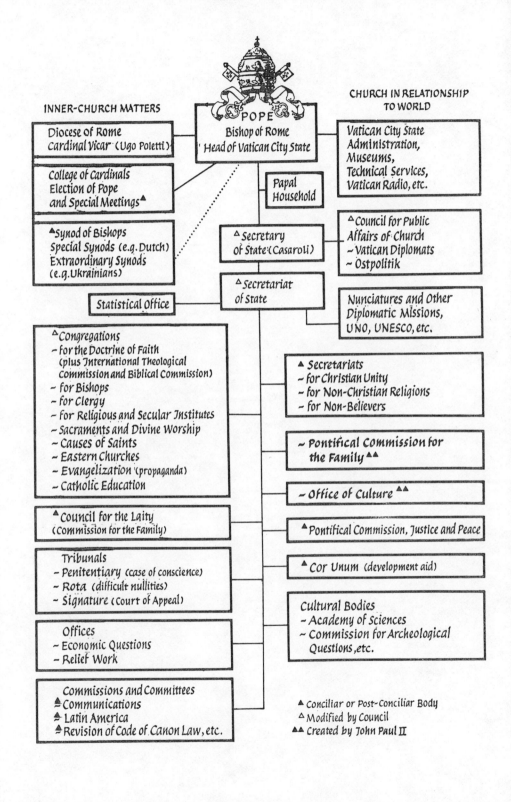

INNER-CHURCH MATTERS

POPE
Bishop of Rome
Head of Vatican City State

CHURCH IN RELATIONSHIP TO WORLD

Diocese of Rome
Cardinal Vicar (Ugo Poletti)

College of Cardinals
Election of Pope
and Special Meetings ▲

△ Synod of Bishops
Special Synods (e.g. Dutch)
Extraordinary Synods
(e.g. Ukrainians)

Statistical Office

△ Congregations
– for the Doctrine of Faith
(plus International Theological
Commission and Biblical Commission)
– for Bishops
– for Clergy
– for Religious and Secular Institutes
– Sacraments and Divine Worship
– Causes of Saints
– Eastern Churches
– Evangelization (propaganda)
– Catholic Education

▲ Council for the Laity
(Commission for the Family)

Tribunals
– Penitentiary (case of conscience)
– Rota (difficult nullities)
– Signature (Court of Appeal)

Offices
~ Economic Questions
~ Relief Work

Commissions and Committees
≙ Communications
≙ Latin America
≙ Revision of Code of Canon Law, etc.

Papal
Household

△ Secretary
of State (Casaroli)

△ Secretariat
of State

Vatican City State
Administration,
Museums,
Technical Services,
Vatican Radio, etc.

△ Council for Public
Affairs of Church
~ Vatican Diplomats
~ Ostpolitik

Nunciatures and Other
Diplomatic Missions,
UNO, UNESCO, etc.

▲ Secretariats
~ for Christian Unity
~ for Non-Christian Religions
~ for Non-Believers

~ Pontifical Commission for
the Family ▲▲

~ Office of Culture ▲▲

▲ Pontifical Commission, Justice and Peace

▲ Cor Unum (development aid)

Cultural Bodies
~ Academy of Sciences
~ Commission for Archeological
Questions, etc.

▲ Conciliar or Post-Conciliar Body
△ Modified by Council
▲▲ Created by John Paul II

THE STORY
SO FAR

1

From the time Jesus said to Simon, "You are Peter. On you I will build my Church," there have been popes. Some were holier than others; many found the office a high-risk occupation. Each of the first eighteen popes was a victim of violence, either crucified, strangled, poisoned, beheaded or smothered to death. Some found no peace even in the grave. Formosus (891–96) was disinterred nine months after burial, his rotting corpse robed in pontifical vestments and placed on a chair to face trial before a religious court presided over by his successor. The corpse of John XIV (983–84) was skinned and hauled through the streets of Rome. Other popes have been imprisoned, exiled and deposed. Some were confronted with rival claimants, faced intense secular interference, heresies, mass defections and schisms.

Yet few institutions in the whole of history have displayed a greater capacity for survival. Roman Catholics often believe this longevity to be striking theological testimony to the divinity of the papacy; much is made of the power of the Holy Spirit for ensuring that the highest office of the Universal Church continues the ministry given by Christ to Peter. The papacy, called by Toynbee the greatest of all Western institutions, exerts a fascination for everybody. Believers find it a comforting symbol of Catholic identity. The rest are mesmerized by its complexities and contradictions.

Popes have civilized barbarians yet encouraged the Inquisition. They condemned torture yet approved it against heretics. Popes, the apostles of peace, have waged war. A few—John XII (955–64) and Alexander VI (1492–1503)—led shocking lives. The papacy, the epitome of unity, has itself been a significant barrier to Church unity.

It remains so in 1978, when Paul VI, the 261st pope to hold the office, is still on the Throne of St. Peter. It is the fifteenth year of his pontificate and 740 million baptized Catholics, whatever else they feel about him, agree he is firmly rooted in the nineteen-hundred-year-old papal tradition. He is as insistently imperious, magnificently monarchic and absolutely absolute as any pope before him. He is also old, waiting to die, he hopes in bed.

But in this year of violence, of urban terrorism and religious fanatics and sense-less brutal killing wherever he looks, not even Paul VI knows with certainty whether his death will be peaceful.

The worry helps to keep him awake at night.

THE JACKAL

Now hatred is by far
The lasting pleasure

—BYRON

11

The creeping gray where night ends and another day begins, 4:30 A.M. by the clock, the moment his mother still calls the first dawn, awakens him.

For a moment Mehmet Ali Agca lies motionless. Only his eyes move, small, red-rimmed, watchful eyes, set deep in a long face. He is nineteen years and five months old on this July morning in 1978. But those eyes make him look at least a decade older. They are the eyes of an insomniac, scanning a room which is all too familiar to him. He was born in it and has experienced all his worthwhile memories so far within the confines of its plain whitewashed walls. Here, he cried himself to sleep after his first street fight. Later he experienced his first sexual fantasy on this bed he has slept in since a boy. And here, too, beneath the small window in the wall, he regularly pleads with Allah to make him famous. Agca is still waiting. In the meantime his mind is filled with other thoughts, ugly and dangerous ideas which excite and frighten him.

His eyes continue to scan. The walls are covered with posters. Many bear the photograph of the same man, Colonel Alpaslan Turkes, leader of Turkey's paramilitary Idealists. Modeled on Hitler's S.S. and equipped with a variety of World War II weapons, the Idealists, better known as the Gray Wolves, are becoming as formidable as some of the more well known terrorist groups in Europe. Turkish law forbids the display of such posters under penalty of imprisonment. But Agca does not care about the risk. He has been a Gray Wolf for two years. So far he has killed nobody. Yet he is willing to do so, and to die, for Turkes.

Agca finds nothing unusual in such fanaticism. He was born and raised with it. There are countless thousands of other Turks like him, all caught up in the Anarchy, the generic term for the appalling violence which sweeps Turkey, Islam's last free society, a democracy of forty-five million persons in a Moslem world of about six hundred million; only the Catholic Church can claim more souls. The Anarchy, for all its tentacles which feed off the interstices of Turkish life, is concerned with one ultimate goal: the end of the present system of authentic elections and multiple parties. Violence, insane and numbing and continuous, has been chosen as the means to do this. Entire cities are now closed citadels controlled by either the right or the left. During the first six months of this year there have been six hundred murders; there is an average of twenty armed bank robberies a day. Nobody knows who is behind the Anarchy; most likely, no single hand any longer controls it, no one voice issues threats, demands, communiqués, chooses the victims. The Anarchy makes no special effort to gouge out the heart of the Turkish state—as the Red Brigades concurrently do in Italy. In Turkey, army officers, judges, politicians and policemen are not specifically singled out; the killing is far more indiscriminate. Nor is it a straight clash between right and left. There are as many as forty-five Marxist revolutionary groups in Turkey fighting each other. The right is dominated by the hard profile of Turkes and his Gray Wolves, who howl when their Leader addresses them. Agca regularly practices the chilling animal sound in his bedroom.

The only furniture in the room, apart from his iron bedstead, is a rickety old table and chair. A strip of carpet is on the bare concrete floor that is icy cold in winter but pleasantly cool in the hot summers. On top of the strip lies a smaller and grander rug. It is handwoven with an intricate pattern of gold and red threads. It belonged to Agca's grandfather; when he died it was passed on, in a family tradition, to his eldest grandson. It is Agca's prayer mat, one of his two most prized possessions.

Above his head is a shelf. It contains a row of books: an English primer, well thumbed, its pages repeatedly folded at the corners to mark important passages; the others are paperbacks, thrillers for the most part, including a reprint of *The Day of the Jackal*. Agca has read it at least ten times, fascinated by the details of how to assassinate a public figure. Beside the books is an old cigar box. It contains his second treasured keepsake, an old Mauser pistol, oiled, wrapped in rags. There are several bullets in the box.

Staring around the room, the dull heaviness he feels is more pronounced. Fear? Expectation? The residue of the malaise which had once again gripped him? He does not know. He is aware only of the tightening in his chest, the queasy feeling in his stomach. But at least he no longer shows any surface anger, no clenching and unclenching of his hands or sudden curling of his lips to expose discolored teeth. His mother has shown him how to control such indications of inner torment, just as she taught him, in the shrill voice people call intimidating but which he finds comforting, that at first dawn he must scramble from bed and recite one of the five daily prayers.

Agca's nervous energy is evident as he gets up, clad in the undershirt and shorts in which he always sleeps. Standing, he is an unprepossessing figure; hands and feet seem out of proportion to his puny body with its concave chest, protruding shoulder blades and thin arms and legs. He looks painfully undernourished. In addition to insomnia, Agca suffers from anorexia nervosa, a severe psychological illness more usually found in teenage girls, and crippling bouts of depression. Not even his mother can fully understand his suffering.

Just as she first showed him years earlier, he now spreads his prayer rug, prostrates himself three times, each time touching his forehead to the ground, murmuring the name of Allah, Master of the World, the All-Meaningful and All-Compassionate, the Supreme Sovereign of the Last Judgment.

Then he begins quietly to recite his long list of hatreds.

The eldest son of the widow Muzzeyene will need a long time to get through his list.

The light is still too diffuse to identify the bleakness of this room. There are four others similarly austere in the house. The largest is his mother's bedroom with its double bed no one has shared since the day her husband died eleven years ago; two smaller bedrooms, one for Fatma, Agca's seventeen-year-old sister, the other for Adnan, his fifteen-year-old brother. There is also the family room, where they eat, squatting on the floor around a potbellied wood-burning stove and, at nights, watch television on an old black-and-white set.

Muzzeyene has painted the living-room walls a sickly green from a tin of paint she found on a local refuse dump she regularly scours. The ceiling is dirty from the stove. There is an outside toilet and water from a pump. For this hovel Muzzeyene pays an absentee landlord the equivalent of one U.S. dollar a week. When he learned the amount, Agca felt it was extortionate. From then on all landlords, absentee and otherwise, were put on his hate list.

The list is extraordinary in its diversity and implication. It includes: all the long-dead Russian tsars and their imperial dreams; NATO, whose bases are scattered throughout Turkey; Sheik Yamani, for refusing to use Arab oil to totally destroy the West. On a more personal level Agca hates hamburgers, ketchup, Levi's, *I Love Lucy*, *Time* and *Newsweek*—anything connected with the most powerful nation in the world, its way of life, values and customs, the very wellsprings of its existence. He needs a full five minutes to remind himself of everything he hates about America.

He especially hates those Americans who buy the staple of village life, and not just the staple of his village, but of hundreds of other villages scattered from end to endless end of Turkey: the poppy. For a thousand years—Agca dates it from the time Alp Aslan defeated the Byzantine emperor at the battle of Manzikert and ancient Anatolia became Turkish—the poppy has been tilled, its oil used for cooking, its leaves in salad, its seeds in bread, its pods fed to cattle, its stalks in building. Only its gum remained untouched by villagers. The Americans have found a special use for it, converting the gum into a morphine base which in turn is refined into heroin.

Officially, this no longer happens. On June 30, 1971, the United States government and the Turkish regime signed an agreement banning all opium-poppy growing in Turkey. The last legal crop was to be harvested in 1972. America paid $37.5 million to Turkey to compensate the poppy growers while they sought replacement crops. President Nixon hailed the agreement as a significant step toward stemming the heroin crisis in the United States. The farmers took the money but went on growing the poppy.

Agca knows what heroin can do. Fresh in his mind is the incident in Istanbul. A drug courier had been caught cheating by his employers. The man was held down and forcibly injected with high-grade pure heroin. The process was repeated every day for a week. By then he was an incurable addict. To complete his punishment his employers arranged that he would receive no further heroin. In another week the demented courier jumped into the Bosporus, drowning in its pollution. Agca finds the episode exhilarating in its violence and deeply satisfying—the way the courier was finally driven to kill himself.

Months afterward the details have lost nothing in his repeated retelling of the story. What he does not add—preferring instead to keep it for this time at dawn when he rekindles all his other hatreds—is his burning resentment for those unknown American drug bosses on the other side of the world. Indirectly, they employ him; he occasionally drives a truck on the heroin trail. He gets only a fistful of Turkish liras for each trip. But it is not that which fuels his anger. It is directly related to his discovery of the vast profits made by the Americans. A poppy farmer might get $15 for a pound of gum. On the streets of New York, refined and processed, the price was $200,000 a pound. All profiteers are now on Agca's list.

So, too, are employers, dating from that day his father was killed in a road accident on a Tuesday and his employer had refused to pay the last full week of salary.

When he thinks of his father nowadays, he can only clearly remember his hands, calloused, broad-fingered and practical; violent, too, suddenly lashing out, sending his mother reeling and the cheap crockery shattering over the floor. Agca remembered how he had smiled at his father's funeral; his mother looked at him and they both understood. Only in deference to her had Agca kept his father off his list.

His death had altered the family's position. Already poor, they plunged still further down the village social scale. All three children, from an early age, were expected to find work. By the time he was ten, Agca sold water by the cup to travelers at a bus stop near his home. It was about this time his eating problems began. He deliberately missed meals or ate no more than he had to when at table. His mother did not seem unduly concerned. Perhaps because she was so busy with other problems—finding the rent money and clothes for the children, scouring the refuse bin for a scrap of window curtain or a usable cooking pot—she did not seriously consider her son's eating habits. Nor did she immediately recognize the psychological changes in him, that he was growing into a young man rather different from his companions. Often he would fall into silent, inactive periods, retreating to his room. When she did think about such behavior, like him, she had no idea of the complex process causing it. Part was associated with the guilt he felt at not loving his father. Yet that same guilt stopped him from speaking about the feeling, let alone seeking help. Instead, all the hostility he had felt toward his father he turned on himself during these periods of depression. Eventually he had come to believe he could only expunge this feeling by hatred. He once mentioned this to his mother, and from then on she encouraged him to hate. And so his list was created.

The light was strengthening now. He could hear the sounds of his mother and sister preparing breakfast, and beyond the window the first stirrings of life in the community somebody had cruelly called Yesiltepe, Green Hill.

Only the largest-scale maps of Turkey pinpoint Yesiltepe, 465 miles due east of Ankara. It huddles on the road the Crusaders trudged to and from Jerusalem. Every thirty years or so the buildings begin to crumble into dust, their dung bricks turning to powder under the fierce heat of summer and the biting cold which sweeps the Turkish steppes from October to April. Yesiltepe has clung for six hundred years to the stony ground that extends to the mountains which ring the community. Eleven hundred people live here in 1978, suspicious insular men in dark suits and flannel shirts and women who cling to their veils as they drive the cattle through the unpaved streets and work the fields. There are a good number of children; even the very young ones smoke and hawk and spit. The small mosque has a tall, tapering minaret. Many of the houses do not have electricity or running water. Restrictive Moslem code keeps all women outside the teahouses where the men spend their days talking and playing cards.

In this remote corner of earth, Agca learned the facts of his life. He was an unusually small child, but gifted: he could read and write at the age of five. Yesiltepe School has no accelerated program for advanced children. Instead Agca was "skipped" ahead by his teachers. At eight he was in the fourth grade, sharing lessons with twelve-year-olds. At first he liked to show off his abilities, but after he had been beaten several times by his classmates he learned to disguise his brilliance. Nevertheless, by the age of fourteen he had learned all the school could offer. He stayed another year, coming and going as he pleased. Almost naturally, because of his impoverished background, he drifted into one of the gangs in the nearby city of Malatya. He found himself running errands for the local crime bosses. He was good. He was recommended to the bigger bosses running the local sector of the heroin trail; when they wanted an extra driver they used him. On a trip to Istanbul he casually made contact with the Gray Wolves; he liked what he heard of their plans to overthrow established government. He joined the group. At the same time he made arrangements to continue his studies at the University of Ankara; young though he was, his grades guaranteed him a place. He spent an uneventful year there. Then the onset of one of his periods of depression cut short his studies. He returned to Yesiltepe and discovered the Gray Wolves had a cell in Malatya. He attended their meetings but found he had little in common with his fellow revolutionaries. He drifted back onto the heroin trail. The money he made from smuggling he gave to his mother. She did not ask where it came from. It was another of their understandings.

In the past five years Agca has owned five handguns. So far his only victim is a neighbor's cockerel whose head he blew off for target practice. His mother had to pay double the market price for the bird; from that moment on the neighbor had been marked down as another profiteer.

Puberty hardened Agca, but his melancholia gave him a curious charm which made him welcome enough in one of Malatya's brothels. Apart from these visits he avoided all contact with the opposite sex. Yet throughout his blossoming process part of him stood off to one side, cold and watchful. It was the part which recognized the ignorance of his teachers, the part which made him constantly replay little vignettes where he had been made to suffer. It was that part which said he must seek revenge.

As a young man he now functions well enough. He is a respected and feared figure among his contemporaries. His affiliation with the Gray Wolves is sufficient to make even the most threatening of Yesiltepe's bullies steer clear of him; Colonel Turkes has shown he can wreak terrible retribution on anybody who dares touch his men.

To Yesiltepe's elders Agca is a strange person. He does not gamble and cannot bear personal competition. Nor does he ever let his feelings get out of control, at least publicly. Though he understands limited aggression objectively, he cannot take part in it. He makes no distinction between friendly competition and total combat to the death. That is why he finds all organized sport boring. The only time he shows real passion is when he is alone, when he is reciting his hate list. It's a year now since he began collecting it, a desperate, confusing catalog no outsider can quantify or explain. It is his only outlet, the one thing which allows him to burn off some of the inner furies. His mental state is dangerously balanced, yet some primeval instinct protects him, ensuring that nobody, not even his mother, realizes what is happening to him.

A doctor would undoubtedly recognize the symptoms as alarming: the withdrawal from food, the frequent escape from normal daily contact, the sudden inner angers that precede the dull pain. A psychiatrist would assuredly probe Agca's self-reproach, his perfectionist behavior—the books on his shelf are lined up in careful symmetry, his clothes are laid out in the same way on the floor by his boots—small clues, but indications of how far his obsessional ideas are expiatory, an attempt to overcome, by a kind of mental magic, deeper distress. And if the psychiatrist were an analyst he might probe Agca about his correct and prudish manners to discover they hid a rather perverse sexuality. He might learn of Agca's compulsion to step over cracks in the ground, to touch wood for luck, to keep a single tune running through his head for days. And all this might, in the end, lead to Agca's telling about his hate list.

But there is no doctor in Yesiltepe and the nearest psychiatrist is in Ankara.

Agca continues with his task, moving steadily through the list, knowing he has time, realizing today will probably pass like any other now that he is again ready to leave the self-imposed isolation of this room. He will spend most of it in the town's tearoom, sipping *çay*, aromatic tea, and catching up on the latest talk.

Nowadays there is much to discuss. Yesiltepe is caught up in the latest sectarian slaughter sweeping Turkey. There have been five deaths in the community, polarizing further the extreme right- and left-wing elements in Yesiltepe. Throughout Turkey hundreds are dead and thousands injured. The victims are clubbed, shot in the stomach, set on fire with gasoline, hacked to pieces with machetes. There have been waves of arrests. In one prison alone, a morning's drive from Yesiltepe, 807 defendants will shortly face a collective trial in the jail yard. Rumor says the guilty ones will be shot in batches of fifty.

Many are Agca's friends, fellow Gray Wolves; most are younger than he is. Killers under eighteen are much in demand among the various factions because Turkish law precludes the death penalty below that age.

Agca also knows most certainly he, too, would now be under arrest but for the depression which has kept him in this bedroom for almost two months, bowed down, withdrawn, refusing anything but the minimum of food. After a time, he has slowly climbed out of his apathy, returning gradually to his present aggressive state.

He is coming to the end of his list. Slowly, in the guttural peasant patois of Malatya province which made city people underestimate him, he reminds himself he hates the queen of England because she symbolizes the worst kind of imperialism; South Africa because of its apartheid and its links with Israel.

Finally only his religious hatreds are left. He keeps them for the end because they are the most virulent, consuming him like a cancer, burrowing into his mind, even capable at times of making him weep. Then, real tears fall down his cheeks, the crying of an unforgiving fanatic who hates all religions save his own. He sees them as threatening, plotting and determined to overthrow the faith to which he subscribes. He has been able to reduce them to one instantly recognizable ideograph. It is that of an old man, dressed in white with a skullcap, who lives in a huge palace far beyond the mountains. He rules like a caliph, issuing decrees and orders many millions must obey. And when he dies another old man takes his place, ruling in the same inflexible manner.

When Agca eventually comes to the end of his hate list, he reserves to himself one final pleasure: to make a wish of who, given the chance, he would like to destroy.

There is nowadays no doubt in his mind. He would like to kill the old man.

All Agca knows about him and the vast kingdom he rules is contained in a school exercise book which he keeps beneath the cigar box holding his Mauser.

This morning, as he does every other morning, as part of the obsessive ritualism which rules his life, Agca rises from his squatting position and reaches for the exercise book. Sitting on his bed he turns the pages. The notes are fragmentary, scribbled in his spidery longhand and difficult to decipher.

The message they contain is both revealing and disturbing. Agca believes the old man is in the vanguard of a calculated campaign to erode the very foundations of Islam. He is doing so by carefully encouraging the introduction of modern life into countries which are the last bastion of the Moslem religion. He is doing so under the guise of progress, pretending to be improving conditions when all the time he is cunningly eroding the essential purity of Islam, making it face compromises which will weaken and ultimately destroy it or, at the very least, transform it into a political ideology which could actually rob it of its deep religious power. Islam, if the old man had his way, would be cast on the religious rubbish heap, little more than an ethnic or cultural irrelevance. Finally it would wither and die, another victim of the extraordinary plotting the old man, his predecessors and all those they represent are capable of. So Agca believes.

Stuck in the exercise book are also faded newspaper and magazine photographs, and stories detailing the old man's travels around the world: to India, to America, to Pakistan, to so many countries, spreading his hateful message, the way his predecessors have done for nineteen hundred years. Surrounded by pomp and glory, rejoicing in even more titles than Allah himself has, the old man is known, variously, as Servant of the Servants of God, Patriarch of the West, Vicar of Jesus Christ, Bishop of Rome, Sovereign of Vatican City, Supreme Pontiff of the Universal Church, His Holiness Pope Paul VI.

Ideally Agca would like to kill Paul. But if, as Agca has written in his exercise book, "the biological solution, death, intervenes," then he is equally determined to kill his successor.

Agca has come to realize that almost certainly he will not be able to achieve this alone. It will require a great deal of careful planning, money and backup. In Agca's mind there are only two possible places from which this support can come: Russia and Libya. He has read that the rulers of these countries hate and fear the pope as much as he does. Agca is positive one of them will help him.[1]

PART ONE
THE LAST DAYS

*He went unterrified
Into the gulf of death*

—SHELLEY

III

For months there has been something missing in St. Peter's Square. From midnight it is closed to traffic and its fountains switched off until the wooden shutters on two corner windows on the top floor of the Apostolic Palace open the next morning. Romans say the time of their opening is a good guide to the current health and temper of the man in the bedroom behind the shutters. If they open before the first rays of the sun pass above the limpid Tiber to light the cross on top of the basilica, Paul would have spent another restless night. If the shutters remain closed until the sun illuminates the vaulted dome of the greatest church in Christendom, then the pope has spent a relatively peaceful one—perhaps with the help of the two vials kept at his bedside. One holds a supply of Mogadon sleeping tablets; the other contains capsules whose contents are a mixture known only to the pope's doctor, the omniscient Mario Fontana. They are to ease his patient's arthritis. Just as they speculate about the shutters, so people do about the medicine.

It is by such means that the mood of the papacy is assessed in this, the sixteenth year of the pontificate of Giovanni Battista Montini, elected in 1963 to be the spiritual leader of the largest church in the world and the bearer of awesome titles, offices and power which, in theory, can reach out from this bedroom in a fifteenth-century Vatican palace and directly affect the lives of

740 million baptized Roman Catholics. In reality, he reigns over a restless church which increasingly pays little more than lip service to his teachings. Many Catholics flout his now-famous encyclical *Humanae Vitae* (*On Human Life*) by continuing to practice birth control; women want to be priests, priests wish to marry, bishops desire to be regional popes, theologians claim a teaching authority even more absolute than the powers vested in the body of the tired and frail old man in the brass bed which faces the closed shutters.

The Vatican's secretary of state, Cardinal Jean Villot, had arranged for the traffic to be halted and the fountains silenced to help Paul sleep.[1] But even Villot felt unable to hush the ringing of the six massive bells of St. Peter's; for three hundred years they have peeled their joy for a new saint and tolled their sorrow at the death of a pope. Now eighty years old, and preoccupied with the physical act of dying—Paul wonders what he will feel, how it will come upon him, whether it will be quick, whether he will be conscious to the very end—the pope could ponder that his four predecessors had lain in this same bedroom waiting for death. He has mused recently, and mentioned it to those of his personal staff who are not excluded by the carapace he has created between himself and the world of ordinary feelings, whether those other popes experienced the feeling he increasingly has: that it will be a blessed relief finally to lay down the heavy burden of being pope.

Nobody will ever know what his first thought is on awakening this particular July morning in 1978. Unlike Pius XII, who kept a diary filled with such private details, and John XXIII, who delighted in telling everybody his inner feelings at the dawn of each day, Paul neither writes down nor speaks about such intimate matters.

Nor, indeed, would anybody know the precise moment he has awoken, or even whether he has slept at all. Years ago he ordered that nobody must come knocking on his bedroom door and wish him good morning. He would emerge when he felt like it. Barring the gravest of crises—in this era it includes a sudden nuclear attack by the Soviet Union or the assassination of an important head of state, such as the American president or the queen of England—almost no one is permitted to enter his bedroom until he says so.

It is a surprisingly small room, square, with a high ceiling. The bed dominates it. Paul brought it with him from Milan, where he was archbishop before the conclave of 1963 elected him pope by a runaway majority. They say —those cynical Romans—the Holy Spirit worked overtime to achieve that result. The bedding is a pastel shade, matching the linen cloth covering on the walls. There is a fine mahogany chest of drawers supporting a beveled mirror and a small desk with an old-fashioned black telephone which rarely rings. Paul does not favor the instrument as a means of communication; he likes to look into a person's eyes when they speak. There is an Afghan rug on the polished wooden floor. The window drapes are pastel. On the wall above the bed is a painting of Jesus' agony on the Cross; it, too, came from Milan, a gift from the priests of the city to commemorate his election. Beside the bed is a table. As well as the vials, there is an old Bible his father gave him the day he made his first Holy Communion on June 6, 1907; seventy-one years later the Bible has been lovingly preserved in a heavy leather cover. Near the table is a prie-dieu where Paul kneels and says his private prayers. Above it a wooden crucifix has been fixed to the wall. Close by, reducing the impact of the Cross, is a fine picture of the Virgin. Crucifix and portrait are also gifts he accepted on the long and lonely journey which brought him to this room.

But there is none of the bric-a-brac a person who has traveled so widely might be expected to have on view: no signed portraits of other heads of state, no photographs to show he has journeyed to places no other pope has ever been. The bedroom is tastefully anonymous. It is as if here, where he now spends a quarter of his daily life, Paul does not wish to be cluttered with his past.

There is one exception, an object that is not a gift, which the pope is almost childishly obsessive about. Wherever he travels it goes with him, carefully packed into his baggage by the senior of his two personal secretaries, Don Pasquale Macchi. This morning it stands in its accustomed place between the Bible and the vials. It is a cheap alarm clock with a lacquered brass frame and roman numerals on its plain white face. It has two stubby brass legs. Every night Paul winds the clock. Every morning, at precisely six-thirty, the alarm gives its tinny summons. He lets it ring for a few seconds and then presses the button on top of the bell, as if concerned not to awaken anybody in the vicinity of the bedroom. It is a ritual he has followed for fifty-five years, from that day in May 1923 when he was made *addetto,* second secretary, to the nunciature in Warsaw. Every night for the seven months he spent there he set the alarm for six-thirty; in those days he slept deeply and the alarm would often shrill its course before he was fully awake. He would rise and do an hour's work before breakfast. This habit of an early start stuck.

Nowadays, he frequently beats the clock, awakening from at best a fitful sleep an hour or more before the alarm rings. Then—he has confided to Macchi—he watches the minutes tick by. Sometimes he silently recites a favorite passage from Shakespeare's *Troilus and Cressida,* the one about "the end crowns all,/And that old common arbitrator, Time,/Will one day end it."

Paul's thin body, clad in a white nightshirt, barely disturbs the bedding. His feet are encased in bedsocks because of his poor blood circulation. Medically, Fontana does not approve of the socks, but the wise old physician —Fontana is seventy and belongs to a different school from the brisk young men of medicine today—recognizes the psychological importance the socks have for the pope.

Physically, Paul has been ill for years. A delicate child, he grew into a far
from robust man. In middle age troublesome bladder and kidney disorders
surfaced. In the end his prostate gland was surgically removed. But in spite of
Fontana's secret capsules, the arthritis in the pope's right knee remains so
painful he often finds it difficult to walk. He has also become prone to bron-
chitis and influenza. Fontana has already treated an attack in the spring with
antibiotics; the side effects of the drugs left Paul's resistance even lower.
Now, in July, another bout seems to be developing. The doctor fears the heat
and humidity of a Roman summer will only further debilitate his patient. He
has urged the pope to go to Castel Gandolfo. Paul demurs: he will only go to
the Papal Palace, the retreat of popes for centuries in the Alban Hills outside
Rome, on the same day he has every other year. His physician can do no more
than visit Paul daily, listen to his chest and silently count the time before the
pope will leave Rome.

Paul now has only one more night to spend in this room high above St.
Peter's Square.

In bed, like anyone else, he appears at his most vulnerable. His skin is taut
on the skull, his hair wispy gray, without vigor. The veins stand out on the
back of his long, thin hands, the fingers tapering to nails which need paring.
Yet, in the depths of his winter of age, there is still something left which the
years have not dimmed: his eyes. Miraculously, they have retained their brilliant blue color, their luminosity and, above all, their look of piercing yet
somehow gentle inquiry. They seem at variance with a face which is lined
and haggard and etched deeply with personal pain.

Shortly after he has silenced the clock alarm, Paul presses one of three buttons on a buzzer system. It is the signal to those waiting beyond the bedroom
that he is officially awake.

Sister Giacomina has been waiting for the sounds of the buzzer in the comfortable bed-sitting-room she occupies close to the pope's room. The two other
buttons link Paul with Macchi's apartment on the third floor of the Apostolic
Palace, and with Franco Ghezzi, the pope's valet-chauffeur, who is married
and lives in an apartment in the rear of the vast rambling building which has
10,065 suites, salons, rooms, reception areas, audience chambers, halls, pas-
sageways and cellars; these are linked by 997 flights of stairs and three elevators, one of which is reserved exclusively for Paul and his personal staff. The
elevator door is near Giacomina's room, a strategic position which allows her
to monitor and, when occasion demands, head off unwanted visitors.

She is one of five sisters who take care of the papal household, washing and
cooking and cheerfully complaining about the electric carpet sweeper when
its cable becomes entangled in their habits as they vacuum the eighteen rooms
of the apartment.

Giacomina is in charge of this domestic retinue. She has served in that capacity for more years than anybody cares to remember. Church regulations stipulate that women who work and live in the households of priests and prelates must be of "canonical age," assumed to mean beyond the age of physical attraction.

Giacomina has filled the requirement for many years. But despite her evident age there is a resilience about her which even the most overbearing of cardinals finds daunting. She knows her position is secure as long as Paul is alive; nobody is allowed to forget that she is more than a mere housekeeper. She combines the management of the papal household with her role as the pope's personal nurse. She is trained in the techniques of mouth-to-mouth resuscitation and how to administer pain-killing and life-support injections. She knows where Fontana is at any moment of the day or night, and she will not hesitate to call him at the first sign her beloved Paul displays of distress. People say she is more formidable than even the legendary Sister Pasqualina who looked after Pius XII. It was she who ended the unwritten rule that the papal household was to be run exclusively by men. But whereas there was endless gossip over the influence Pasqualina had on Pius, there is no doubt about the effect Giacomina has on Paul. With a few well-chosen words she can make light of even the gloomiest of starts to his day.

She knocks once on the pope's bedroom door and waits. When she is bidden to, she enters and greets the pope with words which seldom vary: *"Holy Father, it is going to be a wonderful day."*

Then she walks to the window and opens the shutters.

Two hundred feet below, in St. Peter's Square, a City of Rome policeman who has been waiting for this moment speaks into his two-way radio to tell colleagues on the far side of Bernini's colonnade—a complex of 284 columns and 80 buttresses surmounted by 162 statues each twelve feet high—what has happened. They begin to remove the crash barriers which diverted traffic around the square during the night. Shortly afterward the fountains in the great piazza, 215 yards at its greatest breadth, begin to spout water.

Alone now, Paul gets slowly out of bed and gingerly stands up to test the degree of pain in his right knee; he has been told to do this by Fontana. The pope eases his 130 pounds onto his right leg. The pain is no worse or better than it has been for months. Walking slowly, the way Fontana suggested, Paul reaches the bathroom.

It is as featureless as any bathroom in any luxury hotel; it might have been designed by Hilton or one of the world's other innkeepers. There are pastel tiled walls and a matching suite in lime green. The bath is fitted with a

shower attachment and a nonslip bottom. The pope washes, and shaves with
an electric razor: its make is a secret because the Vatican fears the manufacturer might somehow advertise that Paul uses its model.

While he is in the bathroom Ghezzi enters the bedroom—the only employee allowed to do so without knocking—and lays out Paul's clothes for the
day: a white-linen cassock, caped across the shoulders, white cotton undershorts and vest, white stockings and shoes and a white skullcap. The garments bear no label. They do not need one; there probably isn't a priest in
Rome who would not recognize the distinctive cut of a vestment tailored by
the House of Gammarelli, papal tailors and outfitters for almost two hundred
years. From a tiny workshop in the center of the city they have dressed popes
for mourning and for rejoicing; in the rag trade they are probably the most
exclusive establishment in the world. During the past fifteen years, Gammarelli's cutters and seamstresses have made over a score of cassocks, stoles,
rochets, mozzettas and skullcaps for Paul. But, like any old man, he has developed a fondness for certain clothes: apart from ceremonial occasions he
chooses the comfort of a few old favorite cassocks.

Having laid out the garments, Ghezzi leaves.

Paul prefers to dress in private. He does so slowly; the arthritic stiffness in
his fingers makes it difficult to close the buttons on his cassock. Finally, he
drapes a solid-gold pectoral cross around his neck; it hangs on his chest on a
twenty-four-carat-gold chain. A journalist recently wrote that the cross and
chain could be worth one hundred thousand dollars.

His next move is another of those private little rituals which have always
filled his life. He lowers himself onto the prie-dieu and prays. Then he rises
to his feet and walks to the windows. Standing well in the shadow of the
drapes—he has a genuine concern that some photographer might be lurking
outside with a telephoto lens and snap him off guard—Paul looks out over the
vast expanse of St. Peter's Square, and beyond. It is, understandably, a view
of which he has never tired.

At this early hour it is at its best. Below him, stretching into the distance,
are a hundred and more hooded domes glinting in the sun between the spires,
towers, monuments, palaces and parks. There are streets that run long and
straight, others which are curved and short, broad or narrow. Even up here he
can hear the unique sound of Rome, an echoing hum created as a result of
the city's being built on hardened volcanic ash, the *tufo*.

To his immediate right, about 1,200 feet from his bedroom window, is the
mass of Michelangelo's dome on top of the basilica of St. Peter. Long ago,
when Paul first entered Vatican service, he memorized the proportions of the
basilica. He found the facts useful when later, a fully fledged diplomat, he
spent time making polite small talk at official functions. Nowadays, when he

looks at the basilica, his thoughts may be on that day he will be buried in a vault deep beneath the ground which supports the edifice. Nevertheless, old though he is, and forgetful too, the pope can, if asked, still recite the dimensions of this masterpiece: 651 feet long, 435 feet high, with 77 supporting columns, 44 altars, 395 statues, and a bronze ball on top of the dome large enough to contain sixteen persons comfortably. Nor can he easily forget that, even when the Roman Empire declined and Peter became the Great Fisherman, it still needed a thousand years for his successors—each of them wearing the Fisherman's Ring, which, because of his arthritis, Paul no longer wears—to create this basilica as the focal point of a new empire, Christianity. Though his memory is failing, he will surely not have forgotten that hardly had the last stone been put into place before the Christian world was torn apart by hatred and dissensions.

In the distance he can see the North American College on the Janiculum Hill. If he does not look long in that direction it is understandable. The Church in America is a source of endless problems for him. It is still young and he is old; he does not know, he has told his confidants, how best he can handle the serious challenges from the other side of the Atlantic. But they cannot be ignored.

And over there, to the right of his window, is the roof of the Sistine Chapel—ordinary enough on the outside, affording no clue to the splendor beneath—where, all those years ago, he was elected by his fellow cardinals as the ideal man to govern the Church, reduce the hate, eliminate the animosity, heal the divisions. Some say he has failed to do any of these things. Others ask how it could have been otherwise.

And below, in the still-empty piazza of St. Peter's, is another painful reminder. Early though it is, the square is sprinkled with armed policemen; they have carbines, and radios to call for reinforcements. Their presence is grim evidence of the threat Paul now faces.

Out there in Rome are the persons who killed one of his closest friends, Aldo Moro, the Christian Democratic leader. Moro's life was political conciliation. On the day he was kidnapped, in March 1978, Moro had taken the historic step of bringing the Communists into the Parliamentary alliance to support a Christian Democratic government. Moro's kidnapping personalizes the whole question of urban terrorism for Paul. He repeatedly appealed to Moro's captors to free him, writing a final entreaty in his own neat hand, a few poignant lines imploring the "men of the Red Brigades" on his knees to show mercy. Their response was predictable. Moro was murdered with a circle of bullets around his heart which left him twenty minutes to drown in his own blood.

Paul, some say, has never forgiven the killers. Certainly, what they have done still haunts him as he turns away from the window and shuffles slowly toward the bedroom door ready to begin another long day.

In the corridor outside the bedroom two priests, their severe black soutanes relieved only by the white of stiff Roman collars, stand and make small talk. They respect each other but do not always agree on policies to be pursued. At this hour of the day, by tacit agreement, they confine themselves to noncontroversial subjects: the weather and the holiday from which the younger of the pair has just returned.

The older man is Macchi, Paul's personal private secretary for twenty-three years. His companion is Father John Magee, an Irishman who has served in a similar capacity for three years.

Macchi retains the cultivated hand flourishes of the seminary professor he once was. But over the years an almost permanent scowl has settled on his darkly handsome face. His once-thick thatch of black hair has thinned and grayed. And even here within the papal apartment Macchi is restless. His eyes flicker constantly from the pope's bedroom door back to the corridor. The slightest sound—voices from somewhere else in the apartment, a door opening—tenses him. He has been like this from the day a psychopath tried to kill Paul in the Philippines. Only Macchi's fast reflexes and physical courage in wresting the dagger from a madman dressed as a priest saved the pope from assassination. Macchi, perhaps more than anyone else on the pope's staff, knows of the very real new threats to the pontiff's life. The Red Brigades would like to kill Paul. And the West German government has just secretly informed secretary of state Villot that a unit of the Red Army Faction, a spin-off from the German Baader-Meinhof gang, is in Rome attempting to carry out a plan to kidnap Paul and fly him to Libya. There he would be held hostage, with the Libyan leader's connivance, against the release of all convicted terrorists in Israeli jails. Confirmation of this plan came to the Vatican from the MOSSAD, the Israeli intelligence service. Even now, MOSSAD agents are in Rome trying to locate the Red Army unit. One result of this threat is that plans for Paul to travel by car, as he usually does, to Castel Gandolfo, are canceled. Instead he will fly by helicopter. Macchi has ordered the Vatican Press Office to announce that the reason for the switch is to avoid creating the traffic congestion which inevitably arises whenever the pope drives through the city. Nobody really believes the excuse. Macchi does not care: public relations is not his forte. He is singular, ruthless, impatient, sometimes rude and always totally dedicated to Paul. His enemies, and he has many, say he is a one-man papal Praetorian Guard and presidential Secret Service detail rolled into one. He is the pope's ears, and often his voice. Only Giacomina stands up to him. Some of their clashes have been memorable.

Magee has never been known to exchange a cross word with anybody in the Vatican during the time he has worked there. He is a muscular, well-proportioned man, built like a good hurling player. He has an open face and keen, searching eyes. But it is his voice, the soft lilt of Newry, County Down, where he was born forty-one years ago, which other members of the papal entourage find so attractive. The nuns listen appreciatively to Magee's fluent Italian; they like his unfailing courtesy and humility, his fund of Irish stories and jokes. Magee is probably one of the most popular men in the Vatican. At times he finds this embarrassing. He is still feeling his way; he does not wish to put noses out of joint, particularly the long, sensitive nose of Macchi.

Generally these past three years have gone swimmingly for Magee, mainly because he has ruefully confirmed the validity of many things Macchi explained. He has discovered that cardinals *do* lie, sometimes habitually, often for no reason except they feel the truth can be used as a trade-off, a commodity to bargain with for personal advantage. And cardinals *do* try to manipulate him, though now Magee more easily recognizes the signs of an impending con: the frank and open unblinking look, the smile just that much too accommodating, the casual too-relaxed style of speaking; he knows all the little tricks and has learned that the way to survive is not to become personally involved in the machinations of those who attempt to use him as a stepping-stone to the pope. With these people he maintains a polite, low-key and neutral manner and responds to their wheedling by following one inflexible rule: if a case has merit he will place it before Paul, otherwise nobody can circumnavigate Magee. He's found that his job requires infinite patience, a finicky attention to detail, tenacity and the sheer physical strength to work for absurdly long periods. Magee and Macchi regularly put in a hundred working hours a week, almost all of them under pressure. Both men welcome the month-a-year vacation which frees them from the considerable burden of their office.

Magee has in fact just returned from a holiday in America, flying home through Ireland, where he visited St. Patrick's Missionary Society—the order to which he belongs—in the Wicklow hills. His fellow missionaries at Kiltegan greeted him with pride. Magee is the first member of the order in living memory to serve on the pope's personal staff. Indeed, his whole career has been striking proof of the rapid promotion possible in the Church. Ordained in 1962, Magee was sent to Nigeria as a missionary. Four years later a Vatican talent spotter heard about this young priest in the bush. Magee was brought to Rome. For nine years he worked for the prestigious Propagation of the Faith movement. Then Paul personally picked him to be his English-language secretary.

Magee is saddened to see the deterioration in the pope's physical condition since he has been away from the Vatican. Paul has visibly aged. Magee knows well the signs of impending death; he has seen it many times among the tribesmen of Nigeria. He doubts very much whether the pope will live to see his next birthday, this coming September. Almost certainly he will not be alive at Christmas. Even now, as he comes out of his bedroom toward the waiting secretaries, Magee cannot help but think that the pope walks like a man who has accepted his fate.

First Macchi, then Magee, wishes him a good morning, addressing Paul as *Santissimo Padre*, Holy Father. They fall in on either side of him, matching their pace to the pope's slow, shambling gait.

In the rarefied atmosphere of clerical Rome, the two priests wield immense power. All sorts of people court their favor. The pope consults them on every serious matter. Both are brilliant aides to His Holiness, partly because neither has any compunction about being a thorn in the side of the more senior prelates in the Vatican. In contrast to the ever-calm Magee, Macchi is highly strung. Yet one of his many tasks is to stop the pope from worrying about minor details. Magee, among other things, is Paul's conduit to the world's youth. He also keeps a careful eye on the pope's private charity. Its funds come from many sources. Bishops making their annual reports to the pope will generally present him with a cash gift; the size depends on the wealth of the diocese. American bishops usually give checks for two thousand dollars; Cardinal John P. Cody of Chicago, who rules over one of the richest archdioceses in the Catholic world, habitually hands over ten thousand dollars.

Cody's tangled finances, and indeed his entire behavior, have come seriously to trouble Paul. There are well-founded accusations: that the cardinal is a racist, is in conflict with many of the Chicago clergy, is unpopular with much of the laity and displays some extraordinary political and military views. There are also disturbing reports about Cody's vindictiveness, his obsession with secrecy, his refusal to make annual spiritual retreats. The worst charge of all—the one the Vatican is most shocked about—is that the cardinal has misused Church funds.

But now, moving along beside the shuffling Paul, is not the time for Macchi or Magee to mention such grave matters. Instead, a confidential, detailed report will be prepared, confined only to the facts which can be properly proven. It will make no recommendations. That is not the report's function. But both secretaries can have no doubt what will happen. When Paul reads the report he will almost certainly do what he has threatened to do for some time: dispatch on the first scheduled flight to Chicago the Vatican's troubleshooter, the tough-minded Sebastiano Baggio, prefect of the Sacred Congregation for Bishops and the one man with the skill to forcefully convey Paul's "request" that Cody should give up his office.

The three men reach double doors halfway down the corridor. Paul leads them into his private chapel. Its walls are of white marble, cool to the touch, their hardness softened by diffused light coming through glass mosaics of religious scenes. These are the Stations of the Cross which Paul specially installed at the onset of his pontificate. The three men quickly genuflect toward the wooden cross above the altar. Then, with some difficulty, for the arthritis has affected his hip, Paul bends to kiss the altar and begins mass with the traditional words: *"O Lord, I raise to you my prayer . . ."*

In St. Peter's Square police are setting up barriers which will allow them some control over the crowds expected for the pope's weekly public audience later in the morning. For a very long time Wednesday has been the day of the general audience, when the pope receives people "without rank or name" from the whole world. Since 1971 he has greeted them in the auditorium designed for the purpose by the architect Pier Luigi Nervi. The building stands partially outside the Vatican State boundary, and Rome police fear that somebody—a terrorist, a fanatic, a madman—could enter the hall and attack the pope. All reasonable steps are now taken to minimize the risk. The drably dressed Civil Guards, under the direction of the Central Security Office of the Vatican, are equipped with metal detectors and carefully scrutinize everybody who goes into the hall. There are also armed policemen at strategic points around the building. Their weapons are concealed, in deference to an order from Cardinal Villot, but each Civil Guard is trained in the Rome police armoury to hit a moving target at thirty paces. The city police on duty in St. Peter's Square, even though it is also Vatican State property, have no compunction about displaying their guns. They believe keeping a high profile is one way to reduce the risks.

Paul is back in his bedroom, fortified by the ninety minutes he has spent in the chapel going through the matins, lauds and prime of his daily office. Once more he kneels on his prie-dieu to commune directly with God. The hum from the *tufo* is louder, reinforced by a miscellany of noise from the square below as the tourist coaches arrive in ever-greater frequency. Shortly before nine o'clock, Paul rises from his knees to attend to his frugal earthly needs. He leaves the bedroom and walks the few feet to the dining room where there are a carved walnut table, seating for ten persons, two sideboards and a serving table. A crucifix hangs on the wall. One sideboard holds decanters of liqueurs. The other supports a carved statue of Jesus. There is a twenty-one-inch television set in the corner. Before it was installed the maker promised never to reveal his was the set the pope preferred.

The table is laid with fruit, homemade bread, cheese and butter, all brought in fresh every day. At Paul's place at the head of the table there are a cut-crystal water glass, a plate, cup and saucer. Beside the glass is one of Dr. Fontana's little capsules, placed there by Giacomina.

There are two other place settings, for Macchi and Magee. Apart from

Sundays—when Giacomina and some of the other nuns sit at table, their turn carefully rotated by Giacomina—the pope almost invariably dines only with his secretaries.

They are already seated when he enters and takes his place. For a moment he bows his head in silent prayer, raising it as Giacomina enters the room to serve coffee and bring the pope a selection from the local and international morning newspapers available in Rome. They inclue *Le Monde, Le Figaro,* the international *Herald Tribune* and the Rome *Daily American.* Italian publications include communist ones.

Giacomina stands watchfully until Paul swallows his capsule. Satisfied, she leaves; throughout the day she will regularly make sure he takes his medicine.

The pope begins to read, going first to the editorial page of each newspaper and then moving through the other sections. As he finishes a paper he passes it to Macchi, who, after scanning it, hands it to Magee. There is little conversation. Each is absorbed with the news. It is another of Paul's small rituals, this systematic scrutiny of the print media every morning. Though he will not concede it to anyone else, he has told his table companions the mounting attacks on his pontificate both sadden and hurt him. He can date them from that summer day in 1968 when he published his long-expected encyclical on birth control. It was a catalyst. Everyone in the Church afterward judged him by that pronouncement. Everything he has said before, or since, has been seen in the light of *Humanae Vitae.* The most strident attacks, perhaps not surprisingly, have come from America. He no longer reads them, though he is aware they are still circulated within the Vatican. He does not understand nor wish to know of such disloyalty, just as he cannot understand the process which has made the media feel free to openly criticize the papacy. The son of a newspaperman, Paul now wonders what journalism has come to. He finds it difficult to accept the finite judgments which are beginning to appear; people are already starting to write and speak as though his long pontificate were over. It is a curious feeling, he has more than once told Macchi and Magee, to read of himself in the past tense. Yet that is what is happening. And journalists now regularly trawl through his long life, searching for portents which can explain his actions. They have even gone back to his beginnings, to the village of Concesio in the foothills of the Italian Alps, to see what can be dredged up. But if the clues were there, they have long gone. Concesio is no longer a small farming village; it has become a suburb of the industrial city of Brescia. The Montini family are now shadowy figures. People remember them only vaguely. Paul's father, Giorgio, was a middle-class landowner and newspaper editor. His mother, Giuditta, was a fragile, shy woman, devoutly religious, very like her son. Both parents raised him in a strong Christian rhythm. Early on his thoughts turned to the priesthood. But the prudence, caution and doubts which would haunt him throughout later life had already taken root. Did he have a vocation? Was he physically strong enough to become a priest? A good constitution was essential and he was plagued with delicate health. Did he have the temperament? The stamina and the zeal? Was God guiding him in the right direction? Those doubts had been resolved but others took their place—doubts which had left him awkward about himself and his mission. If he was critical of others, he was even more so of himself. John XXIII had called him, when Paul was archbishop of Milan, "Our Hamlet cardinal." In a way it was true; he did believe suffering was a precondition for overcoming doubt and, with God's grace, reaching a higher certainty and an agreement with those who opposed the cause of good, especially Communists and terrorists. Yet some of those passing judgment on him took little of this into account. They saw him only as the pope who gave moral support to guerrillas in Spain and left-wing parties in Latin America; as the pontiff who allowed himself and his office to be exploited by the communist government of North Vietnam in order to help make their 1968 Tet offensive a reality; as the Holy Father who looked benignly on Castro's Cuba, and allowed Marxist bishops and priests and nuns to say mass in the Church in America, the Third World and Asia; as Paul, who never said a word in protest publicly about the suppression of the Church in Hungary, Romania and Czechoslovakia. They judged him, he would sometimes sigh across the breakfast table to Macchi and Magee, without full knowledge of the facts.

He reads on, moving steadily from one column to the next, the way he devours official documents. Much of the newspapers' contents he finds trivializing, not at all like the serious, sobering writing his father produced. On an inside page of an Italian newspaper is another summation of his pontificate. This one is no more banal nor vindictive than any of the others. He scans it quickly and responds as he so often does to such attacks. He tosses aside the paper and shrugs his shoulders.

Macchi, who has been waiting for such a moment, begins to run through with Paul his list of appointments for the day.

In St. Peter's Square, the atmosphere is Roman carnival. Long lines of visitors wend their way toward the Arch of the Bells, one of the entrances to Vatican City. Beyond the gates is the Nervi Audience Hall. Souvenir sellers batten on the lines offering an astonishing selection of junk: fake papal coins, tin medallions, plastic crucifixes, rosaries, emblems, stamps and postcards of the Virgin, Jesus, the Crucifixion and Paul. There are few buyers for the pope's portrait. It is an old one, taken perhaps five years ago. The coloring is unreal; Paul seems to have been wearing makeup or fallen victim to an airbrush artist. From time to time the police move in and pull a person from the lines. These are pickpockets. On a good morning a score can be arrested. They go quietly to one of the paddy wagons parked beneath the Bernini colonnade.

There is no sign of any other trouble. But the police commander in charge of the square moves busily among his men, who deploy and redeploy themselves in no apparent order around the tourists.

Fully briefed on his appointments, Paul waits in his private study adjoining his bedroom. His official office is two floors below. But he prefers to spend the first segment of his busy, compartmentalized day in this perfectly square room with its floor-to-ceiling shelves filled with books which reflect the wide breadth of his reading. The sciences are well represented, as are the classics. One shelf is given over to the works of major modern novelists: Graham Greene and Saul Bellow each have space on this shelf; Norman Mailer has a place with his *The Naked and the Dead,* a book Paul regards as an important addition to his collection of the more serious antiwar literature of Bertrand Russell and other pacifist writers. There are rows of books on theology and religious subjects of all kinds. The writings of the French philosopher Jacques Maritain are in evidence. On a side table is the Italian edition of Maritain's *Integral Humanism.* Paul, when he was a cardinal, eagerly wrote a preface to the translation. The words, in a sense, sum up his view of the papacy and the Church. He argues it is best to be "a witness by service, and do not think that any other initiative is possible, practical or called for." He is sympathetic, not surprisingly, to integral humanism's premise that all men and women are naturally good, and will readily respond to good and reject evil, when shown the difference. He sees it as the role of the Church to make every effort to identify that difference rather than only to make attempts to Catholicize politics, science, education and literature or any other aspect of life. The call to be a "witness by service" is what the Church must answer before all others. Only then will it keep its rightful place in a world which increasingly excludes any form of Christianity, let alone recognizes the central authority of the pope as the Vicar of Jesus. In Paul's view the papacy and the Church must find a new and more compatible way to attract believers; there is a need to free both the papacy and the Church from their isolation, to recognize past differences and correct them as part of a dedicated new drive to make the twin institutions more palatable to the world.

The words were written before Paul returned to Rome after nine years in Milan. He came south on a train carrying the sort of hangers-on most cardinals acquire. His "Milan Mafia" of designers, architects, financiers and clerics of all kind stamped their authority on his papacy.

Among them was the man Paul now awaits, his doctor, Mario Fontana. The pope is resigned to these daily visits; he accepts them as yet another pinprick from the invisible thicket of thorns which he has allowed to surround him.

Fontana as always is punctual. He enters the study on the first stroke of ten o'clock, a dark-blue-suited figure with a gold fob chain across his vest. Even without his black bag he could be nothing but a doctor; he exudes that special bedside manner which only very successful physicians possess. As papal doctor his official title is *archiatro,* from the Greek *archiatros,* meaning physician to an emperor.

No pope ever had a more devoted doctor than Fontana. He has searched the world for a drug which could ease, if not cure, the crippling arthritis which at times made it almost unbearable for Paul to make the smallest physical movement. His physician has even gone to "fringe" medicine—the world of homeopathic remedies often not recognized by orthodox practitioners—to find a medicament. In doing so he followed a well-established precedent: several popes had used rejuvenating treatments and elixirs to try to combat the ravages of age. Fontana eventually produced his little capsules. The pope has been swallowing them for months. If there are no great signs of improvement, neither has there been a dramatic decline.

Fontana greets Paul with a deeply reverential "Good morning, Your Holiness," placing his bag on a small desk in the center of the room. He does not open it at once but instead starts an innocuous conversation; one morning it is about the weather, another about the tourist season. But the talk is more than polite filling in. Fontana uses it to judge his patient's responses. Is Paul alert? Does he respond with animation? Or is he listless, not really listening? The answers help the doctor decide what sort of night the pope has had. Paul dislikes being questioned on such matters.

The physical examination is quick. Fontana produces a stethoscope from his bag, slips the disk inside the pope's cassock and listens to his chest. It takes only a minute to complete the examination. Fontana does not say anything. Later he will tell Giacomina and Macchi that Paul still needs very careful watching. The doctor intends to travel with the pope to Castel Gandolfo.

Paul and Fontana leave the study and walk to the elevator. They ride down together to the second floor. The elevator is silent and swift, no longer the creaky water-propelled type so common in the Vatican when Paul first arrived. Yet the overall atmosphere is the same: quiet, almost serene, a mood created, he would sometimes say to a visiting dignitary, by the Holy Spirit.

Fontana continues on out to the Courtyard of San Damaso, across which must come all visitors to the papal apartments or the offices of the Secretariat of State.

The Swiss Guards kneel in salute as Paul passes them on his way to his official office, known as the "private library." Each guard carries a sword or medieval pike as his only visible weapon to protect the Apostolic See. Each soldier comes from a good Swiss Catholic family to serve in the Swiss Guard, the sole surviving unit of the armed forces of the papacy. The Swiss Guard is under the direct authority of the pontiff. Paul disbanded the Noble Guard and the Palatine Guard in 1970; he decided that, after years of loyal service, they had no useful role to perform. It is yet another decision which has brought him stinging criticism. Now the Swiss Guard—four officers, a chaplain, twenty-three noncommissioned officers, sixty halberdiers and two drummers, in their billowy Renaissance costume of dark-blue, orange and yellow stripes—are all that remain of ceremonial protocol.

The real protection for the pope is in the hands of men such as the pair of blue-uniformed Civil Guards who stand near the door to his private study. Both are armed with revolvers concealed beneath their jackets. They regularly practice being fast on the draw. They stiffen and salute quickly as the pope passes, but do not bow in case, at that moment, an assassin chooses to strike. A year ago, such an idea would have been preposterous. Now, nobody can be certain.

News of any further threats of violence against the pope, as with previous ones, almost certainly will be first received, and swiftly acted upon, on the floor immediately above Paul's office. Here, on the third floor of the Apostolic Palace, is the Secretariat of State, with its staff of around one hundred, including a dozen diplomats who hold Holy See passports, and about twenty members of religious orders. This is the overcrowded, artificially lit and inadequately ventilated head office of the papal foreign service—the only one in the world which regularly calls upon the Holy Spirit for assistance when faced with a serious political problem. And since the attempt on Paul's life at Manila Airport, the Secretariat has discreetly created a reporting system which allows key members of its staff to be reached day or night by secular governments with news of any new threat to the pope. The system has already been used by the West German and Israeli governments.

Working closely with the pope, the Secretariat is largely responsible for the proper governing of the Holy See and Vatican State. Although they come under the supreme authority of the pontiff, these are separate and distinct entities. The Holy See is the central headquarters of Roman Catholicism. It regulates the religious life of every Catholic, making decisions which affect the faithful in every corner of the world. The Catholic stand on birth control, the Catholic attitude toward Protestantism, the Catholic position on communism, Judaism, Islam—all in the end emanate from the Holy See. Here, too, all kinds of doctrinal questions, from the wording of the catechism to the validity of baptism, are settled. Every aspect of Church policy and practice is formulated on the third floor of the Apostolic Palace. For 740 million baptized Catholics, for 421,839 priests and 986,686 nuns, for 3,700 bishops, for 130 cardinals, for a Church which makes up 18.1 percent of the estimated population of the world; for them all the decisions made in these offices are supposedly binding. It is the Holy See, not Vatican State, which has diplomatic relations with over fifty nations and maintains a diplomatic corps of some forty apostolic nuncios and delegates in various capitals or, in Africa, roving about their territory. Vatican State—a mere 108 acres, a landlocked and walled enclave within the city of Rome, 1,132 yards in length and 812 yards across—is the shell of temporal sovereignty which allows the Church to carry out its mission through the Holy See and the offices of the Secretariat of State.

For the last nine years the Secretariat has been run by Villot, the cardinal everybody likes to label. To journalists he is a xenophobic Frenchman—only Gallic newsmen write with pride that he is God's de Gaulle—pinch-nosed and purse-lipped, whose smile never quite reaches behind his steel-framed spectacles. His detractors postulate that even when he sleeps, Villot's eyes are on guard, staring unblinkingly at the ceiling. A more serious observation is that he has developed his bureaucratic capability after a lifetime of minor victories.

His office is close to a small and beautiful bathroom, designed and painted by Raphael, which is both entrancing and gently salacious. Villot's office, by contrast, is elegantly functional. There is little clutter, but an immediate impression of constant achievement: a variety of paper work comes and goes all the time, passing in and out of the fug of Gauloises which wreathes the room during Villot's working hours. He smokes forty a day. His staff shake their heads and say His Eminence will surely die of lung cancer. Villot gives a Frenchman's shrug: he is seventy-two years old and it is too late to change the habit of a lifetime. Socially, he is a renowned bon vivant; his cellar is said to be the finest in a Vatican of fine wine cellars. He likes small dinner parties, where he listens a great deal to some of the world's leading opinion makers. Listening has always been his strong point in a steady climb to power: auxiliary bishop of Paris in 1954, archbishop of Lyons in 1965 and then the short, sudden leap to this office on the third floor. Here, the world's problems, as perceived in the Vatican, are sifted, analyzed and pronounced upon, but not always for public consumption. Villot is a passionate advocate of the Holy See's renowned skill at low-key, often secret diplomacy. He dreads those times when the Secretariat's role in some delicate negotiation surfaces before a satisfactory conclusion. Then his daily cigarette consumption goes over the fifty mark. Villot is presently involved with the Middle East, Poland and Rhodesia. Moderate success in these areas is keeping him within his usual two packs a day.

For weeks, too, he has been aware of another matter which will likely come to a head shortly. Careful questioning of Fontana has left Villot in no doubt Paul could die soon. When the moment comes, Villot, as secretary of state, would become the camerlengo, or chamberlain, of the Universal Church, in full charge until a new pope is elected, and totally responsible for the organi-

zation of the conclave which will elevate a cardinal to pontiff. Villot has already studied the bulky file on John XXIII's funeral and reminded himself of
Paul's apostolic constitution, *Romano Pontifici Eligendo* (*On Electing a
Supreme Pontiff*), his guidelines for the appointment of his successor. It is
another of those documents which have created dissent. Paul decreed that all
cardinals over eighty years of age are to be banned from the next conclave.
And the strict secrecy of conclave—a tradition which stems from 1903 when
it was deployed to stop the Austrian emperor, Franz Josef, from influencing
the cardinal-voters—has been considerably tightened. Cardinals must solemnly swear before God to keep their mouths shut. The conclave area must
be swept electronically for bugs. Paul, Villot has wryly remarked, is determined there will be no Vaticangate to leak details of the power plays behind
the next papal election. But even Villot could not guarantee the secrets would
be kept. Not anymore. Not the way some of the more ambitious cardinals
have started to behave. Even now, while Paul still lives, they are jockeying
and lobbying, testing the ground for support. It is all illegal and against the
express wishes of the Holy Spirit. But it *is* going on. And Villot senses it
could reach a point where, among other things, he will be forced to increase
his consumption of cigarettes under the nervous strain of coping with some of
the maneuverings of his fellow cardinals.

In the office where he now sits, Paul, two years ago, made a decision which
many still say is one of the peaks of his pontificate. Against all the advice he
received from the Roman Curia—the highly complicated and structured
hierarchical body which is the Holy See's civil service—Paul looked outside
Italy for many of the twenty new cardinals he appointed in 1976. Several of
them—Paulo Evaristo Arns and Aloisio Lorscheider of Brazil, Bernardin Gantin of Benin, Hyacinthe Thiandoum of Senegal, Jaime Sin of the Philippines
and Eduardo Pironio of Argentina—are men for whom the Curia has no special liking; they are progressives, eager for reform, prepared to challenge the
Curia. In promoting them, Paul made his own curial enemies.

He feels the risk was worthwhile and hopes that the newcomers, when
they come to vote for his successor, will look for a candidate who will wish to
continue with the reforms he has introduced. But he does not underestimate
the ability of those in the Curia to manipulate the situation for their own
ends. He has seen them do it before, and he is still trapped in their skillful
snares, this Northern Italian who has never found it easy to get the Romans
to welcome him. Even here, in his inner sanctum, their influence is as tangible
as ever: many of the decisions he will be asked to endorse at the end of the
day will have been prepared, shaped, honed and polished by the Curia. They
will be presented to him as carefully argued memos, papers which have been

written and rewritten to get their meaning right to the very last nuance, documents which have been patiently worked over by many clever minds.

There is no way Paul can change matters. He himself spent thirty years within the curial system. He knows too well how it works. He also realizes that, despite his great achievement in appointing the cardinals he wanted, in the end he cannot beat the system. No pope ever has.

Such thoughts may well have contributed to the sense of failure people now openly detect in Paul. It has been there for a long time, perhaps from that day in 1966, just three years after he became pope, when he visited the grave of Celestine V. Celestine is remembered now only as the pope who resigned in 1294. Paul chose the occasion of the visit to speak of resignation. His words, as always, were open to interpretation. But the consensus was that Paul would abdicate under certain conditions. Already he had become involved in a running battle with the Jesuits; the first shocking whispers of Cody's behavior in Chicago had reached him; the implementation of Vatican II was causing serious difficulties; the Holy See was caught up in Vietnam. Over the years all these crises had deeply troubled him. His sense of failure grew. Even to his secretaries, the discreet and loyal Macchi and Magee, Paul now cuts a lonely and tragic figure—very much the Hamlet cardinal—as he sits and waits for his first official visitor.

More than any of the other rooms he occupies, Paul has taken pains over the decor of this spacious salon with its three windows looking down on St. Peter's Square. He removed the gilt furniture John XXIII favored; gone, too, are his predecessor's predilection for patterned rugs and the busts of dead popes. They have all been taken to one of the cavernous basement stores in the Apostolic Palace to be inventoried, covered by dust sheets and left to await the pleasure of some future pope. From the same cellars Paul ordered up fine Renaissance paintings and wooden statues of the saints and the creamy velours he favors as wall and floor coverings.

He sits at a sixteenth-century desk crafted in the days of Paul IV. It has a hand-tooled leather writing pad, a small clock in a solid-gold frame, a gold-topped roll blotter, a combination scissors and letter opener. Every item is carefully laid out; it is all so neat any visitor knows this is not Paul's real working desk. This is a showcase where he sits and receives a stream of people. Behind him is a shelf with a white telephone. No one can remember when he last used it. No incoming calls ever get this far: they end at the desks of Macchi and Magee. Beside the white telephone are carefully chosen reference books: a Latin Bible and index; a leather-bound volume of Vatican II documents; Paul's celebrated encyclical *Ecclesiam Suam*; a dictionary of missions; a code of canon law; the latest edition of the Vatican yearbook, which has been specially bound for him in white leather. The lighting, the flower arrangements, the position of every piece of furniture, combine to suggest a designer's concept of what a pope's office should look like. It is both overpowering and deadening.

Shortly after ten o'clock, as per Macchi's appointment schedule, Villot comes into the room. He visits it regularly twice a day, more often when there is a particular crisis on which Paul needs special briefing. He stands before the desk and greets and pope in Italian, spoken impeccably with no trace of a French accent. There is nothing in Villot's manner to suggest any truth in the stories written by those journalists who first lampoon his physical features and then go on to report the secretary feels an outsider in the Vatican, that he might even be going to tender his resignation—again.

In the media Villot has been offering his resignation for years. He is supposed to have done so after opposing Italy's referendum on divorce; after failing to convince the United States to allow the Vatican to become more involved in finding a settlement for the Vietnam War; over his continual jousting with the Jesuits. The times he is said to have threatened to go are as legion as the crises alleged to have provoked his reaction. Many of the tales are probably baseless. But there have been occasions—particularly over Vietnam —when Villot found his efforts suddenly torpedoed by those Curia officials who are not above leaking to the press sensitive material. Almost certainly Villot then spoke to Paul about going and the pope begged him to stay.

Paul is not by nature a pleader. No more than he relished symbolically going down on his painful knees to the Red Brigades in a futile bid to save his friend Moro did he like repeating the process each time Villot wanted to quit. But they are both old and weary men; in the end they briefly embraced each other and Villot continued to soldier on.

Yet between them lies an issue which both have spoken about to their confidants—and perhaps their confessors—but have never fully explored with each other. It is the rise and fall and rise again of Giovanni Benelli. Even now, only two years later, the roots of the story have become obscured; those who really know all the facts keep them under careful guard, but the moral of the story is obvious. It all most likely began with Paul anticipating the day when the long-suffering Villot would resign. To prepare for such an eventuality, the pope appointed Benelli as undersecretary of state. Benelli had learned his diplomatic ringcraft in such tricky Holy See postings as Dublin, Paris, Rio de Janeiro and Madrid. Looking much younger than his fifty-five years, with a flashing smile to match his wit, Benelli soon raised Villot's hackles. The pair were simply incompatible. Then, with a swiftness which left even hardened curialists dumbfounded, Benelli was gone—raised to the cardinalate and sent off to be archbishop of Florence, not exactly the wilderness but also not a place for a restless, ambitious prince of the Church. Villot led the coup which ousted him. He had found a ready ally in the pope's troubleshooter, Sebastiano Baggio, and a surprising one in Macchi, who had grown tired of Benelli's abrupt Tuscan manners and high-minded attitudes. The clincher came when Father Romeo Panciroli, who runs a tight-lipped Vatican Press Office, and Bishop Paul Marcinkus, president of the Vatican Bank, supported Villot. Paul had little alternative. Benelli went.

But nobody now thinks sending him to Florence has ended his ambitions. Vatican scuttlebutt openly predicts there is one certain papal candidate for the next conclave, the cardinal in Florence. And rumor adds that if the archbishop is successful in becoming the two hundred and sixty-first successor to the Throne of St. Peter the Apostle, one of his first actions will be to ensure that Villot, Baggio, Macchi, Panciroli and Marcinkus end their days in some of the Church's loneliest outposts. Unless, of course, they resign. It is the sort of scenario which could drive Villot to chain smoking.

This morning there are yet other related issues to make Secretary of State Villot ponder his future. Baggio, having helped to see off Benelli, has begun to make his own play for the papacy. Since May, the man who is known around the Vatican as "Viaggio Baggio," a Curia-created pun meaning "Baggio the Traveler"—an allusion to the endless journeys he takes on behalf of Paul to dampen down some local Church crisis—has been trying to muster support. And the brief alliance between the troubleshooter and the secretary of state is over. Again there are any number of reasons spewing from the rumor mills: incompatibility (always a safe bet in the fiercely competitive Vatican arena); outrage by Villot that anybody should be campaigning as though the papacy were a presidential office; Baggio's view that Villot was just a tired old man who should have resigned years ago. There is as much grist as there are mills. The outcome is that nowadays the pair openly avoid each other. And everybody says the ruptured relationship is yet another sign that Paul will die soon.

It is in this frame of mind that Villot begins to discuss with the pope matters of state. Better than anybody, the secretary knows the Vatican is grinding to a halt.[2] No decision which can be put off is being taken. Everybody is waiting, biding their time and preparing their position for what must follow after Paul is laid to rest.

IV

Almost at the moment Villot concludes his far-ranging presentation for Paul, which as usual incorporated a review of the latest developments in such perennial trouble spots as Beirut, Hanoi, Warsaw and Salisbury, Rhodesia, the door to the salon opens and a prelate enters.

He has neither knocked, been summoned nor sought permission before walking in unannounced. He does not need to. His position and office, prefect of the Prefecture of the Pontifical Household, Casa Pontificia, gives Monsignor Jacques Martin the right to enter the papal presence at any time he chooses. Only the pope's personal valet, Ghezzi, shares this jealously guarded privilege. It allows Martin to keep a proper, and satisfying, distance between himself and the other members of the Pontifical family. As its titular head, Martin is nowadays busier than ever. After centuries of independence, the duties of the Pontiff's Ceremonial Congregation, the offices of the majordomo, the chamberlain, and the Heraldic Commission have all been placed under the control of the Casa Pontificia, where Martin's responsibilities already include running the internal affairs of the pope's household in the Vatican and at Castel Gandolfo, and arranging almost all of Paul's meetings. Martin is also the elderly priest wearing a plain black cassock and simple gold cross who is always close to the pope in the obligatory photographs of important personages who call on Paul. Martin's suite of rooms near the Courtyard of San Damaso is filled with leather-bound albums commemorating hundreds of such occasions. They go well with the frescoed walls and ceilings, the religious scenes, the sportive-looking cherubs and satyrs, the triptych in oils, all of which also help make the prefect's apartment one of the most beautifully appointed among those who work for Paul.

Having entered, Martin stands by the door. His nose is almost the beak shape cartoonists depict when they sketch him as the pope's fixer, the priest who ultimately decides who sees Paul; there is an average of five thousand requests a week for a private, semiprivate or small-group audience. Inevitably, most applicants are disappointed. But those who make it into the papal presence usually come to see Martin as one of the most fascinating men in the Vatican. With some truth, Paul's administration is characterized as "horizontal": it is uniformly competent but short on intellectual giants. Martin is one of the exceptions, and he knows it. Perhaps that is why behind his courtly manners there is a sardonic wit and a glitter in his eye when he detects a worthwhile challenge to his vast knowledge of how the Vatican works. Few offer one. His reputation is renowned for showing up anybody who doubts the astonishing range of facts he possesses.

It was he, using his knowledge of the layout of the Apostolic Palace, who found just the right room to be converted into an infirmary for Paul to have his prostate operation. It is he who knows all about the holy relics on which faith is built: the bones of the Magi, the skull of John the Baptist, the hand of St. Gregory, the robe of Jesus, the Virgin's cloak, Mary Magdalene's foot, even part of the foreskin of Christ, said to be the only known sliver of him, reposing in a ruby- and emerald-studded casket watched over by two solid-silver angels in a shrine in Calcate, north of Rome. And it is Martin, too, who can chart the steady growth in the number of cardinals: the thirty-eight popes who reigned from 1198 to 1492 created 540; during the next three hundred years a further thirty-seven popes named 1,275 cardinals. Some popes, such as Celestine IV and Leo XI, appointed none. Others created them with astonishing rapidity. But until February 1965, the maximum number of living cardinals at any one time remained seventy, the limit fixed to commemorate the seventy ancient scholars of Alexandria who are traditionally thought to be the translators of the Hebrew Bible into Greek.

Paul, the man Martin has come to fetch, raised the number to 101, and then, in 1976, yet again, to a record 136 cardinals.

Martin always has a fresh story, fact or theory to keep his very private dinner parties going right up until the witching hour of midnight when all the gates of the Vatican are closed and no one can leave or enter without a permission which is rarely granted. The Vatican is the only state in the free world which physically seals its boundaries every night. Martin likes the custom; it gives him a chance to get to bed at a reasonable time after spending an hour or so going over Paul's schedule for the following day.

Now, he remains by the door, a precise and self-effacing man with the lightest of blue eyes, the ones which become glacial when something, or somebody, doesn't please him. By some extraordinary means those eyes seem to draw Paul to his feet.

The pope rises slowly, using his desk for support, again feeling the pain in his right knee. Followed by Villot he walks toward Martin.

The three men converse for a moment in French; Paul has a scholar's facility to speak several languages fluently. He has even considered learning Russian so that he might communicate more directly with Soviet leaders; Foreign Minister Gromyko has already paid him four long visits during the last ten years.

Villot makes his farewell, always a formal moment, for both pope and secretary of state are punctilious about protocol, then Martin escorts Paul slowly toward the first of eight antechambers where small groups are waiting.

These are Martin's chosen ones, those he has found a place for on the carefully structured scale of audiences which begin with the large general mass audiences and move on to group audiences, then to semiprivate audiences, *baciamani*, when it is permitted to kiss the pope's hand and engage him in carefully prepared conversation. Finally there are the private meetings, usually held in the salon the pope has just left; these are invariably restricted to heads of state, ambassadors, cardinals or bishops on urgent or important business.

Those waiting in the antechamber are *baciamani*. Each of them—all these men in dark lounge suits and women in long severe dresses—has been able to convince Martin he or she is worthy of this moment: they may have raised funds for their local church, made an outright gift to a Catholic hospital, a Catholic charity, a Catholic mission; perhaps they have a close connection with a powerful bishop or cardinal. Their very presence here denotes special status.

They have been waiting patiently for an hour, shepherded into position by Martin's staff of eight priests who placed them according to a typed list. The most important are in the first room, where, in theory, Paul will spend a little more time; if his schedule runs too far behind, Martin will shorten the pope's stay in the final salons. His aides have been moving among the groupings, reminding them, again, that the ritual demands the most punctilious decorum and protocol. No one must ask the pope personal questions or attempt to obtain a blessing for any object such as a pocket Bible or rosary. All should bend at the knee when the pope comes into their presence. At all times they should address him as "Your Holiness." They may kiss his right hand.

As eleven o'clock approaches there is hardly an empty space in the Nervi Hall. It is filled with twelve thousand people. So many want to see Paul before he dies—though nobody is sufficiently crass to give that as the reason when applying for a ticket to the public audience—that there has been standing room only for months. The endless ranks seem lost in the vast area, causing some people to say that if the hall is supposed to represent one of the entrance halls to heaven, then surely God needs a new architect. Others argue that it is difficult to see what else Pier Nervi could have done, given his brief from Paul to build the largest audience chamber in the Western world. Nervi finally settled for four prestressed concrete walls, an undulating ceiling and a ramped floor running 2,756 feet from the entrance down to the elevated stage at the western wall. There are no frescoes, no canvas reminders of God, heaven, Christ or eternity to soften the vaulted ceiling supported by forty-two white, geminate arches. Set into each of the two long side walls is an oval stained-glass window. Like so much else about the building, the windows have been the object of fierce controversy. Marc Chagall was first asked for designs for them. His sketches were judged too confused and earthly for a setting supposed to suggest heavenly peace. Giovanni Hajnal's impressions of the serenity of God now fill the two windows. Set high in one wall are the glass-fronted booths for television, radio and print commentators. This morning, as usual, they are crammed with journalists; the rumor persists that Paul might yet announce his resignation.

Macchi and Magee have been out to check the microphone standing before the pope's throne; their amplified "Testing, one, two, three, four" has brought ripples of applause.

The massive theater is dwarfed by the largest bronze sculpture on earth, "The Risen Christ." Paul commissioned it in 1965—a full year before workmen began excavating the foundation for the hall, demolishing in the process a number of buildings between the Holy Office and the Leonine Wall of the Vatican. The bronze is the creation of Pericle Fazzini, one of Jacqueline Kennedy's favorite sculptors. The choice of Fazzini was not a universal one; Romans thought Paul should have engaged a local man.

Since June 30, 1971, Paul has come, every Wednesday he is in Rome, to this gargantuan mass of engineering dynamism to speak to the people. It is here he revealed the interpretation and shaping of many of the ideas which have led to endless debate. He has used the audiences both to welcome the test-ban treaty and to indicate that an accommodation with communism is necessary. In this hall he has spoken about the problems of underdeveloped countries, showing a good understanding of the divisive forces currently at work in the world; about the new era of space travel; about the meaning of democracy in an age of increasing totalitarianism.

Yet over the years there has been a shift in emphasis: the sensitive and modest pronouncements of his first speeches have gradually hardened to a more protective attitude, the human-relations aspect has given way to a more authoritarian stand. He is the boss showing he must boss. Never a charismatic or utopian leader like his predecessor, John XXIII, Paul's public pronouncements have become tinged with conservatism. Collegiality, the sharing of power between the pope and the episcopate, which he looked upon with favor during the early days of his reign, now appear to him a dangerous novelty that could usurp traditional papal prerogatives. Inevitably, this change of attitude forged him into an alliance with the conservatives of the Curia. They shrewdly encouraged Paul in his belief that he must say or do nothing which would cause him to go down in history as the pope who presided over the dismantling of the Church. That, whispered those conservatives, would happen if he pursued the initiatives and freedom John had begun to introduce.

Paul was elected at a time when the Church was already seriously divided, polarized between opposing tendencies. He maintained a form of unity by refusing, at first, to push any line resolutely for fear of further weakening the institution. But by following a middle course he came to be seen as indecisive, pessimistic and, some even said, underhand. Few realized he was engaged upon a skillful holding operation. Initially he entered this hall intending merely to restate some of the ancient truths. Gradually, instead of trying to please everybody by making concessions all around, he lost his qualms about favoring conservatives, both religious and political. They came to see him as their own. This had helped ease his Hamletic hesitation and provided the resolve for *Humanae Vitae*. The message of that encyclical was one he continued to convey at his weekly audiences.

Nevertheless, just when he had secured the approbation of the right, Paul had shifted again. He began to argue that the issue of Catholic-Marxist dialogue needed reexamining following the spectacular gains made by the left in various Latin countries; this papal initiative was correctly diagnosed as stemming from fear—the fear the new political situation would adversely affect the Church unless the Church quickly came to terms with it. The result was equally inevitable: there was a right-wing backlash which produced powerful splinter groups. The most publicized is the movement led by the reactionary traditionalist Archbishop Marcel Lefèbvre. To even mention his name in Paul's presence is to draw a stinging rebuke. In part the reporters in the booths awaiting the pope's progress down the ramp are there to see whether Lefèbvre's disciples will stage a demonstration during the audience which will show once more the bitterness of the controversy.

The prospect of trouble and a good story excites the journalists. Many of them have covered the Lefèbvre saga from the day it started, December 8, 1965, the last day of the Second Vatican Council. The reporters spend their waiting time remembering events that, looking back, have an inevitability about them.

At some point in the history of the four-year-long Vatican Council II, Lefèbvre, a French-born archbishop few had heard of, decided the Council was moving the Church dangerously near to a position of "neo-Modernism and neo-Protestantism." On the closing day of the Council he went further. Flanked by two of his priests, the archbishop told a group of newsmen he had legal grounds on which to oppose the decisions of the Council; consequently they were invalid and nonbinding. Lefèbvre had gone on in an androgynous voice which would soon become as famous as Pope Paul's, stating there was nothing in any Church document which said that to disobey the decisions of Vatican II would bring anathema, the ultimate ecclesiastical condemnation for a breach of the true faith.

The reporters who had been there that cool December afternoon still remember how they had reached for their pencils and switched on their cassette recorders. Here was not merely a challenge; here were the makings of a running controversy. Lefèbvre might not be well known, but he *was* an archbishop and senior churchmen didn't usually talk so outspokenly. Lefèbvre's language was uncompromising. The Council, he claimed, had been manipulated by bishops and theologians who "acted in the spirit of Protestantism and neo-Modernism." The basis of this two-pronged attack hinged on his idea that traditional Catholic belief and dogma were being altered fundamentally in an ill-guided attempt to keep up with the changing times. What was happening, argued the archbishop, was "a new kind of Reformation." But unlike Luther in the sixteenth century, who had revolted against the Church of Rome and left it to carry on the fight outside, those behind the "new Reformation" intended to stay in the Church and burrow away from that secure position to collapse well-established patterns.

It was heady stuff, the sort of copy which put the Church back on the front pages.

So it had begun. The headlines were followed by profiles of Lefèbvre, the son of a textile manufacturer from Tourcoing, France, who became a scholarly priest, a valued member of the Holy Spirit Missionary Order, a bishop in Senegal and later archbishop of Dakar. Until the Vatican Council it was a career not exceptional for a talented sixty-year-old who always had ambitions to make his way in the Church. Then, just as suddenly as he had emerged, Lefèbvre dropped from sight. He might have remained forgotten if, in 1969, Paul had not promulgated a new official text for celebrating mass—the Mass Ordinal. It consisted of an Introduction and a new text for both the existing mass and the ceremonial instructions. It was intended as a replacement for the Tridentine order of mass published by Pius V in 1570, which had been in use ever since.

Two Italian priests, sympathetic to the views Lefèbvre had expressed in 1965, wrote a biting criticism of the new Ordinal and Introduction as flying in the face of traditional Catholic beliefs. The priests, following Lefèbvre's example, made themselves available to the media. The tabloids reduced it to: Paul or Pius—it's mass-make-your-own-mind-up-time. Paul asked the Sacred Congregation for the Doctrine of the Faith—previously known as the Holy Office of the Holy Inquisition of Heretical Error, with a history going back more than four hundred years—to examine his Introduction. The Congregation reported favorably. And there the story might have once again stopped.

But Lefèbvre told a journalist he had obtained permission from the Vatican to start his own institute and seminary at Econe in Switzerland. Here was another good tale and the media made the most of it. Lefèbvre helped by launching a series of attacks on the established Church in Europe and the

United States. On November 21, 1974, he published a manifesto castigating the Vatican Council as a "fake," the Pauline mass as "illegal," and the teachings of the bishops "in error." He became an international figure. He quickly opened other seminaries, produced a scathing newsletter and wrote a book, *J'Accuse le Concile*. He became a firm media favorite. Now there was no way the story would die.

Paul—trapped trying to be all things to all persons—hesitated fatally, ignoring Villot's advice to act ruthlessly, crush Lefèbvre and totally destroy his movement. Paul tried to reason with a man who was beyond persuasion. Then, too late, Paul allowed the full fury of the Vatican to fall on the archbishop. Canonical approval was withdrawn from his seminaries. The Vatican Court of Appeals refused to review this decision. By 1976 almost weekly threats, demands and orders from Rome were winging their way to Lefèbvre's mountain fastness to try to bring him to heel. He refused. Instead he took his mission to the United States, stomping around the country, confirming children, preaching against the teachings of Vatican II. He returned to Switzerland in June 1976 and announced he was about to ordain twenty-six young men into the priesthood at his Econe seminary. Legally he still had the right to do so. Then Paul did something no other pope had done for 217 years. He publicly attacked a prelate of the Church. The pope felt he had no alternative. The danger was too real: Lefèbvre could not only ordain priests but also create bishops and even dioceses to compete with the established ones. He could set up his own Church. It was a nightmare.

The day before Lefèbvre was due to ordain his priests, Paul suddenly tried a more direct approach. He sent Cardinal Thiandoum as his special emissary, begging Lefèbvre to desist—in much the same way Paul later beseeched the Red Brigades to spare Moro. Lefèbvre, like the terrorists, did not respond to the plea. He ordained his priests and delivered a sermon about the "traitors of our faith," a reference presumed to be aimed at Paul and the Vatican.

Villot tried. He sent a courier and a letter demanding that Lefèbvre cease. The response was icy. The secretary of state then suspended the archbishop from office. Lefèbvre promptly preached a sermon about the Vatican creating "confusion through bastardization." There were, he thundered, "a bastardized rite [the Pauline mass], bastardized sacraments, bastardized priests." He had one final defiance: "If the pope is in error, he ceases to be pope."

The Church closed its collective doors. Lefèbvre promptly celebrated a Latin-rite mass in a wrestling hall. Six thousand people came to join in the responses. Paul, the same day, drew seven thousand to Castel Gandolfo to hear his appeal: "Help Us to prevent a schism in the Church. Our brother prelate has challenged the Keys placed in our hands by Christ. We will not answer the archbishop in the tone he uses with Us."

The battle raged on, with Paul alternately trying reason and threats, with

Lefèbvre always stubbornly obstinate and maddeningly able to get his point across the front pages. Finally inevitably, when Lefèbvre eventually persuaded Paul they should meet at Castel Gandolfo—"I want to work under your authority, but I must speak to you personally"—the media were on hand to hear the outcome of this historic confrontation.

The reporters would remember the archbishop's appearance that September day. He looked a man possessed by the all-devouring idea that he was right. An hour later he emerged from Paul's summer retreat to give a blow-by-blow account of how Paul had listened while Lefèbvre insisted on his "rights": the right to say the Tridentine mass; the right to ordain more priests; the right to go his own way. Paul had asked whether the archbishop intended to consecrate new bishops. The response was unequivocal: Lefèbvre would do so when he thought it was necessary. He had lectured the pope and Paul had briefly lost his temper. Then they had prayed together, reciting an Our Father, a Hail Mary and the prayer to the Holy Spirit Veni Sancte Spiritus. They made their responses in Latin. Lefèbvre believed it was a sign he was winning.

But peace was still a long way off. The more Lefèbvre denied he was anti-Vatican or "unfaithful" to the pope, or that he had any intention of creating a "Tridente Vatican" or building a basilica to rival St. Peter's, or that he intended to become the latest antipope, a man who the Church decides is not validly elected: the more he denies such charges, the more plausible they become to many of the journalists now waiting for Paul to arrive in the audience hall.

Paul waits patiently while the *sediarii*, the throne bearers, in full morning dress, their starched shirt fronts whiter even than Paul's cassock, approach with the *sedia gestatoria*, the ornately sculpted chair on which Paul is borne into the audience hall.

Surrounding the throne, eyes constantly scanning the tumultuous crowd, security men lead the procession down the aisle. The noise is one continuous roar of singing, cheering, handclapping and crying. This is the time the pope's entourage most fear, when Paul is most vulnerable to attack. Somewhere among the waving hands could be one holding a weapon. Camilio Ciban, head of the security detail, keeps close to the swaying chair, ready to throw himself between the pope and an attacker. Macchi is on the other side of the *sedia gestatoria*, prepared to fulfill a similar function. Magee is in front, eyeing the throng ahead for the first sign of anything untoward. Ciban also has men on either side of Paul's chair. He has told all of them to watch people's eyes; eyes are the giveaway which can provide that vital split second's advantage. None of the security men looks at Paul. His head moves from side to side as he smiles wanly out over the crowds, occasionally leaning down to almost touch outstretched hands. He is careful not actually to make contact for fear he will be yanked from his throne; that nearly happened in India. The procession moves slowly, far more so than Ciban likes. But Paul has specifically ordered there must be no unseemly hurry. People have come from all corners of the earth for this moment and he will not disappoint them. It takes twenty minutes for the chair to reach the dais. There Macchi and Magee help Paul to the throne on the stage. Thunderous applause continues. From the dais the body of the hall seems to be a mass of exploding flashbulbs.

The chair bearers and security detail disappear through a door near the Fazzini sculpture. Now the only protection the pope has are four Swiss Guards, plumed and helmeted, halberds held rigidly before them. To Paul's left sit two rows of visiting cardinals, bishops, Macchi and Magee. The pope looks at them nodding and smiling. The applause roars on. He turns to face the crowd and slowly extends his arms as though embracing everyone. Suddenly, as if drilled to recognize the signal, the crowd becomes silent.

The pope makes the Sign of the Cross and then begins his weekly homily with the words he has always used: "Dear sons and daughters. . . ."

He pauses and closes his eyes. His face is drawn and haggard.

One of the journalists overlooking the scene wonders whether Paul has suffered another sudden spasm of pain. Everybody knows of his arthritis; it has become as talked-about as were Kennedy's back, de Gaulle's liver and Adenauer's pancreas.

A companion shakes his head. The pope, he ventures, is probably wondering what new there is for him to say. He's said it all before, to everybody who will listen.

It's true. No pope has traveled so far to speak to so many.

When all the judgments are in, when his contribution to the Church has been weighed, when the truth is assessed of whether timid by temperament he became brave out of virtue; whether he is right to see tradition not as the dead hand of the past weighing down on the present but as a positive concept of living reality; whether the implementation of so many of the Second Vatican Council's teachings, such a personal triumph for him, ultimately paved the way for a sharing of power while allowing the papacy to be of even greater service to the Church; whether all the liturgical changes he introduced were really only what some critics claimed, more aesthetic than pastoral; whether he too often invoked his personal authority when he should have sheltered behind his fellow bishops; whether, as in the case of *Humanae Vitae*, he was right to pronounce on complex issues of personal liberty about which the world had become so sensitive; whether his well-publicized ecumenism would have been better understood had his utterances been in the form of clear doctrinal statements instead of parables, or what he called "gestures"; when all these and many other matters come to be judged, it is almost certain they will be seen in the context of Paul's most newsworthy achievement—that of being the first modern pilgrim pope, the man who personally brought his message from Rome and, like so many other messengers, found himself not always welcome.

Early on Paul spoke of himself as a pilgrim and of his pontificate as a pilgrimage. All those hard lessons he had learned while a papal diplomat were called in to play when, in his role as the prophet of peace and justice to all men, he made journeys which stirred the imagination. He went to the source of Christian faith, the Holy Land, and embraced Patriarch Athenagoras. He went to India and prayed with the people, receiving in Bombay the most tumultuous welcome the nation has ever bestowed upon a foreign visitor. Fulfilling his description of himself as an "apostle on the move," Paul went to Uganda, where, in Kampala, he made a special effort to speak of the Anglican martyrs. As he stepped from the Alitalia plane on his arrival in Bogotá, Colombia—the first pope to use jet travel—he astonished everyone by kissing the soil of Latin America; that gesture alone ensured that his visit would be a massive personal triumph. In Manila he was attacked by the mad painter dressed as a priest. But it made no difference: everywhere he went he carried his message of spiritual brotherhood. It was part of Paul's dialogue with other religions.

But it was not always easy—in the Far East, in South America, in Central Africa—for the faithful to understand his attitude on birth control, divorce and other inflexible Church teachings. Nor could everyone grasp why large sums of money should be spent on soaring, open-air altars and triumphal arches for parade routes when so many of the spectators were near to starvation.

Wherever Paul traveled he gave the impression that the weight of the world bore down on his narrow shoulders, threatening to crush his diminutive, white-clad figure. Yet when he spoke he had the ears of the world. Only afterward, once he had gone, did some people pause to consider what he had said. They came to see his words as providing no more than a kindly recognition of their existence, a benign acknowledgment of their difficulties, but very few practical solutions.

He addressed the General Assembly of the United Nations, beginning with words he knew assured him respectful attention: "We have a message to deliver to each of you." On that occasion his words had been simultaneously translated into thirty-five languages. He was heard by representatives of almost all the nations on earth. His hopes were compelling: relations between peoples must be regulated by reason, justice and negotiation, not by fear, force or fraud.

The sixty journalists who had flown with Paul from Rome to New York had heard it all before. Some were now listening to it again, in the Nervi Hall, where Paul concludes his homily with a universal blessing.

Escorted by Macchi, Magee, Ciban and his security men, who have silently returned, Paul leaves the throne and walks slowly down to a group of infirm people waiting in a special area to the left of the stage. There are men, women and some children; limbless, wheelchair bound, many bear the unmistakable mark of terminal illnesses.

Paul places his hand on the head of a blind boy. The child looks up sightlessly at the pope, who bends and whispers words he has used before. "Courage, be brave." The boy shakes his head as though he cannot be brave any longer. Paul whispers again. "I will pray for you. Will you pray for me?" The boy frowns, not certain what to answer. Finally he says: "How can I pray for you, Your Holiness?" And Paul answers, very softly, so that Macchi and Magee must strain to hear the words. "You are my son. You can pray for your father." The boy smiles, understanding.

The pope moves to an old woman. She is without arms, a huge goiter on her neck. She is burned reddish black from radiation treatments. The cancer, she says, is still spreading. She knows she must die soon. Will the Holy Father bless her? He quickly places his hand on her head and does so.

It takes almost thirty minutes for him to move among the sick. Clearly the occasion inspires him. His eyes are filled with genuine compassion. He finds the right words for every person. Even the nearby security men are moved.

Other security men are politely urging those in the body of the hall to leave. Barriers stop them from coming close to the pope as he concentrates on his mission to the lame. The crowd begins slowly to drift out into St. Peter's Square.

Paul eventually turns, makes his way painfully up the steps and across the dais, disappearing, without once looking back, behind the bronze sculpture.

The public will not officially see him again until he appears at the special window of his summer retreat this coming Sunday to deliver another homily.

At the rear entrance to the hall, Ghezzi waits with the Mercedes to take Paul and his secretaries back to the Apostolic Palace. During the audience, Ghezzi has polished the car; he does so several times a day. It is without doubt the most cared-for car in Rome. The return journey takes two minutes. It needs only another thirty seconds for the elevator to carry Paul, Macchi and Magee up to the papal apartment.

Paul goes to his bedroom to wash his hands and pray. By the time he returns to the dining room Ghezzi is there—now wearing a white jacket with gold buttons—ready to serve luncheon to the pope and his secretaries.

During the meal they review the morning. The conversation gradually widens to well beyond the audience hall. Magee, in particular, is very good at opening up the talk, bringing the world to Paul's table now that he is too infirm to go out into the world.

The discussion is interrupted by the lunchtime news on television. Paul pushes aside his plate—in any case nowadays he eats very little—and tries to concentrate on the headlines to see whether they have any relevance to the political briefing Villot gave him.

They do. As usual the affairs of the Vatican produce a crop of speculations. There is an item from Hong Kong stating that the delicate maneuvering between communist China and the Holy See is continuing: the Vatican may soon have to accept more government-appointed Catholic priests in China and work within those limits. There is a report from Vienna claiming that Eastern Europe is where the focus of Vatican policy remains. The reporter reminds viewers that recent visits to Paul by Hungary's leader János Kádár and Poland's Edward Gierek were bitterly criticized, that opposition to the pope's global strategy comes not only from known right-wingers but also from those who argue that arrangements in Eastern Europe are reminiscent of the concordats made with fascists before World War II. The story ends with an unnamed Vatican source saying full churches in Poland are clear proof Paul's strategy works. A commentator picks up the theme, arguing that the pope is now so completely committed to rapprochement with Eastern Europe's communist regimes that no successor will be able to reverse the process. The main objective of his activist foreign policy, claims the commentator, is to ameliorate the plight of fifty million Catholics behind the Iron Curtain.

As the news ends Paul rises and leaves the room. Outside, Giacomina waits to escort him to the door of his bedroom. They exchange little conversation, but Paul clearly benefits from the presence of this caring woman who has given her celibate self to him. She opens the bedroom door and stands aside while he shuffles in. Then she closes the door and retraces her steps.

At four o'clock Paul emerges from his bedroom and goes to the chapel to pray once more, saying none and vespers from his breviary. He then returns to his private study and sits at his desk. He fidgets, as he is wont to do nowadays, with the portraits of his mother and father and the three small Byzantine pictures. He has taken to repositioning them from one day to the next, sometimes pushing them to the back of the desk, other times bringing them closer to him. Nobody knows why. No one asks. Paul is not the sort of person to volunteer an explanation.

Giacomina appears with a cup of espresso coffee and another capsule. This is the time of day the nun and the pope exchange domestic small talk. Does His Holiness have a preference for dinner? Will there be guests? She hopes for a response to the latter question other than the brief headshake it draws. Since the death of Moro, Paul has invited almost no outsider to his table. It is another sign of how deeply the crime has affected him. He sees it as a stain which is irremovable and irredeemable. His grief remains obvious. But it has done nothing to soothe the feelings of Moro's family, who saw in his death a terrible object lesson for Paul and his policy of trying to reach an accommodation with Communists. Few of the family attended the elaborate memorial service where Paul publicly upbraided God for not saving his "good, wise and innocent friend."

Afterward the pope retired to the Vatican to brood endlessly on the deeper meaning of the crime. It was more than just another in a long catalog of spectacular and bloody murders. It was a calculated blow to the state and, consequently, to the Church. Almost all of those involved in the Red Brigades' activities had grown up in Italy's two most rigid orthodoxies: communism and Catholicism; a large percentage of the terrorists were basically religious persons who came to politics and violence with the conviction of zealots.[1] For them force was a way of life. In adopting that credo they made Italy the main arena for terrorism in Western Europe. The reason, as Paul has often said, was not hard to see: sapped by social decay, Italy had become a fertile breeding ground because its economic decline had alienated workers and left thousands of well-educated young persons jobless. There was no ready solution; Moro's murder merely showed that no one was immune from the guerrilla warfare being waged in the streets of every major Italian city.

Most ominous of all, in the wake of the killing another figure has been nominated for possible assassination. Repeatedly, the question is now asked: When will there be an attempt to kidnap or kill the pope?

Paul has told his trusted staff on more than one occasion that it would be dangerously foolish to ignore the possibility. As he put it to Giacomina, "We are no longer inviolate."

Not even the optimistic nun has found words to comfort him.

V

It is five o'clock, the hour Villot makes his second formal appearance of the day. He enters Paul's study followed by an assistant, a priest in a soutane who carries a tray filled with papers. The priest leaves them on Paul's desk and departs. Villot remains for a few moments, drawing the pope's attention to various documents in the tray. Paul will initial some, sign others with his formal signature—Paulus PP VI. Satisfied that he has overlooked nothing, Villot once more takes his formal leave.

Paul can now do what he enjoys most: carefully peruse the paper work of his administration. There has probably never been a modern pope so capable of assimilating such a prodigious amount of information so quickly. It was one of the qualities noted when he studied at Rome's Gregorian University. The knack helped shape his destiny; after graduation, and that brief spell in Warsaw where he took his alarm clock and found the climate affected his health, he returned to Rome. Pius XI heard about his wan-faced priest who could read and evaluate at high speed for hours on end. Paul was given a tiny office in the Secretariat of State. He climbed the clerical promotion ladder in a straightforward and successful way, ending as one of two principal advisers to Pius XII. Paul had by then developed an astonishing memory: he could recall totally documents he had seen years before. This remains a tremendous asset as he now studies the contents of the tray before him.

It contains the latest proof that the Holy See long ago accepted that it should deal with politics as well as religion; it has frequently achieved its ends by deliberately confusing spiritual prerogative with political ambition. Popes have challenged emperors, undermined kings and queens, led armies into battle and now, in the case of Paul, passed judgment on Vietnam, disarmament and the problems of the Third World.

Paul does so because he is, in part, speaking from the security of a bedrock of immense secular influence wielded in the name of religion. Perhaps more than at any time in modern history, his pontificate has made its views known on international affairs. Not only has he broken a long tradition by traveling far outside Italy to places ever further removed from the atmosphere of the Vatican, in which he has been formed and nurtured, but in doing so he has created a situation where the Holy See ended the narcissistic provincialism of its daily outlook and squarely faced harsh realities. Although he has done a great deal by way of innovation—while at the same time frequently repeating allusions to the heavy and rather frightening responsibilities of his office, references which often make him seem welcomingly human rather than merely holy—Paul is nevertheless not an innovator. Long years as a bureaucrat have left their mark. The real Paul is now only seen by those very close to him. To the rest he is autocratic on a grand scale, living proof that a pope is absolute and answerable to no legislature; in everything he does he is advised, not constitutionally controlled by lawmakers. In his world there is no such thing as collective responsibility. That may be why he spends so long anguishing over a relatively small matter: the appointment of a new bishop, the moving of a nuncio from one diplomatic post to another, the wording of some minor document. Those around him say, without malice, that he is only really satisfied a decision is right when it is added to his already heavily burdened conscience.

By seven o'clock, about the same time as most nights, Paul is well into the paper work from the Secretariat of State. All three of its departments have made their customary submission.

The first department deals with relations with secular powers and matters arising mainly from concordats. It functions rather like a foreign ministry. The second department handles correspondence with the nuncios, pronuncios and the legates; the latter are specially appointed to represent the pope at specific occasions, such as the dedication of a new cathedral, a religious conference or a minor state funeral. This department also receives all requests from diplomats of the fifty-one nations accredited to the Holy See, and submits names to the pontiff of potential future nuncios. The pope must approve each appointment. The third department, the one whose papers always cause Paul to hesitate longest, is responsible for compiling and transcribing the final drafts of papal briefs from the working language of Italian into English, French, German, Portuguese and Spanish. Paul is fluent in each and is forever concerned about how words prepared for his approval will translate into those tongues. There is less problem when he writes to heads of state. He does so in Latin, the text prepared by the Secretariat of Briefs to Princes.

He has barely finished with the contents of the tray when Macchi appears with another. This contains the day's output from other curial departments which also need Paul's attention.

Cardinal Franjo Seper from Yugoslavia controls the old Holy Office of the Inquisition, established by Paul III in 1542 to combat heresy and still known as the Holy Office in spite of its name's having been changed by papal order in 1965 to the Sacred Congregation for the Doctrine of the Faith. The Holy Office is the most authoritarian of the Church's institutions: the correspondence it submits to Paul about alleged misdemeanors, reports on doubtful theological books and teachings, have a chilling ring about them. With his narrow, obscurantist outlook, the seventy-two-year-old Seper, say liberal Roman Catholics, is perfectly suited for the now-abolished role of the Inquisitor. He writes to the pope most days about the action he wishes Paul to approve against some major infraction of dogma.

Equally regular is correspondence from the Sacred Congregation for the Sacraments and Divine Worship. Much of its work is concerned with granting dispensations for marriages which have not been consummated, and releases for priests who wish to relinquish their orders. There is also a steady flow of paper work from the Sacred Congregation for Religious and Secular Institutes, which settles questions affecting religious orders and examines the status of new foundations. It is now actively concerned with the activities of Lefèbvre. Paul always finds relief in the infrequent reports from the Sacred Congregation for the Causes of Saints, founded in 1588 to handle such pleasurable matters for a pope as canonization and the preservation of holy relics. He reads on, through reports from the Sacred Congregation for Bishops, and those of the Sacred Congregation for the Clergy. He then turns to the crisply clear paper work of Cardinal Gabriel-Marie Garrone, who not only presides over the Sacred Congregation for Catholic Education but is also chancellor of the Gregorian University—the proving ground for all those destined for high office in the Church—and chamberlain of the College of Cardinals. The austere seventy-six-year-old Frenchman, who served with distinction in World War II, includes with his report another of his famous theological conundrums for Paul to ponder. Over the years there has developed an almost continuous intellectual debate between the two men. Paul, as always, will take time formulating a reply; he will end it, as he does each of his letters, with the words "Yours in Christ."

Much of the work near the bottom of the tray requires no more than careful reading and initialing. The Apostolic Penitentiary handles complex problems of conscience: Can a priest kill to protect himself? Should he, as some are doing in Latin America, bear arms? It also advises on the penalties a pope may impose for such a dire crime as a priest saying a black mass. Every year there are a number of such cases; they frighten Paul more than anything else. He regards them as proof the devil is alive and well and hiding inside the Church. Cardinal Giuseppe Paupini, the seventy-one-year-old Italian whom Paul placed in charge of the Apostolic Penitentiary five years ago, is the Vatican's resident expert on sorcery of all kinds. His work is adjudged so important and urgent that he will be the only cardinal allowed during the next Conclave to remain in contact with his office.

There are reports for Paul from the Supreme Tribunal of the Apostolic

Signatura, the tribunal responsible for preparing petitions, usually relating to pardons, for papal approval. Paul has made its main responsibility that of settling conflicts between curial departments. It is the nearest thing to an ombudsman the Vatican has.

Finally, the tray contains the latest reports from the three special secretariats. The Secretariat for Promoting Christian Unity, presided over by one of the undisputed leaders of the Church in Western Europe, sixty-eight-year-old Cardinal Jan Willebrands, archbishop of Utrecht, was created by John XXIII to handle some of the preparatory work for the Second Vatican Council. It made its mark as a vigorous, optimistic and liberalizing body. Paul is now not always happy with some of its recommendations.

Paul himself established the Secretariat for Non-Christians in 1964. It is now in the sure hands of Cardinal Sergio Pignedoli; at sixty-eight he is as energetic as ever. There is a salty flavor to Pignedoli's tongue, a throwback to the days when he was a chaplain in the Italian Navy.

The Secretariat for Non-Believers is under the presidency of Franz König, archbishop of Vienna and one of the Church's few authentic experts on *Ostpolitik*, the détente between Church and communism. The progressively minded König—unlike Willebrands he has never caused Paul concern over a recommendation, as König has an almost uncanny flair for knowing how and when to offer a suggestion for the pope's ear—accepted the job on Paul's assurance that he would not have to move to Rome. With engaging frankness König explained he had no "great desire to be at the head office." Besides, he could better continue to serve Vatican interests by remaining at his strategic post in Vienna, monitoring developments behind the Iron Curtain. Paul likes and respects the courteous Viennese with the mellifluous voice and unrivaled knowledge of the history of religions. Despite his age, seventy-three, König remains a healthy and compelling figure; many in the Curia think they could do much worse than to have him as the next pope.

In St. Peter's Square the tourists have thinned out and the souvenir sellers gone downtown to see who else they can catch. Only the policemen remain in strength. One of them walks toward the seventy-seven-foot-high obelisk in the middle of the most visited square in the world. Another policeman stands at the foot of the obelisk, which took ninety men and four hundred horses to position after it was brought to Rome by the Emperor Caligula. Legend says that on October 13, A.D. 64, Peter was crucified upside down near the spot where the policemen now stand 1,814 years later. The presence of the policemen continues the theme of violence which dominated this place nineteen centuries earlier. They wear flak jackets protecting their chests, crotches, backs and buttocks. They cradle machine pistols. Only a few tourists find incongruous the sight of two heavily armed men standing in the deepening shadow of an obelisk dwarfed by Michelangelo's cupola on St. Peter's Basilica, the very symbol of peace.

At eight-thirty P.M.—the time has never varied in Magee's memory—Paul joins his two secretaries for dinner. Ghezzi stands by one of the sideboards and, like the others, bows his head while Paul murmurs grace. Then the valet serves the meal: thin soup, the way Paul likes it, followed by his favorite veal casserole, vegetables and side salad. Veal alternates with chicken and, very occasionally, steak. Magee, accustomed to the hearty portions of his missionary days, has learned to accept the smaller helpings at Paul's table. But the wine is excellent. And there is plenty of mineral water. Paul uses some to swallow another capsule Giacomina has placed beside his plate.

The dinner talk, as so often recently, hinges on the problems the Church faces in the secular world. Paul is on record as saying he is well aware that he is the principal obstacle to Church unity. Now, years after he made that typically anguished confession, the rifts are wider than ever. What he calls "the forces of darkness"—a generic term for communism, terrorism, the abortion-on-demand movement, the drive against priests remaining celibate, even the antics of Lefèbvre—are wedging themselves ever deeper into the gaps. Moral and ideological schisms have developed to such an extent that they often seem unbridgeable. Everywhere he looks, Paul can see churches destroyed, religious rights curtailed, the blood of his priests and nuns flowing. This is the year the Church is celebrating the eighteenth anniversary of the convocation of the Second Vatican Council and the tenth anniversary of *Humanae Vitae*. Paul had intended the celebrations to help bond the faithful together. Yet what is happening? Dissension on all sides.

Both Macchi and Magee work hard to lift Paul's spirits. Nevertheless tonight is to be no exception. The pope doggedly moves back through half a century of events he has either been directly involved with or observed closely from the wings. Names and incidents drift in and out of his conversation. His memory is impressive but the tone is melancholic. His listeners detect a feeling of betrayal deep inside Paul. But has he himself betrayed the promise of his background—a member of the Northern Italian "liberal wing" of the twenties, a man whose career as an archbishop suggested someone ready to act boldly and imaginatively as a pastoral leader—or has he been betrayed by the more vicious elements of the faction-ridden Curia? Macchi and Magee suspect, and they have told each other as much, that elements of both played their part in taking toll of Paul. But the time has long gone when they might have dared try to lead him away from the abyss he totters toward in conversation. All they can do now is sit quietly and let him ramble on. They feel deep compassion and love for this man who has been, and tries to remain, like a father to them. The secretaries see him not at all as the cold and stern figure of the media, but as a very old and tired man who knows his life is ending and who is inwardly troubled that when the moment comes he may still have left so much undone.

Paul's ruminations end when Macchi switches on the television set for the nightly news. They sit silent, gripped by the flickering images of strife in the world. Macchi, as he has done before, floats the idea of a program devoted only to good news. The senior secretary does not much care for television as such: he believes it frequently distorts by overemphasizing items which happen to be caught on film. He instances an ambush in Vietnam, a shoot-out in some street; it's all far, far too violent for Macchi—but he also feels the day must come when the Vatican will use orbiting satellites to reinforce the faith in every corner of earth. Magee joins in. He is enthusiastic about such global communications; he sees the possibility of unifying the Church by bringing Catholics of South America and Scandinavia together through one satellite. He sees all sorts of benefits. Paul sits quietly, listening carefully, sometimes smiling indulgently at the enthusiasm of the younger men. The flow of bad news from the TV is forgotten. It is the cue for Ghezzi to switch off the set. The valet has come to marvel at the skills the secretaries display nightly in their attempt to distract the pope from the realities of the world.

When the discussion has run its course—both Macchi and Magee are skilled conversationalists and know how far to go and how much to leave for another occasion—Paul rises and returns to his study. For the next hour he will write letters to his family and old friends; he is a loyal correspondent and has been writing regularly to some people for over forty years.

His personal correspondence completed, Giacomina arrives with Macchi— Magee has, by custom, gone to his own quarters to catch up on paper work— and for the next hour they sit with Paul while he listens to his recordings of the classics and opera. Sometimes, when the mood takes him, he will play *Jesus Christ Superstar*. He has a particular favorite from the show, the song Mary Magdalene sings: "I Don't Know How to Love Him." The musical interlude ends, the secretary and the nun leave. Paul once more returns to his desk.

From now until he chooses to go to bed he will be alone. It won't halt the speculation. Reporting the imagined and real thoughts of the pope has become a growth industry. With the Vatican officially more secret than ever over its affairs—always a sign things may not be as ordered as they should— Paul is surrounded, from both within and outside the Apostolic Palace, by those who make a living from conjecture. For a handful of lire, or perhaps a good dinner, they will answer all questions. Does Paul think at times about forgiving those who have wronged him? By any count the list of such offenders is long—and lengthening. Does he worry about the impecunity of the Vatican? The question is hardly original; Paul can still remember, so people say, his sense of shock on discovering that when Benedict XV died in 1922, the Vatican had to float a loan of a hundred thousand dollars from a Rome bank to help pay for his funeral. Does Paul think that, because of what he has encouraged, the Vatican is now in a bigger financial mess than before? The conjecturalists shake their collective head. He would certainly not think about *that*. Not just before going to bed. That would be one guaranteed way to give himself nightmares.

In St. Peter's Square the policemen play the nightly game which helps them while away the hours. They know who sleeps behind every window in the papal apartment. They bet between themselves on the exact moment the light in each bedroom will go out. The stakes are not high because it is not much of a gamble. The household keeps very regular hours. Giacomina's light is the first to be doused. Then Macchi's window becomes dark. Next the light of Magee's bedroom goes out.

It is now after midnight and the three entrances to the Vatican are locked. At the Porta Sant'Anna, the Bronze Doors, and the Arco della Campagna Swiss Guards patrol slowly, caped against the cool night air. Behind them shadowy figures from the Vatican Central Office of Vigilance plod between the various buildings. Many of these guards, rumor has it, are armed and as tough as any antiterrorist squad. In February 1971, Paul placed security on a far more stringent and professional footing when he decreed the members of Vigilance must "maintain awareness of the value of the promise of fidelity to the Supreme Pontiff which implies the strict observance of the orders imparted by superiors, and the responsible and diligent execution of their tasks and special duties attached to them. The tasks of each are not limited materially only to the execution of what they have been ordered to do, but include all that alert and unceasing activity which, by discovering, anticipating and restraining every action contrary to the laws and rules, makes up the singular character of those who are concerned with vigilance and the defense of order, the safety of persons and the safeguarding of material goods." The Vigilance guards do not indulge in such flippancies as betting on lights out. They are a dour and watchful lot, the real muscle behind the fancy-costumed Swiss Guards.

In the square the fountains have been turned off and the traffic diverted. But the light from Paul's study burns on. Then it is gone. A moment later his bedroom light comes on. It is a little patch of brightness against the dark sky. Then suddenly it, too, is no more.

The policemen start a new game. Is the pope asleep? Is he lying awake thinking? About what? There is no betting, but the man who comes up with the unlikeliest answer will be judged the winner. The policemen have good imaginations; the game may run the duration of their shift. Tomorrow it will be different. The helicopter will come and Paul will have gone. The fountains and traffic will run continuously. And the policemen will have to invent new games to play to overcome their boredom.

A detachment of Swiss Guards—in their distinctive steel helmets and starched neck ruffs, the morning breeze making their Renaissance costume seem more billowy than ever—march out of their barracks opposite the pope's parish church, Santa Anna dei Palafrenieri. Built in 1573 for the papal grooms, the oval church is now almost exclusively used only by the guards and the domestic staff of the Vatican. Hardly anyone can remember when Paul last said mass there. The area itself is the tradesmen's entrance to the Vatican. The Porta Sant'Anna, a gate set in the middle of a narrow street, is the way in for produce lorries and vans. It is a noisy spot and, because it is so busy, a magnet for tourists. This morning they stand and gape at the Swiss Guards breaking ranks and boarding a bus which will take them to Castel Gandolfo. They are Paul's advance party, the men who will help protect his summer palace. Everything about the guards seems alien in the essentially Italian environment. This has not helped their relationship with the Vigilance. There is tension between them. The Vigilance looks on the Swiss Guards as little more than toy soldiers. The guards feel the presence of the hard-nosed, drab-blue-uniformed security men is unnecessary; they believe they can do all that is required to protect the pope on Vatican soil. The guards are hardened young men, drilled and honed in the official parade-ground language of their unit, German. Each has pledged to serve for a mini-mum of two years, swearing his oath of personal loyalty to the pope by hold-ing the Vatican standard in one gloved hand while raising the other aloft, two fingers and thumb outstretched to represent the Trinity. It is a highly un-usual unit in which guards need obey only their colonel, one other officer and their sergeant, all of whom wear identically colored plumes. Their other officers can be ignored; so can the Vigilance.

The bus drives out of the gate. Shortly afterward a second, smaller detach-ment of guards, halberds held aloft, march from their barracks and board a couple of jeeps. The vehicles drive slowly along the Via del Belvedere, past the Vatican's printing concern and the separate printing shop of the Vatican's semiofficial daily newspaper, L'Osservatore Romano, and its associated papers and publications. The convoy drives on beyond the Vatican generating sta-tion, its pharmacy, the self-service duty-free store, the health center, the tele-phone exchange and the public offices of the Vatican Bank. In minutes the jeeps are traveling through the Vatican Gardens, wending their way close to the remains of a tower, all that stands of a wall built by Innocent III for a reason only Prefect Martin now really knows.

The gardens are, for all the magnificence of their statues, fountains and grottoes, a mess. Too many effects have been sought after—there are overtones of England, France and the tropics in the landscaping—making the final result a mishmash. Box hedges crowd palm trees, willows stand beside banana plants, rockeries of coral and evergreens are placed side by side. Everywhere there is a jumble of religious artifacts: a representation of the grotto at Lourdes where St. Bernadette saw her vision of the Virgin; a plaster replica of Our Lady of Guadalupe, who appeared in Mexico to an Indian peasant, the Madonna imprinting her image on his work apron. Paul has ordered that this statue, above all others, must be properly tended. It is regularly cleaned with soapy water.

The jeeps are climbing now, past a shrubbery and a flowerbed with the pope's coat of arms picked out in blooms, past the Ethiopian College, and the pseudo palace housing Vatican Radio's director general. The convoy stops by the heliport at the very western tip of Vatican City. The guards get out and take up their positions at the four corners of the pad, specially built to foil any terrorist attempt to kidnap Paul. Another truck arrives bringing a crew of *sampietrini*, skilled maintenance men who normally spend their days repairing and maintaining St. Peter's Basilica. The *sampietrini* have a special place in Vatican affections since that memorable day, during the pontificate of Pius XII, when they discovered a crypt under the basilica filled with a double row of mausoleums, a high altar and the bones of a big man thought to be those of the first pope, St. Peter the Apostle. Today they will do nothing so notable; they will merely roll out the wool carpet they have brought from a storeroom in the Apostolic Palace. The men work carefully to ensure that the carpet will run from the exact spot where Paul will alight from his car to the point where he will board the helicopter.

In the papal apartment Macchi and Magee have been supervising the exodus to Castel Gandolfo. Trunks and chests have been packed and sent down by elevator to the San Damaso Courtyard, once the private garden, *hortus secretus*, of medieval and Renaissance popes. The area is filled with trucks and men loading not only the personal effects of Paul and his staff but boxes from the Secretariat of State and other curial departments; the summer retreat to the Alban Hills southeast of Rome does not mean that even in this almost moribund pontificate the administrative wheels can actually stop turning. From doors around the courtyard frock-coated officials bustle forth to urge that the loading be completed. All sorts of people seem to have business in the area: the pope's almoner is here, chatting to some of the prelates of the antechamber; here, too, are the gentlemen of the pope and the attachés of the antechamber. Prefect Martin, his nose more beaky than ever, seems to be everywhere, checking that each box, case, trunk and chest is loaded in some preordained order only he and his staff seem to know. Suddenly, everything fits into place. The loading is over, the trucks begin to move. Ghezzi arrives with the Mercedes and parks it as close as possible to the elevator. He stands expectantly beside the car, its near side rear door open.

Martin is already riding up to the papal apartment. Moving a pope outside the Vatican is always a difficult task; transporting the aged and infirm Paul demands the very best from the prefect. He emerges on the fourth floor to be met by the two secretaries. Giacomina and her nuns have already departed for Castel Gandolfo; the summer palace has a caretaker staff but Giacomina wants to make the place shipshape in her way. Before leaving she ensured that Paul had taken his morning capsule and that Fontana had pronounced the pope fit enough to travel. Now there is a more than usual air of deadness about the apartment as Macchi and Magee wait for Paul to emerge from his bedroom.

Once Paul has reached the San Damaso Courtyard, still flanked by Macchi and Magee, he pauses to talk to Martin and other members of the household who will be traveling by road to Castel Gandolfo. Villot and Archbishop Giuseppe Caprio, the secretary of state's *sostitutore,* or deputy, are also there. Later each will clearly recall two things: the real reluctance of Paul to leave and his last words before he gets into the car. Caprio bends forward to wish Paul a pleasant stay at Castel Gandolfo. For a moment the pope looks at the *sostitutore.* They are old friends and have remained close. Then Paul speaks, his voice little more than a whisper. "We will go, but we don't know whether we will return"— he pauses again before completing the sentence in the stiffly formal language he still uses in public—"or how we shall return."

Caprio remains numbed by the words as Ghezzi drives off with the pope and his secretaries.

Villot now feels more certain than ever. He walks across the courtyard toward the entrance to the Secretariat of State, head bowed and hands clasped just below the solid-gold cross on his silk soutane; it is a familiar position when he is thinking deeply. The secretary of state has no doubts. Paul has just given the clearest sign yet he is expecting to die soon.

Macchi and Magee instinctively decide—though there is no way they can consult each other, seated as they are on jump seats facing the pope—that they will not pursue the remark.

For his part Paul appears to be concentrating on the scene outside. The car swings around the right side of St. Peter's, past a small door leading down to the tombs of almost all of his predecessors, clustered in no special order around the monument to the Apostle Peter. It is here Paul's body will eventually rest. The Mercedes continues between the Vatican's mosaic factory and the rather overpowering governatorato building, home of the civil administration which runs Vatican City for the pope. In its cellar is the *magazzino,* a veritable bargain basement where those with special permits can buy anything from the latest-model automobile to cigarettes duty-free. It is a privilege jealously guarded and, on Paul's orders, one no insider is encouraged to discuss. He is concerned the concession will be misunderstood in the inflation-ridden secular world outside. Close by is the Vatican's railway station, a branch line from Rome built in the 1930s. The last pope to use it was John XXIII when he made a train pilgrimage to Loreto and Assisi. The Sistine Chapel choir lined the platform singing psalms as the train pulled out of Vatican City. Since then the station has seen no more than a weekly train taking out Vatican mosaics for various churches and bringing in the heavier commercial goods, marble for statues and replacement plant for the print works.

The Mercedes eventually reaches the helicopter pad, Ghezzi parking it precisely so he can open the rear door just where the carpet begins. His passengers alight and he drives off, heading for Castel Gandolfo. With his special Vatican registration plates he knows he has nothing to fear from any Rome traffic policeman as he speeds across the city to pick up the *autostrada* heading into the hills.

There are no ceremonies before Paul, Macchi and Magee board the aircraft. The Swiss Guards go down on one knee and remain in that position as the helicopter lifts off. [1]

Seventeen minutes later, every yard of its flight scanned by Italian Air Force radar at their base beside Rome Airport, where a squadron of Italian fighters stand ready to scramble at the first hint of any attempt to intercept the helicopter, it touches down on the grounds of Castel Gandolfo. Since the seventeenth century popes have come here, to the cool of the Alban Hills, to rest inside an enclave which nowadays provides the main source of income—tourism—for the three thousand villagers who live in its shadow. There are four palaces inside the hundred acres. The Pope's Palace appears the most forbidding, a fortified bastion built for Urban VIII in the early 1600s and extended first by Alexander VII and then by Clement XIII. Compared to its immediate neighbors, the Cybo Palace and the Villa Barberini, Paul's residence lacks architectural character. It looks like a place for a beleaguered man. But his own apartment has an unrivaled view of the lake and hills where the Emperor Diocletian, persecutor of the first Christians, had a villa.

The helicopter comes to a stop between the formal French and Italian gardens and close to a magnificent cryptoporticus, a sheltered walkway decorated with frescoes. Paul, escorted by Macchi and Magee, shuffles its length, oblivious of his surroundings—the splendor of the Roman countryside, the twin domes of the Vatican Observatory brought to Castel Gandolfo by Pius XI in 1935 and still manned by some of those Jesuits Paul has never found easy to handle.

Once upon a time Paul used to visit the observatory regularly and stare through its telescope at some of the hundred billion stars spanning a thou-

sand, and more, light-years across the heavens. He would look up to the Belt
of Orion and at Sirius, the Dog Star, the most glittering of them all, its blinding white light forming the bottom hole in the Belt. When the night was especially clear and his eyes were not tired, he would search for Aldebaran the
Bull, and, beyond, the tiny clusters of stars known as the Pleiades. Then,
turning the telescope westward, he would locate the twins, Castor and Pollux,
so far away in space so vast, his astronomers liked to tell him, that matter was
being formed at the rate of a million million million million tons a second.

Out there, too, was Andromeda, a galaxy very similar to the Milky Way.
They, the dozen or more Jesuit astronomers who manned the observatory, had
first intrigued Paul with the thought that there were billions of stars in the
Andromeda galaxy and then excited him with the idea one of them could be
—if the laws of probability mean anything—a planet like earth, perhaps even
inhabitated by people not unlike earthlings. He had listened, entranced—as
he suspected they knew he would be—while they unfolded to him the secrets
of the galaxies: they were teachers and knew how to arouse and hold his curiosity. His nights with them were one of his few real pleasures. But since his
anger over the general behavior of the Society of Jesus, the order of the
Jesuits, he has deliberately stayed away from the observatory.

Paul had no quarrel with the astronomers. Yet his rigidity insisted that they
must be included as part of the general displeasure he felt toward their order.
Nobody has spoken in Paul's presence for over a year now about the reasons
for the deep rift between himself and the Jesuits. It is another of the taboo
subjects. But everybody knows the crisis is worsening and a solution, however
unpleasant, cannot be put off forever.

Like Cody, the American Church, Vatican finances, the radical priests of
South America, the demands of Catholic Africa and Asia—like so many problems, the question of what to do about the Jesuits lingers on, another festering
issue in the comatose pontificate of the dying Paul.

Inside the palace he takes the lift to his apartment. The Swiss Guards are
already in position. One of their special tasks is to seal this building should
Paul die here.

VI

Throughout July 1978, Pope Paul VI became increasingly weak. His devoted aides grew more concerned. Dr. Fontana saw him twice a day; Giacomina was never far away. On good days the pontiff walked in the garden, either in the early morning or the late afternoon, moving beneath a series of awnings the gardeners had erected to protect him from the sun and the prying lenses of photographers. On those occasions the pope supported himself on the arm of one of his secretaries. He spent much time praying, in either his chapel or his bedroom. He ate very little; Fontana gave him vitamin injections regularly. Only the most essential of papers were brought from the Vatican for the pope to sign. On Sundays he somehow found sufficient strength to greet visitors from his window at the traditional noon angelus. He used the occasions to attack Soviet harshness toward dissidents. He received one special visitor, Mrs. Lillian Carter, mother of the American president. They spent their time together speaking about the infringement of human rights in Russia.

The pope also carefully followed the news, paying special attention to reports of terrorist outrages. The Iraqi prime minister was assassinated in London, seventeen persons were massacred in Rhodesia, a Spanish general was murdered in Madrid, a new wave of bombings engulfed Italy. In all, over five hundred persons were killed or injured in atrocities around the world during July.

There was also other news to concern the pontiff. A newly formed group in the United States, called the Committee for the Responsible Election of the Pope (CREP), urged that the next conclave should be less secretive. CREP was largely the creation of a priest, Andrew Greeley. The pope let it be known he found CREP's ideal unacceptable. That did not stop Greeley from pushing his case.

And the world's first test-tube baby, Patricia Brown, conceived outside her mother's womb, was born in Oldham, England. The pope stated that the Roman Catholic Church had not changed its stance against any form of artificial insemination. Shortly afterward the French National Institute of Applied Sciences announced that after ten years of research the first test-tube fly had been born. The Vatican made no comment.

In the first week of August the weather turned exceptionally humid, causing a sudden flare-up in the pope's already severely painful arthritis. His doctor ordered him to bed. On Saturday, August 5, the Vatican announced that the pope had canceled his next Sunday blessing.

The brief statement heightened the perception of observers both in and outside the Vatican.

VII

A t six-thirty on the morning of August 6, the Feast of the Transfiguration, a celebration to remind Christians that the Risen Christ is always there to give purpose to their lives, a group of listeners outside Paul's bedroom door at Castel Gandolfo hear a familiar sound. It is the tinny summons of his alarm clock. It shrills for a moment and is then silent. There is no other sound from the bedroom beyond the door. Macchi murmurs that the pope is still alive.

It has been an anxious night for all of those grouped in this short corridor which ends at the polished wooden door: Macchi, Magee, Fontana and especially Giacomina and her nuns, who took turns standing near the door in case Paul called for help. But nothing disturbed the long hours of darkness. Since he whispered good night to Macchi eight hours ago, nobody has seen or heard from Paul.

The group still finds it difficult to believe how quickly the crisis developed. The previous day, in spite of agreeing to cancel his Sunday balcony appearance, Paul insisted on getting up for supper. He had sat at the table for forty-five minutes, listening to Macchi expound his passion for modern art. The discussion was interrupted by the television news. There had been another terrorist outrage; this time a PLO bomb had ripped apart the middle of a Tel Aviv market. After the news ended, both secretaries joined the pope in saying the rosary. They then retired to Paul's private chapel and said compline together. Soon afterward the pope said he felt hot and that his arthritis was unusually painful. Macchi escorted him to his bedroom while Magee summoned Fontana. The doctor diagnosed Paul's fever as caused by acute cystitis, which had exacerbated his severe arthritis condition. Fontana ordered total bedrest and began a course of antibiotics. After the doctor left Paul asked Macchi to read him part of Jean Guitton's latest book, *Mon petit Catéchisme: dialogues avec un enfant*. Macchi chose the chapter on Jesus.[1] Guitton had long been one of the pope's favorite French theologians; indeed his intellectual outlook was largely formed through French thinkers such as Pascal, Congar, Bernanos and Simone Weil. Paul said good night and fell asleep. Afterward the two secretaries and doctor met in the palace library to discuss the situation. Fontana left them in no doubt that the prognosis was grave. In a man of Paul's age and weakened physical condition it was quite impossible to predict whether the drugs would work or what side effects they might produce. All Fontana could do was observe closely his patient and ensure that Paul was in no way disturbed. Nobody—and certainly no Church crisis—must be allowed to interfere with this very explicit order of Fontana's. Before parting, the three men had agreed that unless an emergency brought them together sooner, they would meet again this morning outside Paul's room shortly before his alarm clock was due to go off.

Now, in the silence which follows its ringing, nobody in the corridor moves. Paul is still the pope: everybody in the group recalls his clear instruction that no one except Ghezzi is to enter his bedroom unless called. Fontana decides the circumstances are exceptional. He knocks quietly on the door—it is no more than the gentlest of taps—and enters alone, carrying his bag of drugs and needles. After a few moments Macchi follows.

Paul is lying very still in bed. Macchi can see at once that there has been no improvement overnight. The pope's face is flushed, his eyes are red-rimmed and, if anything, more sunken. His skin seems waxy and damp. He looks a very sick man. Fontana examines him fully. The pope has a temperature of over one hundred degrees Fahrenheit, his heartbeat has become weaker and his blood pressure is up several points. Paul complains of increased pain in his right knee, the seat of the arthritis which long ago shrunk him into a prematurely old man. Fontana decides to inject the pope with a heart stimulant and to give him antibiotics intravenously. While he prepares the syringes the doctor makes cheerful conversation, trying to draw Paul out so he can form some assessment of his mental state. Fontana knows the pope's desire to live is going to be a crucial factor in the coming days. The doctor is almost certain the illness has not peaked and Paul's success in coping with that serious time will, in part, depend on how positive he is in his thinking.

The pope, in fact, is quite alert. When Macchi mentions that today is the thirty-third anniversary of the atomic attack on Hiroshima and that the world will be specially praying for peace, Paul reveals that he had intended to touch upon the subject of the perils of atomic weapons during his balcony appearance at noon. Next Sunday, *Santissimo Padre*, says Fontana, maybe next Sunday His Holiness will be strong enough to make an appearance.

The doctor gives the pope his injections and says he will return in a couple of hours. In the meantime His Holiness should try to drink as much as possible. Fontana is worried that the pope's poor intake of fluids could affect his organs.

Fontana goes away to telephone a urologist at Rome's Gemelli Hospital, one of the best medical centers in Europe. He discusses the desirability of the specialist's coming to examine Paul. After reviewing the symptoms the urologist agrees to stand by. Fontana is acutely aware of the very special problems associated with calling in help from outside. Already the fact that Paul's noon appearance has been canceled has alerted the Rome press corps. They are even now setting up camp around the papal enclave, their telephoto lenses trained on its windows ready to capture anything which moves. There is no way the urologist, or any other outside specialist, can reach the pope's bedside without first running the media gauntlet. Calling in a consultant, especially on a Sunday, would immediately suggest that the pope's situation was serious; soon wire service bells would be ringing around the world, causing unease and alarm in the biggest religious bloc on earth. Yet Fontana will not hesitate to do anything to help his patient. Those close to Paul say that these past months the doctor's devotion has scaled new peaks. He has made hundreds of phone calls to distinguished colleagues all over the world; he has pored over the latest literature on the treatment of arthritic conditions. He has done far more than any physician could reasonably be expected to do. Magee has said that if Fontana weren't Italian, he would surely have been an Irish country doctor. It is the highest form of praise Magee knows. Like everyone else in the papal household, the young Irishman is now desperately worried. But he has learned to hide his feelings. It was one of the first things he absorbed from Macchi. A pope's secretary, the suave Milanese had said, is like a barometer; everybody sets their sails by him.

Macchi is himself at his inscrutable best as he stands by Paul while Giacomina and one of her nuns changes the pope's sheets. Macchi then helps Paul back into bed and sits at his side, outwardly as unconcerned as his inner self will let him appear. For years now the senior secretary has been the victim of a vicious press campaign. The scandal sheets portray him upbraiding the pope when he becomes morbid or depressed, sending Paul off to bed when he stays up too late, bullying him to make decisions. And plotting. Always plotting, with Baggio, with Father Virgilio Levi, deputy editor of *L'Osservatore Romano*, with Father Romeo Panciroli in the Vatican Press Office or with Paul Marcinkus—especially Marcinkus—at the Vatican Bank.

Recently these attacks have come from a new source. Greeley, the onetime Chicago parish priest who is the moving force behind CREP, has been writing about the Church and the Vatican for a long time; he is said to be the author of eighty books, a feat explained by one critic as possible only because their author has never had an unpublished thought in his life; and when he produced a book called *Sexual Intimacy,* another critic added that Greeley had now never had an unpublished fantasy in his life. For three years Greeley has been coming to Rome to prepare the ground for his eighty-first work, this one concerned with the making of the next pope, to be written along the lines of Theodore White's books on how recent U.S. presidents were elected. Greeley's trips to Rome have not made the city seem more attractive to him; its plumbing and eating arrangements increasingly irk this quirky man. But he likes the present Vatican even less. He has come to the conclusion that it is out of step with almost everything he holds to be true, though it is never easy to be sure what this Catholic "in good standing" really means, or indeed just who he talks to in the Vatican. He has decided to give pseudonyms to many of them while at the same time somewhat weakening this protection by composing detailed physical descriptions of priests with finely chiseled features and slender aristocratic hands and voices which purr with power. Certainly Greeley's attacks on Macchi are real enough: he blames him for much of what is wrong with Paul, from the way he smiles to the grand designs of his pontificate.

Greeley's Macchi seems far removed from the Macchi who sits by Paul in his spacious bedroom with its decor almost universally beige; chairs, drapes, carpet and silk bedspread are all in this neutral color. In these surroundings the secretary is genuinely caring and attentive to Paul's slightest wish. He gently persuades the pope to sip the glucose drink Giacomina has left. Afterward Macchi offers to read another excerpt from Jean Guitton's book.

Paul wants to know whether there is any news from Baggio. The pope has finally moved against Cody in Chicago by secretly dispatching his troubleshooter with the "request" that the cardinal resign on whatever grounds he chooses. There are any number of factors which decided Paul on this action. There was the confidential report prepared for him by his secretaries. There was another and far more lethal report from Monsignor Agostino Casaroli, secretary of the Council for the Public Affairs of the Church in the Secretariat of State. The sixty-three-year-old Casaroli is known in the Vatican as "our non-Jewish Kissinger," because of his freewheeling style and frequent travels as part of his special responsibility for the more delicate aspects of the Holy See's foreign policy.

Casaroli first learned about Cody from trusted sources in Warsaw. What he heard was sufficiently alarming for him to urge that no matter how great were Cody's past contributions to the Polish Church—a guaranteed way to win the support of Chicago's large Polish community—no matter how powerful a figure he was in the American Church hierarchy, Cody should go, either willingly or by force. Casaroli believed it only a matter of time before the Church's enemies began to exploit Cody's behavior, doing irreparable harm to the Church and the policies Casaroli was helping to further.

From Vienna, Cardinal Franz König had weighed in with a report indicating that the bad news from Cody's diocese had already been gratefully picked up in Eastern Europe. From Latin America, Cardinal Aloisio Lorscheider, showing considerable courage for someone who had only recently been elected to the permanent council of the Synod of Bishops, sent a note bluntly saying Cody's racist image created a poor impression in South America. And even one of Cody's North American colleagues, Archbishop Joseph Bernardin of Cincinnati, also a permanent member of the Synod, let Paul know of his concern in, and beyond, Chicago over Cody.

The precise words in all these alarm signals, Paul has decided, must forever remain secret. He has already told Macchi the reports should be closely guarded and, after he dies, destroyed along with his most private papers. Despite such thoroughness, the allegations against Cody are now becoming public. In part this is due to campaigning by the voice of CREP, Andrew Greeley.

The same wonderfully anonymous sources which allow Greeley to write so enticingly about Vatican affairs have helped him identify the grounds which made Paul send Baggio flying to Chicago with what amounts to a papal demand. No one in the Vatican, where he is cordially disliked, can seriously dispute that this time Greeley has got it absolutely right; there isn't a junior secretary who hasn't heard about the shenanigans of Cody, the most controversial cardinal in the Church.[2]

The first charge against Cody, in Casaroli's view, provides ample ground to act: racism. In his globe-trotting, the tough-minded monsignor has come to see racial discrimination as one of the greatest barriers to Church unity. John XXIII first recognized something had to be done about this blight, but it was Paul, through his journeys, who worked hard to implement racial equality abroad; the impact he had is one of his major achievements. Yet in Casaroli's view there is still a long way to go. During his regular accounts to Villot of his journeys into the Third World, Casaroli reports that the continued racism of America, Australia, South Africa and in some ways in Great Britain has created a gulf which leaves the Church in "the position of trying to dance an Irish jig on a minefield sown by the Chinese." Whenever a prelate comes to Rome it is now virtually mandatory for him to receive Casaroli's lecture against racism. There is not a senior member of the Church who does not know where the Vatican stands on the matter. Yet Cody supported the decision in Chicago to close any number of schools teaching black children in the inner-city ghettoes. Liberal black community leaders called Cody's intervention the worst kind of racism.

Casaroli does not believe Cody is a racist. He simply thinks the cardinal should have known better than to allow the Church to be placed in a position of disrepute. And he hopes Cody will go quietly; Casaroli hates any form of public breast-beating. But he fears that is what Cody will do, for although the evidence is certainly there, not all of it is all that damning. Cody is charged with being in constant conflict with most of his clergy. This the Vatican doesn't normally worry about; it knows there are often disagreements between a strong bishop and his priests and on the whole this is seen as no bad thing: it keeps both sides on their toes. But the situation in Chicago has gone far beyond that. The Association of Chicago Priests publicly condemned their cardinal for lying to them habitually. Some of the most respected prelates in the diocese sent protests to the Apostolic Delegation in Washington and even to the Vatican itself. When asked for an explanation by those in Rome, Cody refused to answer. Paul himself sent a handwritten note requesting that he be more reasonable and cooperative. Cody's reply was typical: he had nothing to answer for. Yet apart from his priests a large segment of the Chicago laity are up in arms. Hundreds of upsetting letters regularly reach Rome containing evidence of Cody's intransigence. Many contain details which suggest that he may be suffering from some mental disorder. The writers document Cody's contact with extreme-right-wing organizations such as the John Birch Society; they instance evidence of his obsession with secrecy and mystery; they tell of a spy network he has set up to keep track of every visiting priest who comes to Chicago; they speak of his personal spite and bouts of uncontrollable pique. The Vatican doesn't think all the accusations are true; there is always a lunatic fringe which writes to Rome about every bishop in every diocese. But these letters from Chicago often come from important and influential Catholics. They can no longer be answered by a polite *pro forma* letter.

Many of the charges, especially from the Catholic business community, accuse Cody of poor management of the diocese; the cardinal, they say, concentrates all the power in his own hands, refuses to delegate, consults nobody except a very small circle of cronies. Important decisions and appointments get shunted aside. But the real nub of the case against Cody, the one charge above all others that finally made Paul act, is perhaps the gravest which can be leveled against a senior prelate—financial maladministration. While treasurer of the American bishops, Cody invested several million dollars of Church funds in Penn Central only days before the railroad went bankrupt. In addition there is the accusation that sixty million dollars of parish funds are on deposit at the Chicago chancery and Cody has refused to account either to the diocese or to the Vatican for what he intends doing with the money or who gets the interest. Again, he has poured millions of dollars into a TV network which operates only in rectories and schools. Even this would not seriously deplete the finances of one of the world's most affluent archdioceses, but coupled with Cody's life-style, the accusation that he uses Church funds to buy expensive presents for those few members of the Curia prepared to look the other way at his behavior, the charge that he refuses to make spiritual retreats, that his rudeness, temper and at times even fury is demonic: all these, together with the reports Paul has studied since arriving at Castel Gandolfo, left him no alternative but to dispatch Baggio to Chicago.

He has been gone now a week. Only Macchi knows what happened. In total secrecy Baggio arrived at O'Hare Airport and was driven to Cody's villa in the grounds of the seminary at Mundelein. Over dinner he laid out the evidence and Paul's "request." There had been a shouting match which lasted into the early hours of the morning. After breakfast Baggio left, his mission to Chicago a total failure. Macchi has been waiting for the right moment to break the news to Paul. Now is not the time. Instead he diverts the pope with the thought that no news from Baggio could only be good news in the end. Paul does not question the excuse. He is too exhausted to do so.

Beyond the sickroom the mood of the household is one of increasing anxiety. Everyone knows the Holy Father's condition has not improved: the domestic staff has seen a grave-faced Fontana huddling with Prefect Martin and then Magee; the gardeners report that the reporters, television and radio technicians are constantly growing in number. Tourists are also arriving by the busload.

During the morning Fontana pays two further visits to Paul. The pope's condition has not altered. Fontana makes another phone call to his colleague at the Gemelli Hospital. They agree that the illness should peak during the next twelve hours; if Paul can survive the day he may yet recover. Fontana's hope that this may happen quickly permeates the household. By midday the staff appear almost happy as they go about preparations for lunch.

Paul has a bowl of soup and sips the fresh lemon drink Giacomina has prepared. The nun and Fontana stand either side of his bed while he drinks. He is lucid and cheerful, thanking them and, through them, everybody else who is so solicitous for his welfare.

When Giacomina leaves the room she is nearly in tears. Macchi, waiting in the corridor for news, is alarmed and asks urgently whether *Santissimo Padre* is worse. The nun shakes her head: no, no, he is being the Holy Father they all knew—only thinking of others.

Relieved, the secretary goes to tell Martin who in turn phones Villot in the Vatican. The secretary of state informs those he has decided should be kept in touch with events at Castel Gandolfo. Calls go to his deputy, Caprio; the dean of the College of Cardinals, Carlo Confalonieri; the vicar general of Rome, Cardinal Ugo Poletti, who tends to the religious needs of the city of which Paul, among his many titles, is bishop. The pope's brother, Senator Ludovico Montini, and his favorite nephew, Marco Montini, are also contacted. Villot knows almost nothing about medicine, but he knows a great deal about the effects even a minor illness can have on someone as old and infirm as Paul; the secretary of state has seen several friends die suddenly in such situations. He asks all those he rings to remain close to their phones. He then makes one more call, to the mayor of Rome, Giulio Carlo Argan, asking him to have police motorcyclists standing by to escort at short notice to Castel Gandolfo the cars of those Villot has previously telephoned. Argan is a Communist, a shrewd and capable man who still resents the way the Vatican interceded against the Communists during the last election. He listens politely, asks few questions but understands fully what could be happening. He gives his orders to the city's chief of police. Motorcyclists are dispatched to wait beside St. Peter's Square and outside the homes of Paul's relatives.

In midafternoon Paul awakes from a restless sleep. Fontana, who has been watching over his patient, slips on the blood pressure cuff and checks the reading: the pressure is up, dangerously so. He checks Paul's pulse. It is erratic. Hiding his alarm as best he can, Fontana listens to the pope's heart. The beat is weak and uneven. He checks Paul's temperature. It is well over the hundred mark. The climax could be coming sooner than Fontana expected.

He gives Paul an injection to steady his heartbeat and presses a bedside buzzer. It brings Giacomina running. Between them the nun and doctor place cooling towels around Paul's forehead and assist him to drink.

The pope's treasured bedside clock, standing beside the Bible his father gave him, helps the doctor count off the minutes as he waits for the first sign of reaction to the injection. Thirty minutes later, Paul's blood pressure has dropped almost to normal and his heartbeat, although weak, is regular. His temperature, too, has been lowered by repeated towel applications and drinks. Fontana cannot be certain, but he hopes the crisis has come and gone. He waits another thirty minutes and, at five o'clock, leaving Giacomina by the pope's bedside, he goes off to make another call to his medical colleague in Rome.

Later the question will be asked—one of many—why Fontana at this stage didn't either have Paul transferred by helicopter ambulance to the Gemelli or request the clinic's mobile intensive care team come to Castel Gandolfo. But Fontana feels that not only is he more than medically capable of handling the situation, there is also the protocol involved. Popes just don't go to hospital, however private or good the facilities may be. The custom dates back to those days when royal personages were treated in their homes because the care there was better than in hospital. When Fontana operated on Paul's prostrate he set up a temporary theater in the room that Prefect Martin found. Calling in the mobile intensive care unit was another matter—one of judgment. Using his considerable experience, weighing the medical and sociological factors involved—the headlines and clamor which would inevitably follow— Fontana decides this is not yet the stage to seek such radical outside help.

The doctor explains his thinking to Martin, Macchi and Magee. They immediately agree with Fontana. The three are still discussing the situation when the buzzer brings them running to Paul's room. Giacomina has noticed the pope's blood pressure has risen. Magee, who has not seen the pope for some hours, is shaken by his appearance: the matted hair, the flushed cheeks in contrast to his general pallor, the tremble in his hand—all signal that Paul is entering another crisis. It passes as quickly as it manifests itself, leaving the pope sunk back on his pillows, Macchi holding one hand, Fontana the other, the others grouped around the bed.

Paul asks Macchi to say mass for him at six o'clock and then requests that his brother and nephew be sent for. Martin hurries from the room, close to tears; Paul has often told him he will know when the end is near and when it is, he will want, if possible, his immediate relatives at hand.

The prefect's phone call activates the plans Villot has prepared for this moment. In minutes cars are speeding out of the Vatican and from the two Montini family residences. Each car is preceded by police motorcyclists who leave the Sunday-afternoon holiday traffic in no doubt of the seriousness of their mission. Their sirens cut a path for the cars as they roar down the *autostrada* toward Castel Gandolfo.

The cardinal secretary of state's limousine is in the lead. Villot sits in the back beside the case which for months he has kept packed for this occasion. It contains his vestments, anointing oil and a small solid-silver hammer.

Less than thirty minutes after leaving Rome, the cars sweep past the press corps and up to the Pope's Palace. The agency reporters note who have arrived and it is the Associated Press man who manages to get off the first flash: "17.55 POPE'S FAMILY JOIN SENIOR VATICAN AIDES AT PONTIFF'S BEDSIDE."

Outside Paul's bedroom Macchi briefly explains the position to the new arrivals. The Holy Father is considerably weakened by his two attacks, but he is conscious and most anxious to follow the mass and take Communion with them. The service will be held in the chapel leading off the pope's bedroom. They should all go in, greet the Holy Father briefly and then move on to the chapel.

If Villot is incensed at being treated in this cavalier way, he does not show it. Macchi is still the pope's closest confidant; he still has more effective power than even the most powerful cardinal. Villot goes in and greets Paul, formal as ever.

At six o'clock Macchi begins the mass celebration. Those present make their responses: Confalonieri, Poletti, Caprio and Villot fill one row of chairs. The Montinis are behind them. In another row Giacomina and her nuns kneel in prayer. Martin and Magee are closest to the open door of the chapel and, like Fontana, who is beside them, the two priests regularly glance over their shoulders at the pope propped up in bed.

Paul follows the mass avidly; during the recitation of the Creed, Magee and Martin clearly hear him twice repeat the words *"Apostolicam Ecclesiam."*

At six-fifteen Fontana suddenly rises to his feet in the middle of a response and goes to Paul's bedside. Instinctively the other worshipers turn, some even half rising to follow him, but Macchi's voice firmly holds them in place. The doctor checks Paul's pulse. It is wild. He places the stethoscope disk on the pope's chest. The heartbeat is irregular. But it is Paul's breathing which is of most concern to the doctor: it is fast and labored. The pope has suffered a heart attack and there is nothing his doctor can do. The effects of the attack pass and Paul lies motionless on his pillow. After some moments he nods toward the chapel and whispers he would like to receive Communion as soon as possible. Fontana conveys the request to Martin. Macchi comes to the bedside and proffers the ritual wafer and wine. Afterward there is a marked change in Paul. He appears totally calm and at peace. He even manages a small wave to those in the chapel. Only Fontana is fully aware of what has happened. The heart attack was not massive but in his opinion it would be decisive. He takes Macchi aside and says the pope can have little time left.

The secretary, observing the protocol, goes to Villot, now standing uncertainly near the chapel door, and tells him the worst. The secretary of state immediately comes to Paul's side and asks whether he would like to be anointed.

The pope nods, "Subito, subito."

Villot goes to his bag and removes the anointing oil. He pours some into a small silver chalice and returns to the bedside to begin administering the last sacraments.

Paul clasps Villot's hand as he prays. Everyone is now grouped around his bed: Giacomina and her nuns on one side, the two Montinis and the Vatican prelates on the other. Macchi and Magee stand at the foot of the bed, watching Villot complete the anointing. The secretary of state steps back as Paul closes his eyes. Fontana bends over him, listening to his heart. He rises and says the Holy Father is still alive. The doctor looks at Paul's bedside clock; in all the years he has known the pope, Fontana has never known it to be too fast or too slow. Its hands point to six-thirty.

There is no sound except the clock's ticking and the steady clicking of the nuns' rosaries.

Shortly after 7:30 P.M., the pope opens his eyes. Magee is not certain but he thinks they have lost their luster, their ability to penetrate deep into a person's soul. They now seem glazed.

Fontana is at once by the bedside, bending down and listening to the sounds of ebbing life filling his stethoscope. Paul's breathing is harsher and shallower. But somehow, between the laboring, he manages to speak.

"We have arrived at the end. We thank . . ."

He is unable to complete the sentence before his eyes close once more.

Villot and the Montinis look toward Fontana. He checks again with his stethoscope. Paul is still alive.

The doctor, Villot, Macchi, Magee and Martin draw to one side. Fontana tells them he is now certain. There is virtually no hope. Barring a miracle the pontificate of Paul VI will be over by midnight. Martin hurries from the room.

In his office in the Pontifical Commission for Social Communications—the Vatican Press Office—its secretary, Father Romeo Panciroli, is grateful to hear from Martin. The withdrawn and precise press aide has been bombarded all afternoon by the world's media. He is totally ill equipped to deal with such an onslaught. He prefers his encounters with the media—when they must occur—to be through those Rome-based correspondents he knows and who, in turn, know how to treat him with proper respect; not at all like the pushy, aggressive, rude and demanding voices which have almost blocked the Vatican switchboard for hours. Martin and Panciroli discuss the wording of a communiqué. They agree it should be brief. That settled, Panciroli has only to decide who shall first have the news. He consults his press directory. The Associated Press is the first name on his list. Moments later its wires carry: "FLASH. AT 18.15 HOURS POPE PAUL VI SUFFERED A HEART ATTACK. HE IS SEMI CONSCIOUS VATICAN PRESS SECRE-TARY PANCIROLI STATED."

It was the AP's Rome bureau's second world scoop of the day.

At nine o'clock the pope once more opens his eyes. He looks around. Nobody knows whether he can see or whether it is only a reflex action.

Villot breaks the silence: *"Santissimo Padre."*

Paul turns to him, nodding. Then he speaks. "Pray for me. . . ." He lapses back into semiconsciousness.

Fontana checks the pope's heart. Afterward he removes the blood pressure cuff. The readings won't make any difference now. The doctor says, quite loudly, that the Holy Father's life is hanging by a thread.

At nine-thirty Paul again opens his eyes. Magee fancies he can see the pope's lips starting to move. He strains forward, trying to catch the words. Villot, closer, can actually make them out without too much difficulty. Paul is reciting, "Our Father." The others pick up the cadence of the Lord's Prayer: ". . . Which art in heaven, hallowed be Thy name. Thy kingdom come, Thy will be . . ."

The pope's eyes close and his lips become still. The others falter through the prayer.

Fontana bends over Paul, listening for an unusually long time to his chest. He feels for the pope's pulse. The doctor straightens and looks at the others. Then he glances at Paul's alarm clock to verify the time. It is 9:40 P.M. There is a distinct tremor in his voice as he pronounces: "It is over."

At that precise moment the ancient alarm clock, which had rung at six-thirty that morning and which had not been rewound or reset, begins to shrill, filling the bedroom with its tinny sound.

Martin is the first to leave the room. The prefect goes to telephone Panciroli. The world must be told.

His departure is a signal for Villot. He is no longer just the secretary of state: he is now also camerlengo, the cardinal who will run the Church, with the help of the College of Cardinals, until the conclusion of the forthcoming conclave. Villot will supervise the funeral preparations, send out the formal invitations and decide a thousand and one matters until a new pontiff is chosen. But first, before he does anything, he must attend to a hallowed ritual.

Villot walks to his case, aware that all eyes in the bedroom are upon him. He removes the small silver hammer and returns to stand over the body. Using the hammer, he taps Paul lightly on the forehead and, in a strong voice nobody can remember him using before, Villot poses a question asked over the corpses of popes for centuries.

"Giovanni Battista Enrico Antonio Marie, are you dead?"

He waits a full minute for any response. He then repeats his action and question. After another minute he completes the ritual a third time. He then turns and addresses no one in particular. "Pope Paul is truly dead."

Villot lifts the pope's right hand. For a moment he stares at it, unbelieving. He looks at Macchi and demands to know where the Fisherman's Ring is. Villot must take possession of it; later, before the assembled cardinals, the camerlengo will use a pair of silver shears to break the ring and Paul's seals of office. From that moment no one can use either to authenticate a false document.

Macchi does not know where the ring is.

Villot's instructions are sharply clear: the ring must be found—and quickly.

Those words signify the transfer of power from Macchi and all the others who have held it for the fifteen years, one month and fifteen days Paul occupied the Throne of St. Peter.

VIII

During the next hours a number of events occurred essentially simultaneously and in no special order. In some cases they were the result of planning. In others they were spontaneous reactions. Some were significant, others less so. All arose directly from what had occurred. Each suggested there was nothing on earth quite like the aftermath of the death of a pope. So, almost simultaneously . . .

Vatican press secretary Panciroli gave the Associated Press its third clear beat on the story by again first telephoning the wire service's Rome bureau. At 9:44 P.M., Italian time, the AP sent a five-bell flash to all its subscribers: "POPE DEAD."

Over four thousand miles away in the Chicago News Center of CBS—where the wall clocks showed the local time as two forty-five in the afternoon—a duty editor dialed Andrew Greeley at his home in Grand Beach to say he was flying a film crew across Lake Michigan for the voice of CREP to explain the pontificate of Paul. The crew arrived while Greeley was saying mass in his garden. He stopped the service to address the camera. He was as critical as CBS may have hoped he would be. But Greeley's views never made the evening news. The tape was lost. Paul's death had not much moved Greeley—nor did the prospect of flying yet again to Rome, although this time he would spearhead the Universal Press Syndicate "task force" covering the funeral and conclave. Greeley would be one of two thousand newspersons to reach Rome in the next seventy-two hours.

By 9:55 P.M. Vatican time, every position on its switchboard was manned. Each nun had a headset clipped over her coif and a cross on a gold chain hung from her neck. Usually the Sunday-night shift was as quiet as each of the three graveyards in the Vatican. But since the AP flash the world had begun to call the Holy See number—Rome 6982—and been answered with the invariable greeting, "Vaticano." In the coming twenty-four hours the nuns would receive and make 27,800 calls.

Macchi was the second person to leave Paul's bedroom. The once all-powerful private secretary had began his first task of the interregnum, the period between the death of one pope and the election of the next. He was trying to find the Fisherman's Ring. Four days would pass before the discomfited Macchi located it at the back of a drawer in the desk of Paul's private study.

The secretary's departure from the bedroom was the signal for the others to leave. Giacomina and her nuns remained behind to bathe the pope's body before it was handed over to the embalmers. The nuns reportedly wept as they worked.

Villot drove back to the Vatican with Confalonieri, Poletti and Caprio. As camerlengo, Villot had already accomplished a great deal since the moment of death. He had ordered Martin and Fontana back to Rome to prepare the preliminary work for the death certificate. He had phoned the papal master of ceremonies, Monsignor Virgilio Noé, and various members of the Apostolic Camera, the body responsible for administering the property of the Holy See during the vacancy. Before leaving Castel Gandolfo, Villot had also symbolically taken possession of its palaces and grounds. During the journey to the Vatican the four cardinals discussed the next steps. Poletti would go on radio and television to tell the people of Rome their bishop had died. Confalonieri would inform the cardinals, the diplomatic corps and the secular governments of the fifty-one nations with whom the Holy See had diplomatic ties. Villot would formally seal the pope's private apartment, in which nobody was allowed to live during the interregnum. He would also take symbolic possession of the Vatican Palace and the Lateran Palace, formally the official residence of the bishop of Rome and now the administrative headquarters of Rome diocese.

Magee remained at Castel Gandolfo to help supervise the arrangements for the lying in state.

RAI, the Italian television and radio network, interrupted its program with the news. Stations all over the Western world did the same. Radio Moscow and Peking Radio, along with most other communist satellites, would wait a further ten hours before briefly noting the passing of the pontiff. Albanian Radio would not report it for three days.

Vatican Radio had closed its offices just off the Via della Conciliazione at 8 P.M. Only engineers were on duty to transmit prerecorded programs. None of them heard the RAI flash. Not that it would have made any difference: the station's director general, Father Roberto Tucci, a Jesuit and the only person with the authority, now the pope was dead, to preempt the schedules, was out of Rome. His team of broadcasters, Jesuits and other missionaries were either at supper or saying devotions in their religious houses throughout the city. They went to bed not knowing the pope was dead or that their station, sometimes known as "the voice of God," was about to face its greatest challenge.

Tailor Anibaile Gammarelli heard the news on the radio. He immediately drove to his shop at 34 Santa Chiara to double-check what he already knew, that the House of Gammarelli had ample cloth for the task ahead.

Tourists started to drift into St. Peter's Square. They stood waiting, they said, for some sort of announcement, expecting a Vatican official to emerge on the balcony of the basilica and say something. When no one appeared they drifted away again.

The first tributes poured in. From the White House, Downing Street, the Elysée

Palace in Paris, the Chancellor's Residence in Bonn, came the verdicts: the pope's contribution to religious harmony had been considerable; he had steered the Second Vatican Council to port; he had strengthened power-sharing in the Church by founding the Synod of Bishops and broken down so many barriers by his trips to all five continents. In Ireland they reminded themselves that he had visited them twice, not as pope but as a senior member of the Secretariat of State. In India, where it was the middle of the night, newspaper editors dusted off obituaries already set in print. Their eulogies were generous. His papacy had been a dramatic turning point in the history of the Roman Catholic Church's relationship with other religions. It was a point of view echoed on a thousand and more editorial pages in the coming days. Later they would be carefully perused in the Vatican as a means of evaluating the Church's position in the world.

Everywhere reporters followed up the AP flash. They reached Hans Küng in Switzerland and asked the Catholic theologian for a comment on a pope who had done nothing to stop the constant harassment Küng had experienced at the hands of the Curia for daring to keep open the debate on the infallibility of the pope. Küng begged time to consider his comment. Lefèbvre also avoided immediate public judgment. But everybody knew it was only a matter of time before both made their positions known.

Religious scholars of other persuasions began to sharpen their prose to deliver verdicts. For those wishing to criticize, the material was there. The Curia was as strife-ridden as ever. The pope's ecumenical gestures had been weakened by this struggle within the Vatican. The Synod of Bishops had not lived up to its promise. Such opinions left a question mark at best. Paul was certainly not the worst pope but he was a long way from being called great.

Some of the ambassadors accredited to the Holy See did not wait for official notification. The British envoy extraordinary and minister plenipotentiary dialed the duty officer at the Foreign Office in London to break the news. The duty officer informed the permanent under-secretary of state. He called the foreign secretary, who informed the prime minister, who decided, as it was the death of a head of state, to inform Buckingham Palace. A court chamberlain brought the news to the Queen at the end of dinner. She immediately asked her personal private secretary to prepare a suitable message of condolence. From the British envoy's call from Rome to the start of drafting formal royal regret needed no longer than fifteen minutes.

Working from an alphabetical list, the staff of the Secretariat of State telephoned and cabled all over the world. The telegrams were in Italian or French. Nobody could mistake the message sent to each cardinal. "THE POPE IS DEAD. COME AT ONCE. VILLOT." The phone calls were equally abrupt, little more than a voice from the Vatican reading out the text of the cable. The hard-pressed staff at the Secretariat had no time to accept condolences or enter into conversations.

At twenty minutes past ten, Austrian summer time, the telephone rang at Woll-zeile 2 in Vienna, the address of the massive Erzbischöfliches Palais, the palace of the cardinal archbishop, Franz König.

The State Secretariat priest double-checked the number on his list—Vienna 532561—to make sure it was right. He was about to put down the phone and send a telegram when the call was answered. . . .

IX

S unday in the archbishop's palace in Vienna's Second District provides a relief from the sounds which permeate even the inner reaches of the thick-walled building during weekday peak traffic hours. In the relative peace of the deserted business quarter of the city on the Sabbath, the palace retains certain features: architecturally it looks like a scaled-down version of the Apostolic Palace, with its courtyard from which floor after floor rises; it has the same faded outer elegance and the same inner magnificence. Yet, unlike the Apostolic Palace, this edifice makes no secret of its security systems. A heavy milled-steel gate bars the entrance. Closed-circuit television monitors anyone who approaches the building. There is a constant guard at the gatehouse. The Vienna police are never far off. In a way it is all a tribute to the power and integrity of the man who has lived here through some of the most tumultuous events in postwar European history. He predicted how the cold war would develop, he warned the Berlin Wall was on the way, he foresaw the Hungarian Uprising and the end of Dubček in Czechoslovakia. He arranged to free Cardinal Mindszenty from his enforced exile in the American Embassy in Budapest and has been a guiding hand in a hundred lesser incidents. The Russians and their satellites both fear and respect Franz König, the cardinal archbishop of Vienna. He is a man some of the communist leaders, in their wilder moments, would like to kill, so the American CIA have told him. König is a prudent man. That is why he has accepted the sort of protection more customary in a high-security prison than in the residence of a religious leader.

Yet König has done more than anyone, with the exception of Agostino Casaroli, to break the massive moral and ideological conflict between the Roman Church and communism. He sees the dangers of a continuing enmity between two solid monoliths. He believes that while the Vatican can never condone communist doctrine, it is not always wise for it to be rigidly dogmatic. König remembers the futility of that during the reign of Pius XII. In the course of his pontificate fifteen countries came under communist rule. Pius's threat to excommunicate all Catholics who willingly remained in the Communist Party or supported its policies had no effect. König long ago abandoned the ingenuous idea that communism would soon be overturned. Instead he argues that the objective should be to win and preserve a better position for the Church under communism.

He has been holding these views since John XXIII's encyclical *Pacem in Terris* (*Peace on Earth*), published in 1963, which provides the intellectual justification for *rapprochement*. No one is more adept at walking this tightrope than König. He knows every subtlety of the encyclical, where and how it distinguishes between false ideas and the historical truths based on them. He played his part in encouraging bishops' delegations from communist countries to attend the Second Vatican Council; later he counseled on how to respond to Khrushchev's encouraging messages to John. And throughout Paul's pontificate, König's advice had been regularly sought. As a result, Paul sent Casaroli to Moscow to sign the Holy See's adherence to the treaty prohibiting the proliferation of atomic weapons. One unlikely effect of the signing is that the Swiss Guards are annually inspected, under the terms of the treaty, to ascertain whether they possess any secret nuclear warheads.

Again, König played an important part in persuading communist satellites to ease restrictions on religious education. And it was his nod which encouraged the Vatican to establish diplomatic relations with Yugoslavia. Many of König's views were reached after a Sabbath of meditation.

He works in his study, when not attending to his own devotions or ministering to others at the regular Sunday masses which are punctuated by the three good meals a day the archbishop still relishes in this, his seventy-third year. He looks not only ten years younger but, even without his cardinal's robes and biretta, there is no mistaking he is a prince of the Church. He exudes that rare mix of deeply pious scholar and very shrewd politician. He is witty and expansive on matters of record, but a staunch keeper of what are known in the Vatican as "the secrets"—all those confidences only very senior cardinals hear. He speaks German with a velvety Viennese accent and can be fluent and amusing in several other languages. He has a face made for sculpting. Even when he is silent, contemplating or listening, he has a habit of sitting with his strong hands intertwined.

König has heard the telephone ringing but has made no attempt to answer it. Instinctively he knows it brings both important and grave news. No one would otherwise call at this late hour. His thoughts immediately go back to the evening television news. There was no hint of a crisis there. Something must have happened suddenly. He feels he knows the answer even before his private secretary walks in. The man is young, but the archbishop sees that he seems to have aged. In a voice König barely recognizes, the priest says the pope died forty-one minutes ago.

The cardinal nods: he had been right about the call. He has expected it, he now remembers, for months. The last time he saw Paul, König knew he was already looking at a doomed man. The cardinal returned to his palace near the Danube and did something he had never done before. He packed a special suitcase for conclave. It contains sufficient personal effects to keep him in confined comfort for a week. If conclave goes beyond that time he will have to send out for more razor blades—or grow a beard.

He gives his secretary an order: reserve the first available airline seat to Rome.

König wants to get there as quickly as possible because he feels intuitively the run up to conclave will be the most decisive in the history of the modern Church. He wants to be in at the beginning so he can play to the full his very proper role as one of the great cardinal-electors.

Shortly after 8:50 P.M. in Dublin—Irish summer time is one hour behind continental Europe—the telephone rings in a secluded mansion on the outskirts of the city. It is one of the operators in the telegraphic section of Ireland's not very efficient telephone service. But nobody can complain about the time this telegram has taken to reach Dublin, a swift twenty-two minutes. The operator reads the message: "DEEPLY REGRET INFORM YOU HOLY FATHER PASSED AWAY. INFORM ALL RELEVANT. YOURS IN CHRIST. VILLOT. CAMERLENGO." The operator spontaneously adds his own condolences and poses the question people will soon be asking all over the world: "What does this mean for the Church?"

"A great deal. Sì, a great deal."

Even this brief response cannot disguise the Sicilian aspect of the man who has spent nine eventful years in this mansion.

It is set in the vast expanse of Phoenix Park. Neighbors include the American ambassador and the president of Ireland. That, some say, is only one of the reasons for the discreet garda presence outside the house. The police are there, it is claimed, to note the unusual callers at the most unlikely hours. Yet, true or not, the man who lives here is certainly sufficiently important to warrant protection. A measure of his position is that he is now the first person in Ireland to be told Paul is dead.

There are those in the British Embassy on the other side of the city, in the Protestant northern enclaves of this troubled island, and certainly across the Irish Sea in the fastness of Whitehall, who would not grieve if this man were no longer in Ireland. They sometimes refer to him disparagingly as "the Green Sicilian," or "the pope's spy." They would pay well to know the contents of the weekly diplomatic pouch he personally seals and sends on the Aer Lingus flight to Rome. As well as details about the work of the Irish Church and its various charities and cultural activities, the pouch frequently contains a shrewd assessment of the people and pressures involved in Britain's battle with the IRA. The man who lives in this mansion is often the first to know details directly from the IRA of some new initiative. In the Vatican's discreet but continuous efforts to bring a just settlement in Ulster, the apostolic papal delegate to Ireland, dean of the diplomatic corps, His Grace Archbishop Dr. Gaetane Alibrandi, has been a key figure. During his nine years at the nunciature he has secretly met many of the IRA leaders. He sees these contacts as part of an intelligence-gathering process which can provide unique insights and information for collation in the Vatican, and eventual study by the pope. Alibrandi's reports on the North often go far beyond what the Vatican learns from its constant contacts with bishops in Ireland and elsewhere. The nuncio is almost certainly the only diplomat in Dublin to deal directly with such prime sources—the political leaders of the men who do the shooting. That is why the Special Branch likes to know who visits this secluded mansion, that is why members of Ireland's coalition rumble that the nuncio should be quietly withdrawn by the Vatican.[1]

The diminutive diplomat—Alibrandi is barely five feet in his old-fashioned lace-up shoes—sees his close connection with those he insists on calling "guerrilla fighters," not "gunmen" nor "terrorists," as yet another way for him to learn of the deeper roots of the Ulster conflict. With a passion even his opponents find mesmeric, Alibrandi argues that most of the IRA act as they do because of the presence of a situation not of their making: that to reject or condemn them, without any attempt to understand them, is simply a different form of violence. To those appalled by this argument, the nuncio serenely responds that any form of killing has a blunting effect.

Alibrandi's involvement in the strife is balanced in his mind by the undisputed truism that ever since Northern Ireland was created, many of its Protestant clergymen have openly and dangerously manipulated the political life of the province to the detriment of Catholics. He is appalled by Orange Order rituals which include calling a football "the pope" and kicking it around a field. He cannot conceive, even in the most Catholic of northern ghettoes, a similar game being played with a football called "the Queen." Alibrandi remains convinced that by refusing to condemn such behavior, the most extreme of Ulster's Protestant clergymen are, willy-nilly, cast as officers in the bitter war which engages their troops; that, quite deliberately, they have allowed religion and politics to meld into a single, potent, all-pervading force; that behind the many other motives for Ulster's peculiar anti-Catholic discrimination lurks one dominant factor: the attitude of these clergymen and their determination to sustain the myths about, and the frenetic fear of, Catholicism.

The nuncio possesses an impressive and depressing collection of Northern Protestant bigotry—all of it abrasive, strident, uncharitable, unyielding and off-putting. It is an effective counter to slip across his dining table when the occasional non-Catholic guest raises a question about some alleged excess of the Church Alibrandi represents in a country which has a long and compliant religious relationship with Rome.

It is this which largely allows him to remain unperturbed by the hostile reaction he attracts from Dublin politicians and members of the diplomatic corps of which he is titular head. It also allows him to be a vigorous defender of the role of Vatican diplomacy in the modern world. He will remind anybody that his functions are clearly defined in a document Paul issued in June 1969: "The primary and specific purpose of the mission of a papal representative is to render ever closer and more operative the ties that bind the Apostolic See and its local Church; the ordinary function of a pontifical representative is to keep the Holy See regularly and objectively informed about the conditions of the ecclesiastical community to which he has been sent, and assert what may affect the life of the Church and the good of souls."

This is enough for Alibrandi. He will go on meeting the IRA if it means he receives a fuller picture of what is happening in Ireland. The papal directive makes this permissible in the view of the sixty-four-year-old diplomat who holds a doctorate in canon law and is an acknowledged expert on ecclesiastical history, international law, sociology and economics. He speaks several languages and began his career at the Secretariat of State by opening and sometimes secretly copying the most private letters of Paul. It is the memory of that misdemeanor which now fills the nuncio's mind when he puts down the phone.

The scene of a few months ago wells up in his memory. Paul was sitting on a couch in his office when the nuncio arrived to make his annual report. He motioned for Alibrandi to sit beside him. They had known each other for nearly forty years and had stayed in touch all the time. Nevertheless Alibrandi detected a feeling of surprise in Paul when he said, "Holy Father, I wish to make a special confession to you." Paul, he remembers, said nothing. Instead his eyes dwelt on Alibrandi, "wonderful eyes, able to make you want to speak." Alibrandi began to talk in little more than a whisper, finding it difficult to admit what he had done so long ago. "Holy Father, do you remember that you gave me sometimes some private letters, very private letters?" Paul answered, "I remember, I remember." Encouraged, Alibrandi continued, "And nobody but the person receiving the letters was to read them?" Again, "I remember, I remember." Then in a surge of words, "Holy Father before I sealed your letters I read them." Paul sat there "not angry, just interested and understanding," as the nuncio completed his confession. "Holy Father those were the best letters I have ever read. And the very best I always copied so I could use the thoughts later in my own letters." Suddenly Paul leaned forward and smiled. "I am very happy that you found my words so useful."[2]

Glad now to be alone with his thoughts, the tiny figure of the nuncio is momentarily a tragic one as the full impact of the news dawns on him. His nut-brown face crinkles with inner pain, his hands pluck nervously at his pectoral cross. Until this moment he has never fully realized how much he will miss Paul, not just as pope but also as a friend.

Alibrandi feels especially sad Paul will never see the splendid new nunciature which is being built for the apostolic delegate. It only has one drawback as far as Alibrandi can tell, now that the need to make the chapel larger than originally envisaged has been agreed on, and that is the new building, out on the busy Navan Road, will make it much more difficult for IRA men to slip in and out.

But, for the moment, the problems of moving to a new home and dealing with members of proscribed organizations will have to take second place to the demands the death of the pope places on the hardworking nuncio.

Paul's death means that in the coming days Alibrandi will be "chained to my typewriter," executing Villot's telegraphed order to "inform all relevant." These will include the president of Ireland, the minister of foreign affairs, the bishops and the nuncio's fellow ambassadors in Ireland. All will receive a personally typed letter. Alibrandi learned to type when acting as Paul's secretary in 1938. He feels it particularly appropriate that the skill Paul encouraged should now be used to inform "all relevant" of his death.

It is teatime in Buenos Aires when the cable from the Vatican confirms what Juan Carlos Aramburu has known for hours. Each of the city's newspaper and TV stations called him for comment following the AP flash. But the sixty-six-year-old cardinal archbishop of the largest Catholic diocese in the world—he is directly responsible for nine million souls—determinedly refuses to say anything until he has Villot's cable in his hands. It is not that he wishes to be unhelpful, it is that he needs every minute to work out the deeper implications of Paul's death. The more he thinks about it, Aramburu will later admit in his pleasant singsong Spanish, the more the situation has the makings of one of those sudden explosive crises which South America itself seems so often able to produce.

Aramburu has a donnish shyness, a throwback to his days as a professor. But it masks a powerful certainty: by the end of the century the numerical power base of the Church will have shifted from Europe to Latin America. There are about 204,100,000 baptized Catholics in South America. There are a further 79,114,000 in Central America and another 17,529,000 in the Caribbean islands. Even these figures are likely out of date, such is the high birth rate. Presently 40 percent of the Church's strength comes from this part of the world. But by the end of the century—at the present rate of one Catholic born and baptized every ninety-three seconds in the area—Latin America will have over 50 percent of that strength. Aramburu believes that in the coming conclave he and his eighteen fellow cardinals from the region, coupled with the Spanish cardinals and perhaps the Portuguese, could provide a voting bloc hard to ignore. Given, that is, that they can agree on a common strategy. Better than anybody Aramburu knows it is a big proviso. Yet it is one for the future. His more immediate concerns are caused by the fact that in every sense Paul's death comes at the worst possible time.

It follows hard on the heels of a calculated snub by Italy's Socialist president, Alessandro Pertini, who decided against sending a message of congratulation to Jorge Rafael Videla, former head of yet another Argentinian military junta and, since five days ago, August 1, civilian president of the country. Pertini felt he could not offer good wishes to a man who has done more than most of Argentina's dictators to abuse human rights.

The fiercely nationalistic Argentinians, 40 percent of whom are of Italian descent, reacted strongly to the slight. Many feel they, too, have been insulted by the motherland they left to begin a new life in Buenos Aires or on the pampas. Aramburu recognizes that the South American Church is likely to be dragged into the controversy: such situations invariably lead to demands for denunciations from the pulpits. In the minds of the masses the issue is simplistically clear: Pertini, an upstart Socialist, has insulted their new president. With a fervor of newfound *patria,* some Argentinians are prepared to see the situation burst into flame; there have already been bomb scares at Alitalia offices and other Italian places of business.

Aramburu fears Paul's death could be the touchfuse. Almost certainly, reasons the cardinal, Videla will wish to attend the funeral and stay on for the installation of the next pope. Aramburu can see how it would provide the president with a badly needed shopwindow, one in which the general with the Clark Gable mustache and thumbs-up gesture he adopted after watching World War II newsreels of Winston Churchill would have a chance to score an important public relations coup; for a man ultimately responsible for the torture and death of thousands, the visit to Rome could be used to make the world think he was, at heart, simply another deeply caring Catholic.

The cardinal feels that if Videla goes he could spark off riots in Rome and mar the solemnities. Yet Aramburu can think of no means of stopping the president. In the three years he has been a cardinal the gifted Aramburu has not faced a tougher problem.

It is one almost as serious as the national malaise which grips Argentina. Inflation is running at 155 percent. Wages have dropped in real terms to between 40 and 60 percent of their level before Videla seized power. Bankruptcies are at a new high. While the remnants of the old Peronist regime are totally discredited, there is no evidence Videla can get the country moving as a modern industrial nation with stable political institutions.

There are other reasons for Aramburu to look with concern on the idea of Videla's going to Rome. In his absence the president might be ousted; his power base is far from secure. Those who seek to replace him could also bring about the one conflict, above all others, which Aramburu privately fears. It would be caused by the dispute over the Malvinas, those near-barren islands five hundred miles off the coast of Argentina which remain almost embarrassingly as one of the last outposts of Britain's once-great empire. Personally, Aramburu has little doubt the islands will eventually become the property of Argentina. But he has always cautioned that the only way to achieve this is by patient negotiation. He fears that in any upheaval following the replacement of Videla the Malvinas could become a burning issue. He knows whenever matters become particularly uncomfortable for a junta—when the protests became more than tolerated whispers about brutalities, about kidnappings, about anything which could precipitate yet another coup—those who currently hold the country down by military force almost inevitably trot out the question of the Malvinas. It is a guaranteed way both to stifle opposition and to unite public opinion.

Aramburu has been telling the Vatican for years that there is the growing possibility of a military offensive by Argentina against the islands.[3] The prospect bothers the cardinal deeply, for he knows that as a prince of the Church he must condemn all violence. Equally, he suspects that if he does, in the case of the Malvinas he would be flying in the face of what his flock wants and, perhaps, even against what he himself believes. But Aramburu is also painfully aware that dictator Videla is probably the worst possible person to go to Rome to put forward any claim to the islands which hinges on moral rights.

In Rome, a member of the African Missionary Order, Father Sean MacCarthy, is dressing in the open-neck white shirt and blue pants he favors for work. MacCarthy is a broadcaster—one of the few in all Rome who do not yet know that the biggest news story since the kidnapping of Aldo Moro has broken.

For the past nine years MacCarthy has hosted Vatican Radio's English-language program to Africa; he also at times broadcasts to Europe. He is fifty-nine, a compact man with a shock of gray hair and a studio pallor. Like his friend John Magee, MacCarthy retains his soft Irish brogue, a well-modulated voice ideal for conveying the Sacred Word on the 16/25-meter shortwave band.

Having breakfasted and driven from his mission house to Vatican Radio headquarters, MacCarthy still has no inkling of what has happened. He casually strolls onto the third floor of the broadcast center where he has his office to find himself caught up in what passes for panic in the usually serene atmosphere of the most powerful religious station on earth: people are almost running; some are even talking a little faster than usual.

Slightly puzzled, MacCarthy goes to his desk in the English-language section and is further surprised when his telephone rings. A radio station in Los Angeles—where it is the middle of the night—is calling for a reaction to the pope's death. Instinctively the broadcaster in MacCarthy surfaces; he begins to speak off the cuff, formulating elegantly interlinked thoughts and offering the sort of careful and balanced judgments long experience has taught him to give. It is a masterly example of the delicate art of avoiding pitfalls. The California station will replay the recording regularly throughout the night, with the billing, "The voice of the Vatican expresses its grief."

It's the sort of hyperbole which makes MacCarthy wince. He just wishes the secular media weren't so tasteless. But he fears that in the coming days he will shudder quite often at such lapses. Those will be the moments he is fervently glad he does not have to compete for a news break or earn his living searching for the next sensation. As a religious, a member of a monastic order, he receives no salary, only expenses and his keep; that's the way he likes it—three good meals a day, a comfortable bed and probably the most faithful listeners a broadcaster could want.

Yet he is no stuffed shirt. He understands the requirements of his calling, the need to play neither up nor down to his audience. He is careful to source everything and his judgments are based on the sort of meticulous research even Prefect Martin would accept.

Having quickly assimilated the basic circumstances surrounding Paul's passing, throughout the morning MacCarthy fields calls from English-language stations around the world, while at the same time preparing his own program for airing from Studio One later in the day. He plans it to be a straight recital of the facts: how and when the pope died, who was there, what his last words were. Nearby broadcasters in thirty-four other languages are preparing their bulletins, from Tamil to Esperanto, from the dialects of the highlands of China to the patois of New Guinea, from the guttural sounds of bush Africa to the resonant growl of the Polish steppes: to almost anywhere there are Catholics ready and able to listen, Vatican Radio will bring its version of the death of the pope.

MacCarthy completes his script. Suddenly he grins. Come to think of it, he is not really going to sound much different from the secular bulletins. Yet no doubt his details will seem more authoritative because, after all, they are being beamed from the transmitters of "the voice of God."

Father Lambert Greenan, editor of the English-language edition of *L'Osservatore Romano,* as usual manages to cope with several matters at once. In one hand he holds a large gin and tonic. In the other he has a newspaper brought along for the Aer Lingus flight to Rome. At the same time, the Dominican is keeping one watchful eye on a particularly powerful cardinal who is dressed as a simple country priest sitting two rows behind him, while his other eye is on a photographer festooned with what the editor thinks must be the entire contents of a camera shop. Greenan wonders how the situation will develop. But nothing will surprise him—not after the events of the past twenty-four hours.

The tall and avuncular Irish-born Greenan—he comes from the same Newry parish as Magee and the pair are close friends, partly because of their dissimilar personalities, and partly because they are members of the "Irish Mafia"—had left Rome to holiday with relations in Ireland. Upon entering Irish air space Greenan suddenly felt compelled to say a rosary for the pope: "I just prayed he wouldn't die while I was on holiday." On Sunday night, home with his family, having uncorked a choice wine for dinner, Greenan felt another compulsion: to catch the headlines on RTE's nine-o'clock television news. He was in time to hear the newscaster announce Paul's death. Greenan spent much of the night arranging to fly back to Rome. As editor of the "almost official" English-language weekly of the Vatican, his presence is mandatory to publish the documentation associated with the funeral and aftermath.

Greenan relishes the prospect of the unremitting pressure ahead; eighteen thousand very select readers in ninety-one countries will look at his paper to provide the plain, unvarnished truth of what has happened and what is going to happen. There won't be a line of speculation—just all the facts the Vatican deems fit to print, translated often from flowery Italian or arid Latin into perfect English by one of the sharpest and finest minds working in the service of the Holy See.

He is also waggish. Greenan once found himself seated beside Archbishop Alibrandi at one of the interminable dinners Irish prelates like to give. Smiling broadly at the swarthy-faced Sicilian, Greenan remarked in mock surprise, "I had no idea we had Arabs in the Church's diplomatic service." The puzzled nuncio looked uncertain, waiting for Greenan to continue. The editor carried on blithely. "Your name. Ali Brandi. That's Arabic for sure in my book." The two didn't exchange a further word during dinner. Greenan tabbed Alibrandi as "a fella who couldn't see a joke."

Behind his daffiness, Greenan is a noted theologian and philosopher of impeccable credentials. He is sixty-one years old, suffers fools badly, but has an unshakable loyalty to a circle of friends which extends through the Vatican into the papal apartment itself. People say he knows almost as many secrets as Macchi and Magee. Greenan keeps them locked behind an ironic smile. He is a formidable man in every sense; those who abuse his trust do so at their peril.

On this Monday morning, sipping his gin and tonic—no easy feat since the plane is being buffeted by a fierce summer storm over France—Greenan wonders why Cardinal Paolo Bertoli is traveling incognito. Greenan knows the seventy-year-old loves his little mysteries; Bertoli has been Scarlet Pimperneling so long that Roman satirists say he should really wear a cloak instead of a cassock. But recently, after a distinguished career as nuncio in Turkey, Colombia, Lebanon and France, Bertoli's star has waned. He had a fierce quarrel with Giovanni Benelli and the two of them simultaneously fell victim of Vatican hatchetry. While Benelli was dispatched to be archbishop of Florence, Bertoli was pressured to the point where he did the unthinkable: he resigned as prefect of the Sacred Congregation for the Causes of Saints. He had gone off, again, as Paul's delegate to try to bring peace between Christians and Moslems in Lebanon. Nobody really felt his heart was in the mission; in any event it failed. Personally, Greenan didn't think such an intervention could work in the political cesspit of the Middle East. Afterward hardly anyone has seen Bertoli for months. Now, here he is, slimmed down, leaner than he has been in years, a glint in his eyes, having boarded the plane at Lourdes. He surely hasn't been to look at the grotto, not dressed like this, in an unadorned black soutane, as unprepossessing as any curate. But it hasn't taken the photographer long to penetrate the disguise. Now, as the plane begins to come out of the turbulence, the cameraman starts to move into position, but hesitatingly: even the brashest of photographers knows Bertoli is explosive over having his picture taken without permission.

Still musing, Greenan is tapped on the shoulder. It is Bertoli, speaking perfect English, a gift Greenan has not known him to display before. Can he borrow the newspaper? Instinctively Greenan replies, "Of course, Eminence." There follows one of those brief conversations which come under the heading "Games People Play." "You know me?" "Of course, Eminence." "How do you know me?" "We meet quite often, Eminence." "Why do we meet?" "I edit the English edition of *L'Osservatore Romano*." "Oh, yes, there are several language editions aren't there?" "Yes, Eminence." "It's terrible news, isn't it?" "Yes, Eminence." Greenan hands over the newspaper, the convoluted conversation at an end, and resumes pondering how his next edition should present its all-important judgment on Paul.

Since 1890 the daily edition of *L'Osservatore Romano*—published at three o'clock every afternoon with weekly editions in English, French, Spanish, Portuguese, German, Italian and Polish—has promulgated the nearest thing the Vatican has to an "official" printed word. Like Vatican Radio and the Press Office, the group of newspapers is owned by the Holy See and answers directly on all editorial matters to a department of the Secretariat of State, the Office of Information and Documentation. The papers' funding comes from the Administration of the Patrimony of the Holy See; its administration is in the hands of a religious order, the Salesians of St. John Bosco.

For nine years Greenan has edited the English-language weekly on a shoe-string; the entire group is in financial straits. Greenan's paper carries little advertising and has no overseas correspondents and just one editorial assistant in a cramped office in a featureless building beside the Porta Sant'Anna. Greenan rigorously follows the editorial line of the parent daily, loyally and, when necessary, pugnaciously upholding the papacy. He provides a valuable record of nearly everything the pope says and does, including publishing the official texts of papal speeches. He also prints occasional articles of real political significance or historical interest. The editorials have a special importance, particularly the unsigned ones. They are usually "inspired" by the pope; sometimes Paul even wrote them himself.

Now, as the plane heads for Rome, Greenan is shaping his thoughts about a man he has both loved deeply and respected. He fears the secular media will once again focus on the *Humanae Vitae* encyclical and miss so much else in the pontificate. Among other things Paul revised the rite of concelebration, that moment the priests of a diocese gather around their bishop to celebrate the Eucharist with him, or when the cardinals congregate around the pope to create visible evidence of collegiality, simple but striking proof all priests and bishops share with him responsibility for the entire Church. While the five meetings of the Synod of Bishops have not been an unqualified success—they could not be since Paul's idea of "open government" in the Church was simply too great a change to absorb in just over a decade—Greenan believes substantial progress has been achieved in the revision of canon law, doctrine, liturgy and the delicate question of mixed marriages. All this he attributes to Paul's commitment to change. And right to the end he remained the pope of ecumenism. Paul seized every opportunity to demonstrate this. Who could forget the moment when Paul once more publicly displayed his innate humility during a historic moment in the Sistine Chapel: the pope had dropped to his knees before Metropolitan Melitone of Constantinople, on a rare visit to Rome, and kissed his feet. And Dr. Michael Ramsey, then the archbishop of Canterbury, had been embraced like a brother on his visit to the Vatican. Such gestures were inspired by Paul's greatest triumph, the bringing to a successful conclusion of Vatican II. This was the pope Greenan will wish to eulogize in print. He is still contemplating the matter when the photographer makes his approach to Bertoli.

Quick as a flash, Greenan is out of his seat and, with a murmured "Excuse me, Eminence," Greenan plucks the newspaper from Bertoli's astonished grasp. Greenan folds the paper to hide the large photo he suspects has galvanized the photographer into action. It is one of Benelli. Above it is the headline "THE NEXT POPE?"

Bertoli smiles tightly. The last thing Bertoli would wish, Greenan suspects, is to be photographed staring at a picture of his old enemy—and undoubtedly a rival in the coming conclave. His good deed for the day done, Greenan sits back and continues planning his commemoration issue on Paul.

Aboard an Austrian Airlines jet converging on Rome, König is also considering the prospects for conclave. He sees himself as something of a veteran, one of the only eleven cardinals still living who attended the 1963 conclave which elected Paul. König has already issued his judgment on the third pope he has served; he remembers Paul as a genuinely holy man whose pontificate set the Church firmly on course toward the next century: no matter who succeeds him, much of what Paul did cannot easily be undone. There are no surprises in König's verdict. Nobody expected there would be. Some, though, are already interpreting König's words as an indication that he will not resist any serious attempt to promote him to the papacy.

Even as the plane is completing its seventy-minute flight from Vienna, speculators have been busy trying to stand up this prospect. They point out that in the last few years König has done a great deal of traveling, presuming he has done so in order that other cardinals may come to know him better; it helps to be a familiar face around conclave. But many cardinals have been traveling lately. The speculators therefore look for another clue. Back in 1975, Sebastiano Baggio and König each wrote articles in support of Opus Dei. Now that *is* interesting. Opus Dei is a right-wing semisecret secular society founded in Spain which wields huge background power in the Church. It is not the sort of fellow traveler in whose company the liberal König would normally be expected to be found; the same can be said of Baggio. Unless, of course, three years ago, both were even then laying the ground for the next papal election. For Opus Dei is a firm favorite with Cardinal Pericle Felici, the influential sixty-seven-year-old prefect of the Supreme Tribunal of the Apostolic Signatura, the person whom Paul placed in charge of settling intracurial disputes but whom many have come to see as the curial cardinal determined to undo many of the progressive initiatives begun by the Second Vatican Council. He fervently follows his passion for filming, shooting sequences which he plays back on one of the few video recorders in the Vatican; the bull-necked Felici, with a Roman Emperor's head and a huge, imperious nose, can sniff out the first whiff of anything faintly liberalizing.

He seems, at first glance, an unlikely person to support König. But, say the experts, the times they are a-changin'. Felici may be better off endorsing König—or, less likely, Baggio, for the two men dislike each other—in the hope that when his man is elected, he will remember who helped put him there. That's how the theory goes. The supposition does not take into account König's own great strength of character and his well-known individualism; it is more likely that if he became pope he would be nobody's man. Popes have a habit of turning out like that. But in the conclave stakes which have now been declared open, few take account of such trifles. The name of the game is to float stories and watch how they develop. It's a time-honored tradition and one the experienced König recognizes.

Sipping coffee with Viennese cookies, aware that everyone on board knows the purpose of his journey, the cardinal archbishop is careful to say nothing to anybody which might indicate what he himself thinks about the future.

At eleven o'clock on this sweltering Monday in Rome, nineteen cardinals, the majority of whom are permanently based in the city, assemble in the Sala Bologna on the third floor of the Apostolic Palace. Several are over eighty, including Carlo Confalonieri, who most people cannot believe is actually eighty-five. The dean of the College of Cardinals doesn't look a day over seventy. He thinks it nonsense that Paul's *Romano Pontifici Eligendo*—the matrix for the next conclave—should bar any cardinal over eighty from voting.

Confalonieri, as tradition demands, takes the chair at this, the first of the general congregations, preconclave meetings when, during the interregnum, the assembled cardinals direct the day-to-day running of the Church. On this occasion they must also decide the funeral arrangements.

It is Villot who quickly takes charge. He is one of the few curial cardinals still holding office. Paul's *Eligendo* demands that most cardinals in charge of departments must automatically resign on the death of a pope so that his successor may have a free hand over whom he appoints. In the *sede vacante*, the period between popes, Villot is the official keeper of the Keys of St. Peter. He is now both secretary of state and camerlengo, only the second person this century to combine the two functions. The first was Eugenio Pacelli in 1939. He became Pius XII. The coincidence is sufficient for Villot's name to be touted as a candidate by all those Vaticanologists who would dearly love to know what is happening in this salon with its frescoes and obligatory wooden crucifix on one wall.

The decisions are few. The funeral is set for Saturday, August 12, five days hence. There would then follow *Novemdiales*, nine days of mourning. Conclave will not actually begin until Friday, August 25, eighteen days away, the latest possible date allowed by Paul's *Eligendo*. Villot reports he has sealed all the palaces he is supposed to seal. He reminds them the next meeting will be the same time tomorrow. This one has lasted a mere ten minutes.

The starting date for conclave decided by these nineteen cardinals and binding on each cardinal elector will produce a welter of criticism, exhortation and raise speculation to fever pitch. But not yet.

Everybody on the outside is presently more puzzled why there are to be six full days between Paul's death and the moment he is placed in his tomb. It's not because that long is required for all the cardinals to reach Rome or for the statesmen of the world to fly in. If necessary they could almost all be here in the next forty-eight hours. Accordingly, somebody starts the story—which spreads like wildfire—that Villot has made his first mistake as camerlengo, that he wants to spin out his moment of glory and preside over the longest papal wake anyone can remember. What else is to be expected, shrug the cynical Romans, from a foreigner—and a Frenchman at that?

It is just the right level of bitchiness to get everybody talking. There's only one thing better than a papal funeral: one with a living scapegoat to mock. The hapless Villot fits the bill perfectly.

Shortly before noon at Castel Gandolfo, Giacomina leads her nuns into Paul's bedroom. They stand around the bed, the only sound the clicking of their rosaries and their prayers.

Paul is covered by a sheet. The drapes are drawn. A powerful fan plays across the room. After one final look, the nuns leave. Giacomina is the last to go. Even so she wants to be away from here well before what will begin to occur in this room at nine-forty tonight—the earliest possible moment under Italian law it can happen. She prefers to remember Paul as she now sees him, a man at peace at last. This is the way Giacomina has been raised to believe a pope should look when he dies.

But Paul must soon become a subject for that very American illusion—making the dead appear approximately alive.

At Dublin Airport, Archbishop Alibrandi looks searchingly into the face of a fellow priest whom he is seeing off on a flight to Rome, already seriously delayed through a strike by French air traffic controllers which has plunged Europe into chaos. Yet Alibrandi's houseguest for the past two weeks, Cardinal Salvatore Pappalardo, remains calm and relaxed. Surely this is another good sign, muses Alibrandi happily. But then there are so many positive things about his fellow Sicilian, the sixty-year-old archbishop of Palermo, to give substance to the scenario the nuncio sees as a distinct possibility. Indeed Pappalardo's entire career is perfect for what Alibrandi envisages. As a seasoned papal diplomat, Pappalardo knows almost all there is to know about the ways and wiles of the Secretariat of State; as former president of the Pontifical Ecclesiastical Academy in Rome, where future Holy See diplomats are trained, he has closely observed the crafty ways of the Curia. And in his pastoral work in Palermo, he continues to perform brilliantly: he fights municipal corruption, helps the poor, stays out of party politics, faces up to the Mafia, denounces anything which smacks of chicanery. Further, Pappalardo is physically strong, cultured, well traveled and absolutely middle-of-the-road in matters of Church dogma. Behind his youthful smile is an iron will. All in

all, Alibrandi believes the next time he sees his closest friend he will happily
kneel and kiss the Fisherman's Ring on Pappalardo's finger—symbolizing acknowledgment that he is the new pope.

During the last sixteen hours, between a brief sleep and planning all else
he must do, Alibrandi's thoughts have constantly dwelt on this exciting idea.
Now, as Pappalardo's flight is finally called, the nuncio gives him one last appraising look. There is no doubt at all: Pappalardo would appear very fine in
papal vestments; he already has the face plus that special aura of authority
and humility which goes with the position.

Driving back from the airport across the city whose newspapers carry pages
of obituaries on Paul, Alibrandi wonders how long it will be before the same
newspapers may be heralding the election of his friend. Yet even the euphoric
nuncio does not minimize the obstacles Pappalardo must overcome. There has
not been a Sicilian pope for over a thousand years. And, like most Italians,
those in the Curia might not easily accept any change in that situation;
there's a degree of racism behind many Italians' thinking. But Alibrandi
remains quietly confident that if anybody can alter this attitude it will be
Pappalardo.

His election could only enhance the career of the nuncio. Alibrandi might
reasonably expect to be made a cardinal, plucked from the turmoil of Irish
politics and brought to Rome to be at the very center of things. It is a prospect heady enough to give added dash to the nuncio's great pleasure, driving.
He speeds on his way, deftly moving in and out of the traffic, almost tingling
with expectation at what the future could hold.

Quickly settling into Rome, absorbing all those sounds and mores which,
Vienna apart, make it one of the most agreeable cities König knows, the cardinal archbishop begins to evaluate the situation. It is more or less what he
expected. Some good judgments on Paul are surfacing. He is emerging not
only as the most-traveled pope in history—even König has to pause to
remember it really was twenty-three pilgrimages in all—but as the pontiff
who contributed a "remarkable corpus of thought" to his times. People are beginning to realize his pontificate was altogether broader and more complicated
than that of a mere social critic and philosopher: he may yet emerge as among
the most intellectually accomplished of world leaders in the past twenty-five
years. Paul had the vision that all roads lead to Rome; through his diplomatic
ties he was more aware of the important trends than almost any other major
modern leader. In a way Paul knew too much rather than too little. He is perceived by his proponents—and König is glad they are at last having their day
—as the man who encouraged the world in its hopes. And now the world is
being reminded of the multitude of milestones along Paul's long road. He

abolished the traditional abstinence from meat on Fridays. He nullified the notorious Index of Prohibited Books, which had included the works of Victor Hugo and Voltaire. He ensured that mass could be celebrated in as many languages as there are people to speak them. He warned that rich nations must share their wealth with impoverished ones or risk "the judgment of God and the wrath of the poor." Now, in death, Paul is being seen as an open-minded conservative guiding a radical reformation; not many reformers have been so hesitant, not many conservatives have wrought such far-reaching change.

It is a verdict König cannot fault. He wishes, though, he could feel the same about the rumors. People, some of whom he thinks should know better, are saying factions have started to form, that groundwork more appropriate to the secular world is already starting to influence the Holy Spirit in deciding the outcome of conclave. In other words the politicking has started. So they say.

König cannot abide this sort of talk. He regards it as demeaning both to the memory of Paul and the serious business of choosing his successor. König also senses how things will develop: every time a pair of cardinals are spotted together it is going to be presented as the makings of a plot.

Yet, he must admit, some cardinals don't discourage speculation. In Florence, Benelli has been telling a radio audience that Villot "had purely formal relations with the Holy Father while I saw him every day," just the sort of words to get the secular press pot bubbling. And of course there is friction: 120 cardinals can't all be expected to like each other; of course there will be dinner parties, very private ones, where the mix of Church guests will be as carefully chosen as any intimate gathering planned by a Parisian or Washington hostess; of course the first table reservations are being made at L'Eau Vive, an agreeable French-cuisine restaurant behind the Pantheon, reportedly one of the places where cardinals like to "consult"—the only sort of lobbying officially permitted under Paul's *Eligendo*. But does it all add up to an orchestrated campaign for the papacy like the contest for the U.S. presidency? Of course not—not in König's view. And he does not wish to get into the semantics of where consultation stops and wheeling and dealing begins.

If there is an answer to that, it doesn't interest König. He has already decided on his opening strategy. He is going to be very careful in whose company he dines. And at all times he will keep his own counsel, listen a great deal and then, in the privacy of his own room in one of the Vatican colleges, he will prepare his next moves.

There is, though, one thought he is prepared to share with others. Having studied the list, surveyed the form, looked at the possible runners, considered their track record, assessed the odds, the cardinal archbishop, not normally a betting man, has a tip: the race is wide open.

Whether he intends it or not, that forecast is going to give rise to the very thing he abhors: further speculation.[4]

Late in the afternoon, seventy-four-year-old Renato Zottich packs five bottles of embalming fluid into a carton at the head office of Zega and Company, Rome's largest funeral establishment. It is not the sort of work the gregarious Egyptian-born professor of mechanics normally does; he is in charge of Zega's fleet of hearses and funeral cars. But Armando Zega himself has entrusted Zottich with this "very special mission," carrying out instructions personally ordered by Villot. The bottles of pinkish chemicals have been imported from the Epic Corporation of America. Zottich has been warned by the Vatican that under no circumstances must the company be informed its chemical was used. Villot is concerned that Epic might use the information to promote their product.

Zottich checks the typewritten cards he has prepared. They contain precise details of how the Epic preparations are to be used. He seals the cards in a company envelope with its distinctive logo—a bold Z on a red background—places the envelope on top of the bottles and Scotch-tapes the carton. He then checks a second package. It contains a huge hypodermic syringe capable of holding half a pint of fluid. He reseals this carton and hands both boxes to a company employee. In keeping with the extraordinary secrecy surrounding the entire operation, the man, at the Vatican's insistence, is only "the Technician."

As with most of Italy, the Vatican is divided on the question of embalming. Zega and Company provide the service mainly for Americans who die in Italy and whose remains are to be shipped home. Few Italians like the idea of their loved ones undergoing the process.

Zottich was surprised and delighted when Zega was contacted by Villot's office and told that Paul was to be embalmed—the decision to do so was taken because of the length of time his body would be on public display—and that the firm should provide "all technical requirements." Zottich feels that in gossipy Rome Zega and Company's role will soon be an open secret; this might encourage others to use the process at five hundred thousand lire a corpse. There is no question of charging the Vatican: Zottich sees "the honor and potential" as beyond recompense.

He tells the Technician the instruction cards must be faithfully followed. The man drives to Castel Gandolfo with Zottich's words in his mind: "No mistakes, Zega and Company depend on you." His van is loaded with equipment which includes a range of ingenious aids to prop and keep a cadaver in place on a catafalque.

The Technician carries the accoutrements in through a side door of the Papal Palace; Fontana and his assistant, Dr. Renato Buzzonetti, escort him to the pope's bedroom. They lay out the equipment and the two doctors study the instruction cards. Fontana and Buzzonetti have only limited experience of embalming procedures, but these seem clear enough. Nothing more can be done before 9:40 P.M.: Italian law insists that even for a pope there must be a twenty-four-hour interval between the moment of death and the onset of embalming to ensure that a person is "medically and legally" dead.

Only when that formality is satisfied do the two doctors and the Technician get to work. They drain all Paul's body fluids. Then they inject a succession of embalming fluids into the corpse. The chemicals harden all the organs and give the skin a firm, pinkish texture. The process takes two hours.

Close to midnight Monsignor Virgilio Noé, papal master of ceremonies, enters the room. Noé carries a silver urn which he has removed from a cabinet under the Altar of the Confession, which itself stands over the tomb of St. Peter in the Vatican Basilica. Noé placed the urn there on June 28, the eve of the Feast of Sts. Paul and Peter. It was one of the ceremonial high spots of his year, the papal blessing of the pallium repositing in the urn. Made from the wool of two lambs—suggesting Christ, the Lamb of God and the Good Shepherd—the pallium was fashioned by Benedictine sisters of St. Cecilia in their convent in the salubrious suburb of Trastévere just beyond the Vatican walls.

Noé now places the urn by the bedside. Then, with the help of the two doctors, he dresses Paul in full pontifical vestments. Noé goes to the door and summons a detachment of Swiss Guards. They enter carring the catafalque. The pope's body is maneuvered into place on the bier. The silent procession then slowly makes its way to the ground-floor Hall of the Swiss Guard. The catafalque is placed in the center of the large salon. The Technician adjusts the rubber neck support and shoulder blocks which help hold the body in position. Noé motions everyone away while he makes the final arrangements to the vestments. Then, with infinite care, he lifts the pallium from the urn and drapes the circular two-inch band of white wool around Paul's neck, arranging it over the chasuble so that the pallium's six black crosses repose above his breast, shoulders and abdomen. Noé kneels for a moment in prayer beside the bier before walking slowly from the hall. As he does so the four-man Swiss honor guard takes up its position, one at each corner of the catafalque. From now until Paul is finally laid to rest, the Swiss Guards will be in constant attendance.

X

In the next four days Rome became the focus of world attention. Nearly all the cardinals had arrived by Wednesday, August 9, when in the evening Paul's body was conveyed by road from Castel Gandolfo to lie in state in St. Peter's. Over a hundred million watched the occasion on television. The endless tributes continued to be published. Still more came as the statesmen of the world arrived to pay their last respects. The Vatican Press Office was under constant siege by thousands of journalists, many of whom complained about the poor arrangements for the media. Among them was Andrew Greeley and the team from CREP. The organization had produced a book, *The Inner Elite,* which supposedly indicated the "mind-set" of the cardinals who would vote in the coming conclave. That very experienced Vatican observer Peter Hebblethwaite noted that the slim volume was "riddled with errors, misleading statements and faulty deductions." But it had sold out by Friday, when Rosalynn Carter and Senator Edward Kennedy made a late but opportune appearance. They got almost as much air time as Paul's will, which the Vatican released in time for the evening television news. The thirteen-page document confirmed the essential goodness and simplicity of the man. It ended with Paul's request for a simple funeral and a plea for pardon from all those he had harmed.

XI

Saturday's dawn reddens the sky, warning of another fiercely hot and humid day, as Macchi enters the Vatican by the tradesmen's entrance—the Porta Sant'Anna. It is symbolic of his new status. The former senior secretary is now just another priest, divested of the power to make or break a man's career. The Swiss Guards still salute him, but they need no longer fear he might find some small fault with their appearance as he has done in the past.

This morning Macchi is too preoccupied to notice how burnished are the guards' boots or how clean are their hands. His mind is on the days which have gone and the task ahead. The past week has etched haggard lines into his imperious face, leaving his eyes black-rimmed from exhaustion and grief. Macchi has hardly slept since Villot ordered him to find Paul's Fisherman's Ring. When he had done so the camerlengo brusquely ordered Macchi to deliver the ring to the Sala Bologna. There, before the assembled cardinals, Villot split the ring with silver shears and shattered Paul's seals of office with the same hammer he had used to tap the forehead of the dead pope.

That was on Wednesday. By then Macchi was in temporary accommodation, living in one of the poky rooms the Vatican always has available around Rome. He had hardly visited it. Instead, by special permission of Villot and under the express terms of Paul's will, the secretary worked from dawn to midnight, when the closing of the Vatican gates drove him out, alone in the papal apartment.

Paul had appointed Macchi executor of his will. The handwritten document, surmounted by the papal coat of arms, was drawn up on July 30, 1965. Macchi could clearly remember the occasion. He had sat with Paul while the pope began to write: "Some notes for my will. In the name of the Father and of the Son and of the Holy Spirit. Amen." The long list of clauses did not read like a last testament. They were more the thoughts of a man who, in that, the third year of his pontificate, was already preoccupied with death. Paul wanted to die *un povero*, a poor man. He wished his funeral to be "pious and simple." He requested no monument over his grave. "Now that the day draws to its close and everything comes to an end and I must leave

this wonderful and turbulent world, I thank you, Lord." Buried in the will is
the reason Macchi has been toiling these past two days in the eerie silence of
the apartment he knows so well. Paul specially ordered in a codicil that
Macchi destroy all personal notes and correspondence. Macchi has been surprised to discover how great is the accumulation. The papers fill a stack of
boxes. Unlike Paul's official papers, which will go to the Secret Archives,
these private ones must remain undisclosed forever. They do not include the
batch of confidential reports on Cody. Villot has confiscated these, telling
Macchi they must be handed to the next pope. The camerlengo regards them
as a time bomb, capable not only of destroying Cody, but also of rending
asunder the Church.[1]

Macchi reaches the San Damaso Courtyard where two Vigilance men
wait with the boxes loaded on a trolley. The cartons have been guarded overnight in the old Vatican jail. In silence the security men follow Macchi to an
elevator. It takes them to the third-floor warren of the Secretariat of State.
There is nobody about at this early hour, which is why Macchi has chosen
this time. The Vigilance men wheel the trolley to a small room. It contains a
large shredding machine. Macchi begins to feed in the very intimate thoughts
of Paul; they come out the other end as unintelligible strips of paper. Even
then Macchi is not satisfied. He orders the Vigilance men to pack the waste
into plastic sacks and have it burned.

Then the secretary leaves the Apostolic Palace for the last time. Now he
has only one further act to perform. He slips through a side door and enters
the vast nave of St. Peter's Basilica. His shoes echoing on the stone floor,
Macchi moves purposefully past some of the twenty-nine altars, the 148
colonnades, the statue of St. Peter whose right foot gleams from constant kissing by the faithful, the huge throne in the tribune with its ancient wooden
chair said to have been sat on by the Apostle, the black-and-gold monument
to Urban VIII teeming with the Berberini bees, the Virgin and Christ, the
"Pietà"—past centuries of work by artisans of every skill. He eventually
stops before the simple bier built by the *sampietrini* in their workshops
behind St. Peter's; they have also constructed the triple papal coffin—the
inner is made of bronze, the second of cedar and the outer coffin is of cypress,
the latter to symbolize the simplicity Paul has requested.

Paul lies in a red vestment over his white garments. The pallium Noé positioned with such loving care is precisely in place. A solitary Easter candle
burns with a steady flame in the still air. The four Swiss Guards stand motionless.

Apart from them there is nobody to see Macchi kneel beside the bier and
pray in silent farewell. Close to tears, he rises and walks slowly out of the basilica, his mind settled. Even if asked, he will not work for the next pope. In-

stead he will take up pastoral duties. It is, Macchi feels, the best tribute he can pay to the memory of the man he loved and revered more than any other.

Greeley has concluded that Paul's lying in state reminds him of "the King Tut exhibit in Chicago." When he viewed the pope's body on Thursday, it appeared to him "very purple and pasty and corpselike"; the passing crowds, muses Greeley, showed "lots of curiosity, but no sign of mourning or grief." His latest observations are added to the ragbag of impressions Greeley has gathered since arriving in Rome. It's been a busy time: some "quick interviews" with those tantalizingly anonymous sources of his; a culling of the Italian media: the news magazines have all been quick off the mark but Greeley thinks it poor taste the way *Gente, Epoca, Oggi* and *Panorama* placed their papal obituaries cheek-by-jowl with more normal fodder—sexual confessions, nude photographs and autoeroticism. He has been sniffing around the cardinals and come to the conclusion that the secrecy, the ban on explicit campaigning and the protocol which forbids cardinals divulging their real differences are all going to affect their decision making.

Greeley's mysterious sources have served him well. Yet he is not happy. In fact, he admits: "I'm afraid I'm going to pieces. I've lost my glasses, I've walked out of the hotel without my wallet, I've forgotten phone numbers, and am in mortal terror of missing appointments." It's nerves, of course, brought on by the thought that tomorrow, Sunday, he is going to publicly unveil his personally conceived, nurtured and so far jealously guarded blinding revelation: just what kind of pope the cardinals should choose if they wish to stay in good standing with Greeley.

One prince of the Church already knows Greeley's intentions. Long ago Cardinal John Cody found it expedient to add the name of the onetime priest in his diocese to the list of those of whom he likes to keep track. Cody sees nothing sinister in this. Greeley is a declared foe and the cardinal thinks it would be foolish not to keep abreast of an opponent's thinking. It is the way he has always operated and it has helped to make him what he is: the most powerful religious leader Chicago has ever had. Cody has seen the likes of Greeley come and go, yet for Cody the priest remains one more prick from his crown of thorns. The cardinal is already savoring the moment he will be asked to comment on CREP's proposals. That may well be the time for Cody to launch a carefully staged counterattack against the insidious smears and aspersions which surround him. No reference to those accusations, naturally, just a short statement indicating that CREP and its cohorts are trying to trivialize the Church. That will be enough. People can always read between the lines.

In any case, nobody but Cody knows the truth behind the accusations, and he has chosen—whether on advice or by personal decision even his closest associates cannot be certain—to maintain total silence in face of the mounting storm. He knows reporters say he's trying to ride it out, that he is behaving like a maddened bull at the Chicago stockyards, almost demanding to be slaughtered at the first opportunity. This does not disturb Cody. People can go on complaining about him to Rome as long as they like, the Vatican can send as many emissaries as it wishes; Cody knows, in the end, there is little anyone can do. To sack him outright would create a scandal which could rip through the American Church, perhaps even cause a few figures to fall in the Vatican. This, too, he knows. So he's going to continue playing it his way. Greeley and his ilk, Cody is convinced, will simply run out of steam. The cardinal has seen it happen before. And, besides, he is a master of the waiting game.

This Saturday morning Cody rises early in his private room in the palatial Villa Stritch, perhaps the finest in a row of fine mansions on the Via della Nocetta. He has slept soundly, shows no sign of jet lag and, since getting up, has been making telephone calls to his network of friends in the Vatican. He has sources in all the right places. With each one he gossips a bit, laughs a little, listens a lot. In a surprisingly short time he has a picture of what is happening. The funeral arrangements do not concern him: he assumes Villot and his functionaries have planned them down to the last amen.

Cody is interested in conclave. He assures a friend in the Irish College out on Via Santa Quattro and traditionally a clearinghouse for such scuttlebutt, that the Americans want a Pope "in the image of Paul," but preferably a non-Italian European who is "definitely not curial." Cody's Irish contact suggests Hume of Westminster as a possibility. The cardinal asks whether his English colleague can speak Italian yet. Hardly a word. Certainly not fluently. Then, pronounces Cody, Hume has no chance: the Italians would never tolerate a bishop of Rome who cannot speak their language. Does his Irish source know of any cardinal who has been taking a crash course in Italian? No, but he'll ask around.

More calls by Cody—who sees them all as the permissible "consultation" allowed under Paul's rules—and he learns there is mounting concern among many of the non-Italian cardinals about the long delay before conclave has been scheduled to start. It's the Italians up to their old tricks, Cody is told, wanting to do what they are best at, preparing their ground at a leisurely pace before conclave begins. Cody can interpret this two ways. It is just the Italians being Italian. Or the Curia thinks it has a potential deadlock on whom it wants to see succeed Paul; if that is the case, those in the Curia need all the time possible to do some very hard "consulting" before the cardinals are locked up.

Cody calls Prefect Martin—with whom when in Rome he likes to mull over Vatican history and also gain some shrewd insights into how the immediate papal family is coping—and he says he favors the view that the Curia may be alarmed. They go on to speak of Cardinal Leo Suenens' recent revolutionary suggestion, the one Vatican Radio reported with the sort of raised inflection which mirrored the shock wave felt throughout the Holy See at the Belgian's proposal, that this time no fewer than four popes should be elected, one to be stationed in each quarter of the globe. Coming from anybody else the thought would have caused an even bigger reaction, but people are becoming used to hearing Suenens' radical ideas. He has also suggested the pope should no longer be chosen only by cardinals who, in any case, have no justification in Scripture, but by a body more representative of the entire Church. Cody considers Suenens' opinions immaterial, especially as he has ceased to be one of the driving forces in that faction the press have come to call "European progressives." Its members include König, Willebrands of Utrecht and François Marty of Paris. Suenens is said to have lost interest in their ideals since becoming an influential member of the charismatic movement. And König himself has just made it clear, though not publicly, that he thinks he is too old to allow his name to go forward as a potential future pope.

Still more calls and Cody gets another slant on how the future could go: while he was flying the Atlantic, Sin, Hume and Lorscheider were having the first of what will become regular meetings—either in the English College or in Lorscheider's room in the Latin American College—to see whether a loose coalition might be formed which would combine the voting power of South and Central America, the Caribbean, Asia and Africa. It could be a very powerful bloc. But who should get its vote in the crucial first ballot? Not even Martin is prepared to go that far.

Within a few hours of arriving in Rome Cody knows more than most curial cardinals about how the land really lies. He likes the look of it. It seems there will be some good old-fashioned politicking ahead—all in the name of "consultation," naturally.

At noon the doors of the basilica close behind the last of an estimated 250,000 persons who have filed past Paul's bier. Outside in St. Peter's Square, on the balustrades of Bernini's colonnade, cameras of Italian television are positioned among the 162 baroque statues of saints. The cameramen rehearse their shots. One pans across the frieze under the drum of the basilica where Latin letters six feet high proclaim: "Thou art Peter and upon this rock I will build my Church and to thee I will give the Keys of the Kingdom of Heaven." Another camera focuses on the great dome of St. Peter's. A third looks down on the square itself where squads of *sampietrini* are setting out over nine thousand seats for the first outdoor funeral in the history of the papacy. A group of Americans have occupied some of the seats, bringing with them a cooler of soft drinks. On the marble steps of St. Peter's, velvet-covered kneelers and chairs are placed for dignitaries of the Church and the secular world. The first of nearly ten thousand City of Rome police, carabinieri and squads of DIGOS, the antiterrorist force, are in position. If the expected crowds materialize, there will be one policeman for every ten mourners. Though street vendors are barred for the day from the square, souvenir shops along the Via della Conciliazione are packed; any fake artifact connected with Paul is snapped up. More Pauline junk mementos have probably been sold during the last five days than in the previous four years of his pontificate.

Elsewhere in the city, U.S. senator Edward Kennedy of Massachusetts places a bouquet on the spot at the street corner where Aldo Moro was kidnapped and then stands silently for two minutes. The only sound is the click and whirr of still and film cameras and the nervous shuffling of the large police detail protecting Kennedy. At the American Embassy Mrs. Carter talks to a CBS correspondent about her impressions and describes how the president's mother, Miss Lillian, prayed for rain in drought-stricken Africa when she visited Paul at Castel Gandolfo, and how the pope told her he would die very soon.

It all seems so irrelevant.

Walking briskly, his soutane swishing softly in rhythm with his stride, Magee enters the Vatican through the Arch of the Bells and on into St. Peter's through a side door. It is pleasantly cool inside the transept, and the barley-sugar columns of Bernini's baldacchino, each ninety-five feet high, soar upward toward the sixteen windows in the dome which filter the fierce sun and give a soft, almost surreal light to the scene Magee has come to observe.

He has no official responsibility here. That is in the hands of Villot and Noé. The secretary is present because, like Macchi, Magee wishes to say a personal farewell to the man who most shaped his life. Outwardly, Magee is not an emotional or sentimental person. But the death of Paul, though he had expected it, has drained him. His is a deeply felt wrench and only his faith has been able to sustain him in genuine grief. Unlike so many who hardly knew the pope, Magee does not choose publicly to share his judgment of the man; it is something too private, this feeling that the world has lost a living saint.

At a nod from Villot, the *sediarii*, who carried Paul on his portable throne throughout his pontificate, now lift his body off the bier and place it in the coffin. One of them drapes an ermine-colored blanket over his body and covers the pope's face with a purple veil. Then the lid of the coffin is positioned and held in place by sixteen solid-gold screws specially made in the Vatican workshops.

Magee turns and walks slowly from the basilica. He does not know what his future will be. He does not much care. Besides, it is much too early to think of such things.

The cardinal who has built his reputation by trying to think of everything, Baggio, troubleshooter by appointment to Paul, arrives in the early afternoon by car outside the imposing portico of the Sacred Congregation for Bishops, whose prefect he has been for five years, and hurries into the building. He has been spotted, of course; there is hardly a cardinal who can now safely move in the city without being observed by one of the tipsters who feed the army of reporters tidbits. And there are any number of good reasons for them to be interested in this squat, muscular man with a wrestler's broad shoulders and hands. Baggio is sixty-five and definitely *papabile*, a candidate for the papacy. He is also perfectly cast to play the role of pope maker. He knows well everybody who matters, the majority of his fellow cardinals and all the most important bishops of the Church: he knows what they think, what they feel about each other; he knows their fears, ambitions, wishes, and often their private desires. Acquiring such secrets is all part of his work as prefect. Nobody wants to be on the wrong side of Baggio. That is why he is so respected and courted.

Until now he has not been seen by the secular world since news leaked about his secret visit to Cody. But lurking in the corner of the Square of Pius XII the Savior of the City, dedicated to that pope's intercession to save Rome from being seriously bombed during World War II, the informer observes that Baggio is carrying a bulky briefcase. There is nothing unusual in this as Baggio is famous for taking with him wherever he goes the most secret papers he is working on; as part of his security system he also never receives visitors in his office for fear they might see a confidential document momentarily removed from the safe behind his desk.

Yet in spite of these measures there is a mole in his ministry—as there are in so many Congregations—who, for money, regularly betrays some of the secrets Baggio labors to protect. And so, by this unsavory route, details surface about the latest contents of Baggio's briefcase.

It is more pay dirt on Cody. There are new and potentially explosive allegations about the long relationship the Chicago cardinal has had with Helen Dolan Wilson, a sixty-eight-year-old divorcee who, since at least 1967, has been a close companion of Cody's. He even brought her to Rome when he was made cardinal. The precise nature of their relationship has produced just the sort of speculation Baggio dreads. Cody and Mrs. Wilson constantly claim they are cousins. But Baggio now knows, after some discreet digging in Chicago—he has relatives in nearby Oak Park—the couple are only distantly related through the remarriage of Mrs. Wilson's father to Cody's aunt. And

Mrs. Wilson has listed Cody's residence as her summer address. Worse, Cody arranged, when he was in St. Louis, for Mrs. Wilson to draw $11,500 a year from the archdiocese; there is no evidence she did much work for this stipend. Finally there is the allegation that Cody is diverting church funds into the private account of Mrs. Wilson; it is rumored that as much as a million dollars has gone in this way.

Nobody outside the Vatican knows whether Baggio put these charges to Cody when they met in Chicago. But they do exist. Yet for the moment Baggio must keep them in limbo. Baggio is many things: aggressive, witty, charming, uncompromising, cheerful and enlightened; he knows all about the "human aspect" of life. Even so, this "Chicago affair" may be something else. He is sure the problem will not go away. It will be carried over into the next pontificate.

And that raises a question not even the prescient Baggio can possibly answer: How will the next pontiff react? Will he weigh it all against the wider effect the removal of Cody could have on the American Church as a whole? A scandal of this nature would assuredly draw worldwide publicity; the harm to the Universal Church could be incalculable. Might the decision be taken not to pursue the matter further? Holy See scandals have been hushed up before. Is this why Baggio, when he leaves the building and is driven off to prepare for Paul's funeral, has a deeply troubled look on his face?

These questions help the rumor mills grind away in the last hours before the moment they, too, must fall silent in face of the awesome ceremony in St. Peter's Square.

Vatican Radio's MacCarthy is one of a couple of hundred broadcasters working the square. Dressed in a black suit and Roman collar, toting a tape recorder, MacCarthy is slowly moving through the crowd gathering impressions, comments and assessments. He is tired, understandably so. Few broadcasters have made such an effort to immerse themselves in the action of the past week. MacCarthy has read almost everything available on papal wakes and funerals; he has found the work of his friend Lambert Greenan in the English-language edition of *L'Osservatore Romano* most helpful. Greenan has just published a caring and authoritative account of Paul's life and times. Commentators around the square are quoting the obituary.[2]

MacCarthy is preparing a pastiche of this climactic day so listeners down through Africa to the Cape of Good Hope will have a feeling for the mood in the square. He describes the scene: "Perhaps as many as one hundred thousand persons, many dressed in black. But this is not merely a time of mourning. It is also a time for thoughtful consideration of the hope for eternal life. There is a mood of silent dignity."

He moves through the crowd toward the white-marble steps. Once more he

speaks into his microphone: "To all of us this scene is new. There has probably never been such an immense congregation for a Christian funeral. It is
another reminder of all His Holiness stood for. He had always sought to meet
his flock in the square on the great religious festivals of the year. He once
said, 'I will make this square an altar.' And so he has."

MacCarthy has now reached the edge of the steps leading up to the doors
of St. Peter's, open again. Away to his right he can see Rosalynn Carter and
Imelda Marcos, wife of the president of the Philippines. Edward Kennedy is
close by. Near him are the former archbishop of Canterbury, Dr. Michael
Ramsey, and the patriarch of Moscow. Around them are crowned heads of
Europe and statesmen of the world. Delegations from over one hundred nations are here. Others can describe their dress and try to interpret the whispers and smiles they exchange; MacCarthy is more concerned to place in perspective what is about to happen: "His Holiness requested in his will a simple
and pious funeral. That has been faithfully adhered to. There is to be no catafalque, nothing to raise his coffin to public view. Instead it will be laid on
the ground. It will be bare and unadorned, except for an open Bible. All this
is another reminder of His Holiness—his very real wish to reduce as far as
possible the symbols of pomp and power which used to characterize the papal
court."

Inside the basilica the procession forms up. The cardinals are paired off according to seniority. Near the front are the primate of Poland, Stefan Wyszynski, and Giuseppe Siri, each of whom has been a cardinal for a quarter of
a century. Close behind follow the Canadian archbishop of Montreal and the
patriarch of Alexandria in Egypt. König is paired with the archbishop of
Dar-es-Salaam. A little further back Cardinal John Carberry, the spunky
seventy-four-year-old archbishop of St. Louis, is close to the august figure of
John Krol, cardinal archbishop of Philadelphia. The lofty Krol and the
diminutive Carberry will make a striking physical contrast for the commentators to seize upon. Another American, Cardinal Terence Cooke of New
York is behind the solid-looking cardinal archbishop of Cracow in Poland,
Karol Wojtyla, whose halting English Cooke does not always find easy to follow. Timothy Manning, cardinal archbishop of Los Angeles, the only one in
the entire procession who speaks Gaelic—he was born in Ballingeary, County
Cork, sixty-nine years ago—is paired with the patriarch of Venice, Cardinal
Albino Luciani. Luciani bridges the conversational gaps with gentle little
smiles. Manning instinctively likes this Italian—which is more than he can
say for some of them. Cody is paired with Felici. They appear to have nothing to say to each other. If Cody's case ever reaches the stage where it must
officially be examined by the Church, Felici, in his capacity as prefect of the
Apostolic Signatura, the highest court of appeal in the Church, will have to

recommend judgment for the pope's final approval. Aramburu of Buenos Aires is beside Sin of Manila. They have come to know and like each other over the years. Aramburu cannot conceal his relief that Argentina's junta leader, Videla, decided at the last moment not to attend the funeral; he has said he may come to the inauguration of the next pope. But that is at least three weeks away. And in the stormy atmosphere of South American politics, anything can happen in the interval. Baggio and Bertoli make another pair. They are outwardly affable.

MacCarthy holds the microphone close to his lips to ensure that his words are not drowned by the singing: "The chair bearers are carrying Pope Paul's coffin down the steps and laying it directly in front of the altar. One of the many new features of this mass is that the cardinals will concelebrate it around the altar. Now they come. The last one, a tall, handsome man, is Cardinal Confalonieri. He will be the main celebrant in today's mass. He is wearing a slightly different-colored robe from the others. Theirs are purple. But his is a bright scarlet—the special color of his office as dean."

MacCarthy has just time to say that the mass proper is beginning when the amplified voice of Confalonieri intones the words of the Confiteor, the prayer for God to pardon the people of their sins and the sins of the Church.

During the brief pause which follows Bible readings in various languages, MacCarthy has time to explain that Confalonieri will next deliver the homily in Latin. MacCarthy lets the first flowing phrases roll before beginning faultlessly to translate them.

He describes the procession which brings bread and wine to the altar for consecration while the choir sings the offertory hymn, Psalm 17. The broadcaster then allows the actual sound of this very solemn moment of the mass speak for itself.

König has been standing almost two hours in heavy vestments in a temperature of over eighty degrees. He is a fit man, but he wonders what the heat is doing to some of the more elderly cardinals. It cannot be easy for them. Then, as the offertory procession returns to the altar, König notices something he will never forget: a gentle breeze has begun to ruffle the open Bible on Paul's coffin; slowly the pages begin to turn. König thinks it symbolic—almost as uncanny as when Paul's alarm clock rang the instant he died.

MacCarthy once more slips in a few sentences, to link the singing of the Litany of the Saints with the closing prayers and the slow procession of the cardinals past either side of the coffin. Then Confalonieri himself describes the final stage of the funeral. In halting English he explains: "The pope now enters for the last time the Vatican Basilica where so often he celebrated the

Eucharist and addressed his word to the Church. The remains of His Holiness will be laid to rest in the tomb in the Vatican crypt. There he will remain in the gentle presence of a Madonna gracefully sculpted by Donatello to await his resurrection in glory."

The moon is rising over the Janiculum Hill, picking out a line of cypress trees, as the choir sing the Magnificat and Paul's coffin, the pages of the Bible still slowly turning, is carried back up the steps to the tolling of the bells of St. Peter's.

Moments later the doors of the basilica are shut.

MacCarthy's microphone catches the sound. And around him the speculation is renewed: which of all the cardinals who have spent the past 159 minutes burying Paul will next emerge on the balcony above these doors as pope?

PART TWO

INS'ALLAH: THE WILL OF GOD.

If this is the way God ordained it,
so it must be

—OLD ARABIC SAYING

XII

T his, they will say, is how it was.

For six weeks Agca led a peaceful life, spending his days for the most part in the company of other men in the tearoom of Yesiltepe. They spoke about the Anarchy, the official executions, the reprisals. But nobody can remember Agca displaying any strong views on the terrorism infesting Turkey. He seemed to be a man apart.

At home he was cheerful, wrestling with Adnan and joking with Fatma that she must not eat so much if she wanted to keep her figure. He was a model elder brother. One day he delighted his mother, Muzzeyene, by returning home with two cooking pots. He planted them proudly on the table before her, grinning, but not saying how he came by them. His mother did not ask; she wished to do nothing to disturb the tranquil domestic atmosphere which had helped to make bearable the furnacelike heat of Malatya province in the middle of summer. That night she cooked him bean curd in one of the pots. He ate a double helping, and there was some gentle joshing from Fatma and Adnan about Agca's newfound appetite. Muzzeyene could not remember being more happy. Allah, she felt, was at last listening to all those prayers she had offered up to him.

And thus it continued until this Sunday evening.

Agca is not a television viewer; too many of the programs are imported from the America he hates, but he recognizes the pleasure some of them give to his mother and Fatma—they especially like soap operas—and so he tolerates the set in the corner of the living room. Normally, out of deference to his views, they wait until he leaves the house before turning it on and giggling over the antics of Lucy and Sergeant Bilko.

Tonight, though, Agca has decided to remain at home. Muzzeyene, sensitive to such matters, detects a familiar restlessness in her son; it is there in the way he abstractedly bites his lip and digs his fingers into the palm of his hands. She hopes it's just a passing phase and not the onset of another full-scale depression.

Thinking it might distract him, and knowing his interest in world events—or so he has often told her—she switches the set on for the late-evening news.

Flickering across the screen is a short clip of the funeral of Paul in Rome.

Agca's reaction even startles his mother. He leaps to his feet, switches off the set with a violence which threatens to topple it from its table, and stands facing his family, screaming. They do not understand his horrifying rage. He looks and sounds like a man possessed. Suddenly, he starts to howl like an animal. It is the call of the Gray Wolves. Still howling, he runs to his room.

None of them can remember ever seeing Agca behave like this. Both Adnan and Fatma are frightened by their brother's behavior. After a time Muzzeyene manages to calm them. By then the howling has died away. She moves to stand outside Agca's bedroom door. Now she can hear him steadily chanting. She is relieved. Agca is going through his hate list. Though she does not know the word, Muzzeyene feels it must be therapeutic for him.

Next morning, at the customary hour of four-thirty, she awakens, expecting to hear Agca reciting the first Koran prayer of the day. Instead, there is not a sound coming from his room.

She checks. During the night Agca has silently slipped away.

Muzzeyene is a practical woman; there is no point worrying where he has gone. He has done this before. On these occasions Muzzeyene has her own routine to follow. She enters his room to see what he has taken. The Mauser and bullets are no longer in the cigar box. This does not unduly disturb her. Her son always carries the weapon and ammunition on him when he leaves home. Muzzeyene does not like the idea, but she has come to accept he is entitled to protect himself; he lives in a violent world, she rationalizes, where it is often kill or be killed.

She checks whether anything else has been removed. Everything seems to be in order. She looks again at the shelf of books. Muzzeyene can hardly read or write, and it is a source of pride to her that Agca has more books on this shelf than are in all the other houses of Yesiltepe combined. She is careful not to touch them; she knows every book has its specially designated place in the collection. Only Agca knows why. If he were to discover she had been in his room during his absence, Muzzeyene feels it could destroy the close bond between them. She studies the spines of the books. They all seem in place. Yet she senses something is wrong. Muzzeyene counts the books, saying the numbers aloud, the way a child or a semiliterate counts.

There are none missing.

Her eyes continue to search the shelf. And then, at last, she realizes. The exercise book beneath the empty cigar box—the one filled with all those photographs and stories about the old holy man of the infidels who has just died—is no longer there.

Muzzeyene wonders why her son has taken it with him.[1]

XIII

She screams at Greeley that he is evil and has sexual problems. He responds that the data on sexual attitudes he has been discussing comes from "sample research," not personal experience. Inwardly he thinks having sexual problems is part of the human condition, but that this woman would surely never cause him any. She is "wild-eyed," young, Italian, and has "Catholic Action written all over her." She is also one of the two hundred or so journalists attending Greeley's press conference to unveil his "job description" of a pope. It is Greeley and CREP's big moment, and they are milking it for all its sociological worth, claiming that the job description is "a contribution of significance to the Church and the cardinal electors."

The reporters scribble furiously as Greeley advances that it does not matter whether the next pope is a curial cardinal or a noncurial cardinal, nor whether he is Italian or not, whether he is from the First, Second or Third World, whether he is an intellectual or a nonintellectual, a diplomat or a pastor, a progressive or a moderate, an efficient administrator or lacking in administrative experience, a "liberation" theologian or a traditional theologian, or how he regards the political issues facing the world.

Barely pausing for breath, in full talk-show stride, well aware of the headlines he is bound to attract, Greeley continues that "doubtless someone in the papal entourage must be an efficient administrator, someone must be a theologian, someone must be a diplomat, someone must be a pastor, someone must understand Italy, someone must be sensitive to the Third World, someone must know how the Roman Curia runs and how it can be brought under control"—a well-timed pause to see how that little broadside has gone over—and then on to the nub of his case: it is not necessary for the pope to have any of these abilities; men with such talents can be found to assist him, consequently they are not needed for the "top position in the Catholic Church."

Greeley has this knack of talking the language of the tabloids, of reducing some of the most complex issues of the religious world to a few pithy sentences. He delivers them. "At the present critical time in its history, faced with the most acute crisis, perhaps, since the Reformation and dealing with a world in which both faith and community are desperately sought, the papacy requires a man of holiness, a man of hope, a man of joy; a sociologically oriented job description of the pope, in other words, must conclude that the Catholic Church needs as its leader a holy man who can smile."

That screaming Italian reporter is not the only one at Greeley's throat. He is accused of trying to merchandise the pope, of attacking the Church, of attempting mass-media manipulation. He fights back, mentally labeling his attackers "pietists and paranoids." Insults are traded. Greeley, throwing caution completely to the wind, says he is not even against a woman pope. "A *papessa* could not make more of a mess of the Church than we men have over the last nineteen hundred years."

Inevitably, the attitude of American Catholics to *Humanae Vitae* is raised; it's a running sore everybody likes to pick. Greeley snaps that the fault lies with the Church: "If an organization fails to communicate, it must assume that *it* has failed, not that the *people* have failed." It's a good note to end on —and another headline for tomorrow. He leaves the press conference, the screams of the wild-eyed young Italian fixed firmly in his mind, convinced she and the rest of the Italian media "will murder us tomorrow; however, it doesn't make much difference."

Precisely. Greeley and CREP are up and running. It's the sort of stage managing even Cody, no slouch in such matters, must reluctantly admire. But Cody has decided, on reflection, that this is not the time to launch a counter-campaign against Greeley's attacks. He is going to ignore them.

Vatican Radio and *L'Osservatore Romano* disregard the wire service reports of Greeley's press conference. Nowadays staff on each of these Vatican organs, in addition to their usual work, are going about the delicate and difficult task of deciding who should be placed on a realistic short list of *papabili*. There are, by this Wednesday, August 16, any number of such lists on offer in Rome; one even presents the entire membership of the College of Cardinals, 130, ignoring the fact that fifteen have reached the age of eighty and are consequently barred from voting under Paul's *Eligendo*, three have not come to Rome due to ill health and one is seriously sick in the city after suffering a heart attack during Paul's funeral; it is highly unlikely any of these nineteen cardinals absent from conclave would be chosen as pontiff. The remaining 111 cardinal electors are now preparing for conclave.

It is from this number that Lambert Greenan is attempting to narrow the choice to a dozen or so names. Each editor in the other language sections of *L'Osservatore Romano* is doing the same. Later the names on these confidential lists will be compared and a final master list of most-favored possible popes drawn up. Special biographies will then be prepared on each cardinal chosen, and a portrait will be selected. An entire series of newspaper editions will be set in advance, each featuring a different candidate. When the name of the next pope is telephoned to *L'Osservatore Romano,* the correct plate will be locked onto the paper's presses and in minutes a special edition will be on sale in St. Peter's Square. That is the theory. The success of the operation depends entirely on accurate prediction at this early stage.

There are few better on the paper's staff for this job than Father Greenan. Long ago, during the days he worked in the Secretariat of State, Greenan learned the rules of Vatican secrecy; consequently, people trust him. They tell him all sorts of things they would never mention to others. He is a receptacle for information on the strengths and weaknesses of those he is now trying to assess.

Greenan looks first at the likeliest source for a new pope: the European cardinals. Fifty-seven of them are eligible to vote. He soon discounts a number of names. Frantisek Tomasek of Czechoslovakia is not only too old at seventy-eight but would also be too daring a choice. Paul made him a cardinal *in pectore,* secretly, not publicly revealing Tomasek's appointment for an entire year for fear of disturbing the delicate *Ostpolitik* of Casaroli. The Czechs have not liked that; they would resent even more Tomasek sitting on the Throne of St. Peter. Antonio Ribeiro, patriarch of Lisbon, is, at fifty, simply too young, even though his career suggests that in the 1990s, should there be a conclave, he could be a serious candidate: he was co-president of the 1977 Synod of Bishops and his fundamental theology is impeccable. For the reason Greenan ruled out Tomasek he now rejects Alfred Bengsch, bishop of West Berlin for the past seventeen years and an implacable opponent of the Wall and communism. Bengsch, muses Greenan, will probably end his days in the city he was born in and to which he returned after being wounded and captured by the Americans at Normandy in 1944, afterward becoming a priest and then cardinal in 1967.

There are four other German cardinals. The most powerful, without doubt, is the forbidding archbishop of Cologne, seventy-one-year-old Joseph Höffner. He is tough, acerbic and conservative; he learned his theology from Pius XII —nothing wrong with that, but is it what the Church now wants? Would the Americans go with such deeply traditional thinking? Höffner is involved —something the Vatican never likes—in fighting with Hans Küng. Küng, in Greenan's view, is wrong: he has a mandate from Rome to teach what Rome approves; that is the end of the matter. But for Höffner to pursue the fight publicly is something else. Greenan passes over Höffner to the next German.

Joseph Ratzinger, the fifty-one-year-old archbishop of Munich, has a career which bears the hallmark of a churchman going places. Almost single-handed, he revitalized the German Church in the postwar years, driving himself and others with uncharacteristic Bavarian energy. He recognized the real challenge lay with the youth: he taught dogmatic theology in Bonn, Münster, Tübingen and Regensburg. His classes were packed. It seemed only natural that Ratzinger should be a *peritus,* an expert adviser, to Vatican II. But there are problems. Ratzinger is not only young but speaks Italian with a thick German accent. He is also cast in the image of Paul—scholarly, reticent, hardly a charismatic figure. Yet Greenan puts a query against the Bavarian's name; he will look again at it later after he has reflected further.

Joseph Schröffer, the seventy-five-year-old West German curial cardinal, is a nonstarter; apart from the age factor Schröffer has been tucked away for much of his life in the Congregation for Catholic Education; important work, certainly, but a post which doesn't offer the breadth of experience a pope ideally needs. Hermann Volk, bishop of Mainz, is seventy-four, and unless Greenan is seriously mistaken, conclave will not be looking for a caretaker pope who will simply keep the Throne of St. Peter warm for a few years while some of the younger cardinals establish their worth.

The Spanish have four cardinals. A very definite possibility is the shrewd and personable archbishop of Madrid, Vicente Enrique y Tarancon. Not only is he the acknowledged leader of the Spanish Church, he has done more than any other Spanish cardinal to lessen the chains which fettered the country's Catholics under Franco. More important, he is in good standing with the Curia and, during the Second Vatican Council, displayed brilliant strategy in a number of crucial debates. Enrique y Tarancon has the ability to reach both progressives and conservatives. His age, seventy-one, his engaging personality, his command of Italian, his understanding of Latin America and the need for the European and American Churches to build bridges there—all these go toward ensuring that the Spaniard is *papabile.*

Greenan discounts the next two Spanish cardinals, José Bueno y Monreal of Seville and Marcelo Gonzales Martin of Toledo—both are virtually unknown outside their own hierarchy—and hesitates over Narciso Jubany Arnau, archbishop of Barcelona. He teaches law at a local seminary and at sixty-five is in the right age bracket. He has a good reputation with his priests and knows how to deliver a sermon. But in the end Arnau is also ruled out. There are so many better possibilities.

The Dutch, despite what's been written in recent months in the Italian secular press, still have, in Greenan's view, a strong contender in Jan Willebrands. It is not just that he is so widely admired and respected: the man has style. Everything Willebrands does has a natural polish about it. And he learned about the Roman Curia's methods from the legendary Cardinal Bea, the scholarly Jesuit who was private confessor to Pius XII: if Bea were alive now, he might have a real chance of being chosen pope by acclamation—that rare occasion in conclave when one cardinal proposes a name and all others accept it at once, so avoiding any balloting. Willebrands is unlikely to achieve that, but he goes on Greenan's list.

Reluctantly he rules out Bernard Alfrink, who retired three years ago from the Utrecht archbishopric which Willebrands inherited. Alfrink is a cautious liberal; he knew how to keep a tight rein on Utrecht and has never let the Curia control him. But he is too old, a shaky seventy-eight. It is virtually the same for the last Dutchman, Cardinal Maximilian de Furstenberg. He was an apostolic diplomat most of his working life before taking over as prefect of the Sacred Congregation for the Oriental Churches; de Furstenberg directed this sensitive body brilliantly. Eventually, though, he found the strain too much and retired. A good and worthy man, his time for high office appears to be over.

Greenan works on steadily, weighing and judging. There is still a long way to go, over one hundred cardinals to assess. He must spend many hours poring over confidential files, searching his memory, telephoning the right persons and holding the sort of cryptic conversations Greenan is renowned for, then thinking some more—all to help him guess "which way the Holy Spirit may be thinking."

Even for the ebullient and very confident editor it is a testing challenge.

The Lancia 2000 with the Venetian registration draws no attention in Rome; there are a thousand cars like it on the streets of this city, in spite of Rome being gripped in *Ferragosto*, the period when everybody who can escapes from the enervating August heat. The Lancia's driver is actually a confidential secretary, Diego Lorenzi. He is only thirty-nine but looks older from the effects of the exhausting past eleven days he has spent chauffeuring the man he is devoted to, and who sits beside him in the car, a sign of their close and informal relationship: Cardinal Albino Luciani, the sixty-five-year-old patriarch of Venice.

Daily, at all hours, Lorenzi has fetched the car from a garage and brought it to the Augustinian College near the Vatican where he and Luciani have modest rooms. He has driven the patriarch to one meeting after another. Luciani is determined to consult with every cardinal voter possible before conclave, exploring with each his views on which way the Church should be going. This is typical of the patriarch; he is dedicated to preparatory work. He says it makes it so much easier to come to the right decision in the end.

Sometimes the meetings continue late into the night. Yet Luciani always manages to smile as he leaves, a full-scale boyish grin which lights up his face, sheds years from it and makes him look almost impish. The smile is his trademark, as recognizable as Cody's back-thumping, Pericle Felici's nervous shuffle and Hume of Westminster's languid good manners.

Only later, when Lorenzi has helped Luciani to his room and there is no one to see them, does the patriarch slump on his bed and admit that the hurt in his legs is at times almost unbearable. He suffers from phlebitis, a painful circulatory disease that is an offshoot from the four minor heart attacks

Luciani has had during the past fifteen years. None have been serious and his doctor in Venice has assured him he has made a complete recovery. Inevitably though, those attacks and the phlebitis have exacted their toll, with the result that Luciani's overall health is not robust. And he is a worrier. This, in part, is why he is taking these soundings among his fellow cardinals: he wants to know how the Holy Spirit—the Word of God which is supposed to "guide the spirit" of each cardinal—may be directing them.

Luciani has kept secret from the Vatican his physical condition. He feared that if Paul heard about it, he might have suggested that he give up his duties. For a man whose life is dedicated to his ministry, such a prospect was unthinkable. His secret is safe with Lorenzi; the ties between them are as close as those of brothers. The secretary, in turn, does everything he can to ease Luciani's physical path. He insists that the patriarch watch his intake of pasta and wine and that he soak his feet twice a day in the herbal preparation Luciani's housekeeper, Sister Vincenza, has obtained. The remedy is from the Dolomites, where Luciani and Vincenza were born. She swears the elixir works. The sophisticated Lorenzi is not so certain. But he will approve anything which may make his employer more comfortable.

The Lancia eases through the noonday traffic this Thursday, August 17, and stops outside the Pio Latino Americano on the Via Aurelia. Luciani has come here to lunch with the Latin American cardinals, many of whom he knows well: Venetians have traditionally emigrated to South America, and the emigrants often have settling-in problems which require Luciani's intercession. The patriarch has brought each cardinal a gift: a signed copy of his book, *Illustrissimi*, a series of make-believe letters Luciani has written to famous authors and characters in history or fiction.

Lorenzi carries the books while Cardinal Aramburu of Buenos Aires, an old friend, leads the patriarch inside. Eighteen cardinals await in the college's main reception room, the entire South and Central American contingent. Their presence in force is a tribute to Luciani. Like him they are dressed in simple black cassocks, the only symbols of rank their scarlet skullcaps. Luciani seems to have a problem keeping his in place; it is frequently askew at an almost raffish angle. The effect, combined with his infectious grin, makes him look more than ever a cheeky schoolboy.

His secretary tactfully maneuvers Luciani to a chair. From there the patriarch distributes the books, nodding happily at the obvious pleasure the gifts create.

Aramburu, while knowing the story well, for the benefit of his fellow cardinals asks Luciani how he came to write the letters in *Illustrissimi*. And Luciani, who has answered the question often, does so now as if for the first time. It is another of his endearing, almost childlike qualities. The reason he gives is engagingly simple, yet holds important truths for all of those present.

"When I preach in St. Mark's, I may have a few hundred listeners. Half of them are tourists who do not understand Italian, and the other half are wonderful people but they are . . . well, getting on in years." He pauses, smiling. "Then the editor of *Messagero di San Antonio* said to me that if I wrote for him, my audience would increase a thousandfold. I was convinced."

There are appreciative chuckles. *Illustrissimi*, Luciani says modestly, is only the result of his desire to reach a wider audience. While doing so, he has frequently used a celebrated name merely as an excuse to develop a serious moral or religious point. He reveals how his simulated letter to the English dramatist Christopher Marlowe, who wrote *Dr. Faustus*, gave him the opportunity to talk about the devil. His listeners nod, captivated by the technique. When he penned his letter to Goethe he was actually exploring the question of *noblesse oblige* in the present-day cinema. His essay to Chesterton was a warning that progress when confined only to materialism could lead mankind to catastrophe.

Luciani explains it is his way of bringing theology to the masses, to try and bolster their faith by relating the Gospel to people and events which everyone can grasp.

The lesson is well received. Aramburu leads the guest of honor into lunch, where much of the table talk is about having *Illustrissimi* translated into other languages.

Aramburu also thinks that "this fine and wonderful man could be a good pope." Such thoughts, of course, do not surface now. They are for later.

The Argentinian does not notice what Lorenzi has seen. Under the table Luciani is using one leg to massage the back of the other. It's a bad sign. It means the pace is once more beginning to affect the patriarch. Thank God, thinks the secretary, it will soon be over and he can drive his beloved cardinal back to the comparative quiet of Venice.[1]

MacCarthy's office in Vatican Radio—a large corner one on the third floor, its size and location indicating his importance in the station—has a wall map of Africa. It reminds MacCarthy, if ever he needs reminding, of the vastly disparate potential audience he broadcasts to every day. There are Boers and Bushmen, jungle tribesmen and desert dwellers; often suspicious or even hostile to each other, they all trust MacCarthy to tell them the truth. For many he also provides almost their only contact with the English language. He never preaches but tries always to inform. For the past twelve days MacCarthy has been preparing his listeners for conclave.

This Friday evening, August 18, he is devoting part of his broadcast to describing what a cardinal is. MacCarthy carefully explains that the word came from the Latin *cardo*, hinge, indicating the pivotal importance cardinals have in the affairs of the Church. Although the title of cardinal goes back well over a thousand years, it was not until 1150 that the Sacred College of Cardinals—consisting of cardinals bishops, cardinal priests and cardinal deacons—came into being. Since 1179 the Sacred College has had the exclusive right to elect the pope. In 1945, Pius XII began to select his cardinals from all over the world. His successors have followed this practice. The aim of the Church is to have each Christian nation represented by a member of the College. Paul decreed that the number of cardinals entitled to vote must not exceed one hundred and twenty. He never disclosed his reason.

MacCarthy pauses, aware that his unseen audience needs time to absorb what he's said. Then he continues, describing how a cardinal is created. It begins, says MacCarthy, when the pope declares the appointment during a secret consistory, a meeting with the cardinals who reside permanently in Rome. Afterward, the promotion is generally made known at a public consistory. And it is then the pope sometimes also announces he has created one or more cardinals *in pectore*, which MacCarthy translates as "in his breast." He explains: "This means their names are not publicly revealed. Such cardinals date their seniority from the moment they are nominated *in pectore*, but all their other privileges begin only on the day their names are revealed. If the pope should die before divulging their names, their promotion is void."

Once more he pauses. He briefly wonders how many letters he will receive asking which living cardinals began *in pectore*. MacCarthy has his reply ready: as far as is known, only Tomasek of Czechoslovakia and Trinh Van Can of Vietnam were elevated this way.

He carries on, explaining that a cardinal has numerous legal and other privileges including the right to use miter and crosier, "to celebrate mass pontifically and to be judged by none other but the pope." Temporally, a cardinal ranks "with the princes of reigning houses." Yet cardinals possess no constitutional rights under the absolute government of the papacy and cannot even meet together without the pope's permission. A cardinal may resign, but he can be deprived of his title for only the gravest of reasons.

MacCarthy goes on to say that in the unlikely event of some nomad in Central Africa coming unexpectedly upon a cardinal, the proper form of address is "Eminence" or "Your Eminence"; the style "Most Reverend Lord" is, suggests MacCarthy *sotto voce*, perhaps a little old-fashioned these days. Before the broadcast ends, he deftly slips in "God's commercial," reminding his listeners that a person of such "eminence" can be as humble as a parish priest, "but I imagine he has a greater cross to bear."

In common with everyone in the Pontifical Household, its prefect, Jacques Martin, is, temporarily at least, out of work. He expects he will be reappointed by the next pope. But nothing is certain. In the meantime he is doing a good deal of thinking and listening.

Martin is not alone in wanting to know which way the wind is blowing. And there is, he is prepared to concede, a lot of interesting chaff flying around. He is not going to say exactly how much reliance he puts on some of it—probably very little—but he doesn't dismiss altogether what secular spectators are saying: conclave will be marked by the presence of many great electors, the euphemism applied to those cardinals who wield the most influence.

König is widely held to be one. Enrique y Tarancon is another. Baggio, Benelli, Bertoli—given they don't think they themselves are in with a chance for the Throne of St. Peter—will each doubtless be influential. But none of these names is new to an old hand like Martin. He is more interested in some of the other cardinals on offer as decision makers.

There is Aloisio Lorscheider. He is fifty-three, too young to become pope unless there is a startling reversal of what has historically been the case. Martin is not altogether surprised the name of the Brazilian archbishop is being put forward by the tabloids as "a pope maker," a phrase the prefect detests. Lorscheider's reputation has gone far beyond the remote corners of the world where he has his diocese. He is a superb theologian and was relator general of the 1977 Synod of Bishops. Paul was much impressed by him—now not necessarily a help in the preconclave mood shaping up. But Lorscheider could emerge as a decisive influence on his fellow Latin Americans and perhaps even the Asians.

Nor is Martin surprised to see the name of Sin of Manila being toyed with; nobody is even remotely suggesting he could become pope, yet Sin's record as a campaigner for human rights, his desire to see the Church more involved in such issues, his astute sense of political timing—all are helping make him potentially an important elector.

And there is Bernardin Gantin, whose behavior during the funeral mass for Paul deeply impressed Martin. There can be little doubt almost every African cardinal will continue to "consult" with Gantin. As chairman of the Commission for Justice and Peace, he is a curial cardinal. He knows the ropes, who is pulling where—and whether that pull can be sustained.

Martin has his own favorite—naturally—but only he knows who. It is almost forty years since he came to work in the city-state. He has experienced its history and is familiar with most of the worthwhile secrets of the period. He's kept all the really good ones to himself. That's how some people survive in the Vatican—acquiring precious information but never revealing it; around the Apostolic Palace it's called "heavenly insurance." The saying goes that the man who knows too much will never be dispensed with; popes come and go but shrewd old retainers like Martin remain securely in their niches.

This Saturday evening, August 19, Martin has invited Macchi to dinner, the last time they will meet before the secretary leaves Rome.

What they discuss remains their secret. The very fact that they have chosen to spend this time together—when at least Martin could expect any number of other invitations to dinner, for, after all, the prefect of the Casa Pontificia is an invaluable sounding board for the possibilities being endlessly discussed—will ferment yet further speculation. Are they planning in some way to use their years of prestige under Paul to influence the choice of his successor? Are they casting themselves in the role of spiritual godfathers about to call in past favors? Are they preparing to float one of those little initiatives, watch it climb and drift over the Vatican walls and then see where it will eventually settle? All—at least for the record—nonsense of course. But the questions are almost as interesting as the fact that they are never answered. The entire scenario fits in very well with the way it is as the first week of the interregnum closes.

same message. In Vatican Radio's main studio, high up on Vatican Hill within the mock palace built by Leo XIII, the team of the prestigious "Four Voices" program prepares to help keep the world informed of developments. The studio looks no different from any other—except that a tiny buzzer has been secretly wired into the control console. It is the receiver for at least one bug which has been secreted into conclave.

The man who carries the transmitter is among the attendants in the Sistine Chapel. The bug is in the shape of a shirt button. To activate the device he merely has to squeeze the button. It simultaneously produces a low-pitched sound in the radio studio's console. He will squeeze the button a prearranged number of times the moment a pope has been elected. The man has been assured there is virtually no risk involved. But listening to Villot he hears what will happen to him should he be discovered.[1]

Villot is reading aloud from Paul's *Eligendo* how his successor must be chosen. The 5,600 Latin words fill sixty-two pages. The camerlengo sternly reminds his listeners that if one of them is found using "any type of transmitting or receiving instrument," that person will immediately "be expelled from the conclave and subjected to grave penalties." It takes Villot a sonorous thirty minutes to read the sixty separate conditions Paul has laid down.

Even then the camerlengo is not done. Villot reads again the solemn conclave oath binding everyone present to accept each of Paul's conditions, to reject outside interference and, above all, to keep the deliberations secret.

The camerlengo consults a list of typewritten names. He calls out the first one. The Egyptian patriarch of Alexandria rises and walks to the purple-draped desk before the altar where Villot is standing. The patriarch places his right hand on a copy of the Gospels and swears to uphold the conclave oath, adding "so help me God and these Holy Gospels which I touch with my hand."

The patriarch returns to his seat and Villot calls the next cardinal to come forward.

In *L'Osservatore Romano*, editorial staff checks the twelve different proofs of the newspaper's front page. Each dummy contains a photograph and potted biography of one of the cardinals the editors have predicted will be the next pope. Eleven they will happily discard. But if all twelve prove to be wrong, their carefully laid plans will come to nothing and there could well ensue the nearest thing to a good, old-fashioned panic of a newspaper trying to meet a deadline.

It needs an hour for the cardinals and their attendants individually to swear the conclave oath.

But Villot is not finished; some of the Italian cardinals—flagrantly breaking the very pledge they have made—will later put it about that the Frenchman now behaves as if he is stagestruck. Yet Paul's *Eligendo* requires that the camerlengo address them further, as he does, on the importance of their deliberations and the need to keep the "good of the Church" uppermost in their minds. It takes him ten minutes. Only then does Villot conclude.

"May the Lord bless you all. Amen."

König has drawn cell eleven in the preconclave balloting for accommodation. It is in a small, partitioned room. On the other side of the plywood divider, he can hear Cardinal Hume walking on the parquet floor. Across the corridor König listens to an American voice telling somebody it's like being back at school. It sounds like either Manning or Krol; König cannot be certain because the partitioning produces a baffle effect which muffles voices.

Walking from the Sistine Chapel to his accommodation, König glimpsed a few of the other cells and knows he is lucky: some of them are really poky, the result of a small salon or office being divided into three and even four living spaces. Each cell—the term goes back to Leo XIII, who was the first pope to decree that cardinals must have separate rooms in conclave so they may meditate in peace—is furnished in virtually the same discount-store manner. There are a bedside lamp, a washbowl and pitcher, a plastic bucket, a hardbacked chair and a stark wooden prie-dieu. Above it is a single wooden crucifix. Beside the pitcher are a bar of soap and two small towels. On the bedside cabinet are a single roll of toilet tissue, a dozen sheets of writing paper and a couple of ball-point pens. Alongside each bed is a strip of floral-patterned carpet. Beneath almost every bed is the result of some intensive searching by Villot's staff, who have combed Rome's monasteries and nunneries to borrow what the Americans call Uncle Joes and the Italians refer to as *vasi da notte*. König prefers the English, chamberpots. His is plain white with a sturdy handle. Villot has decided the walk to the toilets might be too far for some of the older cardinals to make during the night.

Like the other beds, König's has been borrowed from a Rome seminary. It is narrow with a thin mattress over wire mesh, rather different, he muses ruefully, from his splendid inner-spring feather bed in Vienna. Not that König minds. He sees the spartan living conditions as epitomizing the virtues of conclave. He quickly unpacks and kneels to pray at the prie-dieu. All around him other cardinals are doing the same thing.

Watched by Noé—who is most curious to see what might happen—the two electronic surveillance technicians walk through the conclave area. Each man holds a slim black sensor in his hand, rather like a photographer's light meter, which he moves back and forth. The sensors have a range of twenty feet and can penetrate through walls and wooden partitions. The men move unobtrusively, following the signposts at various intersections which indicate the way to the dining hall, toilets, the Sistine Chapel and the various cells.

Suddenly needles on the sensors begin to twitch. The technicians separate to get a cross bearing; their instruments are designed to lock on to each other so as to more accurately pinpoint a target. Moving slowly, eyes on the needles, the technicians pad up the corridor. The needles become steady. There is a buzzing sound from a bedroom. Then the technicians and Noé relax. The sensors have picked up someone using a battery-operated razor. The search continues.

The food is as simple as the cells. It's been prepared by the nuns who operate kitchens for some of the poor of Rome, and are renowned for their gentleness as much as their ability to make pasta seem even more unpalatable to many of the non-Italian cardinals. The sisters have set up a glorified field kitchen in a high-vaulted room in the Borgia apartments. From here they dispense the first meal of conclave—a supper of bread, spaghetti with a meat sauce, bowls of fruit and pitchers of red and white wine. There are also beer and mineral water. The dining room is the Hall of the Popes, once the armory of the Borgia family: thirty-five feet above the refectory tables is a fifteenth-century fresco by Pinturicchio.

König sits opposite Wojtyla. Like the Canadian Paul Léger, the Pole enjoys the simple fare, and he tells his neighbors it reminds him of the trips he regularly makes into the steppes: a bottle of wine and a chunk of bread can be quite enough for a man in those circumstances, he says, grinning hugely.

Wojtyla has one of the smallest cells in the area; it is little larger than a broom cupboard. Yet König has never seen the Pole happier; he is laughing and joking and listening, and doing all at the same time. One moment he is vibrantly strident, the next he speaks in the gentlest of tones. It is an actor's delivery, but there is nothing actorlike in his honesty. Wojtyla radiates sincerity, making König think again that here is a man of exceptional qualities, one who combines high intelligence with a big heart.

Everywhere the conversation is relaxed and wide-ranging. The Latin Americans and the Spanish are at one table. Aramburu prefers to listen, sitting with hands on the table, straight-backed, nodding at the points his colleagues make. His composure hides inner distress. Shortly before entering conclave the aristocratic Argentinian telephoned Buenos Aires to learn that President Videla plans to be in Rome when the next pope is crowned. Videla will be coming at a time when feelings against Italy are running high in Buenos Aires because of the way the Italian president snubbed Videla; inevitably this Argentine reaction has provoked a mood of reprisal in certain Italian quarters:

there have been some very unflattering stories about Videla's bloody background published in Rome's newspapers. It could become very nasty if Videla struts along in the wake of the next pontiff.

Preoccupied by such concerns, it is perhaps understandable that Aramburu has not told his companions why he no longer supports Luciani's candidacy. It may also be that, following the strictures of Paul's *Eligendo*, Aramburu does not wish to exert any influence on their decision making.

Luciani is flanked by Felici and Benelli, while across the table sits the striking figure of Bernardin Gantin, his ebony-black face shining with perspiration in the muggy atmosphere. Within the hall, where at best conditions are hot and stuffy in August, now, with over one hundred cardinals present and without the benefit of air conditioning, they are becoming oppressive.

Ratzinger of Munich shares one of what will become known as the "European tables." He too has entered conclave in a far from ideal frame of mind. The reason is not hard to discern: Rome is plastered with newspaper placards announcing Küng's blueprint for the next papacy. Ratzinger finds almost everything Küng advocates unacceptable. Yet among certain cardinals Ratzinger has detected a measure of cautious support for some of the theologian's ideas. Naturally he will not identify those cardinals who do not completely reject Küng's beliefs, but conclave attendants are whispering that there seems to be a certain coolness between the Bavarian Ratzinger and Willebrands, the Dutchman from Utrecht.

Enrique y Tarancon, the cardinal from Madrid, is among the first to leave the dining hall, his tinted glasses shielding his eyes from the extra lights slung from the ceiling. Shortly afterward the influential Spaniard is seen strolling in the San Damaso Courtyard, deep in conversation with Suenens, the charismatic Belgian.

This sort of details will enable at least one person inside conclave to produce a highly secret and totally illegal diary which he will claim actually to have written while in this forbidden area. It will consist largely of impressions, overheard conversations, trivia about the personal habits of cardinals. More importantly, it will record the results of the ballots in the powerful mystery of a papal election. The diarist is a lowly attendant. He will insist he is keeping his record because he thinks what is happening is "the most historic decision since Pilate washed his hands." Hyperbole apart, he also thinks the secrecy is pointless, that it has no real part to play in the process of choosing a modern man to become the Vicar of Christ, that conclave should be seen for what it is, basically a simple act of election. Commendable though such thoughts may be to those outside conclave, the attendant nevertheless intends to preserve his diary in the security of a Rome bank vault, with instructions that it must not be released until after his death. Since he is only in his early

forties, it could be the next century before the full extent of his jottings surface. However, to substantiate his claim to have written the diary while in
conclave, he will reveal segments that, on cross-checking, seem accurate, so
providing a tantalizing insight into who did and said what in the drama about
to unfold.

The atmospheric fog thickens after dinner as cardinals light up cigarettes,
cigars and pipes. While forbidden to smoke in the Sistine Chapel during the
forthcoming long hours of balloting—though there is no specific ban on
Krol's penchant for chewing on an unlit cigar—they are permitted to smoke
in the adjoining corridors and their cells. This proviso makes the two firemen
attendants nervous; their duties include not only maintaining the ballot-burn-
ing stove, but also keeping wary eyes open for any casually disposed smolder-
ing butts.

Felici is one of several Italians who have brought bottles of *digestivi;* the liqueurs act as a welcome lubricant for the "consultations" which begin in the
cells.

Gantin prefers to keep his discussions on the move. He strides first with
one cardinal, then another, and everyone who listens to this tall, handsome
man cannot but be struck by his intelligence and gentleness—and courage
sufficient for him to have been a threat to the Marxist government of Benin
which forced him into exile. Gantin, like the other black African cardinals, is
only a fourth-generation Christian, but Villot is not alone in thinking the
voices of these men in conclave will provide an important balance to all the
theorizing he has heard these past weeks. In the camerlengo's view there is no
question, having spoken at length to Gantin, that the problems of the Third
World must be in the forefront of the next pope's mind.

Noé and Sin make a second tour of the area; until the end of conclave they
will do so four times a day. The two men reach their last port of call, the Sistine Chapel. They pause in astonishment. There is a lone figure kneeling and
staring up at the majesty of Michelangelo's art, apparently riveted by the
finger of God reaching out to radiate life to Adam. Michelangelo's Adam is
not circumcised—and perfectly right, too, thinks Sin, for Adam preceded
Abraham—but he has a navel, and Sin has always assumed this to be more a
demonstration of the artist's understanding of anatomy than an expression of
any doubt he may have had about the authenticity of the Book of Genesis.
And God—a virile, white-bearded man, old yet ageless in his flimsy pink
nightshirt—is this representing a satire on religion? Such questions about the
"Last Judgment" and the ceiling frescoes have intrigued Sin in the past.
Now, they do not matter. They seem irrelevant in the presence of this kneeling figure. In the dim light of the flickering red lamp in front of the Taberna-
cle, they can see he is in fact not staring at the painting, but praying. He is

motionless, hands before him, head held high, his rosary passing bead by bead through his fingers. It is Albino Luciani.

König awakens to an unaccustomed sound—that of men quietly going about their ablutions; it reminds him of the time he was hospitalized. He can hear Hume pouring water into his washbowl and from across the corridor there is the hum of an electric razor. It is just after 6 A.M. on Saturday, August 26. It is hot and airless in König's cell. Siri was right last night when he said it was like living in a tomb. On the other hand, the ascetic Hume expressed the thought that the primitive arrangements ensure that nothing comes between the cardinals and God. Manning of Los Angeles hasn't seemed to notice the living conditions; he is finding the entire conclave experience novel and exciting. König can well understand the reaction; he still remembers the feeling of awe which gripped him as he entered his first conclave fifteen years ago.

While shaving and dressing he thinks back to that time in 1963 when he personally played a decisive role in persuading Paul to accept office. König and seventy-nine other cardinals had filed into conclave on June 19. Paul—then Cardinal Montini—was the favorite of those who wanted John XXIII's open-window policies continued. On the first ballot Montini had led with about thirty votes, but he was closely followed by two other cardinals, each with some twenty votes. The first, Giacomo Lercaro of Bologna, was the choice of those who thought his simplicity, even more obvious holiness and Franciscanlike poverty, seemed to mirror better John than the cool, withdrawn manner of Montini. The other main contender, backed by Giuseppe Siri, was Cardinal Antoniutti. Deadlock ensued through the second and third ballots. König and Suenens of Belgium had then intervened, arguing that Montini, with his diplomatic and bureaucratic skills, coupled with his very obvious support for John's policies, was the ideal man for both sides. In the fourth and last ballot of the day, Lercaro's votes switched to Montini. It placed him well ahead of Siri's candidate but just short of the two-thirds-plus-one majority of fifty-four needed to win.

At this point a certain Cardinal Gustavo Testa suddenly broke the peace of conclave by standing up in the Sistine Chapel and loudly proclaiming that he would never have been a cardinal but for John. Then he turned to his immediate neighbor, Confalonieri, and asked him to stop blocking Montini's progress. Before the astonished Confalonieri could respond, Testa launched into an impassioned appeal for the conservatives to consider "the good of the Church"—the very phrase Villot used when opening the present conclave—and not to wreck everything John had achieved. With this, Testa had bowled out of the Sistine Chapel leaving his peers openmouthed.

That night König came across Montini in the Galleria Lapidaria, looking anguished. König sat with him, trying to cheer up Montini. He would not be consoled, but kept on insisting he did not want to be pope. König made one last effort: "It's dark now, and you cannot see clearly. But the light will come again and you will see what you must do." Next day Montini became Pope Paul. If König and Suenens had not intervened, the Church could have been ruled by Lercaro, who might even have moved from the Vatican and gone to live in a Rome slum. He had already turned his palace into a hostel for homeless boys. There was no telling what he would have done had he become pontiff.

In the present conclave there was another cardinal very like the saintly Lercaro, Léger of Montreal. König barely knew the French-Canadian; what he did know he admired. It was not every man who could give up the position, the power and the comfort of diocese living to work for the dying in the depths of tropical Africa. The Church clearly needed men like Léger: he was a model for everybody seeking the true meaning of service. But a pope, especially in these troubled times, could not lead the Church cut off from the outside world, however much he might wish to. The next pope must have high ideals, unshakable beliefs certainly. That is why König thinks it may take up to a week to choose him. He doubts there will be a repeat of the one-day conclave of 1939 which swept Pius XII into office; he hopes there will not be the prolonged impasse of 1923, when it took fourteen ballots to elect Pius XI. This time, unlike 1958, when John was preconclave favorite, or 1963, when Paul had such strong initial support, König does not see an obvious choice. In many ways he still wishes his coelectors would look seriously at Wojtyla.

Shortly after eight o'clock, the cardinals troop into the Sistine Chapel. Each genuflects before the High Altar and goes to his seat. They have concelebrated mass and had a quick breakfast of coffee and rolls.

Those attendants so inclined have had a busy time trying to work out what the latest contacts may mean. There has been the intriguing sight of the "pen pal" pacing back and forth with "the traveler," both deep in conversation. Could this mean that Sergio Pignedoli, the nearest thing to a preconclave favorite, is losing ground? Is this why this cardinal who corresponds regularly with hundreds of persons he has met when abroad is trying to persuade Baggio, the globe-traveling troubleshooter, to be supportive? They do make an unlikely pair: Baggio is jowly, tough-minded, as rigid in some of his thinking as his stiff-legged gait; Pignedoli is languid and easygoing, his voice soft and almost sepulchral. But they have found sufficient in common to remain together right up to the moment they enter the chapel.

Felici goes in alone. Yet the watchful attendants, scurrying about the business of making beds and sweeping the corridors, have noticed him well before then. Felici has been spotted using his skills as an advocate to push Luciani's cause. He's been seen entering the cell of Michele Pellegrino, the retired archbishop of Turin. The only question really is why Felici bothered. Almost certainly Pellegrino is already a committed supporter of the Vienna patriarch. Though he has just retired at the age of seventy-five, Pellegrino reflects—perhaps next to Léger—the nearest personality to John XXIII's. He's got the same courage and tenacity, the same simplicity: he prefers to be called "padre" rather than "Eminence"; he wears simple cassocks instead of regal robes; his pectoral cross is wooden rather than jeweled; he has refused a limousine and drives a car even more modest than Luciani's—a Simca 1000. Pellegrino has little in common with Felici. Yet the very fact that Felici has called on him is seen as a sign Felici is leaving nothing to chance. He's drumming hard. Surely that is the reason he has also been with Antonio Poma and Corrado Ursi. The Italians are very different in personality and outlook. Poma is withdrawn, at times almost reclusive; Ursi is expansive and already one of the real mixers in conclave. If Felici has persuaded both men to follow his line on Luciani—goes the whispered scuttlebutt—then he is making serious inroads into the hopes of other *papabili*.

Three of these are seated close together. Willebrands, even in his robes, looks a man with itchy feet; the Dutchman's demeanor suggests he finds the whole business an interruption to what he likes best, traveling. There had been talk just before conclave that the primate of Holland could easily become pope if only he agreed to follow a curial fundamental: never to speak bluntly and passionately and, above all, openly on sensitive Church matters; but the betting is it is too late for Willebrands to change his frank, outgoing approach.

Nobody seems to know how, but James Knox, formerly archbishop of Melbourne and Australia's ranking cardinal, is now on some *papabili* lists. Yet his presence there should not be a surprise. Knox is currently prefect of the Congregation for the Sacraments and Divine Worship. He is the first Australian to hold such high Vatican office. He is sixty-four, superbly fit, and in the parlance of the cricket game he adores, Knox is a very good first-wicket-down bet.

Léon Duval, the cardinal from Algeria who rejoices in the nickname "Archbishop Mohammad," because of his drive to cement Catholic-Moslem ties, has managed to remain an outside possibility. This is partly due to his rigidly orthodox stand on all matters of doctrine. If there is going to be a pope from Africa, then, after Gantin, Duval could be the one.

The eight American cardinals are scattered throughout the two rows of electors. Though some U.S. commentators—notably Greeley and CBS broadcasters—play down their influence, the notion is not shared within conclave.

The feeling here is that the Americans, because of their numerical strength and the fact that they represent some of the most sophisticated Catholics in the world, could exercise considerable sway—and may already have done so. Krol, for instance, has entered into an easy alliance with König, partly because they both think so highly of Wojtyla and partly because they share a common view of where the Church should be going. Cody has also been renewing his links with the Polish cardinals. Carberry of St. Louis and Cooke of New York have proven to be ideal listening posts. They have discounted much of the preconclave waffle and, at their regular briefings in the Villa Stritch, have given their colleagues a very good indication of what other cardinals are thinking. Following Krol's example, the Americans are low-key yet well informed. They are all determined to vote only according to their own dictates; no one has given them anything resembling an instruction on how they should cast their ballots.

Maurice Roy of Quebec and Paul Léger of Montreal have been blessedly free of the debate and discussion which has so preoccupied many of their colleagues.

Still, nobody now seriously thinks of Roy as a candidate. In spite of sound enough liberal credentials, Roy has fallen afoul of some South American cardinals who think he is one of those who continue to drag their heels over condemning torture in Latin America; the accusation is debatable and hardly new, but in the superheated politico-religious atmosphere of that region, Roy has been tabbed at best a fence-sitter on the issue. Some cardinals have also been reminding themselves, and smarting at the memory, that at the 1967 Congress for the Lay Apostolate—a crucial early milestone in Paul's pontificate—Roy had tried to influence the resolution-making process. The memory of his failure is now almost as black a mark against him as was his attempt in the first place to manipulate matters. Both effectively combine to douse any hopes he may have of ever becoming pontiff.

But then, as the cardinals settle in their chairs, no one really knows what may happen. As Felici says, the Holy Spirit moves in a wondrous way.

By eight-thirty the 111 electors are seated. Villot has observed them taking their places. The camerlengo is aware all eyes are once more on him. The most likely will be the third form of election, by "scrutiny," secret ballot.

But equally nobody can say this is certain. That is why Villot waits.

There are perhaps fifteen thousand people already in St. Peter's Square as MacCarthy skirts it on his way to work. Everyone looks frequently toward the Sistine Chapel where the temporary smokestack juts out from the roof.

1 PONTIFF

MacCarthy probably knows more, after his research, than anyone about the chimney. He has mentally locked the facts into place in a smooth-flowing sequence that will form the basis for a commentary script.

Until 1550—the conclave which produced Julius III—voting papers were burned in a *focone,* the touchhole of a gun, lit inside the Sistine Chapel. Julius was an art-loving pope and fretted that the smoke could damage the frescoes. He decreed that for all future conclaves a stove must be installed with its chimney stack extended clear of the building. From that time crowds have appeared in St. Peter's Square to watch the traditional black smoke for an inconclusive vote and white smoke for a successful election. The 1963 conclave had produced its own problems. Klieg lights were beamed at the stack to illuminate it for the television cameras. When the smoke emerged, few could immediately decide its color. An Italian fuel manufacturer subsequently offered to install a foolproof system to eliminate such doubts during later conclaves. Villot refused, still preferring candles of various hues to be burned with the voting papers to enhance the color of the smoke. In many ways, thinks MacCarthy, the camerlengo is engagingly old-fashioned.

Villot is also patient. He sits perfectly still, betraying no emotion, waiting to see whether any cardinal will propose election by acclamation. Ten silent minutes go by. Only then does the camerlengo address the assembly. There has been no intervention by the Holy Spirit; no one suggests delegation. It is time to proceed to election by scrutiny.

Master of ceremonies Noé, who has remained in the chapel with the cardinals for this sole purpose, begins to distribute to each a small pile of identical, rectangular ballot forms. Paul, perhaps during one of those lonely nights he could not sleep, designed them, deciding their size—two inches square—and the legend they carry, *"Eligo in Summum Pontificem,"* "I elect as Supreme Pontiff." He allowed sufficient space beneath the words to write in a name. When Noé completes his task he leaves the Sistine, shutting the door on the cardinal-electors behind him.

What will happen now, beneath the horrors of Michelangelo's version of the Apocalypse—where Jesus is shown as judge and king, shorn of enigma, ambiguity and mystery—is supposed to remain one of the most closely guarded secrets in the world. But this is 1978, when even cardinals find themselves exposed to and influenced by the intense pressures of the Age of Communications. A few cautiously concede that, just as Michelangelo's Christ in the "Last Judgment" fresco towering above their heads has nothing of the subtlety and compassion of the Gospel Jesus, so the ritual of which they are now part fails to take a realistic account of the real role of the papacy on the troubled international stage; there the secular powers, perhaps more than at any other time in history, are genuinely fascinated by the process which produces a new pope. These cardinals, with the best possible motives, will tell their trusted secretaries something of what occurs. The secretaries will compare notes and, in turn, inform their closest friends of what they have learned. In no time the facts will seep down to the level of that conclave attendant who is keeping his diary. While two and two will still sometimes make five, generally speaking the secrets of conclave, inviolate for so long, eventually will out. It is no bad thing. The door, if not exactly wide open, will no longer be shut tight.

Villot asks Sin to check that the door is properly closed. The camerlengo moves to a desk below the altar where Noé has previously placed in a silver chalice the name of every cardinal present. Then Sin, as junior cardinal appointed for the task, joins Villot.

The camerlengo announces the time has come to choose by lot the scrutineers, the three cardinals who will examine and count the votes. As well as these, three *infirmarii* must be selected. If the situation arises, they will go to the cells of any electors who are taken ill and unable to come to the Sistine Chapel. The *infirmarii* will collect their votes and bring them to the scrutineers.

Sin shakes the chalice to mix the folded paper slips. He draws out the first one, unfolds it and reads out the name. It is Wojtyla. The second scrutineer selected is Lorscheider of Brazil. The third is Gantin. The *infirmarii* are then chosen. In the same manner three further appointments are made: The revisers, the cardinals who will check the work of the scrutineers. Once they are chosen Sin tips the remaining slips of paper from the chalice into another receptacle.

Villot calls the scrutineers to the altar. Sin places the now-empty chalice beside a silver plate on the altar. The Filipino returns to his seat. Villot puts the plate over the mouth of the chalice. Next he addresses the cardinals, reminding them again of the very precise procedure Paul laid down for voting, slowly reading out the Latin instructions.

"The completion of the cards must be carried out secretly by each cardinal-elector, who will write down, as far as possible in writing that cannot be identified as his, the name of the person he chooses, taking care not to write other names as well, since this would make the votes null; the folding of the card is done down the center of each card in such a way that the card is reduced to the width of about one inch."

Then Villot too walks slowly to his seat.

The concentration is so intense that a number of cardinals look around nervously at a sudden buzzing. An insect is circling inside the chapel.

König notices that one or two of the men bunched almost elbow-to-elbow around him are staring at the "Last Judgment." He doubts they will find much there to inspire the choice they all must now make; König has always thought the fresco monumentally Roman, weighty and overbearing, intimidating rather than inspiring confidence. He wonders—and is momentarily surprised by the irrelevance of the thought—whether Islam is right when it forbids images or representations of the Divine.

The insect sound is joined by another, equally unfamiliar. It is the scratching of pen on paper.

At the altar Wojtyla is the first to write in his nominee. He folds the ballot in the prescribed form and kneels in prayer, the paper held in his tightly clasped hands. Then he arises and, facing the altar, utters the special oath Paul ordered.

"I call to witness Christ the Lord, who will be my judge, that my vote is given to the one who before God I consider should be elected."

Wojtyla places his ballot paper on the silver plate, pauses for a moment, bows to the altar, then tilts the plate so that the card drops into the chalice.

Lorscheider and Gantin repeat the identical process.

The other cardinals complete their voting forms, endeavoring to disguise their handwriting, looking neither left nor right so as to avoid any temptation to glance at what a neighbor has written. Then, one at a time, they go to the altar to cast their votes. The order of voting is almost militarily rigid: the most senior cardinals go first, with cardinal bishops preceding cardinal priests, who in turn go before cardinal deacons.

König is one of the first to walk down the aisle. His shoes echo on the raised floor, whose felt covering already shows signs of wear. He reaches the altar, kneels and prays for a moment, then rises and pronounces the oath. Having deposited his folded card, he walks quickly back to his seat.

Twenty-six minutes later—Felici is keeping a timetable—the last vote is tipped into the chalice.

König does not think the atmosphere has perceptibly changed. Everybody is certainly very interested in what will now happen, but he does not sense any "special tensions" or "mounting drama." Everyone seems to be very calm. Perhaps Aramburu is right, "the Holy Spirit is making Itself felt."

Wojtyla picks up the chalice and carries it to the scrutineers' table below the altar. Before sitting at the table, he gives the receptacle a thorough shaking, holding it firmly in his strong hands. The sound of 111 slips of paper swishing around inside the chalice carries to all parts of the chapel.

Gantin is seated behind a second, empty chalice. Lorscheider is on the other side of Wojtyla. He sits with arms folded, eyes moving between the two vessels, as Gantin reaches a black hand into the full receptacle to withdraw the voting slips one at a time. As he transfers each to the second chalice,

Lorscheider counts them off aloud. If the total number of cards does not correspond to the number of electors, all the slips will be burned and a second vote taken at once. The numbers tally. The scrutineers can move to the second stage.

Wojtyla switches the chalices so that the full one is once more before him. He dips his hand into the receptacle and takes out a card. He unfolds it and writes down the name on the sheet of paper. He then passes the card to Lorscheider. He, too, writes down the name before passing the card to Gantin. Gantin looks at it for a moment. Then in his captivating voice, he reads aloud the name, as Paul ordered, "in an intelligible manner."

The first vote is for Pignedoli.

Gantin writes down the name he has just read. All the other cardinals do the same.

Wojtyla once more dips into the chalice.[2]

MacCarthy is allowing himself three minutes and fifteen seconds—precisely thirty-two lines of script—to explain the custom of a pope's taking a new name when elected. It will make a nice tailpiece for his broadcast this evening to Africa. He types his thoughts straight onto an old manual typewriter.

"The tradition goes back to the eleventh century. Before that popes simply kept their baptismal name—unless it was of pagan or barbarian origin. The first pope to change his name on election was John II, who governed the Church from 533 to 535. Previously he had been called Mercury, the name of a pagan god. In 955 John XII became pope—changing *his* name from Octavian, the name of a pagan emperor."

MacCarthy reads back what he has typed, checking it against a stopwatch. Satisfied, he continues.

"Gregory V, who was pope from 996 to 999—an easy date to remember!—was the first German pope of the Middle Ages and had 'Brun' as his baptismal name. His motive for changing it to Gregory was that 'Brun' was far too 'barbarous' a sound for the pontiff. Sylvester II, who succeeded Gregory in 999, changed his name from Gerbert, for the same reason."

Another check. He is well within the time he has allowed. He consults his note pad, sorting out the notes he has made, weaving them into the next cohesive thought.

"Pope John XIV, who ruled for eight months in 984, and Sergius IV, who was elected in 1009, both changed *their* names out of a sense of respect and veneration for the *first* pope, since both had originally been baptized Peter. There is a legend, still quoted in the Church today, that only the last pope to be elected will call himself Peter, and after that . . . the end of the world."

MacCarthy pauses. Should he include this? The entire legend is surrounded by controversy. Even the simplest details about the man originally re-sponsible for it are open to heated dispute. Had Malachy O'Morgain actually been born in 1094? Nobody now really knew. Could it really be true he had foretold the identities of ninety-eight popes, from the reign of Celestine II in 1143 to Paul? And had his predictions really looked into the future beyond this present conclave?

But *not*, if St. Malachy is to be believed, *that* far beyond. There are many—as MacCarthy well knows—who do believe the legend of this first formally canonized Irish saint. They accept that Malachy, reputedly born of a wealthy and learned family in Armagh, had been such an astonishing vision-ary that he was able to forecast centuries ago that, after this conclave pro-duced a pope, there would be only three further pontiffs.

Malachy's predictions were supposedly made in 1139 while visiting Rome, where he "saw"—and committed to paper—a series of Latin phrases describ-ing the popes down the ensuing centuries. Except for the final apocalyptic note about Petrus Romanus, the notations are very brief, no more than a few lines for each pope indicating his family name, birthplace, coat of arms or office held before election to the papacy. Some of the phrases contain certain ingenious puns; others are multiple prophecies. Many seem remarkably accu-rate. Adrian IV, the English pope, was designated by Malachy as *de rure albo*, which can be translated as either "the Alban country," a medieval de-scription of England, or "from a white country." Pius III, who reigned for only twenty-six days in 1503, was aptly described as *de parvo homine*, "from a little man." His family name was Piccolomini, Italian for "little man."

Many Catholic scholars maintain that Malachy had nothing whatever to do with the predictions, that they are in fact a sixteenth-century forgery, written with hindsight. But MacCarthy does not think it possible to be so certain and dismissive. If they are faked then the accuracy of the forecasts should fail dra-matically after the sixteenth century. This is not the case. Benedict XV was given the chilling appellation *religio depopulata*, "religion laid waste." He ruled during World War I, which "laid waste" the religious populations of several European countries. John XXIII was designated *pastor et nuata*, "pas-tor and sailor." He was certainly a great pastor and, until he became pope, John was patriarch of Venice, a city full of sailors; and it was he who chose the symbol for the Second Vatican Council: a cross and a ship. The predic-tion for John's successor was *flors florum*, "flower of flowers." Paul's coat of arms depicted three fleurs-de-lis.

And now, if Malachy is to be believed, Paul's successor will be *de medie-tate lunae*. MacCarthy, fluent in Latin, wonders which of the cardinals is best suited to fit "from the half moon." That is the problem with Malachy, muses the broadcaster, he is just too devious at times for full credence to be given his predictions.

MacCarthy looks again at what he has typed about the last pope being called Peter. According to Malachy: "During his reign, the seven-hill city of Rome will be destroyed." MacCarthy understands only too well why the Church repudiates that prophecy. Yet there remains the uncomfortable fact that at least one pope this century had a mystical vision similar to what Malachy foretells. In 1909 Pius X closed his eyes and cried out that he saw a terrifying apparition: "What is certain is that the pope will leave Rome, and in leaving the Vatican, he will have to walk over the dead bodies of his priests." MacCarthy is sure Vatican Radio would never broadcast that. He puts aside his notes on Malachy and goes back to his script.

"From the eleventh century on, only two popes have broken the tradition of changing names, retaining their baptismal names after being elected. The first was the Dutch pope, Adrian VI, who was elected in 1522. The second was Marcellus II, who had one of the shortest pontificates in the history of the Church, just twenty days!"

MacCarthy takes another timing. He has thirty seconds left. He continues to type.

"Originally, if a pope took the same name as one of his predecessors, he was known as 'junior.' If there had been more than one before him with that name he was called 'secundus junior,' and so on. The roman numeral placed after the pope's name was adopted for the first time by Gregory III, who was made pope in 731 and died ten years later. This custom of a roman numeral after the name came into current use around the eleventh century. I wonder whether our next pope will use it."

A final check: exactly three minutes, fifteen seconds.

Wojtyla takes out the last voting card from the chalice, unfolds it, writes down the name, passes it to Lorscheider, who also makes a note before handing it to Gantin. His voice carries clearly. It is another vote for Siri.

Gantin records this and then pierces the card with a threaded needle, as he has all the others. He takes care that the needle—as Paul insisted, though nobody knows why—passes through the word *Eligo*. It takes Gantin only a moment to join Siri's to the other 110 ballot cards already strung on the line. Gantin removes the needle, knots together the ends of the line and places the threaded cards back in the chalice.

The scrutineers each add up the votes they have individually recorded. Other cardinals are doing the same. Felici is the first to finish; he has used a pocket calculator.

Villot commands the revisers to go to the scrutineers' table. They take turns carefully to count the number of ballot papers on the thread, and to check the voting record of each scrutineer. Paul insisted this must be done to ensure that the scrutineers have "performed their task exactly and faithfully."

The revisers return to their places.

All eyes are on Wojtyla. He begins to read out the result of the first ballot. His previous acting experience gives him a natural sense of timing as he delivers each result in a strong baritone voice.

Siri tops the poll. He has twenty-five votes. There is absolutely no audible reaction from anybody. Luciani has twenty-three votes. Felici and Benelli, on opposite sides of the aisle, are seen by other cardinals to exchange quick looks. Pignedoli has eighteen votes.

Wojtyla pauses briefly. Perhaps he is waiting to see if there is any challenge from the floor. He cannot seriously expect one—not after all the checks. Yet he waits. Then his voice picks up the count, which by now most other cardinals already know from their own calculations.

Baggio has nine votes. König has one less. Bertoli has picked up five, the same as Pironio. Felici is limping along with a couple, and Lorscheider also has two. Fourteen other cardinals, including Hume and Pappalardo—on whom Alibrandi, the papal nuncio in Dublin, has pinned his hopes—each have a single vote. No American has one.

Sighs of relief from the tension come from several cardinals. Others look curiously at Siri and Luciani.

Villot rises and formally announces that the ballot is inconclusive. Then, before any discussion can begin, he orders Sin to summon Noé. Afterward Villot walks to the seated cardinals and asks them to hand over any notes they have made. Sin walks behind the camerlengo with a bin which already holds the name slips used when electing the scrutineers, *infirmarii* and revisers. Under Villot's watchful eye the notes are scooped by Sin into the bin. The two men go to the scrutineers' table. Villot takes the threaded votes from the chalice and drops them in the bin. He and Sin then wait in silence for Noé to come into the chapel. When he appears they go to the unlit stove. Villot opens its door while Sin tips in the paper. Noé closes the door. Villot then asks the master of ceremonies to again leave the chapel. Sin checks the door is secured behind him.

Somewhere in the conclave area, the man with the button bug presses it very quickly, twice. It is the prearranged signal that a second ballot is about to begin.

XVIII

By eleven o'clock there are an estimated fifty thousand people in St. Peter's Square. Some try to follow the advice of an Irish friar who makes the Rome front pages this Saturday because he has witnessed the election of every pope since Pius XI in 1922, and who suggests that the best place to stand, "for studying the papal handwriting in the sky, is just in front of the broken clock on the façade of the Basilica so you're sort of gawking over the left shoulder of Taldoni's mighty statue of St. Paul—and watch out for pickpockets: sure they'd steal the freckles off your arm."

Like the crowd, the scores of TV and radio crews and print journalists find the waiting a tedious business. The media mood is not improved by running battles with the increasingly inept Vatican Press Office. No one can remember such journalistic frustration with the Vatican. The Press Office has even received a ringing protest in Latin about the media's *dolore et stupore;* now all this stupefaction and pain is exacerbated by having to hump film equipment about in broiling weather.

Reporters rework earlier copy: only forty-six popes have not been Italian, the last was Adrian VI of Flanders, who was booed on his election day; the last noncardinal was elected 600 years ago—and this time, should there be a long delay, say several hours, between the appearance of the white smoke and that of the new pope on the basilica balcony, it will almost certainly mean an outsider has been chosen, and that the cardinals are waiting for him to arrive, pick a name and put on one of the vestments stitched by Gammarelli.

This sort of flimflam helps the newsmen pass their time cobbling up dispatches that somehow often manage to suggest they know what is going on inside the Sistine Chapel. Yet not even the grossest piece of speculation matches the reality of the high drama developing beneath the slanted roof with its makeshift smokestack which is the focus of attention as noon approaches.

Wojtyla's richly resonant voice announces the result of the second ballot. Luciani has forty-six votes.

A concerted murmur sweeps the cardinals. Most of Siri's original backing must have transferred to Luciani. Wojtyla pauses, like an actor who knows he has delivered a show-stopping line. He smiles.

König thinks there has been a gasp or two. He cannot be certain because, in common with everyone else in the chapel, he is concentrating hard on Luciani.

The patriarch appears like a man who senses danger all around him but can see no way of escape. His face drains of color, the bloodless expression of deeply felt emotion. He looks almost beseechingly at Wojtyla.

Sin wonders, briefly, whether Luciani hopes there has been a mistake. The faces of Benelli and Felici confirm there is no error. Benelli, in particular, has worked hard days and long months for this; he has traveled, discussed and argued. He cannot contain his satisfaction: his knowing, lived-in face has a sharply satisfied look. The bulky heavy face of Felici displays a great flashing smile.

Villot glances sharply at Wojtyla, but otherwise there is no telling what the camerlengo feels.

Wojtyla reads the other votes. Pignedoli now has nineteen, Lorscheider—confounding those pundits who said there would be little support for such a relatively young candidate—has picked up twelve votes, and now has a total of fourteen. Baggio has eleven, two more than in the first ballot. Felici—another small surprise—has picked up seven votes, and now has nine. Bertoli has four and Hume is still there with a solitary vote.

Willebrands, who many thought would make a showing on the second ballot, has not picked up a vote.

When Wojtyla finishes, open conversation breaks out on all sides.

Felici and Benelli both go to Luciani and urge him to face what Felici is heard to term "the reality and the wishes of the Holy Spirit."

Villot firmly asks they return to their seats but, sensing the mood, he allows the general discussion to continue. The calmest and outwardly least involved are the Americans, who sit quietly in their places, content to see what develops.

Ribeiro, the patriarch of Lisbon, turns to Luciani and says in a voice which rises above the babble, "Courage. The Lord gave the burden. He will also give the strength to carry it."

Luciani nods. But nobody knows whether he has really understood or if this is simply a reflex action.

Willebrands, sitting beside him, also offers support. He tells Luciani, "Don't worry. All over the world everyone is praying for the new pope."

This time Luciani does not even nod; he appears to have virtually withdrawn from his surrounds.

Aramburu sits impassively. Though he cast his ballot for Lorscheider—and suspects some of his Latin American colleagues did the same, explaining why the Brazilian picked up those votes—it has all been to no avail.

Pignedoli smiles. Some cardinals will later say it's from relief; others that it is the disappointed reaction of someone encouraged to believe he really would be the best pope the Church could have.

Yet, reflects König, it is not over. There has to be a third ballot. It, too, may produce its surprises.

Villot abruptly gets to his feet and orders Sin to summon Noé. When he appears, the conversations cease. Luciani's face tells Noé what has happened. As he accompanies Villot and Sin to the stove with the second bin of used paper, Noé smiles encouragement at Luciani. The patriarch responds, again with only the merest of nods.

A great cry sweeps the square. *Fumo! Fumo!* A wisp of gray smoke curls from the chimney. Everyone holds their breath. Then there is a collective cry of disappointment as a thick, black column rises from the stack. It dissipates in minutes.

The nuns in the conclave kitchen have exceeded themselves: they offer for lunch roasted chunks of chicken and pork in a bed of rice.

Few cardinals clear their plates. The dining room is a constant hum of excited conversation. Many have decided not even to put in an appearance. They are either alone in their cells—König has glimpsed Hume kneeling on his prie-dieu, head bowed in prayer—or engaged in animated discussion up and down the corridors.

Felici and Benelli and a dozen other cardinals—including Willebrands, Gantin and Sin—have somehow squeezed themselves into Luciani's cell. The patriarch sits on his bed; the others stand or squat around him. In different ways they all say the same: it is the will of God, what is happening to Luciani.

He twines and untwines his hands, an unconscious gesture, just as he is oblivious to the various murmurs and tokens of compassion. He is in a daze, preoccupied with his own thoughts. Gradually, in the face of his lack of response, an unnatural stillness falls over the tiny room, broken when Benelli mutters, with just a trace of exasperation, "You *have* to accept; it's God's way." There are encouraging mutters. Still Luciani sits, isolated, not responding, a man gripped by emotions which even afterward he will not properly be able to explain.

Baggio arrives and he and Felici retreat to the Parrot Courtyard, where they pace to and fro. Even the sharp-eared attendants cannot catch the drift of the conversation. But the outcome is not in doubt. As they separate, Felici gives Baggio a friendly clap on the shoulder and then returns to Luciani.

Pignedoli and Lorscheider are seen to meet briefly in a corridor. A few words and they, too, go their own ways. Lorscheider hurries to Aramburu's cell, where the two men confer privately. Pignedoli calls on Bertoli. They also have a very private discussion: the upshot is that both men arrange to see Benelli in his cell.

Benelli's participation in the brief meeting must be treated scrupulously, for the friction in the past between the three men will be sufficient to produce distortion by their supporters when the details do emerge. In conclave each is under considerable tension and pressure; each is hampered by his own bearing, those small traits of personality which do not make it easy for any of them to accept opposing points of view.

Characteristically, Benelli is intent on coming straight to the point. But normally an experienced and eloquent orator, he is surprisingly awkward, which adds a tone of ungenerosity to his words. He tartly tells Pignedoli that he should not expect to make a further advance in the next ballot.

Everybody knows Pignedoli is an inveterate traveler, perhaps next to Baggio the most globe-trotting of the cardinals. For months now the story has persisted that he's used the trips to mobilize support for a tilt at the papacy. Pignedoli has denied it—repeatedly. Yet the rumor refuses to fade away. Now, with his clutch of nineteen votes, it seems that, like a rolling stone, he *has* been attracting support from various corners of the Catholic world. With a few blunt words Benelli is saying it's all over.

Pignedoli cannot hide his disappointment; his subsequent remarks clearly indicate he hoped for more. Responding with a tartness which matches Benelli's, he says his supporters are loyal and that matters should be allowed to take their natural course. To the astonishment of the others, Pignedoli's style is not his subdued self, full of the hesitancies which nowadays characterize his speech. Instead, there's a distinctly salty air about his words, a reminder of Pignedoli's days as a naval chaplain.

In the end, though, his argument amounts to this: Luciani is a mite too liberal in some areas: being progressive is one thing, verging on the radical is another. He does not specify, but quickly moves on to suggest that Aramburu is not the only one opposed to the patriarch; there are a number of other cardinals who do not like Luciani's supposedly freewheeling ways. This time he throws in one example: the patriarch's well-known relaxed attitude toward his parish priests. Then he fires his final shot. What about Luciani's health?

The question remains unanswered. Is it Benelli's way of dismissing its implications? Or does he simply not wish to get into that sort of debate at this late stage? The issue will produce endless debate. But not now. Now, the two men wait to see what Bertoli will say.

He continues to choose to remain silent. It may be he feels uncomfortable in the presence of Benelli after all their wrangling during those days they were both Vatican diplomats. Or it may be he just thinks Pignedoli should recognize a lost cause. But Pignedoli appears in no way dejected; he seems to have endless ways of introducing new twists to familiar arguments. And, indeed, some of what he says is beyond dispute. There are, without doubt, certain cardinals, Höffner of Cologne being one, who will never endorse Luciani's election. They will either return blank ballot forms, or give Pignedoli what amounts to protest votes.

Yet it is Bertoli who finally speaks the kind of simple truth which brings together all the complexities and reduces them to one telling phrase.

"We must all, for the good of the Church, let the Holy Spirit continue to guide us."

When the discussion ends, it is seen as significant—at least by conclave attendants—that Bertoli goes with Benelli to Luciani's cell. This is taken as symbolic peace between the two cardinals who have battled each other for so long.

Pignedoli repairs to his cell to pray.

König and Suenens of Brussels are with Wojtyla, doing some very basic arithmetic. Luciani is twenty-nine votes short of the seventy-five needed. All three—according to one source close to Suenens—will continue to vote for Luciani. But König remains cautious: while conclave will certainly not last the week he had thought, it may well go beyond a third ballot. Anything can happen; he doesn't like racing terms for such a serious business, but they are still some distance from the finishing post.

In the midst of all this intense activity—nobody can now seriously consider what is happening "consultation," it is high-powered politicking—Krol manages to squeeze in a siesta while Cody has a lengthy discussion with Cooke, one the New York cardinal will later say has "nothing to do with the present business."

At four o'clock, the cardinals return to the Sistine Chapel. Fifty-five minutes later—Felici's timings are useful in pinpointing the progress of events—Wojtyla announces the result of the third ballot.

Luciani has sixty-six votes. Pignedoli has managed to acquire a further two —one is said to be Duval of Algeria and the other Gabriel Garrone, a French cardinal. This gives Pignedoli twenty-one supporters in the chapel. Lorscheider is still there—but fading fast. Thirteen votes have switched from him, almost certainly to Luciani. The Brazilian now only has one; it will be an open secret in conclave that Aramburu is staying with Lorscheider to the end.

Villot calls for an immediate fourth ballot.

It is five twenty-five precisely on Felici's wrist when the first vote of this count is placed on the silver paten and tipped into the chalice. At six-twenty Gantin threads the last card onto the line. A moment later Wojtyla, beaming broadly, announces that Luciani has polled ninety-six votes. In the roar of applause it is virtually impossible to hear that Pignedoli has ten votes—presumably one of them being Luciani's, for cardinals cannot vote for themselves. Lorscheider has completed the course, riding home on the one faithful vote of Aramburu.

Luciani sits with his eyes closed and lips barely moving in prayer.

Villot instructs Sin to summon Noé for the last time, raising his voice above the almost continuous hand-clapping. Then, accompanied by the master of ceremonies and the three scrutineers, the camerlengo walks solemnly to where Luciani is seated, head bowed.

An expectant hush settles over the chapel.

In carefully enunciated Latin, Villot poses the first of two questions.

"Do you, Most Reverend Lord Cardinal, accept your election as Supreme Pontiff which has been canonically carried out?"

Luciani's eyes remain closed. His lips continue to move in prayer. He clasps and unclasps his hands, but whereas in his cell the movement had been an unconscious gesture, now it appears deliberate, as if he is timing himself, judging his moment. His hands become still. Everyone around him strains to see his reaction. At last Luciani opens his eyes.

Noé will have a lasting memory of the "shiny look" now in those eyes. König sees "a certainty" which has not been there before. Gantin senses "strength and resolve." Sin is convinced "it's God's decision."

Luciani's words are all the more stunning.

"May God forgive you for what you have done in my regard."

Villot is flummoxed. He fiddles with his pectoral cross and looks around with what Felici thinks is something akin to despair; Felici doubts that anywhere in the Secret Archives is there the record of a response anything like this.

Luciani suddenly smiles the broad melonlike grin that stretches his skin and exposes those dazzling white teeth over which a Venetian orthodontist has taken such care.

"Accepto . . ."

Villot's relief is so great that he gapes. He is still standing, mouth sagging, as Luciani completes the sentence.

". . . in the name of the Lord."

The camerlengo closes his mouth, licks his lips—and looks warily at the pope.

"By what name will you be known?"

Luciani is in no hurry to respond to Villot's question. Instead he looks at Benelli and Felici. In the interval between the third and fourth ballots, both men had suggested that when this moment came—there were by then, as Felici says, no ifs or buts about the outcome of the election—Luciani might like to consider the influence on him of John XXIII, who ordained him a priest, and of Paul, who made him a bishop.

In a voice strong and certain, Albino Luciani announces what he will henceforth be known as.

"I will be called John Paul One."

MacCarthy is seated before a microphone in view of a monitor filled with a close-up of the smokestack. He glances at the studio clock and continues to read his script about why a cardinal changes his name when elected. Mac-Carthy is keyed to abandon his talk should the chimney suddenly emit smoke. But it remains lifeless. He inserts an ad lib into his text, telling his invisible audience, stretching from the Libyan desert to the lush green of Natal, that they, like the estimated hundred-thousand crowd now in St. Peter's Square, must continue to patiently wait. It is six-thirty P.M.

At that precise moment the attendant with the secret bug goes into action. He first satisfies himself on the whereabouts of the surveillance team who have been repeatedly sweeping the conclave area. He finds them in the Sistine Chapel, standing to one side, eyes on their sensors. The man hurries to the armory of the Borgia Apartments. The nuns in the adjoining field kitchen have either gone to the chapel to watch the celebrations or are busily preparing dinner. No one pays him any attention.

Before coming into conclave he memorized a simple but effective code. It differs only slightly from the one he used when indicating a new ballot had begun; this time the duration of the individual signals will be longer. Each candidate has been given a number. The first name on the man's list gets a single, lengthy buzz, the second two, and so on. He now gives the button eleven distinct squeezes.

There are eleven corresponding bleeps from the receiver wired into the engineer's console in the Vatican Radio studio high up on the western slopes of the city-state.

The employee who has been listening for the signal waits for the buzzing to stop, then writes down one word: Luciani. He holds it up to the sound-proof glass panel dividing the room from the adjoining studio. The broadcasters grouped around table microphones exchange glances. One of them begins to speak.

Vatican Radio has its scoop.

Inside conclave the attendant, as instructed, goes to a toilet and flushes away the bug.

Shortly afterward the surveillance team reports to Noé that the entire area is still electronically clean.

Noé informs Villot.

At six thirty-three—he writes down the time on a scratch pad though he does not know why—Anibaile Gammarelli receives a telephone call from one of Villot's assistants. The tailor hurries to his car and sets off at speed through the back streets of Rome. It will take him six minutes to complete the journey.

The tumult of shouting and honking of car horns pours from MacCarthy's monitor. He smiles ruefully. Moments after he came off the air four puffs of smoke emerged from the stack. The roar continues to rise from the crowd as more smoke is emitted. But though the camera shows the chimney in close-up, MacCarthy is not sure of the smoke's actual color against the pearly white sky. The crowd has no doubt. People are shouting in delight, "È bianco, è bianco!" ("It is white!") MacCarthy's screen cuts from the spectators back to the stack. He sees there is a change. The smoke is darkening. It will continue to behave capriciously, causing doubt where there is no need. His critics will blame Villot—who else?—for not having installed a more reliable system.

Three minutes later—it is now six thirty-seven—the same assistant who phoned the tailor calls Levi at L'Osservatore Romano. The editor listens and relaxes. Levi gives the order to lock onto the press the front-page matrix carrying Luciani's portrait and biography.

Martin waits impatiently at the open door of the Sistine Chapel. He has sent Swiss Guards down to the Arch of the Bells to escort Gammarelli to him. He wishes now he had told Ciban to arrange that Rome police provide a motorcycle escort for the tailor. But there hasn't been time. It all happened so quickly even the experienced prefect is surprised: he thinks four ballots must be close to one of the shortest conclaves in recent history, especially as the last vote seems to have been a formality.

The prefect has heard an intriguing story. Formality apart, the fourth ballot was largely "a confirming one," intended to show how overwhelming was the support for the patriarch. So much so it would effectively silence the dissident Lefèbvre, who previously announced he would not accept the decision of conclave because it did not include the sixteen cardinals over eighty whom Paul's rules excluded from voting.

True or not, Martin is clear that the new pontiff will find Lefèbvre's brand of religious fascism just one of the many nettles he will have to grapple with. Lefèbvre shouldn't be too much of a problem; his reactionary movement is essentially a last-ditch effort of pre-Vatican II nostalgics; their outlook is little different from those diehards who rejected the socioeconomic, political and theological changes which followed in the wake of the great revolutions of the last century. Martin is all for preserving the tenets of Catholic faith, and there are definite lines he will not cross. Yet he has no time for extremists and self-publicists like Lefèbvre who thrive off challenging papal authority. Firmness, in the prefect's view, will see Lefèbvre off.

But it may not be so easy with the rest of the opposition. The avowed aim of many of them is the downgrading of the authority of the Curia and the Sacred College of Cardinals by increased decentralization of the Church, so that laymen, priests and bishops far removed from the ambience of the Vatican can have a greater say in its decision-making process; these revolutionaries march behind a banner which proclaims that the Church and the pope are prisoners of a rigid authoritarian system and that there is an urgent need for liberalization.

The very word is anathema to the crusty old prefect. He knows the new pope will preside over a house divided, polarized between seemingly irreconcilable tendencies. Paul had indeed not wished to go down in history as the pope who oversaw the dismantlement of the Church. But he had left it so weakened, in such an impasse, that it would need a very firm hand to bring it back on course. Was Paul's successor the man to do this? Did he have the talent, the skill, the insight, the wisdom and, Martin had to admit, the essential cunning to cope with the grave challenges of the many autonomous, loosely organized groups of varying religious and political disposition, made up of clergy and laity?

The prefect continues to ponder. Luciani is another northerner; he will be almost unknown in Rome, and in turn will know little of the inner workings of the Curia. Will he be prepared to listen? Will he come south, as Paul did, with his own entourage, to stamp a distinctive Venetian influence on the Vatican? Doubtless he will bring some close and trusted aides. But will he also accept that the best interests of the papacy, in Martin's view, will only be served if the new pontiff reappoints Paul's key nominees—of which Martin is one?

He searches his mind for what he knows about the patriarch. He has seen him around the Vatican when he came to call on Paul. But Luciani always gave the impression that he really couldn't wait to go home to his palace by the water. He's written for the press and produced a book. Martin can't, for the moment, recall which newspaper, or the book's title. Then he remembers: a copy of *Illustrissimi* had been passed around the Secretariat of State, causing some headshakes about its contents: not everybody found it to their taste that a prince of the Church was writing letters to a puppet called Pinocchio. Martin knows he must get a copy, quickly. But that name the new pope has chosen, John Paul I, doesn't it sound a bit cumbersome? Perhaps the Romans, if they like the new pontiff, will familiarize it. Gianpaolo, thinks Martin, might do very well; it has a nice affectionate ring to it.

The prefect is still considering the matter when Gammarelli and his Swiss Guard escort arrive. The tailor carries a small bag. In his dark suit he looks like a doctor.

"Who is he?" asks Gammarelli.

"Papa Gianpaolo." Martin decides to try out the name.

"Gianpaolo?"

"Sì."

Martin turns and walks quickly ahead, discouraging further conversation.

Gammarelli follows closely behind. "Gianpaolo? Is he a cardinal?"

"Sì. What else?"

"Of course. But from where?"

"Venice."

"Ah, Luciani."

Gammarelli's mind is recalling the last time he measured the patriarch as Martin leads him into the sacristy.

Cardinals are milling everywhere; it is like one of those receptions the Sacred College gives in honor of a new member.

Martin cuts through the crowd, nodding and smiling but never slackening speed, Gammarelli in tow.

They finally reach the group around the pope. Martin thinks: yes, he is definitely a Gianpaolo.

Gammarelli recognizes them all except the broad-shouldered Slav with the penetrating eyes. Later, the tailor will remember Wojtyla's worn robe and shoes and wonder who his tailor is. But now he only has time for Gianpaolo.

He is forcibly struck by the contrast with that time, fifteen years ago, he had stood on this very spot and helped Paul to robe. Even then Paul had been distant. In the ensuing years, when Gammarelli regularly measured him, Paul showed increasing impatience with the procedure. Like so much else, clothes seemed to have lost their appeal. Gianpaolo, on the other hand, has always appreciated the tailor's skills. He's been one of those clients who invariably found the time to send a handwritten note of thanks for a new garment. Already he's glanced several times at the portable rack holding the sets of papal vestments Gammarelli has made.

The tailor goes to the rack, now in command. He selects the smallest of the cassocks and turns to Gianpaolo.

"If it pleases Your Eminence." He quickly corrects his mistake. "Pardon, *Santissimo Padre*."

Gianpaolo smiles. "It will take me time as well to become used to this."

Gammarelli helps Gianpaolo remove his cardinal's robe. He hands it to Noé, who takes it away.

The robe will be dry-cleaned, placed in a cardboard box lined with tissue paper and delivered to the papal apartment. There it will be carefully stored until Gianpaolo's death; then, unless he has decreed otherwise, it will be handed over to the senior surviving member of his family.

Gianpaolo stands in his long-tailed shirt and baggy undershorts, still smiling.

The tailor notices his legs. They are swollen around the ankles and the calves are distended. Gammarelli cannot remember them being like this the last time he saw Luciani. But he has too many other things on his mind to give the matter more than fleeting concern. He helps Gianpaolo to don the cassock. The tailor stands back, appraising. It is a poor fit. The hem trails the ground, the sleeves reach below Gianpaolo's fingertips, and the garment hangs loosely on his slight frame.

The pope smiles in sympathy. "You could not have known."

"Grazie, Santissimo Padre."

This is the moment for the tailor when he knows he is in the presence of "a truly wonderful man." Gammarelli drops to his knees, opens his bag and selects an already-threaded needle. Stitching swiftly, he quickly raises the hem. He tucks and sews the sleeves, and then nips the cassock at the back. He again stands aside to run a critical eye over his handiwork.

"It feels very fine," says Gianpaolo.

Gammarelli nods happily. Gianpaolo is not only the most wonderful but also the humblest man he has ever met.

He asks Gianpaolo to sit. The tailor kneels once more and removes the pope's heavy brown shoes and woollen socks, replacing them with the white stockings and red-velvet slippers with their small gold crosses. They are a perfect fit. Gammarelli offers the white papal skullcap. Gianpaolo puts it on, smiling broadly.[1]

Greeley is in St. Peter's Square. The confusing smoke has been pouring from the chimney stack for forty-five minutes. But he thinks "the show" is over. He is about to walk away when a commanding voice booms out over the piazza's powerful address system.

"Attenzione!"

It is Noé uttering his first public word of the new pontificate.

A door of the basilica balcony opens.

Pericle Felici appears, smiling. Martin is behind him, Noé close by. The balcony fills with cardinals as Felici recites the traditional Latin litany.

"Annuntio vobis gaudium magnum!"

A roar greets the words: "We have a pope."

"Eminentissimum ac Reverendissimum Dominium Cardinalem Albinum . . ."

The crowd falls silent. Greeley wonders: Albinum, who in the hell is that? Felici booms on. *"Cardinalem Sanctae Romanae Ecclesiae . . ."*
A pause. Then:
". . . Luciani!"
The crowd goes wild.
Felici roars on. *"Qui Sibi Imposuit Nomen Joannem . . ."*
Greeley thinks: So, John XXIV. That's a good sign.
". . . Paulum!"
Another huge cheer.
". . . Primum!"
There is bedlam in the square.

Greenan is leaving his office when the telephone rings. He hesitates. It's been a long day. But he takes the call.
"Lambert Greenan?"
The accent is American, the voice that of a stranger.
"Who is that?" asks Greenan in the guarded tone he reserves for priests looking for free copies of his paper.
"This is Cody. Cardinal Cody of Chicago. Is that you, Lambert?"
"Yes, Eminence."
"Fine. Fine. Okay. I got your letter. I would have liked to have dinner. But you know, we have a new pope. A nice little Italian fellow called Luciani. A good choice . . ."
"Eminence . . . where are you calling from?"
"From conclave."
"You're calling from *where?*" Greenan cannot hide his incredulity.
"It's all over, Lambert. It's all over. We've got a new pope and the phones are back on in here."
"Yes, Eminence."
"Okay. Well, listen. About your letter. I'd love to have dinner. But not this time. I've got to get back to Chicago, fast, you know how it is . . . ?"
"Yes, Eminence."
"Fine. Fine. But stay in touch, Lambert. You hear me? Stay in touch. Keep the words coming."
Cody puts down the phone.
Dumbfounded, Greenan reflects on the call. He thinks it is one of the most astonishing he has received in his life. Months ago he had written Cody, on behalf of his order, asking the cardinal to dine at their priory when next he was in Rome. There had been no reply. That Cody should have called from conclave was, Greenan thinks, "quite remarkable," but even more so was the cardinal's familiarity. Greenan has never met him, yet Cody behaved as

though they were bosom pals. Greenan shakes his head. He'll never get used to these American ways.

Magee sees Villot emerge onto the basilica balcony. The secretary is watching proceedings from a window overlooking the square. It is almost the first time he has been back to the Vatican these past three weeks. Since Paul's funeral Magee has retreated to the Rome residence of his order. He has spent his days there in quiet contemplation.

In some ways he feels he is at a personal crossroads. In a month he will be forty-two. He knows he has already experienced more than most men can hope to achieve in life. He has sat at the elbow of a powerful pope; he has been privy to some of the most important decision making in the contemporary world: the Vietnam War, the endless horrors of the Middle East, the continuing divisions within his beloved Ireland—all these, and many more conflicts, he has observed from a unique vantage point. He has mixed with ranking statesmen and the merely famous. Some have impressed him deeply, a few shocked him by their venality. Yet he has never shown, by as much as a flicker of an eyebrow, his feelings in public. Long ago this ninth child of a deeply committed Ulster Republican family learned from his Christian Brothers education that outward displays of emotion are unacceptable.

Magee fears it has made him appear almost isolated, sometimes even from old friends, like Greenan and MacCarthy. And these past three years as one of Paul's closest confidants have left their mark. He knows he *is* more reserved, *is* more secretive, *is* more demanding. But there have been compensations. His time in the Vatican has provided invaluable insights into how the Church is really run. He knows most of the important leaders of the Roman Curia. To him they are not a group of faceless men sitting in marble-floored and stucco-ceilinged offices far removed from the pressures of everyday life; instead, they are civil servants who try valiantly to apply high-level Church decisions to local circumstances. And Magee knows a great deal about the workings of the Vatican diplomatic service. Though he does not always find it easy, he has come to recognize that it is sometimes preferable to support an armed regime, usually a right-wing military dictatorship, than accede to the local bishop's understandable desire to denounce the tyranny. He has seen it actually happen in Nicaragua, Chile and Argentina. He knows, too, the unwritten law of papal diplomacy: nuncios are the conduit between a local hierarchy and a dictatorship. If it is overthrown, the nuncio can be posted elsewhere, leaving the hierarchy to build links with the new regime.

Through all of this he has come to understand the reality and the paradox of "spiritual power." He knows it has virtually nothing to do with the accepted view of temporal power; the Church's power is based, in the end, on the experience of the Cross. The Apostle Luke put it so well: "The kings of the Gentiles exercise lordship over them, and those in authority are called benefactors. But not so with you; rather let the greatest among you become as the youngest, and the leader as one who serves." That is the bedrock on which the Vatican's spiritual role is built, one that allows it to follow the instruction given Peter to "confirm the faith of the brethren." The inheritors of Peter, the popes, have, with some exceptions, tried to do that through service, not domination. This is the strong bond which joins the Church to the New Testament.

And it is this thought that is making Magee now wonder whether he should stay in Rome, or whether he might serve the Church better by returning to missionary work in Nigeria. Should he go back to that ill-defined slice of Africa which continues to hold a magnetic appeal for him? He could resume teaching in a bush school, lead the staff and pupils in prayers, learn again to cope with emergencies which have to be resolved through whatever ingenuity is available and, above all, he could remain close to the reasons which had taken him to Nigeria in the first place. It certainly is a temptation to go back.

Like Martin, Magee has been doing some serious thinking about the problems Gianpaolo is inheriting and must overcome. The crisis of authority that began in the mid-1950s still plagues the Church; perhaps now, more than ever, there exist strongly conflicting pressures within a Church looked upon for centuries as the epitome of a solidly based, united and conservative religious organization. With the passing of Paul the call for transformation is once more to be heard. From the United States, in particular, word drifted back to Rome during the interregnum that many lay Catholics were simply not prepared to accept the present order of things.

These protest movements, with their demand for dramatic and drastic change, are different from those that surfaced within the Church in previous times. Those had generally been effectively dealt with by autocratic means. Paul was the first to discover, in the wake of the brief and revolutionary pontificate of John, that such methods no longer worked. He had been reluctantly forced to loosen the reins of papal power. This did nothing to halt the antiauthority protest throughout much of the Catholic world. Even members of the hierarchy were supporting the demand from the laity for more autonomy, freedom and power in all aspects of their religious lives. They were resisting what they saw as authority exercised through domination rather than service. Consequently, the challenges to Paul's authority had left the Church badly wounded.

It is not just Lefèbvre and Küng; it is a galaxy of theologians and teachers bent on creating a surge of Catholic public opinion which will sweep away much of what Magee, for one, holds to be sacrosanct: priestly celibacy, opposition to birth control and abortion and divorce, the ruling out on scriptural and theological grounds the possibility of women being ordained as priests. Yet Magee equally knows there can be no returning to pre-Vatican II Catholicism, as reactionaries like Lefèbvre have demanded. Instead, there must be careful progress on moral, ecclesiastical and theological questions, a balance struck between the demands of the grass roots and the hierarchy; a delicately maneuvered swing away from the right of center—where the papacy was stuck in the last years of Paul—to somewhere which would nevertheless fall short of causing accusations that the new pope was a religious radical. Like Martin, Magee wonders whether Gianpaolo is intellectually equipped to meet the challenge.

And, watching the scene on the balcony of the basilica, Magee can guess what some of those around the new pontiff may now also be wondering. In particular, will they be reappointed? Certainly Gianpaolo will bring with him his own "inner cabinet," one bound to be very different from Paul's. That is to be expected. And even if Magee himself is asked to be a member, how would he slot into the new regime?

He is still contemplating the question when Villot stands aside for Gianpaolo to approach the microphone.

Magee is immediately struck by his smile; it is truly magnificent.

But will it be enough?

As the crowd roars, Magee reminds himself that Gianpaolo is the man people have always liked. He has an impressive pastoral record in Venice; he is popular with his priests and seems to have had no serious problems with the Curia.

Yet things are bound to be different now. Even Paul, in spite of all his curial experience and diplomatic skills, had not found it easy to cope with Vatican bureaucracy, whose exponents Pius XII had once likened to "the Bourbons, who learned little and forgot nothing." Magee feels the judgment unfair—perhaps even harsh. But the system does need careful handling.

He knows through hard-won experience that the successful exercise of power in the Church rests on making proper use of the Curia. Anyone, even a pope, who does not function within the formal and informal parameters of this bureaucracy will find it hard, and often impossible, to operate efficiently in the upper reaches of the Church. Paul discovered it was much easier to work with the Curia than to try to transform it—if only because a pope and his civil service, in harmony, form a winning team. In spite of all his angst with Villot, Paul had remained attached to the Secretariat of State as an instrument of government.

Will Gianpaolo feel the same? Will he realize that if he allows the Curia to slip totally from his control, or permit a strengthened collegial control-sharing with the Synod of Bishops—as some reformers have urged—then gradually he might become little but a figurehead? He will still be publicly loved but to all intents impoverished of power. The only way to keep the papacy potent is to develop a sensible working alliance with the Curia. That will not be easy if Gianpaolo continues, for example, to display a break with traditionalist ideology, as he seemed to do in his pronouncements over Louise Brown, the English test-tube baby. Personally, Magee can find no fault with the sensitive and sensible approach adopted; clearly raised were the question of potential abuse, the risks involved, the possibility of science becoming like the sorcerer's apprentice—controlling instead of being controlled. And indeed, there was a reasoned defense of *Humanae Vitae*. Nevertheless, Luciani's widely reported views brought many a frown to Curial brows. These powerful men would be watching closely and, if the need arose, would act in their own effective way against the new pope. It is a daunting prospect.

Watching Gianpaolo extend his first papal blessing to the crowd, Magee wonders, too, how the pope will cope with the pressures building up on the question of democratization of much of the structure of the Church? The present system of nomination to positions of authority—apart from the election of a pope—functions entirely by cooptation from above; this is under severe challenge and criticism by lower clergy.

Like so much else, Paul shunted aside the question into some backwater; in the end he pretended the problem did not exist. It didn't make it go away. It still vied for attention, demanding a solution. Just like so many issues.

There is, for instance, the vast arena of Christian-Marxist dialogue. In which direction should it go? Paul often encouraged a moderation toward communism far removed from the harsh condemnation of the Pius pontificates. But that very moderation paved the way for radical Catholic forces within the Church to press for reforms well beyond those envisioned by Vatican II, which, in turn, produced the Lefèbvre backlash. And there is the equally explosive question of the Church's long-standing involvement with Italian politics. Paul, like the Pius popes, was an astute politician, committed to the Christian Democrat Party since its birth; indeed, he was one of the right-wing movement's most enthusiastic early backers. He saw the Christian Democrats as the means to hold back hordes of marauding Communists from extinguishing Italian democracy: the possibility was one of the recurring themes in his nightly soliloquys over dinner. During the bitter May–June election campaign of 1976, the Christian Democrats received his full support as they raised the specter of communism at the hustings; Paul even went so far as to threaten excommunication for any Catholic who voted Communist. The bitter residue of that promise still permeated Italy. Gianpaolo must find a way of easing the bonds which hold the Church fast to the Christian Democrats; perhaps he should begin in Rome by opening up a dialogue with the city's Communist mayor.

Again, he will have to take a long hard look at the day-to-day functioning of his financial empire, deciding for a start whether there should be a more humane and less capitalistic use of funds, whether there is any need for the Vatican to make yet more use of its economic power, working even harder to eliminate exploitation, discrimination and oppression. This overview is quite apart from the "local" problems of Marcinkus and Cody and their entangled financial dealings—though they, too, will require serious attention early on in the new pontificate.

So will a whole range of political problems. There is the Holy See's relationship with China. Should it be improved or left in its present ambivalent state? There is the Middle East. Will Gianpaolo do what Paul would never have contemplated and bestow de facto recognition on Israel? Among the strongly ensconced Arab faction in the Vatican the very thought is tantamount to heresy; in some Secretariat of State minds there still lingers a Christ-was-killed-by-the-Jews mentality. There is the spiky issue of the Jesuits. It will need more than Paul's occasional dire warnings, which in the last years gave way to an anguished silence on his part about the matter; the disaffection of the order with the Vatican's way of thinking is a veritable theological minefield. There is the equally contentious affair of the burgeoning Christians for Socialism movement, the self-styled "Critical Christians"; these organized reformist priests and laymen are a recent phenomenon that began in Chile and has now spread to Europe. They are pledged to end what they see as the papacy's involvement with bourgeois political parties and capitalism. Paul pretended they didn't exist. Gianpaolo may not wish to confront them head-on, but there is going to be no way he can bypass them. Coupled with the "Critical Christians" is the liberation theology movement, freely borrowing from Marxism, bent on creating a radically new Catholic doctrine for the Latin American poor. Its priest members carry guns, fight alongside guerrillas, kill in the name of God—and ask the Apostolic Penitentiary to settle any resultant questions of conscience. In the end Paul had refused even to read the shattering reports from the Penitentiary about such shocking behavior.

There are so many—so very many—problems that the tiny white figure on the balcony of St. Peter's must soon begin to contend with.

And, as he watches Gianpaolo wave repeatedly to the crowd, the fiercely dedicated Magee realizes that he cannot leave Rome; that, given the chance, he must stay and use his considerable experience to try to help Gianpaolo to meet all the challenges.

Alibrandi knows his immediate future is settled. He will be staying in Ireland; the nuncio is certain Gianpaolo will have neither the occasion nor the inclination to tamper with his ambassadors for at least a year; new popes generally like to take their time, and soundings, before moving their diplomats. Alibrandi's initial disappointment that his friend Pappalardo was not elected, is eased by his feeling that Gianpaolo will be "a great pope." The nuncio has only glimpsed him on the television screen and barely knows the new pontiff, but he was instantly able to come to one of those decisions that sometimes make other diplomats in Dublin shake their heads in exasperation.

Many of them will shortly receive identical letters from the nuncio which he hammers out on his typewriter. In all he will write a hundred notes to members of the Irish government, his fellow diplomats and the country's bishops, informing them of Gianpaolo's election. Periodically he breaks off typing to make telephone calls to implement the official celebrations which will follow the election.

As the evening wears on, an idea gradually forms in the fertile mind of the nuncio. Fortified by sips of coffee, it grows from a hesitant possibility to a confident certainty.

Shortly his new nunciature will be ready. Sited close to a busy main road, it is geographically exposed for those IRA leaders wishing to slip in secretly to brief Alibrandi on their latest proposals to force Britain out of Ulster, but in every other respect the embassy is a dream come true for the house-proud nuncio.

The finest Irish woods and fabrics have been personally chosen by him for what will be one of the best-appointed outposts of the Holy See's diplomatic service—a mansion certainly more splendidly furnished than the red-brick edifice of the British Embassy, some of whose occupants Alibrandi suspects will look with grave suspicion on the plan he is formulating.

The nuncio hopes to have Gianpaolo as his first official houseguest in the nunciature as part of a triumphant papal visit which would not only include the Catholic South but extend to the Protestant Northern Ireland.

The more he contemplates the idea, the more excited he feels. He gets up, walks around his cozy study, returns to his typewriter, rattles off another letter, gets up again, thinking all the time. The idea is feasible: everything is feasible in the optimistic world of the nuncio; a lifetime of diplomatically getting what he wants has taught him even more wrinkles than he has on his nut-brown face. He knows this is not a matter of sending a handwritten invitation to the pope through the diplomatic pouch; that could easily get delayed or pigeonholed in the Secretariat of State. Curial officials have a habit of doing that if they think a nuncio is going outside normal channels.

Alibrandi realizes he will have to visit Rome to personally put his case to the pope. That, too, is easier said than done. Holy See diplomats stationed abroad, as he full well knows, don't suddenly breeze unexpectedly into the Vatican on some whim. There has to be good reason. Here, at least, the nuncio has an advantage over some of his colleagues in other diplomatic missions.

Since its inception as an independent state, Ireland has always been regarded as having a "special" relationship with the Vatican. Until 1972 the Irish Constitution actually declared that "the State recognizes the special position of the Holy Catholic Apostolic and Roman Church as the guardians of the Faith professed by the great majority of the citizens"; this was deleted by referendum, an olive twig for the Protestant North to grasp. But the Constitution still contained an article which was a pillar of Church thinking: "No law shall be enacted providing for the grant of a dissolution of marriage."

And yet in spite of its close ties to the Church, all is not well in the South. The old patterns of morality are being eroded. With almost half of the country's three-million-odd population under the age of twenty-five, the sober and assiduous faith of former years has given way to a distinct drift away from the fold. The proportion of young adults in the South who are not practicing Catholics has reached an alarming 20 percent of the population. And those who do attend mass are often no more than "lip-service Catholics," reciting their Hail Marys but otherwise paying scant attention to the teachings of the Church. More Irish Catholic girls than ever are using some form of contraceptive—freely prescribed by Catholic doctors for "menstrual irregularities"; more women are traveling to England for abortions; more couples are demanding legal separations. At the same time the number of young people seeking vocations as nuns, priests or monks is declining. Alibrandi thinks he knows what is behind this dismal situation. It is all to do with Ireland's new affluence as a member of the European Economic Community. EEC grants have modernized the country's farms, making them less labor-intensive; foreign investment has attracted young country people to work in the towns. Nearly two hundred years after England's industrial revolution, Ireland is going through a similar process. The result, in Alibrandi's view, is that young, inexperienced adults are being exposed to the dangers of city life: loneliness, unsupervised drinking, drugs, a loosening of sexual standards.

This, then, is the diagnosis he will place before Gianpaolo. Properly argued, supported by reports from the Irish bishops, it will produce a powerful case for the pope's coming to Ireland.

The crucial question remains of when he should make his presentation. Alibrandi knows nothing of the way Gianpaolo likes to do things. But he is certain the pope will need at least a month to settle into the Vatican.

He decides: he will go to Rome in early October. That will also give him sufficient time to contact the two persons who will be invaluable for the successful outcome of his mission. Pappalardo can brief him on Gianpaolo; Magee can smooth his way to the pope's private study.

The nuncio considers the pleasures ahead. It will be mild in Rome in October, a welcome break from the onset of another gray and wet Irish winter; there will be old friends to see around the Vatican, leisurely lunches and dinners, informed gossip to exchange. And at the end of it the plum of being the man to spark off national rejoicing in Ireland with the news that the pope is coming.

The papal visit will have to be carefully promoted as purely pastoral, concentrating on the moral rather than the political problems of all thirty-two counties in the divided island; yet Gianpaolo could have a decisive effect on the violence which plagues the six counties of Ulster. It is a heady prospect which is also fraught with the most delicate of diplomatic difficulties. Alibrandi correctly sees South and North as ecclesiastically one Catholic fief —his own writ extends to all Ireland—and a papal visit which included Ulster would, so far as the Church went, offer no problems. But the nuncio is painfully aware that the more rabid Protestant elements will regard any papal incursion as an attempt to establish a Catholic claim over their domain. The nuncio thinks this is nonsense. But how to convince the extremists? Ultimately, the British government will have to be consulted to pave the way for an "understanding" with the moderate, if not the extremist, Protestant majority.

Alibrandi suspects such a visit would have been unthinkable under Paul: he would have shied away from the idea of walking through Northern Ireland's bitterly divided factions to spread the gospel of peace. But Paul was old and exhausted. Gianpaolo, at least on television, had looked to the nuncio like "an adventuresome schoolboy, a pope who will try anything."

A visit to Ulster would set the style of his pontificate. It would show he is not only ready to carry on Paul's pilgrimages but is prepared to go further. To travel from Rome to Belfast is a mere hop when compared with some of his predecessor's marathon journeys, yet it could be the most dramatic ecumenical gesture of the decade—perhaps even of the century. All these are the arguments which Alibrandi will hone and polish and place before Gianpaolo.

Then a sudden, sickening, jolting thought strikes the nuncio. Despite the most careful planning, the very necessary checks and balances, the prior agreements, the most stringent security, the constant emphasis that it will be only a pastoral visit: in spite of everything, supposing one—just one—Protestant extremist decides that the pope in Northern Ireland is too tempting an assassination target to miss?

XIX

In overcrowded Ankara Agca feels fortunate. He is sharing this fly-blown stinking room in the Yenişehir District of the city with only four other men; they sleep on the floor while he has a narrow truckle bed. The room is one of the Gray Wolves' safe houses and Colonel Turkes, leader of the paramilitary extremists, has passed the word that Agca is to receive favored treatment. Food has been brought to him, and once a girl was sent up; they copulated and she left. The rest of the time he has spent sprawled on the bed reading the exercise book filled with details of Paul's life and travels. Below the last entry he has drawn a dagger in a circle. It is the symbol of the Gray Wolves. When he is not reading, he spends hours patiently aiming his gun. He has heard the hammer click home on the empty chamber hundreds of times. And each time he pulls the trigger he silently mouths a name on his hate list. Yet he no longer finds this rewarding. He is puzzled and dismayed by his lack of feeling but can think of no way of retrieving the loss. Although Agca does not know it, his mental state has taken a significant turn for the worse.

Agca has been told he is being kept here until the time comes for him to kill someone. He now knows enough about Turkes and his organization to realize that spending seven days in a room which bribery has guaranteed is safe from police raids can only mean the intended victim is unusually important. The thought neither excites nor worries him. If anything, he now feels indifferent to the prospect of taking life—or putting his own at risk.

It took him four days to hitchhike from Yesiltepe to Ankara. By the time he reached the city, the uncontrollable rage—which had nearly made him smash the television set because it brought news that he had been denied the chance to kill Paul—had subsided. He now believes it was Ins'Allah—the will of God. And Allah, he is certain, will give him another opportunity. This, too, is only briefly exciting. All that really stimulates him now for any length of time is ugly eroticism; he will speak readily to the other men in this room of his fantasies, describing superhuman sexual feats with a vivid sense of conviction. This aberration is part of the mental change which is evolving and accelerating in Agca's mind.

On Sunday afternoon, August 27, an aide arrives from Turkes with the curt message that Agca will not be required to execute his mission; the intended victim has fled the country.

Hardly has Agca comprehended that once more he has been thwarted when the aide repeats he must leave this safe house and find his own accommodation. As they separate, the man suggests Agca might find work in the *kara borsa,* the flourishing Turkish black market. He gives him a name and address.

Agca's absence of any recognizable response—fury, resentment, disappointment—further suggests how far his latent depressive illness has produced an emotional blunting; a *depersonalization* and *derealization,* the labels of psychiatry which indicate he is increasingly no longer himself, no longer an intact personality, but rather a person who believes the outside world, not he, has altered, has become alien and unreal. Apart from his perverted sexuality, his capacity to experience appropriate social feelings has largely disappeared, and also the primitive prime emotions of hate, fear and anger have withered. It is as if—he will later admit under medical probing—his feelings have become totally unrelated to his environment. He even feels, as he leaves this safe house, that the significance of his life situation is virtually out of his control. He wonders again, though not with any lasting curiosity, whether this is anything to do with the extraordinary secret he has managed to keep from Colonel Turkes, the Gray Wolves and even from his mother. It is so astonishing that even now, just as he has been told to guard it, the secret remains deliberately pushed into his subconscious. And when it does sometimes emerge, though never beyond the confines of his increasingly tortured mind, he thinks the secret belongs to someone else. It is as if, he has said to himself, there are actually two persons living inside his puny body, linked together by a common bond of violence.

Heading on foot across Ankara, Agca passes a newsstand. Several papers carry accounts of Gianpaolo's election. He studies them avidly. There is a new caliph in Rome whose smile only conceals an evil mind dedicated to destroying Islam. Agca must kill him.[1]

Any thought of working in the *kara borsa* is abandoned. Instead, Agca goes to the nearest bar, orders a beer and asks for a telephone directory. For months he has pondered how best to go about what he must now do. In Yesiltepe he could have written, but he had heard the secret police frequently intercept letters addressed to these places. And it was much too risky to telephone long distance to seek an appointment; the telephone exchanges are riddled with informers who listen in to conversations. Here, in the city, it is different. A quick local call, a request for a meeting, would take only moments and even the most sophisticated equipment, he believes, would be unable to trace him.

Agca begins to search for the phone number of the Libyan Embassy in Ankara.

The man who has sworn Agca to secrecy told him the last time they met, that, should the need ever arise, this was the quickest way to contact him.

XX

Gianpaolo knows exactly what is going to happen to him. It's there on the typed schedule Lorenzi has placed on his desk. Every minute of his official day is accounted for. The blocks of time—some fragmentary, others lengthy—now control his life. It is all so different from the easygoing days in Venice. He pushes aside the schedule and joins his secretary at the window.

They both enjoy these private moments together; they are a reminder that what Lorenzi ruefully calls "the system" has not completely taken them over.

For both men the past week has been a learning process. Learning, for instance, to find their way around the large papal apartment: Martin had the place spring-cleaned before they moved in, and the prefect wondered whether Gianpaolo would like it redecorated. He's been smilingly told there's no need; such material considerations have a low priority in the pope's mind, so much so that he's sleeping in Paul's old bed and using his linen. Learning to cope with a daily work load which is endless and daunting—Lorenzi has been keeping track: on an average day Gianpaolo peruses up to two hundred separate documents—more than he would see in a month in Venice. Learning to cope with the isolation: a whole system of checks which begin at the security desk by the Bronze Doors effectively ensures that nobody can drop in, quite the opposite from Venice, where Gianpaolo kept open house. Learning to cope with the formality: Lorenzi still finds it surprising how unbending nearly everybody is in the Vatican. He supposes it's another throwback to Paul's pontificate. Gianpaolo is trying to change this, but it's going to take time. Some of the older curialists are so stiff they almost creak when they speak.

Normally at this hour on Sunday morning—it is barely seven o'clock—St. Peter's Square is deserted. Not today, September 3. Scores of *sampietrini* are busy in the piazza making the final preparations for Gianpaolo's coronation later in the day. And beyond them, ringing the great square, are groups of armed policemen, some with sniffer dogs to check for explosives. Their presence is a reminder that in this respect nothing has changed since the days of Paul. Gianpaolo was stunned to learn how many threats to his life there have already been during the eight days he has held office. Almost certainly all of the telephone calls and anonymous letters are the work of cranks. Yet nobody can be sure. Consequently, Ciban has ordered a further tightening of security. When Gianpaolo queried its need, Villot sent him a file detailing terrorist outrages against the Church, showing that this is not a passing phenomenon but one which grows almost daily as its bishops and priests assert the claims of the underprivileged, the impoverished and the suffering. Gianpaolo affixed to the file a handwritten note asking the Secretariat of State to research one of the initial important questions of his pontificate: did the Church have anything to answer for in shaping the minds of terrorists? He wants the answer ready for the time he will carry out his first overseas visit—to Mexico this coming October for the Conference of South American bishops.

Lorenzi gently reminds Gianpaolo that, like the Vatican workmen in the square, he, too, must put the finishing touches to his coronation preparations: the secretary has managed to juggle the schedule to allow the pope a full hour for this purpose. Lorenzi turns from the window and leads Gianpaolo back to his desk. When the pontiff is seated, and Lorenzi is satisfied there is no more he can do, he leaves.

Gianpaolo resumes drafting the address he will make at his coronation.

Unlike Paul, who almost never committed himself to paper until he had thought out exactly what he would say, and then wrote without hesitation to the end, Gianpaolo writes down a thought, reads it back, amends it, reads it again. It is a slow, laborious process, one perhaps not made easier by the way he constantly consults the mass of papers on his desk. One good thing about being pope, he has told Lorenzi, is that he has unrivaled sources of information at his command. In the past week the Curia has furnished him with any number of facts and figures: from the Secret Archives have come the coronation speeches of pontiffs going back to Gregory VII, who was crowned in 1073 and decreed that the pope had the right to depose emperors and kings, to be judged by no one, and that he alone was entitled to expect his feet "to be kissed by princes." It was Gregory who abolished simony, the sin of buying Church privileges, and ended clerical marriages.

Now, over nine hundred years later, in another briefing paper on his desk, the question of celibacy is demanding Gianpaolo's attention. The Congregation for the Sacraments and Divine Worship has sent him a strongly worded recommendation that it stop handling the hundreds of applications from priests wishing to give up holy orders, generally because they wished to marry, until Gianpaolo considers the entire matter. To help him decide what should be done, the Congregation has made some specific proposals which are far more rigorous than those applied by Paul. Requests for laicization in the future would be addressed directly to the Congregation headquarters in Rome and not to local bishops; they should only be granted in those cases where a "lengthy period" has elapsed since the petitioner "lived as a priest," or if his superiors are able to satisfy the Congregation they made an "initial mistake" in not recognizing that the person in question was unsuited for the celibate life. But even this would do nothing to end the extraordinary situation in the Philippines, where hundreds of priests have "a lasting relationship with a woman," seemingly with no adverse effect on their pastoral duties. Should he make reference in his coronation speech, however obliquely, to the teaching that celibacy is forever—everywhere Church writ runs? To do so would surely require that he should also refer to related issues: the question of priests and nuns who no longer wear suitable religious garb, and those women, especially in the United States, who are demanding the right to be ordained and whose slogans are disapprovingly laid out in the Congregation document: "God is an equal-opportunity employer," "A woman's place is in the sanctuary," "Equal rites for women."

Gianpaolo, in the end, decides a coronation is not the place to begin the task of settling such vexed issues. But he will handle them—and soon.

Equally his speech must strike a response in each one of the 18 percent of the world's population—in total over 740 million souls—for whom he is ultimately responsible in all matters of religion.

Amid the paper work which overflows from his desk onto the floor of his study—the one where he does his serious work, adjoining his bedroom, not the second-floor salon in the Apostolic Palace where he receives his endless flow of visitors—there is one memo which Gianpaolo repeatedly reads. He's plucked it out of the previous night's tray from the Curia. There are two typed sentences. The first states that at 3:42 P.M. on July 9, 1978, the world's population reached 4.4 billion. The second sentence predicts that 73 million people will be born this year, most of them in the Third World.

He finds the statistics mesmeric. He's told Lorenzi that, more than anything, they remind him of his awesome responsibility and the size of the kingdom he now spiritually rules.

On a wall of the study, near one of the speakers through which Paul used to listen to *Jesus Christ Superstar,* Gianpaolo has had pinned a map of the world. He hardly needs look at it to know there are only a few places where there are no native-born Catholics: Afghanistan, Bahrain, the Faeroes, Greenland, Oman, the Maldives, the two Yemens. But elsewhere, numerically the Church has never been stronger. Sixty-three out of every hundred persons in teeming Latin America—from Mexico to Chile—profess the faith. In Western Europe 40 percent of the population is Catholic. The Philippines claim thirty-six million souls. In the rest of Asia and Africa the number of Catholics is growing at such a rate that by the year 2000—when Gianpaolo could still be ruling—almost 70 percent of all baptized Catholics will be in the Third World.

This, he knows, is the area which will in particular be looking to him for strong leadership. In the minutes he has left to complete his coronation address, Gianpaolo makes another important decision. During the past week he has received invitations to visit the old heartlands of European Catholicism—Spain, France, Portugal, and West Germany, where, as a result of a fear of communism, the Church has in recent years gained membership sufficient that now, for the first time since Luther, Catholics outnumber Protestants. There has been a request—slipped in by Cody—to visit the United States. All these are certainly possibilities. But before he makes any such visits he must first travel extensively in the Third World. He knows, after what he has read, that it will not be enough to offer promises at his coronation that the Church will become more involved in the problems of this vast area, with its estimated 400 million unemployed, even more living on the starvation line and with poverty the like of which the First World, Europe, cannot envisage. He must go himself: move among these people, pray with them, make them feel he is part of them.

When Lorenzi returns, he is startled to be told by Gianpaolo that he wants briefing papers on every Third World nation where there are Catholics.

"It could take months," says the secretary hesitantly.

Gianpaolo nods. "It could. But it mustn't." He smiles. "Weeks at the most."

Lorenzi grins. There are going to be some very late nights at the Secretariat of State. No matter: it is time its officials realized that from now on things are going to be very different around the Apostolic Palace.

MacCarthy is conscious he has a privileged role in history in the making. He knows every detail of the coronation service: the timing, the order, the drama of the pageantry, the reason for every ritual, the symbolism behind each of the movements which will shortly unfold in St. Peter's Square on this late Sunday afternoon.

He has immersed himself in the forthcoming ceremony and has no doubt about the importance of the event for the Church, for Vatican Radio and for himself. He also knows the broadcast will fully succeed for him only if those who hear it feel they are participating in a service of great religious significance. He is deeply conscious of the responsibility upon his slight shoulders: for the next two hours or so he will act as one of the many radio voices bringing the events in the piazza to an estimated worldwide audience of six hundred million. MacCarthy's commentary position is high up on top of Bernini's colonnade, with the basilica to his immediate right and looking down on the altar set forward on the rim of the steps, where the great papal throne has been placed before the central door of St. Peter's. Some of the secular broadcasters around him suggest that a papal coronation is an incongruity and an anachronism, unworthy of the 261st successor of Peter the Fisherman. He is disappointed that they do not grasp that the event not only has supreme spiritual importance but is also historically rooted. It was conceived and developed, like so much of the ceremonial of the papal court, in imitation of the first Christian Roman emperors; the coronation is an exaltation of the papacy, a visible proclamation of the ascendancy of the spiritual over the temporal in which the steps of the basilica act as the sanctuary and the immense curving piazza the sweeping nave of the Church. Wisely, it has been decided to begin the ceremony at six in the evening when the shimmering heat of the Roman September day is somewhat abated.

There is an even bigger crowd, MacCarthy reflects, than the previous Sunday when, at noon, Gianpaolo made his first Angelus address from the same third floor window of the Apostolic Palace so long used by Paul. Already, in the public's mind, the memory of the severe pain-racked face of Paul is fading, replaced by the increasingly contagious smile of Gianpaolo. MacCarthy does not know of a more auspicious Angelus address by a new pope. Almost every sentence was punctuated by thunderous applause and appreciative laughter. Even Gianpaolo's first, beautifully timed word—"Yesterday"— received an ovation. He had to pause a full ten seconds before he was allowed to continue.

The next day he took his first administrative decision, reappointing all the officials in the Curia. Martin was back as prefect of the Casa Pontificia and Magee accepted an invitation to work alongside Lorenzi as the pope's other private secretary.

Gianpaolo told a meeting of curial officials and cardinals that he didn't know much about the running of the Church and was counting on their support. His words became endlessly quoted around the Vatican corridors of power: "the Way of the Cross is the way of the popes. I hope the brotherly cardinals will help this poor Vicar of Christ to carry the cross with their collaboration."

MacCarthy was not the only one to note that the pope had dropped the formal and aloof style of the previous incumbent, and used the simple "I" instead of the majestic "we." It was a small but indicative pointer with which to judge the form the pontificate was assuming.

There were others. Gianpaolo had gently chided newsmen he received in audience regarding the dangers of trivializing the papacy, and then, with a grin, added, "The public does not want to know what Napoleon the Third said to William of Prussia. It wants to know whether he wore beige or red pants or whether he smoked." The message to the media was clear: there is a need for balance. Gianpaolo had next talked to diplomats accredited to the Holy See about the function of Vatican diplomacy. Speaking in fluent French, he said: "Obviously we have no temporal goods to exchange, no economic interests to discuss. Our possibilities for diplomatic interventions are limited and of a special character. Our diplomatic missions, far from being a survival from the past, are a witness to our deep-seated respect for lawful temporal power and our lively interests in the human causes that the temporal power is intended to advance." This was correctly seen as a clear statement affirming the separation of Church and state.

After only eight days, it is obvious to MacCarthy that Gianpaolo is making plain what his role will be: that of supreme teacher of the Catholic world, the clarifier of its spiritual and social doctrine, the stout defender of a threatened Christendom. Gianpaolo is suggesting that his will be a pontificate in the Constantine tradition, with less politicking and more praying. In some ways, thinks the broadcaster, Gianpaolo has quickly shown a clear understanding of the real world in which he must now mediate; it is a world where the common man lives in a diversity of races, beliefs, national and cultural backgrounds, where one out of every three persons survives under communism, where one Christian out of every two is not a Catholic. It is still too early, MacCarthy realizes, to put a firm interpretation on all the ideas and aspirations which have begun to evolve. But Gianpaolo's rare gift of holy simplicity should not be seen merely as an absence of complexity; more likely his smiling spirituality is in fact a catalyst for a fusion of important thoughts. This is already clear at the end of his first week as pope. For all his grins and jokes, everything Gianpaolo says and does bears the mark of careful preparation, paving the way for consolidating the very best aspirations of the two predecessors whose name he bears. Yet there are indications that while he recognizes the need to provide continuity in this period of orientation—and knows he requires a seasoned and proven team by him to do so—he will, nevertheless, go his own way. He will do it with that smile, with warmth and friendliness. Even so, there is a steely edge discernible. MacCarthy is certain Gianpaolo will soon start surprising people.

But now, for the moment, both the pontificate and the Church must pause as, in centuries-old symbolism and pageantry, Gianpaolo's papacy is acclaimed with public pomp.

There are nearly three hundred thousand sitting or standing in the square, and MacCarthy uses their mood of expectancy to start weaving his own carefully prepared commentary. He explains how they have been arriving in the piazza from early morning, how they have waited patiently in the heat for perhaps just a glimpse of the new pontiff. He mentions, too, the presence of over twelve thousand police and carabinieri to protect the galaxy of distinguished guests. MacCarthy does not develop the thought: he hopes he will not have to, that all he has heard about the possibility of trouble is really no more than rumormongering.

He begins to describe the procession making its way into the square.

"The Holy Father comes in the procession, like everyone else, on foot. This is another of his many innovations. He has rejected the famous portable throne on which on all such occasions for centuries past, popes have been borne aloft through their congregation with a fanfare of loud trumpets. But for this coronation there will be no trumpets, no escort of Roman nobles. Most of the gleaming uniforms belong to the distinguished guests. Papa Gianpaolo—that is what everyone in Rome now calls him—prefers to walk among his people."

MacCarthy's words match in style and tone the endlessly unfolding scene below him.

"The cardinals, in pairs, venerate the open-air altar. And this inaugural mass is another of the changes the pope has introduced. The liturgy is new. It's been devised by Monsignor Noé, who has been reappointed master of ceremonies, and a commission of experts who have worked all this past week to prepare it. The Holy Father made it clear he did not wish an ostentatious ceremony. Indeed, he has even refused to wear the papal crown, which popes for hundreds of years have received on this occasion. Instead, he wants his insignia, the badge of his office, to be spiritual, a reflection of his pastoral authority. That is why he wears, rather than a crown, the miter, the tall headdress, the emblem of pastoral authority."

MacCarthy does not try to be coldly objective, to remain emotionally outside the event he is describing. To him this is not a procession of quaintly dressed figures: it is a vivid evocation of the true power of the Church.

"The whole world is here. The king of the Belgians. The presidents of France, Austria and Ireland. The prime ministers of Italy and Canada. There are princes and princesses, dukes and duchesses. The vice-president of the United States is here. There are also high officials of state from communist countries. And the representatives of all the major non-Catholic churches. They are all here. But so is the ordinary world; they have come from every corner of the globe. This is truly an United Nations of men, women and children."

He describes the Swiss Guards, the *bussolanti* in their violet cassocks and capes, the penitentiaries in solemn black, the chaplains in red, and then, row after row of white-mitered and caped patriarchs, bishops and cardinals.

"Soon it will be time to surrender ourselves to the mass, to the music, to the singing of the Sistine Choir, to a splendor that some of us may not see repeated. Remember, the last four popes lived into their eighties. That means we can expect the present pontificate to last at least fifteen years."

MacCarthy pauses as spontaneous applause marks the approach of Felici to where Gianpaolo is seated.

"The cardinal removes the pope's miter. What is to happen now is the very central point of the ceremony. It is called the imposition of the pallium. This is the ultimate symbol of a pope's pastoral office, the sign he has entered the fullness of his pastoral ability."

MacCarthy explains the symbolism of the circular band of white wool, with its back and front pendants, which Felici places around Gianpaolo's neck. "It's the sign of the authority which derives from Christ through St. Peter the Apostle, and at the same time it's a sign of service towards the People of God and all our neighbors. The pallium expresses the pope's special commitment to promote with all his might the unity of the Church and his fidelity to the doctrine of the Apostle."

Singing and organ music well up from the square. Then, when the booming voice of Felici pronounces the Latin benediction that concludes the cardinals' role in the coronation, MacCarthy expertly translates into English: "Blessed be God, Who has chosen you to be pastor of the Universal Church, and Who has clothed you with the shining stole of your apostolate. May you reign gloriously through many years of earthly light until, called by your Lord, you will be reclothed with the stole of immortality in the Kingdom of Heaven. Amen."

MacCarthy prepares his listeners for the next part of the ceremony. It is the turn of the cardinals to make their way, one at a time, to the pontiff, and to kiss Gianpaolo's Fisherman's Ring. In return, he embraces them. Some he has to steady as they appear to falter in the heat. A few linger for a word, anxiously watched by Noé.

The long, solemn pontifical mass begins; the Epistle and Gospel are sung in Latin and Greek respectively. There are Scripture readings in nine languages to mark the universality of the Church. Shadows are settling over the square as Gianpaolo begins to read his address. He starts in Latin, switches to his agreeable French and concludes in lilting Venetian Italian. It includes an engaging plea that he will continue to receive the support of those he is pledged to serve: "Surrounded by your love we begin our apostolic service by invoking a resplendent star on our way, the mother of God, Mary. . . ."

Suddenly there is a commotion in the crowd. Angry shouts are followed by leaflets being scattered in the air. Police begin to push through worshipers. From several points around the piazza balloons drift upward. All carry the same legend: "VIDELA—ASSASSINO!"

In the distinguished-visitors' enclosure, President Jorge Videla of Argentina, who has defied Aramburu's last minute appeal to stay away, turns whiter than his bemedaled admiral's uniform. Close by, Aramburu has a mortified look on his face. Videla's presence has cast a pall over the ceremony.

On the fringes of the crowd armored cars inch forward attempting to intimidate the demonstrators. Police move in and there are violent struggles.

Gianpaolo's voice, amplified by a score of loudspeakers, reminds his listeners this "is a day of fraternal union and joy, and let us be guided by Him."

By the time he completes his address, the police have made the first of 282 arrests. Demonstrators are hustled away to paddy wagons while the choir intones the credo.

As the offertory procession begins—the prelude to Communion—the police fan out through the congregation trying to locate those who have released the balloons.

MacCarthy continues to ignore the interruption; his listeners will never know it has happened. He describes the timeless ceremony of the Eucharist, the liturgy of thanksgiving.

"The priests who will distribute Communion to the crowd hold the ciboria, the gold cups containing the bread which will be transformed into the body of Christ."

The police pounce on more demonstrators. There are scuffles. As the protesters are hauled away, the Sistine Choir sing the Lord's Prayer.

"Now, as Communion begins, it will need two hundred priests to distribute it. And the assembly is singing 'Lamb of God, Who taketh away the sins of the world, have mercy upon us.'"

Another fierce fight breaks out beneath Bernini's columns between police and dissenters.

The choir sings the Communion canticle as scores of people run from the square pursued by police. The Te Deum, an anthem of praise and acknowledgment, ends the mass. A squad of police closes in protectively on Videla. The last sight his fellow heads of state have of the Argentinian is of a frightened man being bundled away for his own safety.

Seemingly oblivious to what has happened, Gianpaolo rises and walks into St. Peter's. It's another innovation, this casual, unaffected departure from his coronation. It is also a further sign he intends to break with the past. The historically minded in the square are now certain that a new era is actually dawning.

Shortly before eight o'clock this Sunday evening, a vigorous woman with a strong face uncorks a glass jar of boiled sweets in the kitchen of the papal apartment and begins carefully to select an assortment which she arranges in a cut-glass bowl. This is Sister Vincenza, Gianpaolo's housekeeper and confidante, whose pride in her consecrated virginity she still regards, after a lifetime of chastity, as a special grace from God.[1] In everything she says and does Vincenza embodies the only official Church document on the subject, Pius XII's encyclical *Holy Virginity*, which insists virginity is more perfect than the state of marriage because it transcends the position where "our bodily powers and passions darken the mind and weaken the will."

Vincenza cannot, consequently, begin to understand this movement for change among nuns in many parts of the world. For her it has always been enough to confine the body in order to free the spirit; the core and secret of the deep contentment she possesses is her certainty of the happiness to come. She has offered her life and love to the glory of God because the afterlife is forever. In Venice she was only vaguely aware that not all nuns feel as fulfilled as she does. But this first week in the Vatican has opened her eyes to the fact that after fifteen centuries demands for change can be heard on all sides. Nuns want holidays, the right to dress as they please, to have male friends; she's heard staggering tales that in some American ghettoes nuns are on the pill because of their fear of rape, that nuns wear bikinis and go to public swimming pools and some even ride motorcycles. Centuries of tradition are being heedlessly abandoned in the name of "modernity." The very ethos which has supported her from the day she assumed the cloistered existence— a steadfast belief that the life she has chosen is a preparation and waiting for death, and though there will be purgatory, it will be followed by joyous redemption—Vincenza now realizes is no longer sufficient for her fellow sisters. Every nightly tray that comes from the Curia, the pope has sadly confided to her, contains its quota of petitions from nuns wishing to leave their orders. Ironically, it is those orders—particularly in the United States— which have become the most liberal which are losing the most members. For Vincenza the moral is plain, and when Gianpaolo sought her opinion she urged him to remember it: too many sudden freedoms could erode the very basis of an institution which has served the Church and human needs for fifteen hundred years. He promised to remember her warning.

Having filled the bowl, she recaps the jar and places it back on the shelf. Nobody else, Vincinza has ruled, is to touch its contents. Apart from the sweets on the shelf, there are other little delicacies the pope likes: a variety of nuts, tins of his favorite coffee, a pot holding brown sugar.

In her full-length black habit—Vincenza is thankful her Order of Maria Bambini has not introduced the modish calf-length habit some orders now favor—and her headdress, she has a timeless look, like a figure from a medieval manuscript. She is somewhere between her fiftieth and her sixtieth birthdays, but like so much else about her, she keeps the exact year secret. She knows some people around the Apostolic Palace find her sharply discouraging about any personal questions about herself or the man she now finds it strange, after all their years together, to call Holy Father. She still lapses back to Padre Albino. Prefect Martin, she realizes, does not like to hear such familiarity, but young Padre Magee, though he sometimes speaks so softly she has to strain to catch his words, has said it's all right, that everybody can see how devoted and loving she is toward the pope. And friendly-sounding though the name Gianpaolo is, Vincenza finds the appellation hard to get used to; in a way it reminds her of those distant days when she made her final, solemn, binding vows, taking on a new identity, accepting that from then on, for the most part, she would merely be called "Sister." Gianpaolo has always addressed her, from the first day she came to cook and clean for him, "my little Vincenza."

Then, she never dreamed of one day effectively being the mistress of the most important household in the Church. When Gianpaolo phoned her in Venice and asked whether she would move to the Vatican, she was too overwhelmed except to whisper "*Sì.*" That was a week ago.

Now, she feels fully able to cope with the papal apartment. The marvelous thing is how easy she finds it to run. She has three nuns to help her and the sort of labor-saving gadgets the patriarch's palace did not possess: here, there are a waste-disposal unit, a fully automated laundry, the very latest electric ovens and equipment to take away the ache of bread making and food preparation. There is even a vacuum cleaner so silent she hardly knows when it is working. For someone who has been nurtured in the sternness of monastic simplicity—she well remembers those long hours on her knees as a postulant polishing floors to a fine finish by hand because her mother superior insisted the only way for a nun to get to heaven was on her knees, be it praying or scrubbing—the modernity of the apartment is almost overpowering.

Yet she has already stamped her own personality and authority on many of its eighteen rooms. Even if the pope doesn't want the place redecorated—she could have told Martin before he had made the suggestion that Gianpaolo just wasn't interested in such things—Vincenza has set about brightening up the uniformly neutral beige and gray tones Paul so cherished.

As she marches out of the kitchen carrying the bowl of sweets on a silver tray, she can see everywhere evidence of the changes she has so far introduced. Striding down the central corridor of the apartment which eventually leads to Gianpaolo's bedroom, she glimpses through open doors—the pope insists they remain open to give the apartment a more homely atmosphere—her handiwork: colorful cushions on chairs and settees, familiar ornaments and oil paintings from Venice and everywhere photographs of the pope's relatives. There are family snaps on the dining-room sideboards, more in the drawing room and, on his study desk, a striking portrait of his favorite niece.

Passing the study, Vincenza sees it is occupied by Magee and Lorenzi. Both are so intent on their paper work they do not even look up. She admires their ability to concentrate on an immediate task to the exclusion of all else. She's also glad of the rapport between the two secretaries. She had thought at first it might be difficult for Lorenzi. He had done everything in Venice except pay the domestic bills, which she had settled. Here Prefect Martin takes care even of these, after he's carefully checked each item. Vincenza doesn't like the arrangement but Magee has soothed her. He is a born diplomat: he just knew how to handle everybody. Only tonight he gave another demonstration, this time in the wake of the violence which marred the closing stages of the coronation. Vincenza had seen the demonstrators being rounded up from her bedroom window. She felt the police were right: a papal coronation is no place to protest. Shortly after Gianpaolo arrived back in the apartment, Villot and Aramburu had come to say how upset they were. That, at least from what she'd overheard, was their intention. But Magee had quickly intervened. Following a few whispered words, the secretary of state and the Argentinian cardinal left, apparently satisfied. Though he has only been back in the apartment for a few days, Vincenza realizes Magee is very attuned to Gianpaolo's ways. One of the things the pope dislikes is pointless inquests. To discuss the scenes in the square would be in that category.

Vincenza reaches the pope's bedroom door, the only one that is closed. He is in the second-floor salon, receiving more dignitaries. The nun enters.

Here, too, her touch is discernible. There's a rug which matches the color of the lampshade on the bedside table. Both come from Venice, but the settee she found in that Vatican warehouse filled with centuries of discarded papal artifacts. Vincenza thinks there is sufficient furniture stored there to equip all the palaces of the cardinals, and her well-developed social conscience wonders why better use is not made of it instead of simply storing the furniture from one pontificate to another.

She places the bowl of sweets beside the short stack of books on the bedside table. For as long as she can remember the man she must now call *Santissimo Padre*—at least in front of others—likes to suck boiled sweets while he reads before going to sleep. Every evening at this hour she places a fresh bowl by his bedside.

Vincenza turns back the sheet and lays out his pajamas. Then, her work in this room completed for the night, she goes to a window and stares out through the parted curtains. Almost miraculously, the square has virtually returned to its usual empty grandeur: carpets have been rolled up, the altar moved back into the basilica, thousands of chairs stacked away, crash barriers removed. Only the patrolling policemen remain. She still can't believe what she has heard: that there are people somewhere out there who would kill Gianpaolo, not because of anything he personally has done, but because he is pope. It's beyond her comprehension that anyone can hate to this extent.

The nun starts to wonder, not about such possibilities, for there is nothing morbid about her. Nor is she normally introspective. But still she wonders how much time Gianpaolo may have left.

Twice in the past week he has called her to his bedroom, asking her to bring a bowl of hot water and the bottle of herbal elixir they both feel is so beneficial for his phlebitic condition. In Venice she regularly sat with him while he soaked his feet and ankles, and she sometimes knelt and used a cloth to bathe the calves below his rolled-up cassock. She has done the same here in the Vatican. But whereas in Venice the swelling at least temporarily receded, here it has not done so. His ankles and calves have remained puffy.

Vincenza asked him to consult Dr. Buzzonetti. The pope simply shook his head and gently told her there was nothing to worry about, that it's probably caused by no more than a change of location, and when his body adjusts to the Rome climate everything will be all right. He sounded so convincing that she accepted this. Only later, after looking in a medical book, has she learned that phlebitis is not affected by climatic conditions.

Magee and Lorenzi look up this time as Vincenza pauses by the study door on her way back to the kitchen. The men smile when she says dinner will be on time. During this settling-in period of the pontificate meals have rather tended to be taken by Gianpaolo and his secretaries at all hours. Frequently the pope has eaten from a tray at his desk to try to keep up with the sheer volume of paper work. The fare is simple: soups and puddings with a nutty flavor. Gianpaolo is a poor eater, "a nibbler" Magee calls him. But, like the Irishman, the pope cleans his plate. It's a common legacy from their childhood, when each learned the virtues of waste not, want not. Vincenza moves on, her habit swishing from her brisk pace as she hurries to the kitchen.

The secretaries consult their list of the pope's appointments for the remainder of the evening. In a few minutes the elevator should bring him back to the apartment after his last public engagement of the day, a ten-minute meeting with a group of American bishops. They are fortunate to have been given even this amount of time. On the pope's tight schedule some people are granted literally only a brief moment to greet Gianpaolo, exchange a few words, pose with him for an official photograph and receive his blessing before Martin escorts them out and ushers in the next visitors. If it weren't for the photograph, Magee thinks wryly, some might later have trouble convincing themselves they had actually been in the presence of the pope. It is nobody's fault: there are just so many people demanding to see Gianpaolo— the requests for personal audiences received this first week have doubled from the five thousand Paul received weekly at the height of his popularity. Martin has worked wonders sifting the requests and squeezing in audiences between more serious papal meetings. But even so, Gianpaolo's daily schedule extends far beyond that of Paul's.

Tonight, at the end of a day which has already lasted fourteen crowded hours, there are two further appointments.

Benelli is scheduled to arrive with the pope and spend thirty minutes with him. But because of his status as a close adviser to Gianpaolo, the cardinal from Florence often ignores the clock and goes beyond his allotted time; not even Martin's freezing stare has always been able to pry him away from the pontiff before Benelli was ready to go. Tonight, after seeing Benelli and following dinner, a forty-five-minute item on his schedule, Gianpaolo will return to the study to confer with Felici, who, even more than Benelli, is now firmly entrenched as the pontiff's most trusted adviser. The space allotted for him is open-ended. Thankfully, at least there are no curial trays expected tonight; the coronation has temporarily halted the flow of paper. Tomorrow it will be business as usual.

Lorenzi leaves the study to wait by the elevator for Gianpaolo and Benelli. This custom of one of the secretaries meeting the pope every time he returns to the apartment is another of the changes that Magee recognizes set the domestic side of this pontificate apart from its predecessor's. Even excluding Vincenza's innovations, the life-style within the papal apartment is dramatically different. Gone with Paul's vials of Mogadon and those mysterious capsules of Fontana's—the old doctor has retired, leaving the medical care of the pope in the hands of Buzzonetti—is the deadening silence which permeated the place during Paul's long months of dying. Now it is generally filled with the cheerful voices of the nuns; the only time they become respectfully silent is when visitors arrive. And even then the sounds of their occasional giggling from the kitchen gives a homely touch. Perhaps most important of all for Magee has been the way Vincenza and Lorenzi have integrated him into this new order. They regularly draw on his experience of the previous pontificate and, in turn, brief him on Gianpaolo.

Magee finds the pope delightfully informal around the apartment. He calls his entourage by their first names, something Paul never found easy to do, and frequently stops his staff to inquire how they are settling in. During the evenings, when his official day is done, he likes nothing better than to sit in this study listening to Magee describing the inner workings of the last pontificate.

Initially, the secretary was surprised by what Gianpaolo wanted to know: he is not deeply interested just in everything Paul did, but how he did it: what parts of his daily routine he enjoyed most, which he disliked. Magee apologized that he could not be as helpful as he would like, explaining that he entered papal service when Paul was already an old man, his eyes, sunk into his head, often looking out at the world with a look that appeared pleading or helpless. Gianpaolo asked what had made Paul like this, and Magee explained, with compassion and love, about the inner torment which had racked the old pope, eventually making Paul a man who retreated almost totally into the privacy of his own mind. Interposed were the moments when Paul whispered, "I am alone too much," in the voice of someone both puzzled and intimidated by the world. Change was often the hardest thing for him to understand.

Gianpaolo had nodded sympathetically and continued with his quietly probing questions, explaining that it was important for him to understand so he could better see where he must introduce change, revise procedures and make decisions which Paul, for all the reasons Magee gives, failed to implement.

Everything he has heard from Gianpaolo suggests to Magee that the papacy is about to take a dramatic change of direction.

There are the small pointers. The way Gianpaolo publicly addresses people as "brothers and sisters," instead of Paul's "sons and daughters." The way he canvasses the widest possible opinions on almost every matter: lowly members of the Curia who never spoke to Paul suddenly find themselves encountering Gianpaolo during one of his prowls through the Apostolic Palace and having their views on a subject earnestly sought. There is the tremendous attention he gives to all his public speeches: it has sometimes taken him a dozen drafts to get the right tone, which is becoming very much stamped by seemingly spontaneous asides that have in fact been carefully rehearsed. Gianpaolo is very much the writer-actor.

There are larger indications. Though it is clear the main thrust of his mission will be pastoral, he is quickly coming to terms with the political-spiritual strength of the papacy. The signs are that he will use it to make the Church less authoritarian and more responsive to progressive ideas.

But only so far. The purpose of this meeting with Benelli is an indication of that.

The meeting is very much part of the most significant pointer of all: how he intends to handle the Curia. Gianpaolo has made it politely clear to his civil servants that he is fully aware of their power, that he respects their right to exercise it and does not intend to resurrect the sort of innovations John XXIII introduced which had led to the crisis over ideology and organization that Paul, despite his reforms of the Curia in 1967, failed to solve. Having said that, Gianpaolo has gone on to indicate that there should be a shift in emphasis, more consultation with the local bishops, more meaningful dialogue between the Curia and those whom it serves. It has all been very low-key, punctuated with the now-familiar smile. Yet the curialists have been left in no doubt as to what the pope expects.

It is too early yet to see if it will work. But the signs are good.

Magee is still buoyed by such thoughts when Gianpaolo and Benelli arrive with Lorenzi. He closes the door behind him, a sign of the sensitive nature of what is to be discussed.

Benelli wants to settle the Küng Question. He feels the matter has dragged on far too long. Eight years of bitter wrangling have ensued since the Swiss theologian first described Paul's decisions on birth control, celibacy, and mixed marriages as "efforts to restore a preconciliar theology." Since then, in spite of the plainest of warnings, Küng has continued his assault through a series of articles and books. Even the full weight of *Mysterium Ecclesiae*—issued by the Congregation for the Doctrine of the Faith, successor to the Holy Inquisition—has not stopped Küng. The document was published specifically to counter his rejection of papal infallibility. It is the most that could be done to punish such heresy, now that burning at the stake is no longer permissible. According to some accounts of this meeting between Gianpaolo and Benelli—one thing which has not changed in the new pontificate is the number of moles willing to spill some of the beans in exchange for money, preferably American dollars[2]—Benelli genuinely regrets that it's no longer possible to cast to the flames the likes of Küng.

The cardinal explains that at Paul's behest the Vatican tried to have Küng repudiated by his peers. This failed. Next, Küng was "invited" to Rome to explain his views before the Congregation for the Doctrine of the Faith. But he avoided that. And, since the theologian was a diocesan priest employed by a secular university, he has also been able to shrug off any Vatican threat to his income. Paul—and Benelli produces these facts more in sorrow than in anger—felt Küng's popularity, coupled with his scholarly reputation and the ecumenical importance of the views he expounded—Paul was very sensitive to anything that could make the Church appear to be trampling on ecumenical advance—had combined to make it difficult for the pope to intervene more forcibly. But Paul's death did not mean Küng was going to stop his challenge. Far from it: Benelli's sources have told him the theologian is winding himself up for another tilt at the papacy. What's particularly distasteful to Benelli is that Küng shows every sign of enjoying his ecclesiastical skirmishing. In the cardinal's view there is only one answer. Gianpaolo, through the Congregation for the Doctrine of the Faith, should publicly and unswervingly condemn Küng.

Gianpaolo says he will review the entire case. He agrees Küng's views are divisive and promises Benelli his answer in a month. He makes it clear there is no more to be said for the moment.

After dinner Felici is shown into the study. Once more Lorenzi closes the door and the two secretaries start to take notes while the cardinal argues that the time has come for Gianpaolo to end the defiance of Marcel Lefèbvre. Felici is well briefed; his review is masterful and authoritative. He ends by saying Gianpaolo should either pronounce a sentence of formal excommunication or hand the case over to the Congregation for the Doctrine of the Faith for trial under canon law.

The pope listens carefully until Felici finishes. Then he asks questions, each posed in a gently inquiring way. Has not the Vatican's canonical endorsement of Lefèbvre's seminary at Econe been withdrawn? Has not the archbishop already been suspended *a divinis,* forbidden to exercise his priestly and episcopal functions? Had not Paul already censured him in a way no other bishop has been condemned by a pope this century? And yet what has all this achieved? Is there not a danger that further punitive action will merely endow Lefèbvre with an importance he does not deserve? Should he not be left to fade into perspective and oblivion, remembered only perhaps as *l'incident Lefèbvre,* a tiny footnote, insignificant when measured against any proper reckoning of Paul's pontificate?

The four men in the study know no answers are expected now. It is not because the hour is late. It is because the questions have been posed so Felici can go away and ponder them at leisure. When he feels he can answer them, he should return.

This is part of the style of the new pontificate.

Noé realizes there is another and, for him, unwelcome aspect when he picks up the phone in his apartment on Monday morning, September 4. He can't remember when he was last disturbed so early in the day, barely dawn. Yet it is not that Ciban is calling at this outlandish hour which upsets Noé; he gets on well with the security chief. One of the qualities the master of ceremonies likes in Ciban is his calmness: in the past he has always sounded and behaved as though nothing could shake him; not even his failure to track down the culprits who bugged conclave had ruffled his composure. But now Ciban's voice is shaky as he recounts what has happened.

The master of ceremonies arranges to meet Ciban and Martin—who has already been informed—behind the Pinacoteca, the papal art museum.

Hurrying from his apartment through the Vatican grounds, Noé thinks over what Ciban has said. It all fits a pattern; perhaps manifestation would be a better word to describe some of Gianpaolo's behavior. During the past week the pope has become almost eccentric in the eyes of the protocol-steeped and staunchly traditionalist Noé.

There was his insistence on having the coronation mass rewritten: the mass which had bound each pope to the Church since the Treaty of Westphalia in 1648, when the nations of Europe were allowed to go their own religious ways; the mass that was said for Clement V, the only pope to be crowned in Lyons, France; the mass seven other successive popes received during the long exile of the papacy in Avignon; the mass which had remained virtually unchanged since the papal crown was placed on the head of Leo X with the words: "Receive the tiara adorned with three crowns and you know that you are father of princes and kings, victor of the whole world under the earth, the Vicar of Our Lord Jesus Christ to whom be glory and honor without end."

Gianpaolo dispensed with such terminology—because he also refused to wear the crown pontiffs wore even before the days of Hannibal and Charlemagne.

Noé sees the crown as a potent symbol which helped the Church rise triumphant from the pillaging of Alaric the Hun, Genseric the Vandal, Barbarossa of Prussia, Napoleon of France. Leo I wore it when he assumed the old Roman title, *Pontifex Maximus,* Supreme Pontiff. Boniface VIII placed it on his head the day he made his immortal declaration: "The Church has one body and one head, Christ and Christ's Vicar, Peter and Peter's successor: in his power there are two swords, a spiritual and a temporal sword; both kinds of power are in the hands of the Roman Pontiff."

Further, Gianpaolo had virtually dispensed with the plural majestatis, "we"; it had been the way popes from Silvester I to Paul had spoken; it was another way for them to show they thought of themselves as kings, and of the Church as their kingdom. Even John XXIII, who introduced so many other ideas Noé found difficult to accept, had not gone so far as to speak in the singular "I."

But then, the master of ceremonies can reflect as he hurries to meet Ciban and Martin, most previous popes were nurtured and shaped almost exclusively by the Roman Curia, that kingdom within a kingdom which knew how to prepare potential pontiffs.

Gianpaolo is not an "insider," someone who has spent his working life in and around the Vatican. Therefore, in Noé's view, he is not properly grounded in what is permissible and what is not. There is no question about it: papal infallibility doesn't extend to a pontiff's doing what he likes. Gianpaolo is as bound by rules and regulations as those who serve him. If only he realized that, there would be no need for Noé to come trotting up to Martin and Ciban behind the museum.

The prefect looks nonplussed. What has happened is outside his experience. He listens dolefully as Ciban explains the events to Noé.

One of the Vigilance men had called the security chief with the news that shortly after daybreak the pope had walked past a dumbfounded Swiss Guard on duty at the Porta Sant'Anna, and stood for some minutes on Italian soil looking up and down a thankfully deserted street. Then he had just as casually strolled back through the gates, wishing the guard a cordial good morning before going on his way. The man had been so thunderstruck by what had occurred that when Ciban subsequently questioned him, he was barely coherent.

Ciban's immediate concern is security. If just one member of the Red Brigade happened to have been passing . . . He does not need to complete the thought.

As well as this nightmarish possibility, Noé and Martin are concerned with another aspect: the diplomatic gaffe the pope caused by walking onto Italian territory. As head of state, says Noé crossly, Gianpaolo should know he is simply not permitted to stroll into another country unannounced, and especially unescorted. This sort of behavior must stop; others can decide how far the pope can go on matters of dogma, theology and doctrine. When it comes to throwing protocol out of the window, then it is very much Noé's business to halt the slide. He asks where Gianpaolo is now.

Ciban says one of his guards is trailing the pope through the Vatican gardens. He speaks into a handset, puts the receiver to his ear and listens to the crackling response. Gianpaolo is walking on one of the upper terraces.

Noé and Martin brace themselves and with Ciban set off in pursuit.

They find Gianpaolo talking animatedly to one of the gardeners. The pope waves cheerfully as the trio bear down on him.

The gardener backs away. In all his years of Vatican service he has never encountered such a distinguished gathering at such an early hour. The man continues to stay within earshot, and later will recount how Noé takes Gianpaolo firmly by the elbow and lectures him on the personal risks he has taken and the diplomatic rumpus his action could have triggered—and might yet, if word leaks.

The Italians are very sensitive about such things, says Martin morosely. He rocks back and forth on his heels, a sure sign he is agitated. Ciban has a hurt look; it's as though he thinks the pope is personally determined to make his life a misery.

Gianpaolo nods thoughtfully. In the gentlest of voices he says he had not meant to create problems. Then he bestows a winning smile. No harm has been done. And think what has been achieved.

Achieved? Noé repeats the word, as if he thinks he must have misheard what was said.

Gianpaolo positively beams. Yes, *achieved*. He doubts any of them have been out of bed this early. They should look upon what has happened positively: it has given them the perfect start to their day.

With another cheerful wave he begins to walk back to the Apostolic Palace.[3]

"He's vanished!"

Ciban cannot believe what Martin is saying. He's barely over Gianpaolo's dawn escapade. Now this.

"What do you mean 'vanished'?" The security chief has difficulty in forming his words.

"He was here. Now he's gone." Martin is impatient. "You must find him."

"Where are you?"

"In the apartment."

"And the Holy Father was there?" There is something almost reproachful in Ciban's question. This really cannot be happening to him. He asks Martin to explain further.

There is little more to say. After breakfast the pope went to his study to listen to the morning radio news. Magee saw him there. A little while later, when Martin arrived to escort Gianpaolo down to the second floor salon for the first meeting of the day, the pope was no longer there. Lorenzi had gone to stall the visitors, some African bishops. Martin has searched the apartment, without success.

Ciban pulls himself together. He tells the prefect he will telephone his guard posts around the Apostolic Palace. Within minutes he is satisfied. The pope has not slipped past his men.

In the meantime Martin is leading a search party from the apartment. The prefect says gloomily it could take days to check every room in the rambling palace. Vincenza brims with good humor: she says Gianpaolo has done this before, popping out of the palace in Venice without telling anybody. Many a time he'd slip into an old cassock and a pair of sandals to spend an evening incognito in his favorite restaurant eating seaweed pizza.

Martin is openmouthed at the revelation.

The posse rides down in the elevator to the third floor, where the Secretariat of State warren is coming to life. Its staff looks curiously at the pope's personal aides peering around doors.

Vincenza finally locates Gianpaolo in the room where Macchi fed Paul's personal papers into the shredder.

By now word has reached Villot. He lopes from his office to find the pope and his staff standing by the shredder.

Gianpaolo smiles at the secretary and explains, almost apologetically, that none of his aides can make the machine work. Can Villot help?

Thoroughly bewildered, the most senior diplomat in the Vatican begins to feed in paper.

Like Ciban he can't quite believe what is happening to him.[4]

It is eight o'clock on Tuesday morning, September 5, when Gianpaolo arrives in the spacious salon on the second floor of the Apostolic Palace with its three windows overlooking St. Peter's Square. Here, where Paul took such careful pains to stamp his authority, Gianpaolo has almost casually asserted his personality. There are snapshots of his relatives on the sixteenth-century desk, a series of smiling faces in simple wooden frames standing between the gold-topped roll blotter and the scissors letter opener which Paul was never known to touch, but which Gianpaolo uses to prepare the slips of paper he utilizes as markers to insert between the pages of important files.

One of the files is a slim, buff-colored folder containing his handwritten notes of everything Felici and Benelli have told him about the financial operations of the Vatican. The pope informed his secretaries over breakfast that for the next ninety minutes he does not wish to be disturbed while he reviews the file. Its contents have a bearing on his first meeting, scheduled for nine-thirty sharp.

Gianpaolo has no real head for figures, even less for an easy understanding of the complexities of international finance. But he instinctively recognizes the smack of scandal, and the sordid saga Benelli and Felici have previously unfolded wiped away his smile and left him wrinkling his nose in disgust; once or twice, at some particularly shocking revelation, he smacked his hand on the desk and asked, "Why?" It was his only audible reaction during the several sessions the two cardinals had needed to brief Gianpaolo.

First they detailed the tangled financial dealings which have bound the IOR—Vatican Bank—to Sindona even after the Sicilian's financial empire collapsed in 1974 in New York. The latest news from there is still alarming for the Vatican. Sindona is trying every legal move available in the American courts to avoid being extradited back to Italy; at the same time he is dropping dark hints that if he is returned, he will detail precisely how far Marcinkus was aware of, and had condoned, his own crooked dealings.

Felici and Benelli fear Marcinkus might have known far more than he has ever admitted. Both cardinals are equally satisfied that Marcinkus has not been involved in any direct financial chicanery, that he has not acted for personal gain and does not have a bank account somewhere. Felici's verdict is that Marcinkus is "greedy for the Church and overambitious"; Benelli's judgment is "incompetent and inexperienced."

Now, in the wake of *il crack Sindona,* another scandal is brewing. Potentially even more dangerous than Sindona for the Vatican—for its financial credibility and moral authority—is the astonishing way Marcinkus has blithely allowed Vatican Bank to become entangled with Roberto Calvi.[5]

Ironically, Sindona introduced Calvi to Marcinkus. They were immediately drawn to each other, sharing a similar passion for secrecy and financial wheeling and dealing. Shortly after meeting with Marcinkus in 1971, Calvi and Sindona set up Banco Ambrosiano Overseas in Nassau. Three years later, as Sindona's world collapsed, so Calvi's fortunes rose. He became president of Banco Ambrosiano, with its holding company based in Luxembourg and branches throughout Italy and abroad. The Nassau bank was only a single tentacle of this vast financial octopus spreading over fifteen countries. But it is unusual in at least one respect: on its board of directors is a certain "Mr. Paul Marcinkus."

Vatican Bank took up 4 percent of the Ambrosiano Luxembourg stock and 8 percent of the Nassau stock—and began to act closely with Calvi's Italian-based banks. In its immune position, Vatican Bank could move abroad millions of lire, circumventing strict Italian laws designed to restrict such transfers. The laws did not, of course, apply to Vatican Bank, protected by the sovereignty of the city-state. But now, the Bank of Italy is about to begin an extensive audit of Calvi's financial empire. Both Benelli and Felici fear it will uncover not only serious breaches of Italian law but also show how extensive are the complex interlocking relationships between Vatican Bank and the increasingly dubious-looking Calvi empire. Even if Marcinkus is shown to have been at best naïve and at worst rashly incompetent, the ensuing scandal will cause the greatest harm to the Church.

At the same time, apart from Sindona, there are currently two other financial time bombs ticking away in the United States which could detonate at any moment with further devastating results for the Vatican.

The first concerns the possibility that the U.S. Justice Department might make public its so far highly secret report on investigations in 1973 into organized crime. Justice Department agents have uncovered a plot by the Mafia to use European businessmen to borrow vast sums of money against counterfeit stocks and bonds of American corporations. The investigators privately interviewed Marcinkus in his office in the Vatican; so secret was their visit that not even Ciban knew of it. The investigators wanted to know whether Marcinkus had any suspicion the Mafia was planning to launder the best part of nine hundred million dollars' profit from the counterfeit-securities swindle through Vatican Bank. Marcinkus's answers had so far remained a secret of the Justice Department. One suggestion is that President Nixon himself ordered that the report must not be published. But with Nixon disgraced, there is no guarantee it will remain so.

The second time bomb is Cody. It is not so much the amount of money involved: compared to the Vatican's estimated loss in *il crack Sindona*, the Chicago cardinal's caper runs to probably no more than a couple of million dollars. It's the salacious background which most worries Benelli and Felici: the whiff of moral lapses, a touch of *la dolce vita* that can only evoke unhappy memories of earlier princes of the Church who strayed. Coupled to all this is the way the Internal Revenue Service is stalking the financial doings of the Chicago archdiocese. Not to mention the journalistic pack sniffing in Cody's wake. It all bodes ill.

Gianpaolo continues to ponder over the notes he has made during meetings with Benelli and Felici. They explained that the Vatican's entanglement in such unsavory financial affairs had come at a time when it was—and it still is —reeling from a succession of other monetary blows. There has been a fall in the number of financial bequests to the Church; during the past five years the amount has slumped by 30 percent. The annual contribution of Peter's Pence has declined steadily since the days of John. Allowing for inflation, in true worth the amount collected is now only 60 percent of what it was a decade ago. Against this, salary raises for curial employees—whose numbers have tripled these past fifteen years—had to be given just as Italy's inflation peaked, creating a domino effect.

And only now, three years later, is the full extent of the financial disaster of the Holy Year of 1975 clear. The Church had invested huge sums trying to attract pilgrims to Rome. They did not come. As a result the Vatican was forced to dip heavily into emergency contingency funds to meet a deficit equal to some six million dollars. This position has worsened despite the most stringent cuts. The projected deficit for 1978—quite apart from the expense of Paul's funeral and the ensuing conclave and coronation—is expected to be eleven million.

Now, eight years after Paul launched his angry attack on critics who spoke disturbingly of the Vatican's "fabulous wealth," it is the Church's deteriorating investment position which most worries Gianpaolo. Holdings in real estate, art, rare books and all the other treasures the Vatican possesses still makes it in a sense one of the richest organizations in the world. But the capital it has available to invest is dropping all the time—because of bad management. It began when Paul signed that secret deal with Sindona taking the Church's portfolio outside traditional Italian markets, where the Vatican could exercise rigid control over its investments, into the financial markets of Europe and the United States.

Gianpaolo learned that plunging, often as a major shareholder, into multinational conglomerates had resulted in a diminishing of the Vatican's influence in the financial world. No longer could the Church wield the power it previously possessed when it held sway over companies and could ensure that they did not engage in dubious practices; there had been mistakes made then, too, but nothing on the scale that has happened in the last five years.

Close to nine-thirty, Gianpaolo finishes reading. His thoughts at this moment remain his alone, shared with no one.

Yet already Felici and Benelli have told several people of that earlier moment when the pope looked at them and, in a voice they had not heard before, said this must stop; an end must be put to policies which left the Vatican financially defenseless and at the mercy of profiteers, speculators and high-flying con men like Sindona and Calvi.

For the moment, he decides, Marcinkus will remain at the helm but, like Küng and Lefèbvre, the future of the banker is under review. In the meantime the Church must urgently seek new ways to make use of its funds.

Exactly at nine-thirty Martin ushers in Bernardin Gantin. Gianpaolo leads the tall black African cardinal to a sofa and sits beside him. Gianpaolo comes quickly to the point. He outlines what he has learned and what he wants to do.

Gantin is frank—and will later make no secret of it. Paul, possibly partly because of his own financial experience, had, in the closing years of his pontificate, developed an entrenched fear of the Italian left. This, coupled with his increasing conservatism, had decided him to move the Vatican's money beyond the reach of those in Italy he felt might one day grab it. He had acted from the highest motives and no one, least of all Gantin, wanted to see the Church's money put at risk in unstable Italian stock. Equally, if the Church is to continue to be seen as the church of the poor, especially in the Third World, it must ensure that it does not appear blatantly materialistic and divert some of its still-considerable financial resources to more humane causes. Gantin urges that the Vatican use its investment, wherever possible, to help stop socioeconomic injustices and exploitation. Vatican finances should be used to support worthwhile redevelopment schemes in Africa, Asia and South America. There could still be acceptable profits—and such a policy might also virtually put an end to the growing criticism from Catholics and non-Catholics about how the pope's financial empire functions.

For the first time Gianpaolo smiles. There *are* going to be changes. For a start he wants Gantin to take charge of Cor Unum, the Church's powerful organization for international aid. Until now this important and delicate position belonged to Villot.

Gantin accepts.

When Gantin emerges from the pope's salon, Martin, waiting in its crowded anteroom, sighs. His carefully prepared schedule is already overrunning. It really is so irritating, the prefect has complained to Magee and Lorenzi, the way the pope simply refuses to keep to time. Martin has tried everything. He has come in and stood pointedly inside the door. Gianpaolo either ignores him or cheerfully waves him away. He has tried to devise a "fifty-minute hour," allowing a ten-minute interlude between appointments. That hasn't worked either. The pope simply runs on.

Martin finds all this upsetting enough. But matters are exacerbated because there often seems no good reason why the pope uses his valuable time talking to people who, really, in the end, are relatively unimportant. For instance, Gianpaolo has had in some of his former archdiocese priests for a chat which ran on well beyond the allotted span. Again, between meetings that are important, Gianpaolo sometimes wanders off and talks with anybody he comes across in the corridors of the Apostolic Palace or the San Damaso Courtyard.

The prefect has needed his considerable tact and experience to smooth the ruffled feelings of several cardinals making their farewells before leaving Rome, who found themselves kept waiting beyond their appointed time. Cody, for one, was not pleased. Nor was Aramburu. Others, like König and

Sin, were more philosophical: they felt running late was just part of the papacy shaking down.

Martin feels relieved that the imposing figure he has been engaging in polite conversation while waiting for Gantin to finish seems in no hurry.

Everything about Metropolitan Nikodim, archbishop of Leningrad and Novgorod, reminds Martin of a bear. The man has a huge bearlike head, thick bear-shaped neck and shoulders, a bearlike belly and hams of arms which he uses to fan himself like a bear swatting flies. And even in the voluminous regalia of the Russian Orthodox Church there is no disguising that the metropolitan is a hairy man. He has a full, flowing beard which extends from just below his eyes to the start of his ample stomach; there are tufts of hair in his ears and on the backs of his broad fingers and hands; when Nikodim strips off for his regular swim in a Rome hotel pool, the thickly matted hair on his body causes heads to turn; he stands close to six feet and weighs about three hundred pounds.

Born in a small town a hundred miles outside Moscow, he has clung to his native peasant patois. Nobody is really fooled. Nikodim's mind is sharp enough to make more than one member of the Soviet Politburo—so Casaroli has informed Gianpaolo—ponder anxiously the strength of Christianity under communism. In the Vatican, Nikodim is also seen as a powerful bridge maker between the Church and non-Catholic Christian churches. The metropolitan has been allotted a full fifteen minutes in which to speak privately to Gianpaolo about the problems of religious worship in Russia.

Martin finally leads him into the salon. While introductions are made Vincenza enters with a tray bearing a coffee set. The prefect leaves with her.

Gianpaolo will now be the only witness to what happens. He will recall precisely the sequence of events and, natural reporter that he is, pare them to the essentials for the subsequent benefit of Magee, Lorenzi and others. It won't change anything.

For a moment he talks to his visitor. Then he pours two cups of coffee. He offers the metropolitan cream and sugar: Nikodim accepts a little of each. They are standing by the pope's desk. Nikodim takes a sip from his cup. Gianpaolo is about to do the same when he pauses, startled.

A stricken look crosses Nikodim's face. Cup and saucer drop from his hand. The saucer shatters on the desk top; the cup spills coffee on the carpet, which the thick pile quickly absorbs. Nikodim clutches his chest, makes a choking sound, and then topples backward, crashing to the floor. His mouth and eyes remain open. But Gianpaolo knows instinctively his guest is dead.

The pope picks up the white telephone and dials Lorenzi, telling him to get a doctor.

Almost immediately Martin and Magee rush into the room. Buzzonetti quickly arrives.

The doctor kneels beside the body, listens for a heartbeat, checks for a pulse. He stands up, shaking his head.

Martin suggests that Gianpaolo cancel the rest of the morning's appointments.

"No!"

Magee is startled by the sharpness of the pope's response.

"No. These people have come to see me. They will." Gianpaolo looks down at the body. "That is what this good man would have wished."

The corpse is still warm when the rumor starts: Nikodim is the victim of a confusion with poison; he had sipped lethally contaminated coffee which was actually meant for the pope.

It is both vicious and untrue. The metropolitan died from a massive coronary. But the story continues to spread.

Behind Gianpaolo is the towering figure of the Risen Christ in a mass of jagged bronze, the dominant feature of the Nervi Audience Hall. Facing him, only held in check by steel crush barriers patrolled by anxious security men, are some twelve thousand men, women and children, all gripped in high emotional fervor. There may be more. Shortly before the doors closed, there was a final surge of people into the Nervi, and now there may be so many crammed into this vast indoor arena that public safety laws are being broken. Nobody seems to care. The fifty or so television and still-camera men encroaching on the huge stage where Gianpaolo sits on his throne; the two hundred reporters in their gallery set into one wall; the radio broadcasters in the adjoining booths; the forty cardinals and almost a hundred bishops seated with them on the stage; and, above all, the public who stretch row after jam-packed row so far back that from the throne the faces meld and blur—all are totally absorbed by the extraordinary performance Gianpaolo is giving during his first Nervi audience, on Wednesday, September 6.

People who have been coming here for fifteen years cannot remember Paul, at his most relaxed, behaving like this. Indeed, there may be nothing quite like it in the entire history of the papacy. Two months ago Paul spoke to them in terms often obscure, his dogma impeccable but frequently so hedged with caveats that many could not follow his meaning.

The journalists came then expecting—perhaps even half hoping—there would be trouble: that the supporters of Lefèbvre might disrupt Paul's words; that somewhere in the crowd would be followers of Küng. But now the newsmen are almost all here for a very different reason. They simply want to see what Gianpaolo will say and do after their own close encounter with him at their special audience a few days ago. He offered the evocative thought that the Church is "like a clock," its "hands give certain rules to the world," and "the Church itself needs winding up, which is the Curia's job." He asked and answered the question as to what distinguished him from every other pope since the year 914: he was the first for over a thousand years entitled to add a "One" after his name. The journalists decided he was going to be a most quotable pope. This is why they are here: to witness the captivating performance Gianpaolo has put on since coming into the Nervi, skullcap askew, face lit up with irrepressible humor.

It has taken him thirty minutes to walk from the rear of the hall to the throne beneath the Risen Christ. Along the way he has shaken hundreds of hands, exchanged even more greetings and behaved, one reporter noted, "like a humble, godly man, his skullcap askew suggesting a degree of lovable incompetence which is in no way threatening."

From the moment Gianpaolo speaks the entire gathering is in his hands.

He begins by saying he intends to "imitate Paul, in the hope that I, too, will be able, somehow, to help people become better."

It is straight to the point, not stuffy theology, more like crisply spoken journalism.

"We must feel small before God. When I say, 'Lord, I believe,' I am not ashamed to feel like a child before his mother. One believes in one's mother. I believe in the Lord, in what He has revealed to me. The commandments are a little more difficult to observe, but God gave them to us not to satisfy a whim, not in His own interest, but solely in our own interest."

He pauses and looks at them all in turn: his cardinals and bishops, some smiling uncertainly, for they, too, have witnessed nothing like this; at the film crews and the reporters high up in their gallery. They respond by recording his smile, the way he gives his cap an even jauntier angle. Then he looks out over the great mass of people and, with an aplomb a stand-up comic would envy, says he is going to tell them a story.

"A man went to buy a car from the agent. The latter talked to him plainly. 'Look here, it's a good car. Mind that you treat it well. Premium gas in the tank and oil for the joints. The good stuff.'"

He pauses; his timing is perfect.

"The man replied. 'Oh, no, for your information, I can't stand the smell of gas or of oil. I'll put champagne, which I like so much, in the tank, and I'll oil the joints with jam.'"

Appreciative laughter sweeps the Nervi. A quick wave of Gianpaolo's hand and there is silence for the punch line.

"The agent said, 'Do what you like. But don't come and complain if you end up in a ditch with your car!'"

Another burst of laughter. Then the point of the story, delivered with a surge of feeling.

"The Lord did something similar with us. He gave us this body, animated by an intelligent soul, a good will. And he said, 'This machine is a good one. But treat it well.'"

Thunderous applause. He silences it by beckoning a choirboy to join him on the platform. His name is James and he is just ten years old, an angel-faced child. With him Gianpaolo reveals another gift: his sure way with children.

"James, have you ever been ill?"

"No."

"Ah, never?"

"No."

"Never been ill?"

"No."

Chuckles come from all over the hall.

"Not even a temperature?"

"No."

"Oh, how lucky you are!"

Another burst of delighted laughter. Gianpaolo pats James on the head. The child has paved the way for the moral he wants to convey.

"When a child is ill, who brings him a little broth, some medicine? Isn't it his mother? That's it. Afterward you grow up, and your mother gets old. You become a fine gentleman, and your mother, poor thing, will be in bed, ill. That's it. Well, who will bring the mother a little milk and medicine? Who will?" He waits for James to digest the scenario.

"My brothers and I."

Gianpaolo beams. "Well said!" He addresses the audience. "'His brothers and he,' he said. I like that. Did you understand?"

A mighty roar of agreement.

"But it does not always happen. As patriarch of Venice I sometimes went to homes. Once I found an elderly woman, sick."

Gianpaolo pauses, looks at James, smiles, prepares himself to play the part of both the visiting clergyman and the ailing woman.

"How are you?"

The pope subtly changes his voice. He sounds like a frail old woman. "Well, the food is all right!"

"Are you warm? Is there heating?" He's the caring cleric.

"It's good."

"So you are content?"

"No." He adds another voice to his repertoire, that of a neutral observer. "She almost began to cry."

He switches again, back to the concerned priest. "But why are you crying?"

"My daughter-in-law, my son, never come to see me. I would like to see my grandchildren."

In the hall people are actually crying.

Gianpaolo raises his voice. "Heat and food are not enough. There is the heart. We must think of the hearts of our old people. The Lord said that parents must be respected and loved, even when they are old. And beside the parents, there is the state, there are superiors. May the pope recommend obedience? Bossuet, who was a great bishop, wrote, 'Where no one commands, everyone commands; where everyone commands, no one commands any longer but chaos.' Sometimes something similar is seen in this world too. So let us respect those who are our superiors."

He smiles at James, gives him a final pat on the head and sends the boy back to his place.

He is not finished. Gianpaolo tells them charity is the soul of justice, but that he has always recommended not only great acts of charity, also little ones.

He says he wants to repeat a story he read in Dale Carnegie's *How to Win Friends and Influence People*.

"A lady had four men in the house: her husband, a brother, two grown-up sons. She alone had to do the shopping, the washing, the ironing and the cooking. Everything, all alone. One Sunday they came. The table is laid for dinner, but on each plate is only a handful of hay."

Another perfectly timed pause. As the laughter erupts, he quells it.

Gianpaolo spreads his hands expressively. " 'Oh!' the others protest and say. 'What? Hay?' And she says. 'No, everything is ready. Let me tell you. I prepare your food. I keep you clean. I do everything. Never once have you said, "That was a good dinner you made for us." Say something! I'm not made of stone!' "

Now he lets the applause come. He bides his time. Then he quickly delivers the message. "People work more willingly when their work is recognized. These are little acts of charity. In our homes, we all have someone who is waiting for a compliment."

As the applause eventually dies, Magee thinks Gianpaolo has done more in ten minutes than some Church leaders achieve in a lifetime. He has created a means by which he can funnel his teachings, knowing they will be warmly received. It has been a tremendous performance—perhaps one powerful enough to make his opponents pause.

XXI

The opposition grew.

Within his city-state—with its thirty squares and streets, parish church, grocery store, post office, car pool, garage and bookstore—the voices of dissent became more vocal, more malicious and more bold in their rejection of what the pope said and did.

When he smiled and laughed, they smirked. When he quoted not only Dale Carnegie but also Jules Verne, Mark Twain, Napoleon and St. Bernard, they said he culled his philosophy from the *Reader's Digest*. The more his audiences were attracted by his direct, commonsense approach, the fiercer grew the opposition; the more the crowds cheered, the more the Curia growled.

They picked over Gianpaolo's words, looking not so much for hidden meaning —there was almost none—as for a chance to ridicule and repudiate with that special kind of subtle viciousness curialists can use when they feel most threatened; these were the gibes of single-minded men whose outlook had been shaped in part by grappling with such travails as birth control, premarital sex and the increasing threat of women being ordained as priests.

These were men who had come to believe in the closing years of Paul's pontificate that, unless the slide was halted, by the end of the century there would no longer be a religious institution which they, in any event, recognized as the Roman Catholic Church. All around them they perceived opponents tearing at the very fabric they held sacred in order to achieve that change even sooner. There were priests in open rebellion against their bishops; bishops in revolt against the authority of the Vatican; black, yellow and all shades of brown, Catholics all, insisting that their will be done in the name of their brand of racism and under threat of separation from the parent Church; nuns who refused to wear habits or even work alongside priests because it offended their newfound religious women's liberation. There were Catholic gay churches, Catholic yogis, Catholic Pentecostalists, Catholic Processions; they are to these men in the Curia what the dancing dervishes are to mainstream Islam.

For years—say the curialists—the deviates have had sympathizers in high places in the hierarchy; any number of cardinals who should know better continue to pay at least lip service to the demands of those determined to bring about change and the havoc their opponents fear.

They had almost welcomed the passing of Paul. For them, he had become simply too feeble to handle the crisis of communism, contraception and theological revolt. Not only had he finally failed to walk alone on the peaks of decision, he had lurked in the foothills, pleading and scolding, and trying to please all sides. Under him papal authority had reached a new nadir. The Church had been eviscerated by his weakness, his indecision, the lack of real authority that greatness demanded. Paul, in their eyes, became a pygmy pope leading the pygmy masses to the abyss.

They had expected, they said, so much from his successor: that he would refute moral support for terrorists in Latin America and elsewhere; that he would temper sympathy for Third World causes; that he would voice his objection to Marxism in all its many guises; that he would stamp—hard—on the concept of a "people" church where everyone was allowed to go their own way; that he would tell Catholic homosexuals and divorcees they could never be allowed full religious rights; that he would denounce all those priests and nuns hell-bent on the destruction of the social order which the Church must have to survive. This, at the very least, they had hoped for.

Instead, Gianpaolo gave them parables about Pinocchio and, perhaps even harder for these archconservatives to accept, photographs of himself shaking hands with the Communist mayor of Rome.

In the embattled world of the diehards, this was tantamount to a declaration of war between them and the pope. He was, they shuddered to one another, almost certainly going to realize their worst fantasies: there *would* be more homosexual marriages; *would* be more denials of the Virgin Birth and the Resurrection; *would* be an increase in tactile prayer, Satan-Jesus cults, masses celebrated by women in living rooms, nude altar boys, rock masses, black revolutionary Christs, female Holy Spirits; there *would* be a burgeoning of clerical posturing and theological absurdities.

They all had hoped for a successor in the mold of Pius XII, a true Prince of Power, imbued with a real feeling for traditional values, a model—they added—all popes should aspire to follow. Instead—they went on—they had acquired a pope who insisted he was more of a mere man than even John had proclaimed, who had, within a few days of being elected, indicated that change was inexorable, and that the Church had already passed through a momentous trapdoor—the Second Vatican Council—from which there could be no turning back. In all Gianpaolo said and did—for his opponents—he seemed to be suggesting that the Church was out of date and the only way it could contribute to the immense problems and possibilities it faced was to "adapt." The very word was anathema.

When he told the College of Cardinals in the first week of his pontificate that he had no real idea how the corporate structure of the Church worked, they had not objected. There had been popes in the past content to leave everything to the Curia and virtually rubber-stamp what it ordered. It had worked very well. But Gianpaolo was different: he poked his smiling face around every door—so much so that Villot, for one, always so exasperatingly courteous in the French way, and so tolerant of human failings, was tearing at his full head of hair. So they said. And the husky, balding Benelli—whom entrenched curialists unfailingly called "the Gauleiter"—was being allowed to flex his muscles. That might not, in the end, have mattered: after all, they had seen Benelli off once already. What really distressed the diehards was that, in spite of all his happy wanderings up and down the corridors of power, Gianpaolo still did not seem really to understand what his priorities should be.

He spent long hours preparing his apparently spontaneous homilies and Sunday Angelus asides. It got him a great deal of publicity. But the curialists fretted that even in his third week as pontiff, he appeared uncertain how many Sacred Congregations there were and seemed to have little grasp of the subtleties of interrelationship among those which he knew. While the maze of congregations, tribunals, secretariats, commissions and offices of the Curia might indeed appear cumbersome to a newcomer and in need of streamlining, they insisted this complicated labyrinth was well integrated and worked because everyone recognized the demarcation lines. No pope—said the men who manned the lines—could possibly ignore the recommendations of his civil service and hope efficiently to rule the Church. But that was what Gianpaolo was doing: he was falling behind with his paper work.

They said he appeared to have only a hazy notion of the many splits in the Church: the rift between the bishops of Latin America and the United States over the need to coexist with, or continue to reject totally, communism; the division within the intellectual life of the Church over what was acceptable and what was not; the argument over what could be done to halt the steady drift away from the priesthood. In so many ways Gianpaolo had taken over a house divided.

Even his most implacable enemies conceded he could not simply sit back and do nothing; that would assuredly have allowed the dam which Paul's policies had cracked to be totally breached. So: something had to be done.

What Gianpaolo did—they insisted—was something worse than doing nothing. He increasingly showed he had little patience with the daily grind, the decision making and the politicking, while at the same time he liked to be involved in everything. He was, in the words of one Irish curialist, "a messer."

The criticism was both unfair and untrue.

Even before September 6, when *Il Mondo*, Italy's leading financial journal, published a detailed exposé of the Vatican's financial morass, almost confirming what Gianpaolo had learned from Benelli and Felici, he had already begun to untangle the machinations of Marcinkus, who had been firmly asked for an accounting. And Baggio had been put back on the Cody trail.

Casaroli, for one, was quickly impressed by Gianpaolo's grasp of the Church's relationship with the regimes of Eastern Europe. Casaroli placed seven crucial questions before the pope; Gianpaolo answered five of them promptly and asked for time to ponder the other two. Paul had never been so positive.

The inescapable truth was that Gianpaolo had deliberately decided to take a long view. He did not feel it mattered that he was not grasping such trifles as who did what, where and why; what concerned him was that he could be the pope who led the Church into the third millennium. In the year 2000 he would be eighty-seven, not an unknown age for a ruling pontiff. To guide the Church into the next century successfully he must function less as a monarch and more as a colleague and pastor. He must bring the full promise of Vatican II to fruition, making it an instrument of genuine reform and reunion. This called for a new kind of papal leadership, less rigid, more open. That was why, when speakng to a group of visiting American bishops, he had not only warned of the dangers of divorce but also admitted there were many questions on the issue yet to be discussed. In other words, the door was not firmly closed. He used his Angelus talks on Sundays and his Wednesday audiences—both with their frequent references to Pinocchio, surely his favorite character—as a genuine attempt to foster a rekindling of faith. He was going unashamedly for mass appeal: this was the basis of his remarkably effective catechetical style, his polished microphone manner, his powerful attraction for the ordinary people of the world. He was a magnificent communicator and the papacy gave him a platform which had never before been available to him.

He used it shrewdly from the outset. He identified one crucial issue as collegiality; it was essential for power and decision making to be more widely diffused, and there must be a genuine increase in the sharing of responsibility between himself and his bishops. He said—and meant it—that he needed the collective wisdom of the episcopate to resolve the pressing questions facing the Church. He was more than willing to decentralize authority and at the same time give greater autonomy to episcopal conferences and diocesan councils. And he wanted this sort of cooperation to permeate all levels of the Church. In no way, he said with his usual winning grin, was he ceasing to be head of the Church, the ultimate arbiter. Far from abrogating his responsibilities, he was showing a new understanding of them by emphasizing that he saw his role as someone who ruled within, rather than over, the Church. Enforced imperialism had no place in his pontificate.

He quickly demonstrated, too—which may explain much of the opposition—that the Curia held no fear for him. He would build from where Paul had left off, internationalizing the Curia still more. He planned to introduce foreigners in increasing numbers into middle-management posts; eventually there might even be non-Italian nuncios. And he wanted younger people in the Curia: the average age of his civil servants was currently 60.2 years. He also saw a need to increase the number of religious and lay women from the present paltry few; while it would require a great deal of "understanding"—another of his words which drove opponents to reach into their office cupboards for drink—the day could soon come when women held important executive positions in the Curia. It would all fit in with his overall concept that the Curia must be more pastoral, more service-oriented and much more in keeping with the requirements of the Church he wanted to lead.

Gianpaolo revealed an immediate ease with his prime responsibility of preserving the unity of faith and communion. And he was always willing to try to capture the popular imagination to do so. He studiedly remarked that God was "even more our mother than our father." When he was challenged—as he full well knew he must be—he gave the perfectly correct response that the idea was not his, but Isaiah's. More important, it was yet another way for him to stimulate debate on such issues as Christology, Mariology, the sacraments and communal absolution. It became quickly clear he would pay the most careful attention to the responses to such serious theological issues. He warmly embraced the concept that, "free from anxiety," he would give positive guidance in all decisive questions affecting life and death, good and evil, including matters where human sexuality was involved. Nor would he be a doctrinaire defender of ancient bastions. Rather —and always paying proper attention to consistency with the Church's teaching— he would be a pastoral pioneer, encouraging responsible religious debate and ready to guide and correct when necessary.

In his inaugural address he has set another measure of his pontificate: "The danger for modern man is that he would reduce the earth to a desert, the person to an automat, brotherly love to a planned collectivism, often introducing death where God wishes life." He made it clear he would use his greatest asset—the morality and the inspirational authority of the papacy—to correct this situation. He would do everything he could to move the minds and hearts of people through exhortation and example. The wounds society inflicted on its members—and he was thinking, in these first weeks of his pontificate, of the Middle East and Iran— could be healed by love, hope and truth: all offer the only way to create a new sense of spiritual brotherhood. He intended to foster this feeling by traveling; he hoped his journeys would further demonstrate his visible solidarity with other faiths and creeds.

Gianpaolo made it plain in his first speeches that he was painfully aware that of the four billion plus people on this planet, 60 percent of them lived below the level of subsistence. He would, in all humility, like to be their spokesman, the pope who would plead for this voiceless majority; he would say and show, wherever possible, that the dispossessed, the oppressed, the disadvantaged and the poverty-stricken should regard him as their advocate. He was determined to sensitize the consciences of the wealthy and powerful and encourage them to develop a worldwide economic and political system based on justice and not on exploitation. In saying this he had not forgotten the words of Bernardin Gantin.

Nor indeed had he overlooked that, as leader of the largest church in the world, he could exercise unique moral suasion to further ecumenism. Close to a quarter of a million people in St. Peter's Square and an estimated hundred million around the world heard his clear-cut credo: "we intend to dedicate our prayerful attention to everything that would favor union. We will do so without diluting doctrine, but at the same time without hesitation." Here was clear notice that Gianpaolo meant to foster evangelical spirit, reject authoritarianism, unite Christians and improve existing ties between Jews, Moslems and the peoples of other religions.

In all he said and did he struck a universal chord. He received more attention and coverage than even John had managed at the outset of his reign. It continued like this through the sunny weeks of September. In the process it seemed as though his opponents, like so much else, were being swept away; their angry voices were lost in the roar of the crowd.

People began to say this could be the beginning of perhaps the most triumphant pontificate this century.

At his Wednesday audience, on September 27, sixteen thousand people somehow manage to squeeze into the Nervi Hall. He stuns them by speaking in excellent English on a subject he knows a great deal about: love.

Even his opponents admit that he is expert at dispensing it.

"*Mon dieu.*"

Magee waits, giving Villot time to collect his thoughts.

"Have you told anybody else?"

"No. But his nun found him, Eminence."

"Keep her there, outside his room. Nobody is to talk to her until I arrive."

"Yes, Eminence."

Villot again pauses. Then he issues orders.

"Stay in the bedroom. Lock the door. Phone Buzzonetti. Wake up Lorenzi. Get him to call Confalonieri and the others. There's a list, isn't there, from last time?"

"There's a list, Eminence."

"Good. Get Lorenzi to do that. I'm coming straight over."

Villot breaks the connection. Magee recognizes that already the secretary has once more donned the mantle of camerlengo.

At twenty minutes past five Magee unlocks the bedroom door and Villot strides in. He has managed to shave and comb his hair. He looks immaculate. He is carrying the same small bag he brought with him to Paul's deathbed.

The camerlengo is faced with a ticklish problem. His question to Magee about when the pope died is linked to absolution, the granting of the forgiveness of sins. The much-debated theological point is how long after death total absolution may be granted. It revolves around the vexing question of how durable a soul can be. There are some Catholics who argue that if a Catholic succumbs following a long wasting illness, cancer for example, the soul might leave the body relatively quickly, possibly within thirty minutes of death. But if a person has been healthy before being fatally struck down, his soul could remain in the body three or four hours, perhaps even longer. To non-Catholics the proposition may appear fanciful, but it can afford great comfort to Catholics.

In Villot's judgment, the soul of Albino Luciani, Pope John Paul I, the 261st successor to St. Peter, had not yet departed.

He reaches into his bag and removes a vial of holy water. Villot opens it and presses it to his thumb. He places the vial on the side table and then turns to the bed. In a hoarse whisper, Villot begins to chant.

"*Si capax, ego te absolvo a peccatis tuis, in nomine Patris, et Filii, et Spiritus Sancti. Amen.*"

"*If it is possible, I absolve you from your sins, in the name of the Father, and of the Son, and of the Holy Ghost. Amen.*"

He makes the Sign of the Cross on Gianpaolo's forehead. Then he rapidly moves his thumb up and down, back and forth, touching the pope at each Station of the Cross.

"Per istam sanctam Unctionem, indulgeat tibi Dominua quid-quid deli-quisti. Amen."

"Through this holy anointing, may God forgive you whatever sins you have committed. Amen."

Villot then administers the Apostolic blessing.

"Ego facultate mihi ab Apostolica Sede tributa, indulgentiam plenariam et remissionem omnium peccatorum tibi concedo, et benedico te. In nomine Patris, et Filii, et Spiritus Sancti. Amen."

"I, by the faculty given to me by the Apostolic See, grant to you a plenary indulgence and remission of all sins, and I bless you. In the name of the Father, and of the Son, and of the Holy Ghost. Amen."

Villot steps back from the bed, recorks the vial and places it back in his bag.

Buzzonetti arrives. The doctor is ashen-faced and tieless. As he closes the bedroom door, Magee hears Lorenzi making another telephone call from Gianpaolo's study. He has placed Vincenza in there.

Confalonieri arrives with Martin and Noé as Buzzonetti completes his medical examination. He turns from the bed and addresses the others. "A coronary occlusion. He felt nothing."

"When?" Villot's question is flat and expressionless.

Buzzonetti clears his throat, thinking. "I estimate the time of death between ten-thirty and eleven o'clock last night."

Villot bends down and opens his bag. When he straightens, he is holding the tiny silver hammer Magee last saw him produce in Paul's bedroom at Castel Gandolfo.

Villot stands by the body and carefully removes Gianpaolo's spectacles. He folds them and places them on the side table.

Then, just as he did with Paul, Villot taps the pope on his forehead with the hammer and solemnly inquires whether he is truly dead. When he has asked the question three times and received no reply, he informs those present, according to the rites of the Holy Roman Catholic and Apostolic Church, that Albino Luciani is dead.

He places the hammer in the bag, closes it and addresses Magee. "Bring in the nun."

Magee fetches Vincenza.

She is dry-eyed and totally composed as she stands before Villot and recounts what she has seen and done. Villot thanks her and asks her to return to Lorenzi.

When Magee has once more closed the bedroom door, the camerlengo stands with his back to the group and makes decisions that are going to have a devastating effect.

Villot decrees that the world must be told a story which departs from the truth in several places.

Vincenza's involvement is to remain secret. She and the other household nuns are to be returned as soon as possible to the mother house of their order, where they are to remain, away from any public contact, for the rest of their lives.

The official Vatican version will be that Magee, waiting to escort the pope to early-morning mass, discovered him dead in bed. And, says Villot, indicating the document chastising Arrupe, no mention must be made of it. The world will be told that Gianpaolo died reading *Imitation of Christ*. Villot explains the astonishing camouflage is to avoid "unfortunate misunderstandings."

Next Buzzonetti makes his contribution. He says he cannot straighten the body. Villot orders that Armando Zega and Company be contacted. Martin uses his bedside telephone to call the firm of morticians.

At ten minutes past six the Zega employee known as the Technician arrives with an assistant. The Technician carries a small suitcase. He opens it and the others are amazed to see it contains several lengths of rope.

The Technician explains what he and his colleague must do.

"Then do it," orders Villot.

The morticians take up positions either side of the bed. The Technician knots a rope around Gianpaolo's ankles and another across his knees. He and his assistant grasp the ends of the ropes. The Technician nods and they pull steadily. Gianpaolo's knees unbend. The men tie the ropes to the bed frame. They place a different rope around the pope's chest and pull it taut to straighten the trunk. Each man then takes an arm, straightening it by physical force so it rests at the side of the body. Each limb is now held in place by rope. The restraining cords will stay until rigor mortis has passed and the body is pliable once more. The men move to the head, one firmly grasping it while the other slowly manipulates the jaw to a normal position. They cover the body with a bed sheet, tucking it neatly into the side of the mattress, leaving only the head exposed. They close its eyes and mouth. Gianpaolo appears to be sleeping peacefully.

Magee escorts the men from the room and arranges for their return next morning to embalm the body.

The secretary will not be here to meet them. He is about to find himself caught up in a staggering twist to the drama of the death of a pope who has ruled for only thirty-three days. It will involve the KGB, the Soviet intelligence agency, and the chilling charge that Gianpaolo was murdered by poison.

XXIII

It's Saturday morning, September 30, and Franz König's mood matches the Roman weather: heavy. He's reeling from what he has just learned. That is why he's closely watching each of his fellow cardinals as they drift into the Sala Bologna. He keeps wondering which of them might have swallowed the carefully prepared and cunningly dangled bait. Even now, as he sits here in his purple-silk mourning robe, well inside the Vatican, König is sure the sophistry is still working its deadly effect far beyond the Leonine Walls. Reporters are clearly devouring it: König thinks grimly that this is to be expected. The material is so temptingly prepared it's a gift horse for sensation seekers.

But members of the press are not the only ones deceived. Some of the radical voices in the Vatican can be heard in the corridors and courtyards saying that for the first time in history, there should be an autopsy performed on a pope: that Gianpaolo's body should be opened and his organs removed for laboratory analysis to see if he has been poisoned. The very idea makes König shiver.

If it was only members of the Curia who were suggesting the postmortem, that would be quite bad enough. But a meeting of the Sacred College of Cardinals, the first of this interregnum, is about to begin in this salon to consider whether there should be an autopsy to try to quell all the rumors. This is what König finds especially disturbing. This is why he continues to watch the other cardinals for signs any of them has swallowed the simulacrum and will be pushing for an autopsy—so falling into the trap which has been prepared by the Soviet organization above all others that König hates and despises, Komitet Gosudarstvennoy Bezopasnosti, the KGB.

König is one of the few cardinals in the room who have seen at first hand the machinations of the KGB, and everything he has learned confirms this is one of their operations. He is certain he recognizes the agency's *modus operandi;* the footprints, invisible though they may be to others, in his mind lead all the way from Rome to Moscow, to the building in Dzerzhinsky Square where the KGB shares its headquarters with the infamous Lubianka. Very possibly the importance of the operation means it was cleared, perhaps is even being directed by, the agency's chairman, General Yuri Andropov.

König knows how efficient the general can be: over the years Andropov has done his share of besmirching the Church. And just forty-eight hours ago, when König was in Helsinki on "Church business," he had heard of yet another KGB drive being prepared against the Church behind the Iron Curtain.

But even that pales against this—a full-scale plot to destabilize the entire Church through the smear that the pope was murdered by his trusted aides. The very concept of the plot is so staggering that even now, with the evidence of its success so far only too clear, König cannot quite believe the KGB hopes to get away with it. But it has—and it is. If it hadn't, there would not be this meeting. There would not have happened so many of the things which have since König heard Gianpaolo was dead.

His secretary woke him in his Helsinki hotel with the news. Even a strong mind like König's can absorb only so much. He simply refused to believe, hoping against hope, refusing to think the unthinkable, clinging to the thought that there had been a mistake. Then it hit with a force which made him physically gasp: a promising pontificate was cruelly over and the Church was again vulnerable until a new choice is installed. He had sat on his bed and prayed. By the time he was being driven to the airport, König was again his composed self. As the taxi pulled into the terminal, he heard the Finnish radio announce there were reports the pope had been poisoned by "persons unknown." That was the beginning. By the time he reached Vienna—staying only long enough to pack for conclave—König's staff was fending off newsmen following wire-service reports from Rome on the same theme. That was when his suspicions hardened. But only when König reached Rome and discovered that people inside the Vatican were suggesting that an autopsy would "prove" the pope died of natural causes did he become certain that what was happening bore the hallmark of the KGB.

That was yesterday.

Today he knows the plot has a firmer grip than he could ever have thought possible. The very credibility of the Church, the Vatican and the papacy is being eroded. It is truly frightening.

Looking around the Sala Bologna, König wonders what support he can expect for his plan to stop the KGB's machinations.

He has been one of the first to arrive and occupies the same seat he had during the last interregnum, when the Sacred College met here every morning to settle important Church matters. The salon is just as grandly impersonal as he remembers it: the frescoes and the fine art collection almost casually hanging on the walls of this high-ceilinged room do nothing to hide the fact that the Sala Bologna is almost never used except on such momentous occasions as interregnums.

The long table at which König sits is standard multinational-boardroom length; the chairs might have come from any conference supplier. König wonders whether the drinking water in the glass jugs placed at regular intervals on the table has been changed since last he was here.

Most of the cardinals are in shock so severe that they sit in numbed silence waiting for the meeting to start. König is positive none of them anticipated Gianpaolo's death. That is what makes the evil campaign so horrific.

König is even sure he knows which section of the KGB spawned it: it bears the malevolent mark of Department D—for *dezinformatsiya*—of the First Chief Directorate. Only Department D can move so swiftly, be so well organized, calling upon its vast experience in the area of grand deceptions designed to mislead, confuse or influence world opinion against the Church. What has occurred reeks of the opportunism which has in the past seen other Department D provocations grow to monstrous proportions. The Vatican has been thrown into panic.

The KGB success and the attendant repercussions both stem largely from decisions taken by Villot. König and the other cardinals who see the specter of Department D—they include Joseph Ratzinger of Munich, Joseph Höffner of Cologne, Giuseppe Siri of Genoa and the Poles, Stefan Wyszynski of Warsaw and Karol Wojtyla of Cracow—find it virtually impossible to make sense of the camerlengo's behavior. They feel that from the moment Villot invented the nonsense about Magee finding Gianpaolo in bed reading *Imitation of Christ*, the camerlengo has played into the hands of Department D. This criticism is both carefully restrained and further muted by compassion. The years had taken their toll on Villot even before he assumed the intense pressures of the last interregnum and conclave. And, if only because of his close contact with the pope, the shock of Gianpaolo's sudden death has been all that much more traumatic for him. It has left his decision-making process fatally flawed.

This may account for the strained, almost haunted look about the camerlengo. Seated at one end of the table, Villot appears a very old man who realizes he has lost his grip on events, but cannot quite understand how. And even König, despite his certainty that the KGB is behind the plot, finds it hard to provide satisfactory answers to all aspects of the calumny.

For whatever reason—whether he is in fact recoiling in shock, whether there is something close to hysteria behind the tightly controlled mask of a face—Villot has not been his normally careful and farseeing self since he made the first extraordinary decisions in the pope's bedroom.

To attempt to hide that Gianpaolo was reading the indictment of the Jesuits is understandable; the pope's death effectively puts into limbo the crisis with the Society of Jesus.

But to try to excise the presence of Vincenza from the timetable of Gianpaolo's death and place discovery on Magee borders on the irrational.

In any event, shortly after Villot made these decisions, a sequence of happenings occurred which, within a matter of hours, torpedoed whatever thinking might have induced him to attempt such fabrications in the first place.

This much is known:

Around 7 A.M. on Friday—when word is officially given by Vatican Radio that Gianpaolo is dead—Franco Antico receives the first of many calls he will accept and make during the rest of that day.

Antico is the secretary general of Civiltà Cristiana, the aggressively right-wing organization which plastered Rome during August with posters demanding: "ELECT A CATHOLIC POPE." It supports Lefèbvre, opposes many of the changes introduced by Vatican II. More important for what is to follow, Civiltà Cristiana believed Gianpaolo to be "a good man" bent on a project dear to its own heart: reforming the Curia, which the organization identifies as the enemy of Lefèbvre's traditionalism. The international media briefly spotlighted Civiltà Cristiana during the last interregnum. But since then it has virtually dropped out of sight. Membership is beginning to fall from a claimed peak of fifty thousand in forty-one countries. Civiltà Cristiana badly needs something to get it back to those heady days when *Time* and other news magazines gave it space and the contributions came rolling in.

To the journalists who interviewed him in August, Antico seemed someone who would have been a success with the Medici popes. He is a romantic and trustingly naïve. He also sees conspiracies where most people don't. Antico is very responsive to what the press likes to hear: he's the sort of man some journalists simply can't do without. These qualities are about to have a disastrous effect when he takes that first early-morning call.

With the stubbornness which is another of his traits, Antico will go to his grave refusing to name his caller. He will merely contend he is "a person with good Vatican connections." In the scenario which now develops, all the cardinals who insist this is a KGB plot determinedly cast Antico's caller in the role of agent provocateur for Department D. Later Casaroli, Martin, Magee and Noé, people not usually given to wild words, will also insist the man is a KGB agent.

Antico is shocked by what his caller tells him.

By the end of their conversation—Antico thinks it may have lasted twenty minutes—he has a very clear picture of what must be done. With his penchant for conspiracies, the secretary general has not needed much convincing that, in the name of Civiltà Cristiana, he should immediately call for an autopsy, and that the reason for doing so is to establish whether the pope was murdered "by persons unknown."

Since 1959, when Department D was formed, it has achieved its most conspicuous successes by distributing its fabrications through a gullible medium most unlikely to be thought associated with Soviet duplicity. The devoutly Catholic Antico perfectly fits the department's requirement.

Who his caller is must remain a matter of speculation. KGB disinformation operations have always differed from conventional Soviet propaganda insofar as extraordinary care is taken to conceal the true originating source. In this case, as König accurately perceives, the plan has been well laid, suggesting that careful fieldwork established the pipeline to Antico. Almost certainly there are several cutout points between Department D officers and the person who actually telephoned Antico. In the event of a subterfuge going wrong at any stage, tracing it back to the KGB would be a near-impossibility. Perhaps it is as König says, a matter of recognizing the footprints.

In this case the fuse has been laid but remains to be lit.

It is the Vatican Press Office which applies the match. About the time Antico is having his momentous conversation, Father Romeo Panciroli clears with Villot the official announcement of Gianpaolo's death: "This morning at about 5:30 A.M., the private secretary of the pope, Father John Magee, entered the bedroom of Pope John Paul I. Not having found him in his chapel as usual, he was looking for him in his room and found him dead in bed with the lights on as if he were reading."

At seven-thirty on Friday morning, Panciroli telephones this statement to major foreign and Italian news agencies in Rome.

About thirty minutes later, Ansa, an Italian wire service, receives a call from Antico. He reads out a statement which states categorically that Vincenza found the pope and that she "dashed down the corridor" to awaken Magee. Gianpaolo had "a few sheets of paper in his hand," which Antico identifies as "highly secret documents."

The Ansa reporter's excitement is understandable. In almost every respect Antico's version contradicts the Vatican's.

Shortly after eight o'clock Ansa begins to transmit Antico's staggering demand for an autopsy to ascertain whether the pope has been poisoned.

By then other correspondents in Rome are being called by Antico with the same astounding tale.

Few, if any, stop to ask basic questions. What is the nature of the evidence? Has it been handed over to the Italian police? Are there sworn statements and witnesses? No such challenges are offered. It is simply enough that Antico is an official of an organization which was taken seriously in August. His utterances are now accepted at face value again.

The reporters begin to call Panciroli. He is still bruised from his abrasive encounters with the media during the previous interregnum and conclave, and reacts badly: he is cooler than usual. It makes him no new media friends; the reporters accuse him of covering up. Panciroli calls Villot. The camerlengo orders the press secretary to put up the shutters. The suspicion of conspiracy gains strength.

Nobody will know whether Villot stops to think how it is that the perfectly accurate account of Vincenza's involvement has emerged so quickly.

By midmorning on Friday, Antico and Civiltà Cristiana are firmly back in the spotlight. He is taking media calls from all over Europe. If the reporters suspect the real status of his imposing-sounding organization—a small, fading institution that clings to the hem of Lefèbvre's cassock—it does not trouble them. As the press has built up the archbishop, so it now endows Civiltà Cristiana with a significance it does not deserve. Perhaps then it is inevitable that Antico, with his heady blend of romance and suspicion, should soon be claiming, "We have concrete evidence to back our demands for an investigation. But we can't release it at this time. We want to preserve the legal niceties and work through channels."

He helpfully suggests that the reporters call Vincenza and Magee.

Faced with Panciroli's freezing refusal to comment, journalists try to reach the nun and the secretary.

They are too late. On Villot's orders, three hours after she found Gianpaolo, Vincenza and her nuns were bundled out of the Vatican and driven away into the Church's equivalent of purdah. When the Vatican switchboard contacts Magee and says reporters wish to speak to him, the secretary prudently calls Villot first. Magee is stunned by the camerlengo's reaction. Villot instructs him to pack at once, leave the Vatican for a seminary well outside Rome, and to stay there until further notice. The bewildered Magee follows the nuns into exile.

It does not take long before Antico is calling the press with this latest news. The reporters check. The Vatican Press Office says Magee has "left the country," and that the nuns are "inaccessible."

So the conspiracy theory has grown to the point where the Sacred College is having this Saturday-morning meeting.

Of all the many questions which deeply trouble König as he sits in the Sala Bologna, one in particular predominates: how was Antico's caller so well informed so quickly? Accepting he was a Soviet agent provocateur, an even more shattering question remains to be answered: Is there somewhere within the Vatican a KGB mole?

It is unthinkable. But as König knows too well, this is the era of the unthinkable.

Felici is the last to enter the Sala Bologna. For the past month he has been virtually at Gianpaolo's elbow, every kilo of his bulky frame fostering his appearance of being the confident confidant. Now Felici seems to have physically crumbled: his huge head and neck look too large for his body.

Benelli also appears to have shrunk. His eyes are hollow, his cheeks caved in: he seems a man who has recently done a great deal of crying.

Nobody doubts both Felici and Benelli will recover; it's not in their nature to do otherwise. But for the moment their world has collapsed.

It is difficult to gauge the mood of Siri of Genoa. Behind his horn-rimmed spectacles he is more inscrutable than ever. Perhaps he is mulling over what his sources in the Italian intelligence service have told him about the KGB's operation. Or maybe he feels like someone who has been given a second chance at the papacy—which, at the age of seventy-two, Siri must surely expect to be his last tilt. It may also be that his twenty-five years as a cardinal has taught him to maintain an expressionless face on such uncertain occasions as this.

Beside Siri sits Salvatore Pappalardo. He seems to be concentrating solely on his writing block; one has been set before each cardinal for any notes he cares to make. Pappalardo arrived on an early-morning flight from Palermo and is still mildly perplexed over having been buttonholed by Baggio about the need to resist any move to conduct an autopsy. This was the first Pappalardo had heard of the proposal. He finds the suggestion repugnant. Not only does it fly in the face of precedent, a postmortem will cause further offense to all those Italians who disliked the idea of Paul's being embalmed.

There are thirty-four cardinals in the salon when Villot, at precisely eleven o'clock, starts the meeting. The remainder of the Sacred College have yet to reach Rome.

Carefully eyeing Felici, Villot first asks those present if they have each received their letter, signed by him, requesting that they take part in conclave. Villot is not going to allow Felici the chance to attack him again for his lapse at the outset of the last conclave. Only after he gets an affirmative nod from each cardinal does Villot continue.

He repeats, almost word for word, the bald nonsense of the press statement he approved, adding that at the pope's bedside was a copy of *Imitation of Christ* and that Buzzonetti concluded death was from a massive heart attack which probably occurred around eleven o'clock the previous Thursday night.

There are no questions.

Villot proposes that the funeral should be in five days' time, Wednesday, October 4, the feast day of St. Francis, the patron of Italy.

There are no objections.

Everybody is waiting. The lengthening silence is broken from an unexpected quarter. Few can have expected the dean of the Sacred College to be the one to raise the subject. But Confalonieri says there is a need to act decisively to end the malicious campaign that is now well under way. Distasteful as it may seem, it is nevertheless now necessary to have an autopsy. Oblivious to the reaction to this—there are a number of surprised gasps—he goes on to say the world must accept what everyone in this room most assuredly knows: that Gianpaolo has been peacefully called home; brief though it has been, his pontificate was not uneventful. Secure in that knowledge, it would be both sensible and desirable to take the only possible course to end this dastardly campaign of vilification. He will support any vote for a post-mortem.

König waits while the others consider what they have heard. He is himself as astonished as any at the line Confalonieri has taken. The dean's view will, undoubtedly, have a powerful effect on those who are still undecided. It will be all that much harder for König to win them over—let alone change the minds of those already committed to Confalonieri's point of view. Not for a moment does König think the dean has been influenced by anything other than the highest of motives. Certainly there is no question of anybody in this room—let alone a KGB mole—being able to nobble Confalonieri. He has clearly come to his decision after the most careful consideration. The fact that König thinks Confalonieri is wrong in no way alters his respect for the cardinal.

König begins to speak, slowly measuring his words. There is the matter of a lack of precedent. So far as he knows, there has never been an autopsy on a pope. Therefore, would it not be best to wait for a vote of the full College to make the decision? Will not a postmortem fan the fires they all want to douse? Though the time left before the funeral is short, is it not better to reflect further and consult quietly among themselves over the weekend? Surely this is too grave a decision to rush.

It is the familiar König technique, this posing of carefully enunciated questions. He moves on, calm and deliberate, confident of his argument.

There is the matter of secrecy. How could an autopsy be concealed? Outsiders would have to be involved. However trusted they were, there is no certainty there would not be a leak. And if there was an attempt at secrecy, and it was discovered, wouldn't the damage be all the greater?

Further, assuming that prior notice is given, think how it could be exploited. Would it not be easy for the KGB to say it was no more than a cosmetic operation? Look at the outlandish lies they are already successfully spreading without any basis. Imagine, then, how much more effective their propaganda would be if they actually had something tangible to hang it on? And when the result is known, and the outcome is as irrefutable as they all know it must be, what then? Will the attacks cease? Assuredly not. More lies will follow. He finishes as he began, suggesting again that at the very minimum they should wait until the full College is assembled.

There is another silence. Villot waits to see whether anyone else will speak.

It is Felici who causes the second surprise. He argues that the presence of all the cardinals will not resolve the issue. There are likely to be just as firmly held opposing views then as there are now. Besides, it is possible some of the cardinals will not reach Rome until the day of the funeral. In view of the lying-in-state which is mandatory, it is impossible to wait until then. Nor, indeed, can the matter be delayed beyond Monday at the latest for "practical reasons."

Felici has been speaking to the Technician, and he now knows a great deal about the bodily chemical changes which occur after death.

He proposes that three doctors externally examine the pope's body. Afterward they should prepare separate reports on the "medical advisability" of an autopsy. These ought to be available for the next meeting of the cardinals on Monday.

He suggests the names of a Rome pathologist and two physicians.

Villot pauses a moment and then asks for a vote.

Twenty-nine of the cardinals support Felici.

Under the polite but watchful eyes of two Swiss Guards, Lorenzi leads a team of Vatican workmen on a tour of the papal apartment. It is early Saturday afternoon and they are making a final check that no personal effects are left.

Before going, the nuns removed all evidence of their presence. Vincenza has taken her stoup of holy water, the black wooden cross over her bed, her small collection of well-read books, a picture of the Virgin, the vacuum flask she kept by her bedside during the night in case she was thirsty.

In the past twenty-four hours the workers have also emptied the apartment of any sign that Gianpaolo lived here. Rubber-wheeled trolleys moved from room to room, gathering up boxes and chests which Lorenzi, often close to tears, had packed. One holds Gianpaolo's wardrobe of Gammarelli cassocks and other clothes, some so new they have not been taken out of their tissue paper. Another box contains his modest collection of shoes, well-worn uppers, heels that need repairing; among them is a pair of felt carpet slippers, the sort an old-fashioned gentlemen's haberdashery sells. Two chests hold his personal papers, the letters from his family and friends, old birthday and Christmas cards, notes from world leaders congratulating him on his election, letters from bishops and priests wishing him the long pontificate that was not to be, laboriously written requests from children in his old diocese asking whether they might visit him in the Vatican. There are his books, among them a surprising number of contemporary novels, a popular history of the world, several volumes of nature study, and of course the classics of philosophy and theology which helped him write *Illustrissimi*. There are magazines and the files of clippings from newspapers which he collected as part of his research material for those speeches which so captivated the world. There are a casette recorder and the tapes he sometimes used to try out a phrase or a whole section of a particularly important speech: he would play them back, listen, and continue to record until he was completely satisfied he had his delivery and timing word-perfect. There are his family photographs, each individually wrapped by Lorenzi in old newspapers that Gianpaolo liked to keep. There are the paintings and etchings, the ornaments and colorful cushions Vincenza so carefully displayed, a small chest which holds the tins and jars from that special shelf in the kitchen where she kept his nuts, coffee and sugar. Everything had been methodically packed and labeled, and taken down to a storeroom in the basement of the Apostolic Palace. In all it comes to some thirty containers. They will eventually be handed over to the pope's family.

Lorenzi leads the workmen into the pope's private study. Here, more than anywhere so far, he has learned the hard facts of papal death. The secretary still remembers that particularly painful moment when, shortly after formally pronouncing Gianpaolo dead, Villot walked into this study holding the Fisherman's Ring, which he had removed from the pontiff's finger. He asked Lorenzi for an envelope, into which he casually dropped the ring. Later it would be ceremonially broken before the cardinals. The camerlengo brusquely informed Lorenzi that Secretariat of State officials would soon arrive to remove all official documentation of the pontificate. They had taken away three large chests.

The desk at which Gianpaolo worked in such a clutter is now bare-topped; the overflow of paper has been removed from the floor, the wall map taken down. The study is as dead as a showroom.

To make doubly sure nothing remains, the men open and close drawers and cupboards. They work, as they have done since starting their task, in almost total silence. At first Lorenzi thought this was out of respect, or perhaps awe at being able to handle the intimate objects of a pontiff. But gradually he has concluded the workmen are merely indifferent: they have been in Vatican service much of their working lives and the routine of fetching and carrying for popes and powerful prelates has long lost its fascination. The men are mostly bored. There is nothing to say, so they say nothing.

Satisfied that the study is cleared out, Lorenzi conducts the men to the pope's bedroom.

The secretary still finds it difficult to enter the room, the very hub of activity in the immediate aftermath of Gianpaolo's death. Here throughout Friday morning came an endless procession: the vicar for Vatican City, who blessed the mortal remains; the president of the Council of State, who stared at the corpse and left as silently as he entered; the prelates of the Antechamber; the almoner of His Holiness; cardinals and bishops. Lorenzi finds it astonishing how many persons had a need, if not a right, to come and stand at the bedside and look and whisper to each other. Noé, Martin and Villot have been in and out, conferring, planning, deciding, not so much reverential, more quietly businesslike.

Contrary to an arrangement made with Magee, the Technician and his assistant returned to the apartment around midmorning Friday; by then Magee had gone. Their arrival was the signal for Villot to order everyone from the bedroom. Lorenzi already knew there would be no autopsy until the Sacred College ruled on the matter. He also knew it would be impossible to conduct a postmortem once the body was drained and filled with the Epic Corporation's embalming fluids. An hour after they entered the bedroom the Technician and his aide leave.

The secretary was one of the first to return to the room. He found Gianpaolo lying on the bed, fully dressed in papal vestments, a miter on his head, arms neatly folded, wrists lightly dusted with powder to hide the chafe marks where the restraining ropes had held them until rigor mortis passed. The face had also been carefully made up. But without his spectacles and with lips tightly pursed, Lorenzi thought the pope bore little resemblance to the smiling twinkle-eyed man he has served and loved.

Shortly afterward the body was carried on a stretcher by Swiss Guards through the apartment to the high-ceilinged Sala Clementina. Here, in the vaulted vestibule to the papal apartment, beneath the priceless artwork of Giovanni and Cherubino Alberti and Paul Bril, Gianpaolo was placed on a bier and the death vigil of the Swiss Guards began.

That was twenty-six hours ago.

Now, the bedroom has a desolate air. The horsehair mattress on its ancient frame is covered by a single sheet. The bedside lamp and rug have gone. The prie-dieu stands forlornly in a corner. The bowl of sweets has been removed. From the bathroom Gianpaolo's toiletries have been packed and taken away.

But there remains one item, to Lorenzi the most symbolic of all, that he has yet to remove. He goes to the wardrobe and opens its door. Reaching to the top shelf he takes down the cardboard box which contains the dry-cleaned cardinal's robe Gianpaolo changed out of in the Sistine Chapel. Lorenzi cradles the box under his arm and walks sorrowfully from the bedroom.

Behind him one of the men closes the wardrobe door. A Swiss Guard waits until all have left the bedroom, then closes its door and follows the group down the corridor.

Villot and Martin are waiting at the entrance door to the apartment. They stand aside, saying nothing, as Lorenzi and the workmen pass. The guards take up position on either side of the door. Villot removes a key from his robe

Felici has come here straight from the meeting of the cardinals. He is certain his memory has not failed him; somewhere in this labyrinth among the millions of rare books and documents he believes is one which will prove König wrong: there *is* a precedent for a papal autopsy.

Stored away in Felici's prodigious recall is the memory of coming across the hint that a postmortem was performed on Pius VII.

It is not much of a clue, and Antonio Samorè, the cardinal archivist, has said so. But it has been enough to spur on Felici; his sheer energy and enthusiasm persuaded Samorè and his staff to join the thrill of an intellectual hunt over a course which is 150 years old.

Nobody is better at finding their way round the obstacles to this plunge into the past than the two monsignori Samorè has called upon to assist: the prefect of the archives, the gentle and erudite Martino Giusti, and the senior archivist, Charles Lamb, who, after twenty years in Rome, still retains his Scottish burr.

Between them they have combed for clues the most likely of the 684 indexes, many handwritten and barely decipherable; these offer the only guide to the contents of this cloistered storehouse of astonishing secrets.

The hunt has been made that much more difficult because the life and times of Pius VII, like those of other popes, are not contained in one section but are scattered under various headings: parts are secreted in the *armadii*, the closets of the Miscellanea whose index uses the coded letters of the Greek alphabet; parts are in the *fondi*, various collections of documents which possess only onomastic, by-name, indexes.

But Felici, with a gambler's instinct, has brushed aside the difficulties. He *knows*, he repeats, that somewhere in this building is what he wants.

It is Lamb who suggests that a search be made of the Chigi family library. The Vatican acquired it early in World War II, when many of the great private archives of Europe were handed over for safekeeping because, in common with the cities of refuge in ancient Hawaii, the Vatican is inviolate from war. The Chigi family, like that of the Borghese, has for centuries been part of the papal court, collectors and discreet chroniclers of the secrets of successive popes.

Unlike many of the others, the library is well cataloged and sensibly arranged.

In no time the four men are once more immersed in that period onward from July 6, 1809, when Pius walked out of the papal apartment and down the great staircase into the Court of Honor, which the soldiers Napoleon had sent to arrest him had already desecrated. The Chigi papers detail the forty-two days of forced travel which took the prisoner-pope from Italy over the Alps to Grenoble, Avignon, and then back past Nice to the tiny fortress town of Savona on the Gulf of Genoa. For two years Pius VII languished there.

Then, continues the Chigi diary, in June 1811, Napoleon discovered the English fleet's plan to rescue the pope. In frail health—Pius VII had a mysterious stomach malady, Felici reads with quickening interest—the pope was unceremoniously carted off in the dead of night northward to Fontainebleau. Here he languished a further three years.

It was not until Napoleon was exiled to Elba that Pius VII could recuperate in the peace of the Vatican.

Felici is certain he remembers: it's not enough, but it's coming back. He's been here before—to these well-ordered papers of the Chigis. He still can't quite recall the reason, nor does it matter. Not now. He tells the others the search could soon be over.

They too begin to concentrate on the area Felici is trawling through, the closing stages of the life of Pius VII.

It remains a laborious process. There are cross-references to follow up which send Lamb and Giusti hurrying to collect yet more folders. Nobody minds. Caught up with Felici's relentless pursuit, they enjoy the spirit of the chase.

Felici reads on; his excitement is contagious as he comes to the long account of the death agony of a pope who has already suffered so much. His pontificate of twenty-three troubled years closed with an ever-present Chigi to record his last words. Pius VII died mumbling: "Savona and Fontainebleau."

And at the end of the report is the probable cause of his death: a weakened heart.

Felici is nonplussed. It is simply not possible: his memory, he is sure, has not played tricks. He turns the file over. There, on the back, is yet another maddening cross-reference, pointing him toward a new *fondo*.

Lamb returns with files from it, silently placing them by Felici's lectern.

The cardinal is more perplexed than before. These *buste* cover part of the brief papacy of Pius VIII, who reigned for less than two years.

Then Felici *really* remembers. He was wrong. His memory has played a trick. But now all that matters is that his instinct has finally given him the answer. All those years ago, when he first stumbled upon the clue which has kept him and his helpers poring over papers for the last six hours, he came here to read the history of papal medals. Paul had wanted the information and for some reason insisted that Felici personally obtain it for him. Felici discovered that Pius VIII had created the *benemerenti*, the medal popes award to those they decide have given outstanding service to the Church. And there, in this file which contains much about the life of a pope who had been largely dull and blameless, is that elusive clue. It is another cross-reference on the inside cover of the *busta*.

Now, Felici has no doubts. It takes only minutes for Lamb to return with the file. He is smiling. Felici suspects the archivist has looked inside and knows. No matter: Lamb is also entitled to feel triumphant.

They gather around Felici as he opens the *busta*. It contains the original diary of Prince Agostino Chigi, who had been marshal of conclave after Pius VIII's death.

Felici begins to read out Chigi's graphic account of the pope's "frequent convulsions" before he died. He turns another yellowing page, his finger moving over the lines which Chigi's quill pen scratched onto the parchment paper.

And at last he finds what he seeks. It is Chigi's detailed account of how an autopsy was secretly carried out on the pope the day following his death to establish whether he had been poisoned. The doctors who opened up Pius VIII found: "the organs healthy; the only thing noticed was some weakness in the lungs and some said his heart was weak."

Felici smiles triumphantly. He has his precedent.

It may be that Benelli is unaware or perhaps he no longer cares. But he is being overheard and his words will be touted to some of the newsmen arriving in Rome to cover Gianpaolo's funeral and the ensuing conclave.

Cardinal watching is back in vogue. There isn't a member of the Sacred College who can safely expect, between now and the moment he enters the Sistine Chapel, to escape surveillance by tipsters.

Media interest in the Holy See started relatively recently. Fifty years ago few newspapers outside the strictly Catholic press carried regular Vatican news; it was not until 1927 that even *L'Osservatore Romano* reported directly a pope's remarks. The Press Office opened in 1945 and remains a place where a reporter cannot ask real questions and expect answers. Nor does it as a rule arrange interviews with Vatican staff. Consequently a system of informers has sprung up. All kinds of people, including clerics, regularly accept gratuities for information.

Some informers are on retainers. Some, like Paolo Rossi, make a decent living. Rossi is the man who once got hold of an advance copy of Annuario Pontificio, the red-covered yearbook which lists the current Church hierarchy throughout the world and is an invaluable Who's Who to those in the Curia. The Annuario has been published since 1716, and the pope receives the first copy of the new edition, printed every January. Rossi beat him one year because he had inside information that the latest directory showed that the head of the Orsinis—who have served the papacy longer than any other Rome family—had no longer retained his traditional post as assistant to the throne. It was the pope's way of showing his displeasure that Prince Filippo Orsini, one of Rome's more attractive married playboys, was too close a friend of a famous actress. Rossi spilled the beans in advance of publication. He has been twenty years in the business of gathering such tidbits. He boasts all sorts of Church connections. Certainly he is a grafter. And clearly one reason for his success is intelligent anticipation.

This Saturday night he's booked a table for himself and a companion in the one restaurant in Rome where he can reasonably expect to uncover at least one cardinal. It's L'Eau Vive in the Via Monterone, a nondescript back street near the Pantheon which tourists tend to ignore. For more years than anybody can be certain, this is the place senior members of the Vatican dine; 90 percent of the clientele come from the Church. The prices are much too steep for a mere parish priest; even monsignori have to save before paying a visit to one of the culinary showplaces of Rome. It is not only the delectable food and vintage wines which attract bons vivants. It is the service provided. Many guests at L'Eau Vive believe that the waitresses are nuns, but actually they are members of the Travailleuses Missionaires de la Conception (Missionary Women of the Immaculate Conception), a secular "family." Each girl is young; most are tall and strikingly beautiful, and they all wear gold crosses on neck chains. Their soothing voices and soft smiles are often long remembered even after the agreeable food fades from memory. For the appreciative prelates this is pleasure without temptation.

Rossi has obtained a table in the coveted back room of the restaurant—where cardinals always dine—by a ruse he has used before. He wears a clerical black suit with a gold cross in his lapel. If challenged he will say he is a religious editor. He looks the part and has never been stopped in the years he has been coming here to listen and afterward peddle what he has heard.

Tonight, he had not expected such a windfall.

A corner table is occupied not only by Benelli but by two other cardinals, Suenens and Willebrands. They are members of that loose coalition people like Greeley say set Luciani's bandwagon rolling.

They have dined well, but have confined themselves to generalities during the meal. Only when coffee, laced with fragrant anise, is served does the conversation become more serious and worthwhile for Rossi.

Suenens begins by suggesting that the problems of the Church are once more where they were at the time of Paul's death: there is still a need to settle the role of the Synod of Bishops, to overcome the confrontation between the Church's moral principles and the modern ethics of lay society, to resolve the special problems of the Third World, to stabilize relations with the governments of Eastern Europe—and, perhaps most important of all, to find a means to end the falling off of religious fervor within and without the Church itself. It is barely a month since Gianpaolo began to handle these problems. He had shown signs he would tackle them; yet no one could seriously argue he had left a heritage which was much more than a promise of things to come. Gianpaolo had indeed given every indication of being different. But there is now no way of knowing just how different. Equally the Church must not slip back to the era of Paul. The dialogue Gianpaolo began must continue.

Benelli nods periodically. Rossi decides this is only out of politeness, that it's Suenens "clearing the ground."

The amplified voice of the restaurant hostess stops further discussion. She orders the waitresses to take up their position before the large statue of the Virgin which stands in its grotto in a corner of the restaurant. Hands clasped in reverence, the girls stare shiny-eyed at the plaster Mary. Then the voice of the hostess, coming from hidden loudspeakers, invites the diners to join the waitresses in the speciality of L'Eau Vive, singing a hymn over coffee.

The rich voices of the three cardinals lend authority to the timeless words of "Ave di Lourdes."

Afterward Willebrands picks up the thread of the discussion. There must surely be an expanded role for the Synod of Bishops in the next papacy; it is the one most effective way for the pope to handle the problems Suenens had indicated. Given greater authority, the bishops could effectively end the rebellion of Lefèbvre and Küng, hopefully without a need for further theological bloodletting. It could not be done at once and there would have to be give-and-take. But none of this could be achieved before a strengthened working relationship is established between the Synod and the next pope.

Benelli's balding head continues to nod in agreement. Then, in the aggressive voice that people often resent or are intimidated by, he intervenes: What about the Jesuits? Look how Arrupe has responded to Gianpaolo's death: the briefest of statements, not so much tinged with sadness, more with stoicism. Wasn't this an indication that the Society of Jesus would continue as before? Shouldn't the next pope come down once and for all on them and, if needs be, frog-march Arrupe back into line—and be seen to be doing it?

Rossi is all ears: this really is news—Benelli laying down rules on how the Jesuits should be tamed.

The cardinal from Florence is in full flow now. The next pope must be "vigorous," appeal to the progressives, "but not offend the conservatives." He must move Vatican II appreciably on, and do it early in his pontificate. But he "must not disinherit the Curia." They, too, have their part to play in bringing "the malcontents" to heel.

Rossi has no doubts: this is not only very salable material, it is Benelli signaling that he's most ready and willing to go forward as a candidate for the papacy. Rossi's basis for his conclusions may be too subtle for many people, but he has spent sufficient time eavesdropping on prelates to recognize the often obscure language of cardinalspeak. Rossi is satisfied he has heard enough to peddle the story that once more the archbishop of Florence, the mercurial Giovanni Benelli, is back on the ramparts and ready to defend his right to go for pope.

Shortly before eleven o'clock on Monday morning, October 2, eighty-five cardinals assemble in the Sala Bologna. Their mood is tense and expectant. They know about the widespread calls for an autopsy and the campaign of calumny which many readily accept is KGB-inspired. What else, they have asked each other en route to this meeting, can explain the way suspicions have been fanned? One of Italy's most responsible newspapers, *Corriere della Sera,* has just stated that Gianpaolo's death raised such grave doubts that "we cannot understand why an autopsy was not performed, especially since the Vatican constitution does not explicitly forbid this."

Felici has been busy thoughout Sunday calling his media friends to campaign for a postmortem. He really believes it is the only way to end the terrible smears. More and more newspapers and radio commentators are lending their authority to this view. Many point out that the world has lost confidence in official versions of events—citing Watergate, the assassination of President Kennedy, the Aldo Moro murder investigation, the Lockheed scandal: *ipso facto* the Vatican version Villot approved should not be believed. Indeed, the original scenario for the death is in tatters, and the camerlengo's prestige has suffered a severe blow both in and outside the city-state.

Villot has before him a file filled with evidence of how the campaign is escalating. Antico's Civiltà Cristiana continues to rampage through the media. But Villot has decided that to censure him publicly would only attract even more odium to the Vatican, and to approach Antico privately is too unthinkable for the camerlengo to consider. Consequently the secretary general of this recently obscure organization is continuing to receive the sort of attention usually reserved for ranking statesmen. Antico appears to be relishing every moment. And the more his views are reported, the more support he acquires.

One of Lefèbvre's aides, the French abbot Ducaud-Bourget, rants, "It's difficult to believe that the death was natural considering all the creatures of the devil who inhabit the Vatican."

A Spanish organization, Fuerza Nueva, semireligious, pro-Franco and hitherto almost unknown, attracts wide media attention with its ridicule of the Vatican's press statement.

An obscure philosophy professor in Madrid gets huge coverage by postulating how the pope could have been murdered.

Edition by newspaper edition, bulletin by radio bulletin, newscast by television newscast, the dreadful story spreads: anything and anybody is dragged in: the Borgias, the Renaissance popes with their penchant for hemlocking opponents—it's all grisly grist for the rumor mills. No wonder even the most level-headed of the cardinals in the Sala Bologna come to accept that the KGB is masterminding it all.

At eleven o'clock the doors of the salon are closed and Villot starts the meeting.

He announces that the three doctors have submitted their reports. In a toneless voice he reads out the first.

It is signed by the two physicians. Their conclusions are largely based, they admit, on the original medical findings of Buzzonetti, who examined the body "within seven hours of death." He had found there was no discoloration of the face, no suffusion to suggest a stroke; rather the skin was "white as chalk," indicating blood/oxygen starvation. In their considered opinion Buzzonetti had been correct in his diagnosis of a myocardiac infarct, probably preceded by fibrillation, an arrhythmic heart action and swift death. In their view there is no need for an autopsy.

Their pathologist colleague disagrees. Speaking "purely medically," there is no way, almost forty-eight hours after death, the lapsed time before he examined the body, for him to be positive that death resulted only from a massive heart attack. He is quite willing to accept this as the most likely cause. But to be clinically positive there should be an autopsy.

Villot says the majority medical vote is *"negative et amplius,"* a clear rejection. Unless he hears to the contrary he proposes to call for a vote on this expert opinion. He pauses and looks meaningfully down the table at Felici.

For the second time in two days Felici surprises his colleagues. He sits, arms folded, saying nothing. He has decided—he will say later—there is no point flying in the face of expert testimony. It will be the only comment, brief though it is, he will permit on the matter; it will become another enigma in the Felici legend.

Villot continues to wait.

Some cardinals, such as Krol, Cooke, Cody and Carberry, have just arrived in Rome. They and the rest of the North American bloc are firmly with König: there is no need for an autopsy. Krol is confident: "If there had been any reason to suspect foul play, the Vatican would have investigated it fully. There wasn't. Hence there isn't any need for formal denials. They wouldn't satisfy the people clamoring loudest for an autopsy; nothing would."

Enrique y Tarancon and the other Spanish cardinals are equally emphatic: a postmortem will only pander to the public appetite for sensationalism.

There is murmured agreement around the long table.

Sensing it, eager to catch this favorable wind, to steer himself and the Vatican free of the unholy mess his original mishandling of the situation is responsible for, Villot quickly calls for a vote.

It is virtually unanimous. There will be no postmortem; there is quiet confidence that the rumors will fade and wither as nothing fresh emerges to feed them. But König has a new fear.

Now that the KGB has scored such a success it will surely want to try again.

XXIV

To the end it maintained its simplicity, the wake and funeral for Gianpaolo. Over six hundred thousand ordinary people—the same kind as those who attended his Wednesday audiences—filed past his body before the coffin lid was closed prior to the funeral on Wednesday afternoon, October 4.

The words of the mass were essentially the same as the ones expressed over Paul's coffin. The setting was identical: the piazza of St. Peter's. But the pomp and the glory, the presence of the high and mighty, was markedly absent this time. Jimmy Carter sent his mother to represent the United States. Mayor Edward Koch represented New York. Everybody was relieved that President Videla of Argentina stayed home to watch the outdoor service on television. Thirty-one countries took the pictures from the square. But the major networks weren't inclined to send their star commentators to Rome. As a CBS executive said, "We did this show last month."

The funeral was a damp affair. It rained on and off for most of the ninety-minute ritual. Several times the tall candle seemed about to flicker out in the wind. But the water-soaked pages of the Bible stayed open at the Gospel of St. John.

At precisely five-fifty Rome time, twelve frock-coated pallbearers bore the coffin into the basilica and afterward on down to the grotto. There it was placed in the sarcophagus which already carried his name. The tomb was covered by a heavy stone slab. Above it two fifteenth-century marble bas-reliefs of flying angels watched over the pope. They had smiles on their lips.

PART THREE

CONSPIRACY

Cursed be the heart
that thought the thought,
And Cursed be the hand
that fired the shot.

—BALLAD (UNDATED)

E ven if he begins to suspect and wants to unravel the carefully conceived manipulation, the nurtured exploitation of his strengths and weaknesses and the deadly way his condition was recognized and seized upon; even if he grasps any of this, the road along which Agca is traveling on this Thursday morning, October 5, is not the place to try to begin to understand.

For a start, the truck he is driving demands all his attention. The 1960 Dodge is well beyond its normal life-span and has been sorely neglected. Its tires are balding, its gears crash and grind; there is a disconcerting knocking sound in an engine which should have been replaced a hundred thousand miles earlier. Apart from the speedometer and odometer, the dashboard instruments no longer function. The brake linings are worn and the lights out of alignment. In most Western countries the vehicle would not even interest a rapacious scrap dealer. But in Turkey the truck is unexceptional. Its one functioning gauge confirms what Agca has carefully noted on a piece of paper he taped beside the indicator at the outset of his journey—that since then he has driven this decrepit truck over one thousand kilometers. The instrument cannot reveal that covering this distance has meant a numbing, jolting lonely week in the cab, continually fighting a stiff steering wheel to avoid the worst of the pitted road surface. His route has brought him across the Cappadocia, that eerie volcanic district which extends for hundreds of miles southeast of Ankara; a surrealist landscape of towering stone cones and plunging ravines. He has passed the rock chapels of Göreme, the troglodyte village of Avcilar and the ancient underground cities of Kaymakli and Derinkuyu. Later he turns east into that part of Turkey which was once Upper Mesopotamia, where, two thousand turbulent years before Christ, man struggled to survive in this still-hostile landscape.[1]

Like the truck, Agca blends easily into his surroundings. He wears heavy army-style lace-up boots which he uses constantly on brake and accelerator. He is dressed is rough serge trousers and a faded flannel shirt, old-fashioned enough to have a hole for a collar stud. A cloth cap is on his head, its greasy peak pulled well down on his forehead so no one can easily see his eyes. He does not like people to stare into them; this is another of his recent peculiarities. His beard and mustache are a thick stubble. Agca looks what he wants to be taken for: a countryman about his business.

At the start of his long journey considerable care was taken by others to enhance this impression. The Dodge's license plates were rubbed with mud, obscuring the numbers, giving an appearance common enough in the empty hinterland beyond Ankara. On the run down to Haran, the truck was filled with rickety furniture: if he was stopped Agca would have said he was delivering it to a family in Haran whose relatives had died in Ankara. At Haran the chattels were off-loaded and replaced by a consignment of maize and chickens. Many will die before Agca reaches his next destination. He does not care. In a way this is symptomatic of what is happening to him.

During the five weeks since he left the safe house of the Gray Wolves in Ankara, the changes in Agca have been so insidious he himself barely recognizes them. But they are there, subtly altering his personality, making him more malleable and receptive. All Agca senses, apart from his eroticism, is that he feels increasingly dead; he is in fact no longer locked in to his environment by the repertoire of emotional responses that have sustained him for years.

The reason which has brought him on this bone-jarring journey across Turkey to the Syrian border initially excited him—this possibility of getting help to kill the new pope in Rome. But long before he reached his first destination, Haran, he heard that this pope, too, was dead. News which once drove him nearly to smash the family television and to retreat howling to his bedroom to chant the mantra of his hate list, this time he received with indifference. It was *Ins'Allah* at work, and if *Ins'Allah* wills it, he will be given another opportunity. That possibility, at least, has not lost its appeal.

In this frame of mind Agca is continuing his journey. Now and then he recites his hate list. Yet for the most part the old rewards—the feelings of elation, domination and intense physical pleasure—have largely gone; he really feels only the familiar excitement, a rekindling of anger and hate, when he reminds himself of all the evils his imagination places at the door of the pope and the Roman Catholic Church.

And another part of Agca's mind also functions as clearly as ever; it is his well-developed sense of secrecy and cunning. He wrapped his treasured Mauser and bullets in oilskin; then, along with the exercise book filled with details about Paul, the first pope Agca wanted to kill, he concealed the items in a flap he cut under the truck seat. It is one of the tricks he remembers from that period which he still manages to keep hidden even from his mother. And now he is certain that she—and also Turkes and the other Gray Wolves—have no idea he is actually here, on the road from Haran.

Yet, despite the precautions he has taken, Agca knows he will need all his wits and prayers to avoid arousing the suspicions of the Turkish Army, which patrols this border area with Syria. The last of the summer tourists have long gone; for another year there will be no sightseers gawking at the sacred carp in the pool beside the Mosque of Abraham at Urfa, four hours away in the Dodge bouncing noisily through one mountain pass after another. Anybody who moves along this ancient trail—two thousand years ago King Antiochus I traveled this very route to conquer the local tribes—is automatically frowned upon by the patrols during the long months of autumn and winter.

For here, above the gorges, well concealed from any tourist cameras, between where the Euphrates and the Tigris have their sources, the U.S. Central Intelligence Agency has its listening posts; radar dishes beam northeast and south, sufficiently sensitive for their attendant computers to isolate and identify individual telephone calls in Damascus, Tehran and even further afield, deep inside Russia. And beyond the gorges are the massive black-basalt walls of Diyarbakır, the provincial capital of this desolate area, with its modern air base from which black-painted American spy planes take off to photograph military movements in Syria, Iraq, Iran and the Soviet Union. The American presence confirms the strategic importance of Turkey in the overall NATO defense plans for southern Europe and eastern Mediterranean. It is this entire system which Agca and the countless members of the Anarchy wish to overthrow.

With his blinkered vision, Agca has no difficulty believing implicitly what he was told in Haran: that the Americans, for whom, like the Church, he has not lost his hatred, are powerful enough in this area to have persuaded their Turkish allies—Europe's largest land army—to deal swiftly and harshly with anyone acting even remotely suspiciously. The dreaded military prison at Diyarbakır is full of men being detained only for this reason.

Agca has also been told that if ever he comes under suspicion, both his Turkish and his American enemies will use all available means to extract from him everything he learned from the man at the meeting which brought them together briefly in Haran, the biblical village of strangely domed dwellings where Abraham lived for several years and which is mentioned in the Book of Genesis. As a result of that meeting, Agca is now driving a further five hundred miles northeast to another Old Testament shrine, Mount Ararat, where Noah's Ark rested until the Flood subsided. There, close to that part of Turkey which borders Iran and Russia, Agca hopes for more news from the one other man who has had such a complete influence on his life for the past eighteen months.

Both the man he met in Haran and the one he will meet at Ararat form the crucial human elements in the secret Agca has kept for all of this time.

But even without the hazardous driving conditions—several times he has barely avoided minor landslides caused by the sound of the truck's protesting engine echoing around one of the narrower ravines, bringing shale tumbling down onto the road—and the constant threat of encountering army patrols, it is still hard, because of the psychological changes he is experiencing, for Agca to have a sustained and clear recall of how it all began.

The events, it will later emerge, are deeply rooted in his subconscious. When Agca does think of them he has the feeling they really involve another person, one he has permitted to inhabit his body for reasons he cannot explain, even to himself. This inner world is not equipped with the normal guidance system which would allow him to clearly differentiate for himself between what really happened and what was delusion.

His condition will subsequently make it that much more difficult for the psychiatrists and interrogators to understand and accept his motives. They will note his predominating mood, the long periods of morose and unproductive silence, and they will wonder how long he has lived in this halfway house between normality and psychosis. They will realize that, as part of his condition, he has no real insight into it, and that he does not see himself as disturbed.

They will also discover that driving along this Turkish road, Agca is content. His future is being decided by others. This is how it must always be from now onward, said the man he has just secretly met in Haran before he faded back across the border into Syria. He is Sedat Siri Kadem. They have been friends for a long time.

This much will become known:
For five years Kadem sat at the desk adjoining Agca's in Yesiltepe School. He was older than his classmate by almost three years, a short, muscular

figure with crinkly black hair and coal-black eyes. Kadem was one of the few boys who did not tease or beat up Agca because of his scholastic abilities. In return Agca helped Kadem with his lessons. Both graduated the same year with equal marks. It was Kadem who paved the way for Agca to get a job driving for the local Mafia. They remained friends, but after Agca enrolled in the Gray Wolves, Kadem suddenly dropped out of Malatya's small but thriving underworld. Nobody was very interested in why or where he has gone; already the Anarchy was seeding itself through the land and it was assumed that Kadem joined one of the roaming bands of killers, intent, for whatever reason, on disestablishing Turkish democracy. In January 1977, Kadem reappeared in Yesiltepe, called on Agca and resumed their friendship as casually as he interrupted it. One night in Kadem's room in Malatya they became lovers. Agca found the experience exciting. The eroticism had already taken root; sexuality, accompanied afterward by unpleasant accusatory thoughts, would torment him. Pledging Agca to secrecy, Kadem told him where he had been during the past year: a training camp in Lebanon. There he learned the latest techniques for "liberating" Turkey, ending the hateful system of corrupt Western democracy, removing the country from its position as NATO's farthest outpost in the Middle East and returning it to a closed Islamic society. Kadem expressed perfectly the driving force which had sustained Agca for some time. He offered to take Agca back with him to the school for terrorism near the road to Damascus.

They Dodge safely passes through Diyarbakır. There are soldiers everywhere. But they give no more than cursory glances at the battered truck, its driver and the bags of maize and crates of clucking chickens. Beyond the city the threat from army patrols recedes with every mile the protesting truck covers on the windswept, barren road to Bitlis. There are no CIA bases out here amid the snow-capped mountain vastness.

The Romans and the Parthians, the Byzantines and the Sassanids grappled to occupy this place of howling gales. None of them succeeded: they were driven from their freezing forts by sweeping sheets of rain and snow.

Even now the weather is seasonal: a blistering wind buffets the truck, chilling to death the weaker chickens, forcing the others to huddle together.

Agca grips the wheel harder, hunches himself against the dark, glowering skies on all sides. Soon the peaks are lost beneath a canopy of cloud and mist which swirls so low it often reduces visibility to feet. Even in the cab, with a padded jacket buttoned to the neck and the heating full on, Agca feels iced to the bone. He shouts the names on his hate list and, whether from the cold or because his hatred is once more burning brightly, tears trickle down his cheeks.

He will remember this journey well. Just as he will never forget the last time he entered this impregnable area.

This, too, is known:

On March 10, 1977, a Thursday, Agca and Kadem board a bus in Malatya, the first of several they will travel on to bring them, two days later, to Mardin, a southern Turkish city as dazzling white as the surrounding snow peaks. From there they walk for an entire frozen night farther south, crossing the border into Syria during the small hours when the Turkish guards huddle in their pillboxes. They walk another half day to the Arab shantytown of Senyurt. A waiting truck takes them to the training camp. After reaching its perimeter Agca seldom sees Kadem. He has no time to think about this. There are hundreds of recruits in the camp who are drilled from dawn until far into the night. After a month Agca is transferred to an inner compound within the main complex. He receives intensive training with a variety of weapons, Russian and American. He is coached in sniper tactics and learns how to carry out assassinations under various conditions.

Psychiatrists will wonder whether with total confidence they can know anything more. They will note Agca's memory gaps, his compression of events, his constant lack of emotional response, and they will ponder whether, in their jargon, this is all associated with "a loss of the ego boundary," whether in fact the essential and the nonessential, the relevant and the irrelevant have become equal in Agca's mind.

His interrogators will request that the psychiatrists get names and descriptions which can be checked against those in computers of a dozen intelligence agencies. The doctors will return with more questions. What names did the instructors have? What did they look like? What accents did they use? Arabic? Turkish? Maybe—Russian? They will pose hundreds of questions, taking him back and forth through his time in the camp. And so by this careful process they will come to the name of the man Agca is now driving to meet.

Again, known:

It is Saturday morning, April 30, 1977. Agca's last day in the camp. His bag is packed; he is returning to Turkey with no more than he came with. He is thinner and fitter than he has ever felt. He is called to the camp office. Kadem is there. They briefly embrace, then Kadem leaves the room. Moments later Teslin Tore enters. He has one of those easy-to-label faces. Jaw, eyes and nose all convey the same enveloping hardness. It extends to his neck, shoulders and barrel of a chest, and to his biceps and thighs. He wears the same battle fatigues as the last time they met, in the Sinan Hotel on Malatya's Kisla Caddesi. Then, Tore was distant and dismissive as he paid Agca for a successful drug run. Now, he is cordial and effusive. Tore drives Agca westward, across Syria, toward the Mediterranean. At dusk they reach the frontier post of Ciivegozu. The Syrian soldiers wave them through. Two hundred yards up the road, at the Turkish checkpoint, the barrier is raised without the cars having to stop. Tore drives them into Turkey. Two hours later the car reaches the regional capital, İskenderun. They spend the night in separate rooms at the Guney Palas, a second-class hotel on Temmus Caddesi. Next day Tore drives them to the airport, fifteen minutes from the hotel. He buys a one-way ticket to Istanbul on THY, Turkish Airlines. He gives the ticket to Agca, embraces him, but more formally than Kadem did, and leaves. Four hours later Agca is back in Istanbul.

The psychiatrists and the interrogators will pounce. How can he remember this sort of detail? When, precisely, did he go to the Sinan Hotel? Did he see anyone else there? How long did he work for Tore in Malatya? Did he not wonder what Tore was doing in the camp? Was he an instructor? A recruit? Why did he drive Agca hundreds of miles? What time exactly did they cross the border? Could he identify the faces of the guards if they showed him pictures? Where did they buy gas? What time did they reach the Guney Palas Hotel? Could he recognize any of the staff from photographs? Did he register in his own name? And Tore—did he use an alias? How did Tore pay the bill? How did he pay for the ticket?

The questions will come: flat, doubting questions; clever, pliant questions; harsh, threatening questions.

They will all be to no avail.

It is dark when the Dodge drives along the sweeping curve of the highway to Bitlis, its worn tires humming on the highway, suddenly asphalt. Agca can relax his concentration, think once more about the little book, no thicker than a passport, which, as part of his secret world, he has kept tucked inside his shorts. This book is as precious as the exercise book and the gun and bullets hidden under his seat. He realizes his mother knows about them: she has not been as clever as she thinks; he knew every time she had disturbed the books on the shelf in his bedroom. But she will never know of the little book. No one must. Kadem made him promise this before he handed it to him.

Desperate for a breakthrough, the psychiatrists and interrogators will reveal to Agca that they know about the little book; that it is a passbook for the main Istanbul branch of Türkeye Is Bankasi, a bank; that on December 13, 1977, an initial forty thousand liras—about three thousand American dollars—was put on deposit in the name of Mehmet Ali Agca.

But who had forged his signature? Why? What was the money for? Where had it come from?

Why? Why? Why?

The truck passes through Bitlis around midnight. Agca has driven almost two thousand kilometers since leaving Ankara. Beyond the sleeping town he pulls off the road, and, as on previous nights, he sleeps in the cab. Behind him the few surviving chickens cluck feebly. By morning they will almost all be dead, either from thirst or from the biting cold.

Two hours later he awakes. He is not refreshed. But he cannot sleep longer. He has this strange compulsion to go on and on. He can't explain it—and certainly didn't to that official from the Libyan Embassy when he met him in Ankara.

As he had been instructed, he used Tore's name when his call to the embassy was answered. After a brief hesitation he was asked to wait. Then another voice came on the line, suggesting a meeting at the bus terminal on busy Hipodrom Caddesi. It had been a brief meeting, merely long enough for Agca to explain he wanted to see Kadem or Tore as soon as possible. The Libyan suggested they should meet again at the terminal in two days. When they did, he handed Agca a wad of liras and told him to collect a vehicle from a garage on Atatürk Boulevard.

It is the Dodge that now, well before dawn, Agca guides around the icy shore of Lake Van near Turkey's border with Iran.

He is ahead of schedule. Kadem estimated he would not reach here until sunrise. Steering with one hand he chews *yufka*, unleavened bread, and swigs from a bottle of raki, aniseed-flavored spirit potent enough to make his eyes smart. It has been his only nourishment for days.

Agca can still recall the burning intensity of Kadem's promise. It was after he had explained—again—about all the names on his hate list and why he had felt impelled to come on this long and dangerous journey, to seek help to kill a pope who is no more. It was then that Kadem made his vow. He had held Agca's hands in his and said that soon those other enemies will be dealt with, that the demanding hatred he carries in his head will be quenched.

This prospect still sustains Agca as he continues his lonely journey.

In two days' time, at the location Kadem gave him, Agca will meet Tore on Mount Ararat.

Like Kadem, Tore is under the direct control of the KGB.

XXVI

Villot sighs irritably. One of the African cardinals wants to be able to see the moon. Noé sympathizes with the camerlengo's exasperation: this really is too much.

It is Monday morning, October 9, and they are in Villot's office trying to finalize the arrangements for conclave, due to start this coming Saturday. The opened windows do little to reduce the fug of Gauloises around Villot. He is already well into his first pack of cigarettes, though it is only just nine o'clock, and by the end of the day he'll be close to emptying three. His normal forty-a-day limit has consistently been broken this past week. The usually fastidious Villot now resembles an even sadder and seedier version of the xenophobic Frenchman journalists portray: he is more pinch-nosed and purse-lipped; when he does smile, rare enough in itself nowadays, it clearly comes nowhere near reaching behind his spectacles. And ash sprinkles his wool soutane—it's autumn now and the old camerlengo has given up his fine silk cassock of summer—from the Gauloises which droop one after another from a corner of his mouth.

Villot is still badly rattled—there is no other word for it—by some of the excesses of the Italian press. They are not letting up with their innuendos about Gianpaolo's death. The autopsy issue lives on, abetted by a call for all cardinals eligible to vote to have a medical examination before conclave—and that the results should be circulated before any balloting. There is even the rumor that Karol Wojtyla had an electrocardiogram before coming to Rome.

The point which concerns Villot about the health issue is not so much that it flies in the face of tradition and papal dignity, but the expense. To give 111 mainly elderly men a thorough check-over would mean sending them all to the Gemelli Hospital; it would cost a great deal. Villot knows only too well that the forthcoming conclave and its attendant coronation are financial burdens which the Vatican can ill afford at a time when its expenditure is going up while income declines. There has, naturally enough, been no provision made for a second conclave coming so quickly. Consequently, Villot has had to do his share of barrel-scraping to distribute the cost of Gianpaolo's funeral and find the cash to meet the considerable expense of electing his successor.

It's not been easy, the camerlengo querulously tells Noé, trying to balance

everything, satisfy everybody and still stay within budget. The same amount
of money as before has been allocated for this conclave. But since August,
prices have risen, to be sure only a few lire for this item, a few for that. But
on the scale Villot operates on—accommodating and feeding some three hundred persons for an indeterminate period—the increase is bound to be substantial; he has calculated that overall this conclave may in the end prove a
whopping 15 percent more expensive. To juggle successfully with it all
needs the combined skills of a quartermaster, accountant and hotelier.*

Noé clucks sympathetically and helpfully suggests that this time the African cardinal should be allowed to have his moon: it would save both labor
and materials if conclave windows were not painted over.

Villot agrees. They move on to another request, one of a small pile before
him which have come from cardinals who, two months ago, filed into conclave willing to accept what they were given. Now they are seasoned cam-
paigners, and ready to display their princely power. Carberry of St. Louis has
been telling the Rome press corps that, in August, "we felt as though we were
going into a dark tunnel; now it is as though we are entering a bright room."

But clearly not bright enough for Cody. He's sent a handwritten request on
bond Chicago archdiocese note paper for the whole lighting system in conclave to be improved.

Villot flatly rejects the idea. That would cost even more than full medical
examinations. The camerlengo turns to another suggestion. It is from Felici.
He thinks each cardinal should have a proper bedroom, not the thinly partitioned salons of August when, Felici writes, he was unable to sleep because of
the snoring from the cubicles on either side.

The camerlengo and master of ceremonies consult the floor plan of conclave. The usable area around the chapel has been considerably extended.
Sleeping accommodations will be on three floors. Felici can have a corner
room on the upper floor; it has a bathroom attached. That should keep him
satisfied.

Noé picks out another request. One of the Americans wants a bedside ashtray; last time, he complains, he had to use his chamberpot. Villot checks one
of the many lists which his staff have prepared. In August twenty-five ash-
trays were allowed for. He sees no need for this number to be increased. The
camerlengo dictates a brief note to a hovering priest-secretary suggesting that
the cardinal bring in his own ashtray.

He moves on. A European cardinal has complained about the mattress and

* The thought of Villot's equal in a secular government, a foreign minister, being personally involved in such pettyfogging detail is clearly preposterous, but it is an indication of the
endearing Ruritanian atmosphere which pervades the upper echelons of the Holy See. Senior
Vatican staff frequently settle very minor matters which in other administrations are dealt
with by junior members of a department.

bed he had last time. There will be the same narrow beds and slim mattresses this time, along with the same well-laundered sheets and the same one thin blanket for each cardinal. There is a request for more writing paper. This is also refused. Each cardinal will still get only five sheets on which to scribble his thoughts—or, as Wojtyla and König did in August, to use for playing tick-tacktoe between their "consultations."

Noé checks a memo. It is from one of the French cardinals. Can he have Vichy water, preferably two bottles a day? Villot refers to a price list. Vichy costs more than Italian mineral water. But he approves the request. The camerlengo is partial to Vichy himself.

Ratzinger of Munich wonders whether it's possible to have a shaving mirror. Noé remembers that one of the conclave staff, chasing up chamberpots, came across hundreds of tiny plastic-framed mirrors in a Rome convent. They would do. Each cardinal will have one for shaving.

Manning of Los Angeles wants to know if there will be a bar kitchen where the cardinals can make themselves coffee and tea, or perhaps collect a snack from a well-stocked refrigerator.

Noé checks another list. A fridge from the pope's kitchen had been temporarily moved down to the conclave area before the papal apartment was sealed.

Aramburu asks whether there can be more South American dishes on the menu; he is one of those who became bored with the endless diet of pasta last time.

Villot consults the produce list. This is where he has made a substantial saving. In August supplies had been bought for a week. But with that conclave lasting little more than a day, there had been a huge surplus which the Vatican distributed free to the poor of Rome. Villot this time has allowed food for only four days, nearly a 50 percent cut in costs; if the need should arise, more can be sent in through those revolving drums—the only links with the outside world during conclave. And the camerlengo has gone further, substantially reducing the amount of rations for each person. Their beer-and-wine allocation has been cut by half.

Regretfully, he dictates to Aramburu, there is no way to include regional dishes on the conclave menu.

A German cardinal has a query about the infirmary. The room set aside last time had electric lights but no proper wall socket, let alone modern monitoring equipment. Could not adequate power be laid on and a basic resuscitation trolley provided? Ideally there should be oxygen and ECG facilities. Surely these could be rented.

Villot shrugs. They could, but the cost is beyond his budget. He dictates an explanation to the German. It will be hand-delivered, like all the other notes, before the day is over, to cardinals scattered throughout Rome. Some things will not be curtailed—among them the courier service of priests Villot uses on these occasions.

He and Noé begin to check shopping lists. The hundred toilet rolls have still to be bought. A similar number of table place settings—a single knife, fork and spoon for each cardinal and conclave attendant—must be rented. Richard Ginori, one of Italy's leading crockery manufacturers, has offered to provide the china. A sample plate is enclosed with the offer. It is a tasteful beige. Villot dictates grateful acceptance.

More lists. To be rented: trash cans, clip-on reading lamps. To be borrowed from convents and monasteries: tablecloths and napkins, prayer stools and night tables.

Villot picks out yet another letter. It's from one of the Italian cardinals, Corrado Ursi of Naples. He politely wonders—his diffidence can be sensed in his prose style—whether there can be a little extra elbow room in the Sistine Chapel this time to help preserve the secrecy Paul's *Eligendo* requires.

The camerlengo gives another weary sigh. He sympathizes with Ursi. But there is no way of making more space in the Sistine.

And once again it will be possible for leaks. Whatever else has changed since August, Villot is sufficiently realistic to accept that the human frailties of some of those directly involved in the forthcoming proceedings will not have altered.

Nor will the role change of the Vaticanologists. They blissfully continue to interpret the uninterpretable, judge the unjudgable, put flesh and blood on the Holy Spirit and perhaps even give It shoes to see where the Spirit goes in order to postulate why. The experts are legion: the priests in the pay of newspapers; the religiosociologists under contract to those television networks that thought Gianpaolo's funeral wasn't worth sending a team to Rome for but have decided conclave is good for their ratings; the religious editors with mysterious pipelines which need a lot of expense-account maintenance; the specialist writers who handle the event as though it's just another routine assignment; the hard-news reporters who hold court in the bars of the Rome Hilton and decide among themselves which rumor is floatable and which should be sunk with large gin and tonics. Nearly a thousand of them have registered with the Vatican Press Office; this entitles them to pick up the cardinals' biographies left over from last time.

Like all other ologists, Vaticanologists are really no more than outsiders peering in, attempting to penetrate the unpenetrable. In between they squirrel around Rome, listening to anybody with a rumor to peddle, a fact to sell.

Paolo Rossi, the doyen of the tipsters, has made more money these last ten days than in the previous two months. A score of journalists have bought his account of what happened at L'Eau Vive. Now he has another Benelli story for sale. This past Sunday, Rossi has learned, the cardinal's secretary lunched at the Polish Church of St. Stanislaus near the Piazza Venezia. Also present were Wojtyla and two Polish bishops, Andre Deskur and Ladislaw Rubin. It may not sound like much of a tidbit, but in Rossi's experienced hands it is transformed into high-value intrigue. Benelli's secretary, claims Rossi, was sent along to enlist Wojtyla's vote in return for the assurance that in a Benelli pontificate the Synod of Bishops would be given much increased importance; Rubin is the Synod's secretary general and Wojtyla has been a member of its permanent council since 1971. The item is fleshed out, Rossi-style: who sat next to who, what they ate, who drank what, even how much. It *sounds* authentic. But it has to be taken on trust—and Rossi's reputation for worming out such details.

Most of the cardinals are now back in Rome after a long weekend outside the city when all kinds of pacts, deals, schemes, agreements, bargains and plots were hatched. So runs the scuttlebutt.

Not even the indefatigable Greeley can check them all out. The last time around he and CREP had their moment with the job definition for the papacy. Now Greeley—of whom Cody has increasingly been heard to plaintively ask whether no one will rid him of this meddlesome priest—has come up with another gee-whiz wheeze. He and his associates are going to preempt conclave by telling the cardinals, and the world, who, according to their complicated calculations, the next pope should be. For, as well as CREP, Greeley is associated with another acronym, NORC, the National Opinion Research Center in Chicago. NORC has used computer models to simulate conclave. Data on the "attitudes and behavior" of each cardinal elector, gathered from "people in a position to know"—none of whom, in the Greeley way of doing things, are named—have been acquired. Further, "a number of experts on the College of Cardinals rated each of the cardinals on a scale of relative influence from one to five, five indicating a highly influential cardinal and one a cardinal with relatively little influence on others."

Felici, Benelli and Lorscheider scored five, suggesting that they held the greatest sway over their fellows. Siri, Baggio, Arns of San Paolo and Madrid's Enrique y Tarancon received four. Among those rating three were König, Gantin, Sin, Suenens and Willebrands.

In addition: "using a complex decision-making model," the creation of NORC, "a weighted profile which calculated the attitudes and behaviors which would be most typical of the College was constructed from the data. Each of the cardinals was then assigned a score based on his deviation from that profile, a score on a scale running from zero to two hundred."

And this was how it was done. With hey-presto verve Greeley has his order of "profile deviation."

It's bad news for Benelli. Greeley and NORC have him at twelve on their papal hit parade. Bertoli can do no better than come in at eleven. Felici is at ten. Poletti sticks at nine. König, whom last time Greeley elected beforehand as an "interim pope," is now well out of the running, at eight. Pironio, a curial favorite, is one place above. Pellegrino, another Italian, makes it to the number six spot. And at five—certain to be a real headline grabber for all the English newsmen in Rome—is Hume. Immediately above him is Baggio. Willebrands is third from the top of this astonishing list. If only he knew, there's little doubt nuncio Alibrandi would be close to clapping his hands in delight because his close friend, Pappalardo, has such a small "profile deviation" that he's come second. And at the number one spot, the first pope in history to be chosen by a NORC computer, is the cardinal who wrote so politely to Villot asking for more elbow room when the votes which really matter, those cast in the Sistine, are made. It is Corrado Ursi.

Greeley means to release this list on Thursday. Not only is it perfect timing to get him more useful publicity, he has this idea the cardinals will look seriously upon what at best seems about as tasteful an exercise as the betting book Ladbroke's ran on the first conclave.

Greenan has no patience with gimmicks like computer forecasts; he sees them as part of the journalistic tomfoolery which this conclave is attracting. Equally, the sharp-minded, and sharp-tongued, editor has to prepare his own in-house list of *papabili* so that *L'Osservatore Romano* can preset another batch of front pages which, he hopes, will include the cardinal to be selected at the upcoming eighty-third conclave.

This Tuesday afternoon, October 10, he is at his desk, which is covered by the jumble of papers he finds both reassuring and rewarding. They form, he can reflect, the proof that old-fashioned methods still pay off best.

Greenan has acquired copies of everything all the cardinals have said publicly since assembling in Rome: their sermons, the occasional press conference the Americans and some of the Europeans give, newspaper accounts, transcripts of their radio and television statements. He has coupled reports from these with the genuine network of contacts he has within the Sacred College and the Curia. For Greenan—trained in that most skillful of Vatican techniques, how to differentiate between an event and its interpretation—the result has been some important discoveries.

The sermons preached at the *Novemdiales* masses are especially revealing. Basil Hume, in his own careful English way, suggests—Hume is not one to make dogmatic assertions at any time, let alone on such a sensitive issue as this—that there should be no temptation, having buried Gianpaolo, to forgo all the hopes and expectations which his pontificate had indicated. The move toward a collegial style of Church government must continue. And yet the astute Greenan detects that many cardinals want to redraw the one outstanding memory of Gianpaolo's reign: its pastorality.

It is now no longer enough, as it was in August, to merely define pastoral as "from a diocese." That had created its own problems for the Curia on how divisive issues could be settled. It might well be illusory, but the image had been forged, and it stuck, that Gianpaolo was little more than a happy-go-lucky pope who adored children, cared about the poor and vaguely saw his mission to be in the Third World; he was the world's favorite small man, battling against strong opposition. Like his beloved Pinocchio he was always getting into trouble—in his case with the Curia.

In their subtle and wily ways, which Greenan, an old trouper in this baroque circus, long ago learned to spot, some cardinals are saying there is nothing wrong, as such, with the next pope's being "pastoral"—given one important proviso. The meaning of "pastoral" should not be taken to suggest that their choice of pontiff be restricted to again plucking somebody from a diocese, especially someone who might not grasp, or may not care to learn, how the infracture works of an organization as complex as any multinational.

Krol offers the intriguing thought that a cardinal who works in the Curia and is involved in settling divorce questions can be "profoundly pastoral"; Dearden of Detroit goes further: *all* curial cardinals are men of compassion, which is Dearden's way of saying "pastoral." Gantin reinforces this with the attractive idea that "all the cardinals are in some sense pastoral men—and many of them have been in a diocese, including myself."

Is Gantin declaring, by way of cardinalspeak, that he's ready to become the first black pope? Greenan thinks surely not. Gantin is not that naïve.

The editor senses what lies behind this determination to make "pastoral" a broken-backed word. Redefined, it can now be applied to every one of the cardinal electors. Nobody this time will be able to get a bandwagon rolling by promoting the "pastorality" of a *papabile*, as had happened with Luciani.

Greenan continues to work his way through the sermons. He has read them several times already, underscoring passages which offer him important clues as to how the campaigns—all naturally called "consultations," all cleverly within the limit of what Paul's *Eligendo* states is permissible—are developing.

Confalonieri, though himself well past the voting age limit, is determined his fellow cardinals will know what sort of pope he hopes they will choose. The dean of the Sacred College has spelled it all out. In an oblique tribute to the cosmetic skills of the Technician and his embalming aids, Confalonieri has spoken about Gianpaolo's smile, "hovering on his lips even in death," a reminder that he was "a meteor which unexpectedly lights up the heavens and then disappears."

Greenan has already underlined the words. He sees them as a clear indica-

tion—indeed remarkably so, in the otherwise often obscure prose of the sermon—that the dean wants a second, similar shining star to emerge smiling
from conclave. But, and here there is another clue for the prescient editor to
ponder, the next pontiff must not only have faith and the perfection of Christian life, he must also understand and know how to come to terms with "the
great discipline of the Church."

There it is again: what amounts to a call for a curial cardinal, one who will
smilingly put a stop to liturgical abuses and get back to good old doctrine.

But who?

Siri, with his clutch of votes which Greenan thinks are probably as committed to him now as they were back in August, is very much in the running.
He has paid his public tribute to Gianpaolo—nicely formed phrases delivered
to full effect. But the overall impression of Siri's real judgment—carefully
buried beneath the layers of politeness—is that Gianpaolo might not have
proven such a good pope when judged against the themes the conservative
archbishop of Genoa holds sacred: "primacy of the spiritual," "ecclesiastical
discipline," "separated spirituality." Greenan interprets the code phrases as
Siri suggesting that the next pontiff would do well to remember these catch-
words.

And, in spite of his obligatory denial, Siri is *papabile*. Everybody knows
this. He goes onto Greenan's list.

So does Felici—if only because he virtually declared his own candidacy
during a remarkable sermon largely devoted to reminding everyone how close
he was to Gianpaolo; who better, then, than the man who has been a pope
maker to become pope? That's the message wrapped up in all the references
from Corinthians and the Gospels which Felici used as essential ballast to
give a weighting for something very basic. Felici would love to be pope.

But where does this leave Gianpaolo's other great advocate, Benelli? Not to
mention the possible non-Italian *papabili*?

Greenan realizes he has a lot more reading to do before he can type his
final list. To help him along with his task he goes to a dull-gray metal office
cupboard. When he opens it, his eyes take on an anticipatory gleam. Facing
him, neatly arranged so their labels can be read instantly, is a selection of bottles. Each one contains a vintage Irish whiskey. Greenan selects a bottle and
pours himself a generous measure. Then he continues reading. It is going to
be a long day and he knows he will need to make several visits to this place,
which the few who are aware of it have dubbed Greenan's Cupboard of the
Holy Spirit.

One after another, spaced throughout Wednesday, October 11, arriving
and departing between their other engagements, a large number of cardinals
come to the Collegio Pio Latino Americano on the Via Aurelia. Here, where

Albino Luciani presented copies of *Illustrissimi* and spoke movingly about his reasons for writing it, these cardinals now discuss the very different style of another author. The well-stocked Latin American College library is one of the few places in Rome which still have ample copies available of *Segno di Contraddizione*. This is the Lateran retreat which was preached in 1976; each year, and at the request of the pope, a version of the retreat is presented before him and the Curia. Traditionally the discourse is given by an Italian Franciscan or another Rome-based bishop. Two years ago, Paul invited Karol Wojtyla to write and deliver the retreat.

All the cardinals coming to the Collegio Pio Latino Americano are non-Italian. They include Enrique y Tarancon, who is already familiar with, and approves of, this particular retreat. But he goes to the college late in the afternoon because here is a chance for him to hear how other visitors are reacting. The senior Spanish cardinal is gratified. Aramburu and Arns, San Paolo's archbishop, both of whom are carefully monitoring reactions, say the response has been unanimous. The Dutch cardinals are particularly impressed by what they have read. The German cardinals—all five of them—have been equally complimentary. The Asians and the Africans, especially the Polynesian, Pio Taofinu'u, who still hobbles after his boating accident off Samoa just before Paul's funeral, appear undivided in their enthusiasm. The seven French cardinals have been led in praise by no less than the chancellor of the Gregorian University, Gabriel-Marie Garrone, who used to send Paul intellectual teasers, now says that what he's read in the College library is as theologically impeccable as anything he has studied during thirty years of Church service. Garrone is conservatively minded. What interests Enrique y Tarancon is the reaction of François Marty, archbishop of Paris. He's a liberal, far across the religious spectrum from Garrone. Yet Marty, too, seems completely satisfied and, like Aramburu and Arns, the other seventeen Latin American cardinals have also found much to appreciate in Wojtyla's words.

The visits to the Collegio Pio Latino Americano library have come about through König. He has been studiously casual over the whole matter, murmuring the idea to one cardinal as they strolled into a meeting of the Sacred College in the Sala Bologna, dropping the thought into a conversation with another while they walked through the Vatican gardens, König is adamant that he is not running any sort of campaign. Indeed, the very idea, he will patiently insist, is quite absurd; such politicking is fine for the Morris West novels Wojtyla likes to read, but things are rather different in reality. König maintains he is merely being "helpful"; no cardinal, he argues reasonably, can know all there is to know about his peers. All he is doing in Wojtyla's case is offering some useful pointers they may care to think about. Just that, and no more.

No doubt responding to such a courteous approach, the cardinals have been equally receptive to König's suggestion that, having read Wojtyla's retreat, they might find the time to dip into his other writings. These have been neatly flagged in the Collegio library, all in the cause of being helpful, naturally.

There is the speech on the liturgy Wojtyla made in a Vatican II aula on November 7, 1962; it is an erudite call for a more biblical and less clerical approach to the Church. The address is as carefully balanced as another, this one on the sources of revelation, which he delivered at another Vatican Council session, on November 21, 1962. Even a quick perusal of his writing shows Wojtyla is no peasant pietist clinging to outmoded ideas. Nor is Garrone the only cardinal to believe that here is impeccable theology, very much in tune with current curial thinking, delivered with a reality in keeping with the ethical philosopher which Wojtyla is by training.*

And there is still more to make these busy cardinals pause and ponder and, in some cases, cancel appointments so they can continue to read. Here is Wojtyla on communism and atheism; Wojtyla's rejection of theologians who sow seeds of doubt by questioning such fundamentals as the Trinity, the evidence of Christ, the real presence of Jesus in the Eucharist, the indissolubility of marriage; Wojtyla on the importance of Mariology; Wojtyla on the need for a strong Catholic identity, a call for a ringing proclamation of faith in a world which is increasingly losing its religious way.

It is all here in the library of the Latin American College, clearly referenced, so cardinals can easily discover where this Polish bishop stands on issues they hold dear: ingenuous statements which reveal a fidelity to traditional commitments and yet leave sufficient room for the more liberal cardinals to feel a warm glow of approval.

For instance, there is Wojtyla's grappling with atheism. He shows a refreshing openness which appeals to the likes of Suenens, Sin and Willebrands. Wojtyla is not in favor of an outright condemnation of atheism because this would end any hope of dialogue on the matter. Instead he leans toward the "heuristic approach," aimed at finding common ground with unbelievers. It is an attitude which extends throughout Wojtyla's thinking; he begins and ends with the idea that everything stems from the thick of human experience, that the Church itself is involved in a continuous process of search, that there is no room for pointless moralizing "or the suggestion that we have a monopoly of the truth," and that, above all, the Church must never appear as an authoritarian institution. He first said this on October 21, 1963, and he has been restating the view regularly ever since.

* Cardinal Wojtyla was one of the most prolific writers in the Sacred College. Polish history and culture provided him with an endless stock of references and symbols which he consistently drew upon. In the past two years his work had become increasingly known to his fellow cardinals.

It is indeed, as König indicates, all very interesting. Something to keep at the back of a cardinal's mind. But not too far back. Not with the growing indications by this Wednesday night that the Italian cardinals are hopelessly divided on whom they should support. For the first time in 455 years there is a feeling—small and subdued though it is—that this time a non-Italian has at least a chance of being chosen pope.

Kite flying, MacCarthy tells a Vatican Radio colleague dismissively, "it is all pure kite flying." They are on the station's second floor beside the bank of wire-service teletypes churning out stories on Greeley and NORC's forecast of who will be pope.

MacCarthy is hard put to recall the former Chicago priest among the scores of other observers who for the past two weeks have been constantly drifting in and out of the building, seeking the help of Vatican Radio staff in understanding the many mysteries surrounding the election of a pontiff. MacCarthy is almost certain not one of his colleagues would have any part in this caper. But there it is, the Associated Press, cheekily date-lining its story "Vatican City"—perhaps to give it more credibility when the actual office of the agency is in downtown Rome—boldly stating: COMPUTER PICKS URSI AS NEXT POPE.

A messenger tears off the message and adds it to a pile of others in a tray marked "Conclave."

Though it is only midmorning of this Thursday, October 12, the basket is filled with the outpourings of the wire services. It has been like this all week, evidence of continuing, and increasing, media interest in the forthcoming conclave.

MacCarthy tells his colleague the "whole thing is being overplayed; there's this idea something quite extraordinary can happen. I don't buy it."[1]

Much of what rests in the basket is assuredly pure speculation, often reflecting the attitude of reporters who, unlike MacCarthy, cannot accept that the Holy Spirit has an incalculable role to play.

Yet, Greeley's computer caper aside, the basket also contains proof that there is no letup in a concerted effort by the Italian press to get Siri elected. It has been forging ahead for three days, printing flattering profiles and glowing assessments of the archbishop of Genoa. To suggest that this has any connection with "consultation" is nonsense; what is happening is nothing less than a well-organized offensive, a determined bid to concentrate wonderfully the minds of the cardinal electors. This very Thursday morning, RAI, Italian state radio, broadcast a ten-minute eulogy about Siri, displaying the sort of unctuousness RAI in the past has reserved only for an elected pope.

MacCarthy's colleague, in fact one of the radio team which last time scooped the world with the help of the conclave bug—he himself will insist he had no prior knowledge of the affair—sees the entire Siri operation as permissible psychological warfare; if successful, it could rule out any desire to electronically and illegally penetrate this conclave. The man points to yet another wire service report clattering off the teletype. It claims Siri has a "packet" of fifty committed votes.

He thinks, as do many others, that behind this sustained press campaign is the Curia once more intervening in the choice of a pope. The curial cardinals are trying to stampede those still-uncommitted electors to throw in their lot with Siri, who has been given an editorial face-lift in the media, so much so that he is barely recognizable. The theory is plausible, given the "soft center" of the present Sacred College, evinced by how quickly these "centrists" jumped on the bandwagon which swiftly put Gianpaolo into office.

MacCarthy remains skeptical. Assuming any of this is true, could it not be, he ponders, a cunning ruse by Siri's opponents? Perhaps they have arranged to focus all this attention on Siri on the basis of "setting him up to knock him down," phenomenon not uncommon in the politics of MacCarthy's birthplace. His enemies will have realized Siri's record of archconservatism cannot stand up to the intense publicity he is getting; the more the lily is gilded, the more inevitable it is that an ab-reaction will set in. Indeed, continues the shrewd Irishman, indicating a UPA story, there is more than a hint that this has already started. "Informed sources"—MacCarthy smiles wryly at the words, wondering whether once more they indicate flummery rather than facts—are starting to remind people who Siri really is: the cardinal who detested John XXIII and Paul, the bishop who maligned the Second Vatican Council as "the greatest disaster in recent ecclesiastical history," the prelate who drags his feet in the face of anything remotely "liberalizing." Is this the man, then, the agency story quotes those "informed sources" as asking, who should be the next pope—no matter that Siri now calls himself a "centrist," a "moderate" and, even more whimsically, an "independent"?

Reminded of this, MacCarthy's suddenly crestfallen companion thinks not. He rifles through the basket, pausing at an Agence France Presse story. The French agency claims the French cardinals believe it will be a short conclave; "no more than three days" is the reported confident prediction of Marty of Paris. AFP suggests that the "collective French view," drawing another wry smile from MacCarthy, is, should Siri's bid fail, that Felici will be the "acceptable" compromise Italian candidate. No named source is given for this. Nor can MacCarthy divine who are the "high sources" in another agency story which states that if the split in the Italian ranks continues, Hume, Willebrands and Gantin could all become candidates.

"So could everybody else in the Sacred College," he growls.

MacCarthy, molded by the inviolate rule of Vatican Radio, that nothing can be broadcast unless it is properly sourced, repeats it is all kite flying. He and his colleague walk away from the teletypes.

Martin is entertaining Noé to lunch on Friday, October 13, in the prefect's handsomely furnished apartment near the San Damaso Courtyard. The actual *cortile* has been boarded off in preparation for conclave: this time the deliberating cardinals will have the benefit of striding over flagstones which the Renaissance popes first trod.

The elderly prefect asks again—indicating the newspaper open between them across the dining table—what will the cardinals make of *this?* It is a prominently displayed article in *L'Osservatore della Domenica,* a popular weekly illustrated companion of *L'Osservatore Romano.*

The article carries the staid headline PROPHECY AND REALITY. But the clue to its potential impact, the reason for Martin's question about how the cardinals will react, is its author. Monsignor Corrado Balducci is a senior official in the Sacred Congregation for the Evangelization of Peoples, the old De Propaganda Fide. Around the Vatican, Balducci is known, not altogether facetiously, as the resident demonologist, the prelate who has made a study of the supernatural and in particular predictions of disaster. This time Balducci has been doing research which closely patterns that which MacCarthy did on the eve of the first conclave. But whereas MacCarthy was then certain that Vatican Radio would never broadcast some of the direst predictions of the Irish saint, Malachy, Balducci has had no problem publishing Malachy's apocalyptic portrait of the next pontificate: "There will be a great disaster, which could very likely be World War III." In support of Malachy he cites the mysterious Third Secret of Fatima, the one only a new pope can see. Balducci ends his article with the warning, "God cannot prevent such a scourge if mankind does not deserve it."

Dire though the warning is, it is the relevancy to the papacy of what Balducci is saying which fascinates Noé and Martin. Coming as it does on the eve of conclave, published in a most impeccable outlet, the article is bound to be seen as a timely reminder that in a threatened world, only a strong-minded pope can lead the faithful from such a disaster. This is no time for mere "pastorality," for trading jokes with children, for making analogies with Pinocchio or some other character. This is very much the time to go back to the hellfire-and-brimstone days, to remind the faithful what sort of faith is needed to ward off the evil eye. Unwritten though it is, the message is very clear to Noé and Martin: the cardinals must elect a man sufficiently resolute to take the Church through the stormy days ahead.

Balducci's position in the Curia and the timing of the article indicate that the Siri faction has far from given up hope of having him elected. It is as clear as the sunlight streaming into Martin's dining room that Balducci's piece is meant to suggest that apocalypse soon can only be averted by electing Siri now.

But he is about to commit an astonishing act of *felo-de-se*.

König cannot believe it. Yet there is the evidence: a couple of thousand self-inflicted mortal words which must effectively put paid to Siri's chances of *ever* becoming pope.

It is breakfast time in the German-Hungarian College on Saturday, October 14. This is normally the quietest period of the day, when the cardinals and their entourages munch cold sausages and cheese and say little to each other.

Now, the room is awash with incredulous voices trying to make sense of what Siri has gone and done. By any yardstick it is incredible—this most astonishing interview the archbishop of Genoa has given to *Gazzetta del Popolo*. He has trampled all over the memory of Gianpaolo by venomously shredding the late pope's inaugural address. He has hit out at Villot and the way his Secretariat of State is run. Then, hardly pausing for breath, Siri has swept aside any idea of serious collegiality among bishops during the next pontificate. The hapless reporter who sat through the tirade describes how he himself suffered Siri's wrath. Politely asked a question, the cardinal had bristled, "It is one I would only take from my confessor." Asked another, Siri thundered, "I don't know how you could ask such a stupid question. If you really want an answer, you will have to sit there and shut up for three hours."

König reads the story a second time. It appears even more incredible.

What can Siri have been thinking? The intemperate tone, the shocking personal abuse shown toward the reporter, this surely cannot be typical of a man who throughout the week has been running surefootedly, so sweetly reasonable through the media? Above all, why permit the interview to be published now, only hours before the cardinals go into conclave, allowing no time for any of the heat to cool, when every damning word is at its most lethal?

König does not know the answer.

But, just as Siri's outburst is so extraordinary, so are the reasons for its publication. Siri gave the interview yesterday on the strict understanding that it would be embargoed for at least forty-eight hours, by which time all his fellow cardinals would be safely locked with him in conclave and therefore unable to read what he'd said. The reporter agreed to Siri's proviso. Then, later on Friday, Siri gave a Genoa radio station an interview which was a watery version of what he had told *Gazzetta del Popolo*. It was broadcast within the hour, as, curiously, Siri had made no embargo request of the station. Ansa, the Italian news agency, carried a brief account of the broadcast. Their wire service teletype was seen in the newsroom of *Gazzetta del Popolo*. The editors concluded that Siri had himself broken the embargo and decided to run their far more explosive interview this Saturday morning.

Even before König reads it, Siri puts out a denial that he gave the interview. The newspaper reporter immediately offers to make public his tape recording of their meeting. Siri backs off. He has done himself even more damage.

As König prepares to participate in the mass for the election of a pope, he delivers a final prediction on Siri. In his most velvety of tones, the Viennese murmurs to other cardinals waiting for the mass to begin that if Siri were elected pope, he would "have a simple, humble ceremony in St. Peter's Square, but then afterward, in private, he would have a marvelous coronation with all his friends present and incense billowing all over the place."

They are *mots* which spell the coup de grâce for Siri. His chances are dead.

But Benelli's live on. Is this why, wonders Felici, the archbishop of Florence is taking in a typewriter to conclave—so that he can type out his acceptance speech?

Dining alone on Saturday night does nothing for Greeley's spirits. For a start there is the attitude of the American cardinals: "absolute pushovers for curial propaganda." He is especially aggrieved with Carberry, not just because he's taken into conclave ten chocolate bars, or because he's apparently told the American press now isn't the time for a non-Italian pope. That's fine by Greeley: he's still clinging to the hope Ursi will win. What irks him about Carberry is that "the good cardinal of St. Louis does not seem to comprehend that people are not expecting a Xerox copy" of Gianpaolo as the next pontiff.

And, nothing new in this, he's angry too: "All right, we lost John Paul"—Greeley tells himself after dinner—"*why* is God's problem. If John Paul is replaced by business as usual, the people will be profoundly disillusioned. That's where lots of Catholics are today. They went through an interlude of being proud of Catholicism and had it snatched away from them; they want it back. Yet many of these clowns who are doing the voting don't perceive that."

Some of these "clowns" might also be hard put to understand why Greeley appears unable to refer to the last pope as everybody else does—with affectionate sadness, as Papa Gianpaolo.

Perhaps his attitude might stem from a confession he has put on tape about his sources.[2] There just don't seem enough of those unidentified yet wonderfully described figures he gives such colorful pseudonyms to. In fact there might be only one, Deep Purple, alias the Cincinnati Kid, the prelate whom some Vaticanologists think is Greeley's main informant, the archbishop of that city, Joseph Bernardin.

Right now the archbishop is back home. Which also might explain why, when Greeley returns to St. Peter's Square and stares up at the moonlit outline of the Sistine Chapel in the sealed-off conclave area, he asks himself plaintively one question. What's going on up there?

XXVII

Over dinner in the Borgia Apartments—altogether too grand a setting for the modest fare of *fettuccini* and *gelato* or *frutta* washed down with pitchers of wine—several cardinals venture that conclave might go into Monday. The observation is solemnly noted by the minor attendant who is once more keeping a secret diary.[1] Late into Saturday night he watches the "factions" forming. The Italians, all twenty-seven of them, loosely divide their allegiance between four candidates: Benelli, Ursi, Felici and, in spite of his gaffe, Siri. Some of the Africans and Asians, if the free exchange of views in the corridors is any guide, are drawn either to Ursi or Benelli. Aramburu and some of the other South Americans also lean toward the archbishop of Florence. No other trend is discernible.

König, who right up until entering conclave had worked so assiduously promoting Wojtyla, retired early without appearing to have "consulted" with anybody. The last cardinal is asleep by midnight.

Before breakfast next morning, Sunday, October 15, Wojtyla in cell ninety-six was already engrossed in the latest statement from the government minister responsible for Church matters in Poland; under communism, religion has a special political department in that country to watch over it.

Suenens of Belgium had an early meeting with Enrique y Tarancon of Spain; they spent the time talking about the state of the Spanish Church after Franco and the crucial duty that the Spanish cardinals have to ensure that their country's newfound *democracia* does not lead to undesirable excesses.

Both men can only have been too well aware of the role the quiet and thoughtful Enrique y Tarancon had created for himself. In previous conclaves the influence of Spain's cardinals was, at best, minimal. Almost invariably they were firmly placed with one of the Italian "factions." But Enrique y Tarancon, during the nine years he had been cardinal, had been preparing his country for the momentous events which would follow the death of Franco. To make the transition from dictatorship to democracy more bearable, he had encouraged his bishops and priests to look beyond Rome. By doing so, he told them, they would be able to find what was good and could be adapted to the new mood of freedom in the Spanish

Church. It had been a genuine voyage of discovery which was not always fully appreciated by Spanish traditionalists, who were set in the religious mortar Franco used to bind the Church to him. Along that journey, Enrique y Tarancon had discovered Wojtyla. He found that the Pole's vision of how the Church should develop was close to his own. When König, an old friend, suggested that the time had come for a non-Italian pope, Wojtyla came naturally to mind. During the past week, with all the instinctive good manners which made him such an engaging figure, Enrique y Tarancon had been pushing the Polish cardinal. It had been a discreet and dignified campaign.

Lorscheider of Brazil, following doctors' orders and as part of his recovery from recent heart surgery, walked steadily through the corridors, pausing to speak to everybody he met.

Two Africans, Bernardin Gantin and Joseph Malula, archbishop of Kinshasa, strolled back and forth across the San Damaso Courtyard. Malula told Gantin what he had already told *Time* magazine: "All the imperial paraphernalia, all that isolation of the pope, all that medieval remoteness and inheritance that makes Europeans think that the Church is only Western—all that tightness makes them fail to understand that young countries like mine want something different. They want simplicity. They want Jesus Christ. They want change."

"That's why we're here," said Gantin cheerfully. "To make change happen."

Breakfast was quickly over. The coffee was as dreadful as Sin remembered from last time. Along with the other 110 cardinals he hurried to the Sistine Chapel, eager to start. There, the formalities—the election of scrutineers, infirmarii and revisers—were swiftly completed. Noé departed and voting began.

The expected Italian challenge was obvious well before the last card was pierced by the threaded needle through the word *Eligo*.

As in August, Siri topped the poll, this time with twenty-three votes. When news of this reached the general conclave area, it caused considerable speculation. Siri's brutally frank interview, coupled to Balducci's call for an iron-fisted pope to ward off Armageddon—or something very close—was interpreted as indicating that the conservatives, far from running scared, were going all out for a quick victory. The twenty-three votes provided a respectable platform from which the Siri campaign could grow, attracting those "soft centrists" willing to overlook some of his wilder pronouncements in the hope that Siri would be the salve for the doom-laden future Balducci had signified was waiting around the corner. Difficult though it may be to accept in a secular sense, Balducci's article had a marked effect on the minds of some cardinals. Many brought copies with them into conclave, where Balducci's warnings were a source of lengthy debate. The outcome had been this remarkable support for Siri.

Benelli received twenty-two votes. Nobody was very surprised; a good Benelli showing early on was a foregone conclusion. The question was whether his supporters would stay with him for the next ballot, when a more definite pattern might begin to emerge, or desert him for all the old reasons: the unease, suspicion and even distrust the archbishop of Florence could still evoke among his peers.

Ursi had eighteen votes. The general consensus among conclave staff was that he was well placed, although not exceptionally so. Depending on continuing "consultations," support could drift to him from Benelli, or vice versa.

With seventeen votes, Felici surprised a number of people. Their interpretation —even allowing for conclave's glasshouse atmosphere where so many opinions were forced to the surface before they could properly mature—had a certain fascination. Felici was almost as conservative as Siri. Perhaps Felici was making a showing as an alternative in case it should emerge that, after all, Siri would remain unacceptable even on the Day of Judgment for some cardinals.

A genuine surprise was the fifteen votes recorded for Pappalardo. What indeed could this mean? Nobody was quite sure, but the feeling was that he was a genuine compromise candidate, somebody to rally behind if the four Italian front-runners locked horns.

Wojtyla had five votes. The word was that his only visible response was to crease his broad Slav forehead with a frown. Such a modest return for all the hard work König had put in may account for what some attendants insisted was barely disguised disappointment on the face of the archbishop of Vienna.

Among the remaining contenders receiving votes in this ballot were Poletti, who got four, and Gantin, who had three.*

Everybody agreed that by midmorning on Sunday it looked like a straight fight between the Italians.

The second ballot shortened the field. The results produced the first murmurs of real astonishment. Siri had suddenly fallen away. Only eleven cardinals, the very core of the curialist diehards, stayed with him. But it was all over; there was no way Siri could come back. The speculation on why he had failed would come later. There would be talk of deals and promises, of, as the secret diarist would write, "the Holy Spirit and reality intervening." It would all be irrelevant. The salient point was that shortly before noon, Siri was out of the running.

Ursi clung doggedly to his eighteen votes. His bolt was also shot. He had made no progress. In the next ballot his supporters would assuredly transfer their loyalties. Pappalardo's had already done so. He was no longer a contender.

Felici had climbed strongly with thirty votes. Almost all of them, it was assumed, came from Siri supporters. Not only was Felici the cardinal the majority of the conservatives were indicating could be the man to ward off Balducci's predicted almost-end of the world, he might also achieve the equivalent of a miracle: bringing enough of the liberals over to him to get a quick victory.

There was only one flaw in this attractive scenario. Benelli had leaped ahead

* One source insisted that both Hume and Sin each received a vote.

with forty votes. There will be talk that all his traveling, all his careful preparations, all those dinners at L'Eau Vive—all were beginning to pay off.

But he was still thirty-five crucial votes short of the seventy-five needed to win.
There was a long way to go.

Wojtyla trailed with nine votes. This time he did not frown. He looked astonished. So they said. Many conclavists found his modest advance puzzling. Who
were those nine cardinals who felt compelled to support him?

König was certainly one. In half a dozen separate conversations this Sunday
morning he had made it very plain where his loyalty lay.

Enrique y Tarancon was another. Yet only a few people found his support for
Wojtyla significant. They were the ones who became aware of a brief meeting
after breakfast between the Spaniard and König. The alliance between the Viennese and Enrique y Tarancon was a bridge to the all-powerful voting bloc of
South America, Africa and Asia. Enrique y Tarancon was not only the undisputed
leader of the Spanish Church, he had tremendous influence in the Third World.
Even the autocratic Aramburu was prepared to listen to him. With the Spaniard
committed from the outset to Wojtyla, the way was open to garner in the forty-
four other votes available from Spain, Latin America, Asia and Africa. It would
also be reasonable to assume that Australia, New Zealand and Western Samoa
could be persuaded. But the evidence of common attitude between König and
Enrique y Tarancon largely escaped notice.

So, too, did the equally crucial support of Krol. Almost certainly he had been
one of the initial five who supported Wojtyla. The archbishop of Philadelphia
knew his fellow Pole well, had entertained him in America and had begun quietly
to tell others that here indeed was a person of impeccable credentials. On this second ballot, Cody and Cooke came in to support the candidacy of Karol Wojtyla.

But it did not look very serious. How could it? In spite of the fact that König,
Enrique y Tarancon and Krol had the closest possible connections and between
them considerable influence over more than half of the cardinal electors, they had
apparently so far been able only to marshal six others in the Sistine Chapel to
vote for Wojtyla.

During lunch—a heavy meal of macaroni and similar pasta dishes accompanied
by rather fruity red wine—there was some speculation about whether the Aus-
trian-Spanish-American triumvirate had tried and failed to influence their colleagues or were actually waiting to see how and where the Italian challenge would
develop in the next ballot before they again took the initiative.

After lunch, Cody, Krol, König and Enrique y Tarancon were repeatedly seen
walking back and forth across the San Damaso Courtyard, deep in conversation.
Later they were joined by Suenens and Marty. They subsequently returned to the
Sistine Chapel for the third ballot.

Its result showed a further narrowing of the field.

Felici had been stopped. His total tally had slipped to twenty-seven. He sat in his seat, drumming his fingers, a set, determined look on his face. So they said. Felici felt "total acceptance." So he said.

Eighteen voters remained loyal to Ursi. The question was not only why but for how long.

Siri somehow still had five supporters. Nobody could understand this senseless squandering of votes.

Wojtyla's nine maintained what looked like a lost cause. The feeling was that they must soon leave this Pole alone with his charisma. There seemed no way he could improve his position.

Poletti and Gantin had dropped from view.

It was Benelli's round. He had forty-five votes.

Villot suggested there should be a thirty-minute pause before the fourth and final ballot for the day was cast.

Several significant meetings occurred during the break.

Enrique y Tarancon, Willebrands and König met. Then the Spaniard had a meeting with Aramburu. At the same time König was talking to both Sin and Gantin, key members of the Asian-African bloc. These meetings attracted interest, and there was speculation that König was going to throw in the towel and accept the fact that Wojtyla was now an also-ran. But for once there was no leak; nobody really knew what was afoot.

Villot and Baggio met with Pignedoli in the bar kitchen. Sipping coffee, they were overheard expressing their determination to stop the unthinkable from happening: having to swallow the bitter past and, in the colorful words of that secret diarist, "kiss the Florentine's Fisherman's Ring." They would, of course, do precisely that if Benelli was elected. But equally, they were determined to do everything possible to see it did not happen. Villot was deputized to call on Felici. While the camerlengo shambled off, inevitable cigarette in mouth, yet another "consultation" was under way.

Pappalardo, Poletti and Ursi met Benelli. The only sure thing about this encounter was that it was short. The four Italians separated, with Benelli apparently having failed to get his companions' agreement to come over to his side.

It did not seem to much matter. In the next ballot, Benelli acquired a further twenty votes, giving him a total of sixty-five—a mere ten short of victory.

And Ursi's supporters had finally done what was expected of them hours earlier. All but four had left the agreeable archbishop of Naples.

It was where Ursi's erstwhile supporters went which surprised so many.

Wojtyla suddenly had twenty-four votes. The significance of the quiet "consultations" König, Enrique y Tarancon and Krol had initiated became clear. Yet their real sway had only just started. Whether it could gain momentum at this late stage —with Benelli in sight of the Throne of St. Peter—was anybody's guess.

The speculation this caused was matched only by the buzz of astonishment which followed the announcement that a new contender had entered the list. He was Cardinal Giovanni Colombo, the seventy-six-year-old archbishop of Milan. He had not been thought *papabile* when he came into conclave. But with some firm persuasion from Villot and Felici—the outcome of their meeting had evidently been a strengthening of the stop-Benelli movement—Colombo had agreed to be cast in the role of the Curia's compromise candidate. He would take up the mantle originally meant for Felici. Colombo was, in the convoluted language of one curialist, "a conservative moderate." He was somewhat to the left of Felici but nowhere near Benelli, who was characterized as a captive of the non-Italian cardinals, as the Italian who would destroy the Italian papacy, and as the old foe of the Curia who had already caused havoc by imposing an inexperienced Gianpaolo on the Church's civil service.

Colombo was there to stop Benelli. That he was old, frail and not too bright did not matter. He was Italian and quite possibly the only candidate able to halt Benelli. Colombo would keep the papacy well and truly in the family.

Fourteen cardinals had voted for him.

It was a fitting end to a remarkable day in the Sistine Chapel.

After supper—*pasta in brodo, insalata* and beer or wine—König, Enrique y Tarancon and Krol were busy stressing to various cardinals that there really was no basis for the somewhat desperate countermeasure against Wojtyla which had emerged from the Benelli camp: namely, that to elect a pope from behind the Iron Curtain would have extraordinary political consequences for the Church. The risks, König patiently and quietly insisted, could be far outweighed by the benefits.

Each of Wojtyla's three advocates had their own very different approach for promoting his cause.

König correctly gauged that, in Europe, the support of the five German cardinals was crucial; any wavering among the French and the Dutch would almost certainly cease once the Germans were fully committed. And the German Church was heavily involved in supporting the Third World: Ratzinger and Höffner in particular could be expected to lend their considerable authority to round up any remaining Third World candidates. König intuitively pitched his arguments on a level his listeners could hardly resist. He reminded them that Wojtyla was a resilient enemy of communism, itself a perpetual bogey in a country which bordered Eastern Europe and whose populace firmly believed the day might come when the Russians would roar up the *Autobahn*, overrunning West Germany on their way to conquering all of Free Europe. As pope, Wojtyla would be able to call upon his already vast experience of the communist menace, as well as make the best use of his formidable strength to face the challenge of religious persecution behind the Iron Curtain. Finally, König shrewdly reminded the Germans that Wojtyla had publicly asked the German Church to forgive the Polish Church for "whatever offenses" it had committed. It was the clincher—and placed all five Germans in the Wojtyla camp.

Krol stressed the qualities of the man he knew well: Wojtyla's fearlessness, his physical prowess, the way he could ski, fish and run with the best of them; his poetry, his modesty, his "sensible attitudes" to Church dogma as a firm middle-of-the-roader; in short, he was the sort of person who, but for an accident of birth, could have been a typical, and ideal, American. Krol's fellow Americans were impressed.

Enrique y Tarancon looked into the future. Wojtyla's background, he told colleagues from Latin America, would make him the perfect type to deal with the problems of the Third World. They listened attentively.

The lobbying was low-keyed and relaxed; so much so that some of the Americans—Manning, Carberry and Dearden—would later insist there had been no electioneering. Several cardinals retired early on Sunday night to read copies of Wojtyla's *Segno di Contraddizione*, the Lateran retreat which König had thoughtfully brought into conclave. It was all part of the careful light-touch strategy.

Conclave was barely stirring on Monday morning, October 16, when news swept the enclave that Colombo, after a night of prayer and reflection, no longer wished to be considered.* It was sensational enough for Felici to hurry to Colombo's room. The two men spent a short time together, perhaps no more than five minutes. Felici emerged, according to one eyewitness—not a cardinal—even more set-faced than he was when his own candidacy had collapsed in the Sistine Chapel. Felici then went to Villot. They were still together when breakfast was announced. By then most people knew Colombo was out. He was himself one of the first to sit at table; an observer said the old man looked ten years younger.

Wojtyla appeared with the senior Polish cardinal, Stefan Wyszynski. They took their places opposite König and Krol. König raised his coffee cup in silent salute. Krol smiled warmly at Wojtyla and said, in Polish, "It's okay."

There was no response. Wojtyla sat, head down, eyes fixed on his plate. Nobody could really tell what he thought.

The Benelli camp occupied the long center table in the dining room. The predominantly Italian faction was accompanied by some of those outsiders whom the curialists accused the archbishop of Florence of selling out to: there were Owen McCann, the archbishop of Cape Town; Lawrence Picachy, a Jesuit, archbishop of Calcutta and president of the Indian Bishops' Conference; Antonio Ribeiro, patriarch of Lisbon; Franjo Seper of Yugoslavia; Stephanos Siderouss of Egypt. It was a mixed bag but one capable of exerting itself vigorously.

With Colombo departing as swiftly as he had been press-ganged into entering, his fourteen votes would have to be redeployed.

The possibility for even more drama was clear to everybody. It was likely that

---

* One source insists that Colombo made his decision on Sunday evening after he was visited by Benelli. Benelli denied any such meeting took place.

the four votes for Ursi would now switch to Benelli. There was a mood among the increasingly gloomy Italians that even Benelli, in the last resort, was better than losing the papacy to a non-Italian. If the switch did occur, then it would need just six of those fourteen Colombo votes to see Benelli elected. The feeling was that even among the diehards six might be persuaded to endorse their old enemy, if only for the sake of Italian continuity in the papacy.

Amid considerable expectancy and some tension, the cardinals filed to the altar to cast their first votes of the day.

Benelli moved up to seventy votes, just five short of victory. Wojtyla had forty.[2]

Villot ordered a break of fifteen minutes for those who wished to take coffee or other light refreshments.

Wojtyla promptly went to his room and pointedly closed the door, a clear sign he did not wish to be disturbed.

Wyszynski huddled with König and Enrique y Tarancon outside the Sistine Chapel. The Pole and the Austrian spoke German, which König translated into Spanish for Enrique y Tarancon.

There was no need for König to translate Wyszynski's vigorous assertion, "Es wird passieren."

Enrique y Tarancon agreed, "Sí, esto ocurrirá."

Certainly it could happen. But Benelli was very, very close. The next ballot might well see him elected.

It was not to be. In the course of fifty-five momentous minutes, no fewer than eleven votes switched from Benelli to Wojtyla. The tally was now fifty-nine for Benelli and fifty-two for Wojtyla. It was all over for the archbishop of Florence. But this did not guarantee that Wojtyla would win. He still needed at least twenty-three more votes.

The cardinals broke for lunch. Hemmed in by supporters determined that he should not now retire to his room, Wojtyla was led into the dining hall.

Wyszynski took him by the arm and whispered in Polish, "The Holy Spirit demands that you accept what is happening."

König quickly translated the words into German and Spanish. Encouraging responses were directed at Wojtyla. He seemed to König "a good example of pale and pensive." The Viennese poured himself some wine from one of the pitchers on the table and raised his glass toward Wojtyla. This impromptu toast led to others. Soon cardinals as far up the table as Basil Hume of England, ten places from Wojtyla, were turning and toasting the Pole. For a while he remained silent. Then, in a low and intense voice, he said, "No, no, no."

Enrique y Tarancon, fearful of any disruption to the newfound momentum, quickly intervened: "Sí, sí, sí." Pointing at the food, cannelloni, the Spaniard said, "Buen provecho!"

Wojtyla grunted, "Smacznego." He began slowly to stuff forkfuls of the rolled pasta into his mouth.

The Benelli table—not a strictly accurate description, for his supporters were scattered all around the room—was downcast.[3]

Lunch was an unusually lengthy one: nobody seemed anxious to leave in case he should miss a new development. When dessert was served, a straight choice between ice cream and fruit, Willebrands and Baggio came over to Wojtyla. They simply stood close to him, saying nothing, lending him their silent approval.

Finally, when the nuns began rather pointedly to clear the tables, the cardinals drifted out, many heading for the sunny confines of the San Damaso Courtyard.

There Ratzinger and Höffner quietly concentrated on any Third World cardinals they thought might still be hesitating. During the course of the next hour the archbishops of the Dominican Republic, Guatemala, Sri Lanka and Indonesia were all gently spoken to.

In the meantime König and Wyszynski were closeted with Wojtyla in his room. Wojtyla sat on his bed, hands clasped between his knees, head bowed. Wyszynski perched on the edge of the only chair in the room. König leaned against the closed door, effectively barring entry to anyone who might wish to come in.[4]

Wyszynski spoke first. Gripping the arms of the chair he said to Wojtyla, "You will have to accept." He turned to König. "You tell him."

König shrugged. "I have." He loked at Wojtyla. "You simply must face the truth. This *is* what the Holy Spirit wishes."

"It is a mistake." Wojtyla's response was barely audible.

"There is no mistake. Look at the figures. There is the proof." König's deeply felt compassion for Wojtyla softened the words.

Wyszynski rose from his chair and stood over Wojtyla. The old cardinal reached out and gently touched the younger man's bowed head. "Please, Karol. This *is* right. For the Church. For Poland. For you."

There was no response.

"Please, Karol. Do not resist what is right."

This time there was the tiniest of head movement, so slight König could not be certain what it meant.

"You will accept?" König's voice was uncertain.

"If that—" Wojtyla did not complete the sentence.

"It is. It *is* right," insisted Wyszynski.

This time Wojtyla's nod was more discernible. "Let us see what happens this afternoon."

König moved away from the door, lowering his voice. "That is right. But you must prepare yourself now for the outcome."

When it became clear Wojtyla was not going to respond, König continued. "You must be called John Paul Two."

Wojtyla raised his head and looked at König.

König smiled. "Do not look so worried. You have been chosen for this. That is clear. You *are* going to be elected pope. And you *must* be called like that because that is a mark of the continuity we *all* want."

Wojtyla asked that they now leave him so he could pray alone.

"We shall all pray," promised König.

The first ballot of the afternoon was decisive.

Wojtyla had seventy-three votes. Benelli's support had dropped to thirty-eight.

At twenty minutes past five in the afternoon, the result of the eighth and final ballot was read out.

Wojtyla had ninety-seven votes.

Thunderous and sustained applause swept through the Sistine Chapel. Then Villot rose and began to walk toward the slumped figure of the archbishop of Cracow. Wojtyla sat, head in his hands, tears running between his broad fingers, a suddenly lonely and isolated figure beneath Michelangelo's apocalyptic "Last Judgment."

XXVIII

The door of the Sistine Chapel opens and Noé stands there, looking inside. He is transfixed by what he sees.

Behind him, craning their necks, are a group of openmouthed attendants who have been drawn here by the thunderous noise. Within minutes the corridor is completely filled by supporting players in the drama which has occurred. Nuns come rushing from the kitchen; the barber and the electrician, the bedmakers and the floor sweepers, even the counterelectronic surveillance men with their sensors, are pushing and shoving to see what is happening.

Noé remains in the doorway, overwhelmed. He is certain there have never before been scenes quite like this in the Sistine. Here, where Philibert of Orange once casually stabled his horses while his army pillaged and raped its way through the Vatican, bringing a fear not since equaled, there is on this sunny Monday evening four hundred years later a joy also unequaled.

Most cardinals are on their feet, still clapping wildly. Others, the Africans and South Americans, are using their clenched fists to hammer the tabletops. Polynesia's Pio Taofinu'u is swaying gently to his own rhythm. Several of the Italians are shouting "Viva!" "Viva!"

König, architect of the victory, alternately takes off his spectacles, polishes them, and puts them on again—only to have to remove them once more when they mist up. If he is not crying, it is something remarkably close.

Enrique y Tarancon also displays a repetitive reaction. He stands up, sits down, and stands up again, applauding and smiling nonstop; no one has ever seen this serious-faced Spaniard so happy in public.

Krol is talking animatedly to some of the other Americans, communicating to them his "elation and exhilaration." In all the hubbub his listeners can hardly hear him.

Felici has balled one fist and is pounding it into the other; he looks more than ever like an emperor bestowing his accolade.

Siri manages a wintery smile. Yet his applause is as sustained as any of the cardinals.

The Germans are ecstatic. Not only are they congratulating each other with formal handshakes, but Ratzinger, in a totally unexpected demonstration of emotion, cries out that the Holy Spirit has prevailed.

Basil Hume shows more restraint. His smile is reserved, but his approbation is genuine.

Benelli is gracious in defeat, grinning and nodding toward where Villot now towers over Wojtyla.

He remains a bowed and isolated figure, hands locked tightly together, apparently oblivious to the noise.

The camerlengo extends his arms, slowly dipping them in an ungainly movement, like a tired old bird flapping its wings. It is his way of asking for silence.

Noé turns and motions the crowd in the corridor to stand back. They reluctantly retreat a few feet. There are excited whispers of "Who is it?"

Ignoring them, Noé moves inside to Villot.

The ovation continues. Villot's movements become more agitated; his arms seem to be moving on their own. He looks around, beseechingly.

Gradually the clamor dies. The cardinals resume their seats, staring at the isolated figure of Wojtyla.

Noé nudges Villot. The camerlengo coughs.

Wojtyla's head remains bowed.

Villot taps him lightly on the shoulder.

At last Wojtyla raises his head.

König, seated a few feet away, is relieved. Whereas in Albino Luciani's countenance there had been "a certainty," there is in Karol Wojtyla's "a firm resolution, the face of a man who has come to terms with what God wants of him."

Krol thinks he is witnessing "not the loneliness of the long-distance pope but a strong man taking up a great task."

Hume's reaction is equally interesting. He feels "desperately sad for the man. Yet somebody has to carry the tremendous burden."

Clasping his hands before him, Villot peers down at Wojtyla.

Cody is not the only person present to realize the significance of the moment: "This is no eyeball-to-eyeball; this is the abnegation of the old order, the end of the Italian domination of the papacy, the start of the new order from Poland."

For a long moment—Felici thinks it may have been a full thirty seconds—Villot and Wojtyla continue to stare wordlessly at each other.

Then, in Latin, Villot poses his first question.

"Do you, Most Reverend Lord Cardinal, accept your election as Supreme Pontiff, which has been canonically carried out?"

The tears which Wojtyla wiped away before raising his head well up once more.

Felici is deeply moved. He thinks it takes an unusually balanced personality to display emotion so freely: "This is not a neurotic response, it is a man responding from the heart about what he feels."

Wojtyla quickly blinks his eyes. Then in a steady and resonant voice, carefully pitched to reach all corners of the Chapel, he makes his response, also in Latin.

"With obedience in faith to Christ, my Lord, and with trust in the Mother of Christ and the Church, in spite of great difficulties, I accept."

Tumultuous applause sweeps the Sistine. It is taken up by the conclave staff bunched in the chapel doorway.

Villot flaps his arms. But it is now just a meaningless gesture. The old camerlengo is smiling as hugely as everybody else.

Finally, undoubtedly eager to hear the answer to Villot's next question, the cardinals subside. Noé glances toward the doorway. It is enough to stop the excited whispering there.

Villot asks: "By what name will you be known?"

König glances at Wyszynski. He is staring intently at Wojtyla. Wyzsynski's lips are trembling, whether in prayer or excitement König cannot tell.

In a voice even more declamatory, Karol Wojtyla announces his decision.

He will be known as John Paul II.

Villot smiles, turns to face the altar and then, departing from protocol, he impulsively swings back to embrace the new pope.

Noé, mindful of the need to adhere to precedent, goes to the door and gives his first instructions of the pontificate. He orders an assistant to have the conclave area opened, to give Martin the news, to have the prefect summon Gammarelli, to remove the seals on the papal apartment and to request that a team of nuns dust off and air the place. Then Noé hurries back to Villot. John Paul is receiving one joyful cardinal after another. Villot respectfully intervenes and, accompanied by König, Krol and Enrique y Tarancon, he takes the pope to the sacristy to await the arrival of the tailor.

John Paul walks directly to the rack holding the vestments the House of Gammarelli delivered just before conclave. He inspects them briefly and then makes his choice.

"I don't need anyone to dress me," he says jovially to König, in German.*

The pope dons the white-linen cassock and secures its white sash. The robe is a reasonably good fit. When moments later Gammarelli is ushered into the sacristy by Martin, the tailor can immediately see that it will take him only minutes to make the minimal adjustments required.

"*Un* polacco?"

Greeley fancies he hears the word repeated endlessly across crowded St. Peter's Square. The disbelieving whisper rustles through the throng that the

---

* John Paul converses in a mixture of Polish, German, Italian and a little French. Many present in the sacristy well remember how even there he switched from one language to another with ease.

first non-Italian pope since Adrian VI died on September 14, 1532, is a Pole. Greeley, putting behind him the confident prediction that Ursi would be the man shortly to step past the glass doors opening onto the central balcony of the basilica, senses the "angry, confused and sullen" mood of the crowd. They continue to stare incredulously up at Felici, who has just made the historic announcement: "*Habemus papam. Carolum Sanctae Romanae Ecclesiae Cardinalem Wojtyla.*"

Felici is joined by Noé and together they drape a red-bordered white papal tapestry over the balustrade. It still bears the coat of arms of Gianpaolo.

Someone asks Greeley whether the pope is a black.

"No."

"*Asiatico?*"

"No. *Un polacco.*"

"*Un* polacco?"

Felici and Noé leave the floodlit balcony briefly, then they are back, standing on either side of the door, looking expectantly into the basilica. There is movement there. But nobody in the square can actually see what is happening.

It is Gammarelli making a final adjustment to John Paul's cassock. Satisfied, the tailor steps back. There is no doubt about it, he murmurs to Martin, no pope has looked finer in his vestments.

John Paul's red-velvet mozzetta is a perfect fit, resting comfortably on his broad shoulders, its gold-trimmed front falling cleanly over his chest. The white-silk skullcap is firmly in place, enhancing his strong, broad face.

In the past few minutes, between the walk from the sacristy to where John Paul now waits to step onto the balcony, his tailor has detected a definite change in the pope's demeanor.

There is a look in the deep-set eyes which was not there before; it was present when Gammarelli made that final adjustment: almost a warning that this is not a man who wants to be bothered with the trifles of life. There is now also an impatient thrust to John Paul's strong chin. He really wants to get on with it, thinks the tailor; he is clearly anxious to get down to the real business of being a pope.

John Paul stands a few feet from the doors to the balcony. Straight ahead is the towering obelisk of Caligula, where Nero burned the Christian martyrs, where St. Peter was crucified and St. Paul beheaded. Beyond runs the Via della Conciliazione, lined with the buses which have brought the faithful and the merely curious to the great piazza.

Close behind John Paul are Villot and other cardinals. But most have retired to their rooms to rest before dinner.

The pope begins to move onto the balcony when Noé motions him back.

John Paul hesitates for the merest fraction. Then, picking up stride, he brushes aside the master of ceremonies with one impatient flick of his hand.

At 7:21 P.M. precisely he steps into the spotlight.

MacCarthy feels a sudden tension. He is in Vatican Radio's mobile studio atop Bernini's colonnade. It offers a near-perfect vantage point from which to view the scene on the balcony. But for once there is almost nothing for the broadcaster to do. A Vatican Radio microphone is on the balcony to pick up the first public words of the pope for transmission live around the world.

Waiting for him to appear, MacCarthy has tried to place the election in some sort of perspective. He sees the pope's choice of name as significant, a clear-cut statement that the papacy will continue a line which did not have time to be consolidated during the short pontificate of Gianpaolo. The relative youth of the new pope, fifty-eight, removes any thought that he was elected only as a transition pontiff; instead he could be reigning at the start of the next century. Yet now, in the first minutes of his reign, John Paul might stumble.

Looking down on the piazza, MacCarthy senses this is predominantly a Roman crowd, one used to Italian popes. A slip now, and this newcomer will be lost, perhaps forever. The word would spread. Everything John Paul would subsequently do or say could have appended to it the pejorative *"un polacco."* The Romans can be very cruel to their own, as Paul learned. With an outsider they could be vicious. This is why MacCarthy continues to feel tense as John Paul steps forward to the microphone.

The pope stands directly under the name of the Borghese Paul V, emblazoned across the façade above the balcony. He lifts his arms in a gesture of greeting and acknowledgment, a shy smile on his lips. Then in a strong voice he gives his first blessing to the city and to the world.

"All honor to Jesus Christ," he chants.

"Now and forever," responds the crowd.

He lowers his hands and grips the top of the tapestry. For a moment he waits. There is nothing nervous about the pause. It is the action of a man who knows the effect he wants to create. When he speaks there is a surprised and delighted roar from the piazza. He looks *un polacco,* but his Italian is almost perfect.

"May Jesus Christ be praised."

"Now and forever," roars the crowd.

"Dearest brothers and sisters . . ."

There is wild cheering. The throng does not need reminding that this was how Gianpaolo used to address them.

"We are still all grieved after the death of that most beloved pope . . ."

John Paul waits, content to let the applause roll on.

MacCarthy relaxes. It's going to be all right, he tells himself, it really is going to be all right.

The pope's voice booms out and the crowd obediently falls silent.

"Behold, the most eminent cardinals have called forth a new bishop of Rome, called him from a far-off country, far, but still so near, because of the unity of faith and Christian tradition."

Huzzahs of encouragement rise from the square.

"I was afraid to receive this nomination . . ."

Another pause. Sections of the crowd shout out that he has nothing to fear.

John Paul's voice changes. It becomes deeper and more vibrant.

"But I . . . but I accepted out of love and veneration for Jesus Christ and the Holy Mother. . . ."

He stares down at them. They stare back.

"I don't know if I speak your"—a suspicion of a chuckle—"our Italian . . ."

A delighted burst of laughter.

"Our Italian well enough. If I make a mistake you will correct me."

The ecstatic cheering of the crowd continues unchecked for a full half minute.

John Paul's arms are extended again.

"Thus I present myself to you in our mutual faith and confidence in the Mother of Chirst and our Church. And, also, to start on that road, the road of history and the Church, beginning with the help of God and the help of men."

Now there is no stopping the crowd. The joyous tumult nearly drowns the sound of the six great bells of St. Peter's ringing out their jubilation.

The pope stands perfectly still. He spreads his arms wide in embrace. Almost magically the noise stops.

"Blessed be the name of the Lord," he chants.

"Now and forever," responds the crowd.

"Our help in the name of the Lord," intones the pope.

"Who has made heaven and earth."

With a majestic sweep of his arms, John Paul traces his first papal blessing in the Roman night air.

"May the blessing of Almighty God, Father, Son and Holy Spirit, descend upon you and remain forever. Amen."

He turns and leaves the balcony as the huge ovation continues.

Lambert Greenan is relieved that he is not involved in the production of the special edition of *L'Osservatore Romano* to commemorate the election. The possibility of a Polish pope was never seriously considered by any of the editors asked to submit short lists. The result is confusion.

Thankfully, thinks Greenan, the panic is happening well away from his quiet enclave. There are still two days to go before the press date for his weekly English-language edition. The timing of the new pope's election suits him perfectly: there is time to think, time to shape those elegant phrases Greenan is famed for, time to make a more mature assessment.

Sipping a whiskey—he's chosen a twelve-year-old Irish to mark the occasion—Greenan sits at his desk, Roman collar unbuttoned, sleeves rolled up, glasses perched on the end of his nose, alternately reading and pondering before occasionally making a brief, cryptic note.

He is convinced that not only is the election of a Polish pontiff in itself an event of extreme importance, but in choosing the first non-Italian in almost five centuries the normally cautious College of Cardinals displayed an imaginative rashness which has moved the papacy from the conventional certitude of the old Roman order to somewhere potentially far more exciting—yet possibly fraught with dangers.

Greenan expects that John Paul, simply because of his background, must possess a very particular experience of some of the greatest problems confronting the Church.

He's a Pole, the editor reminds himself, and Poles have their own special national attitudes stemming from that country's historic and geographical situation.

"The Irish of Middle Europe?" he scribbles. Greenan sips whiskey and adds, "Perhaps not. But close."

The editor ruminates. Above all John Paul will undoubtedly have been raised in the tradition that the Polish Church remains, in spite of communism, the true custodian of Polish nationhood. Greenan knows that during the long dark period of foreign occupation, first under the Germans and then the Russians, the Polish Church had been directly responsible for preserving the identity of the country. It continues to do so. Despite brutal pressure from Poland's Communist Party, the Church has managed to keep itself an intact institution without whose consent the nation cannot properly be governed.

In recent years—Greenan makes another note that coincidentally this is the period during which John Paul's own career in the hierarchy developed—the Polish Church has reached a more stable understanding with the Polish government; there is cautious realization on both sides of the need for coexistence. The pressures are still there, but the Church in Poland flourishes. Either despite persecution or because of it, the churches are full; in terms of faith, the Holy Roman Catholic and Apostolic Church of Poland is stronger than in any Western country.

Once more Greenan reaches into his own background for a comparison. He makes another jotting: "Stronger even than Ireland where religion and nationalism go hand in hand."

Greenan wonders whether this could be one of the underlying reasons John Paul was elected. Is this the Sacred College's means of coping with the undeniable problems of Eurocommunism, the way its creed has even eaten into the Catholic strongholds of Western Europe? Is not John Paul's own success in battling with communism a shining example showing that the doctrine is not invincible, that in the competition for the confidence and support of his people, the Church not the Party has emerged victorious?

It is very possible that John Paul's experience of living under communism has not only tested his faith and his courage and given him the inner strength which comes only to those who have learned to resist, but it may also have convinced him a godless authoritarian structure can only successfully be resisted by a God-fearing one. It would be good if this were so, Greenan decides; firmness is a valuable quality in these times when Christian values are being eroded on all sides.

Yet the real issue, the editor thinks, may be a more subtle one: can a pope who has been schooled in the direct confrontation between an embattled Polish Church and an atheist government possibly possess the subtlety and flexibility of thinking needed to cope with the many more challenges—far more varied than any Poland can throw up—which the Church faces throughout the world? Geenan slowly sips his whiskey, lost in contemplation. Overnight the entire Church has been set on a journey the end of which cannot be known. The Polish regime, and behind them the Russians, will undoubtedly not like the idea of a Polish pope, one whose election is bound to have the effect of strengthening still further religious faith under communism. Equally, oppressed Catholics throughout communist Europe will see John Paul's election as confirmation of the Church's continued concern for them; it will be a beacon which will point them forward. But where could all this ultimately lead? Bold and brave though the decision to elect a Polish pope was, Greenan is suddenly aware that it has also created a situation where dangerous human, political and religious forces alien to the Church could be unleashed.

The phone interrupts Greenan's meditations.*

"Lambert?"

"Cardinal Cody?"

"Who else? How you been?"

"Fine, Eminence."

"Well, I got bad news for you."

"Not again, Eminence."

Cody has previously provisionally accepted Greenan's second invitation to dine with him this evening at his priory.

---

* Greenan will remember this call just as vividly as his earlier one from Cody; he thinks it "may be because it isn't every day I get called by an exalted cardinal."

"The pope wants us to eat and pray with him. Very Polish."

"Also very Irish, Eminence."

"Polish. Irish. Same thing where I come from," growls Cody. "Okay. You ask me again. Understand?"

"Perfectly, Eminence."

A sudden thought strikes Greenan. The Chicago cardinal has a large number of Poles in his archdiocese. It's worth a try.

"Eminence, what's the new pope like?"

"Huh?"

"You've met him of course?"

"Sure. Lots of times. A great man. Let me tell you a few things. . . ."

For the next twenty minutes Greenan listens to one cardinal's very personal view of the new pontiff. The editor will decide that what he hears is too privileged ever to reveal.

The riveting call ends on a high note.

"Lambert, you listen to me. This is going to be the greatest pope ever. You got that? Ever."

Without waiting to say good-bye Cody rings off.

During dinner in the Hall of the Popes, John Paul moves among his cardinals.

He has a friendly word for each, physically embracing many. When Wyszynski struggles to rise from his place, the pope gently eases him down and bends to whisper in his ear. The old warrior nods. Both are close to tears.

John Paul moves on. As he reaches Villot he quietly inquires whether any champagne is available.

Villot grins. *"Oui, Santissimo Padre. Mais oui!"*

Tight though his budget has been, the camerlengo presciently purchased three crates of champagne to be brought into conclave. He somehow had a feeling the wine might be needed.

He passes the request on to Noé.

The master of ceremonies is dumbfounded. "Champagne? Here?"

"Oui! Et tout de suite!" replies the delighted Frenchman.

Soon afterward nuns arrive with bottles and trays full of fluted glasses. They hover, uncertain.

The pope beckons them to him. He takes a magnum and expertly uncorks it. He tells Noé to begin opening the others.

Then, tray-bearing nuns in tow, John Paul moves around the hall, pouring each cardinal a glass. When a bottle is emptied he hands it to a nun and takes another from Noé. Caught up in the spirit of the occasion the master of ceremonies is soon drawing corks with the aplomb of a wine steward.

As John Paul gives Krol his champagne, he says, "I must return to Philadelphia soon so you and I can sing together again."

Krol replies, "Anytime, any day."

Perhaps it is overhearing this which gives Terence Cooke, archbishop of New York, the idea. He turns to Krol.

"Why don't you sing now?"

Krol hesitates. "Sing here? What?"

"Anything. Something appropriate."

Krol sips champagne. "Perhaps something they like in Poland?"

"Good. That would be very good."

Krol rises. Gradually his rich voice can be heard around the room, quelling all conversation. He is singing the Latin lament *"Plurimos annos plurimos,"* a wish for a long life.

Other cardinals begin to join in. They stand.

John Paul grins and continues pouring champagne with, if anything, more verve.

Krol comes to the end. There is applause. The pope beams approvingly, clearly enjoying the impromptu celebration.

"Sing 'The Mountaineer,'" suggests Cody, expansively waving his glass. "Sing 'The Mountaineer.' It's a great favorite of His Holiness."

"In Polish," adds Wyszynski. The old cardinal has a look of triumph and anticipation in his eyes. Possibly more than anyone else in the hall, he recognizes the deeper implications for both the Church and the secular world of having a Polish pope. In fractured German he tells König, "Everything is going to be different, very different."

König nods in agreement.

Wyszynski repeats that Krol should sing the words in Polish.

Clearing his throat, the archbishop of Philadelphia launches into the traditional *"Goralu, czy ci nie za."*

There is silence as people begin to lower their glasses and listen to Krol's powerful voice. Few of them understand the words: "Mountaineer, why are you leaving your beautiful hills and silvery brooks? —For bread, Lord, for bread." But the words do not matter; the feeling conveyed by Krol transcends any need for translation.

He comes to the end of his rendition.

There is quiet applause as people look toward the pope.

In the gentlest of voices John Paul speaks. "That was beautiful. Would you please sing it again?"

Wyszynski has a suggestion. "Instead of singing 'For bread, Lord, for bread,' sing 'For You, Lord, for You.'"

Krol nods. Again his voice fills the chamber.

While he is singing, John Paul quietly continues pouring champagne. When Krol finishes his second version, the pope has another request.

"Sing it once more." It is not a command, more a plea.

"And I will join in," says John Paul.

Krol launches himself for the third time into the evocative ballad.

Martin shakes his head disbelievingly at Noé. The prefect probably knows as much as anyone present about papal elections but he has never seen or heard of anything remotely like this. As Martin watches, the pope, still singing in accompaniment with Krol and having finished dispensing champagne to the cardinals, now begins to serve the nuns.

For Noé, steeped in the stifling tradition of the Italian papacy, this is simply incredible. The pope is casually pouring champagne for nuns and singing as though he's been doing both all his adult life.

"It must be the Polish way of doing things," says Martin in wonderment.

When the song ends, amid the applause Krol and the pope embrace. They converse happily in Polish. Some of the Italian cardinals, whose language has so often dominated such occasions, are seen to exchange wan smiles with each other. They have no idea what is being said.

Jaime Sin is not the only one in the hall to be overheard wondering whether this is the Italian way of putting on a brave face—or whether it may possibly signify something else.

Agca has been back in Istanbul a week—back in this stinking rented room off Orou Caddesi, behind the great Mosque of Sultan Suleiman the Magnificent.

Before they parted on the freezing slopes of Mount Ararat, Teslin Tore told him a further thirty thousand lire would be credited on this Monday to his account at an Istanbul branch of the Türkeye Is Bankasi.

A few hours ago, as Tore had instructed, Agca went to the bank with his passbook. A teller took it from him and he was asked to wait. When the teller returned he handed back the passbook to Agca. It contained the new entry.

Agca had returned to this room, to flop on its rickety bed and endlessly study the passbook. On paper, by Turkish standards, he was now a wealthy man. He has the equal of almost five thousand American dollars to his name, more money, he is sure, than anyone in Yesiltepe can ever dream of possessing.

But Tore was adamant. Agca must not withdraw any of the money until told. Tore explained that was "a test."

Agca understands. In the Gray Wolves there are constant tests, designed to measure a member's loyalty, his strengths and weaknesses.

It is the instructions Tore has given him about the Gray Wolves which

Agca finds puzzling. Tore ordered no one in the organization must become aware of their secret meeting on Mount Ararat. Yet he also insisted he has the same goal as Colonel Turkes: to drive out of Turkey all hated Western influence and return the country to the "old ways."

Turkes, Tore claims, is personally ambitious and extremely dangerous to anybody who recognizes him for what he is: someone simply not powerful enough to carry out such a cleansing operation. That, Tore adds, is yet another reason for Agca to keep from Turkes and his Gray Wolves any hint of their secret meeting. Agca agrees.

Nor does his disoriented and disassociated mind find any difficulty accepting what Tore has said his new role must be within the Gray Wolves. To the organization Agca must appear as enthusiastic and fearless a member as ever. At the same time he must take the greatest care not to attract the interest of Turkey's authorities; he must stay away from his old criminal haunts and lead an exemplary life.

Agca agrees to it all.

Chaotic though his attitude may seem, psychiatrists will subsequently conclude that these are recognizable responses. They go with Agca's vague feeling that his willpower has been weakened, that his thoughts and sometimes even his words are all being imposed from "outside"—and are largely beyond his control. The psychiatrists will speak of *personality ambivalence*. But only later.

This Monday night it is enough for Mehmet Ali Agca to recall, as he lies in this fetid room contemplating his bank passbook, trusted Mauser beneath his pillow, that Tore has promised the time will soon come when he can begin to kill some of those enemies whose names he carries in his head.

After he listens to the news on a radio in the café below his room, a new name has been automatically added to his hate list. It is that of John Paul.

XXIX

In the aftermath of John Paul's election all sorts of attempts were made to get into his mind: to define and explain, elucidate and exemplify the reasons for his election and the direction of his mission.

The very fact that he was Polish was seized upon. The choice of a pope from that crucible, and the cautious acceptance of his election by the Polish state and the wider Soviet orbit, was taken as an admission that even within the communist empire there were things which were Caesar's and others that were God's.

By choosing him, the Church was entering with new vigor the gavotte between Christianity and communism. His election was interpreted as a decisive advance not only in Rome's claim to the leadership of Christendom but as a major step toward an understanding with all sorts and conditions of men.

Here was a pope who, having lived through decades of confrontation between his own Church and a communist regime, could create a real impact on relations with Marxism throughout the world; who could lead from the front the Holy See's search for a *modus vivendi* with the governments of Eastern Europe; who, coming from one of the historic frontiers of the Church's encounter with the modern world, could provide a new image of Catholic universality, a revitalized sense of the Church's involvement in the actual passions of ordinary people; whose message need not be the comfortable one of bourgeois Catholicism but an appeal for all Catholics to find their human dignity through fidelity to the crucified and risen Lord.

When John Paul II announced, as one of his early administrative decisions, that the Latin American bishops' conference—twice postponed because of the death of his predecessors—would take place in the coming January, immediate debate began on how a pope who recognized certain praiseworthy elements in the Marxist ideology of social transformation would regard the theology-of-liberation movement so strongly supported in parts of South America. His intellectual consistency, speculated Vaticanologists of all persuasions, should at least ensure that he did not indulge in Paul's fire-and-brimstone threats to excommunicate Catholics who aided the movement. They pointed to lessons of John Paul's past, to Cracow, for instance, where he had won important concessions from the government for the building of more churches and the improved religious education of children; his promise in return that Cracow Catholics would stop killing policemen had not meant he had sold his congregation short or compromised himself. Equally, he had been one of the leading supporters of the strikes in 1976 which led to the Student Solidarity Committee in Cracow; when one of its members died in suspicious circumstances he had vigorously pursued the authorities. He had encouraged the now-famous "flying university" of historians and scientists who taught aspects of subjects banned from the official curriculum.

Nor had he been afraid to condemn those most unsavory skeletons in the Polish Church's own cupboard, racism and, in particular, anti-Semitism. His denunciation was discerned to have been markedly stronger than the Polish Church's official position required. His own life of suffering, endurance and hardship was undeniably imprinted on his face. That he had, in contrast to most Catholic prelates, attended a secular university, that he was an accomplished author, linguist, philosopher and traveler—he made repeated trips to North and South America and even voyaged as far as New Zealand—all these suggested to Vaticanologists that he was likely to move the emphasis of papal activity away from theological debate and concentrate more on the social responsibilities of the Church. So ran the speculation.

John Paul had once said: "We cannot be Christian and materialist." Where, then, did this leave the growing number of people committed to the theology of liberation? Surely with the hope that here, at last, was a pope whose own background had demonstrated—impeccable though his anticommunist credentials were —that he had come to terms and could coexist with Marxism; here also was a pope who, by one of those elisions of opinion, was instantly seen not only as the spiritual leader of Eastern Europe but also as the pontiff for Africa, for Asia, and for Latin America. There Marxism and Catholicism had been forged to prepare for revolution. If he would not actually lead it, would John Paul at least condone it?

He would not.

In the plainest of language he warned those who were attempting to "mold Christ, to adapt Him to their own dimensions," that they would find naught for their comfort in his pontificate. Commentators began to book their plane tickets for Puebla, the site in Mexico for the bishops' conference. The whiff of a coming confrontation was in the air.

In the meantime there was much else of more immediacy to consider—Puebla was still four months away—and ponder upon. In his first message to the world, again delivered directly and succinctly, blessedly devoid of ecclesiastical obscuration, John Paul made it clear his being Polish was "of little importance"; no one should be distracted from the universal character of his office and the message he had to proclaim. With an actor's delivery, judged to win unstinted enthusiasm from the quarter of a million people in St. Peter's Square, he promised to be "the witness of the divine tool, reserving to all the same benevolence, especially to those being put to the test."

That, said the Vaticanologists, was most definitely political, was assuredly directed at the continuing destruction in Lebanon and Cambodia and every place on earth where there was strife. He would use the full influence and authority of his office to end it.

Yet in the same homily he also spoke of his intention to avoid interference in temporal politics. The fact that the Holy See had diplomatic relations with many countries should not be taken as implying approval for a given regime. In turn, Holy See diplomacy must have "an appreciation of possible temporal values; an interest in, and help for, human issues. These must be prompted, sometimes by direct intervention, but above all through formation of consciences, bringing a specific contribution to justice and peace on the international plain."

The words were examined endlessly. Clearly they did not suggest a political quietness in this pontificate; they were also anything but a supine respect for temporal power: John Paul's goals in this area were plain. He was determined to make any wayward regime with whom the Holy See had diplomatic ties, recognize the true worth of "liberty, respect for life and for the dignity of persons—who are never instruments—fairness in dealings, professional conscience in work, and the loyal search for the common good, the spirit of reconciliation and an openness toward spiritual values."

Some said that Paul's *Ostpolitik* had just been updated. And that, in spite of John Paul's wish to minimize the importance of his background, only a Pole could have expressed it so feelingly.

But while his utterances were being dissected, for many in the Vatican this first momentous week of his pontificate was virtually a holiday as staff made good use of the two hundred dollars' equivalent granted each of them by the pope to celebrate his election. The bonus to mark a new regime was an old custom. So was John Paul's reappointment of all heads of departments, with the exception of the ailing American cardinal John Wright. Yet there was one important difference: the reappointments would not necessarily run for the normal five years. Curialists could expect changes after the pope had time properly to assess his civil service. There was immediate uncertainty and even alarm around the Curia. No other pope had ever treated them like this before.

Questions were added to all the suppositions. In particular could such a powerfully dominating personality satisfy another early promise: to bring the world's Catholic bishops into the sharing of responsibility for governing the Church, the collegiality which was so much discussed during the Second Vatican Council? John Paul had spoken of shared responsibility, but he had yet to reveal how he saw it actually working. Did he envisage more power for the Synod of Bishops? Or more decision making on a local level, with a consequent general reduction in the need to refer to Rome? Nobody was certain. They comforted each other, saying that this was all part of the exciting style of the new pontificate. Camelot had come to the Vatican. Most questions were lost amid the admiration for John Paul's sheer drive, most marked in his frequent reiteration of the fundamental relationship between Christ and Peter, and the unbroken line that had made him the 262nd successor to the throne of the Apostle. And yet, of course, his inheritance was more than the tradition of nearly two thousand years. It was also the lessons of the past six weeks, when the catalytic effects of Gianpaolo's pontificate had created a new kind of papacy. It was Gianpaolo's short reign which prompted a new self-awakening in the Church; it was Gianpaolo whose thirty-three days had purged the pessimism, the admonitions and laments of Paul's pontificate; it was Gianpaolo who had tilled and sown the ground with new compassion and hope.

But swept up in John Paul's great charisma, this was largely forgotten. The new pope was endowed with magic. He became the object of fan-magazine hero worship. A typical reaction was that of Archbishop Derek Worlock of Liverpool, who reportedly described John Paul as "the greatest intellect I have ever met . . . he has a wry, wrinkled smile and is a man of wonderfully exuberant good spirits. He possesses a fantastic ability to analyze and weigh up everything."

No doubt that was all true—but it sounded more appropriate as a eulogy for the Beatles than an assessment of how the new pontiff would shape up.

Besides, "wry, wrinkled smile" apart, no clear picture had emerged of how different in everyday, human terms John Paul was from the predecessors whose names he now bore.

At exactly five o'clock in the morning of Sunday, November 19, 1978, the lights on the top floor of the Apostolic Palace come on. The policemen in St. Peter's Square stamp their feet and move around, trying to look busy. It is still dark and the great piazza is deserted. But the patrolmen can never be sure when "Monsignor Gee-Whiz"—they latched on to the name when they overheard Marcinkus use it on the very first day of the pontificate—might come stalking past the Bronze Doors to see whether they are keeping a proper watch.

This is day thirty-four of the new reign—the policemen keep count though they half joke that after Gianpaolo there will be no betting between them on the length of John Paul's pontificate—and Gee-Whiz goes on giving people a hard time. He is everywhere and at all hours, a glint-eyed, black-soutaned figure with an imperious nose and a sharp tongue which can lash out equally well in Polish, Italian, French and German. The men think it uncanny the way he is able to sniff out anything not in keeping with the new order. Twice already this past month they have seen Gee-Whiz lope along in the darkness behind the chipped supports of Bernini's colonnade. What did he expect to find? the policemen grumble. Despite the Red Brigades and talk of Rome's being now one of Europe's breeding grounds for urban terrorism, this is still Vatican City to these hardened patrolmen; in their view there is no need for Gee-Whiz to behave like this. It makes everybody nervous.

The patrolmen have been told by their commander to be particularly vigilant. His orders came from the Italian minister of the interior. The minister had been asked by Villot to tighten up security in the piazza. Gee-Whiz made the demand to the secretary of state. The question which intrigues the policemen in the square is, did Gee-Whiz first consult the pope, or was it another of his unilateral actions?

This, the policemen grumble, is very possible. Nothing they have heard, either from inside the Vatican or at police headquarters, suggests that the pope is in any more danger than his predecessors. Nevertheless, now that the lights burn brightly in the papal apartment, they move purposefully around, their automatic weapons and flak jackets making their movements ungainly, their hands cupped around their cigarettes; Gee-Whiz doesn't like people smoking on duty.

The policemen have made it their business to learn all they can about Gee-Whiz. They know his real name is Stanislaw Dziwisz. He is barely thirty-four years old, is now the pope's senior private secretary; he has been with him for the past thirteen years. They have seen that the relationship between the two men is the close one of a father and son. The patrolmen believe John Paul indulges Dziwisz; that the pope is letting his secretary run loose through the Vatican to roust out the lethargy and deadwood. The policemen don't mind that: after all, they chuckle, wasn't it John XXIII who, when asked how many people work in the Vatican, had said, "About half"? It is the way Dziwisz goes about his duties which annoys the patrolmen. He expects to be instantly obeyed and can be brutally frank and dismissive, in a way not even Macchi was. Whenever he gets the chance, he lapses into Polish, much to the consternation of the Italians in the Vatican. In manner and style, the policemen have recently heard Villot whisper, Dziwisz appears like a reincarnation of one of Richard Nixon's aides; Villot is believed to be again seriously wondering whether it isn't time to step down and avoid all the angst Dziwisz seems to thrive on.

And just look at the way he's tamed Martin, the policemen tell each other as they circle the square, regularly glancing up at the brightly lit papal apartment. Although the prefect has been reappointed, it's said things are different. While he still has the privilege of walking in unannounced and uninvited on the pope, now he almost never does so. Not after Dziwisz sharply told him John Paul doesn't like this sort of interruption. And the daily list of appointments has first to be approved by Dziwisz; it is he, not Martin, who goes over them with the pope. Again, when the prefect is present, Dziwisz has the disconcerting habit of speaking Polish—leaving Martin frozen-faced and effectively frozen out of the conversation.

Yet this is nothing, the policemen remind each other, compared to the way Noé is treated. He has again been appointed master of ceremonies. But several of the patrolmen have bets among themselves for how long. Some wager Noé will be gone within a year, fast by Vatican standards. Others think he might last a little longer; that removing Noé too soon would be seen as an anti-Italian bias in the new pontificate. Most certainly Noé's days are numbered—perhaps were from that moment he tried to shoo back the pope from the balcony of St. Peter's. Since then they have repeatedly clashed. When the pope appears in public, Noé positions the microphone one way and John Paul invariably changes it; during a procession, the master of ceremonies will attempt to stride almost beside the pope, who will curtly motion him away; at a reception, Noé hovers at the pontiff's elbow and is studiously ignored. Only the previous Wednesday, as the pope was about to enter the Nervi Hall for his weekly audience, Noé had fussed over the position of John Paul's skullcap. The pope angrily upbraided him. The policemen, from their own experience, know Noé cannot and will not change; it is in his nature to fuss and be a stickler for perfection. Frail old Paul and easygoing Gianpaolo tolerated his attentions. But John Paul clearly will not. Behind his smile there is an explosive temperament. One day, think the policemen, Noé will go too far. That's what makes the betting so interesting—knowing that the moment may not be all that far off. In the meantime they can still tell their families and friends how different things are now in the papal apartment.

Thirty minutes after the policemen saw the lights come on in the apartment, the pope had shaved with an old-fashioned open razor and showered, running the water ice-cold for the last rinse; he has recommended this to his personal staff as a way to maintain good blood circulation. Then he dressed himself in a white-linen cassock, a white skullcap on his head, his feet shod in sturdy size ten shoes. He is ready to start another of his eighteen-hour days.

As he does every morning after his ablutions, he returns to his bedroom and prays before a striking portrait of the Madonna hanging on the wall above the prie-dieu. The picture has come from John Paul's bedroom in Cracow. It is the only visible link with his past throughout the entire apartment. There are no discernible mementos, souvenirs or keepsakes; some visitors wonder if this is an extension of the pope's desire to play down his background.

Yet his devotion to Mary is very much a part of his Polish heritage. During the few weeks he has been pontiff, John Paul has constantly reminded the world that the Marian shrines of Poland loom large in his own life and piety. He plans to return to the theme later today, at his noon angelus: it is so natural for him to do so he would assuredly be surprised if anyone should remark on it.

At five forty-five he rises to his feet and strides from the bedroom.

Dziwisz and Magee are waiting for the pope inside the apartment's private chapel. It is now three weeks since Magee was summoned back from his enforced exile. John Paul personally sent for him, appointing the Irishman as his English-speaking private secretary. The pope knows Magee is ideally suited for the delicate task of building bridges between the new papal family and the Curia. But in a conversation with Dziwisz Magee made it plain—insists the Vatican's still-thriving "Irish Mafia"—that he wouldn't tolerate any interference. Dziwisz promptly responded in Polish. Magee coolly interrupted him and apologized for not being fluent in the language; he suggested that in the future Dziwisz and the other Poles on the pope's personal staff should try to use the common language of the Vatican, Italian. Or, with Magee, they could try English or French. But Polish was pointless. The Irish Mafia relished the story.

This morning both secretaries greet John Paul with the traditional *Santissimo Padre*. Then they follow him to the altar to celebrate the first mass of the day.

At seven-thirty, the pope leads his secretaries into breakfast. Already present is the pope's Polish doctor, Mielyslaw Wyslocki. He is a member of the entourage John Paul has imported from Cracow, Warsaw and other Polish dioceses; in all some forty Polish priests and nuns are scattered throughout the Vatican. They report directly to Dziwisz.

Wyslocki's presence reminds Magee of the unhappy position of Buzzonetti, who attended two previous popes and, though he is the Vatican health commissioner, has yet to be reappointed physician to the papal household. This is upsetting enough for Buzzonetti, but what concerns him more is that his efforts to give the pope a thorough physical examination have been thwarted. Dziwisz has repeatedly said John Paul has no time and, besides, he is in robust health. Buzzonetti accepts that this is probably the case, but he understandably wants to check for himself. And, try as he might, Buzzonetti has not been able to see John Paul's medical history.

Magee realizes he is going to have to tackle Wyslocki about all this. But now is not the time. The doctor is tucking into a plate of Polish ham and sausage. Every week the Polish airline LOT, on flight 303 from Warsaw, flies in quantities of provisions including Polish beer, *chleb*—Polish bread—and the buckwheat to make *blini,* the pancakes served with sour cream which the pope relishes.

The kitchen invariably serves traditional Polish peasant food. Magee finds it palatable enough, though after the frugal tables of Paul and Gianpaolo the portions are often too substantial for him to complete.

John Paul, however, has a healthy appetite; he frequently takes second helpings. Over breakfast this Sunday, as usual, he confines himself to domestic talk.

He wants to know the reaction to his latest edict: that all the papal staff should give up their afternoon siesta and work "a normal day." Dziwisz reports there have been no problems.

What about the tennis court? The pope has requested that one be renovated for his use. Dziwisz looks at Magee. He says the matter is in hand. John Paul has another question. Could a swimming pool replace the cleverly concealed roof garden Paul had installed? He would like nothing better than to get in a dozen lengths first thing in the morning. Magee explains that a previous survey showed it was impracticable to install a pool atop the Apostolic Palace. The pope persists: in that case, couldn't one be built at Castel Gandolfo? Then at least he could swim throughout the summer.

Dziwisz intervenes. He speaks rapidly in Polish to the pope. Magee waits patiently until the exchange is finished and then asks Dziwisz for a translation. It is all very relaxed. But no one can deny there are undercurrents at work.

At eight-thirty John Paul takes the private elevator—the one nobody else can use unless invited to do so—to the third floor. The Swiss Guards on duty drop to one knee. The blue-uniformed Vigilance outside the pope's official study noticeably stiffen. When they do so the outline of shoulder holsters becomes more visible under their jackets.

For the next three hours the pope works at his desk on the final draft of his angelus address. He writes slowly, thinking deeply about everything he pens; it is part of his intellectual makeup, part of the scholastic discipline which imbues him. He writes on a large writing block; the penmanship is bold and distinctive.

At eleven-thirty Dziwisz enters the study with Noé. The master of ceremonies carries a red-velvet cloth etched with gold.

They move quietly past the pope to the central one of the study's three windows. Dziwisz opens the window. From the square below come cheers and applause. Dziwisz thinks there must be close to two hundred thousand people down there. It has been like this for each of John Paul's angelus addresses. The secretary helps Noé neatly drape the velvet over the window ledge. Next they clip into place on the ledge a heavy glass lectern. Finally Noé positions the microphone. The two men stare for a moment longer down at the piazza, at the rows of television cameras, at the enclosure filled with still photographers, at another packed with reporters.

Behind them John Paul is reading aloud, rehearsing his speech. Key words have been underlined. The delivery is measured, the place for pauses noted. On one level this is the natural actor determined to give a good performance; on another the words are a further indication that in this pontificate papal theology and policy seem to be swiftly intermixing, while the range of pastoral solicitude is ever expanding.

At one minute to noon the pope rises from his desk and walks to the window. Noé and Dziwisz stand well clear.

John Paul begins to speak.

His words, like everything else he said publicly in the coming weeks, were examined, given their place in the chronology of pronouncements and directives which flowed from the pope. They were related to the personal predilections, attitudes and convictions which were rooted in his youth. When John Paul stressed the dignity of men, Vaticanologists who had traveled to Poland to further disinter his past reminded themselves that as a young man he had heard the cries of those randomly rounded up by the Gestapo; he came of age with the terror on his own doorstep in Cracow's Debniki Square, the entrance to a specially built Jewish ghetto. Auschwitz, symbol of modern technological genocide, is in a corner of his old archdiocese. Was this, then, why he felt compelled to remind everybody he still believed, regardless of the horrors he had been privy to that there was an inherent dignity in man; that just as the Nazis had failed to extinguish it, so, too, would their successors in spite of their more sophisticated modalities of dehumanization? Was he putting Russia and its satellites on notice? Was he warning them in particular that though he had placed behind him his Polish background—a valiant effort which proved impossible—he could not, would not, stand idly by if communist oppression passed a certain stage in Poland? It sounded very much like it, and Vaticanologists were not the only people who sensed the shivers in the Vatican. Several ambassadors attached to the Holy See informed their governments that this was showing signs of being the most politically explosive papacy since the days of Pius XII.[1]

And certainly John Paul was more direct than his predecessors. Not even Gianpaolo, for all his Pinocchioisms, had been so assertive. John Paul was determined that there could be no doubt about the emerging motifs of his pontificate. Nor was there any indication of corporate thinking in what he said, no suggestion of many hands laboring over various drafts. Instead there were a personal resonance and style, quintessential idioms and syntax, an individual selection of terms and scriptural loci—all combined to identify the pope as sole author. Even his inaugural homily and his first encyclical, *Redemptor Hominis*—the latter written first in Polish and then translated by himself into Latin—were preeminently personal testimonies.

It became quickly apparent that his assertions were meant to underpin a deep conviction about the irreplaceable worth of life from "within the womb to natural death." In this world abortion was too unthinkable even to be mentioned as something always to be rejected. It was a clear warning that he would have no time to hear any pleas for change. The same would apply to divorce and birth control: they were not matters for debate.

John Paul was making vivid the timeless and awkward truths about the Church: that it had survived because of its core of strong convictions; that to continue to do so required him to nurture, defend and transmit those truths. A diluted faith could not compete with the distractions of the modern world: a reluctance to accept authority rooted in tradition should be seen as the sin of pride, the foolish assumption that there was nothing to learn from previous experience.

Three months after his election, it was clear that a cardinal who, in Poland, was a tenacious adversary of an overbearing state had become, in Rome, a vigorous enforcer of orthodoxy. No one should have been surprised.

Behind the smile, the warmth of his personal contact, the way he found the time to return to his original role as a parish priest and solemnize a marriage, his ability to don an unadorned black cassock and sit in one of the confessionals of St. Peter's giving penance, his sudden and unexpected visits to the sick in Rome hospitals, the way he lifted up a child and looked lovingly into its face, his easy communion and fraternal relationship with his fellow bishops, his inborn sense of dignity which came from being energized by his own experiences, his overall image as a Supreme Pastor who was determined to resist the usual deadening institutionalization of the papacy—behind all this was an implacable traditionalism. In his doctrinal attitudes, in his views on worship and pastoral care, on every contentious issue his pontificate faced, he was rigidly orthodox. He would not move from well-prepared ground. He was not going to be an innovator; he was going to be a constant reminder of the old Catholic truths. There were some who wondered whether he drew too much comfort from the cheers which greeted him in the Nervi Hall on Wednesdays and from his balcony overlooking St. Peter's Square on Sundays; whether he realized that beyond his immediate horizons there were Catholics who were beginning to stir uneasily.

Yet he could still surprise.

Shortly before half past two on the sunny afternoon of November 21, 1978, a Mercedes sedan drives down the military-straight Via della Conciliazione, cruising slowly between the stone benches and imitation obelisks which border the road, bunching together the constant stream of traffic honking and crawling toward St. Peter's. The car's silver paintwork is coated with the mud and dust of some four hundred miles' travel.

Almost two days have passed since the driver—a member of an elite corps known as Chauffeurs de Monseigneur, specially established for the sole purpose of transporting one person around Europe, the man in the back of the Mercedes—set out on the tiring journey. When they had started from the remote Swiss village of Riddes, the old man had sat bolt upright. Now, thirty-six hours later, with brief stopovers for food and rest, having been driven out of Switzerland over the Alps, into Italy down through the wine valleys of Lombardy and finally along the helter-skelter *autostrada* to Rome, seventy-two-year-old Archbishop Marcel Lefèbvre still sits proudly and defiantly erect. He has barely spoken to his chauffeur during the drive. The man does not mind; for him it is a privilege just to be in the presence of a prelate he venerates even more than the pope. He is one of twenty drivers ready, willing and able, at any time and at their own expense, to carry Lefèbvre anywhere in Europe he wishes to go in order to voice his objections, celebrate his illegal masses and to continue to challenge the authority of the man he will shortly face, John Paul. It is a confrontation which makes the chauffeur tingle with apprehension. He is both bewildered and overawed that his passenger can remain so stoically calm. Not even since joining up with their two-car escort on the outskirts of Rome for the last stage of this historic journey has the archbishop shown a flicker of emotion. His face, for all his frailty, is set and resolute. No one, thinks the chauffeur, not even the Polish pope, will shake the determination of Marcel Lefèbvre.

As the Mercedes turns left into the Via del San Uffizio, the escort cars follow closely behind. Seated in the first, in full regalia, is Cardinal Giuseppe Siri. This is his first time back in the Vatican since he left conclave, the sound of champagne corks popping and Polish songs still ringing in his ears. His face, too, is a mask. The passenger in the second car is Silvio Oddi. He is a curial cardinal; some say he is even more of a Catholic extremist than Siri. Between them they have exerted considerable pressure for this meeting to take place. Yet the two cardinals remain surprised that the pope has agreed to it. They can see no way there can be compromises, no possibility of Lefèbvre retreating. Indeed, when they met just now on the other side of Rome, the archbishop made it icily clear that he had come here to listen; for him this was not a peace mission.

At the Arch of the Bells news-film cameramen, photographers and reporters await their arrival. Informed of the meeting, they have assembled, as they have so often in the past thirteen years of Lefèbvre's rebellion, in the confident expectation that when he emerges from the Vatican he will tell them how he trounced this pope—just as he so many times defeated Paul and would undoubtedly have triumphed over Gianpaolo had he not died.

Lefèbvre motions the driver to stop. The archbishop rolls down the back window, ignores the reporters' questions and stares bleakly into the cameras. Satisfied that the moment has been recorded, he closes the window and orders the chauffeur to drive on. As the car bounces over the Vatican cobblestones, Lefèbvre disregards the salutes of the Swiss Guards.

The cortege drives around the back of the basilica, crossing the Parrot Courtyard and on into the larger Cortile San Damaso. The cars park on the far side, near the elevator to the Secretariat of State and the papal apartment.

Dziwisz and Magee greet the visitors. Then, preceded by the two secretaries and flanked by Siri and Oddi, Lefèbvre is escorted to the salon where John Paul conducts most of his audiences.

The pope is standing in the center of the salon, fingers entwined, when his visitors arrive. He moves forward quickly and embraces first Lefèbvre and then the two cardinals before leading them to a side table where coffee and biscuits await. The secretaries act as waiters. The talk is small and stilted.

Siri and Oddi have not only sponsored this meeting, but they have advised the archbishop what he should say, and how and when he should say it. They are his champions in every sense. But they will not be allowed to take part. That was made clear to them before the pope agreed to the meeting. Gradually and discreetly, Dziwisz and Magee move them from the salon. Magee closes the door behind him.

For fifteen minutes it remains shut. Then it suddenly opens. John Paul stands there. He is holding Lefèbvre by the elbow. The archbishop looks dazed. As they stand in the doorway the pope once more embraces the arch-

Based on the evidence available, mostly reports funneled to the Secretariat of State from Eastern Europe, no one could be certain.

It was decided to include König in future deliberations. Better than anybody, with his unique experience of Soviet intentions, his unsurpassed connections behind the Iron Curtain, the cardinal in Vienna was ideally placed to know what the Russians might be intending to do.

Casaroli undertook to continue tapping the CIA connections he had nursed along since coming into office.[7]

There remained one other issue to be discussed. Everyone quickly agreed John Paul must go ahead with his most taxing journey so far, the forthcoming twelve-day, eighteen-thousand-mile tour of Brazil. During it he would deliver forty-seven addresses, each of which he was writing in the Portuguese language, which he had learned specially for the occasion. Using language-laboratory discs and a tutor, for the past few weeks the pope had studied a couple of hours daily, between midnight and 2 A.M., so that he could communicate directly with Brazil's one hundred million Catholics, the largest single Catholic population in the world.

At the end of June he set off. Special arrangements were made to keep him informed of developments in Poland.

Arns and Lorscheider were on hand to conduct the pope through a seemingly endless land filled with nightmarish social problems. The contrasts visibly disturbed John Paul: slums and skyscrapers side by side; incredible wealth and unimaginable poverty; above all a smiling military government ruling a country in which, during the past decade, the pope knew nine bishops had been arrested, thirty-four priests tortured and at least eight killed.

As usual John Paul tailored his words for the occasion. After dealing with what a member of his entourage called "the old faithfuls"—divorce, abortion and birth control—the pope spoke brave words about the need for land reform, the rights of minorities and, significantly, at Manaus on July 10, on the rights of workers, including their right to strike.

The day before, he had received word from the Apostolic Palace that Solidarity was mobilizing itself for confrontation. Walesa had said he would call a national strike unless he got what he wanted.

The pope's tour continued, during which he stressed the primacy of the spiritual and the need for priests to stay out of politics. There was nothing in his voice to show how poignant and ironic were his words.

The tour closed on a down note. John Paul sharply rejected any thought of the Brazilian bishops' being allowed to ordain married men from the *favelas*, the shantytowns, despite a belief that this was the only means to strengthen the Church's influence in these places. The pope was not even swayed by the thought that it would ease the hold in the slums which the theology-of-liberation movement had.

During the long flight back to Rome, John Paul barely discussed the Brazilian trip. His mind was on events in Poland. There was nothing he could do publicly.

Casaroli had warned that such a course might well delay, if not defeat, the very thing the pope wanted achieved—the peaceful creation of Solidarity. This John Paul accepted. Equally, he refused to consider any suggestion that Walesa should be told to put an end to his plans. After a year of covert papal support, that would be too severe a blow for the young trade unionist to bear; Walesa was already under considerable pressure in Poland.

John Paul moved for the summer to Castel Gandolfo. The secret meetings continued in the summer palace in the Alban Hills. Increasingly the question narrowed down to how best the pope could intervene.

On Monday, August 4, came the news he most feared. König's finely attuned ears in Vienna had picked up alarming signals that the Russians were seriously considering ordering the Polish regime to conduct a purge of Solidarity's leadership while at the same time warning the population that if there was any further rebellion, martial law would be imposed. If that provoked resistance, the Red Army would roll into Poland. It was a dire situation.[8]

Only John Paul knows precisely when he finally decided that he, and he alone, had to act—and act urgently. It may have been during one of those early-morning walks around the gardens of Castel Gandolfo; it may have been over a meal with his secretaries; it may have been during one of those times he was swimming his daily dozen lengths of the pool. It may even have been when he knelt in prayer in the small private chapel attached to his bedroom where Paul had died two years before to the very week. Somewhere, sometime, in the first week of August 1980, John Paul decided he must write the most extraordinary letter any pontiff had ever penned.

John Paul wrote, in Russian, a single handwritten page on his personal stationery with the papal coat of arms in one corner, to President Leonid Brezhnev of the Soviet Union.[9]

The pope told the president he believed Poland faced a Soviet invasion. John Paul warned Brezhnev that if this did happen, he would relinquish the Throne of St. Peter and return to stand at the barricades beside his fellow Poles.

The pope concluded the letter, "Yours in Christ."

He addressed the envelope in his own handwriting to Brezhnev in the Kremlin.

There remained the decision as to who should courier the letter to Moscow.

There was no question of using one of the Secretariat of State priest-couriers. The matter was far too delicate, far too politically explosive for such a course.

König would have been a good choice. But his absence from Vienna could cause comment. It would have to be someone from the Vatican.

Dziwisz was excluded because of his comparatively lowly rank. The aim was for the letter to be delivered personally to Brezhnev. A monsignor, even if he was the pope's secretary, was of insufficient importance to impress the president of the most powerful communist nation on earth of John Paul's earnest intention to resign his office and help lead his people's resistance against the Red Army.

Casaroli was a possible choice. He spoke Russian and knew the Soviet mind. The secretary would be a powerful emissary, one who could without doubt make those in the Kremlin sit up and take notice. But the absence from the Vatican of the Holy See's equivalent of foreign minister might also lead to what John Paul so badly wished to avoid: any hint of what he was doing surfacing.

There was another possible person: Marcinkus.* The IOR governor had impressive qualifications. He was a close confidant of the pope; his advice during the whole affair, like Casaroli's, had been a great help; he also spoke Russian; he was not a man to be awed by Brezhnev; and, as the Vatican's banker, it would not be unusual for him to travel anywhere in the world at short notice on the pope's business. But was he reliable?

The letter was reportedly hand-delivered to Moscow in the second week of August 1980. There followed two months of intense, highly secret shuttle diplomacy between Warsaw, Moscow and Rome, paving the way for the historic agreement signed early in November 1980 between Solidarity and the Polish regime.

On November 12, the pope told a crowded Wednesday audience in the Nervi Hall of his "joy at this wise and mature agreement." He went on, in the only public reference to everything that had happened, to state that the "maturity which in the last few months has characterized our fellow countrymen's way of acting will continue to be typical of us."

The Russians had not invaded. But neither could Brezhnev forgive or forget John Paul's position on Solidarity; the defiant Polish pope was indeed a man of immense influence and real power. He might prove even more troublesome to the Soviet authorities in the future.

* The use of Marcinkus would go some considerable way toward explaining why, after all the financial disasters the IOR experienced under him, Marcinkus would, at least for some considerable time, remain in office. The pope is not one who easily forgets great personal favors, and this may have helped Marcinkus when there were demands in 1982 for John Paul to rid himself of the banker.

XXXII

Agca has taken to wearing a *kaffiyeh*, the flowing Arab headdress held in place by a single knotted cord. It provides protection both against the cold of the Libyan night and scorching daytime sun. He also wears a pair of desert boots which Teslin Tore bought for him in Beirut. They go well with Agca's faded U.S. Army fatigues, part of a surplus consignment for the Vietnamese War that, after years, found its way to this training camp forty-five miles south of Tripoli City. It is on the road to Al-Qyaddahiyal, where Colonel Muammar al Qathafi,[1] ruler of this desert nation, was born in a goatskin tent not unlike the one Agca has shared these past two months.

Once, he had seen Qathafi's helicopter hovering over the camp. His instructor, the short burly American everybody simply calls "Major Frank," told Agca that Qathafi likes to be flown out regularly and look down on this place. It's here, Major Frank likes to boast, that "the cream"—the most promising terrorists—are put through their paces. This, the major never tires of saying, is "the graduation class."

Frank is the first American Agca has ever met. The experience initially confused him. For years Americans and the United States have had a position high on his hate list. That remains so. But Agca nevertheless finds Major Frank likable. He decides it is mainly because of the very factual way the American talks of killing. Major Frank has told Agca he has killed over twenty men, and in the past month he has been demonstrating just how to do so with a variety of weapons. Agca has been deeply impressed. He would like to know more about Major Frank. But the rules of the camp forbid his asking. It is a necessary precaution in the event that any of the students here are afterward captured. Major Frank has told Agca chilling stories of what the Israelis do to the terrorists they catch.

Major Frank should know. For a spell he trained Israeli officers in counterterrorist methods. That was when Frank Terpil was a CIA field officer, one of the agency's experts on sabotage. Now he is a fugitive from American justice. A grand jury in Washington indicted him for supplying explosives to Libya, conspiring to assassinate one of Qathafi's opponents in Cairo, recruiting former American military pilots to fly Libyan aircraft and recruiting Green

Berets to help him run the training camp Agca is now in. Terpil is far more dangerous and deadly than any of the hundred men he and his team are instructing. That also makes Terpil attractive to Agca.[2]

The camp is very different from the one Agca went to in Syria more than two years ago. Here he is not subjected to political lectures on the history of the PLO and its long struggle for a Palestinian homeland, or on the evils of Zionism or the threat of Western imperialism. Here such discussions are taboo. Agca soon discovered why. In this camp there appear to be terrorists of all political persuasions. They come to receive training and then they depart. Nobody asks where they have come from or where they are going. It is another firm rule of this place that such questions are never put.

Now, Agca himself prepares to move on. He removes his headdress, desert boots and fatigues and changes into a three-piece suit manufactured in East Germany, as were his cheap suitcase and other clothes. He is given a one-way tourist-class ticket for the Lufthansa flight which will take him to Sofia in Bulgaria. He has been told that Tore will meet him there.

Agca's mind can no longer recall in any logical manner everything that has happened to him since Tore took them through the mountain pass east of Erzurum out of Turkey and into Iran, at the end of 1979. Some incidents remain vividly clear, others contain gaps. The psychiatrists will later wonder whether, in a clinical sense, this is one of those periods when he was "lost" in a catatonic stupor. That could explain the memory gaps and the astonishing detail which Agca will remember about certain of his experiences: whole conversations, who had been unkind to him, who was helpful.

The initial trip south from Iran into Syria was a blur; it may have taken a month or more. But by February 1980, Agca and Tore were in Damascus. There they had met Kadem. He and Agca resumed their homosexual relationship until Kadem left the city, telling Agca he was going to Libya. At the end of April, Tore showed up in the room he had rented for Agca with a two-day-old copy of *Milliyet*. It contained news that Agca had been sentenced to death in absentia by an Istanbul court. Agca remembers how he shrugged and giggled for hours over the report. This, too, was in keeping with his mental state.

The next memory he has is of Tore arriving in June with an Indian passport, which he gave to Agca. Tore said, "From now on you are Yoginder Singh." Just as he had spent hours in Turkey staring at the bank passbook, so Agca took endless pleasure studying this imperfectly forged document.

On July 3, Tore arrived once more in Agca's room with a travel bag and five hundred dollars. He spoke carefully to Agca, making sure his instructions were clearly understood. He made Agca repeat them back. Then they took a

taxi to Damascus International Airport. There Tore gave Agca a ticket to
Sofia. Agca can remember Tore complaining about having to pay the airport
tax of ten Syrian pounds.

From Vrajdebna airport Agca took a taxi for the six-mile journey to the Vitosha Hotel in Sofia's downtown area. He checked into room 911, which had
been prepaid. A note from the management on the bedside table informed
Agca that he had been given credit facilities to dine in the Vitosha's restaurant and use the hotel's room service.

On the evening of July 5, 1980, he received two visitors. The first said his
name was Omer Mersan. The other identified himself merely as "Maurizi."
They quickly convinced Agca they knew Tore and Kadem. The three of
them then spent, Agca will recall, several hours together.

Maurizi asked Agca about his life after leaving Yesiltepe. He made him
repeat his hate list, in full. He carefully questioned Agca about his religious
attitudes and asked to see his scrapbook on Paul. Maurizi leafed through it,
asking Agca to explain some of the entries. He asked him why he felt compelled to kill a pope. Agca had given his reasons and then ordered dinner to
be sent to his room. During the meal Maurizi had continued probing. He
went back over Agca's religious attitudes. But he gave no sign whether he
approved or disapproved of them. Finally he had sat back. Mersan then asked
Agca to produce his Indian passport. He flipped through it, shaking his head,
saying how lucky Agca had been to cross any frontier with such a clumsy forgery. He handed the passport to Maurizi, who pocketed it. Mersan then produced another passport. It was Turkish, number 136635, made out in the
name of Faruk Ozgun, and already bore immigration stamps for London
(Heathrow), Paris (Charles de Gaulle) and Munich (Riem). The passport
contained a photograph of Agca and details which aged him five years, giving
his year of birth as 1953. Mersan handed Agca the passport. He told him to
use it for all future travel until otherwise instructed.

The two men left. For Mersan, a Turkish smuggler based in Munich, his
part of the operation was over.[3]

But Maurizi is known to Western intelligence services as Maurizi Folini, a
senior KGB agent in the Balkans with good connections to extreme left wing
elements in Italy's Red Brigades.

In the next four months, Agca met Folini on two further occasions. The
first time Folini gave him five hundred dollars' spending money. The second
time he informed Agca he would be going to the training camp in Libya.
Kadem was there when Agca arrived but left shortly afterward. It was the last
time they would see each other.

At the camp Agca met four other men who are to play an important role in his life: Ali Chafic, Omer Ay, a Turkish-born terrorist and member of the Gray Wolves, Ahmed Jooma and Ibrahim El Haya.*

Like Agca they have been coached in the art of assassination, car bombings and urban mayhem of every kind. Special training has been given to them all in the skills needed to carry out a successful "operation," Terpil's generic word for murder in crowded public places. They have been taught the importance of groundwork, positioning and anticipation, and how to create a diversion. They have studied film of the assassination of President Kennedy in Dallas and successful attacks on politicians in Spain and other countries. Finally, they have worked together as a team under the watchful eyes of their instructor.

Now, while the others are to remain at the camp, it is time for Agca to travel. He is even physically fitter than he had been in the Syrian camp. And during his stay in Libya he has regularly seen a doctor who asked many of the questions Folini posed: about Agca's hate list, his religious obsessions, his compulsion to kill a pope. The doctor prescribed antidepressant drugs: largactil and phenelzine. The latter has produced side effects from which Agca continues to suffer: a dryness of the mouth, constipation, sudden waves of dizziness, a lowering of sexual feelings, difficulty in urinating. Worst of all to bear are the sudden pounding headaches that come and go without warning. The doctor has told Agca these pains are also common side effects from phenelzine, but that he must continue to take both medicines. Agca accepted this and a six-month supply of the drugs is packed in his suitcase as he leaves the camp. It is the only indication he has that he will not be returning here until well into 1981. But even of that he cannot be certain. Nor can Agca possibly know as the Libyan Airways 737 climbs away from Tripoli airport that he has finally begun his journey into the history books.

Cardinal Sin can barely contain himself. For weeks he has been assailed on all sides. From their fortified palace President and Mrs. Marcos—the famous "conjugal dictatorship"—have used every ploy to exploit the pope's presence in the Philippines. The formidable pair have asked to fly aboard the pope's jet; they have wanted to say mass privately with him; in a dozen different ways they have tried to turn the visit into a papal endorsement of their authoritarian regime. Sin has successfully resisted them. At the same time he

* In December 1981, Chafic, Jooma and El Haya were named by the U.S. government as members of a Libyan hit squad on its way to the United States to assassinate President Reagan. There was a worldwide alert for the men. In January 1982, Omer Ay was arrested by West German police in Hamburg. Turkey demanded his extradition. The German authorities refused to hand him over until he had been dealt with for crimes in their country.

has faced a running battle with his own clergy. Many oppose the visit not only because it could comfort the regime but also because they fear John Paul's own views do not fit the local scene. The Church in the Philippines is trying to divest itself of its image of being the acquiescent supporter of the wealthy and the powerful. Even more than in Latin America, Filipino priests and nuns are openly militant.

It is against this background that the papal party jets into Manila on February 17, 1981. From the moment John Paul rises from kissing the ground at the airport, he finds himself in a tense situation. Remembering the attempt on Paul's life when he visited Manila, the regime has hemmed John Paul in behind a security cordon reminiscent of the way he was guarded in Turkey. Sin remains his moon-faced impassive self. The cardinal is waiting for the moment when the pope will say what he thinks.

That moment comes later in the afternoon of the first day of the visit when John Paul pays an official call on the Marcoses and members of the government. The world's press is on hand, sensing confrontation. It is swift in coming. His voice steady and measured—signaling to veteran Vaticanologists that there is trouble on the way—John Paul reminds everyone this is a pastoral visit, that he is here "in the name of Jesus Christ." The pope turns and looks squarely at the president and his wife. He fixes them for a long moment with his eyes. There is a steely look in them. Noé, standing almost at the pope's elbow, knows the look well. He has seen it in John Paul's eyes when he is angry. This time, the pope's passion is the more formidable because of the cold way he delivers his attack. He reminds everyone—and as he does so he glances quickly at the suddenly uneasy president, his wife and their officials —that nothing can justify violation of human rights. He then delivers a drubbing of all the regime represents. He ends with a direct appeal to the ministers present "to see enacted those reforms and policies that aim at bringing about a truly humane society, where all men and women and children receive what is due to them, to live in dignity, where especially the poor and underprivileged are made the priority concern of all."

Sin is content. He has advised the pope that the only way to make the visit work is to speak out, to take sides, to let the Marcos regime know exactly where the pope stands.

The pope and the cardinal leave the crestfallen administration behind. There are further home truths to be uttered. John Paul intends to make the clergy understand their position. He tells hundreds of them in Manila's cathedral: "You are priests and religious, you are not social or political leaders or officials of a temporal power."

He goes further in his next address. He warns another great assembly of priests and nuns about resorting to violence: "The road toward your total liberation is not the way of violence, class struggle or hate. It is the way of love, peaceful solidarity."

Marcinkus and Casaroli can recognize that the words are also a warning signal to the other side of the world. It is John Paul's way of telling Lech Walesa and his Solidarity movement not to push too hard. Not now, when they have achieved so much.

Here, in the Philippines, the pope feels he has delivered two telling blows. He has put both the regime and the episcopate on notice that they had better mend their ways if they are to remain Catholics in good standing.

On February 23, it is time for John Paul to fly north to make his contribution to a wider issue. He goes to Japan, to speak first in Hiroshima and then in Nagasaki about the perils of nuclear war. His words are among the finest of his pontificate. Realizing that the pope knows the contents of the third secret of Fatima, and remembering the article by Balducci published on the eve of the conclave that elected John Paul, some of those in his entourage wonder whether the pope believes a nuclear holocaust is closer than many realize. It is a somber note on which to end the Asian sortie.

On Good Friday, April 17, 1981, the first day of the Easter holiday, Istahak Cahani, the recently appointed defense attaché at the Israeli Embassy in Ankara, receives a telephone call from a contact in MIT, Turkish military intelligence.[4] Cahani learns that, using the name of his false passport, Agca has enrolled for a language course at the University for Foreigners in Perugia, Italy. A Turkish "casual"—MIT parlance for a member of the network of informers it maintains throughout Europe's Turkish community—has recognized Agca. It is the description of his two companions which at first excited Cahani's MIT contact and now produces the same response in him: Agca was seen in Perugia with one man who looked like Tore: the other's description fitted Folini.

Cahani is a resourceful professional intelligence officer. One of the functions of his profession, he has been known to quote, is "hearing voices through the noises." As the senior member of the Israeli intelligence team in Turkey, Cahani has problems extracting those "voices" from some very distorted "noises." The various factions of the Anarchy tend to lie as a matter of course; so do the regime's security forces, including MIT. But, in spite of his caution, Cahani has come to believe, because of everything he now knows, that Agca is not just another run-of-the-mill Turkish terrorist.

His own growing file on Agca confirms this. There is the fact that Agca was sprung from his Istanbul prison in an operation which bore all the marks of a professionalism MOSSAD itself could not fault. Though the escape had been carried out by Turks, they almost certainly were advised either by the

KGB or another Eastern-bloc intelligence agency. That suspicion alone had been enough for Cahani to be aroused. But there was more. Despite being the subject of an Interpol red alert—the most serious arrest-on-sight order the international agency distributes to its member police forces—Agca remains free. Yet in the past three months he has flitted in and out of West Germany and Switzerland. Each time he disappeared through that most famous of bolt-holes, Checkpoint Charlie in East Berlin. Cahani had listened sympathetically as his MIT source explained the chagrin of other MIT officers who tailed Agca on these trips. On the German leg the Turks were accompanied by a team from BND, the German secret service. The BND had apparently told their Turkish counterparts they would not allow Agca to be arrested on German soil for his two murders; they feared it might provoke a revenge reaction from one of the many Turkish terrorist groups which have based themselves in West Germany.[5] Besides, the BND might well find it more interesting to let Agca come and go virtually as he pleased in order to see where eventually he might take them. This situation has caused friction between the two intelligence services, contributing to the reasons Agca remains free. Yet Cahani suspects there are other reasons. On his trips through Europe Agca has stayed in good hotels, appears to be well funded. Only a very generous paymaster provided such cash. Cahani knows this also points toward a KGB involvement.

But the final "voice" had come to Cahani from a MOSSAD agent stationed in Sofia. Alerted by Tel Aviv, the Israeli agent had quickly picked up Agca's trail when he arrived back in the Bulgarian capital from Libya. A few days after again settling in to the Hotel Vitosha, Agca received Abuzer Ugurlu, known throughout the Balkans as "the Godfather" of the area's thriving underworld. Ugurlu's smuggling activities into Turkey produce an annual turnover of millions of dollars. His total Eurowide connections have made him a multimillionaire. He has an imposing home in the most select quarter of Sofia; his neighbors are senior members of the Bulgarian Communist Party.

The reason for Ugurlu's power and position is known to Western intelligence agencies. Their files on him all indicate the same story: he has been allowed to build up his personal fortune and acquire his privileges in return for the invaluable service he provides. For years Ugurlu's smuggling network has been the most effective way to distribute huge quantities of weapons to Turkish terrorists, of all persuasions, as part of a deliberate attempt to dismantle Turkey, NATO's vital outpost. The computers of the CIA, MIT and Britain's SIS confirm what the MOSSAD agent in Sofia has told Tel Aviv: Ugurlu has the most direct and closest of links to the Bulgarian secret service. In turn, no other Eastern-bloc intelligence agency is more closely tied to the KGB.

The fact that Ugurlu called on Agca not only strengthened, at least in the view of MOSSAD analysts, the conclusion that Agca had connections with Soviet intelligence, but was also a clear indication of his growing importance to the KGB.

Still interpreting those "voices," Cahani had made a number of deductions. Ugurlu's network is the one Agca has used to travel so successfully around Europe. The purpose of the journeys, Cahani decided, is so that Agca can become familiar with the area in which he will sooner or later carry out some mission. At first the defense attaché thought Agca would be used for an attack against a Jewish installation in either West Germany or Switzerland: an embassy, legation, El Al office, a Jewish bank—anything with an Israeli connection. Warnings were sent out from Tel Aviv, security tightened on all Jewish property in both countries. MOSSAD passed on their fears to the BND and Germany's other counterterrorist force, the BKA. The response was cool.

Then Agca disappeared once more through Checkpoint Charlie. For weeks Cahani has waited patiently for news.

This latest sighting in Perugia is important. With Tore and Folini seemingly in tow, Agca could be going to strike at one of the many Jewish targets in Italy.

Cahani goes to the embassy's cipher room and begins to encode a telex to MOSSAD in Tel Aviv.

On Saturday April 18, the DIGOS office on the third floor of the Rome police headquarters receives news that a possible terrorist squad is in Perugia. MOSSAD is given as the source. The squad is identified as "Mehmet Ali Agca alias Faruk Ozgun, Teslin Tore and Maurizi Folini." After Agca's name comes a copy of the Interpol red alert. Tore and Folini are identified imprecisely as "Soviet intelligence." DIGOS is Italy's justifiably famed anti-terrorist squad, set up to fight the Red Brigades. It is overworked and under-staffed. It does not have a good working relationship with MOSSAD; like the German BKA, harassed DIGOS feels the Israeli agency has a penchant for sending out too many fliers.

The duty officer in Rome calls the local police in Perugia. Their inquiries meet with a blank response. This is the middle of the Easter holiday weekend. The University for Foreigners is closed. There is no way the Perugia police can easily run checks on something which anyway sounds rather unlikely: the idea that a terrorist squad would find anything suitable to attack in Perugia seems rather farfetched. There is little more to be done until Tuesday.

Then, when checks are completed, the Perugian police are not surprised to have found no trace of Agca and his companions. Although a Faruk Ozgun had indeed registered at the university, he had not turned up for classes. No one has even heard of the other names. It is not an uncommon situation; a great deal of police work is foot-slogging investigation. The Perugia police inform DIGOS in Rome. The message goes back up the line to Interpol in Paris—the clearinghouse for all such traffic—and on to Tel Aviv: if the terrorist squad has been in Perugia, it is not there now.

DIGOS in Rome thinks none of the team may even have entered Italy.

Tel Aviv again telexes Cahani in Ankara to continue listening to his "voices." He does not have much hope. But he goes on listening. Something tells him Agca is set to strike soon. And while he cannot know where, Cahani is confident of who the target is going to be: either a Jewish person or a building. The attaché is not a betting man, but he would bet a month's paycheck on that.[6]

On Wednesday, May 6, John Paul allots two full hours—10 A.M. to noon —to discuss an issue his staff think is beginning to vie with Poland for his attention. It is the delicate question of the Holy See's relationship to the People's Republic of China.

Casaroli heads a group half a dozen strong at the Secretariat of State who have been working on the problems for months. Some of them traveled with the pope to the Philippines and Japan so they could renew informal contact with the Chinese Church; a year earlier, in March 1980, John Paul had sent König to Peking to report on the situation. König returned after ten days pessimistic: Catholics in China, to survive in a religious sense in a basically hostile climate, had to keep a distance from Rome. They were allowed to practice their faith only under the auspices of a government-sponsored organization called the National Association of Patriotic Catholics. The association has since 1949 elected its own bishops without the approval of the Vatican.

The elections are illicit but not invalid. Though they do not have the seal of Holy See approval, they do represent the all-important continuity of ordination. And the Chinese bishops have the support of Marcel Lefèbvre in his mountain redoubt in Switzerland because they say the Latin Tridentine mass for China's three million Catholics.

They are the product of three centuries of relationship between China and the Church. It began when the Jesuits walked into Peking in the sixteenth century. They were warmly received. Then, in a momentous blunder, Rome rejected the Jesuits' idea of integrating Chinese and Catholic culture. Had this been allowed, China might very well have become a Catholic country. But when the proposal was turned down, Catholic influence faded; the Chinese Catholics remained a small minority, sometimes tolerated, more often persecuted, but always tenacious of their faith. Since coming to office, John Paul had uttered several conciliatory statements toward the Chinese Church.

But he longed to do more.

This morning's meeting in his salon is to discuss the possibility of a full-scale pastoral visit to China, in which he would be the first pontiff to celebrate mass in Peking's nineteenth-century French-Gothic-style cathedral, and to say other masses in Canton and Shanghai. It would not only be a splendid act of bridge building between two of the oldest powers in the world, but also an open declaration of the Holy See's recognition of the vast importance of China. And if that was seen in Moscow as an indication of what the pope felt about the Soviet brand of communism, so be it.

Casaroli reports that one seemingly insurmountable problem remains: Taiwan.

The Peking government will not consider allowing a papal visit until the Holy See ends its diplomatic ties with the Chinese Nationalist government of Taiwan.

Everybody in the room knows the dilemma: the Church flourishes on Taiwan. It has two hundred thousand Chinese Nationalist Catholics. They have a laudable education system which includes the world's only Chinese Catholic university. Just as the United States in the secular world had been pledged not to turn its back on Taiwan, so the Holy See is committed to maintaining its spiritual support.

This, John Paul insists, cannot change. And yet, he adds, a way must be found to reach Peking.

Casaroli says there are a number of possibilities to consider.

There should be a follow-up to the meeting John Paul had in Manila with a hundred Chinese Christians who had flown from Peking specially for the occasion. The pope told them the past was over: mistakes had been made; this was freely acknowledged. But what mattered was the future. The thoughts had been guardedly received in Peking. Now, suggests Casaroli, is the time to capitalize on this reaction and make another approach to the government-approved bishop of Peking. An appropriate letter could be sent from the secretary inquiring about the possibility of a personal meeting. Casaroli is himself prepared to fly to Peking for talks.

John Paul gives his approval.

Next there is the more delicate matter of the Chinese Jesuit who had been released after twenty-two years in prison the previous September. This was clearly, in Chinese eyes, an olive branch. Why not then, suggests the secretary, reciprocate? Would it not be appropriate, he asks the pope, to elevate the Jesuit to be archbishop of Canton? This could only be seen in Peking as a genuine desire on the part of the Holy See to once more be allowed to become involved directly with the Chinese Church.

The pope agrees.*

This Wednesday afternoon John Paul drives from the Vatican in his now-familiar white-painted jeeplike *campagnola*, the popemobile. There are some fifty thousand people in St. Peter's Square to greet him. Smaller than the crowds were in the early stages of his pontificate, they are nevertheless numerically far larger than those his predecessors generally attracted. It continues to be a constant headache for security chief Ciban. Today, for the first time, his Vigilance men have some real support. As well as the Rome police, there is a squad of DIGOS agents spaced apart and moving watchfully near the popemobile as it crawls around the piazza with the pope smiling and tending his blessing.

John Paul's outstretched arms embrace those widely separated points of the crowd where five men watch the popemobile's progress. They leave the piazza without showing the slightest sign of recognition of each other. They have been particularly warned against this by Maurizi Folini and Teslin Tore, their KGB controllers. The five men are Ibrahim El Haya, Ahmed Jooma, Omer Ay, Ali Chafic and Mehmet Ali Agca.

* In June 1981, the Holy See announced the appointment. The National Association of Patriotic Catholics attacked it. Next came a strong denunciation by the Chinese government of the Holy See's illegally interfering in the internal affairs of the Chinese Church. The door was once more closed. But only for a time. By 1982, the dialogue between Rome and Peking was again in full flow, part of potentially the most significant contemporary advance in Church-state relations. Nobody doubts that what is happening is of immense significance. The Soviet Union views the Church's Chinese connection with the deepest of misgivings. It has aroused barely dormant fears in the Soviet communist psyche, the idea that the combination of Chinese and Holy See cunning is too strong a match for any secular power. It is yet another reason for Moscow to regret the appointment of John Paul.

THE POPE
AND THE JACKAL

If it were done when 'tis done, then 'twere well
It were done quickly: if the assassination
Could trammel up the consequences, and catch
With his surcease success; that but this blow
Might be the be-all and the end-all here,
But here, upon this bank and shoal of time,
We'd jump the life to come.

—MACBETH (I: vii 1)

Absolutism tempered by assassination.

—DEFINITION:
THE RUSSIAN CONSTITUTION
(COUNT ERNST MÜNSTER)

XXXIII

The solitary night-duty operator in the Vatican telephone exchange, an elderly nun, puts down her book and looks at the rows of buttons and lights on the switchboard which runs the length of this beige-colored room. From dawn to midnight the exchange is run by shifts of half a dozen sisters who daily handle thousands of calls. But this is almost three o'clock in the morning of Wednesday, May 13, 1981, and outwardly the Vatican sleeps. The nun knows better. That is why she has put down her book. Her headset is clipped over her coif and a cross on a gold chain hangs from her neck. Her face is composed. But her eyes remain watchful. The nun is waiting for a signal.

Before her, on a typed card, is a list of emergency telephone numbers. They begin with Ciban's bedside extension. Next on the list is the night extension of Buzzonetti, now reinstated as papal physician. Then comes the number of Casaroli's bedroom telephone and the bedside extensions of Dziwisz and Magee. They are followed by the numbers for Martin and Noé. At the bottom of the list are two numbers written in longhand. The first is the general number of Rome police headquarters. The next is the main number of the Gemelli Hospital. They have both been on the list since the end of April.

The nun suspects, but cannot be certain, that their presence is connected with a noticeable increase in security in and around the Vatican. She has seen how the Swiss Guards now ask for identification from even long-serving Vatican employees, how the Vigilance has increased its patrols of the grounds, how there are more policemen on duty in St. Peter's Square. The precautions have puzzled her. And everybody else she has spoken to—her fellow operators, clerical workers in the Apostolic Palace, the staff in the duty-free store—seem equally mystified by the sudden increase in security.

There is nothing prescient about it. Casaroli has designated the Gemelli as the hospital which will handle any serious medical emergency involving John Paul. The secretary has told the others privy to this decision—Marcinkus, Buzzonetti, Dziwisz and Magee—that in the event of the pope's becoming ill he wished to avoid the criticism which arose from the way Paul's final illness was handled and the extraordinary aftermath of Gianpaolo's death. This time, Casaroli has ordered, at the first sign of any medical complication, the pope is to be sent to the Gemelli. The listing of city police headquarters is also innocent enough: the presence of its number in the Vatican exchange is merely part of Ciban's regular review of standard security procedures. He has received no sudden tip that trouble is in the offing; indeed, the latest information from his contacts at headquarters suggests that the relentless, but unpublicized, combined efforts of the police, carabinieri and DIGOS are at last making Rome too hot for the Red Brigades.

The nun, of course knows nothing of this. All she knows is that at three o'clock—the appointed time—the signal she expects every hour comes. One by one the Vigilance night patrols call in from various posts inside the Vatican. The nun switches each call through to the guardhouse behind the Arch of the Bells. When all the calls are in, she picks up her book. She hopes she can get in another hour's reading before the process is repeated.

Shortly after four o'clock a shadow detaches itself from the darker mass of Bernini's colonnade. It is a Rome policeman, one of twenty-four now stationed around the silent piazza. The patrolman walks toward the obelisk. A colleague waits there. They light cigarettes and stare, bored, at the darkened Vatican buildings. They hate night duty; nothing ever happens.

An hour later, the first light appears in the papal apartment. Thirty minutes later there are lights everywhere on the top floor of the Apostolic Palace. The policemen extinguish their cigarettes. One of them, a lapsed Catholic, asks his companion a familiar question: whether it is a life of celibacy which makes everybody in the pope's entourage get up so early. Just as he had hoped, the question stimulates his companion to begin another discussion about the private habits and foibles of the pope. Does he bathe or does he shower? Sing Polish hymns or pop songs as he goes about his ablutions? Does he still eat all that Polish stodge for breakfast or has he gone Roman and settled for coffee and a bread roll? They continue in this vein to the end of their shift. As they go off duty they promise each other they will tap their contacts around the Apostolic Palace for the answers.

At eight o'clock John Paul returns to the private study down the corridor from the dining room. His eating habits have not changed: a substantial breakfast, a light lunch and then a good dinner. More than anywhere else in the apartment, the study reflects his tastes and personality. There are photographs of his parents in wooden frames on his desk. The titles in the bookshelves are predominantly Polish. Where Paul's copy of Mailer's *The Naked and the Dead* had stood, there is now the latest Morris West confection, *The Clowns of God*. It is all about a pope who claims he has received a private revelation of the end of the world and the Second Coming of Christ; he resigns his office to save mankind. Curialists who have read the book think it's clever nonsense. They, of course, have no knowledge of how closely it parallels John Paul's letter to Brezhnev.

A maid pauses outside the door of room 31 on the third floor of the Pensione Isa. It is a small, clean hotel near one of Rome's railway stations. Most of its clients are students or tourists of limited means. The hotel provides reasonably priced, comfortable accommodation for those who wish to make the fifteen-minute walk to St. Peter's Square. Most guests leave early, breakfast in one of the nearby coffee shops and return in the early evening to freshen up before going out again for dinner. It is a routine which allows the hotel to get by with a small cleaning staff: since all the rooms are generally vacated for the day by around nine o'clock, the handful of maids employed at the Pensione Isa can go about their work uninterrupted.

For the past two days the maid who services room 31 finds its occupant has spoiled her routine. He comes and goes at all times, then returns to spend hours in the room. Sometimes she has heard him muttering away in a foreign language. She wonders whether it has anything to do with the bottles of tablets she has noticed he keeps on his bedside table. The maid thinks he must be quite ill to be taking so many medicaments. He arrived on Monday, carrying a briefcase and flight bag. He paid in advance for three nights. That means, thinks the relieved maid, he will be gone by the morning and she can return to her well-ordered ways.

She listens outside the door, her basket of cleaning cloths and sprays in her hand. There is no sound from within. Perhaps he slipped out when she was servicing one of the other bedrooms. The maid knocks lightly and enters the room. She is wise in the ways of hotel guests; nothing surprises her anymore. Nevertheless, she is still astonished by the reaction she gets. The man in the narrow single bed leaps to the floor and stands facing her in his vest and shorts. He is crouching as if expecting to be attacked, elbows tucked into his waist, fists clenched in front of his face. He is shouting at her in a language she cannot understand. But his meaning is clear. He wants her out of the room.

Uttering excuses, the maid backs toward the door and closes it behind her.

Agca turns and climbs back into bed.

At noon John Paul and Casaroli meet in the pope's private study to discuss the latest crisis in Northern Ireland—one that placed the Holy See on a collision course with the British government of Prime Minister Margaret

Thatcher.[1] Both the pontiff and the secretary have been told there was at least some circumstantial evidence that Mrs. Thatcher may have allowed her foreign secretary, Lord Carrington, to destroy what was meant to be a highly secret Holy See initiative to try to save the life of IRA prisoner Bobby Sands.

His hunger strike in the notorious Maze Prison in Belfast had focused world attention on the entire matter of Britain's involvement in Ulster. While imprisoned, Sands had been elected a member of the British House of Commons. He had vowed to die for the cause he had espoused all his adult life—an Ulster free from what he saw as British domination. From the day he went on hunger strike there were widely expressed fears that his death would spark more such actions and create a serious general escalation of violence in the province.

The pope had asked Magee to act as his coordinator over what was happening in Northern Ireland. Magee remained in close contact with Alibrandi and O Fiaich. All three had the uneasy feeling their telephone calls may have been monitored—perhaps by one of the agents of Britain's Secret Intelligence Service who were widely thought to have been operating on both sides of the Irish border for some time. In the Republic they were suspected of working directly out of the British Embassy in Dublin. In the North, O Fiaich's palace —his friends say—may be under electronic surveillance if only because, like Alibrandi, the cardinal felt it essential to talk to all those involved in the sectarian conflict—and that naturally included those with affiliations to proscribed organizations whose every activity is of interest to the security forces. Consequently, the conversations between Magee's office, Alibrandi's study and O Fiaich's palace had been necessarily cryptic.

But toward the middle of April, with Sands weakening daily, Magee was in no doubt that the messages he was getting from Ireland came down to one matter: it was time for the Holy See to intervene.

On Thursday, April 23, Magee had raised the idea with John Paul. The pope listened carefully but gave no decision. Next day, Friday, he discussed the question with Casaroli in Magee's presence. The secretary had steepled his fingers in that familiar gesture and made a suggestion: the Holy See should not only intervene but Magee himself should travel to Belfast to make a direct appeal to Sands to call off his hunger strike. At the same time Casaroli would try and persuade the British government to make some concessions to the IRA prisoners in the Maze H-blocks.

Throughout the weekend, April 25–26, Magee remained in close contact with Alibrandi and O Fiaich while Casaroli had several meetings with the British Minister to the Holy See. The secretary also called Cardinal Hume in London and the pope's apostolic delegate to Great Britain, Archbishop Bruno Heim. Between them they kept Downing Street informed of developments; there was a desire in the Vatican that there should be no misunderstanding of what it was trying to do. In particular Hume and Heim both stressed that this initiative should not be seen as in any way offering comfort to those who committed violence; the Holy See was intervening solely on humanitarian grounds. Hume and Heim reported back to Casaroli that they were satisfied that this message had got across.[2] That the response in Whitehall appeared cool was, they counseled, understandable. What was being proposed required a great deal of thought. To make it work would need much give-and-take on both sides. But if the will was there it might just succeed—provided a spectacular triumph for what the Holy See had always been good at: patient and secret negotiation.

By Monday, April 27, the situation had hardened to the promising point where the Sands family, through O Fiaich, had indicated that they would welcome Magee and that Bobby Sands would see him in his prison cot, seriously weak though he was. A ticket was booked for Magee to fly to London and then on to Belfast. The British minister to the Holy See informed the Foreign Office in London. This was normal procedure. Magee would travel on a red-covered Holy See diplomatic passport and would expect to receive all the courtesies normally shown to an important papal envoy. But there was one specification about the trip that the Secretariat of State felt worth restating to the British minister: secrecy was of paramount importance; there must be no leaks at any stage. The Sands family had pledged their cooperation and O Fiaich was satisfied that for once the IRA would not try to capitalize on the visit. So concerned was Casaroli with letting as few people as possible know exactly when Magee would be traveling that Hume and Heim were not given his flight times. There was really no need for them to know. London was merely a short stopover to Belfast. But the British minister was given full details: Magee would fly on Tuesday morning, April 29, on Alitalia to London and would then take the British Airways shuttle to Belfast. The details were passed to the Foreign Office in London.

It is what John Paul and Casaroli have been informed happened then which continues to infuriate them.

They have been told there was a deliberate leak of Magee's movements from the Foreign Office. The circumstantial evidence—the result of some very fast Casaroli-initiated inquiries in London—does imply that the leak, if not actually authorized, "had the agreement of Carrington," and that "Mrs. Thatcher herself most certainly knew what was being done."[3]

True or not, one thing was very clear: Magee was still on his way to London when the British media knew he was coming. Numerous reporters had called Northern Ireland's Protestant leader, Ian Paisley, to ask his views. They were predictably outraged. He saw Magee's visit as "the unacceptable involvement of the Roman Papacy" in the affairs of "Protestant Ulster."

Magee's carefully conceived secret mission was in shreds even before he touched down at London's Heathrow. There he was met by Peter Blaker, Lord Carrington's deputy, and Michael Alison, minister of state at the Northern Ireland office. They made it clear the British government was not prepared to make concessions to IRA inmates—they wanted to be allowed to run their own affairs in prison in much the same way as prisoners of war do —while under duress. Magee found both men icily formal. He found the headlines dismaying: there was no way, ran the reports, that Ulster Protestants would help save Sands if it meant the British government having to give ground to "terrorists."

For two days Magee shuttled to and from Sands' prison bedside. In the end Magee had been unable to extract a single concession from the Thatcher government. He left Belfast convinced that the Holy See had been "doublecrossed" by London. If there had not been what he perceived as a carefully managed publicity storm it might have been possible to have avoided the impasse. But in the superheated glare of the media there had been little chance of Magee's successfully carrying out John Paul's wishes and finding the compromise solution the pope had sincerely hoped existed.

Immeasurably sadder—and, he told his friends in the Irish Mafia, "wiser to the wiles of the Brits"—Magee had continued to do all he could from the Vatican to diffuse the hunger-strike crisis. He was still trying when Bobby Sands died.

Now there has been a second hunger-strike death. More are expected.

After reviewing the situation John Paul and Casaroli call in Magee and tell him that the Holy See cannot involve itself further in such a public way. It will continue, however, to work behind the scenes.

Magee leaves to inform O Fiaich and Alibrandi.

This much will become known.

Agca spends most of the morning in room 31. He rereads notes he has made. They detail the final instructions he received from Teslin Tore when they last met, this time in Milan. Tore does not know Agca has made these jottings, which, if discovered, could compromise all the months of training and planning that have gone into the forthcoming operation. Agca, in his willful way, which all the medicaments he has been taking cannot change, nevertheless went ahead and wrote down his instructions.

Folini has given Agca two million Italian lire to cover his expenses in Rome. Folini also repeated what he had almost certainly been instructed to say by the KGB: when Agca had completed his mission he would receive three million Deutschmarks, yet another identity plus sanctuary in Bulgaria. Agca did not doubt any of this. Ever since that first deposit of forty thousand Turkish liras in his name on December 13, 1977, in the Türkeye Is Bankasi, he had received ample proof that those who now controlled him had the finances and resources to back up Folini's words.

In Milan Agca had also received further proof of how careful Tore and Folini always are to avoid anything which would directly implicate them. Tore's final instruction to Agca was that he should go to the Milan railway station and collect a packet left there in the name of Faruk Ozgun, the alias Agca was still using. Then, after quick handshakes, Tore and Folini had left him. They were due to meet Agca in the Vitosha Hotel in Sofia this coming weekend.

He had gone to the left luggage office, produced his passport and collected his packet. It was surprisingly heavy for its size. He had gone to the station toilet, locked himself in a cubicle and opened the packet. It contained a Belgian-made Browning 9-mm. semiautomatic pistol and bullets. The gun had been bought in Austria, with money almost certainly provided by Folini, by yet another sinister figure in the conspiracy that had been forged. This man is Horst Grillmeir, an old associate of smuggler Omer Mersan and the Bulgarian Godfather, Ugurlu.[4]

The instructions Agca received tell him what he must do with the gun at this stage. He now places it in his flight bag.

Some instructions he has disregarded. He will not dye his hair. Nor will he wear a cross to pretend he is a Catholic pilgrim. Even the idea of placing around his neck the symbol of a person he hates passionately is enough to make him feel physically ill.

Just before two o'clock, Agca takes his antidepressant drugs: in Milan Tore gave him a further supply, sufficient to last until he reaches Sofia. Agca plans to begin the journey this very evening, taking a train to Florence and flying from there to Geneva, where there are connections onward to Sofia. His coterrorists will go their separate ways to their predetermined destinations.

Agca is not concerned about them. He knows they are merely supports for what he will do. He only wishes his headache would go away.

He strips and shaves and washes. Then he settles back on the bed and quietly begins to recite his hate list, glancing frequently at his watch.

By three o'clock there are about eighty thousand people in St. Peter's Square. They include an elderly American woman, Ann Odre, from Buffalo, New York, and a pert Jamaican woman, twenty-one-year-old Rose Hall. They have chosen their positions with care. They are right at the front of the fenced-off route the popemobile will travel and both are also quite close to the platform from which John Paul will deliver his weekly address. The women stand a few feet apart, with their backs to the right-hand curve of Bernini's colonnade as they look toward the basilica. Behind them, and just in front of the colonnade, are two trucks. One is a mobile first-aid post, the second is selling Vatican stamps. An ambulance edges its way through the crowd and parks beside the post-office trailer. The women notice there are plenty of policemen around, but security seems very lax. The checks seem casual on those with passes to enter the special pens immediately below the dais.

The crowd is even larger than the women expected. Though they do not know each other, there was a common thought in their minds when they chose their positions: they are ideally placed to leave the square quickly when the ceremonies are over.

Standing on an upper edge of one of the square's fountains, another American, Lowell Newton, also thinks he is well positioned. He can see over the heads of the crowd and the light is right for what he wants to do.

Like everybody else in the ever-filling piazza, the three Americans wait patiently.

At four o'clock John Paul goes to his bedroom and changes into a freshly pressed pristine-white-silk cassock. It has a tailored cape that Gammarelli has cleverly modified to enable the pope to wear a flak jacket beneath the cassock. The tailors' skills have been wasted. The pope not only continues to refuse wearing any protection but has ordered that the flak jacket be removed from the apartment. The very thought of it, he has angrily told his secretaries, goes against all his office stands for.

John Paul leaves the bedroom and joins Dziwisz in the nearby study. The secretary will accompany him in the *campagnola* during its customary two-circuit drive around the square. Then Dziwisz plans to hurry back to this study to prepare yet another brief on what is happening in Poland. Just as Magee is determined to keep before John Paul what is occurring in Ulster, so Dziwisz makes every effort to keep the pope informed on the latest maneuverings between the Polish Church and the regime in their homeland. And Dziwisz can take satisfaction in that he has even managed to persuade the pope to slip in some references about Poland in his homily this afternoon. Both he and the pope agree the words will be a further welcome boost for Solidarity.

Dressed in a sports jacket, white shirt open at the neck and a pair of black trousers and shoes, Agca edges his way past where Lowell Newton is standing to a position almost facing Ann Odre and Rose Hall. He carries his flight bag on his right shoulder. Its zipper is closed.

Minutes later Omer Ay makes his way through the crowd to stand at Agca's right elbow. His body masks the flight bag.

Neither man gives any sign of recognition.

Some distance away, quite close to Newton, waits Ali Chafic.

On the other side of the piazza, near the Arch of the Bells, Agca knows that Jooma and El Haya should now be in position.

At ten minutes to five, John Paul and Dziwisz arrive in San Damaso Square, where the popemobile waits. Casaroli is there. So are Martin and Noé. The pope takes the secretary aside for a brief conversation no one can overhear. Then John Paul turns to Martin and reminds the old prefect he wants time set aside in the morning to review "papers." Martin promises to re-arrange the schedule.

Dziwisz climbs into the *campagnola* and sits in the white-leather padded seat immediately behind the pope.

John Paul takes up his accustomed position. He stands and grips the steel white-painted handrail. The papal photographer is there, sitting opposite Dziwisz; he is there to get some action shots the pope wants to send to close friends at Christmas.

At five o'clock precisely, the popemobile drives out of the courtyard.

Ahead, from the square, though nobody there can yet see anything, the cheering begins. The crowd knows he is coming. On these occasions his time-table and route never vary.

As the *campagnola* approaches the Arch of the Bells, Vigilance men, DIGOS agents and uniformed Rome city policemen begin to walk ahead and immediately behind the vehicle. Their presence, if anything, makes the small popemobile appear more vulnerable. As it emerges into the piazza the noise rises to a roar. There are now well over a hundred thousand people in the square and they are cheering wildly.

John Paul waves and smiles. The *campagnola* moves past Jooma and El Haya.

With a couple of hundred yards to go before the *campagnola* reaches him, Newton raises his camera and readies himself.

Ann Odre finds the sun is reflecting off her glasses. It is difficult for her to see. She thinks: It's crazy; I've come all this way and now the sun's going to blot out things.

Rose Hall has never heard so much noise. She tries to tell a neighbor it is not even like this at carnival time in Jamaica. Her companion shakes her head. Rose cannot be heard above the tumult.

Agca and Ay smile and wave toward the pope, as they have been told to do. They can glimpse the white figure in the popemobile greeting those standing at the bottom of the square.

The vehicle moves at two miles an hour. John Paul is now facing inward, waving and smiling at the tens of thousands surrounding the obelisk in the center of the piazza.

As the *campagnola* approaches, Newton lowers his camera. The pope has his back to him. Then he remembers: on the vehicle's next circuit around the square the pope will be facing outward, toward him.

Following orders, detective Vito Ceccarelli continues to work his way through the crowd. He is following his nose, heading for those parts of the square where experience has taught him he might make an arrest. Ceccarelli is a member of a plainclothes detail of Rome City policemen on the lookout for pickpockets. He dislikes the work because of the way he has to shove and elbow his way through the throng; he gets a lot of hassle and very little thanks when he makes an arrest. As the *campagnola* passes, Ceccarelli is facing the basilica, near one of the square's fountains. He begins to shoulder his way up toward the right-hand side of the colonnade. The area is a favorite spot for pickpockets as it offers an easy escape route into the surrounding maze of streets.

Like Newton, Ann Odre and Rose Hall can see only John Paul's broad back as the popemobile passes. They know that next time around he will be facing them.

It is exactly five-fifteen when the *campagnola* begins its second circuit.

John Paul moves to the other side of the vehicle and faces outward, partially blocking Dziwisz's view. Photographer Felici, having taken several rolls of film over the pope's shoulder, has dropped off the popemobile and is now among the security men walking ahead of the vehicle. Felici is taking pictures of the crowd's rapturous reception and the pope's obvious happiness.

At eighteen minutes past five, the popemobile passes Newton. John Paul appears to be waving directly into his camera. It's a better photograph than Newton ever imagined he would get.

The popemobile continues along to where Ann Odre and Rose Hall wait. They are both cheering and laughing, as is virtually everybody around them.

Nobody notices the flight bag being unzipped and a hand reaching inside. It emerges holding the Browning Agca has brought to the square.

Detective Ceccarelli is still doggedly working his way through the crowd as John Paul passes. Ceccarelli notes, almost automatically, that the pope gives a particularly broad smile to a group of people waving a Polish flag.

After the popemobile passes, the detective continues on up the square. He is heading toward the post-office trailer. That's where, with a bit of luck, he'll nab a pickpocket, so giving himself some satisfaction for his tiring afternoon in the piazza.

Dziwisz sees there are about sixty feet to go before the *campagnola* completes its second circuit.

Impetuously, John Paul does something which always makes the secretary nervous. The pope reaches into the crowd and plucks up a child being held at arm's length. It is a little girl, with tousled blond hair. He hugs and kisses her and then hands her back to her ecstatic mother. Dziwisz is always worried that a child will somehow wriggle clear of the pope's grasp and fall, creating a nasty accident. But whenever he mentions to John Paul the possibility, the pope only grins. Now, as Dziwisz continues to watch nervously, the pope bends down and leans out of the *campagnola* to give his hand to another little girl, dressed in Communion white. He straightens and looks about, wondering who else he might personally embrace or greet. It's his way of bringing the papacy to the masses in even the largest of crowds.

John Paul is now no more than twenty feet from Ann Odre and Rose Hall.

The first shot rings out.

Various individuals hear it differently. Ann Odre believes it is a car backfiring. She looks toward the two parked trailers and the ambulance.

Rose Hall thinks someone has let off a firecracker. She thought they only did such things at Kingston carnivals.

Ceccarelli instinctively identifies the sound as gunfire. But even then he is confused. His experience is limited to the Rome City police range with its excellent acoustics. Here, in the crowded square, the direction the sound came from is not easy to locate. The detective begins to cast around, ruthlessly elbowing people out of his way. Other policemen stationed in the crowd are doing the same.

Even before the first echo fades, Dziwisz knows what has happened. There has been a shot. For a fleeting second—too short for the secretary subsequently to measure—he does not know who, or if anyone, has been hit.

John Paul remains upright, gripping the handrail.

Dziwisz is about to yell "Sit down!" when the pope starts to sway.

Agca's first bullet has penetrated John Paul's stomach. It has produced multiple wounds in the small intestine, in the lower part of the colon, in the large intestine and in the mesentery, the tissue which holds the intestine to the abdominal wall.

Instinctively, John Paul places his hand over the entry wound to try to stop the spurting blood.

The papal photographer sees the shocked and bewildered look in the pope's eyes and instinctively lowers his camera.

John Paul starts to falter and crumple, desperate though he is to remain upright. He uses his left bloodstained hand to grip the handrail for support. His right hand is bunching the cassock in a futile attempt to stanch the flow of blood. His face grows increasingly contorted with agonizing pain. He begins slowly to collapse onto Dziwisz.

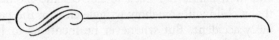

Extending his right arm, Agca draws a new bead with the Browning. His feet are placed firmly on the ground, a foot apart, the best position, he has been drilled, to keep him rock-steady in a crowd. He remembers what his instructors in Libya had drilled into him: *Take your time. Line up the target. Remember you have surprise on your side.*

Agca fires again.

A second 9-mm. shell hits the pope, in his right hand. It falls uselessly to his side.

Agca can see bright-red blood spurting onto the white cassock.

He pulls the trigger once more.

The third shot hits John Paul in the right arm.

The *campagnola* driver twists in his seat. His mouth is open. But no word comes.

Dziwisz cradles the pope in his lap. John Paul is saying, "Thank you. Thank you."

The secretary starts to scream at the driver in Italian. "Move! Back and forth! Move! Get us out of here!"

All around there is madness.

Dziwisz is shielding the pope with his body and screaming at the driver to go faster.

The phalanx of security men are whirling, guns drawn, shouting orders and counterorders.

The crowd itself is beginning to sway as if being buffeted by a great wind. One shocking sentence is repeated from mouth to mouth, rippling ever outward from the scene of carnage. In a dozen different languages the same thing is said: "The pope has been shot!"

The papal photographer crosses himself. As he does so, a policeman bundles him aside.

The popemobile continues at an agonizingly slow speed through the throng. Its interior is a place of deepening horror. Blood continues to fountain up through John Paul's cassock, staining his cross, spattering all those around him; blood is soaking into the white leatherwork and dripping onto the floor.

The pope is barely conscious. His eyes open and close. He is whispering in Polish. Dziwisz holds him tight, murmuring words nobody around can understand. The secretary is saying a Polish prayer for the dying.

Ann Odre turns in the direction of the shooting. Another shot rings out. She is hit squarely in the chest. She collapses, seriously hurt.

Another shot.

The bullet hits Rose Hall in the left arm. She falls to the ground.

Two innocent bystanders have now been badly wounded.

Agca glances to his right. Ay has gone.

Agca, gun in hand, sets off after him. He is heading in the direction of the trailers and ambulance parked in front of the colonnade.

The third shot gave Ceccarelli a bearing. He is moving, bulldozerlike, even before the sounds of the other shots. Head down, arms flailing, he beats a path through the crowd. He, too, is heading for the trailers and ambulance.

Newton has left the fountain and is moving in the direction of the gunfire. As he does so, he sees a young man burst from the crowd, running very fast and holding a black revolver in his right hand.

Fearing he himself might be shot, Newton quickly turns away from the terrorist, hoping to give the impression he hadn't noticed him. The man passes within ten feet of Newton. The intrepid cameraman swings around and photographs him fleeing.

It is Ali Chafic.

On the far side of the square, Jooma and El Haya—placed there for the very purpose of providing an effective cover-up—have run from their post well before the *campagnola* approaches.

Like Chafic and Ay, these other members of a hit squad trained in part by a renegade CIA officer in a Libyan school for terrorism and financed by the KGB, believes Agca has totally succeeded in a mission that has been conceived as a suitable response to a pope who has dared to challenge communist Russia.

Agca is almost there. The crowd continues to open before his waving gun. As he reaches the post-office trailer he tosses the Browning away, sending it skidding under the trailer.

At the same moment his legs are cut from underneath him.

Detective Ceccarelli has made his arrest.

The popemobile lurches through the Arch of the Bells. An ambulance is parked there, engine running. Its crew swiftly transfers John Paul to a stretcher and lifts him into the ambulance.

Dziwisz goes with him.

Lights flashing and siren wailing, the ambulance heads off at speed for the Gemelli Hospital.

Inside, John Paul repeatedly whispers the one word that both the Italian ambulance crew and the Polish secretary can understand.

"Madonna. Madonna. Madonna."

During the desperate twenty-minute drive to the hospital through nearly two miles of twisting city streets crowded with rush-hour traffic, behavior patterns emerge in the ambulance which will be endlessly repeated as news of the shooting spreads.

The two attendants riding in the back reflect an attitude which becomes common. As they bend over the pope, making him as comfortable as they can, the men are filled with incredulity and outrage that this has happened to one of the most revered figures in the world. They are also themselves so shocked they partially forget to follow their training. Instead of keeping the pope quiet, they allow John Paul to go on repeating his beseeching, *"Madonna."*